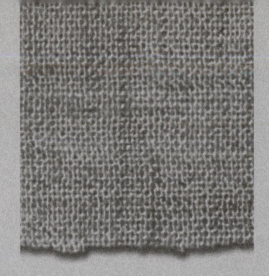

CULTURAL ANTHROPOLOGY

SEVENTH EDITION

Marvin Harris

Late, of the University of Florida

Orna Johnson

University of California, Los Angeles

PEARSON

Boston   New York   San Francisco
Mexico City   Montreal   Toronto   London   Madrid   Munich   Paris
Hong Kong   Singapore   Tokyo   Cape Town   Sydney

Series Editor: *Dave Repetto*
Series Editorial Assistant: *Liz DiMenno*
Marketing Manager: *Laura Lee Manley*
Editorial Production Service: *Omegatype Typography, Inc.*
Composition Buyer: *Linda Cox*
Manufacturing Manager: *Megan Cochran*
Electronic Composition: *Omegatype Typography, Inc.*
Cover Administrator: *Joel Gendron*

For related titles and support materials, visit our online catalog at
www.ablongman.com.

Between the time website information is gathered and then published, it is not
unusual for some sites to have closed. Also, the transcription of URLs can result
in typographical errors. The publisher would appreciate notification where
these errors occur so that they may be corrected in subsequent editions.

Library of Congress Cataloging-in-Publication Data

Harris, Marvin
    Cultural anthropology / Marvin Harris, Orna Johnson.—7th ed.
      p.   cm.
    Includes bibliographical references and index.
    ISBN 0-205-45443-7 (paperback)
    1. Ethnology. 2. Anthropology. I. Johnson, Orna. II. Title.

  GN316.H36   2007
  306—dc22

                                        2006043405

Printed in the United States of America

10 9 8 7 6 5 4 3   CIN   11 10 09 08 07

Credits appear on pages 383–385, which constitute an extension of the copyright page.

CULTURAL ANTHROPOLOGY

Contents

Marvin Harris cared deeply about the problems facing U.S. society. He believed there is an intelligible process that governs the way cultures evolve, and he felt that a cultural materialist framework is best equipped to help us draw generalizations that can be used to solve the problems we confront. His work revealed how different cultures adapt in contrary ways to specific economic and ecological realities. One of his main concerns was how cultures respond when the demands of a growing population exceed natural resources, leading to a decrease in the efficiency of production and quality of life. He firmly believed that warfare results from population pressure and is the price our ancestors paid to prevent the lowering of living standards.

In the years since Marvin Harris first published his theory of **cultural materialism**, the world has not become a safer and kinder place. If anything, the main problems that confront us in this new century are just those that arise out of a steady set of developments in the infrastructure: population growth; intensification of production leading to deforestation, the collapse of fisheries, and pollution; income disparity; and economic integration leading to greater globalization of the economy and the depersonalization of work. Harris's books, and indeed his life's work, offer us a set of theoretical and methodological tools with which to increase our understanding of and ultimately our ability to influence the direction of the changes we are facing today.

GOALS OF THE BOOK

This textbook explains the theory of cultural materialism in a clear and concise manner and shows how cultural behavior makes sense within a cultural materialist framework. My commitment to this textbook is not just to keep Marvin Harris's memory alive but to provide students with a scientific theory of culture whose findings can be accepted on logical and evidentiary grounds. For Marvin Harris, science had two great strengths: first, as a communal enterprise in which agreement among a community of scholars is based on evidence that is rigorously tested and challenged; and, second, as a source of strong theories that make specific predictions that can be supported (or refuted) with reference to evidence. These are not esoteric scholarly matters. A scientific anthropology holds the promise that we can build knowledge on which to base effective action. Science is the predominant system of knowledge that can claim to build reliable knowledge that accumulates over time. While art and philosophy may change over time, it is always possible to argue that ancient arts and philosophies are as true today as they ever were. Not so with science, which identifies past errors and moves on.

The hope that science brings to anthropology inspired one of Harris's most eloquent passages in *Cultural Materialism*:

> No other way of knowing is based on a set of rules explicitly designed to transcend the prior belief systems of mutually antagonistic tribes, nations, classes, and ethnic and religious communities in order to arrive at knowledge that is equally probable for any rational human mind . . . the real alternative to science is not anarchy but ideology; not peaceful artists, philosophers, and anthropologists, but aggressive fanatics and messiahs eager to annihilate each other and the whole world if need be in order to prove their point. (pp. 27–28)

Elements of structure (e.g., political relations to the state) and superstructure (e.g., ideology and political rhetoric) are intrinsically linked to the infrastructural process. It is up to us to figure out how the parts of the universal pattern are related. In the years since *Cultural Materialism* first appeared, the world has not become a safer and kinder place. If anything, the main problems that confront us in the new century are just those that arise out of a steady set of developments in the infrastructure: population growth; intensification of production leading to deforestation, the collapse of fisheries, and pollution; and economic integration leading to greater globalization of the economy and the depersonalization of work. Cultural materialism offers us a set of theoretical and methodological tools with which we can increase our understanding of, and ultimately our ability to influence the direction of, these changes (Johnson and Johnson 2001).

New to This Edition

The most prominent new feature in the textbook is the incorporation of cases from the twelfth edition of *Conformity and Conflict*, a reader edited by James Spradley and David W. McCurdy. This is intended to help instructors apply a theoretical perspective to ethnographic cases. Thirty articles are analyzed at the end of chapters in features called Through the Lens of Cultural Materialism. The articles are briefly summarized and then analyzed from an emic/etic perspective and/or organized by their universal pattern components in order to help the reader better understand the case material. This analysis provides insights into how cultural materialism helps explain sociocultural phenomena. This is achieved in two ways:

- It outlines emic and etic components of ethnography by showing which information is derived from the participants—representing the "native" point of view—and which information is based on the anthropologist's (or researcher's) understanding of the culture.

- It organizes the case material according to infrastructure, structure, and superstructure (mode of production and reproduction, domestic and political organization, and ideology).

The goal of this feature is to help students identify the three components of the universal pattern and show how they are interrelated. It also helps students distinguish the different ways of attaining cultural descriptions: using information based on an informant's viewpoint or using information derived from researcher observations. Sometimes emic and etic data may be identical but, more often than not, beliefs or ideology may obfuscate an empirical perspective. For example, the article "The Kayapo Resistance" by Terence Turner shows how the universal pattern helps organize ethnographic material.

- The Kayapo faced outside threats to the sustainability of their mode of production (gold mining and plans for a hydroelectric dam) that threatened their existence. This is the *infrastructure* component of the case.

- Although lacking in political clout, the Kayapo came together and pooled resources to patrol their borders. They also demonstrated in Brasília and attracted attention and financial support from international groups that ultimately helped them protect their environment. These actions make up the *structure* aspect of the example.

- Environmental activists helped disseminate information about the disastrous effects of the proposed dam, swayed public opinion, and effectively convinced the World Bank to withdraw funding for construction. This is the *superstructure* of the Kayapo story.

A second new feature consists of 11 diagrams outlining the universal pattern as it applies to ethnographic profiles in Chapters 5 through 11. This feature helps students consistently tie the theoretical framework to the ethnographic case studies described in the Profiles. It reinforces the importance of understanding culture in terms of the three-part division of cultural institutions and how infrastructure, structure, and superstructure are interrelated in each case.

Statistical data throughout the textbook has been updated.

Chapter 2 contains expanded information about cultural materialism. It discusses the *primacy of infrastructure* and clarifies the notion of infrastructural determinism. The chapter also contains two new diagrams: one outlines the principle of cultural materialism to provide students with a visual chart of the components; the other gives an overview of the diversity of anthropological theories.

Chapter 3 contains a discussion of cultural transmission and shows how culture allows for continuous adaptations that make it possible for humans to develop new technologies and more complex societies. Increased emphasis is placed on human adaptation.

Chapter 5 more clearly outlines the different modes of production and provides a chart that clearly identifies the conditions and ethnographic examples associated with each type.

Chapter 6 adds a discussion of the mode of reproduction in China that shows how cultural attitudes are influenced by changes in infrastructure (decreased land availability) and structure (government monetary incentives).

Chapter 16 contains an extended discussion of religion and society, including the moral force of religion and symbolic representation of groups.

CHAPTER 1

INTRODUCTION

The diversity in the United States is demonstrated by these children wearing ethnic clothing.

The Five Fields of Anthropology

What Is Distinctive about Cultural Anthropology?
Holism
Fieldwork and Participant Observation

Ethnography
Ethnology
Anthropology and Science

Why Study Anthropology?

Anthropology is the study of humankind—of ancient and modern people and their ways of living. Different branches of anthropology focus on different aspects of the human experience. One branch focuses on how our species evolved from earlier species. Other branches focus on how we developed our facility for language, how languages evolved and diversified, and how modern languages serve the needs of human communication. Still others focus on the learned traditions of human thought and behavior, how ancient cultures evolved and diversified, and how and why modern cultures change or stay the same.

People from different continents who speak different languages and possess different values and religions find themselves living closer and closer together in a new global village. To all members of this new community, anthropology offers a unique invitation to examine, explain, and celebrate human diversity. At the same time, anthropology reminds us that, despite our different languages and cultures, we are all members of the same species and share a common nature and a common destiny.

[handwritten: studies people]

The Five Fields of Anthropology

Departments of anthropology in the U.S. colleges offer courses in five major fields of knowledge about humankind: cultural anthropology, archeology, anthropological linguistics, physical anthropology, and applied anthropology.

- **Cultural anthropology** (sometimes called *social anthropology*) deals with the description and analysis of cultures—the socially learned traditions of past and present ages. It has a subdiscipline, *ethnography*, that describes and interprets present-day cultures. Comparing these interpretations and descriptions can generate hypotheses and theories about the causes of past and present cultural similarities and differences.

- **Archeology** and cultural anthropology possess similar goals but differ in the methods they use and the cultures they study. Archeology examines the material remains of past cultures left behind on or below the surface of the earth. Without the findings of archeology, we would not be able to understand the human past, especially where people have not left any books or other written records. *[handwritten: studies things]*

- **Anthropological linguistics** is the study of the great variety of languages spoken by human beings. Anthropological linguists attempt to trace the history of all known families of languages. They are concerned with the way language influences and is influenced by other aspects of human life and *[handwritten: history of languages]*

with the relationship between the evolution of language and the evolution of our species, whose scientific name is *Homo sapiens*. Anthropological linguists also study the relationship between the evolution and change of languages and the evolution and change of cultures.

- **Physical anthropology** (also called *biological anthropology*) connects the other anthropological fields to the study of animal origins and the biologically determined nature of *Homo sapiens*. Physical anthropologists seek to reconstruct the course of human evolution by studying the fossil remains of ancient human and humanlike species. They also seek to describe the distribution of hereditary variations among contemporary human populations and to sort out and measure the relative contributions to human life made by heredity, the natural environment, and culture.

- **Applied anthropology** uses the findings of cultural, archeological, linguistic, and biological studies to solve practical problems affecting the health, education, security, and prosperity of human beings in many cultural settings. *[handwritten: uses all]*

What Is Distinctive about Cultural Anthropology?

The common thread that ties the fields of anthropology together is the broad focus on humankind viewed across time and space. The purpose of anthropology is to understand what it means to be human by studying all aspects of human behavior and ideas. Anthropologists recognize that immense differences lie between people—differences in physical traits, language, lifestyles, beliefs, values, and behaviors. By studying these differences, we come to understand that ways of behaving and believing are intelligible in terms of the overall context in which they occur. By adopting this broad view of the human experience, perhaps we humans can tear off the blinders put on us by our local lifestyles. Thus anthropology is incompatible with the view that a particular group—and no one else—represents humanity, stands at the pinnacle of progress, or has been chosen by God or history to fashion the world in its own image.

[handwritten: Holism — big picture]

The distinction of anthropology among the social sciences is that it is *holistic*; it tries to understand the processes that influence and explain all aspects of human thought and behavior.

Anthropologists at Work

A. Ethnographer Nancy Scheper-Hughs with the engineer of the Aguas Pretas Sugar Mill in Timbauka, Brazil.   B. Ethnographer Napoleon Chagnon charts kinship relationships among the Yanomami.   C. Jerald T. Milanich, archeologist, Florida Museum of Natural History, with prehistoric (A.D. 200 to 900) Native American bird vessel.   D. Linguist Francesca Merlin with the speakers of a previously unknown language near Mt. Hagen, New Guinea.   E. Biological anthropologist Joan Silk records baboon behavior, Amboseli, Kenya.

 Holism is an approach that assumes that any single aspect of culture is integrated with other aspects, so that <u>no single dimension of culture can be understood in isolation.</u>

Other disciplines in the social sciences are concerned with particular segments of human experience or particular times or phases of cultural processes. In contrast, anthropology seeks to understand all the components and processes of social life—for example, the physical environment, methods of food production, the organization of family life, the political system, religious customs, and artistic endeavors. Because anthropology studies the interaction between biological and cultural differences, it is strategically equipped

to address key issues concerning the origins of social inequality in the form of racism, sexism, exploitation, poverty, and international underdevelopment. Thus anthropology has much to contribute to our understanding of the major issues that divide contemporary society and threaten national and ethnic conflict.

Fieldwork and Participant Observation

In the early twentieth century, researchers studied cultures with the goal of describing them in as much detail as possible. In recent decades, anthropologists have been focusing more on problem-oriented research. Some are committed to scientific and causal research to explain aspects of culture that sometimes seem "unexplainable" (Murphy and Margolis 1995), such as why some cultures prohibit eating certain foods for religious reasons. Other anthropologists favor more intuitive research that avoids hypothesis testing and favors evocative interpretationist descriptions in search of symbols, motivation, and meaning—for example, how apparently elusive conceptions of personhood are revealed in ceremonial conduct (Geertz 1973).*

> **Fieldwork** refers to firsthand experience with the people being studied. It involves integration into a community through long-term residence and knowledge of the local language and customs while maintaining the role of observer.

Cultural anthropologists collect their primary data through **fieldwork**, an extended period of involvement that typically entails living in the community and immersion in the culture being studied. The fieldworker typically gathers information through various methods of ethnographic field research that involve living close to the people and participating in their lives as much as possible.

> **Fieldnotes** are the data collected by anthropologists.

Fieldnotes include journals, daily logs, diaries, interviews, behavioral observations, and transcriptions of audiotapes. Some fieldnotes include everything the anthropologist writes down as she or he sees or hears it, as a source of background information, while others are devoted to more systematic records such as household census, life histories, gift exchange, land tenure histories, and direct, systematic observations of behavior (Johnson and Sackett 1998).

> **Interviews** rely entirely on research subjects as sources of knowledge.

Research subjects (or informants) can provide cultural interpretations and report events they have witnessed (or heard) firsthand.

> **Participant observation** places the ethnographer at the scene where a combination of direct observation and interviewing provides the evidence from which ethnographic accounts are constructed.

Just as children learn a great deal by observing family members, anthropologists learn about a culture by observing the behavior of others and participating in

*See the first page of the References for an explanation of the system of citations used in this book.

routine activities. However, coming from another culture, anthropological fieldworkers must keep an open mind and not let preconceptions get in the way of understanding the culture they are studying (Dewalt et al. 1998).

> **Direct systematic behavior observations** refer to the study of activity patterns that show patterns of action and interaction of the people we study.

Systematic observation is structured by explicit rules that include:

- Who we observe (adult heads of household or children under age 5)
- When and where we observe them (at random times throughout the day at home or in the evening during mealtime)
- What we observe (speech acts or specific physical actions)
- How we record our observations (descriptive notes or a checklist of behavior)

Interviews and questionnaires involve gathering verbal data through guided conversation. In an open-ended interview, the researcher encourages the respondents to take the lead in the conversation to reveal themes and issues that are important to them. Questionnaires and surveys involve prepared formal interviews with structured topics of inquiry that can be used for comparisons between groups—for example, household composition, material possessions, norms and expectations for relating to friends and relatives, and the like.

Many cultural anthropologists try to complement systematic observations with formal interviews and questionnaires to compare what people do and how they perceive their actions. For example, people in a workplace setting may tell the anthropologist that they have friends among their co-workers who are of different ethnicities, yet observations of lunchtime behavior show that most people sit next to and converse with people of their own ethnic background. The voluminous data collected in the field generally require many hours of analysis for each hour spent collecting them (Sanjek 1990).

During the beginning of new fieldwork research, anthropologists and other strangers to the culture commonly feel awkward and unsure.

> **Culture shock** is the feeling of anxiety and disorientation that develops in an unfamiliar situation when there is confusion about how to behave or what to expect.

Anthropologists commonly have persistent feelings of uneasiness and anxiety that occur when one shifts from one culture to another. Once the initial period of adjustment passes, anthropologists often develop lifelong friendships with individual members of the community and may be adopted into local families through a relationship known as *fictive kinship* (see Chapter 9). The anthropologist often forms complex relationships with the people being studied. The researcher must see things from the other person's point of view and still see patterns and processes that may not be consciously understood by the people in the culture being studied.

Anthropologists refer to the people who share information about their language and culture as *informants, participants*, or *respondents*.

 Informants are people through whom the anthropologist learns about the culture through observation and by asking questions.

The process of working with informants is a painstaking effort to sort out information and knowledge. It is important to choose informants who are knowledgeable and articulate; moreover, no matter how reliable the source, anthropologists find it advisable to explore the same topics with several informants and to use a variety of interview techniques and methods appropriate to the goal of the study (Weller 1998).

Besides talking to informants, anthropologists commonly undertake **direct observations of behavior** as a traditional method of fieldwork. Although expensive in terms of field and analysis time, making systematic observations is the only way to obtain accurate data on what people are doing and how much time they spend in various activities. Informant recall—or even the researcher's writeup of fieldnotes at the end of the day—will be shaped by selective remembering or forgetting that make descriptions based only on memory highly inaccurate (Johnson and Sackett 1998).

Ethnography

 Ethnography is a firsthand description of a living culture based on personal observation.

Ethnography literally means "a portrait of a people." It is a written description of the customs, beliefs, and behaviors of a particular culture based on information collected through fieldwork. Anthropologists have tried to study small-scale societies before they have had disruptive culture contact with modern societies. The resulting ethnographies have often consisted of descriptions of traditional cultures as if they existed in the present. Ethnographies are still often written in the ethnographic present, and readers are cautioned that most cultures described may no longer exist.

Today anthropologists no longer restrict themselves to studying small, traditional societies. Moreover, traditional anthropological approaches and methods are now used to study communities in complex nation-states. Today's research also tends to be more specialized and often focuses on more specific topics of interest. A few topics covered in this book are

- *Ecological anthropology,* which considers the interaction between environment and technology to study human adaptation and change
- *Economic anthropology,* which studies how goods and services are distributed through formal and informal institutions
- *Political anthropology,* which focuses on political integration, stratification, methods of conflict resolution, leadership, and social control
- *Medical anthropology,* which studies biological and sociocultural factors that affect health and illness
- *Psychological anthropology,* which is concerned with how culture affects personality, child rearing, emotions, attitudes, and social behavior

Nonetheless, the discipline tries to retain its holistic orientation. For example, people who identify themselves as political anthropologists are concerned with the effects of environments or economies on political behavior or on how people raise their children.

More recent social changes, resulting from increased globalization, have led ethnographers to describe local cultures as embedded in the regional and global economy. This movement has led to the concept of transnational research, which recognizes that the world is not a mosaic of isolated cultures but a network of communities linked by immigration, tourism, media, and now cyberspace. This situation may require multisited field studies; for example, migrants must be studied both at home and abroad to understand the diverse cultural influences they experience (Hannerz 1998).

Ethnology

Anthropologists use the comparative method to understand patterns of thought or behavior that occur in a number of societies.

Anthropologists insist first and foremost that conclusions based on the study of a particular culture be checked against the evidence of other groups. In this way anthropologists hope to control biases and generalize their findings to specific kinds of societies.

> **Ethnology** is a study of a particular topic or problem in more than one culture, using a comparative perspective.

Whereas ethnography presents the details and particulars of a single community or culture, **ethnology** is the comparative study of customs and beliefs that tries to formulate theories about the similarities and differences between cultures. Comparative research can provide answers to a number of theoretical questions. For example, certain customs and practices, such as writing systems, tool use, and folktale motifs, tend to recur in different societies. Sometimes this recurrence is the result of geographical proximity, but in other cases, where there has been no known contact, we find independent occurrences of certain traits due to similar governing conditions. Cross-cultural comparisons provide evidence for such patterns and help explain them.

Anthropology and Science

Anthropology is handled as a social science by some and as one of the humanities by others. The humanistic side of anthropology focuses on the rich, complex descriptions of human experience through life histories, personal narratives, and the contemplation of religious and aesthetic meanings.

> A **humanistic approach** aims to describe and interpret each culture on its own terms; it believes comparisons distort the unique qualities of a given culture.

> A **scientific approach** aims to explain cultural differences and similarities; it believes that regularities exist across cultures and can be discovered through empirical data collection and systematic comparison.

As a science, anthropology looks for patterns and interrelationships to create possible explanations or hypotheses that explain the phenomena being observed.

A **hypothesis** is a proposition or tentative explanation of the relationship between certain phenomena that can be validated (or invalidated) by evidence collected according to explicit procedures. The social sciences, however, lack the ability to yield precise and reliable long-range pre-

dictions. Scientific truth is not absolute but states what is considered to be the most probable explanation and then tests to see if the interpretation is correct.

> Science does not yield certainties or laws; it yields probabilities.

As our knowledge expands, some theories may prove better than others, and sometimes old truths are discarded as new theories become more probable.

Why Study Anthropology?

Most anthropologists make their living by teaching in universities, colleges, and community colleges and by carrying out university-based research. But a substantial and increasing proportion of anthropologists find employment in nonacademic settings. Museums, for example—especially museums of natural history, archeology, and art and folklore—have long relied on the expertise of anthropologists. In recent years, anthropologists have been welcome in a greater variety of public and private positions in government agencies concerned with welfare, drug abuse, mental health, environmental impact, housing, education, foreign aid, and agricultural development; in the private sector as personnel and ethnic relations consultants and as management consultants for multinational firms; and as staff members of hospitals and foundations (see Box 1.1).

In recognition of the growing importance of these nonacademic roles as a source of employment for anthropologists, many university departments of anthropology have started or expanded programs in applied anthropology. These programs supplement traditional anthropological studies with training in statistics, computers, and other skills suitable for solving practical problems in human relationships under a variety of natural and cultural conditions.

Despite the expanding opportunities in applied fields, the study of anthropology remains valuable not so much for the opportunities it presents for employment as for its contribution to the basic understanding of human variations and relationships. Just as most students who study mathematics do not become mathematicians, so too most students who study anthropology do not become anthropologists. For human relations fields, such as law, medicine, nursing, education, government, psychology, economics, business administration,

BOX 1.1 | An Anthropological Scorecard

Anthropologists frequently identify themselves with one or more specialized branches of the five major fields. The following is only a partial listing. Starred items have strong applied focus.

Cultural Anthropology

Ethnography. Description of contemporary cultures.

*Medical anthropology. Study of biological and cultural factors in health, disease, and treatment of the sick.

*Urban anthropology. Study of city life, gangs, drug abuse, and so on.

*Development anthropology. Study of the causes of underdevelopment and development among less developed nations.

Archeology

Historical archaeology. Study of cultures of the recent past, using both written records and archeological excavations.

Industrial archeology. Historical archeology that focuses on industrial factories and facilities.

*Contract archeology. Conduct of archeological surveys for environmental impact statements and protection of historic and prehistoric sites.

Physical (Biological) Anthropology

Primatology. Study of the social life and biology of monkeys, great apes, and other primates.

Human paleontology. Search for and study of fossil remains of early human species and their ancestors.

*Forensic anthropology. Identification of victims of murders and accidents; establishing identity of criminals.

Population genetics. Study of hereditary differences in human populations.

Linguistics

Historical linguistics. Reconstruction of the origins of specific languages and of families of languages.

Descriptive linguistics. Study of the grammars and syntaxes of languages.

Sociolinguistics. Study of the actual use of language in the communication behavior of daily life.

*Applied Anthropology

Also, see page 313.

---

and communication media, anthropology has a role to play that is as basic as mathematics. Only by becoming sensitive to the cultural dimensions of human existence and learning to cope with them can one hope to become really effective in any of these fields.

Anthropology has much to contribute to the educational philosophy known as *multiculturalism,* which stresses the importance of viewing the world from the perspectives of all the cultures, races, and ethnic groups present in modern nations. As part of their attempt to broaden the cultural horizons of their students and combat ethnocentrism, many colleges have developed required "cultural diversity" courses. Cultural anthropology is the original multicultural approach to human social life, and it remains by far the most systematic and comprehensive alternative to traditional curriculums that view the world primarily in terms of "dead, White, European males." In anthropological perspective, multiculturalism consists not merely of the knowledge that cultures are different and worthy of respect but also of a commitment to analyzing the causes of similarities as well as differences (Paredes and Pohl 1995).

According to Gary Ferraro (2000), people with training in cultural anthropology are able to use their observational and analytic skills in a variety of ways in both the public (government) and private (business) sectors of the economy. Students are finding their way into areas of employment such as aging, criminal justice, cultural resource management, family planning, human and civil rights, medical systems and patient care, museum, program evaluation, refugee settlement, substance abuse, and welfare policy, to name only a few. You won't see many positions specifically advertised for anthropologists, but the research skills that anthropologists acquire can be used in a variety of employment environments (Schwartz 2000).

SUMMARY
and *Questions to Think About*

1. Anthropology is the study of humankind. Its five major branches are cultural or social anthropology, anthropological linguistics, physical (or biological) anthropology, archeology, and applied anthropology.

2. Anthropology is distinctive in its commitment to holism and to understanding all factors that influence human thought and behavior.

3. Through fieldwork, cultural anthropologists participate in social activities, directly observe behavior, and conduct interviews to understand human thought and behavior.

4. An ethnography is a published account of a particular culture. Ethnology is the comparison of ethnographic information from two or more cultures.

5. A humanistic approach to anthropology describes the unique aspects of a given culture; a scientific ap-

proach seeks to find probabilistic explanations for cultural differences and similarities.

6. Anthropology has much to contribute to understanding multiculturalism; it is committed to understanding the processes that underlie cultural similarities and differences.

Questions to Think About

1. What does it mean to say that anthropology is *holistic?*

2. What are some goals of anthropological research?

3. How can anthropologists be useful outside of academic settings?

THROUGH THE LENS
of Cultural Materialism

Conformity and Conflict • Reading One

Ethnography and Culture

James P. Spradley

James Spradley describes how ethnographic fieldwork collects information by asking questions to understand the native's perspective and by making systematic observations of behavior and events. (See discussion of *emics* and *etics* in Chapter 2.)

- An anthropologist *elicits the native's point of view* to describe a culture different from his or her own.

- An anthropologist *observes the behavior* of others to identify patterns that are culturally significant to both the anthropologist and to members of the culture.

The first perspective describes how people define, classify, and evaluate their physical and social environment including nature, relatives and friends, and the supernatural. This allows the anthropologist to understand the cultural meaning of actions and events and how people understand and feel about cultural rules and expectations.

The second perspective is studied by observing what people do. This involves participating in activities, observ-

ing behavior and events and recording what is said and done.

Ethnography focuses on the following aspects of culture:

- Cultural knowledge (traditions that people have learned). Culture is a shared system of meanings that enables people to interpret and evaluate situations.

- Cultural behavior (how people behave in given situations). This refers to the patterned behavior people follow, regardless of whether they are conscious of the rules.

- Cultural artifacts (including tools, structures, and art). Artifacts consist of the things people make and how they are used by members of a culture.

Culture consists of both *explicit* and *tacit* knowledge. *Explicit* culture is what people know and can readily communicate, such as kin relations and cultural rules of behavior. *Tacit* culture is knowledge outside of people's awareness. It consists of behavior we recognize only when norms are breached—for example, when another person stands too close or otherwise makes us feel uneasy.

CHAPTER 2

THE NATURE OF CULTURE

Navaho rug makers are made, not born.

n this chapter, you will find alternative definitions of culture and of other key concepts such as society and enculturation. You will also encounter certain general processes that help explain why customs, traditions, and behavior are both similar and different around the world. Then we will embark on the difficult but necessary task of identifying the principal parts of the system of behaviors and thoughts that constitute human social life. Finally, we will set forth the theoretical viewpoint of cultural materialism and the universal pattern of culture that guides the organization of this textbook.

Definitions of Culture

> **Culture** refers to the learned, socially acquired traditions of thought and behavior found in human societies. It is a socially acquired lifestyle that includes patterned, repetitive ways of thinking, feeling, and acting.

The definition of _culture_ as consisting of patterns of acting (behavior) as well as patterns of thought and feeling follows the precedent set by Sir Edward Burnett Tylor, the founder of academic anthropology in the English-speaking world and author of the first general anthropology textbook:

> Culture . . . taken in its wide ethnographic sense is that complex whole which includes knowledge, belief, art, morals, law, custom, and any other capabilities and habits acquired by man as a member of society. The condition of culture among the various societies of mankind, in so far as it is capable of being investigated on general principles, is a subject apt for the study of laws of human thought and action. (Tylor 1871:1)

> Some anthropologists prefer to view culture as a purely mental phenomenon consisting of the ideas that people share concerning how one should think and act.

The view that culture is "pure idea" has been compared to the notion of culture as a computer program—a kind of "software" that tells people what to do under various circumstances. According to Clifford Geertz (1973:44), "Culture is best seen . . . as a set of control mechanisms—plans, recipes, rules, instructions (what computer engineers call 'programs')." This view implies that ideas (knowledge, rules, and meaning) guide and govern behavior. The drawback to this concept of culture as "pure idea" is that it excludes reference to repetitive patterns of behavior, which are part of culture even when people are not conscious or fully aware of their existence. Behavioral components of culture include the things people regularly do and how they habitually act—whether or not they are fully conscious or aware of such patterned behavior.

> Behavior can guide and cause ideas and behavioral events can affect the evolution of sociocultural systems even though people may not be fully cognizant of these events or actions.

The effect of behavior on cultural development can be seen in times when cultures change rapidly, as is happening today in most of the world. For example, before the 1970s, many women who had husbands and school-age children in the United States believed that wives should depend on their husbands for family income. Pressured by rising prices and a desire to maintain or raise their standard of living, increasing numbers of married women with school-age children abandoned this "program" and joined the wage labor force, even though traditional family values still prevailed. Women left home to work because their earnings made the difference between getting by or falling into poverty. Today, the majority of married women with school-age children are in the labor force, and this change in behavior has brought forth a change in people's shared ideas and expectations about women's capabilities and their right to equal job opportunities. (See Chapter 14 for a more detailed look at how and why the program governing marriage and the family in the United States changed.)

Another drawback of viewing culture as a mental program, rather than as having both mental and behavioral aspects, is that many of the most pressing social problems of our times are not programmed at all. The traffic jam, for example, is a highly patterned cultural phenomenon that occurs despite the programming that drivers receive to keep moving.

Society, Subculture, and Sociocultural System

The term **society** refers to an organized group of people who share a homeland and who depend on each other for their survival and well-being. Each human society has an overall culture, but all societies contain groups of people who have lifestyles that are not shared by the rest of the society. In referring to patterns of culture characteristics of such groups, anthropologists often use the term _subculture_.

Members of a **subculture** share certain cultural features that are significantly different from those of the rest of society.

Even small societies have subcultures associated with males and females, children and adults. In larger and more complex societies, one encounters subcultures associated with, for example, groups based on ethnic, religious, and class distinctions. People may also change and renegotiate their affiliations and identities as they move from one social context to another.

Finally, the term *sociocultural* is a useful reminder that society and culture form a complex system of interacting parts (more about the components of sociocultural systems in a moment).

Enculturation

The culture of a society tends to be similar in many respects from one generation to the next. In part, cultural continuity is maintained by the process known as *enculturation*.

Enculturation is a partially conscious and partially unconscious learning experience whereby the older generation invites, induces, and compels the younger generation to adopt traditional ways of thinking and behaving.

Thus Chinese children use chopsticks instead of forks, speak a tonal ("sing-song") language, and worship their ancestors because they have been enculturated into Chinese culture. Enculturation is achieved through the control that the adult generation exercises over the means of rewarding and punishing children. Each generation is programmed to reward thought and behavior that conforms to the patterns of its own enculturation experience and to punish, or at least not to reward, behavior that does not so conform.

The concept of enculturation (despite its limitations, as discussed later) occupies a central position in the distinctive outlook of modern anthropology. Failure to comprehend the role enculturation plays in maintaining each group's patterns of behavior and thought lies at the heart of the phenomenon known as *ethnocentrism*.

Ethnocentrism is the belief that one's own patterns of behavior are always natural, good, beautiful, or important and that strangers, to the extent that they live differently, live by savage, inhuman, disgusting, or irrational standards.

A.

B.

C.

How, What, and When We Eat: Culture at Work
A. Midday meal, Yangon, Myanmar. Food is good to touch as well as to eat. B. Fast food, the United States' most notable contribution to world cuisine. C. The correct way to eat in China.

People who are intolerant of cultural differences usually ignore the following fact: Had they been enculturated within another group, all those supposedly savage, inhuman, disgusting, and irrational lifestyles would now be their own. Recognizing the fallacy of

A.

C.

B.

Passing Culture On

A. In Bali, a man reads to his grandchildren from a script on narrow bamboo strips.   B. In India, a Sikh father teaches his child how to wrap a turban.   C. In Mission Viejo, California, young people learn the culturally approved manner of eating artichokes.

ethnocentrism leads to tolerance of cultural differences and a desire to learn more about them.

A certain degree of ethnocentrism is natural for people raised in a single culture; their values and ways of behaving appear desirable and superior to all others. Ethnocentrism is potentially dangerous, however, when it leads to intolerance of other cultures and is used to justify the mistreatment of others. Taken to the extreme, it leads to the belief that people who are different from us are not worthy of basic human rights and therefore their mistreatment or annihilation is morally justified.

Cultural Relativism

Members of different human groups have always been curious about the customs and traditions of strangers. The fact that people who live in different societies build different kinds of shelters, wear differ-

ent kinds of clothing, practice different kinds of marriages, worship different spirits and gods, and speak different languages has always been a source of puzzlement. The most ancient and still most common approach to these differences is to assume that one's own beliefs and practices are normal expressions of the true or right way of life, as justified by the teachings of one's ancestors and the commandments or instructions of supernatural beings. Most cultures have origin myths that set forth the sequence of events leading to the beginning of the world and of humanity and to the adoption of the group's way of life. The failure of other groups to share the same way of life can then be attributed to their failure to be true, real, or normal human beings.

Anthropologists place great emphasis on the viewpoint known as *cultural relativism*. This concept has several meanings. To some anthropologists, cultural relativism means not passing judgment on the moral worth of such cultural traits or institutions as cannibalism, first-cousin marriage, or eating insects. It means disavowing any absolute, universal moral standards that can be used to rank cultural beliefs and practices as good or evil, superior or inferior, right or wrong.

Probably the majority of anthropologists, however, would argue for a more provisional kind of relativism. Namely, they would hold in abeyance any moral judgments until they have learned what the world looks like to people in different cultures.

Cultural relativism stipulates that behavior in a particular culture should not be judged by the standards of another. Yet it is evident that not all human customs or institutions contribute to the society's overall health and well-being, nor should they be regarded as morally or ethically worthy of respect.

Like everybody else, most anthropologists make ethical judgments about certain kinds of cultural patterns, but they seek to minimize the effect of these preferences and beliefs on the conduct of their research so they can understand why people think and act as they do. Ethical and moral decisions should be based on the best available knowledge of what is happening in the world. This knowledge is gained through reliable scientific methods that tell us who is doing what to whom and who is responsible for the suffering and injustice that needs to be remedied. If anthropologists want to tackle politically controversial issues such as the spread of AIDS in Africa and the plight of landless peasants in Latin America, they need to understand social institutions and practices in objective scientific terms that will reveal possibilities for improving the moral outcome.

Science and the Relativity of Truth

It is important to distinguish clearly between the relativity of *values* and the relativity of *truth*. Values relativism says there are no universal moral values because values should be evaluated in terms of the cultural context; relativism of truth says objective truth about human thoughts and actions is unobtainable because all research is biased. Objective truth is unobtainable, according to some anthropologists, because all observers, even those who use scientific methods, are influenced by their own culture-bound experiences and their interpretations are affected by the values and perspectives associated with their nationality, ethnic group, class, and gender.

The position we adopt in this textbook is that anthropologists do not need to reject their values in order to carry out an objective study of cultural phe-

nomena. They can disapprove of pollution, genocide, sexism, racism, poverty, child abuse, and nuclear war and still maintain scientific objectivity about these phenomena. Nor is there anything antiscientific in setting out to study certain cultural patterns because one wants to change them.

Scientific objectivity does not arise from having no biases—everyone is biased—but from taking care not to let one's biases influence the results of research. Scientists seek to control bias by telling one another as clearly as possible what they have done to gather and analyze their data and by formulating coherent theories that can be tested and retested by other researchers. People who assert that scientific methods cannot be applied to sociocultural phenomena commit a basic error: They assume that objective truth means the absolute, final, unquestioned truth. Instead, science results in temporary and provisional objective truth. Even when theories have considerable evidence supporting them, no theory is unquestionably true because scientific knowledge is only partial, and the progress of science follows the ability of humans to test new theories that predict what one would expect to find if a particular interpretation is correct.

Science involves a never-ending process of formulating and testing new and better theories.

Although theories cannot be proved, they are subject to falsification.

Falsification entails the rejection of a theory because the prediction is not supported by the data.

This view of science derives from the positivist empiricist tradition that makes no claim to being value free but proposes to overcome inevitable biases of knowledge by using methodological rules that are open to public scrutiny. Just because the final, absolute, objective, certain truth can never be reached does not mean that all truths are equally arbitrary and biased (D'Andrade 1995; Haraway 1989; Harris 1995; Holton 1994; Lett 1991; Watson 1990).

Limitations of the Enculturation Concept

It is easy to see that enculturation cannot account for a considerable portion of the lifestyles of existing social groups. Old patterns are not always faithfully repeated in successive generations, and new patterns are continually being added.

The replication of cultural patterns from one generation to the next is never complete.

In fact, the rate of innovation and nonreplication in the industrial societies has reached proportions alarming to each successive generation. Margaret Mead was among the first to call attention to the profound worldwide significance of the resulting "generation gap." Her description of the generation gap was written over two decades ago, but her words are as pertinent now as then:

> Today, nowhere in the world are there elders who know what the children know; no matter how remote and simple the societies are in which the children live. In the past there were always some elders who knew more than any children in terms of their experience of having grown up within a cultural system. Today there are none. It is not only that parents are no longer guides, but that there are no guides, whether one seeks them in one's own country or abroad. There are no elders who know what those who have been reared within the last twenty years know about the world into which they were born. (1970:77–78)

Enculturation can account for the continuity of culture, but it cannot account for the evolution of culture.

Even with respect to the continuity of culture, enculturation has important limitations. As indicated, not every replicated cultural pattern results from the programming that one generation experiences at the hands of another. Many patterns are replicated because successive generations adjust to similar conditions in social life in similar ways. Sometimes the programming received may even be at odds with the actual patterns; people may be enculturated to behave in one way but be obliged by conditions beyond their control to behave in another way. We have already mentioned traffic jams, which exist even though people try to avoid them. Poverty is another example. As we will see in Chapter 12, many poor people find themselves living in houses, eating food, working at jobs, and raising families according to patterns that replicate their parents' subculture, not because their parents trained them to follow these patterns but because poor children confront educational, political, and economic conditions that perpetuate their poverty.

Diffusion

Whereas *enculturation* refers to the passing of cultural traits from one generation to the next, *diffusion* refers to the passing of cultural traits from one culture and society to another—for example, Americans eat sushi, the Japanese play baseball, and the whole world wears Levis.

 Diffusion takes place when culture contact leads to borrowing and passing on of culture traits.

This process is so common that the majority of traits found in any society can be said to have originated in some other society. One can say, for example, that much of the government, religion, law, diet, and language of the United States was "borrowed" or diffused from other cultures. Thus the Judeo–Christian religions come from the Middle East; parliamentary democracy comes from Western Europe; the food grains in the American diet—rice, wheat, and maize—come from Asian, Middle Eastern, and Native American civilizations, respectively; and the English language comes from the amalgam of several different European tongues.

Early in the twentieth century, diffusion was regarded by many anthropologists as the most powerful explanation for sociocultural differences and similarities. The lingering effects of this approach can still be seen in popular attempts to explain the similarities among major civilizations as the result of their derivation from each other—Polynesia from Peru or vice versa; the New World (the Americas) from the Old; and so forth.

In recent years, however, diffusion has lost ground as an explanatory principle because the adoption of new cultural traits requires that these traits be integrated into the recipient population. It is true that, in general, the closer two societies are to each other, the greater will be their cultural resemblance. But these resemblances cannot simply be attributed to some automatic tendency for traits to diffuse. Societies that live close together (in location) are also likely to occupy similar environments; hence the similarities between them may be caused by the effects of similar environmental conditions. Moreover, numerous societies that lived in close contact for hundreds of years retain radically different ways of life. For example, the Incas of Peru had an imperial government, whereas the nearby forest-dwelling societies lacked centralized leadership of any kind. Other well-known cases are the African Ituri forest hunters and their Bantu agriculturalist neighbors and the "apartment house" Pueblos and their marauding, nomadic Apache neighbors in the southwest United States.

Resistance to *diffusion* is as common as acceptance.

If this resistance were absent, Catholics and Protestants in northern Ireland would not differ; Mexicans would speak English (or U.S. citizens, Spanish); and Jews would accept the divinity of Jesus Christ (or Christians would reject it). Furthermore, even if one

A.

B.

Culture, People, and the Sun

The relationship between people and the sun is mediated by culture. A. Sunbathing is a modern invention. B. On the beach at Villerville in 1908, only "mad dogs and Englishmen went out in the midday sun" without their parasols. As the rising incidence of skin cancer attests, sunbathing can indeed be hazardous to your health.

accepts diffusion as an explanation, the question still remains of why the diffused item (say, monotheism or agriculture) originated in the first place.

> *Diffusion* cannot account for many instances in which people who never had any contact with each other invented similar tools and techniques and developed remarkably similar forms of marriage and religious beliefs.

Dramatic examples exist of such inventions and discoveries that occurred not only independently but also at approximately the same time (see Box 2.1).

In sum, diffusion is no more satisfactory than enculturation as a mode of explaining cultural similarities. If only diffusion and enculturation affected social life, then we should expect all cultures to be the same and to stay the same; this is clearly not the case.

It would not be accurate to conclude, however, that diffusion plays no role in sociocultural evolution. The nearness of one culture to another often does influence the rate and direction of change as well as the specific details of sociocultural life, even if it does not shape the general features of the two cultures. For example, tobacco smoking originated among the native peoples of the Western Hemisphere and after 1492 spread to the most remote regions of the

BOX 2.1 | Old and New World Independent Inventions

All items listed were present in both the Old and New Worlds prior to 1492.

Textiles

Purple dye
  Prepared from coastal mollusk
  Elite connotation of purple
Scarlet dye (cochineal/kermes)
Resist dyeing

Loom
Cotton
Clothing
Turban
Nightcap
Pointed-toe shoes
Long robes
Sash, mantle, sandals, loincloth

(continued)

BOX 2.1 | Old and New World Independent Inventions *(continued)*

Weapons, armor

Kettle-shaped helmet
Sling
Thickened textile armor

Metallurgy

Lost-wax casting
Smelting, alloying, forging, hammering,
    gilding, and so forth

Ceramics

Paper

Lime sizing of writing surface

Architecture

Colonnade, aqueduct, canal, cement-lined
    reservoir, highway
Corbeled arch
True arch
Walled city
Fired brick
Pyramids

Mathematics

Place value notation
Zero concept
Zero sign
Astrology and astronomy
Articulated lunar, solar, and stellar calendar counts 360
    days plus 5 extra days
Cycle of 7 days
Day measured sunset to sunset
Observatories
Eclipse records
Day names

Writing

Hieroglyph system
Ideographs, rebus

Social organization

Merchant class or caste
Organized trade, caravans
Corvée labor
Kingship complex
King concept
Divine mandate

Throne
Canopy
Umbrella or parasol as sign of dignity or rank
Scepter
Crown or diadem
Tomb in elevated structure
Burial chamber with hidden entry
Royal tombs (conspicuous display)
Dedicatory sacrifice, subfoundation burial of children
Gold necklace, sign of office
Heraldic devices
Litter
Deference of bowing, downcast eyes

Religion and ritual

Paradise concept
Underworld, concept of hell
Dualism (good and evil)
Earth, air, fire, water as basic elements
Deluge motif
    Produced by rain
    A few persons saved in a vessel
    Bird sent forth to check drying
    Pyramid tower built for safety against deluge, de-
        stroyed by being blown down by wind

Sacrifice complex

Animals slain
Human sacrifice
Offerings burned on altar in ceremonial area
Communion in consumption of part of the sacrifice
Parched grain or meal as offering
Blood offered as sacrifice
Blood scattered over area and participants
Snake symbolism
    Signifying wisdom, knowledge
    Signifying healing
    Signifying fertility
Incense
    Incense mixed with cereal one type of offering
    Accompanying most rituals
    For purification
    For offering to gods—sweet, attractive
    Symbolizing prayer
    As route for ascent of soul

Source: Adapted from Riley et al. 1971.

globe. This diffusion could not have happened if the Americas had remained cut off from the other continents. (The tobacco plant did not grow outside the Americas.) Yet contact alone obviously does not tell the whole story. Hundreds of other Native American practices, such as living in wigwams and in matrilocal households (see Chapter 8) did not diffuse even to the colonists who lived next door to Native American peoples.

Fieldwork and the Mental and Behavioral Aspects of Culture

Cultural anthropologists employ many kinds of methods to learn about cultural patterns. These include survey questionnaires, censuses, life histories, genealogies, formal and informal interviews, filming, videotaping and audiotaping, and notetaking (Bernard 1994; Sanjek 1990). The anthropological method of *participant observation* involves living for extended periods among a people and participating as much and as closely as possible in their daily round of activities—talking, listening, and just plain looking. The aim of the fieldworker is to obtain knowledge of both the mental and behavioral aspects of a culture. The mental aspects consist of thoughts and feelings that exist at various levels of consciousness:

1. *Unconscious rules.* People may have a culturally prescribed body language and not be aware of it. For example, they may not be able to state the rules that govern the distance that they maintain between each other while holding a conversation, just as they are unaware of rules of grammar when they speak.

2. *Partially formalized rules.* Other culturally patterned ways of thought exist closer to consciousness; people may not routinely talk about certain cultural rules but can express them when questioned by the fieldworker. Thus they can usually state the values, norms, and proper codes of conduct for activities such as weaning babies, courting mates, choosing leaders, treating diseases, entertaining guests, categorizing kin, worshiping, and performing thousands of additional commonplace behaviors.

3. *Formal rules of conduct.* Cultures also have many fully conscious, explicit, and formal rules of conduct and statements of values, norms, and goals that people talk about during ordinary conversations, write down in law codes, and announce at public gatherings (rules about littering, making bank deposits, playing football, trespassing, and so on).

4. *Rules for breaking rules.* Finally, to make matters more complex, cultures have rules not only for behavior but also for breaking rules of behavior, such as when you park your car in front of a sign that says "No Parking" and gamble on not getting a ticket.

Knowledge of this inner world is not the only product of fieldwork. In addition, anthropologists observe, measure, film, and take notes about what people do

A.

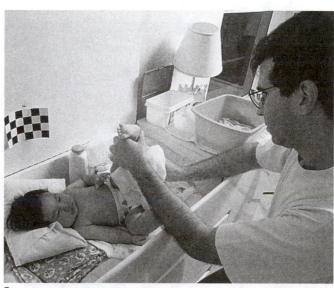

B.

The Limits of Enculturation

A. Before the 1970s, fathers spent less than three minutes a day interacting with infants.   B. This cultural pattern was not passed on to today's generation.

during their daily, weekly, or annual rounds of activities. They watch births take place, attend funerals, go along on hunting expeditions, watch marriage ceremonies, and attend hundreds of other events and activities as they unfold. These events and activities constitute the behavioral aspect of culture.

Emic and Etic Aspects of Culture

The fieldworker can describe both mental aspects and behavioral events and still not offer a satisfactory description of culture. The problem is that both the thoughts and behavior of the participants can be viewed from two different perspectives: that of the participants themselves and that of the observers. In both instances, scientific and objective accounts of the mental and behavioral fields are possible (see Box 2.2).

> **Emics** describe culture from the participants' viewpoint; the observer uses concepts and distinctions that are meaningful and appropriate to the participants.
>
> **Etics** describe culture from the observer's perspective; the observer uses concepts and distinctions that are meaningful and appropriate to the observer.

The first way of studying culture is called *emics* (pronounced *ee-miks*), and the second way is called *etics* (pronounced *et-iks*). (See Chapter 4 for the derivation of these terms from the linguistic concepts phonemics and phonetics.)

> The aim of *emic* descriptions is to produce a view of the world that the native participants accept as real, meaningful, or appropriate.

In carrying out *emic* research, anthropologists seek knowledge of the categories and rules one must know in order to think and act as a native. They attempt to learn, for example, what rule lies behind the use of the same kin term for mother and mother's sister among the Bathonga, or when it is appropriate to shame house guests among the Kwakiutl, or how to ask a boy or a girl out for a date among U.S. teenagers.

> The aim of *etic* descriptions is to generate scientific theories about the causes of sociocultural differences and similarities.

Rather than employ concepts that are necessarily real, meaningful, and appropriate from the native point of view, the anthropologist interested in the etic aspects of a culture uses categories and rules derived from the vocabulary of science—categories and rules that are often unfamiliar to the native. Thus etic studies may involve the measurement and juxtaposition of activities and events that native informants find inappropriate or meaningless (Headland et al. 1990).

Emics, Etics, and Sacred Cows

The following example demonstrates the importance of distinguishing between emics and etics when trying to describe and explain cultural differences and similarities. In the Trivandrum district of the state of Kerala in southern India, farmers say that they obey the Hindu prohibition against the slaughter of cattle and that they never knowingly do anything to shorten the lives of their animals. Yet in Kerala, the mortality rate of male calves is almost twice as high as the mortality rate of female calves. In fact, male cattle (oxen) 0 to 1 year of age are outnumbered by female cattle (cows) of the same cohort in a ratio of 67 to 100. The farmers themselves are aware that male calves are more likely to die than female calves, but they attribute the difference to the relative "weakness" of the males. "The males get sick more often," they say. When asked to explain why male calves get sick more often than females, some farmers suggest that the males eat less than the females. A few farmers even explain that the male calves eat less because they are not allowed to stay at the mother's

Traffic Jam in New York City
Despite having clear traffic rules, traffic jams are a cultural pattern.

A.   B.   C.

Diffusion

Can you reconstruct the diffusionary history of the objects and activities shown in these scenes?
***A.** A Sambura warrior in Kenya makes a call on a cellular phone.   **B.** A Mongolian metropolis.*
***C.** A Brazilian woodsman uses a chainsaw.*

teats for more than a few seconds. But no one says that male cattle are not as valuable in Kerala as they are in other regions of India, where they are used for plowing dry fields. In Kerala, where rice, the principal crop, is grown in postage-stamp–size fields, oxen are at a disadvantage. They tend to get stuck in the

---

BOX 2.2 | Emics and Etics Represent Two Perspectives for Viewing Cultural Phenomena

Emics	Etics
Emics is derived from *phonemics*—sounds that native speakers recognize as being distinct and significant in distinguishing meaning (see Chapter 4).	*Etics* is derived from phonetics—sounds that are distinguished by linguists but may or may not be meaningful to native speakers (see Chapter 4).
Emic knowledge represents views of thoughts and behavior from the perspective of the participants.	Etic knowledge represents views of thoughts and behaviors from the perspective of the observer/ researcher.
Emic descriptions are regarded as meaningful and appropriate by members of the culture being studied.	Etic accounts and descriptions are expressed in terms of categories that are regarded as meaningful and appropriate by the community of scientific observers.
Emic knowledge may not be applicable for generating scientific theories.	Etic knowledge is obtained through direct observation or elicitation or through participants trained to be observers.
Emic knowledge achieves the status of emic by passing the test of native consensus.	Etic knowledge must be applicable for generating theories of cross-cultural differences and similarities.
Emic descriptions describe what is culturally meaningful, rather than what is theoretically significant.	Etic descriptions do not have to be meaningful or appropriate to native informants to be deemed valid.

mud and break their legs. Water buffalo have no such problems and are thus preferred over oxen to prepare the fields for planting. The emics of the situation are that every calf has the "right to live" regardless of its sex. But the etics of the situation are that cattle sex ratios are systematically adjusted to the needs of the local ecology and economy through preferential male "bovicide." Although the unwanted male calves are not slaughtered, many are more or less starved to death by selectively restricting their feed.

The comparison of etic and emic versions of culture gives rise to some of the most important and intriguing problems in anthropology. Of course, emic and etic descriptions need not always differ from each other. And even in this case, if one gets to know Indian farmers very well, some of them may reluctantly discuss the need they feel to cull animals of the unwanted sex. But only an etic perspective can lead one to understand why in northern India, where oxen are used to cultivate the soil, etic bovicide is practiced more against female than male cattle (resulting in some states in an adult cattle sex ratio of over 200 oxen for every 100 cows), whereas in the wet rice region of southern India, just the opposite takes place—bovicide is practiced against male cattle. Sex ratios are thus systematically adjusted to the needs of the local economy. (See Chapter 16 for more discussion on the emics and etics of cattle in India.)

Four viewpoints (Box 2.3) can be formulated from the data collected in southern India (Harris 1979b:38).

BOX 2.3 | **Four Views of Cattle Slaughter in Southern India**

The farmers' emic mental view confirming the rule against the slaughter of cattle.	"All calves have the right to life."
The farmers' emic view of their behavior.	"No calves are ever starved to death."
The observer's etic inference of the farmers' mental beliefs based on the lopsided sex ratios.	"Let the male calves starve to death when feed is scarce."
The observer's etic view of the farmers' behavior based on the statistics of calf sex ratios.	"Male calves are starved to death."

The Universal Pattern

Anthropologists agree that every culture has patterns of behavior and thoughts related to making a living from the environment, raising children, organizing the exchange of goods and labor, living in domestic groups and larger communities, and expressing the creative, playful, aesthetic, moral, and intellectual aspects of human life. However, anthropologists do not agree on how many subdivisions of these categories should be recognized or what priority each should be given when it comes to doing research.

To compare one culture with another, the anthropologist must collect and organize cultural data in relation to cross-culturally recurrent aspects or parts of the sociocultural system.

 The **universal pattern** is a set of categories that is comprehensive enough to afford logical and classificatory organization for a range of traits and institutions that can be observed in all cultural systems.

In this book, we will use a universal pattern consisting of three major divisions: infrastructure, structure, and superstructure (Box 2.4.)

1. **Infrastructure** consists of the technologies and productive and reproductive activities that bear directly on the provision of food and shelter, protection against illness, and the satisfaction of sexual and other basic human needs and drives. Infrastructure also embraces the limitations and opportunities placed on production and reproduction by a society's natural habitat, as well as the means employed to increase or decrease population growth. For example, a sketch of the infrastructure of modern-day Japan might include Japan's electronic computerized and robotized information and manufacturing economy, its dependence on imported raw materials, the effectiveness of its public health system, its reliance on abortion as a means of population regulation, and the extensive damage that has been done to the natural habitat by various forms of industrial pollution and economic growth.

2. **Structure** consists of the groups and organizations present in every society that allocate, regulate, and exchange goods, labor, and information. The primary focus of some groups is on kinship and family relations; others provide the political and economic organization for the whole society; still others provide the organization for religious rituals and various intellectual activities. To continue to use Japan as an example, structural features would include a domestic economy based on small, male

Body Language
People have unconscious cultural rules for maintaining space between them when greeting and conversing.

BOX 2.4 | Components of the Universal Pattern*

Infrastructure

Mode of Production
The technology and the practices employed for expanding or limiting basic subsistence production, especially the production of food and other forms of energy, given the restrictions and opportunities provided by a specific technology interacting with a specific habitat.

- Technology of subsistence
- Technoenvironmental relationships
- Ecosystems
- Work patterns

Mode of Reproduction
The technology and the practices employed for expanding, limiting, and maintaining population size.

- Fertility, natality, mortality
- Nurturance of infants
- Medical control of demographic patterns
- Contraception, abortion, infanticide

Structure

Domestic Economy
The organization of reproduction and basic production, exchange, and consumption within camps, houses, apartments, or other domestic settings.

- Family structure
- Domestic division of labor
- Domestic socialization, enculturation, education
- Age and gender roles
- Domestic discipline, hierarchies, and sanctions

Political Economy
The organization of reproduction, production, exchange, and consumption within and between bands, villages, chiefdoms, states, and empires.

- Political organizations, factions, clubs, associations, and corporations
- Division of labor, taxation, tribute
- Political socialization, enculturation, education
- Law and order
- Class, caste, urban, and rural hierarchies
- Discipline, police and military control
- War

Superstructure

- Art, music, dance, literature, advertising
- Values
- Meaning
- Symbols
- Religious rituals, myths, and beliefs
- Sports, games, hobbies
- Science

*Remember, each of these components can be viewed from an emic, etic, behavioral, or mental perspective.

wage-earner, urban-dwelling nuclear families; a political economy that is characterized by global corporations regulated and assisted by the state; and a moderately democratic parliament. It would also include organizations such as universities, Buddhist temples, and art museums.

Obviously the focus of a given social group may overlap with the focus of another. Multinational corporations, for example, do more than produce and sell commodities; they also foster or create beliefs about free trade and consumerism. Gov-

ernments may contribute to the regulation of every aspect of social life; established churches may regulate sexual and reproductive behavior as well as spread religious beliefs. To study these connections, we must begin with some preliminary map of a society's structure, based on the primary focus of its most important groups.

3. **Superstructure** consists of the behavior and thought devoted to symbolic, ideational, artistic, playful, religious, and intellectual endeavors as well as all the mental and emic aspects of a cul-

A.

B.

C.

D.

Rules for Breaking Rules

*Cultural behavior cannot be predicted from knowledge of a simple set of rules. In **B.**, a handicapped driver is taking down the license number of a car that has parked against the rule. **A.**, **C.**, and **D.** tell their own sad stories.*

ture's infrastructure and structure. This would include, in the case of Japan, such features as the Shinto and Buddhist religions; distinctive forms of Japanese painting, theater, and poetry; penchants for baseball and wrestling; and a belief in teamwork as a source of competitive advantage.

The Diversity of Anthropological Theories

The kinds of research that anthropologists carry out and the kinds of conclusions they stress are greatly influenced by the basic assumptions they make about the causes of cultural evolution. Basic assumptions made by anthropologists of different theoretical persuasions are called *research strategies* or *paradigms*.

No textbook can conceivably be written so as to represent all the current research strategies with bias toward none and equal coverage for all. In this book, we have made a conscious effort to include alternative viewpoints on controversial issues. However, the research strategy followed most closely is that of cultural materialism.

Cultural Materialism

The point of view followed throughout is known as **cultural materialism**.

Cultural materialism is a research strategy that holds that the primary task of cultural anthropology is to give scientific causal explanations for the differences and similarities in thought and behavior found among human groups.

Cultural materialism approaches anthropology as a science that seeks to understand and explain sociocultural phenomena. The goal of scientific research is to account for observable entities and events and their relationship to one another by using a theory that is subject to correction and improvement through empirical testing (Harris 1979b:26). Scientific theories are accepted in accordance with their relative powers of predictability. Because science cannot guarantee absolute truth, free of error, we can only assert that our predictions are probable rather than certain. *Probabilistic determinism* seeks to make generalizations that are expected to be applicable more often than not.

Materialist theories aim to explain the probable causes of sociocultural differences and similarities by giving theoretical priority to infrastructure.

Cultural materialism makes the assumption that sociocultural explanations can best be carried out by studying the material constraints and opportunities to which human existence is exposed. Material constraints and opportunities arise from the need to produce food, shelter, tools, and machines and to reproduce human populations under conditions set by biology and the environment. They are called *material* constraints and opportunities in order to distinguish them from constraints or opportunities presented by ideas and other mental or spiritual aspects of a society's superstructure, such as values, religion, and art.

For cultural materialists, the most likely causes of variation in the mental or spiritual aspects of human life are the variations in a society's infrastructure that refer to how people make a living and maintain a healthy population in a given environment.

A fundamental assumption is that human beings have the capacity to adopt a wide range of beliefs and behaviors, and that these patterns are molded by the influence of culture. To understand how culture molds behavior and beliefs, cultural materialism assumes the **principle of primacy of infrastructure** (Harris 1994).

The **principle of primacy of infrastructure** states that infrastructural variables are more determinative of the evolution of sociocultural systems.

But this does not mean that belief systems do not affect social and economic changes. In looking for causal explanations, this approach begins with infrastructural determinants and tries to identify how ecological, technological, and reproductive factors affect how people make a living and meet survival needs. It is also important to note that cultural materialism does not predict the behavior of individuals or the peculiarities of ideology; it is concerned with aggregates of individuals within a cultural framework (Lett 1997).

Thus infrastructure, structure, and superstructure are not equally effective in determining the retention or extinction of sociocultural innovations:

- Innovations arising from the infrastructural level (industrial robots, for example) are likely to be preserved and passed on to future generations if they enhance the efficiency of productive and reproductive processes.
- Adaptive infrastructural innovations are likely to be selected even if they do not conform with the

preexisting structural and superstructural components (unionized, labor-intensive assembly lines; fear that robots will cause unemployment).

- In contrast, innovations originating in the structural or superstructural sectors (for example, new religions) are likely to cause substantial changes in other sectors, but it is unlikely that they will be retained over time if they are not compatible with material constraints (that is, if they substantially impede the system's ability to satisfy basic human needs and drives).

This approach does not mean that the mental and spiritual aspects of cultures are somehow less significant or less important than production, reproduction, ecology, and other infrastructural aspects of sociocultural systems. Moral values, religious beliefs, and aesthetic standards are in one sense the most significant and most distinctly human of all our attributes. Their importance is clearly evident. The issue that cultural materialism addresses is why a particular human population has one set of values, beliefs, and aesthetic standards, whereas others have both similar and different sets of values, beliefs, and aesthetic standards. See Figure 2.1 for a review of the assumptions that underlie cultural materialism.

Anthropology's Origins

The discipline of anthropology originated in the late nineteenth century as Western colonists and travelers began to write about the briefs and customs of native people to make sense of the so-called savage ways of life. By studying these non-Western "primitives," scholars tried to reconstruct the stages through which human culture progressed and understand how natives are different from civilized folk.

Nineteenth-Century Evolutionism and Social Darwinism

The idea of cultural progress was the forerunner of the concept of cultural evolution that dominated theories of culture during the nineteenth century.

According to *evolutionism,* cultures were usually regarded as moving through various stages of development according to different levels of rational knowledge, ending up with something resembling the Euro-American lifestyle.

It was believed that evolution led from small communities of people who knew each other's faces to large, impersonal societies; from slave to military to industrial societies; from animism to polytheism to monotheism; from magic to science; from female-dominated horticultural societies to male-dominated agricultural societies; and from many other hypothetical earlier and simpler stages to later and more complex ones. One of the most influential schemes was that proposed by the American anthropologist Lewis Henry Morgan (1877) in his book *Ancient Society.*

Morgan divided the evolution of culture into three main stages: savagery, barbarism, and civilization. These stages had figured in evolutionary schemes as early as the sixteenth century, but Morgan subdivided them and filled them out in greater detail and with greater reference to ethnographic evidence than had anyone else.

The success of Charles Darwin's biological theory of the survival of the fittest (he called it *natural selection*) greatly enhanced the popularity of the view that social and cultural evolution also depended on biological evolution.

After the publication of Darwin's (1859) *On the Origin of Species,* a movement known as *social Darwinism* appeared, based on the belief that cultural and biological progress depended on the free play of competitive forces in the struggle of individual against individual, nation against nation, and race against race.

The most influential social Darwinist was Herbert Spencer, who went so far as to advocate the end of all attempts to provide charity and relief for the unemployed and impoverished classes and the so-called backward races on the grounds that such assistance interfered with the operation of the law of the survival of the fittest and merely prolonged the agony and deepened the misery of those who were unfit.

Marxist Evolutionism

Although the writings and thoughts of Karl Marx were diametrically opposed to social Darwinism, Marxism was also heavily influenced by the prevailing nineteenth-century notions of cultural evolution

Basic Assumptions of Cultural Materialism

Cultural materialism assumes that the various parts of society are interrelated (the universal pattern) and that when one part of the sociocultural system changes, other parts will also change. *Infrastructure*, however, has theoretical priority as a research strategy. Cultural materialism advocates that the first step in understanding a widespread practice or belief is to look at infrastructural practices.

Infrastructure refers to how people make a living without depredating the environment and without causing destructive increases or decreases in population size (how populations strike a balance between population size and the consumption of energy from a finite environment under a given technology).

Infrastructure is divided into two parts:

- The mode of *production* (derived from Karl Marx—but without dialects) relates to people's ability to utilize natural resources and technology to satisfy basic needs.

- The mode of *reproduction* (derived from Thomas Malthus but without the pessimism of ultimate doom) relates to the behaviors that stabilize population growth (or decline) in relation to the availability of the food supply.

Structure refers to the organized patterns of social life involved in the economic processes that allocate labor and the products of labor to individuals and groups.

Structure is divided into two parts:

- The *domestic economy* refers to household activities, family relations, and the division of labor by age and sex. This includes domestic hierarchies, discipline, sanctions, voluntary organizations, and some religious groups.

- The *political economy* consists of groups and organizations that regulate production, reproduction, consumption, exchange, and defense between groups. These groups include political organizations, redistribution organizations, education, taxation, stratified hierarchies, and the military.

Superstructure refers to ideational, normative, and symbolic processes that influence the patterned ways members of society think, conceptualize, express, and evaluate behavior.

Superstructure is divided into two parts:

- *Behavioral superstructure* includes artistic expression (art, music, dance, narratives), rituals, sports and games, and science.

- *Mental superstructure* refers to beliefs such as ideology, kinship, ethnobotany, subsistence lore, ethnic and national identity, magic and religion, and taboos.

There is feedback among the components of the universal pattern.

- *Change:* The most effective sociocultural change releases more, rather than less, energy from the environment and affects individual cost–benefit decisions regarding work, family size, and living standards.

- While infrastructure is considered to have primary influence on sociocultural process, social structure and superstructure are not mere reflections of infrastructure. Changes in structure and superstructure may not always be compatible with infrastructure, but they are unlikely to be retained over time if they impede the efficiency of the infrastructural process.

Figure 2.1
Basic Assumptions of Cultural Materialism

and progress. Marx saw cultures passing through the stages of primitive communism, slave society, feudalism, capitalism, and communism. Moreover, like many of his contemporaries, Marx stressed the importance of the role of struggle in achieving cultural evolution and progress.

All history, according to Marx, is the outcome of the struggle between social classes for control over the means of production.

The proletarian class, brought into existence by capitalism, was destined to abolish private property and bring about the final stage of history: communism.

On reading Morgan's *Ancient Society,* Marx and his associate Friedrich Engels thought they had found a confirmation of their idea that during the first stage of cultural evolution, there was no private property and that the successive stages of cultural progress had been brought about by changes in the mode of production.

Morgan's *Ancient Society* provided the basis for Engels's (1884) *Origin of the Family, Private Property and the State,* which until the middle of the twentieth century served as a cornerstone of Marxist anthropology.

Historical Particularism

Early in the twentieth century, anthropologists took the lead in challenging the evolutionary schemes and doctrines of both the social Darwinists and the Marxist communists. In the United States, Franz Boas and his students developed the dominant theoretical position, which was known as *historical particularism.* According to Boas (1948), nineteenth-century attempts to discover the laws of cultural evolution and to schematize the stages of cultural progress were founded on insufficient empirical evidence. Boas argued that each culture has its own long and unique history.

To understand or explain a particular culture, the best one can do is to reconstruct the unique path it has followed.

The emphasis on the uniqueness of each culture amounted to a denial of the prospects for a generalizing science of culture. Another important feature of historical particularism is the notion of cultural relativism, which holds that there are no higher or lower forms of culture. Such terms as savagery, barbarism, and civilization merely express the ethnocentrism of people who think that their way of life is more normal than those of other peoples.

To counter the speculative "armchair" theories and ethnocentrism of the evolutionists, Boas and his students also stressed the importance of carrying out ethnographic fieldwork among non-Western peoples. As the ethnographic reports and monographs produced by the historical particularists multiplied, it became clear that the evolutionists had indeed misrepresented or overlooked the complexities of so-called primitive cultures and that they had grossly underestimated the intelligence and ingenuity of the non-Caucasoid, non-European peoples of the world.

Boas's most important achievement was his demonstration that race, language, and culture are independent aspects of the human condition.

Since both similar and dissimilar cultures and languages are found among people of the same race, the social Darwinist notion that biological and cultural evolution were part of a single process had no merit.

British Functionalism and Structural Functionalism

In Great Britain, the dominant early twentieth-century research strategies are known as *functionalism* and *structural functionalism.* According to the functionalists, the main task of cultural anthropology is to describe the recurrent functions of customs and institutions, rather than to explain the origins of cultural differences and similarities.

According to one of the leading *functionalists,* Bronislaw Malinowski, cultural institutions function to meet the basic physical and psychological needs of people.

Once we have understood the function of an institution, argued Malinowski, then we can understand how cultural beliefs and practices contribute to the smooth functioning of society.

A. R. Radcliffe-Brown (1935) was the principal advocate of structural functionalism. According to Radcliffe-Brown, the main task of cultural anthropology was even narrower than that proposed by Malinowski. Whereas Malinowski emphasized the contribution of cultural elements to the biological and psychological welfare of individuals, Radcliffe-Brown and the structural functionalists stressed the contribution of the social structure and kinship to the maintenance of the equilibrium of society.

Thus, the *functionalists* and *structural functionalists* evaded the question of the general, recurrent causes of cultural differences, while emphasizing the general, recurrent functional reasons for similarities.

Culture and Personality

In turning away from the nineteenth-century notions of causality and evolution, many anthropologists, influenced by the writings of Sigmund Freud, attempted to interpret cultures in psychological terms. The writings of Freud and the antievolutionism of Boas set the stage for the development of the approach known as *culture and personality*. Two of Boas's most famous students, Ruth Benedict and Margaret Mead, pioneered the development of culture and personality theories. Many advocates of the culture and personality approach stress the importance of early childhood experiences in the formation of a basic or modal type of adult personality or national character.

Some *culture and personality* theories attempt to explain how shared experiences produce a common basic personality that creates and sustains cultural differences and similarities.

In general, however, culture and personality advocates do not deal with the problem of why the beliefs and practices that mold particular personality types or national characters occur in some cultures but not in others. They have also been faulted for overgeneralizing about cultural patterns based on stereotypes and ignoring the variations among the people they study.

Cultural Ecology

After World War II, increasing numbers of anthropologists became dissatisfied with the antievolutionism and lack of broad generalizations and causal explanations characteristic of the first half of the century. Under the influence of Leslie White (1949), an effort was launched to reexamine the works of the nineteenth-century evolutionists such as Lewis Henry Morgan, to correct their ethnographic errors, and to identify their positive contribution to the development of a science of culture.

Leslie White was a pioneer in postulating that the overall direction of cultural evolution was largely determined by the quantities of energy that could be captured and put to work per capita per year (see p. 74).

At the same time, Julian Steward (1955) laid the basis for the development of the approach known as *cultural ecology*, which stressed the interaction between natural conditions such as soils, rainfall, and temperature with cultural factors such as technology and economy as the cause of both cultural differences and similarities.

Julian Steward was interested in discovering general laws of culture. He proposed that cultures in similar environments would tend to follow the same developmental sequences and would develop similar features in response to environmental challenges.

According to Steward, cultural features most closely associated with subsistence practices were termed the *cultural core*. These culture types were then sorted into a hierarchy of political complexity: band, tribe, chiefdom, and state.

Biological Anthropology and Evolutionary Psychology

Biological anthropology is a research strategy that attempts to explain some sociocultural differences and similarities in terms of *natural selection*. It is based on a refinement of natural selection known as the *principle of inclusive fitness*. This principle states that natural selection favors traits that spread an individual's genes by increasing not only the number of an individual's offspring but also the number of offspring of close relatives, such as brothers and sisters, who carry many of the same genes.

Biological anthropology holds that evolutionary processes produce change that helps us understand why organisms develop different adaptive behaviors in different environments.

Selection does not necessarily bring about a one-to-one correlation between genes and behavior but does between genes and tendencies to behave in certain ways rather than others. For example, evolutionary anthropologists hold that the tendency for humans to forage in a manner that optimizes energy produced per unit of time invested is selected because it maximizes reproductive success (Lewontin et al. 1984; E. O. Wilson 1975, 1978).

Evolutionary psychology is centered on the idea that human behavior and thought processes are a result of natural selection because the neural framework of the brain evolved to solve problems faced during our species' evolutionary history.

Evolutionary psychologists believe the key to understanding the modern mind is to realize that its circuits were not designed to solve day-to-day problems of modern Americans—they were designed to solve the day-to-day problems of our hunter-gatherer ancestors.

It is believed that the neural circuits of the brain were designed through natural selection to help our hunter-gatherer ancestors survive better in harsh environments and produce viable offspring. Characteristics such as avoidance of disease-causing agents, selection of mates with good genes, and defense against aggression helped people survive and were consequently passed on to future generations.

Symbolic and Interpretive Anthropology

Symbolic anthropologists view culture as a mental phenomenon and examine how people create and understand reality.

Symbolic anthropologists view public *symbols* and actions as a manifestation of culture that is formulated through the construction of reality.

Clifford Geertz analyzed culture as an organized collection of symbolic systems that are acted out in public displays. The interpretation and analysis of these public symbols is intuitive and involves "thick description," which uncovers the layers of meaning of an event (1973:6). Another pioneer of symbolic and interpretive anthropology, Victor Turner (1967), viewed ritual symbols as instruments for maintaining social order. Ritual symbols are essential in renewing social order because they "instigate social action."

Because the interpretation of cultural symbols is highly speculative, symbolic anthropology does not provide a theoretical framework for analyzing cultures universally. It lacks a methodology for explaining cultural symbols and critics claim the credibility of symbolic interpretation is closer to literary criticism, based on the explanatory skills of the anthropologist, rather than social science.

Postmodernism

Mention must also be made of the fact that many anthropologists are known as *postmodernists,* who challenge the discipline and reject all general causal viewpoints, holding that the chief aim of ethnography ought to be the study and interpretation of the emics of different cultures—their world views, symbols, values, religions, philosophies, and systems of meanings. During the 1980s, these approaches grew in popularity and were characterized by rejection of the distinction between the observer and observed, etics and emics, and science and nonscience.

Postmodernists question whether anthropology is or should be a science. They believe that knowledge is shaped by culture, and therefore anthropologists cannot be unbiased in their research.

One recent manifestation of this line of development is called *deconstruction.* It focuses on the hidden intentions and unexpressed biases of the author of an ethnography, rather than on the question of what the culture being described is really like.

Because postmodernists believe that anthropologists cannot be objective in their research, they focus on self-revelation and the interpretation of their own personal experiences (and the viewpoints of other unheard voices) in a given culture.

Although postmodernists make valid points about the need to expose biases and prejudices in scientific descriptions, their flat rejection of scientific truth as a goal of ethnography results in fragmented, contradictory, and essentially nihilistic notions about the human condition.

See Table 2.1 for an overview of all the previously discussed anthropological theories and their proponents.

SUMMARY
and *Questions to Think About*

1. Cultures, as defined in this book, consist of socially acquired ways or traditions of thought, feeling, and behavior.

2. Cultures maintain continuity by means of the process of enculturation. In studying cultural differences, one must guard against the habit of mind called *ethnocentrism,* which arises from a failure to appreciate the far-reaching effects of enculturation on human life. Enculturation, however, cannot explain how and why cultures change.

Table 2.1

Anthropological Theories and Their Proponents

Theory	Assumption	Advocates
Nineteenth-century evolutionism and social Darwinism	All societies evolve through a series of stages as a result of rational thinking. It was assumed that cultural evolution depended on the principle of natural selection.	Tylor, Morgan, Spenser
Marxist evolutionism	Stresses the role of class struggle in bringing about changes in the mode of production.	Marx, Engels
Historical particularism	Stresses the uniqueness of each culture and the need for in-depth ethnographic fieldwork.	Boas, Kroeber
British functionalism and structural functionalism	The task of anthropology is to understand how cultural institutions meet the needs of individuals and contribute to the functioning of society.	Malinowski, Radcliffe-Brown
Culture and personality	Anthropology's task is to show the relationship among early childhood experiences in creating a common personality that impacts cultural variables.	Benedict, Mead
Cultural ecology	Cultures evolve in direct proportion to their capacity to harness energy; cultures in similar environments have similar features in response to environmental challenges.	White, Steward
Cultural materialism	Theoretical priority is given to material conditions (infrastructure) in explaining cultural differences and similarities.	Harris
Biological anthropology and evolutionary psychology	Cultural traits are selected if they maximize an individual's reproductive success; the neural circuits of our minds are the product of natural selection and designed during the course of human evolutionary history.	Cosmedies and Tooby, Boyd, Richarson
Symbolic and interpretive anthropology	Public symbols and rituals represent important aspects of culture.	Geertz, Turner
Postmodernism	Interpretation is introspective and a form of individualized understanding based on narrative and listening to and talking with others; theory and methodology are invalid because objectivity is an illusion.	Foucault, Marcus, Fisher

3. Not all cultural recurrences in different generations result from enculturation. Some result from reactions to similar conditions or situations.

4. Whereas enculturation denotes the process by which culture is transmitted from one generation to the next, diffusion denotes the process by which culture is transmitted from one society to another. Diffusion, like enculturation, is not automatic and cannot stand alone as an explanatory principle. Neighboring societies can have both highly similar as well as highly dissimilar cultures.

5. Anthropologists use many kinds of methods for studying cultures, but they are best known for participant observation. Unlike other social animals, which possess only rudimentary cultures,

human beings can describe their thoughts and behaviors from their own points of view.

6. In studying human cultures, therefore, one must make explicit whether it is the native participant's point of view or the observer's point of view that is being expressed. These are the emic and etic points of view, respectively.

7. Both mental and behavioral aspects of culture can be approached from either the emic or etic point of view. Emic and etic versions of reality sometimes differ markedly but usually correspond to some degree.

8. All cultures share a universal pattern. The universal pattern, as defined in this book, consists of three main components: infrastructure, structure, and superstructure. These components in turn

consist, respectively, of the modes of production and reproduction, the domestic and political economy, and the creative, expressive, aesthetic, and intellectual aspects of human life. Such categories are essential for the organization of research and differ according to the research strategy one adopts.

9. Anthropology encompasses many alternative research strategies; the one followed in this book is cultural materialism. The aim of this strategy is to discover the causes of the differences and similarities in thought and behavior that characterize particular human populations by giving theoretical priority to infrastructure—a society's mode of production and reproduction.

Questions to Think About

1. Why is it important to distinguish between behavioral and ideological aspects of culture?

2. Why do anthropologists use the viewpoint of cultural relativism to understand cultures that are different from their own?

3. What does it mean to say that "all research is biased"? How can science try to overcome culture-bound biases?

4. Why is it important to distinguish between emic and etic perspectives when describing cultural phenomena?

5. Why does cultural materialism attempt to explain the probable causes of sociocultural differences and similarities by giving causal priority to infrastructure (the mode of production and reproduction)?

6. Under what conditions are ideological innovations most likely to cause changes in other sectors that will be retained over time?

THROUGH THE LENS
of Cultural Materialism

Conformity and Conflict • Reading Three

Shakespeare in the Bush

Laura Bohannan

An anthropologist retells the story of *Hamlet* to Tiv elders in West Africa, assuming that the story is universally relevant. She discovers, however, that the Tiv interpret the story in terms of their own cultural perspective. They believe Hamlet's madness is the result of witchcraft and cannot understand why Hamlet is upset that his uncle has married his mother so soon after his father's death.

Structure

- In Tiv society, each king has several wives and many sons, whose labor is essential to prepare food for guests so that the king will be loved for his generosity. In English society, a king has one wife, many servants, and subjects who pay taxes.

- Among the Tiv, a woman must remarry quickly after her husband dies because she needs a man to provide manual labor to prepare the land for cultivation. Also, the Tiv practice polygyny, which is common in horticultural societies where women and children are responsible for planting and harvesting. In English society, a queen is not expected to remarry quickly; she is wealthy and does not require a husband to provide for her.

Superstructure

- Tiv superstructure is based on beliefs in omens and witchcraft, whereas the English believe in ghosts.

- In Tiv culture, a woman remarries quickly so she can grow crops, whereas among English royalty, it is disgraceful for a woman to remarry immediately after her husband's death.

Emic Interpretation

- The Tiv elders believe that Hamlet's madness is the result of witchcraft. There is no other way they can explain Hamlet plotting violence against a senior relative.

- The Tiv believe Hamlet should have gone to a diviner to learn the truth about how his father died and called on the elders to settle the matter.

- Ophelia's madness is also believed to result from witchcraft because the elders cannot see any other explanation for a person drowning. The Tiv believe Ophelia's brother is responsible for her death because he had many debts and wanted to profit by secretly selling her body to the witches.

- The anthropologist cannot get the Tiv to understand the concept of a ghost, a spirit of a dead person that is still on Earth. The Tiv claim that the ghost of Hamlet's father must be either an omen sent by a witch or a dead body that the witches have animated to sacrifice and eat.

Etic Interpretation

- The Tiv have different political and spiritual beliefs due to their social structure and superstructure; they cannot comprehend Hamlet's madness or why Hamlet is upset that his mother married his father's brother.

- The anthropologist is unable to prove her assumption that "human nature is pretty much the same the whole world over." The Tiv elders' refusal to accept her version of *Hamlet* and their reinterpretation of the story shows that the Tiv cannot comprehend the story as written because of differences in family structure and spiritual beliefs.

THROUGH THE LENS
of Cultural Materialism

Conformity and Conflict • Reading Seven

How to Ask for a Drink

James P. Spradley and Brenda J. Mann

Emic and etic methodology is used to study speech events at Brady's Bar.

Emic Perspective

Informants (employees and regulars) recognize and report on a number of speech acts, enabling the anthropologists to construct a folk taxonomy for ways people normally ask for a drink.

Etic Perspective

The anthropologists observe and record speech acts used in the bar. These observations provide additional information on how people ask for a drink as well as the "rules for breaking rules."

Example: To avoid being carded, two underage boys enter before the bouncer goes on duty and sit at the bar. Each of them confidently asks for a beer and once served, they move to table where they later order another round. The waitress, who would normally cards minors, does not override the bartender's decision to let them buy drinks.

How people are served depends on who they are (whether they are regulars or not) and their performance in asking for a drink. Regulars receive drinks without even having to ask; they take their place at the bar or table and a drink appears. If they have the same drink repeatedly, they may receive a drink on the house. Underage regulars are not carded whereas "off the street" customers avoid being carded by knowing how to perform. They ask for a drink in a manner that changes their status from "underage off the street customer" to someone who has a right to drink at the bar.

CHAPTER 3

THE
EVOLUTION
OF THE
CAPACITY
FOR CULTURE

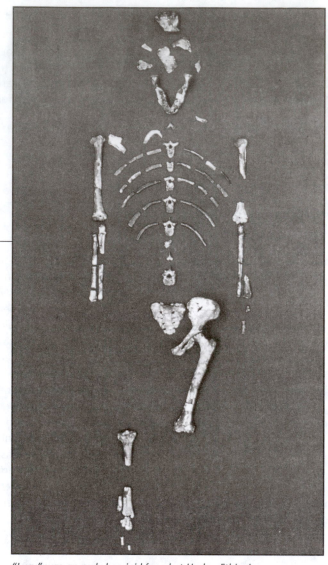

"Lucy" was an early hominid found at Hadar, Ethiopia.

Human culture consists of the patterned, socially acquired traditions of thought and behavior found in human societies. In this chapter we will explore the capacity for culture as it evolved from rudimentary beginnings among our ape-like ancestors. Once these ancestors passed certain biological thresholds under the influence of natural selection, cultural behavior underwent its own form of evolution, resulting in an increasingly complex social life and an increasing dependence of human beings on cultural practices for survival. This leads to the question, How much capacity for culture exists among nonhuman species? To answer this question, we will examine evidence for the use of tools and language among chimpanzees and other primates—the species that most resemble humans. A point to be emphasized is that the biological processes that account for biological evolution and the learning-based processes that account for cultural evolution are quite distinct, even though biological evolution shaped the learning processes that made cultural "takeoff" possible.

Genes and Natural Selection

The principal process responsible for biological evolution is known as *natural selection*. The theory was proposed by Charles Darwin in 1859 after spending five years studying the flora and fauna of South America and the Galapagos Islands. Darwin noticed that finches on different islands had different beaks that corresponded with different environments and feeding habits. They appeared to have come from the same ancestor, yet the different configurations of their beaks were suited to their diverse feeding habits. Darwin believed that a similar selective process takes place in nature; some members of a species are wiped out by nature's challenges, while others have certain qualities that make them less likely to die. The survivors will reproduce, while the badly adapted ones will die and gradually disappear from the population.

 Natural selection refers to changes in the frequencies of certain genetic traits in populations due to the differential reproductive success among individuals.

The theory of natural selection is based on three basic postulates:

1. All species are capable of producing offspring at a faster rate than they can increase the food supply and other necessities of life.
2. Variation among organisms affects their ability to survive and reproduce.

3. This variation is genetically transmitted from parents to offspring. Advantageous traits that are inherited by offspring will become more common in the population. Less favorable traits will cause offspring to die before they reach reproductive age and will eventually disappear.

Over time, those organisms that can better survive and reproduce in a given environment will increase their reproductive success and eventually will replace organisms that are less well adapted.

 Reproductive success refers to the number of offspring an individual rears to reproductive age.

Reproductive success is correlated with traits that are resistant to selective pressures. These include the organism's ability to resist disease, to gain or hold territory more securely, to obtain energy in larger or more dependable amounts to avoid or escape predators, and to reproduce more efficiently and dependably. Natural selection occurs when there is a mutation in DNA (genes) that is beneficial to survival. This trait is passed on to the individual's offspring, which in turn increases their survival. Natural selection can increase the frequency of the favored *genotypes* (types of genes) in a few tens of generations. Individuals who possess favorable traits will contribute more offspring to the next generation, so that over time these traits will become more common in the population.

The power of natural selection to raise the frequency of even a rare gene variant can be seen in the evolution of penicillin-resistant strains of bacteria. The variants conferring resistance are present in normal populations of bacteria but in only a small percentage of individuals. As a result of the differential reproductive success of such individuals in the presence of the antibiotic, however, the rare resistant genotype soon multiplies and becomes the most common genotype. So far, medical science has been able to develop new antibiotics to take the place of the ones that have lost their effectiveness. But the race between the effects of natural selection and the ingenuity of medical science is a close one and full of potential danger for humankind.

Natural Selection and the "Struggle for Survival"

Charles Darwin and Alfred Wallace formulated the basic principles of how **biological evolution** could result from natural selection. Under the influence of the prevailing philosophy of economic competition, however, both Darwin and Wallace accepted Thomas Malthus's concept of a "struggle for survival" as the main source of selection for reproductive success. Thus, in the nineteenth century, natural selection was pictured incorrectly as the direct struggle among individuals for scarce resources and sexual partners. Even more erroneously, it was interpreted as consisting of aggressive behaviors such as organisms of the same species preying on and destroying one another. Nothing in Darwin's theory, however, holds that successful competition for resources must necessarily consist of aggressive encounters.

Today, biologists recognize that natural selection favors cooperation within species as much as it favors competition.

Although within-species killing and competition sometimes do play a role in biological evolution, the factors promoting differential reproductive success do not necessarily relate to an organism's ability to destroy other members of its own population or to prevent them from obtaining nutrients, space, and mates.

In social species, the perpetuation of an individual's genes often depends as much on the reproductive success of its close relatives as on its own survival and reproduction. Many social insects even have altruistic sterile "castes" that assure their own genetic success by rearing the progeny of their fertile siblings.

Altruism is the act of maintaining the well-being of an individual's close relatives and their offspring to ensure their survival so that their genes will be continued in the next generation.

As we will see, primates, although capable of murderous violence, also perform complex altruistic behaviors that are beneficial to both their own reproductive success as well as that of close relatives.

Natural Selection and Behavior

Natural selection shapes not only anatomy and physiology but also behavior. Traits are adaptive when they present a selective advantage in relation to a particular set of environmental circumstances. An adaptive strategy leads to biological or behavioral adjustments that are selected for because they contribute to improving the health, well-being, and reproductive success of the innovators.

Adaptation refers to biological and cultural traits that improve opportunities for individuals of a population to survive and reproduce.

Adaptation is used in several different contexts, all of which refer to an organism's accommodation to its environment. One form of adaptation involves the acclimatization to a sudden change in environment. Another kind of adaptation occurs during the slow course of evolution and is the result of the competition among individuals of a particular species over many generations in response to ever-changing environmental conditions. Third is cultural adaptation, which is unique to humans and based on their capacity to produce and reproduce culture from one generation to the next. **Cultural adaptation** refers to the knowledge and behavior that enable people to survive and thrive in a given environment. Cultural adaptation balances the needs of a population and the potential of the environment under a given level of technology.

Science recognizes that in every organism, behavior is the outcome of a highly complex combination of factors resulting from the interaction between genes and environment. An organism behaves in a particular way because of its genetic makeup and the characteristics of its environment. Nevertheless, we can say that behaviors range from extremely stereotyped, inflexible responses that are determined by genetic factors to those that are highly flexible and dependent on learning. For example, when they try to avoid a hungry bird, some species of fruit flies fly upward and others downward. Some wasps lay their eggs in a particular species of caterpillar and in none other. Genes also largely determine the mating rituals of fish, the web building of spiders, the feeding of queen bees by workers, and countless other behavioral expressions of drives and instincts characteristic of different animal species. These behaviors evolve as a result of copying errors (mutations) in the replication of genotypes. The wasp's preference for one species of caterpillar, for example, was an error that was selected for because it increased the wasp's reproductive success. Thus a new pattern of behavior, based on a new genotype, became part of the wasp's instinctual program.

Although it is very useful for organisms to be equipped with a program of detailed behavioral responses encoded in their genes, there is another type of behavior that is not programmed in the genes and that has many advantages. This is behavior that is learned and programmed in the organism's neural network and brain. For example, seagulls learn to recognize and follow fishing boats; they learn the locations of fast-food restaurants, town dumps, and other sources of garbage; and they learn all these behaviors without a single change in their genotype. Although the ability to learn to locate novel foods is genetically encoded, the behavior itself is not encoded in the genes or the genes of their offspring. Future generations of seagulls can acquire this knowledge only by learning it on their own.

The ability to acquire new patterns of behavior through learning is a fundamental feature of all multi-celled animals.

The capacity for learning has been widely selected for because it leads to a more flexible and opportunistic pattern of behavior than instinctual programs. Learning enables individuals to adjust to or take advantage of novel opportunities (such as feeding on french fries spilled in parking lots) without having to wait for the appearance and selection of mutations.

Nonhuman Culture

Selection for increased learning capacity set the stage for the emergence of culture.

The capacity for learning has depended on the evolution of larger and more complex brains and of more intelligent species. The great evolutionary novelty of culture is that capabilities and habits are acquired through *learning,* which is socially transmitted, rather than through the more ancient process of biological heredity. (It must be stressed, though, that actual cultural responses always depend in part on genetically predetermined capacities and predispositions.)

Many animals possess learned traditions that are passed on from one generation to the next and that can be thought of as rudimentary forms of culture. As we will see in a moment, chimpanzees and other primates possess rudimentary learned traditions. However, only among the *hominids* (members of the human family) has culture become as important a source of adaptive behavior as biological evolution based on changes in gene frequencies. Able to stand and walk erect, their hands freed entirely from locomotor and support functions, the earliest hominids probably manufactured, transported, and made effective use of tools as a primary means of subsistence. Apes, in contrast, have survived nicely with only the barest inventory of tools. Hominids, ancient or modern, have probably always depended on culture for their very existence.

Tools and Learning

Experimental approaches to behavior show that most birds and mammals, and especially monkeys and apes, are intelligent enough to learn to make and use simple tools under laboratory conditions. Under natural free-ranging conditions, however, the capacity to make and use tools is expressed less frequently. As a result of the process of natural selection, these animals have become adapted to their environment through such body parts as snouts, claws, teeth, hooves, and fangs.

Although primates are intelligent enough to make and use tools, their anatomy and normal mode of existence disincline them to develop extensive tool-using traditions.

Among monkeys and apes, the use of hands for tool use is inhibited by the importance of the forelimbs in walking, running, and climbing. That is probably why the most common tool-using behavior among many species of monkeys and apes is repelling intruders with a barrage of nuts, pine cones, branches, fruits, feces, or stones. Throwing such objects entails only a momentary loss of the ability to run or climb away if danger threatens.

Among free-ranging monkeys and apes, the most accomplished tool user is the chimpanzee. Over a period of many years, Jane Goodall and her associates have studied the behavior of a single population of free-ranging common chimpanzees in the Gombe National Park in Tanzania. They have discovered that the chimpanzees "fish" for ants and termites. Fishing for termites involves first breaking off a twig or a vine, stripping it of leaves and side branches, and then locating a suitable termite nest. Such a nest is as hard as concrete and impenetrable except for certain thinly covered tunnel entrances. The chimpanzee scratches away the thin covering and inserts the twig. The termites inside bite the end of the twig, and the chimpanzee pulls it out and licks off the termites clinging to it. Especially impressive is the fact that the chimpanzees will prepare the twig first and then carry it in their mouths from nest to nest while looking for a suitable tunnel entrance (Goodall 1986).

"Anting" provides an interesting variation on this theme. The Gombe chimps "fish" for a species of aggressive nomadic driver ant that can inflict a painful bite. On finding the temporary subterranean nest of these ants, the chimps make a tool out of a green twig and insert it into the nest entrance. Hundreds of fierce ants swarm up the twig to repel the invader. "The chimpanzee watches their progress and when the ants have almost reached its hand, the tool is quickly withdrawn. In a split second the opposite hand rapidly sweeps the length of the tool catching the ants in a jumbled mass between thumb and forefinger. These

Jane Goodall
Making friends with chimps Prof and Pax in Gombe National Park, Tanzania.

are then popped into the open, waiting mouth in one bite and chewed furiously" (McGrew et al. 1979:278).

In addition, chimpanzees can manufacture "sponges" for sopping up water from an inaccessible hollow in a tree. They strip a handful of leaves from a twig, put the leaves in their mouth, chew briefly, put the mass of leaves in the water, let them soak, put the leaves to their mouths, and suck the water off. A similar sponge is employed to dry their fur, to wipe off sticky substances, and to clean the bottoms

Chimpanzee Termiting
The chimpanzee inserts a stick carefully stripped of leaves into the nest. Then the chimpanzee withdraws the stick and licks off the termites that cling to it when it is withdrawn.

of chimpanzee babies. Gombe chimpanzees also use sticks as levers and digging tools to pry ant nests off trees and to widen the entrance of subterranean beehives.

Observers in other parts of Africa report similar types of behavior—variants of fishing for ants, dipping for termites, and digging up insect nests or prying them loose. They have watched chimpanzees pound or hammer tough-skinned fruit, seeds, and nuts with sticks and stones. The chimps of the Tai forest of the Ivory Coast open the hard shells of the panda nut with rocks that serve as hammers. They search the forest floor for a suitable hammer stone, which may weigh anywhere from 1 to 40 pounds. Then they bring the stones back in the crook of their arm, hobbling on one arm and two legs, from as far as 600 feet. They place the nuts on thick tree roots or exposed rock that serve as anvils and skillfully pound away (Boesch and Boesch 1984, 1991; Whitesides 1985). In West Senegal, chimps use stone hammers to pound open the fruits of the baobab tree (Bermejo et al. 1989).

Inspired by these and other feats of chimpanzee ingenuity, Nicholas Toth and Kathy Schick of the University of Indiana have been teaching a chimpanzee named Kanzi how to make stone tools (Gibbons 1991; Savage-Rumbaugh and Levin 1994). Ultimately, Toth and Schick hope that Kanzi will teach his fellow chimps to do the same. (See the later section headed "Apes and Language" for more about Kanzi.)

Is It Culture?

There appears to be no specific genetic information that is responsible for chimpanzee termiting and anting. True, for this behavior to occur, genetically determined capacities for learning, for manipulating objects, and for omnivorous eating must be present in the young chimpanzee. But these general biological capacities and predispositions cannot explain termiting and anting. Given nothing but groups of young chimpanzees, twigs, and termite nests, termiting and anting are unlikely to occur on their own. Thus, although chimpanzees acquire complex skills such as anting and termiting, they have only a rudimentary form of culture.

Unlike humans, chimps and other social animals do not experience continuous cultural change. Their cultures remain rudimentary and do not evolve.

Extensive studies of nonhuman culture have been carried out with Japanese macaques. Primatologists of the Primate Research Institute of Kyoto University have found a variety of customs among macaques that are based on social learning. They have even observed the process by which behavioral innovations spread from individual to individual and become part of a monkey troop's culture independently of genetic transmission.

To attract monkeys near the shore for easier observation, Kyoto researchers set sweet potatoes on the beach. One day a young female began to wash the sand from the sweet potatoes by plunging them in a small brook that ran through the beach. This washing behavior spread throughout the group. Nine years later, 80 to 90 percent of the animals were washing

Japanese Monkey Culture
A female monkey of a Koshima troop washing a sweet potato.

their sweet potatoes, some in the brook, others in the sea (Itani 1961; Itani and Nishimura 1973; Miyadi 1967).

The limitation of primate learning is that it generally does not allow for the development of cumulative knowledge or complex culture. New behaviors such as potato washing are simple enough to be learned independently through trial and error by each macaque, and it takes a long time for the behavior to spread through the group. It is unlikely that a macaque from one group could teach macaques from another group, where they have not been exposed to the same conditions, to wash potatoes. Primate-learned behavior is individually acquired through a process of trial and error that leads to successful discovery (Galef 1992; Tomasello 1994).

Jane Goodall (1971:161) describes young chimpanzees as they learn tool-use techniques to "fish for termites." They learn through trial and error; each chimp invents the technique anew as his interest is drawn to the activity. At about 18 to 22 months they begin to termite on their own. At first their behavior is clumsy and inefficient. Novices often retrieve discarded sticks and attempt to use them on their own. They become proficient at termiting when they are about 3 years old. Fishing for ants, with the risk of being bitten, takes longer to learn; the youngest chimp to achieve proficiency was about 4 years old (McGrew 1977:282).

The conclusion that anting is a learned cultural trait is strengthened by the fact that chimps at other sites do not exploit driver ants, even though the species is widely distributed throughout Africa. At the same time, other groups of chimps do exploit other species of ants and in ways that differ from the Gombe tradition. For example, chimps in the Mahale mountains 170 kilometers south of Gombe insert twigs and bark into the nests of tree-dwelling ants, which Gombe chimps ignore (McGrew 1992; Nishida 1987). Similarly, there is cultural variation in tool use. Throughout the area, chimpanzees sometimes peel the bark from the twigs or vines they use for termiting; in some locations, they then discard the bark, whereas at Gombe, after they peel the twigs or vines, they use the bark itself as a tool for termiting (McGrew et al. 1979).

People who are skeptical about the existence of nonhuman culture claim that "culture is what humans do." Yet if we are willing to define culture more broadly as "group behavior that is acquired, at least in part, from social influences," then we can say that culture is present in nonhuman species (McGrew 1998). There is little evidence for teaching in nonhuman primates. But much human learning also takes place without systematic instruction.

A.

B.

Japanese Monkeys Washing Wheat

A. Members of a Koshima troop separating wheat from sand by placing the mixture in water.
B. A central figure is carrying the mixture in its left hand. Two monkeys in the foreground are floating the wheat and picking it up.

Apes and Language

In recent years, a revolutionary series of studies has revealed that the gap between human and ape language capacities is not as great as had previously been supposed. Yet these same experiments have shown that innate species-specific factors prevent this gap from being closed.

Many futile attempts were made to teach chimpanzees to speak in human fashion before it was found that the vocal tract of apes cannot make the sounds necessary for human speech.

Attention has shifted toward trying to teach apes to use sign languages and to read and write. Chimpanzees and gorillas trained in laboratory settings have acquired communication skills that far exceed those of animals in the wild. Experiments with a chimpanzee named Washoe soon demonstrated that apes could learn to communicate in Ameslan (American Sign Language). Washoe used sign language productively; that is, she combined the signs in novel ways to send many different messages. For example, she first learned how to sign the request "open" with a particular closed door and later spontaneously extended its use beyond the initial training context to all closed doors and then to closed containers such as the refrigerator, cupboards, drawers, briefcases, boxes, and jars. When Susan, a research assistant, stepped on Washoe's doll, Washoe had many ways to tell her what was on her mind: "Up Susan; Susan up; mine please up; gimme baby; please shoe; more mine; up please; please up; more up; baby down; shoe up; baby up; please move up" (Gardner and Gardner 1971, 1975).

Koko, a female gorilla trained by Francine Patterson, acquired a vocabulary of 300 Ameslan words. Koko signed "finger bracelet" for ring, "white tiger" for zebra, and "eye hat" for mask. Koko also learned to talk about her inner feelings, signaling happiness, sadness, fear, and shame (Hill 1978:98–99).

A remarkable achievement of more recent studies is the demonstration that signing chimpanzees can pass on their signing skills as a cultural tradition to nonsigning chimpanzees without human mediation. Loulis, a 10-month-old chimp whose mother had been incapacitated by a medical experiment, was presented to Washoe, whose baby had died. Washoe adopted the infant and promptly began to sign to him. By 36 months, Loulis was using 28 signs that he had learned from Washoe. After about 5 years of learning to sign from Washoe and two other signing chimps, but not from humans, Loulis had acquired the use of 55 signs. Washoe, Loulis, and other signing chimps regularly used their sign language to communicate with each other even when humans were not present. These "conversations," as recorded on

Koko the Gorilla
Koko, shown here with Francine Patterson, learned sign language and could talk about inner feelings.

Kanzi, the Chimpanzee
Kanzi learned 150 words by merely listening to conversations since infancy.

remote videotape, occurred from 118 to 659 times a month (Fouts and Fouts 1985, 1989:301).

But it was Kanzi, the pygmy chimpanzee genius who learned to make stone tools (see section "Tools and Learning"), who captured everybody's attention. Without training, Kanzi developed a true comprehension of 150 spoken English words. Like a human child, Kanzi acquired his comprehension of spoken words merely by listening to the conversations that surrounded him from infancy on (Savage-Rumbaugh and Levin 1994:247ff.). With the help of a keyboard and voice synthesizer, Kanzi could carry on extensive conversations in English. Every precaution was taken in testing Kanzi's comprehension of symbols to make sure that no unconscious prompting or scoring bias was introduced by his guardian teachers (see Box 3.1).

A vast gap still remains between the language performances of humans and apes.

Despite all the effort being expended on teaching apes to communicate, none has acquired the linguistic

BOX 3.1 | Kanzi's Accomplishments

Kanzi's comprehension of spoken English has led to a variety of tests of his understanding of vocabulary and syntax. In a vocabulary test, Kanzi listened to words presented over earphones and had to match them with one of three pictures presented to him. The person testing him could neither hear the word nor see the pictures that were presented. He responded correctly at 75 percent or better performance to 149 of the 194 words presented with natural speech and 103 of 150 words produced by a speech synthesizer that had no intonation. When 24 pairs of similarly sounding words were presented (*orange–onion* or *shot–shirt*), Kanzi correctly discriminated among 21 of the pairs. In a recent comprehension test, Kanzi was presented with more than 700 novel commands asking him to do things with objects or people in a way he had never done before. These novel sentences were presented by an experimenter who was out of sight, and the responses were evaluated by observers wearing headphones playing music so that they could not hear the commands. Kanzi responded correctly on more than 90 percent of these trials, indicating an ability to understand the symbolic referents of the words and the way in which the relationship between words was encoded by syntax. Because each sentence was novel, there is no possibility that rote learning accounts for the results.

Source: Charles T. Snowden. 1990. "Language Capacities of Non-Human Animals." *Yearbook of Physical Anthropology,* pp. 221–222. Copyright © 1990 John Wiley & Sons. Reprinted with permission of Wiley-Liss, Inc., a subsidiary of John Wiley & Sons, Inc.

skills we take for granted in 3-year-old children. Still, what all these experiments have shown is that natural selection could easily have given rise to the human capacity for semantic universality by selecting for intellectual skills already present in rudimentary form among our apelike hominid ancestors (Lieberman 1991; Parker 1985:622; Savage-Rumbaugh 1987; Snowden 1990).

Cultural "Takeoff"

At about 35,000 years ago, culture entered a period of cultural "takeoff." In the next 10,000 years, the cultures of western Eurasia changed more than they had during the previous million years. Technological and artistic creativity greatly increased, signifying the emergence of the first culture that observers today would recognize as fully human, marked as they were by unceasing invention and variety (Bar-Yosef and Vandermeersch 1993:94).

 Cultural "takeoff" occurred once the capacity for language and language-assisted thought developed. A vast number of cultural differences and similarities appeared independently of changes in genotype.

Prior to this time, cultural and biological evolution seem to have occurred at comparable rates. There is little evidence of substantial technological or material innovation during the million years prior to 35,000 years ago, and cultural and biological changes seem to have been tied together. After cultural "takeoff," the rate of **cultural evolution** increased dramatically without any concurrent increase in the rate of human biological evolution. The occurrence of cultural "takeoff" justifies the contention of most anthropologists that to understand the last 40,000 years of the evolution of culture, primary emphasis must be given to cultural rather than biological processes. Natural selection and biological evolution lie at the base of culture, but once the capacity for culture became fully developed, a vast number of cultural differences and similarities could arise and disappear entirely independently of changes in genotypes.

Closely linked with the capacity for cultural behavior is the uniquely human capacity for language and for language-assisted systems of thought. Although other primates use complex signal systems to facilitate social life, modern human languages are qualitatively different from all other animal communication systems. Most or all of our distinctly human traits, including our large brains, were probably established well before the development of language. The unique features of modern human languages undoubtedly arise from genetic adaptations related to both the development of the larynx and increasing dependence on social cooperation in culturally acquired modes of subsistence.

The anatomy of the larynx makes takeoff possible by enabling humans to exert fine control over spoken sounds and therefore engage in more complex forms of communication.

The fact that modern great apes are capable of learning symbolic communication systems suggests that the cognitive basis may have already existed in humans and that it was the physiological modification of the larynx that provided humans with a distinct advantage in producing the wide range of sounds used in language. Humans therefore were superb "hosts" for language because natural selection had already laid the basis for increasingly efficient modes of concept formation and their linguistic expression.

Scientists believe that modern human infants are born with the kind of neural circuitry that makes learning to talk as natural for them as learning to walk (Bickerton 1990; Pinker 1994). This circuitry in turn represents the kind of mental "wiring" useful for a species that needs to acquire and transmit large amounts of new information during its lifetime. Note, however, that no one knows for sure when fully modern forms of languages were acquired by our hominid ancestors or what sequence of development was followed.

Cultural Transmission

Most anthropologists agree that there is continuity between the cultures of other animals and human culture. If much of the behavioral variation found in animal populations were observed among humans, it would certainly be regarded as cultural (McGrew 1992). Similarly, the function of cultural transmission in humans may well be related to the function of cultural transmission in other species. The main difference between animal and human cultural transmission is that only humans show evidence of cumulative cultural evolution.

 Cumulative cultural evolution refers to behavior or artifacts that are transmitted and modified over many generations and gain complexity as they evolve.

Cumulative cultural evolution is not present in animal culture because animals, for the most part, learn new behaviors on their own, without deliberate teaching. Although it is commonly believed that monkeys and apes are good at mimicking what others do, they are not good imitators compared to humans. Apes are capable of emulating behavior by observing how tools are fashioned, but they do not pay attention to details. They do not acquire sufficient information through observation and attempt to copy behavior through a process of trial and error (Boyd and Silk 2006).

Humans, on the other hand, utilize social learning techniques, such as teaching and imitation, that allow them to obtain knowledge at much lower cost. The ability to directly imitate the behavior of others allows individuals to acquire knowledge without incurring the time and effort needed for discovery. Additionally, the human capacity to approve or disapprove of an offspring's learned behavior allows parents to evaluate behavior and make it more accurate (Castro and Toro 2004). Yet imitation by itself does not increase an individual's ability to adapt in the long run. Approval or disapproval transforms cultural learning into a hereditary system whereby cumulative cultural transmission takes place, thereby accumulating and passing on new innovations to the next generation.

> Cultural transmission, through cumulative improvement, allows individuals to acquire their parents' behavior after it has been improved through the acquisition of new innovations. Such improvements are then passed down through the generations, allowing for further innovation to take place.

The evolutionary potential of culture thus allows for continuous adaptation, making it possible for humans to develop new technologies, increase reproductive success and population density, and develop complex societies based on cooperation among large groups of unrelated individuals.

As we have seen, the capacity for culture fundamentally transforms many aspects of the evolutionary process. Individuals rely on imitation or some other form of cultural transmission or can invent completely new solutions as a result of their experiences. Also, unlike genetic transmission, cultural transmission makes it possible to learn not just from one's parents but to acquire new ideas and behaviors from a vast number of sources.

During times of rapid environmental change, it does not make sense to copy what worked in the past. When an environment changes or a population migrates, people must choose the advantage of following practices learned from the previous generation or try alternate solutions. Cultural evolution allows for the acquisition of better strategies for adaptation to local environments without having to wait for genetic changes to take place (Richerson and Boyd 2005).

Because many aspects of human psychology are shaped by natural selection, people generally—but not always—learn to behave adaptively. It is assumed that humans try to maximize well-being and fitness, that they are rational actors, and that in most cases, they will adopt cultural traits that are efficient. Efficiency is measured in terms of the amount of energy obtained (i.e., nutritional value) per unit of time, relative to caloric expenditure. Individuals and families therefore seek to maximize benefits that improve material conditions, health, and well-being, so they can thrive and reproduce offspring for future generations.

SUMMARY
and *Questions to Think About*

1. The human capacity for culture is a product of natural selection. Natural selection alters the frequencies of certain genotypes in a population through differential reproductive success, but it is not synonymous with a struggle for survival between individuals. Fitness in humans results as often from cooperation and altruism as from struggle and competition.

2. Both anatomical and behavioral traits are shaped by natural selection and encoded in the genes. However, learning is a process of behavioral change that is entirely different from the behavioral change induced by natural selection. Learning permits organisms to adjust to or take advantage of novel contingencies and opportunities independently of genetic changes and is the basis of cultural traditions.

3. Although the capacity for acquiring traditions is shaped by natural selection and took off only with the evolution of brainier species, culture is acquired through social learning and is not transmitted through genes.

4. Cultural behaviors such as tool making and tool use occur in many nonhuman species, especially

monkeys and great apes. Yet even among monkeys and great apes, tool-using traditions remain rudimentary. One reason for this is that monkeys and apes use their forelimbs for walking and hence cannot readily carry tools.

5. Learning among monkeys and apes is based on social facilitation (not teaching or observation and imitation). This kind of learning is not cumulative but based on behaviors that individuals are able to learn on their own.

6. The human capacity for culture accelerated dramatically about 35,000 years ago when culture "took off." Vast numbers of traditions began to evolve at a rapid rate without any significant changes in the size of the brain. A vital ingredient in this takeoff was the development of the human capacity for semantic universality.

7. As shown by numerous experiments, chimpanzees and gorillas can be taught to use signs. Compared with 3-year-old children, however, apes have only rudimentary capabilities for language.

8. Unlike biological transmission, cultural transmission makes it possible to learn new behaviors from a variety of sources and to efficiently pass on adaptive cultural traits.

Questions to Think About

1. What is the difference between biological and cultural adaptation? What role does each play in human evolution?

2. What is the basis for the claim that nonhuman primates have the capacity for culture? What are the limitations on primate acquisition of complex culture?

3. What is cultural "takeoff," and how was it facilitated by semantic universality?

CHAPTER **4**

LANGUAGE

AND

CULTURE

שמור על רכושך;
אל תשאיר חפצי ערך במכונית

لا تترك أغراض ثمينة
في سيارتك

TAKE GOOD CARE OF YOUR POSSESSIONS —
DON'T LEAVE VALUABLES IN YOUR CAR

VEUILLEZ NE PAS LAISSER
VOS OBJETS DE VALEUR DANS LA VOITURE

DAS EIGENTUM BEHUETEN WERTVOLLE SACHEN
NICHT IN AUTO ZURUECKLASSEN

CUIDE SUS PERTENENCIAS.
NO DEJE OBJETOS DE VALOR EN EL COCHE

ATTENZIONE AGLI OGGETTI DI VALORE.
NON LASCIATELI INCUSTODITI IN MACCHINA

Linguistic diversity is common in many nations.

Language serves an instrumental role in coordinating infrastructural, structural, and superstructural activities and thus belongs to all three domains. Moreover, communication is the basis from which emic structure and superstructure are built. We begin this chapter by describing the design features of language that make semantic universality possible. We then review the basic analytic concepts that are employed in *formal linguistics* (also called *structural linguistics*), which is the systematic study of language. We then move on to questions directly relevant to *anthropological linguistics,* such as the relative value and efficiency of different languages, the effect of language on culture, the relationship between language and gender, and the extent to which different languages are associated with different ways of seeing and understanding the world. Another issue to be discussed is the universal occurrence of change in a language's features. Ultimately, all languages are "corruptions" of parent languages, as we will see from an examination of the processes responsible for linguistic change. A remarkable feature of languages is that they maintain their structural coherence through centuries of change without native speakers being aware of the changes taking place.

Universal Features of Language

In the last chapter we saw that although animals can communicate, there are fundamental differences between animal and human communication. Among humans, cultural "takeoff" coincided with linguistic "takeoff."

The acquisition of language is an instrumental force in the creation of increasingly complex social activity.

Language is the medium by which ideas, inventions, and memories outlive individuals and generations. Linguistic competence makes it possible to formulate rules for appropriate behavior for situations that are remote in space and time. Language allows individuals within and across generations to replicate activities and maintain social traditions. Conversely, language also facilitates social change. And as people invent new patterns of social activity, they invent corresponding rules to fit the new practices. These rules are stored in the brain and passed on through language. With verbal rule–governed behavior, humans easily surpass all other species in the complexity and diversity of social roles and in the formation of complex cooperative groups.

Semantic Universality

 Semantic universality is a unique aspect of human communication. It refers to the communicative power of language—the fact that language provides for nearly infinite combinations that express different experiences and thoughts in different ways.

By carefully studying language, linguists have determined that all human languages have the same potential for effective communication because they share the same fundamental properties. Semantic universality is achieved through three distinctive features: productivity, displacement, and arbitrariness (Hockett and Ascher 1964).

- **Productivity** refers to the infinite capacity of human language to create new messages—never before uttered—to convey information about an infinite number of subjects in greater and greater detail. Animals, in contrast, cannot efficiently increase the amount of detailed information they convey when they increase the length of their utterances. For example, with a characteristic call, a gibbon can communicate "Danger." By screaming or by repeating the message several times, the gibbon can even emphasize the degree of danger, but this does not increase the information conveyed in the message. In contrast, the productivity of the human language makes it possible to convey specific and detailed information. We can say, "Be careful . . . there is movement over there . . . in the acacia tree . . . I think it is a leopard."

- **Displacement** refers to the ability to send or receive a message without direct sensory contact with the conditions or events to which the message refers. Among animals, vocalizations or sounds are closely tied to specific types of stimuli. Thus a growl is made as a warning only when there is a direct perceived threat. Humans have no difficulty communicating information about displaced domains. We can talk about past events long after they have taken place, as well as future events and imaginary events. Displacement is the feature we have in mind when we refer to human language as having the capacity to convey "abstract information." Some of the greatest glories of human life—including poetry, literature, and science—depend on displacement, but so too do our most shameful achievements: lies and false promises.

- **Arbitrariness** refers to the fact that there is seldom a connection between the abstract symbols employed by humans and the events and properties they signify. There is no inherent physical reason why *water* signifies a clear liquid constituted of H_2O molecules. Human language is constructed out of sounds whose physical shape and meaning are not programmed in our genes. There are no genes that make English speakers say *water* and Spanish speakers say *agua*. Animal communication, in contrast, consists of genetically stereotyped signals and decoding behavior, such as when dogs emit chemical signals as a sign of sexual receptivity or chimpanzees use facial expressions or hand gestures that are recognized by all members of their species. Because the assignment of meaning to sound is arbitrary, sounds are not tied to what they refer to and therefore become flexible units of meaning. (See the discussion on language and symbolic thinking on p. 47).

Linguistics: Elements of Language Analysis

As with other areas of scientific inquiry, linguists try to discover the underlying rules that govern language.

Linguists have discovered that although surface forms may differ, all human languages are composed of the same basic elements.

The following discussion gives a brief description of the components linguists have identified. These elements, taken as a whole, are known as *grammar;* however, the "rules" of linguistic grammar differ from the prescriptive (do's and don'ts) of grammar taught in the classroom. An English teacher, for instance, would say the sentence "I are going to school" is incorrect grammatically, pointing out that standard English calls for a singular verb to match the singular subject *I*. A linguist would only be interested in the facts that the sentence is understandable and that it contains a subject and verb. A linguist's grammar is therefore called *descriptive* because it doesn't judge how a language should or should not be used; it describes how people talk.

Linguists describe how language is constructed, not proper usage.

Speaking and hearing language are largely unconscious processes. We perceive language as a smooth, mostly continuous stream of sound and do not pay attention to the minute distinctions that make it comprehensible. The job of the linguist is to figure out the patterns and rules that make the language work. As you will see, unraveling and segmenting language into individual units of analysis is a complex process. Like other scientific classification systems, structural linguistics breaks language down into hierarchical levels, which proceed from the smallest to broader, more inclusive categories. We begin here with the smallest unit, called a **phone,** and proceed to how sentences are formed and have meaning, which is called **syntax.**

Phonetics and Phones

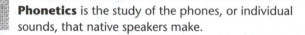

Phonetics is the study of the phones, or individual sounds, that native speakers make.

The sounds used by languages differ from one another; phones that regularly occur in one language may not occur in another. For example, the "click" sounds that occur in several languages spoken in Africa and the sing-song tones of Chinese are not found in other languages. The smallest number of phones known in a natural language is 13 (Hawaiian), and Quechua has about 30. No matter how many phones are used, human language can combine sounds to produce complex meanings. A repertory of only 10 phones, for example, can be combined to produce 10,000 words consisting of 4 phonemes (defined in the next section) each.

Linguists have identified all the phones in known languages. Because in most languages pronunciation of the sound may differ depending on where it is positioned, linguists have developed an International Phonetic Alphabet (IPA), which consists of 81 symbols. For example, linguists would represent the "ph" of *phone* and the "f" in *farm* as [f] no matter what language they occur in. The IPA solves another problem in that it includes sounds not represented in most alphabets—such as the "click," which is shown by [!].

Phones represent etic occurrences. They occur due to variations in the location of the tongue and lips and the stress, pitch, and tone of the sound. They can be observed and identified in speech without having to question the speaker.

Phonemics and Phonemes

Phonemic differences are derived from patterns of sounds that are meaningful to native speakers.

Phonemes are units of sound (phones) that lack meaning in themselves; they are the smallest sound *contrasts* that distinguish meaning for native speakers.

In English, the words *ban* and *van* mean different things. Yet the differences in sound between the two words are slight because the vocal mechanics involved in saying "b" and "v" are very similar. Because "b" and "v" make a difference in meaning, they are classified as phonemes in English. No two phones "naturally" contrast with each other. If we are able to distinguish one phone from another, it is only because as native speakers we have learned to accept and recognize certain phones and not others as being clearly distinguishable and contrastive.

Although the phonemes /b/ and /v/ in the preceding example make a difference in meaning, for Spanish speakers, this distinction does not exist and it is difficult for a native Spanish speaker to distinguish between the words *berry* and *very*. Likewise, in Spanish there is a rolled "r," and a distinction is made between a short or long roll. Thus, the words *pero* (the conjunction *but*) and *perro (dog)* are not readily detected by English speakers.

Phonemes thus represent the fact that not all variations of a given sound result in differences of meaning. Another example makes this notion clearer: In English, the sound of "l" in *lake* is considered quite different from the sound of "r" in *rake*—the two sounds belong to different phonemes because they are *recognized as different* by English speakers. However, to Chinese, the two sounds are not meaningful and do not appear to contrast with each other. English speakers laugh at "rots of ruck" yet do the same thing with "t" and "d" in the middle of a word when pronouncing the word *letter* as "ledder" instead of using a crisply articulated [t].

The phonemic system—all the phonemes in a given language—thus consists of sets of phones that are arbitrarily but habitually perceived by the speakers as contrastive.

It is native speakers who perceive whether subtle contrastive differences between *phones* are *phonemically* significant.

Morphemes

 A **morpheme** is the smallest part of an utterance that has a definite meaning.

A *morpheme* may consist of a single phoneme ("a") or of strings of phonemes in different combinations and permutations. You may be asking yourself, "But isn't this the definition of a word?" and you would be partially correct. But if we examine words, we find that some are assembled from parts, each hav-

ing meaning. For instance, the word *speaking* is really formed from two parts: the word *speak* and the suffix *-ing*. Some morphemes can stand alone, whereas some can occur only in conjunction with other morphemes. *Hello, stop,* and *sheep* are called *free morphemes* because used by themselves, they can constitute the entirety of a well-formed (understandable) message. For example, to the question *Are those goats or sheep?* the answer *Sheep* constitutes a perfectly understandable message. In contrast, *bound morphemes* are embedded within words—such as the suffix /-ing/, the past-forming /-ed/ of *talked* or *looked*, and the /-er/ of *speaker* or *singer.* These and similar constructions are called *bound morphemes* because they can never constitute well-formed messages on their own.

Words, then, are free morphemes or combinations of morphemes that can constitute well-formed messages. As a unit of analysis, *morphemes* are a useful comparative tool because languages vary widely in their reliance on free or bound morphemes. Chinese, for example, has many free morphemes, whereas Turkish has many bound morphemes.

A linguist's grammar, as mentioned earlier, is not the same as the prescriptive rules for speaking English. Linguistic grammar has many facets: the rules for combining *phonemes* into *morphemes* (**morphology**) and the rules for combining morphemes into words and sentences (syntax), which will be discussed next. The existence of rules governing the formation of permitted sequences of phonemes is largely unconscious but can readily be seen in the reaction of speakers of English to common names in Polish, such as *Zbigniew Brzezinski*. English, unlike Polish, does not permit sound combinations such as "zb" and "brz." Similarly, speakers of English know by unconscious rule that the words *btop* and *ndak* cannot exist in English because they involve prohibited sound combinations.

Syntax

 Syntax consists of the unconscious rules governing the arrangement of words in sentences and phrases.

Syntax involves sentence structure, how words are ordered, and the relationship of the component parts. The unconscious rules of syntax arrange words into categories corresponding to basic features of the world—nouns (things), verbs (actions, events), and adjectives (qualities)—and govern the formation of sentences. They allow a listener to figure out what the speaker intended to report about the relationships among things, qualities, and actions. Native speakers can distinguish between grammatical and ungrammatical sentences even when they have never heard particular combinations before. Here is a classic example:

1. Colorless green ideas sleep furiously.
2. Furiously sleep ideas green colorless.

Most speakers of English will recognize sentence (1) as a grammatical utterance but reject (2) as ungrammatical, even when both seem equally nonsensical. Still, native speakers can seldom state the rules governing the production of grammatical utterances. Even the difference between singular and plural nouns is hard to formulate as a conscious rule. Adding an *s* converts *cat* into *cats* and *slap* into *slaps,* but something else happens in *house* when it turns into *houses* and yet another when *rose* changes to *roses.* (Try speaking these aloud to gain a sense of how the *s* varies in pronunciation.) Three different variations of the same morpheme *s* have been used according to a complex rule that most native speakers of English cannot state yet use with ease.

Language and Symbolic Representation

Language is only one medium through which humans interpret, express, and transmit culture. The capacity for language is part of the more generalized human capacity for symbolically representing objects, actions, and relationships.

> **Symbolic thought** occurs when a person simultaneously associates two or more complex ideas that evoke a reaction.

The response to complex symbols is usually emotional and has meaning that most members of the culture understand. This is why people are intensely moved in the presence of a culturally meaningful symbol, such as a war memorial or place of worship. Humans use complex symbols that represent associations not necessarily related to their *referent* (what the symbol stands for). For example, the clothes a person wears can symbolize class, occupation, sexual orientation, religion, or ethnicity.

- Several layers of symbolic meaning may be embedded in objects, words, or actions. A sports event, for example, can simultaneously represent several cultural ideals, such as team spirit, sportsmanship, courage, endurance, and defense of territory.
- The relationship between a symbol and its referent is arbitrary. Symbols are given meaning within a cultural context. (Sacramental wine may be physically the same as table wine; it is considered sacred because it represents the blood of Christ.)

Symbols Communicate Complex Meaning

At the 1968 Olympics in Mexico City, gold medalist Tommie Smith and bronze medalist John Carlos, both Americans, gave the "Black power" salute during the playing of the U.S. national anthem. They were barefoot, wore black gloves, and bowed their heads. They said that the clenched fists represented Black strength and unity, the bare feet were reminders of Black poverty, and the bowed heads showed that expressions of freedom in the national anthem did not apply to African Americans.

- Symbols can arouse passion and evoke thoughts and emotions that can lead to extreme behavioral responses, particularly when found within the context of political and religious structures.

The national flag is a common example of a symbol that has many associations, such as unity, political loyalty, national pride, and a host of other emotionally provocative meanings. Its symbolic value has led to codified rules concerning how it should be placed and disposed of. Confrontations over its proper treatment have often resulted in violence and may even inspire people to sacrifice their lives. For many Americans, the famous statue of four soldiers struggling to raise the flag at Iwo Jima symbolizes this implicit understanding of what the flag symbolizes. Thus symbols are not mere substitutes for objects but are vehicles for conceiving the meanings that objects have come to symbolize. As a public symbol, the flag is capable of evoking a response that can be mobilized into action; a protestor burning a flag may evoke an emotional response that can lead to aggressive and violent behavior among onlookers.

Language Issues and Theories

How is it possible for humans to create so many different messages and still be understood? No one is quite sure of the answer to this question.

Innate Grammatical Knowledge

One theory that explains how modern human beings acquired linguistic competency has been proposed by Noam Chomsky. According to Chomsky (1973), human language is possible because of the existence of an innate capacity for grammar. Every utterance has a surface structure and a deep structure. Surface structures may be dissimilar—indeed, they often are—but the deep structure will be the same. For example, "Meat and gravy are loved by lions" is superficially different from the sentence "Lions love meat and gravy," yet listeners understand their meaning to be the same. However, if we look at a third sentence, "Lions love meat and lions love gravy," we can see that the first two sentences are actually modeled from the information in it. Both are actually superficial transformations of the third sentence, which more closely reflects the deep, or underlying, structure.

An essential feature of Chomsky's notion of grammar is that at the deepest levels, all human languages share an inborn species-specific structure that is "hard-wired" into neural circuitry.

According to Chomsky, the human brain contains a genetically transmitted blueprint for building words into sentences. It is the existence of this inborn structure that makes it possible for children to learn to speak at an early age and for adults to translate any human language into any other human language. Because of this hard-wired aspect, Chomsky's approach is called an *innatist*, or *rationalist*, explanation of the human capacity for language.

Are There Superior and Inferior Languages?

Linguists of the nineteenth century were convinced that the languages of the world could be arranged in a hierarchical order. Europeans invariably awarded the prize for efficiency, elegance, and beauty to Latin, the mastery of whose grammar was long a precondition for scholarly success in the West. Linguists thought that languages spoken by contemporary "primitive" people were, in fact, intermediate between animal languages and modern civilized languages. They were forced to abandon this idea when they discovered that complexity of grammatical rules had no relationship to levels of technological and political development.

Simple human languages, with limited vocabulary and grammar, do not exist. Groups with simpler technologies or social organizations do *not* have simpler languages.

Although no language is logically superior to another, each speech community develops a specific vocabulary that is equipped to express the ideas and experiences that are significant in its cultural context. For example, the Agta of the Philippines have 31 verbs meaning "to fish," each word referring to a particular type of fishing. Yet they lack a simple generic word meaning "to fish." In the Tupi languages spoken by Native Americans in Brazil, numerous words designate separate species of parrots, but no general word exists for "parrot." Other languages lack words for specifics. They have separate words for numbers 1 through 5; thereafter, they simply rely on a word that means "many."

Today linguists realize that the failure of a language to have a general or specific word has nothing to do with its evolutionary standing. It simply reflects culturally defined needs to be specific or general. The Agta, who depend on fish for much of their subsistence, never have any need to refer to "fishing" as a general activity; what is important to them is that fish can be obtained in many specific ways. Similarly, speakers of the language of preliterate societies need to know about the distinctive properties of plants. On average, they can name and identify 500 to 1,000 separate plant species, whereas the ordinary speakers of the languages of urban industrial societies can name only 50 to 100 such species. Not surprisingly, the urbanites do more lumping and get along with vague concepts such as *grass, tree, shrub, bush,* and *vine*. Speakers of languages that lack specific numbers beyond five also get along very well because they seldom have to be precise about large quantities. If an occasion arises when they have to be precise, they cope by repeating the largest term an appropriate number of times (Witowski and Brown 1978, 1985).

No, There Are No "Primitive" Languages

Speakers in preliterate societies often lack specific words for colors. Lacking control over dyes and paints, they seldom need to be color conscious. But if the need arises, they can always adapt to the occasion by referring to "the color of the sky" or "the color of milk." Even parts of the body get named in conformity with the cultural need to refer to them. In the tropics, people don't wear much clothing, and they tend to speak languages that lump "hand" and "arm" under one term and "leg" and "foot" under another. People who live in colder climates and who wear special garments (gloves, boots, sleeves, pants, and so on) for different parts of the body more often have separate words for "hand" versus "arm" and for "foot" versus "leg." None of these differences therefore can be interpreted as evidence of a more primitive or intermediate phase of linguistic evolution. All of the 3,000 or so languages spoken in the world today possess a common fundamental structure and need only minor changes in vocabulary to be equally efficient in storing, retrieving, and transmitting information and in organizing social behavior.

Language, Thought, and Causality

For many years, linguists have investigated to what extent languages influence how native speakers perceive and structure the world. At the center of this controversy are ideas set forth by Edward Sapir in 1929 and developed by Benjamin Whorf, known as the **principle of linguistic relativity**, or the **Sapir–Whorf hypothesis**. According to Whorf, when two language systems differ radically in their vocabularies and grammars, their speakers live in wholly different thought-worlds. The reasoning for this is that the experiences of native speakers of different languages are "filtered" through the grammars and categories of their respective languages. This "filter" has the effect of structuring the world in a particular way for its speakers. Thus, learning a new language causes a person to enter a new social reality based on the language habits of the group.

> According to the **principle of linguistic relativity (Sapir–Whorf hypothesis),** speakers of different languages will construct reality differently because language affects how individuals perceive reality.

Whorf believed that even such fundamental categories as space and time are experienced differently as a result of the linguistic "molds" that constrain thought. According to Whorf, English tense structures encourage English speakers to think of time as a divisible rod that starts in the past, passes through the present, and continues into the future—hence, the English language's past, present, and future tenses. Hopi grammar, however, does not locate events with reference to time; it has no equivalent of past, present, and future tenses. Does this mean that a Hopi cannot indicate that an event happened last month or that it is happening right now or that it will happen tomorrow? Of course not. But Whorf's point is that the English tense system makes it easier to measure time, and he postulated a causal connection between the tense system of Indo-European languages and the inclination of Euro-Americans to read timetables, make time payments, and punch timeclocks.

> Although language and thought are reflected in culture, it is incorrect to assume that language "causes" or "restricts" thought or that language "determines" culture.

No one would deny that the absence of calendars, clocks, and timetables must have given preindustrial societies such as the Hopi an orientation to time very different from that of industrial-age societies. But we have no evidence to support the view that one kind of grammar rather than another is responsible for the sense of time scarcity that comes with postindustrial existence. The way Westerners think about time is clearly influenced by an accelerated pace of life, in which time is of essence.

Linguistic Naming Categories

Whorf's idea that people who speak different languages see the world in fundamentally different ways has been tested in the domain of color categories. Some languages have separate terms only for brightness contrasts, such as those designated by *black* and *white*. Others have up to a dozen basic color terms. This difference would seem to indicate a highly relativistic or culture-specific form of color perception. Yet there is considerable evidence that even when their language contains only two or three basic terms, people actually tend to see the same parts of the color spectrum as those whose languages contain many color terms. When a language has only a few color words, distinctions can still be made by combining words (such as *pale red* for *pink* or *almost black* for *gray*) to describe colors that do not have separate color terms.

Berlin and Kay (1991) have found definite regularities in the assignment of color terms in 30 different cultures. The number of basic color terms in a language increases with technological complexity, such that color terminology is most developed in languages where people have a history of using dyes and artificial coloring. Moreover, color terms tend to be added in a definite sequence. If a language is to have more than two basic categories, the third term will be *red*. If there is a fourth category, it will be either *green* or *yellow;* then *yellow* or *green;* then *blue;* then *brown;* and finally *purple, pink,* or *orange* (Berlin and Kay, 1991). Unfortunately, we can find exceptions to this scheme, and the basic question of why different cultures have different color terms remains unresolved (Hewes 1992; MacLaury 1992; Witowski and Brown 1978; but see Agar 1994).

Is a language that has only two or three color terms at a disadvantage with respect to those that have a dozen or more? It seems unlikely, because one can always refer to additional colors by saying something is the color of some familiar object. In English, for example, *orange* was initially distinguished as that color found on the skin of oranges.

Sociolinguistics

Linguistic anthropologists have also taken a keen interest in the social context of language. Alessandro Duranti defines _linguistic anthropology_ as "the study of language as a _cultural resource_ and speaking as a _cultural practice_" (1997:2). To understand how language is used and what people do with it, you have to venture into the world of social action, where language is part of specific cultural activities such as telling a story, showing respect, asking for a favor, giving directions, and so on (Duranti 2001:1).

 Sociolinguistics is concerned with how language is used in different social contexts and what it tells us about social relationships.

Sociolinguistic data obtained in real-life social interactions provide important clues about structural and superstructural patterns such as status, class, and gender differences. Speakers may tailor their words for a particular audience. "Please lower your voice" and "Quiet down!" are linguistic options available for saying the same thing—in this case, asking for less noise (Bonvillian 1997). Similarly, the way language is used in group activities such as storytelling reveals the dynamics of group membership; it displays patterns of deference and asymmetry, how gender is manifested, and how individuals are aligned within the group (Goodwin 1990).

Dialects may be used to create and maintain social boundaries between individuals in social groups. Groups maintain their identities through linguistic distinctions. For example, the Native American Tewa of Arizona have had three centuries of contact with English, Spanish, and Hopi language speakers. Yet they continue to speak their ancient Tewa language, which marks their ethnic identity and maintains the social boundaries associated with Tewa traditions (Kroskrity 2001).

Language and Gender

Certain obligatory categories in standard English reflect a pervasive social bias in favor of male-centered viewpoints and activities. The traditional (although waning) use of the marriage announcement "I now pronounce you man and wife," which labels the male by his humanness and the female by her relationship to him, is an example of such bias. Many nouns and pronouns that refer to human beings lack gender—_child, everybody, everyone, person, citizen, American._ However, teachers of standard English once prescribed masculine rather than feminine pronouns to refer to these words. Thus it was once considered correct to say "Everyone must do his homework," even though the group being addressed consisted of both males and females. Newspaper columnists were fond of writing "The average American is in love with his car." Obviously, a perfectly intelligible and sexually unbiased substitute is readily available in the plural possessive pronoun _their._ In fact, nowadays almost everybody uses the word _their_ in their [sic] everyday conversation (Hill and Mannheim 1992; Lakoff 1990).

Gender differences are also found in the speech styles of men and women. Nancy Bonvillain (1997: 249–259) documents several studies that show the following gender-specific speech styles:

- _Pronunciation._ Men exhibit greater use of nonstandard pronunciation (such as—_n_ in _runnin_) than do women of similar age, and social groups.
- _Intonation._ Men use a more narrow range of pitch and more even volume and velocity in their speech patterns than women.
- _Verbosity._ Contrary to the belief that women are talkative, men in fact talk more than women.
- _Grammar._ Women use "tag questions" much more frequently than men—sentences in which the speaker makes a statement and adds a "tag" in the form of a question: _It is hot today, isn't it?_
- _Vocabulary._ Women tend to use intensifiers such as _very, terribly,_ and _extremely_ and empty adjectives such as _wonderful_ and _lovely._ They also tend to use "hedge words"—expressions that mark the speaker's uncertainty about the validity of the statement, such as "I've been _sort of thinking that it would be nice_ if you came with me."

Some linguists believe men and women have different goals that reflect a difference in subculture, with different ideas of friendship and norms for communicating. Others argue that differences in men and women's speech reflect women's nonassertive and powerless position in society (Lakoff 1990). This is clearly a process that deserves further research.

Linguistic anthropologists have drawn attention to how men and women use language for different purposes. Typically, women use language to establish closeness in private settings, whereas men use language competitively in public settings (Tannen 1990). Initial insight came from observing children's play, which showed that children tend to play in gender-segregated groups, where gender differences in communication are first established (Maltz and Borker 1982; Wood 2005);

- Boys play in fairly large groups, their games are competitive and structured by rules, and they use communication to get attention and compete for status.

- Girls play in pairs or in small groups, they engage in cooperative role-play that does not have rules or clear cut goals, and they spend more time talking than doing anything else.

As adults, men and women not only have different conversational styles, but they also misinterpret each other's intentions. Such miscommunication is known as **cross-talk.**

> **Cross-talk** takes place when listeners miss or misinterpret cues in communication.

Maltz and Borker (1982) identify some of the ways American men and women come into conflict when they engage in casual conversation:

- Women use communication to create and maintain relationships, whereas men use communication to assert their ideas and opinions.

- Women explicitly acknowledge what has been said, whereas men do not refer to preceding comments but rather pick up the conversation where it left off.

- Women discuss problems with one another to share experiences and they offer assurances and support to facilitate closeness. Men, however, hear women and other men who present them with problems as making explicit requests for solutions. Men respond by using conversation to show their knowledge by giving advice.

- Women feel that men disregard their emotions when men offer solutions, whereas men feel they are showing support by suggesting how to solve problems.

"Father Knows Best." Despite apparent strides in gender equality, gender hierarchy is implicitly reinforced in many middle-class families. In studying family conversations videorecorded during dinnertime, Ochs and Taylor (2001) show that gender asymmetry is firmly rooted in everyday activities, whereby mothers act as initiators of family interactions while fathers act as evaluators and "family judges." This asymmetry is repeatedly played out in what the authors call a "Father Knows Best" scenario, which is a covert reproduction of male dominance in American culture.

In most of the families studied, fathers play a less active role in their children's lives, so mothers encourage the children to "fill in" their fathers about their activities. Although most of the stories told at

the dinner table are about the children, mothers are the most likely to be "problematized," or described as problematic because of an action, thought, or feeling. Fathers frequently criticize their spouses yet are rarely in the position of being criticized themselves. This asymmetry is also reflected in the children, as boys do 50 percent more problematizing than girls.

During dinnertime, a family member typically initiates a story that puts the protagonist in a vulnerable position. For example, the mother introduces a story about how her son's chair broke earlier in the day when she sat on it. The entire family takes part in scrutinizing the mother for breaking the chair. The father admits that he knew the wood was split (but did nothing about it), the children take a closer look at the chair, the father jokingly says that "It is a real sign (the mother) needs to go on a diet," and the child to whom the chair belongs becomes upset because he does not want to use the chair anymore (even though it has been fixed).

When women direct their narratives to their husbands, they disadvantage themselves by unwittingly "exposing their experiences to male scrutiny and standards of judgment" (Oaks and Taylor 2001:446). This power differential in family interaction reproduces gender hierarchies in the home and contributes to the formation and perpetuation of gender roles. Ochs and Taylor (2001) conclude that when women and men work together to inquire about and control their children, women become part of a dominating force; but when parental alignments occur wherein one spouse dominates the other, women may contribute

Gender Differences in Conversational Style
Men and women attach different meanings to what is said and often have misunderstandings about intentions.

to (and become a model for) the dynamic in which women are dominated by men.

Language, Social Class, and Ethnicity

It is not uncommon for certain linguistic styles and dialects to be considered inferior to others. Earlier we discussed language differences between cultures and saw that preliterate people with simple technologies do not have correspondingly simple languages. Here we will see that dialect differences within speech communities likewise do not reflect substandard or inferior language structure.

Language superiority in complex, stratified societies is associated with social and political motivations—specifically, maintaining the subordination of certain segments of society. Members of the elite strata often assert that the dialects of those in the lower strata are substandard. This judgment has no basis in linguistic science. Labeling a dialect spoken by a segment of a larger speech community substandard is a political rather than a linguistic phenomenon (Gal 1989). The demotion of dialects to inferior status can be understood only as part of the general process by which ruling groups attempt to maintain their dominant position (see Chapter 12). Linguistically, the phonology and grammar of the poor and uneducated classes are as efficient as those of the rich, educated, and powerful classes.

This point should not be confused with the problem of functional vocabulary differences. Exploited and deprived groups often lack key specialized and technical words and concepts as a result of their limited educational experience. This lack constitutes a real handicap in competing for jobs but has nothing to do with the adequacy of the phonological and grammatical systems of working-class and ethnic dialects.

Well-intentioned educators often claim that poor, inner-city children are reared in a "linguistically deprived" environment. In a classic study of the speech behavior of Blacks in northern ghettos, William Labov (1972) showed that this belief reflects the ethnocentric prejudices of middle-class teachers and researchers, rather than any deficit in the grammar or logical structure of the ghetto dialect.

The nonstandard English of the Black ghetto, now called **African American Vernacular English** (AAVE, also known as *Ebonics*, derived from *ebony* and *phonics*), contains certain features that are unacceptable in White, middle-class settings. Yet the use of these features in no way prevents or inhibits the expression of complex thoughts in concise and logically consistent

Standard English Is Combined with AAVE to Establish Bicultural Identity

The language features of African Americans are not homogeneous but vary according to class and social setting.

patterns (see Profile 4.1). The grammatical properties of AAVE are not haphazard and arbitrary variations of standard English. Nor is AAVE "bastardized English" or "fractured slang," as some have called it. On the contrary, it conforms to rules that produce regular differences with respect to the standard grammar and pronunciation. In fact, all languages, if they have enough speakers, have dialects—regional or social varieties that develop when people are separated by geographic or cultural boundaries.

The language used by African Americans is not homogeneous but is characterized by heteroglossia (Box 4.1). Many middle-class African Americans refuse to accept AAVE as representative of African American culture, while others try to be "bicultural" by integrating AAVE with standard English (M. Morgan 1995). The use of AAVE is more common among the working class than the middle class, among adolescents than among the middle aged, and it is generally used in informal contexts rather than formal ones (Rickford 1997). Nevertheless, linguists assert that AAVE is a systematic, rule-governed language and recognize its use as a marker of cultural identity.

Code Switching

Bilingual speakers often use another form of speech known as *code switching* (see Box 4.1), in which the speaker switches back and forth from one language to another during a conversation. Sometimes this is

PROFILE 4.1 | African American Vernacular English (AAVE)

AAVE is an English dialect used by many African Americans in the United States, in familiar and informal settings. The term *vernacular* refers to the first form of language that a person learns to speak, one that is used among family and friends. Like other native languages and dialects, AAVE has a well-formed grammar that allows its speakers to express any logical statement or complex chain of reasoning.

Some linguists thought that African Americans in the southern states learned a nonstandard English from people who spoke other rural dialects, particularly Irish plantation workers. But as research progressed, scholars discovered that narratives told by former slaves lacked many features of contemporary AAVE, thus casting doubt on the theory that all these features originated among slaves. At the same time, linguists have found that many features of AAVE developed after rural Blacks from the South moved to the large cities of the North from the 1930s onward.

AAVE has certain unique features:

- In indirect questions, AAVE preserves the order of a main question: "I asked him did he know."

- Modal auxiliaries such as *may, can,* and *might* often come in pairs, as they do in other southern dialects: "He might could do that."

- Double negatives occur more often in AAVE than in other dialects, often with inversion: "Can't nobody tell," "Don't nobody care."

- The absence of an *-s* on verbs in the third-person singular—as in "He walk home"—is a characteristic feature of AAVE, although speakers often pronounce the *-s* in formal speech.

Another typical features of AAVE is the grammatical use of *be* and *been* as a means of expressing a habitual action, as in "He be sayin' that" or "It don't be like that." AAVE often lacks contracted forms of the verb *to be*, as in "He tired," but all speakers of AAVE occasionally use the full and contracted forms as well. For example, the *be* in "He be doin' that" conveys the meaning that he habitually or usually does this, a meaning not present in

"He doin' that." When *been* occurs before the verb, it indicates that the situation described has gone on for some time and still continues, as in "I been had that coat" or "It been busted." Similarly, *done* intensifies the verb it precedes, as in "You done done it now." Before the verb, *be done* can express the inevitability of a future result: "If you listen to them, you be done went batty."

Other features differentiate AAVE from mainstream English concern patterns of style and rhetoric:

- Intricate patterns of ritual insults—known as *busting, woofing, sounding, chopping,* or *snapping*—which are not intended to be taken as true. For example, one person might put down another by saying, "Your mother plays dice with the midnight mice."

- Indirect ways of offering criticism called *signifying.* For example, a pregnant woman who swore she was not going to have more children, and now claimed to be just putting on a little weight, was told by her sister, "Now look here, we both be standing here soaking wet and you still trying to tell me it ain't raining."

- A form of mocking, sometimes called *marking,* which involves the precise imitation of another person's way of speaking.

The AAVE community has also developed elaborate patterns of excuse and pretense, known as *shucking* or *jiving.* For example, in his autobiography, Eldridge Cleaver describes how he dealt with a police officer after he ran a red light: Putting on a big smile, Cleaver explained that he thought he could make it but his old car was just too slow. Some observers have noted that when African Americans are most interested in what a speaker is saying, they frequently begin speaking themselves, rather than following the mainstream pattern of becoming silent.

Source: Adapted from William Labov. 1972. "The Logic of Nonstandard English." In *Report of the 20th Annual Round Table Meeting on Linguistics and Language Studies: Linguistics and the Teaching of Standard English to Speakers of Other Languages or Dialects [Monograph Series on Languages and Linguistics, No. 22],* James E. Alatis, ed., pp. 214–215, 229. Copyright © 1972 Georgetown University Press.

done midsentence, and sometimes it is done when there is a change in subject. Code switching reflects a desire to retain an ethnic identity. As with AAVE, it is not haphazard or "lazy" speech but instead requires a thorough command of syntax in both languages and an ability to integrate them smoothly into a conversation. A unique example of code switching is found in New York among Puerto Rican Americans who speak "Nuyorican" (New York Puerto Rican), as they struggle to retain their identity while moving back and forth between Puerto Rico and the United States (Zentella 1990).

BOX 4.1 | Sociolinguistic Terms

Speech community: A group of people who speak the same language and who share norms about the appropriate use of language.

Diglossia: A pattern of language use in a bilingual community, where two languages or dialects are used according to social circumstances.

Heteroglossia: The use of multiple dialects or language styles based on the social setting (such as formal, casual, professional) and social context (status and role relationships) of the speakers.

Code switching: The practice among multilingual speakers of selectively alternating between languages or dialects within a single conversational segment—for example, *Me voy* (I am going) *to the mall.*

Ethnography of speaking: The study of speech interactions in different cultures and of the interrelationships between language and other aspects of culture.

Communicating Respect in Interethnic Encounters

Interethnic tension between Koreans and African Americans in cities like Los Angeles has gained national attention. One aspect of potential conflict is rooted not only in miscommunication but in different cultural assumptions of politeness that reinforce stereotypes and racial tension between the two groups. Research by Benjamin Bailey (2001) shows that to overcome cultural prejudice, individuals must not only share the same language but also share the same assumptions of how to interpret and understand what's being said.

Korean storekeepers and African American customers have distinctly different ideas of what it means to be polite and respectful. Both groups name rudeness as a primary grievance with one another and feel that more respect and courtesy should be accorded to them, yet each group thinks it is generally respectful of the other. Despite good intentions in both groups, there are fundamentally different ways of showing respect in different cultures. These differences in speech and gesture can lead to serious misunderstanding because a perceived lack of respect is often interpreted as aggression.

Bailey outlines two distinct strategies for conveying politeness in public encounters with strangers:

- *Restraint politeness.* Restrained actions, which are nonimposing and demonstrate politeness through respect of another's privacy. This includes refraining from asking questions, not engaging in personal conversations, and making frequent use of apologies. These interactions are observed more frequently among immigrant Korean retailers and immigrant Korean customers.

- *Involvement politeness.* Engaged interactions, which express the approval of the personality of the other. This strategy includes showing interest in the other person by engaging in personal conversation, offering compliments, making jokes, and so forth. These interactions are observed more frequently among African American patrons.

Bailey argues that Korean shopkeepers and African American customers have distinctly different notions about their encounters because they each have fundamentally different expectations of what it means to be polite:

- Korean forms of exchange involve *socially minimal encounters,* which are limited at most to a greeting, a negotiation of the transaction, and the closing of the transaction. This type of interaction helps create co-membership in a relationship through respect for another's privacy. Korean storeowners feel pride in being able to know what their regular customers want before the customer requests the item. For the storeowners, an interaction that requires no necessary verbalization is the most respectful—it represents a good shopkeeper who *knows* the customer. Unfortunately, it was precisely the resistance to engagement that is cited by African American customers as insulting and as evidence of racism on the part of immigrant Korean storekeepers.

- African American forms of exchange are *socially expanded encounters* with extended interaction between the customers and storekeepers. Interactions are characterized by small talk and sharing personal information that helps create an interpersonal relationship between customers and storekeepers. Yet this form of communication—which often involves sharing personal information, use of high volume, and use of profanity—is perceived as disrespectful by Korean storeowners.

Thus, while service encounters between storeowners and customers may appear overtly friendly, their distinctly different forms of communication tend to reinforce pejorative stereotypes of storeowners as unfriendly and racist and of customers as selfish and poorly bred. This mutual misunderstanding often results in hostility as each participant exceeds the other's tolerance for what he or she perceives as disrespect and outright rudeness (Bailey 2001).

Linguistic Change

Like all other parts of culture, <u>language is constantly undergoing change</u>. These changes result from slight phonological, morphemic, and grammatical variations. They are often identifiable at first as dialect differences, such as those that distinguish the speech of U.S. Southerners from the speech of New Englanders. If New Englanders and Southerners were to move off to separate islands and lose all linguistic contact with each other and their homelands (no TV or radios), their speech would eventually cease to be mutually intelligible. The longer the separation, the less resemblance the languages would have.

Dialect formation and geographical isolation are responsible for much of the great diversity of languages. Many mutually unintelligible languages of today are "daughter" languages of a common "parent" language. This can be seen by the regular resemblances that languages display in their phonological features. For example, English *t* corresponds to German *z*, as in the following pairs of words:

tail	Zagel	tin	Zinn
tame	zahm	to	zu
tap	zapfen	toe	Zehe
ten	zehn	tooth	Zahn

These correspondences result from the fact that both English and German have a common parent language known as Proto-West Germanic.

In the 2,000 years that have elapsed since the Roman conquest of Western Europe, Latin has evolved into an entire family of languages, of which French, Italian, Portuguese, Rumanian, and Spanish are the principal representatives. If linguists did not know of the existence of Latin through the historical records, they would be obliged to postulate its existence on the basis of the sound correspondences among the Romance languages.

The anthropological linguist can see clearly that every contemporary spoken language is a transformed version of a dialect of an earlier language and that even in the absence of written records, <u>languages can be grouped on the basis of their derivation from a common predecessor.</u> Thus, in a more remote period, Proto-West Germanic was undifferentiated from a large number of languages, including the earliest forms of Latin, Hindi, Persian, Greek, Russian, and Gaelic, each of which is a member of the Indo-European family of languages. Inferences based on the similarities among the Indo-European languages have led linguists to reconstruct the sound system of the parent language from which they all ultimately derive. This language is called *Proto-Indo-European* (see Figure 4.1).

Many non-Indo-European languages spoken in Asia, Africa, and the Americas have also been shown to belong to linguistic superfamilies that originated in a single language thousands of years ago and were taken to their current territories by migrants (Renfrew 1994). The question now being debated among

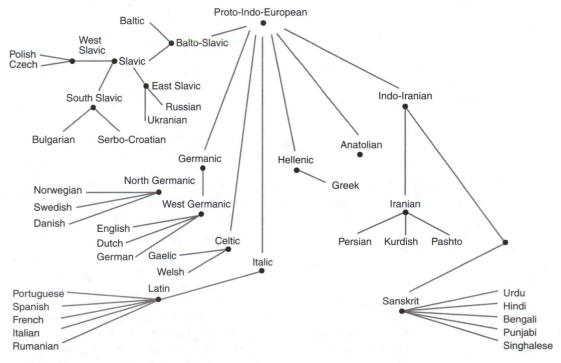

Figure 4.1 Indo-European Family of Languages

linguists is whether these protolanguages can in turn be traced to a small number of still more ancient tongues or perhaps even to just one—the original language of the first anatomically modern humans (Ross 1991).

Languages may also change without any geographical separation of portions of a speech community. For example, within 1,000 years, English changed from Old English to its modern form as a result of shifts in pronunciation and the borrowing of words from other languages. The two languages today are mutually unintelligible. As these changes illustrate, Modern English can be regarded as a "corruption" of Old English. Indeed, all modern languages are corruptions of older ones. This does not prevent people from forming committees to save the "King's English" or to protect the "purity" of French.

SUMMARY
and *Questions to Think About*

1. The communicative power of language is due to semantic universality, which is enabled through three features: productivity, displacement, and arbitrariness.

2. Structural linguistics has identified universal patterns in language. Languages are based on etic sounds known as *phones*. The basic code elements, *phonemes,* consist of phones that are emically contrastive. Different languages have widely different repertories of phones and phonemes, neither of which conveys meaning by itself. The smallest units of meaningful sounds are called *morphemes.*

3. The ability to send and receive messages in a human language depends on the sharing of rules of grammar. There are two different aspects of grammar: *morphology,* or rules for combining phonemes into morphemes, and *syntax,* or rules for combining morphemes into words and sentences. Knowledge of the rules of grammar makes it possible to produce completely novel utterances yet be understood.

4. Language ability, which consists of the ability to symbolize objects, actions, and relationships with words, is an instrumental force in the transmission of culture but is not the only medium through which culture is transmitted. Humans also extend meaning to objects other than words. This is because language is part of a more general capacity for symbolic representation.

5. The capacity to manipulate complex symbols may have preceded language development. Humans endow virtually every aspect of the world with multiple layers of meaning. This is also a powerful means of communicating cultural practices, norms, and beliefs.

6. Noam Chomsky, explaining how language speakers can produce and understand an infinite number of new sentences, states that all languages have a deep structure to which various superficially dissimilar utterances can be reduced. Novel sentences are transformations of these deep structures; at their core, all languages share an innate species-specific structure that is hardwired in the brain.

7. All human languages are mutually translatable, and no one language has a more efficient grammar than another. Grammars and vocabularies differ widely, but these differences do not indicate any inherent defect in a language or any intellectual inferiority of the speakers. General and specific categorizations, as with numbers, plant classifications, and color terms, reflect the practical need for making general or specific distinctions under particular cultural and natural conditions. Moreover, the view that certain dialects of standard languages are inferior forms of speech reflects class and ethnic biases. Dialects such as African American Vernacular English do not in and of themselves inhibit clear and logical thought.

8. Attempts to show that linguistic differences determine how people think and behave in different cultures have not been successful. All humans, for example, probably have a similar set of perceptions of time and color differences, despite the different ways in which their languages indicate such differences. Few, if any, correlations other than vocabulary can be shown between language and the major forms of demographic, technological, economic, ecological, domestic, political, and religious aspects of sociocultural systems.

9. Language is always found within a social and cultural context, and studying language use can provide clues about structural and superstructural patterns within cultures. Sociolinguists study how language is used in different social situations, as well as other aspects of linguistics that offer a glimpse into the unconscious processes that shape sociocultural systems.

10. Linguistic anthropologists have found interesting differences in men and women's speech which result in "cross-talk," expressions of dominance versus subordination, and women's inadvertent exposure to scrutiny and judgment.

11. Some dialects in complex speech communities are considered substandard. Such claims are based on political rather than linguistic grounds. Obligatory linguistic categories such as those concerned with gender may play a role in the maintenance of various forms of hierarchical relationships.

12. Ethnic groups have different practices for displaying respect. Misunderstandings during interactions can lead to tension and ethnic conflict, as seen in the case of immigrant Korean storekeepers and African American customers.

13. Languages, like all other aspects of culture, are constantly being changed as a result of both internal and external processes. Thus all languages are "corruptions" of earlier parent languages.

Questions to Think About

1. Why do linguists describe how language is used in different social contexts?

2. In what ways is writing a cultural, not a biological, adaptation?

3. How does symbolic thinking affect human emotion and behavior?

4. What do linguists mean when they say "There are no simple languages"?

5. How do new behavior patterns lead to the adoption of new vocabulary or speech patterns?

THROUGH THE LENS
of Cultural Materialism

Conformity and Conflict • Reading Six

The Sapir–Whorf Hypothesis: Worlds Shaped by Words

David S. Thomson

Do speakers of different languages construct reality differently? Benjamin Lee Whorf and Edward Sapir theorized that people can only understand the things that their language can explain or describe. Whorf supported his theory by studying the Hopi language, in which time is only thought as objective, things that exist now, or subjective, things that can be thought about and belong to a state of becoming. He compared the Hopi's conception of time with that of the English language, in which time is divided into units and viewed on a linear scale. Westerners abide by deadlines, whereas the Hopi do not measure the future in terms of days or months but believe everything has its own rhythm according to its nature.

Infrastructure

- The Hopi are a horticultural society that depends largely on harvests of crops such as wheat and corn.

- Whorf claimed that the essence of Hopi life is preparing in the present so that those things that are capable of becoming can in fact come to pass. This frame of thinking is beneficial in an agricultural society, where the community believes in praying and preparing the earth, seeds, and plants in order to reap a good harvest. Thus, past and future tenses are not necessary.

Superstructure

- The Hopi have elaborate festivals, rituals, dances, and magic ceremonies that are designed to facilitate a good harvest. The Hopi prayer pipe is smoked to channel good thoughts toward the growing crops.

- The Hopi's general mindset is that they must aid the crops to grow so that the harvest will be successful; their ideology focuses on controlling the unpredictable forces of nature required for a good harvest, which is crucial to survival.

Emic View

- The Hopi do not have a future tense because they believe that things will reach a final state when nature ordains it. They have faith in nature to provide for the future.

- The Hopi also believe that their rituals will give the crops the mental preparation necessary to help nature allow them to grow properly.

Etic View

- The scarcity of rainfall and geographic isolation of the Hopi make them dependent on a good harvest. Their rituals are aimed at facilitating the harvest through their thoughts and activities.

- Their conception of time is well suited to a society where future outcomes are crucial but unpredictable. Success in food production does not require the explicit concept of chronological time; nature has a will of its own, and rituals are practiced to prepare for an outcome (by concentrating on good thoughts), rather than control it.

Additional Examples Supporting the Hypothesis

- Languages vary in the number of terms used to distinguish colors. Some languages have different names for shades of color (for example, *purple, mauve,* and *lavender*), whereas others do not. People can remember a color better when their language has a familiar term for it. This suggests that people's ability to differentiate reality is affected by the names offered by their language.

- The Hanunoo of the Philippines have ninety-two names for *rice* and can easily distinguish between all varieties. Americans, on the other hand, recognize only one kind of *rice* but have many terms for *automobiles*.

Examples Negating the Hypothesis

- An obvious problem is the notion of causality. It could be argued that people's experience affects the way they use language. For example, in the case of the Hopi, it is likely that their harsh environment has taught them not to dwell on the past or future but to prepare for what is to come.

- In terms of color perception, there is nothing in the physics of color that suggests particular segmentations of the color spectrum, yet it has been confirmed that human neurophysiology influences how people perceive colors. Even when a language contains a small number of color terms, people see the same parts of the color spectrum as people whose language contains a large number of color terms.

THROUGH THE LENS
of Cultural Materialism

Conformity and Conflict • Reading Nine
Conversation Style: Talking on the Job
Deborah Tannen

Workplace conflicts between men and women can be attributed to miscommunications that stem from etic differences in conversational styles. Men tend to engage in oppositional interactions, such as banter and put-downs. Women, on the other hand, strive to maintain equality; they take other people's reactions into account and downplay positioning in the authority structure. These gender differences are especially significant when it comes to asking questions: Men are much less likely to ask questions in public settings because they do not want to be cast in the subordinate position of not knowing. On occasion, however, not asking can have serious consequences.

Women's Conversational Style
(from the Researcher's Perspective)

- Women try to avoid appearing boastful and do not try to assume a one-up position.

- Women try to take other people's feelings into account.

Male View of Women's Conversational Style
(from Men's Perspective)

- Men see women as less confident and less competent because they behave in a less assertive manner.

- Men often misinterpret the conversational style of powerful women because they do not assert a one-up position.

Consequences of Gender Differences in Conversational Style

- In a medical setting, a physician's failure to ask questions for fear of receiving a negative evaluation can be detrimental to a patient's health.

- Amateur pilots who won't ask for help because they can't admit they are lost run the risk of disaster if they run out of gas before they can land.

- People jump to the wrong conclusions regarding interpersonal conflict because they do not recognize differences in conversational style. For example, a man may incorrectly assume that a woman does not like him or that he is incapable of getting along with women. Being aware of conversational style differences is essential for understanding gender differences, and being ignorant of these differences leads to the assumption that women possess inferior communication or personality skills.

Villagers harvest their rice crop in Bali, Indonesia.

CHAPTER 5

PRODUCTION

To provide a coherent framework for understanding the causes of sociocultural differences and similarities, we focus first on the principal varieties of infrastructures. In this chapter, we will be considering primarily the aspects of infrastructure that make up a society's mode of production. The focus is on different modes of food production, such as hunting and gathering, horticulture, pastoralism, and industrial and postindustrial forms of agriculture. Cultures engage in many kinds of production besides food production (manufacturing tools, handicrafts, mining, and the like), but food production systems—the technology and practices used for expanding subsistence production—have been the main focus of productive effort throughout history and prehistory. We will use energy, measured in terms of caloric input and output, to look at how the resources are expended in producing food using different forms of technology under different environmental conditions. Although the intensification of production can lead to diminishing returns, diminishing returns can also lead to new and more productive technologies. What, then, is the long-range result of technological innovation? The answer may surprise you.

The Evolution of Energy Production

Human life and culture cannot exist unless societies capture and transform the energy available in the environment for the production of goods and services. The method of production and the amount of energy captured depend in turn on an interaction between the *energy-capturing technology.*

 Energy-capturing technology refers to how people apply human labor and technology to natural resources.

 Features of the environment consist of sunlight, rainfall, soil quality, forests, and mineral deposits.

Because neither technology nor the features of the environment can be changed limitlessly, a society's mode of energy production provides a powerful set of constraints and opportunities with regard to a people's entire way of life (Moran 1999; D. Price 1995).

During the time of the earliest hominids, all the energy that was used came from food. The first great step in the evolution of energy production was the use of fire. We do not know exactly when hominids began to use fire. Early hominids may have achieved partial control over fire, but full control may not have been achieved before the appearance of modern *Homo sapiens.* Certainly by the time of cultural "takeoff" 40,000 years ago, fire was being used for cooking, warmth, protection against carnivores, driving game animals over cliffs or into ambushes, and possibly favoring the growth of desired plant species (Goudsblom 1992).

By 10,000 years ago, animals began to provide energy in the form of muscle power, harnessed first to sleds and then to plows and wheeled vehicles. At about the same time, humans began to use high-temperature charcoal fires, first for making ceramics and later for smelting and casting metals. We do not know with certainty when wind power was first used (probably to propel small canoes), but modern humans were sailing in large ships by the time the earliest states arose. Not until the medieval period in Europe was the energy in falling water tapped extensively. And only in the last 200 or 300 years have fossil fuels come to dominate production.

 Fossil fuels consist of materials such as coal, petroleum, and natural gas derived from decomposed remains of prehistoric organisms over a period of hundreds of millions of years.

Today, fossil fuels supply nearly 90 percent of all the energy consumed by industrially developed nations. New deposits continue to be discovered, but the reserves of the principal **fossil fuels** remaining in the earth are limited.

New sources of energy have followed each other in a logical progression, with the mastery of later forms dependent on the mastery of earlier ones. In both the Old World and the New World, the sequence of inventions that led to metallurgy depended on the prior achievement of high-temperature wood fire ovens and furnaces for baking ceramics. In turn, the development of this technique depended on learning how to make and control wood fires in cooking and heating. Low-temperature metallurgical experience with copper and tin almost of necessity had to precede the use of high-temperature iron and steel. Mastery of iron and steel, in turn, had to precede the development of the mining machines that made feasible the large-scale use of coal, oil, and gas. Finally, the use of these fossil fuels spawned the Industrial Revolution, from which the technology for today's nuclear energy derives.

The dependence of later forms of technology on earlier forms acts as a powerful constraint on the evolution of sociocultural systems. This is not to say that all technological change has to occur in a single definite sequence throughout the world (Pfaffenberger 1992). The earliest known ceramics, for example, were figurines fired in special kilns 27,000 years ago in Czechoslovakia. Presumably, the artisans who made these small statues possessed sufficient knowledge to make pots. But ceramic pots were too heavy to be lugged from one campsite to another. Hence the full development of ceramic technology was put on hold until more sedentary villages developed toward the end of the last ice age. Similarly, the wheel was invented in pre-Columbian Mexico but used only as a toy, given the absence of appropriate domesticated traction animals and the prevalence of steep and rocky trails that were better managed by human bearers.

Throughout history, technological advances have steadily increased the average amount of energy available per person.

The demand for increased investment in technology arises from the need to increase the range and quantity of food a population can produce in a given environment. As a population grows, it increases its need for production. To produce more food, a society must increase its per capita use of energy. This can be done by expending more per capita physical energy (working harder or longer hours) or harnessing energy from the natural environment (from draft animals or nonrenewable resources, such as irreplaceable fossil fuels). More technologically advanced cultures may harness more energy per capita, but increased energy consumption does not mean a culture is better adapted, especially when the primary energy is based on nonrenewable resources or pollutes the environment.

Increased energy use does not necessarily bring a higher standard of living, nor does it mean that energy will be produced or used more efficiently.

Less advanced cultures may be better adapted to their environments than high-energy cultures, and social systems based on high-energy consumption may seem more secure than they actually are. Many great civilizations have fallen in the midst of material plenty because they depended on a primary energy base that was not renewable.

The Influence of the Environment and Ecology

Humans learned to live in many different environments, ranging from deserts to tropical rain forests to arctic floes. People are able to live in these differ-

ent environments through cultural adaptation; they select cultural patterns of behavior that best enable them to provide for their basic needs. For example, the Inuit living in the Arctic, where there is seasonal variation in game and fish, adapt to their environment by living in small, nomadic groups linked by kinship and marriage and by using technologies such as dogs and sleds for transportation. They schedule their movements to adjust to the availability of resources in their environment. They have also developed extensive social ties that allow them to shift about in both short-term and long-term visits and to adjust the makeup of their groups according to the seasonal availability of resources.

Many strategies are used for coping with environmental problems. As we saw in Chapter 2, evolutionary theory emphasizes that individuals and groups adapt to their environments by making adjustments that increase their well-being and the likelihood of their survival. We would therefore expect individual acts and beliefs to respond to a broad range of environmental characteristics, such as the following:

- Fluctuations over time in the availability of resources
- Activities of other groups in competition for these resources
- Introduction of new technology that changes the way food is produced

Ecological anthropology sees the human population as an integral part of the ecosystem and focuses on human adaptation, including physiological, cultural, and behavioral relationships (Moran 1999).

 Ecological anthropology is concerned with cultural and biological responses that affect or are affected by the survival, reproduction, and health and spatial distribution of human populations.

Ecosystems tend toward homeostasis—that is, they tend to resist change and remain in equilibrium (Odum 1971). Yet predictable patterns of change do take place. Change comes from a variety of sources that disrupt the ecosystem (Netting 1986):

- Climatic changes, such as those associated with drought or flooding or leading to migration or internal conflict
- Technology that is transformed or replaced by more effective tools or by the diffusion of a new food crop
- Social organization that features new patterns of domestic organization or political institutions

Carrying Capacity and the Law of Diminishing Returns

The abundance of game, quality of soils, amounts of rainfall, and extent of forests, in combination with a particular form of technology, set an upper limit on the production of food and hence on the number of human beings who can live in a particular environment.

 Carrying capacity is the upper limit on production and population in a given environment under a given technology, without degrading the resource base.

Note that for humans, carrying capacity must be defined relative to the given set of infrastructural and sociocultural conditions. If these conditions change—for example, as a result of deforestation or the introduction of new technologies—then carrying capacity will also change (J. Cohen 1995). Although carrying capacity sets the upper limit to production and reproduction, most societies maintain their production and population below that limit.

To understand why this gap between carrying capacity and the actual level of food production and population occurs, we must identify another crucial feature of food production called the *point of diminishing returns* (see Figure 5.1).

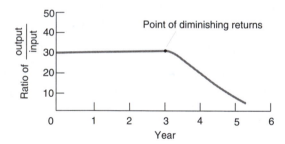

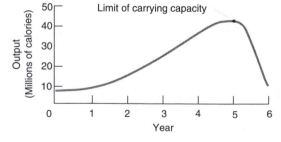

Figure 5.1 Production, Carrying Capacity, and Diminishing Returns

The point of diminishing returns is reached in year 3, but the limit of carrying capacity is reached in year 5. Production is intensified and continues to increase until year 5, and then it crashes.

 The **point of diminishing returns** is the point at which the amount of food produced per unit of effort begins to fall.

Slash-and-burn farmers, for example, bring on diminishing returns as they increase the number of years they consecutively plant in the same garden. They have to work harder in order to produce the same amount of food to maintain the same-size population. The reason most food production systems maintain themselves below carrying capacity is that diminishing returns set in before carrying capacity is reached. No one willingly wants to work more for less. As a result, production and population will remain below carrying capacity.

However, unless population growth is also regulated, the temptation to maintain or even increase production will be very great. This can be done by intensification—that is, by increasing the time and energy devoted to production.

 Intensification refers to an increase in labor output (i.e., using more people, working longer hours, or working faster) to produce greater yields without expanding the amount of land used.

Through intensification, a mode of production can be pushed far beyond the point of diminishing returns all the way to and beyond carrying capacity, thereby irreversibly damaging the resource base.

It is inevitable that intensification will lead to the depletion of nonrenewable resources.

The present condition of ocean fisheries in many parts of the world illustrates what happens when production passes the point of diminishing returns. In general, the rate of return per unit of fishing effort has declined by almost half. And some local fisheries, such as haddock in the Gulf of Maine, have been completely destroyed (L. Brown et al. 1991; Royce 1987). Between 1950 and 1989, the annual world fish harvest increased from 22 to 100 million tons. This rise was made possible by intensifying fish production through the use of bigger boats, better electronic gear, bigger nets, spotter airplanes, and other technological advances. Since 1989, however, total production has leveled off, and production per capita has started to decline. Additional fisheries will soon collapse if these trends continue (L. Brown et al. 1994; Weber 1994).

In seeking to avoid depletions, environmentalists must consider the importance of maintaining production at a given level in order to feed and provide income for a particular population. This requirement has led to the concept of **maximum sustainable yield.**

> **Maximum sustainable yield** is defined as the level of production immediately prior to the point of diminishing returns.

No one has yet demonstrated that maximum sustainable yield is a realistic goal for resource management. Indeed, some environmentalists flatly deny that scientists can reach a consensus on the maximum sustainable yield of any resource and assert that resources throughout history and prehistory have often been overexploited (Ludwig et al. 1993:17).

Law of the Minimum

Environmental restraints on human food–energy systems are not always immediately apparent, even to the experts. Extreme caution must be exercised before concluding that a particular culture could "easily" raise its total energy flow by increasing the size of its labor force or by increasing the amount of time put into food production. Allegations of untapped environmental potential are especially dubious when based on short periods of observation. Many puzzling features of human ecosystems result from adaptations that are made to recurrent but infrequent ecological crises, such as droughts, floods, frosts, and hurricanes, and to cyclical epidemics of animal and plant diseases.

A basic principle of ecological analysis states that communities of organisms adapt to the minimum life-sustaining conditions in their habitats, rather than to the average conditions. One formulation of this principle is known as **Liebig's law of the minimum.**

> According to **Liebig's law of the minimum,** a population will be limited by critical resources that are in the shortest supply.

This means that growth is limited by the minimum availability of any one necessary resource, rather than by the abundance of all necessary resources. The short-term observer of human ecosystems is likely to see the average condition, not the extremes, and is likely to overlook the minimum factor when confronted with apparently unrestricted abundance. Liebig's law applies as well to seasonal minima such as the availability of water among the !Kung San (see Profile 5.1). The populations of many subarctic North American hunter-gatherer groups were closely adjusted to the amount of fish available during the winter months, rather than to land animals available throughout the year.

Depletion and New Modes of Production

What happens to a society when its modes of production are pushed beyond diminishing returns and into environmental collapse? Various scenarios may unfold: The people may migrate to a new habitat, or they may die off through hunger and disease.

> In the past, environmental depletions have sometimes stimulated the adoption of new modes of production.

As suggested in the work of Ester Boserup (1965), when hunters and gatherers deplete their animals and plants, they are likely to begin to adopt a mode of production based on the domestication of animals and plants. When slash-and-burn agriculturalists deplete their forests, they may begin to cultivate permanent fields using animal fertilizer. And when rainfall agriculturalists using permanent fields deplete their soils, they may shift to irrigation agriculture. The shift from preindustrial to industrial and petrochemical forms of agriculture can also be seen as a response to depletions.

The depletion of ocean fish stocks illustrates this point. *Aquaculture*—the raising of fish in nets and ponds—is rapidly overtaking fishing in many parts of the world as a mode of fish production, just as agriculture and animal husbandry once replaced the hunting and gathering of terrestrial plants and animals. We have reason to believe, therefore, that if we deplete additional natural components of the industrial mode of production, new and still more productive infrastructures may yet arise. However, technology alone will never provide a long-term guarantee of high levels of production and consumption for the majority of human beings. No matter what the next mode of production may be, its increased efficiency will soon be strained to the limits if population growth is not checked. Ocean fisheries again provide an example of what this means. Even though production increased from 22 to 100 million tons from 1950 to 1990, world population has grown so fast that per capita production of fish has actually begun to decline (L. Brown et al. 1994:181).

PROFILE 5.1   Hunters and Gatherers—The !Kung San

Location: The Kalahari desert of Botswana and Namibia in Africa

Production: Collecting mongongo nuts and plant foods and hunting wild game

Density: Less than one person per ten square miles

Land Ownership: Communal; use rights acquired by belonging to the group

Time of Research: 1960s

The !Kung San (! designates a click sound; see Chapter 4, "Phonetics and Phones") are a hunter-gatherer people who live in the Kalahari Desert on both sides of the border between Botswana and Namibia in Southern Africa. With at least two qualifications, they may be taken to represent simple band-organized, mobile hunter-gatherers. The first qualification is that the description that follows pertains to the way the !Kung lived in the 1960s. Since then, they have changed greatly and become involved in new commercial and political relationships. Although we will use the present tense, it should be understood as referring to what anthropologists call the *ethnographic present*—how things were when the ethnographers did their fieldwork. The second qualification is that even before the 1960s, the !Kung had intermittently been more or less intensely involved with nearby groups of cattle-herding peoples with whom they traded and for whom they sometimes worked. Nonetheless, the !Kung of the 1960s practiced a way of life that was quite distinct from the cultures of their nearest neighbors in almost every respect (Lee 1993; Lee and Guenther 1991, 1995; Soloway and Lee 1990; Wilmsen and Denbow 1990).

Like most hunter-gatherers who inhabit sparse environments, the !Kung San move about a great deal from one camp to another in search of water, game, and wild plant foods. They build only temporary shelters and have few possessions, yet they are well nourished and moderately long lived. As occurs almost universally among hunters and gatherers, !Kung San men specialize in hunting and !Kung San women specialize in gathering, although on occasion, women will bring small animals back to camp and men will help carry heavy loads of nuts.

The number of people in a !Kung camp varies from 23 to 40, with an average camp size of 31 (20 adults and 11 children). During a four-week study period, Richard Lee (1979) calculated that 20 adults put in an average 2.4 days per week in hunting and gathering. On any particular day, the number of people hunting or gathering varied from zero to 16. About 71 percent of the calories consumed by a !Kung camp are provided by women's gathering activities. Women range widely throughout the countryside, walking about 2 to 12 miles a day round trip for a total of about 1,500 miles a year each. On an average trip, each woman brings back from 15 to 33 pounds of nuts, berries, fruits, leafy greens, and roots, whose proportions vary from season to season.

Studies of the !Kung and similar band-organized hunter-gatherers have dispelled the notion that the hunting-gathering way of life, even in adverse environments, necessarily condemns people to a miserable hand-to-mouth existence, with starvation avoided only by dint of unremitting daily effort. About 10 percent of the !Kung are over 60 years of age (compared with 5 percent in countries such as Brazil and India), and medical examination shows them to be in good health. Judged by the relatively large quantity of meat and other sources of protein in their diet, their sound physical condition, and their abundant leisure, the !Kung San have a relatively high standard of living. The key to this situation is that their population is low in relation to the resources they exploit. They have fewer than one person per 10 square miles on their land, and their production effort remains far below carrying capacity, with no appreciable intensification. (See Chapter 19 for a discussion of more recent changes among the !Kung San.)

!Kung Woman Gathering Mongongo Nuts
The mongongo is rich in protein and provides up to 58 percent of the calorie intake.

Table 5.1

Major Modes of Production

	Hunting and Gathering	Horticulture	Pastoralism	Agriculture with Plow	Agriculture with Irrigation	Industrial Agriculture
Example	!Kung	Matsigenka	Turkana	Northern India	China	United States
Environment	Desert with sparse resources, including water	Tropical forest; gardens relocated every 3 to 5 years	Arid grasslands unsuitable for agriculture and waterholes	Arid region with irregular monsoon rains	Fertile plain with perpetual growing season	Fertile land with intensified mechanized production
Settlement	Migratory and live in temporary camps	Semi-sedentary hamlets	Highly mobile in search of food for livestock	Sedentary villages with permanent gardens	Large villages with access to river	Rural regions exclusively devoted to farming
Population	Low population density	Low population density	Low population density	Increased population density	High population density	Only 3% of workforce are farmers
Production	Adequate wild vegetable food and meat for small population	Cultivation of root crops supplemented by hunting, fishing, and wild foods	Nomadic herding and trade with agriculturalists	Intensive rainfall cultivation of grains; livestock provides traction and milk	Intensive rice cultivation; double cropping; domesticated animals; communal water resources and ditches	Mechanized equipment powered by fossil fuel; use of fertilizer and pesticide; indirect labor exceeds direct labor
Land Use	Communal territory and waterholes; access willingly granted	Communal ownership of land claimed through individual use	Grazing land owner of corporate kin group with exchange networks throughout region	Half farmland owned by wealthy farmers who hire other farmers to work land	Land owned by households with some tenant farmers	Private and corporate ownership of land; used for profit

Major Modes of Production

The six modes of production described in this chapter are outlined in Table 5.1. It is important to note that these categories are not mutually exclusive because more than one strategy is utilized in many societies. Furthermore, there is considerable variation in each category of food production due to differences in environment and technology, which determine population density and the efficiency of food production. For example, some horticultural societies have communities of only 30 people, whereas others living along large rivers or with animal domestication may have several hundred. As technology changes, so does the efficiency of food production, which enables a segment of the population to produce for the entire community. This frees up community members to become non–food producing specialists. These specialists may produce manufacturing tools, pottery, and other inventions that will lead to more efficient food production, increased population density, and more complex social structure.

Hunting and Gathering

Hunting and gathering was the only mode of food production from the time of the first humans to about 12,000 years ago. Most of the living hunter-gatherers who have been studied by anthropologists or who are known through historical documents occupy regions that are unsuited for agriculture: the lands close to the Arctic Circle or deserts such as Kalahari of Africa or the interior of Australia. Most of these hunter-gatherers are organized into small groups called *bands,* numbering from about 20 to 50 people. Bands consist of individual families who make camp together for periods ranging from a few days to several years before moving on to other campsites. Band life is essentially migratory; shelters are temporary and possessions are few. Yet hunters and gatherers are known for their relative "prosperity," leisure, and autonomy. When the !Kung San of Botswana were asked why they did not take up plant cultivation, they replied, "Why should we plant when there are so many mongongo nuts in the world?" (Lee 1968:33) (see Profile 5.1).

One must be careful, however, not to overgeneralize about hunter-gatherers and their environments. Even in recent times, some hunter-gatherers lived in lush environments that provided the infrastructural basis for relatively complex sociocultural systems. Archeological evidence from both the Old and New Worlds indicates that in favorable environments, complex, sedentary villagelike settlements long preceded the appearance of domesticated plants and animals. Thus anthropologists generally agree that recent band-organized hunter-gatherers cannot be regarded as typical of hunter-gatherers of the remote past, when no agriculturalists or pastoralists existed anywhere and when every kind of habitat was available for occupation by hunter-gatherer peoples (R. L. Kelly 1995).

Despite their dependence on wild plants and animals, hunters and gatherers do not eat every edible species in their habitat. They pass up many edible plants and animals even when they encounter them while searching for food. Of some 262 species of animals known to the !Kung San, for example, only about 80 are eaten (Lee 1979:226). This pickiness also occurs among animals that, like human hunter-gatherers, must forage (search) for their food. To account for this selective behavior, ecologists have developed a set of principles known as **optimal foraging theory** (Box 5.1).

Optimal foraging theory predicts that hunters or collectors will pursue or harvest only those species that give them the maximum energy return for the time spent foraging.

At least one species will always be taken—namely, the one with the highest rate of energy return for each hour of "handling time," or time spent in pursuing, killing, collecting, carrying, preparing, and cooking the species after it is encountered. The foragers will

BOX 5.1 | An Intuitive Explanation of Optimal Foraging

Imagine that you are in a forest in which some trees have a $1 bill and other trees have a $20 bill hanging from the topmost branches. Should you climb every money tree you come across, or should you climb only the $20 trees? The answer depends on how many $20 money trees there are. If there are a lot of them, it would be a mistake to climb $1 trees. On the other hand, no matter how scarce $20 trees might be, if you happened to find one, you would always stop to climb it.

take a second, third, or fourth species when they encounter it only if by doing so it raises the rate of caloric return for their total effort (Hawkes 1993; Hawkes et al. 1982; E. Smith and Winterhalder 1992). Of course, foragers do not actually measure how many calories they expend or obtain. But through repeated trial and error, they achieve a rather precise knowledge of whether it is worth their while to take a particular species. (If lions and wolves can develop this selective behavior, so can humans!)

Optimal foraging theory helps explain foraging strategies; foragers tend to maximize the time spent collecting food that has higher nutritional value. They will add items to their diets only as long as each new item increases (or does not diminish) the overall efficiency of their foraging activities.

This prediction is especially interesting with regard to the question of how the abundance of a food item, such as a food species, influences its position on or off the optimal diet list. Items that lower the overall rate of energy return will not be added to the list no matter how abundant they become. Only the abundance of the higher-ranked items influences the breadth of the list. As a high-ranking item becomes scarce, items previously too inefficient to be on the list get added. The reason for this is that the scarcity of the top-rated item means that more time must be spent before it is encountered. Therefore, the average rate of return for the whole list shifts downward so that it is no longer a waste of energy to stop for items that have a lower rate of caloric return (Hawkes et al. 1982).

A word of caution is needed here. Energetic efficiency is not the only factor determining the diet of human hunter-gatherers. Many other factors, such as

!Kung Women Returning to Camp
They have been out gathering wild vegetables and are carrying digging sticks.

the protein, fat, mineral, and vitamin composition of foods, may also determine which species are favored. But energetic efficiency is always an important consideration and is the factor that has thus far been measured most successfully by anthropologists.

Horticulture

Horticulture, also known as *slash-and-burn, shifting,* or *swidden horticulture,* is the farming of domesticated plants and is practiced mainly in tropical regions.

Horticulturalists tend to live in more permanent settlements, close to their gardens. But again, not all horticultural societies are alike. Many groups depend on a mixture of hunting and gathering, farming, and raising livestock. And of course, many kinds of farming and animal raising exist, each with its own ecological and cultural implications.

Horticulture utilizes naturally occurring rainfall. This creates the perpetual problem of replenishing the nutrients taken from the soil by erosion and successive crops. One of the most ancient methods for solving this problem, still widely practiced to this day, is **slash-and-burn farming.** With this method, a patch of forest is cut down and left to dry; then the vegetation is burned and crops are planted among the ashes, which contain a rich supply of nutrients.

Slash-and-burn farming requires large stretches of fallow land because long periods are necessary for the soil to be replenished.

Despite the lush vegetation of the tropics, the soil quality is poor because the heavy precipitation causes nutrients to filter deep into the soil (a process known as *leaching*), and it washes away the topsoil. In regions of heavy rainfall, a slash-and-burn garden cannot be replanted for more than two or three seasons before the nutrients in the ashes become depleted.

A.   B.

Hunters
A. Drawing a bow.   B. Returning from the hunt with a shotgun and a slain peccary. Animal protein is a major limiting factor in the Amazon. Today, up to 80 percent of the game is killed by shotgun, further reducing the game population.

Planting in a Swidden (a Slash-and-Burn Garden)
This Machiguenga woman is planting tubers while nursing her child in a recently burned garden.

Slash-and-burn thus requires a large amount of land awaiting the regrowth of vegetation suitable for burning and planting.

Slash-and-burn farming produces high yields for relative low labor inputs.

The amount of labor input or energy expended per acre for slash and burn is much lower than for more intensive forms of farming, such as irrigation, hoe, or plow agriculture.

In the long run, slash-and-burn ecosystems use up a considerable amount of forest per capita, but in any particular year, only 5 percent of the total territory may actually be in production (Boserup 1965:31). Horticulturalists, such as the Machiguenga (Profile 5.2), who live in small hamlets of 15 to 30 people, remain in the same location for an average of four years until they have exhausted the best land. Then they build new houses within easy walking distance of new fields cut from virgin forest. In more densely settled societies, communities tend to remain in the same place for longer periods and people have to walk farther to their fields.

The Problem of Meat

Another problem with tropical slash-and-burn modes of production is the vulnerability to depletion of animal species. This problem is especially acute where the main staples are protein- and fat-deficient root crops, such as sweet potatoes, plantains, yams, manioc, and taro.

The animals that inhabit tropical forests tend to be small, furtive, and arboreal. As the human population density rises, these animals quickly become very scarce and hard to find. Although plant foods can provide nutritionally adequate diets if eaten in variety and in large quantities, meat is a more efficient source of essential nutrients than plant food, kilo for kilo.

Like virtually every other human group, the Tsembaga highly prize animal food, especially in the form of fatty meat. However, in the tropical regions of New Guinea, all the wild animals have been depleted. According to Rappaport (1984) the population density of the Tsembaga is 67 people per square mile, compared to one per square mile among the Matsigenka. Pigs are an important domesticated animal because hunting is no longer viable, but they are costly to maintain because they consume the same food as humans. When a pig herd is at its maximum, almost as much time and energy is devoted to growing food for pigs as for people. When the effort needed to care for pigs becomes excessive, a pig feast is held, resulting in a sharp decline in the pig population.

Furthermore, because of increased population density, agricultural land is badly depleted and overused. The Tsembaga, like many other tropical forest people, confront the specter of "eating up their forest" (Condominas 1977) by shortening the fallow period to a point where grasses and weeds replace trees

Plow Agriculture

A totally different solution to the problem of maintaining soil fertility is to raise animals as well as crops and to use the animals' manure as fertilizer. This system, known as *plow agriculture,* once characterized the European and American small family farm. With the advent of the industrial era, soil fertility came to depend primarily on chemical fertilizers, eliminating the need for raising animals and crops on the same farm (but introducing a whole new set of problems associated with the toxic effects of the chemicals employed).

Plow agriculture turns and replenishes the soil and involves significantly shorter fallow periods than does slash-and-burn agriculture. Fields are left fallow

PROFILE 5.2 | **Slash-and-Burn Horticulture with Hunting and Gathering—The Machiguenga**

Location: Amazon headwaters of Peru

Subsistence: Slash-and-burn horticulture, hunting, gathering

Density: Less than one person per square mile

Time of Research: 1972 to 1973 and 1980

The Machiguenga (also known as Matsigenka) are tropical horticulturalists in southeastern Peru who live in small, scattered hamlets averaging 15 to 30 people. They live high in the rain forest, at a population density well below one person per square mile, where they practice slash-and-burn horticulture and hunt and collect wild foods. Root crops such as manioc, yams, and taro provide a surplus of starchy foods that are stored in the ground until needed. After being planted for one or two years, the fields are depleted of soil nutrients and become overgrown with weeds. Banana and papaya trees are left standing, and the remaining manioc crop is left to lure wild game that is trapped or hunted on moonlit nights. After three years the entire garden is abandoned as it reverts to natural vegetation.

The Machiguenga are selective in choosing a location for a new garden. A central concern is to be near a good source of water, such as a stream that feeds into a river, and where the soil is soft and easy to cultivate. People are careful to avoid conflict over resources when new plots are staked out. They choose their sites well in advance to let their intentions be known. If no one objects and the land "clears title," then the process of cutting down forest begins. A general pattern is that the Machiguenga maintain "dual residence," moving back and forth while a new house is built and the garden starts producing (A. Johnson 2003).

About 10 percent of the diet consists of wild foods such as game, fish, and insects. Although only a small part of the diet, these represent foods rich in high-quality protein, fatty acids, and nutrients that are essential to nutritional well-being (Baksh 1984; A. Johnson 1989). The Machiguenga have adapted to the scarcity of wild game and fish by maintaining a dispersed population, with small widely scattered family groups that move to a new location about every three to five years.

Machiguenga households are capable of living alone for long periods. A husband and wife are a complementary team that is self-sufficient in food production and manufacturing. The Machiguenga do not band together for defensive purposes or for hunting. In fact, individual families periodically leave their hamlets to camp out in "less crowded" areas where temporary shelters serve as "vacation homes" and wild food is more abundant. Or when the river is low, families move down to the beach where fishing is easy. This pattern of dual residence also helps avoid disputes. People are afraid of confrontations and will disengage rather than risk violence. During the early 1900s the Machiguenga were able to survive the effects of Western diseases and forced labor capture on rubber plantations by escaping farther into the jungle to live in isolated family households.

For slash-and-burn horticulturalists such as the Machiguenga, cooperation between households always has its costs as well as benefits. Sociability, sharing a windfall of wild food, and collaboration on fishing projects that require coordination in damming the river all make cooperation attractive. But such activities do not last long, and when the specific event is over, people return to the autonomy of the family household (O. Johnson 1978, 1980). The exception is when a shaman, charismatic leader, or more recently, a schoolteacher is able to attract several hamlets within an hour's walking distance. He brings people together by hosting feasts, after which the guests reciprocate by clearing a garden or planting crops. This provides the host with an abundant harvest to feed visitors and ample food for future feasts. Overall, however, the shortage of meat and fish limit population growth and keep people from aggregating in large village communities, where fish and wild game are rapidly being depleted. (See Chapter 19 for a discussion of more recent changes among the Machiguenga.)

for no more than a year; green manure and animal manure are used to add soil nutrients while the plow breaks up the soil so that oxygen can release the soil nutrients more quickly. This increases the productivity of the land and results in higher annual production per acre, which means that the land can support larger communities (see Profile 5.3).

Plow agriculture is more labor intensive than slash-and-burn agriculture but requires less farmland to support a given population.

Although domesticated animals, such as horses, oxen, and water buffalo, provide heavy draft labor, more human labor is required to restore soil fertility under plow

PROFILE 5.3 Plow Agriculture in Northern India

In the arid climate of northern India, wheat is cultivated with the help of ox-driven plows. About half of the farmland in India is cultivated by farmers who own less than five acres of land; the remainder is owned by relatively wealthy landlords who hire landless farmers to work for wages. Agricultural production faces occasional declines because of irregular monsoons that cause flooding and disrupt the economy.

Few Indians eat meat, yet livestock plays an important role in the agricultural economy. The native breeds are capable of surviving for long periods without food or water. Besides providing traction for plows, the ani-

mals are used for transport of people and farm products. They provide dung for fertilizer, cooking fuel (made from dried dung cakes), and floor plaster; leather for baskets and thongs; and milk for cheese and other dairy products. Cattle that are sick or outlive their usefulness are sent to special homes that are maintained through charity or are allowed to roam the countryside as strays. And when the animals die of natural causes, the meat is eaten by members of meat-eating castes. For the average small-scale farmer, however, the animals perform vital functions, given that substitutes such as tractors are not readily affordable.

agriculture than with slash-and-burn systems. Moreover, as densities grow and regions become more populated, land must be kept under cultivation longer in order to extract increasingly larger quantities of food.

Two-thirds of the world's population raise both animals and plants. Although many environmentalists regard raising animals as an inefficient source of food, a distinction must be made between specialized industrial animal production for meat or milk and generalized animal production that provides nonhuman sources of energy for farming and a variety of animal products. In the latter case, as with India's mixed farming system, meat is just one of the benefits and usually the least important. In many cultures,

animals also function as the only available "bank," in which savings can be held for future emergencies. Under preindustrial conditions, feeding root crops or grain to animals may be the only alternative to letting a harvest go to waste. In other words, writes Constance McCorkle (1994:4), the question is not whether people can afford to eat hamburgers. Rather, it is whether—without the incorporation of livestock into their farming systems—the majority of the world's agrarian producers and the urbanite consumers will have anything to eat at all!

Using Animals to Provide Energy

These oxen provide energy-efficient means of plowing fields in Indonesia.

Using Animals to Provide Food

This Nyinba man is milking a cross-breed between a cow and a yak. Cross-breeds provide better dairy products, such as butter and cheese, and their hair is used to make tents. They are, however, sterile and do not reproduce.

Irrigation Agriculture

Irrigation agriculture depends on artificially constructed dams and ditches. Soil fertility is a lesser problem because irrigation water contains silt and nutrients that are automatically deposited on the fields. Under favorable conditions, *irrigation agriculture* yields more food calories per calorie of effort than any other preindustrial mode of food production. And among irrigation farmers, the Chinese have excelled for thousands of years. The high population density in the irrigated parts of China is characteristic of societies that practice large-scale irrigation agriculture. It results from the fact that if the amount of water sent to the fields is increased, more labor can be applied to production without diminishing returns.

Under favorable conditions, irrigation agriculture yields more calories per unit of land than any other preindustrial mode of production.

Initially, the main impetus for irrigation was not to increase average yield but to have water available in areas where rainfall was unpredictable. As irrigation systems spread, it was apparent that differences in productivity became greatly magnified. Fields that used irrigation and drained well produced far more than those that were not suited to irrigation. The wet rice fields of Asia are perhaps the most productive of all preindustrial agricultural systems. Plots of wet rice cultivation are capable of yielding a harvest year after year, with no fallow. Where water availability and drainage are especially good, the same plot can yield two or three harvests in a single year.

Whenever there is agricultural intensification, human societies grow in numbers and increase in technological and political complexity.

Managing a common water resource is critical to irrigation agriculture. Consequently, centralized decision making developed with respect to mobilizing labor to build and maintain waterways and rights of access. With increased production, segments of the population became full-time specialists, making crafts, tools, and other items that could be traded for food produced by others. Because of the efficiency of irrigation agriculture, villages such as Luts'un (Profile 5.4) produced five times more food than they consumed. What happened to the surplus? The villagers exchanged it through markets and money for nonfarm goods and services, they used it to pay taxes and rent, and they used it to raise large numbers of children and to sustain a high rate of population increase.

A.

B.

Irrigation Agriculture

This form of agriculture occurs in many varieties, each with a special influence on social life.
A. *Massive Chinese water works.*   **B.** *Terraces cover much of Javanese croplands.*

PROFILE 5.4 | Irrigation Agriculture—Luts'un

Location: South China, Central Yunan Province

Production: Plow, fertilizer, irrigation—highly labor intensive

Density: 896 people per square mile

Time of Study: 1938 to 1943

Chinese villages provide a sharp contrast to the hunting, gathering, and horticultural people we have discussed so far. A detailed study of the labor inputs and weight yield of agricultural production in precommunist times was carried out by the anthropologists Fei Hsiao-T'ung and Chang Chih-I (1947) in the village of Luts'un, Yunnan Province. There the villagers obtained over 50 calories for each calorie of effort they expended in the fields.

The village is a typical Chinese farming community, located in a densely settled fertile plain and supported by intensive rice cultivation. Each household is an autonomous economic unit that holds property in common. Most village households own their own land, but some landless tenant farmers are either forced to sell their land to pay off debts or come from large families that did not have enough land to be subdivided for each son to inherit. In 1939 to 1940, the village had a population of about 700, living in 122 households; of these, 38 did not own land.

Land parcels are less than an acre, but the land is intensely cultivated so that each parcel yields a high re-turn. The soil is fertilized using animal manure or human waste (known as *night soil*). The land is then plowed with the use of buffaloes. Irrigation is provided through the use of several large water wheels that draw water from the local river. As the river water flows over the dam, buckets attached to the wheel are filled. As the wheel turns, the water is emptied into a ditch that runs into the fields. The local irrigation council makes sure the water wheels and the ditches are kept in good condition.

The mild climate permits a perpetual growing season with double cropping. First rice is planted. The women take rice shoots from nursery beds and transplant them into the fields. Women also harvest the rice, and the men are responsible for threshing and taking the rice to the storehouse. Then men immediately dig trenches so that two varieties of beans can be planted. Certain vegetables (legumes) improve the fertility by adding nitrogen to the soil.

Those without land or with little land work as tenant farmers or hired workers for people who can afford to pay for their labor. People with sufficient skill or means become part-time craft specialists or merchants. According to Fei and Chang (1947), villagers need only 40 percent of the total yield of rice they produce, leaving 60 percent that can be sold to obtain other necessities and to pay taxes. These taxes cover the salaries of local administrators as well as government officials in distant cities.

Pastoralism

If one feeds grain (wheat, barley, or maize) to animals rather than to people and one then eats the meat, much of the energy available in the grains will be lost. Thus, for cattle in feedlots, it takes about 7 kilograms of grain to add 1 kilogram of live weight to each animal (L. Brown et al. 1994:192). The loss in efficiency associated with the processing of plant food through the gut of domesticated animals accounts for the relatively infrequent occurrence of cultures whose mode of food production is that called *pastoralism.*

Pastoralists are peoples who raise domesticated animals and who do not depend on hunting, gathering, or planting their own crops for a significant portion of their diets. Pastoralists typically occupy arid grasslands and steppes where precipitation is too sparse or irregular to support rainfall agriculture and where water for irrigation is not available.

There are two basic types of pastoralists. The first type consists of those who move their livestock in a regular seasonal pattern in relation to seasonal changes in the available pasture. This strategy is called **transhumance.**

Transhumance is a form of pastoralism organized around the seasonal migration of livestock between mountain pastures in warm seasons and lower altitudes the rest of the year.

In some transhumant adaptations, as formerly practiced in the Swiss Alps, for example, only a small number of herders take the animals to the high pastures. In other cases, such as the Basseri of Iran (Barth 1961), people and animals stay close together during the entire migration.

The second major type of pastoralism does not involve movement back and forth along a traditional migration route. Instead, people and animals try to find the best pastures wherever they may be located. This strategy is called **nomadic pastoralism** (see Profile 5.5).

 Nomadic pastoralism is often associated with migrations that follow established routes over vast distances.

Pastoralists seldom kill their animals for meat because they provide greater net return through the production of milk, blood, wool, and traction. Pastoralists are not nutritionally self-sufficient. They need to supplement their animal foods with plant foods obtained through trade with their sedentary farming neighbors. In fact, nomadic pastoralists normally have some kind of symbiotic relationship to agricultural groups in order to acquire goods they cannot produce themselves.

Successful pastoralists can increase their holdings at a faster rate than agriculturalists. Herding, however, is much more risky because animals are susceptible to disease, drought, and theft and herds can be wiped out almost overnight. The advantage, however, is that pastoralists can exploit the vast areas that are unsuitable for agriculture and are able to move in response to changing economic and political conditions. People live together by choice, rather than

Transhumant Pastoralists
These Basseri of Iran are on the move.

by coercion, and can simply move apart to minimize conflict (Bates 1996:95).

Pastoralists frequently attempt to improve their position by raiding the sedentary villagers and carrying off the grain harvest without paying for it. They can

PROFILE 5.5 Pastoralism—The Turkana

Location: Arid grasslands of Northern Kenya

Production: Nomadic herding of domestic livestock

Density: 3.3 persons per square mile

Times of Study: 1949, 1970s, early 1980s

The Turkana are nomadic, like the !Kung. But unlike the !Kung, the Turkana travel with their food supply in the form of livestock; their movements depend as much on the needs of their animals as on their own. The advantage of owning domestic livestock in an arid climate is that animals convert otherwise inedible plant life into food for human consumption. This makes it possible for the Turkana to extract food value from animals in an environment that is too marginal for anything else.

The vegetation in the region consists of annual grasses and shrubs in the plains and perennial grasses and trees in the northern mountainous areas. The Turkana have adapted to the variability in the vegetation, terrain, and climate by herding five kinds of livestock and by moving quickly from one location to the next.

According to Gulliver (1955), the frequent moves make it possible for the Turkana to make maximum use of the vegetation in the area by first utilizing areas that dry out early in the season and then moving on to better grazing where the vegetation lasts longer. The major livestock are cattle, sheep, goats, camels, and donkeys; the latter are used mainly for transport. In the dry season the Turkana divide up their herds; cattle and sheep require grass for grazing, whereas camels and goats can do well in drier bushy areas.

During most of the year the Turkana are deliberately scattered to avoid competing with each other for pasture. Kinship and friendship networks are used to exchange information, labor, and livestock and to ensure against herd loss in case a natural disaster decimates a family herd. Each homestead can turn to friends in another region for food and livestock to replenish their herd (Dyson-Hudson and McCabe 1985). In the past, these networks were also used to mobilize support in response to raiding and warfare with enemies from outside the group.

often do this with impunity because having animals such as camels and horses makes them highly mobile and militarily effective. Continued success in raiding may force the farming population to acknowledge the pastoralists as their overlords. Repeatedly in the history of the Old World, relatively small groups of pastoral nomads—the Mongols and the Arabs are the two most famous examples—succeeded in gaining control of the large agricultural empires on their borders. The inevitable outcome of these conquests, however, was that the conquerors were absorbed by the agricultural system as they attempted to feed the huge populations that had fallen under their control (Barfield 1993; Galaty and Johnson 1990; Khazanov 1994).

Energy and the Evolution of Culture

According to anthropologist Leslie White (1949:368–369), a basic law of energy governs the evolution of culture: "Other factors remaining constant, culture evolves as the amount of energy harnessed per year is increased, or as the efficiency of the means of putting energy to work is increased." The first part of this law seems to be supported by comparing the per capita output of Chinese irrigation agriculture with the per capita output of the !Kung, and Tsembaga, as Table 5.2 shows.

> If one considers only human labor inputs, the ratio of output to input does go up in efficiency as technology increases in complexity.

But as can be seen in Figure 5.2, enormous increases in the per capita use of energy have occurred during the past century, as people have gone from draft animals, to steam engines, and on to internal combustion machinery.

The validity of the second part of White's law—that more highly evolved culture would be better adapted—is therefore not so clear. If one considers only human labor inputs, the ratio of output to input does go up in efficiency as technology increases

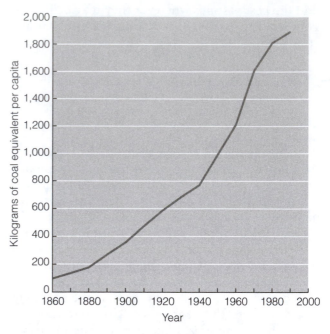

Figure 5.2   Worldwide Energy Consumption
There has been a sharp increase in the per capita consumption of coal during the last century.

Source: Adapted from D. Price. 1995. "Energy and Human Evolution." *Population and Environment,* 16(4):311. Reprinted with kind permission from Springer Science and Business Media.

in complexity. For example, the ratio of output to labor input measured in calories ranges from 11:1 for the !Kung to 18:1 for the Tsembaga to 54:1 for the Luts'un. But these figures do not include the nonhuman energy that is consumed—the energy that the Tsembaga use in the combustion of trees to make their gardens and the considerable amount of energy they "waste" in converting vegetable foods to pork. Nor do the numbers for Luts'un include the considerable energetic cost of milling rice. As Timothy Bayliss-Smith (1977) has shown in an attempt to test White's law, South Sea communities drawn into participating in aspects of modern industrial modes of production produce much more food energy per capita, but their efficiency in terms

Table 5.2

Per Capita Energy Production

Culture	Total Output in Calories (in thousands)	Population	Per Capita Output in Calories (in Thousands)
!Kung	23,400	35	670
Tsembaga	150,000	204	735
Luts'un	3,790,000	700	5,411

of energy output to input shows no clear upward trend.

> If we consider the total energy inputs and outputs of food production in advanced industrial societies, the trend in efficiency of putting energy to work runs counter to White's prediction. When we include other sources of energy input, such as fossil fuels and machinery, we find that advances in technology have actually resulted in decreased efficiency of food production.

Industrial Agriculture

Estimating the input–output ratio of industrial agriculture is difficult because the amount of indirect labor put into food production exceeds the amount of direct labor (Box 5.2). An Iowa corn farmer, for example, can produce 81 bushels of corn in 9 hours with an energy equivalent of 8 million calories (Pimentel et al. 1975). This gives a nominal ratio of 5,000 calories of output for every calorie of input! But enormous amounts of indirect human labor are embodied in the tractors, trucks, combines, oil and gas, pesticides, herbicides, and fertilizers used by the Iowa corn farmer.

Industrial Farming

A rice harvest near Yuba City, California. Consider the amount of energy it takes for food in industrialized societies to reach the dinner table.

In the United States, 15 tons of machinery, 22 gallons of gasoline, 203 pounds of fertilizer, and 2 pounds of chemical insecticides and pesticides are

BOX 5.2 | Energy Input in Packaging and Processing Industrial Food

Food Package	Energy Required to Produce (kcal)	Food Product	Energy Required to Process (kcal/kg)
Wooden berry basket	69	Instant coffee	18,948
Styrofoam tray (size 6)	215	Chocolate	18,591
Molded paper tray (size 6)	384	Breakfast cereals	15,675
Polyethylene pouch (16 oz)	559	Beet sugar (assumes 17% sugar in beets)	5,660
Steel can, aluminum top (12 oz)	568	Dehydrated foods (freeze-dried)	3,542
Small paper set-up box	722	Cane sugar (assumes 20% sugar in cane)	3,380
Steel can, steel top (16 oz)	1,006	Fruit and vegetables (frozen)	1,815
Glass jar (16 oz)	1,023	Fish (frozen)	1,815
Coca-Cola bottle, returnable (16 oz)	1,471	Baked goods	1,485
Aluminum TV-dinner container	1,496	Meat	1,206
Aluminum can, pop-top (12 oz)	1,643	Ice cream	880
Plastic milk container, disposable (1–2 gal)	2,159	Fruit and vegetables (canned)	575
Coca-Cola bottle, nonreturnable (16 oz)	2,451	Flour (includes blending of flour)	484
Polyethylene bottle (1 qt)	2,494	Milk	354
Polypropylene bottle (1 qt)	2,752		
Glass milk container, returnable (1–2 gal)	4,455		

Source: Adapted from D. Pimentel and M. Pimentel. 1985. "Energy Use for Food Processing for Nutrition and Development." *Food and Nutrition Bulletin,* 7(2):36–45. Reprinted by permission of United Nations University Press, Tokyo, Japan.

A.   B.

The Hidden Costs of the Industrial Mode of Production

A. An abandoned hazardous waste dump. The pit is 5 feet deep and covers 34,000 square feet.
B. Times Beach, Missouri. Floodwaters spread soil contaminated with dioxin, previously concentrated near highways, all over residential neighborhoods. Cleanup crews collect samples for analysis.

invested per acre per year. This represents a cost of 2,890,000 calories of nonfood energy per acre per year (Pimentel et al. 1975), a cost that has increased steadily since the beginning of the century.

Before 1910, more calories were obtained from agriculture than were invested in it. By 2000, it took ten calories in the form of fossil fuels to produce one calorie of food. Today, vast quantities of energy are used simply to process and package food.

In recent decades, scientists and technicians have altered their assessment of the ability of technology to dominate the environment. Increasingly, we have seen that industrial modes of production have not liberated human social life from the constraints of nature. For example, we now realize that we have ignored or silently passed on many costs of industrial production to generations yet unborn. Specifically, we have depleted irreplaceable resources and polluted air and water in many parts of the world. Efforts are now underway in many industrial nations to reduce air and water pollution and to prevent the depletion and poisoning of the environment. The costs of these efforts testify to the continuing importance of the interaction between technology and environment. These

costs will continue to mount, for this is only the very beginning of the industrial era. In the years to come, the inhabitants of specific regions will have to solve problems such as those listed below, as well others yet to be calculated:

- Pesticides are becoming less effective over time and there has been a tenfold increase in the amount and toxicity of pesticides since 1940.
- Fertilizers pollute the groundwater and are washed downstream into lakes, ponds, and bays, where they kill fish and other wildlife.
- Farm machinery and transport consume vast amounts of irreplaceable fossil fuels.
- New varieties of high-yield genetically engineered seeds are fatal to the genetic diversity of plants and have destroyed a number of varieties of fruits and vegetables available in the early twentieth century (Kimbrell 2002).

Postindustrialism

The mode of production in the United States is an advanced, increasingly high-tech form of industrialism. Industrialism denotes the mass production of

An Information Factory

Rows of Internal Revenue Service workers process information.

goods, services, and information by means of a highly detailed division of labor in which workers use electronic and other kinds of petroleum-driven machines in routinized, repetitive ways. This detailed division of labor involves the separation of production tasks into many tiny steps carried out by different workers.

The United States remains the top-ranking industrial manufacturing country in the world. Nonetheless, three-quarters of all employees produce information and services rather than tangible objects. Most employed adult Americans work in offices, stores, restaurants, schools, clinics, and moving vehicles rather than on factory assembly lines. They wait on customers; repair broken machines; keep accounts; write letters; transfer funds; and provide grooming, schooling, training, information, counseling, and therapy

to students, clients, customers, and patients (Swasy and Hymowitz 1990). Farming, which once occupied the vast majority of U.S. workers, now occupies only 3 percent of the workforce.

The rise of the service and information sectors has led to the characterization of the United States as a **postindustrial** society (Bell 1973). The shift to services and information processing has merely resulted in extending the detailed division of labor and the use of mass-production machines—office computers, word processors, duplicators, supermarket bar code scanners, electronic mail, automatic dialing machines—into additional kinds of production (D. Harris 1987; Sanderson 1991). Offices are factories whose product is information; this blurs the distinction between blue-collar and white-collar workers.

SUMMARY
and *Questions to Think About*

1. In the comparative study of modes of production, we consider the quantitative and qualitative aspects of energy production and of ecological relationships. Most of the energy flowing through preindustrial energy systems consists of food energy. Moreover, the technology of energy production cannot readily be altered. It has evolved through successive stages of technical competence,

in which the mastery of one set of tools and machines has been built on the mastery of an earlier set.

2. Through technological advance, the energy available per capita has steadily increased. However, technology never exists in the abstract but only in the particular instances where it interacts with a specific environment.

3. Technology, interacting with environment, determines carrying capacity, which is the upper limit of production and consequently the upper limit of human population size and density as well. When a population exceeds its environment's carrying capacity, the resource base will deteriorate and production will decline precipitously.

4. The fact that a food energy system is operating below carrying capacity, however, does not mean that ecological restraints are absent. Production may be cut back after reaching the point of diminishing returns. But it may also be increased by intensifying the production inputs. Still, intensification, if continued without technological change, will result in irreversible damage to the habitat.

5. A common human cultural response to declining efficiency brought about by intensification is to alter technology and thereby adopt new modes of production.

6. Hunting and gathering was the universal mode of food production until the end of the Stone Age. Depending on the kind of technology and the environmental conditions, several types of hunter-gatherers can be distinguished.

7. The !Kung San are an example of the simple, band-organized, mobile variety found in less favored habitats. Their output-to-input efficiency is low, especially for the male-dominated activity of hunting. However, by maintaining a low population density and avoiding intensification, they enjoy a relatively high standard of living (good diets, unpolluted environments, and lots of leisure time). Energy efficiency plays an important role in the selection of the species that hunter-gatherers use for food.

8. According to optimal foraging theory, foragers stop to take only those species whose handling time adds to or does not decrease the overall efficiency of their foraging effort.

9. Slash-and-burn horticulturalists, such as the Machiguenga and Tsembaga, satisfy their caloric needs with greater efficiency than the !Kung San, but the Tsembaga have depleted the game animals in their habitat and must rely on costly domesticated pigs for their animal proteins and fats.

10. Plow agriculture uses draft animals as a nonhuman source of energy to break up and replenish the soil so that the same plot of land can be used more often—without long fallow periods. This method supports higher productivity for larger communities.

11. By using irrigation agriculture, the people of Luts'un produce a large surplus. Their output–input ratio for human effort is three times higher than the output–input ratio of the Tsembaga.

12. Pastoralism, another preindustrial mode of food production, is practiced only in areas that are unsuitable for agriculture because feeding plant food to domesticated animals, rather than consuming crops directly, results in a 90 percent reduction in the efficiency of converting sunlight to human food.

13. As Leslie White predicted, the amount of energy harnessed per capita in the long run has steadily increased. Energy efficiency has also increased as measured by the return for human labor input. But when other sources of energy are included in the calculation of efficiency, advances in technology have resulted in decreased efficiency of food production, as demonstrated by the enormous energy inputs that characterize industrial agricultural systems.

Questions to Think About

1. What influence do environment and technology have on the mode of production?

2. What impact do intensification, carrying capacity, and the law of diminishing returns have on production? What is likely to happen just before carrying capacity is reached?

3. What does optimal foraging theory teach us about hunters and gatherers?

4. What are some of the differences between slash-and-burn and irrigation horticulture in terms of technology, population density, yields per calorie of effort, and resource management?

5. Pastoralists make a living by exploiting areas that are unsuitable for agriculture. What kind of special advantages do livestock offer pastoralists? How is herding a sustainable adaptation in arid environments?

THROUGH THE LENS
of Cultural Materialism

Conformity and Conflict • Reading Ten

The Hunters: Scarce Resources in the Kalahari

Richard Borshay Lee

The author argues against the common 1960s' misconception that hunter-gatherer societies are dependent mainly on game animals and live arduous, uncertain, hand-to-mouth lives. His study in the Dobe region has revealed that the !Kung have adapted well to their mode of production and lead sustainable lives. Research has shown that the low-technology subsistence methods used by the !Kung are highly efficient. They provide adequate food for relatively few hours of work.

Infrastructure

Emic

- "When a Bushman was asked why he hadn't taken to agriculture, he replied: 'Why should we plant when there are so many mongongo nuts in the world?'" (p. 112).

Etic

- The !Kung inhabit the semiarid northwest region of the Kalahari desert and rely on a hunting and gathering mode of production. They reside in camps that are self-sufficient subsistence units, whose members move out each day to hunt and gather and return in the evening to pool the collected foods in such a way that every person present receives an equitable share.

- Each camp is associated with a permanent waterhole and "each waterhole has a hinterland lying within a six-mile radius that is regularly exploited for vegetable and animal foods" (p. 109). Lee does not use the term *band* to describe the !Kung due to the fact that camps are "open aggregates of cooperating persons which changes in size and composition from day to day" (p. 109). Trade between camps is minimal, although people move freely between camps.

- The !Kung move their camps about five or six times a year, once each camp has reached the point of diminishing returns, or when the amount of food return per unit of effort begins to fall. Once !Kung members begin traveling farther and farther for resources, they will most likely move to another camp in order to increase the efficiency of food return. The abandoned land is then left to regenerate.

- Since there is rarely more than two or three days' supply of food on hand at any time, the !Kung work every third or fourth day to gather food. The mongongo nut is the most important food source, as it accounts for 50 per-

cent of the vegetable diet by weight. The !Kung's production effort remains well below the carrying capacity.

- An "output of 2,140 calories and 93.1 grams of protein per person per day may be compared with the Recommended Daily Allowances for persons of the small size and stature but vigorous activity regime of the !Kung Bushmen. The RDA for Bushmen can be estimated at 1,975 calories and 60 grams of protein per person per day. Thus it is apparent that food output exceeds energy requirements by 165 calories and 33 grams of protein" (p. 118). This proves that the !Kung can satisfy nutritional requirements with only two or three days' worth of modest subsistence effort. There is a high degree of security in gathering, which accounts for 60 to 80 percent of the annual diet by weight.

- Game animals, by contrast, are scarce, mobile, unpredictable, and difficult to catch. Meat is considered as a "special treat" and is never depended on as a staple, so no one goes hungry when hunting fails.

Structure

Etic

- The !Kung way of life is primarily embedded within their subsistence economy. Within the domestic economy of their culture, the !Kung practice a sexual division of labor. "Vegetable foods comprise from 60 to 80 percent of the total diet by weight and collecting involves two or three days of work per woman per week. The men also collect plants and small animals, but their major contribution to the diet is the hunting of medium and large game" (p. 110). Thus "although men's and women's work input is roughly equivalent in terms of man-day of effort, the women provide two to three times as much food by weight as the men" (p. 110).

- Although it has been claimed that hunter-gatherers do not live long lives, Lee found that "in a total population of 466, about 46 individuals were determined to be over sixty years of age, a proportion that compares favorably to the percentage of elderly in industrialized populations. Furthermore, the aged hold a respected position in Bushmen society and are the effective leaders of the camp" (p. 115).

- Young people are not expected to provide food regularly until they are married. As a result, the people in the 20 to 60 age group support a surprisingly large percentage of nonproductive young and old people. About 40 percent of the population in a camp contributes to the food supply. This allocation allows for a relatively carefree childhood and adolescence and a relatively relaxed old age.

- In terms of the political economy, the !Kung live in a rather self-sufficient egalitarian society with no effective hierarchy.

Superstructure

Emic

- The !Kung view both hunting and illness as unpredictable and subject to magical control. Men engage in trancing, which enables them to reach a state of enhanced consciousness and access energy from the realm of their spiritual ancestors.

Etic

- "Over 50 percent of the men have learned to trance and regularly enter altered states during the course of the all night dances. Those who have entered trances rarely go out hunting the following day. . . . In a camp with five or more hunters, there are usually two or three who are actively hunting and several others who are inactive" (p. 117).

THROUGH THE LENS
of Cultural Materialism

Conformity and Conflict • Reading Eleven

Adaptive Failure: Easter's End

Jared Diamond

Infrastructure

- The first Polynesian colonists who inhabited Easter Island found themselves in "a pristine paradise," with all the prerequisites for comfortable living: a rich subtropical forest full of plant and animal food resources, fertile soil, and bountiful building materials. They prospered and their population grew.

- Easter Island's population cut down the forest faster than the forest could regenerate itself. "The destruction of the island's animals was as extreme as that of the forest: without exception, every species of native land bird became extinct."

- Intensification generated a chain of events that depleted the native flora and fauna and thus led to the depletion of all basic resources, as the carrying capacity was greatly exceeded.

- Disaster progressed slowly, so that the inhabitants hardly noticed what was happening until it was too late.

- A population must adapt to the minimum availability of any one necessary resource, rather than by the abundance of all necessary resources (Liebig's law of minimum). The population on Easter Island overlooked the minimum factor and became used to the average condition, due to the seemingly unrestricted abundance of resources.

- The scarcity of resources impacted the people's mode of production; the environment could no longer sustain such a large population. "People also found it harder to fill their stomachs, as land birds, large sea snails, and many seabirds disappeared. . . . Crop yields also declined, since deforestation allowed the soil to be eroded by rain and wind, dried by the sun, and its nutrients to be leeched from it."

- Overproduction ultimately led to the people's demise.

Structure

- Coming from Polynesia, the early inhabitants brought with them a complex stratified political system based on the redistribution of locally available resources and regional economic integration. Stratified redistribution intensifies production in order to accumulate wealth and prestige.

- Stratification creates a high consumption economy. Non–food producing individuals provide manufactured goods and services that enhance the prestige of the ruling segment of society. On Easter Island, such specialists erected stone statues on platforms that became larger and larger over time in an escalating spiral of one-upmanship, as rival clans tried to surpass each other with shows of wealth and power.

- As resources were depleted, the population suffered and "local chaos replaced centralized government and a warrior class took over from the hereditary chiefs." Eventually, rival clans toppled the heads of other clans' statues, symbolizing the collapse of the political economy.

Superstructure

- Huge stone statues on the island symbolized political power and prestige.

- A perceived abundance of resources led to overconsumption and was used to establish and sustain stratification.

- As resources became more scarce, rival clans competed with one another through displays of wealth and power.

- Continued rivalry led to warfare and to the further destruction of the environment and culture.

CHAPTER **6**

REPRODUCTION

These parents and their infant are among the San of the Kalahari Desert.

We will now focus on the reproductive aspect of infrastructure. Given the potential that human beings have to increase population, how is population brought into balance with production and carrying capacity? We will see that preindustrial societies affect population growth through such means as sexual abstinence, prolonged nursing, abortion, and direct and indirect infanticide. Then why do people in poverty-stricken parts of the world persist in having large families, whereas people in rich industrial countries have fewer and fewer children? What explains rates of population growth is not the possession of contraceptives or abortifacients but the costs and benefits of raising children under different modes of production.

The Relation between Production and Reproduction

Reproduction is a form of production—the "product" being new human beings. Under optimal conditions, women can have between 20 and 25 live births during their fertile years (which last roughly from age 15 to 45).

In all human societies, women on the average have far fewer children than they are capable of having.

The record, 8.97 children per woman, is held by the Hutterites, a communitarian sect in western Canada

Large Families Preferred in Developing Countries
Having a high fertility rate improves people's standard of living in the short term.

(Lang and Gohlen 1985). If all children born live to reproduce, any number of births greater than two per woman would potentially result in population increase (holding death rates constant and without emigration). Even small rates of increase can result in enormous populations in a few generations. The !Kung, for example, have a growth rate of 0.5 percent per year. If the world had started 10,000 years ago with a population of two and if that population had grown at 0.5 percent per year, the world population would now be 604,436,000,000,000,000,000,000. No such growth has occurred because through various combinations of cultural and natural factors, reproduction has been kept within limits imposed by systems of production (Box 6.1).

Much controversy surrounds the nature of the relationship between production and reproduction. Followers of Thomas Malthus, the founder of the science of *demography* (the science of population phenomena), have long held the view that the level of population is determined by the amount of food produced.

 Malthus believed that population would always increase more rapidly than the food supply; in fact, he believed that population growth would tend to rise faster than any conceivable rise in productivity, thereby dooming a large portion of humanity to perpetual poverty, hunger, and misery.

However, evidence from many nonindustrial societies shows that populations maintain their levels of production well below carrying capacity, as discussed next, and that Malthus was wrong in assuming that population growth would necessarily lead to scarcity and misery. Moreover, as advocated by Ester Boserup, we could turn Malthus upside down and see the amount of food produced as being determined by the level of population growth.

BOX 6.1 | The Human Crop

The arithmetic of global population growth has become numbingly familiar: 1 billion in 1800, 2.5 billion in 1950, and 6.3 billion today. In the past four decades, more people have been added to the globe than in all of history before the middle of the twentieth century. And growth continues unabated. The world's population is now expanding at the unprecedented rate of approximately 1 billion per decade (Bongaarts 1994a, 1994b:771).

Ester Boserup has proposed an alternative view that holds that food production tends to rise to the level demanded by population growth. As population expands and the point of diminishing returns is reached, people invent or adopt new and more efficient modes of food production.

In light of recent anthropological research, the position that seems most correct is that production and reproduction are equally important in shaping the course of sociocultural evolution and that to an equal extent, each is the cause of the other. Reproduction generates population pressure (psychological and physiological costs such as malnutrition and illness), which prompts efforts to increase production through technological improvements.

Population pressure often leads to intensification, diminishing returns, and irreversible environmental depletions. Depletions, in turn, often lead to new technologies and to new modes of production.

Population Pressure versus Population Growth

Population pressure and population growth are not the same thing. **Population growth** is birthrate minus mortality, not counting migration in and out of a territory, whereas **population pressure** refers to pressure on resources that forces people to work harder to obtain the same amount of food. Under favorable environmental conditions, population size and density can increase, at least temporarily, without lowering a people's standard of living. During the nineteenth century, the settling of the American West was accompanied by high fertility rates and a rapidly rising population, and because the landscape was fertile, there was a rising standard of living among pioneer farm families.

Moreover, population pressures may exist even if a population is not increasing. For example, a stable population may deplete local resources if it is unable to expand into new territory. To prevent the erosion of their standard of living, people often employ physically and emotionally costly means of reproductive controls, such as **infanticide** and induced abortion, to continue to keep their population growth at a low level. For example, Arctic hunter-gatherers live at very low population densities and virtually zero rates of population growth. They practice female infanticide as a means of keeping their population within the limits that can be sustained by their mode of production (E. A. Smith and S. A. Smith 1994).

The key to understanding population pressure is not population density but the number of people in an area relative to its resources.

Population pressure might even exist among people who are experiencing a population decline. Many Native American communities in the Amazon have declined in number because of epidemics yet find it increasingly difficult to maintain their standard of living using their traditional mode of production because they have been forced, by more politically dominant groups, to occupy marginal environments that are less capable of sustaining them, given their level of technology. Perhaps the best way to envision population pressure is to regard it as present with varying intensity among virtually all societies (the exception being societies that are expanding into uninhabited frontiers). Even in high-tech industrial countries, where fertility rates have fallen below replacement levels (see later in this chapter) largely by using modern methods of birth control, population pressure has a role to play in phenomena such as unemployment, crime, homelessness, child abuse, and pollution.

Given the finite nature of our capacity to produce energy, population growth can only drive up the price of energy and the goods and services energy makes possible. At best, population pressure is a destabilizing force. It interacts with natural sources of instability, such as changes in climate, to bring about both small- and large-scale shifts in modes of production. Thus, although production limits population growth, population pressure provides a perpetual motivation for overcoming such limits (Graber 1991, 1992; A. Johnson and Earle 1987; Keeley 1996).

Population and technology have a feedback relationship: Populations grow because new sources of food are discovered as new technology is used to increase production; technological change is invented or accepted because it enables people to intensify production and better adapt to their environment.

Preindustrial Reproductive Practices

Much evidence supports the view that preindustrial cultures reduced or controlled population pressure by keeping reproductive rates low. How did they do this in the absence of condoms, diaphragms, pills, spermicides, effective abortion drugs (Riddle and Estes 1992), and knowledge of the human ovulatory cycle? Four categories of practice have had the direct or indirect effect of regulating population growth:

- Care and treatment of fetuses, infants, and children
- Care and treatment of girls and women (and to a lesser extent of boys and men)
- Intensity and duration of lactation (the period of breastfeeding)
- Variations in the frequency of coital intercourse

Before describing these practices, we should point out that many anthropologists and demographers regard only conscious attempts to limit reproduction to a targeted number of children as evidence of population regulation (Wood 1990). Our view is that effective limits on population growth can be achieved both by direct, conscious efforts and by indirect and unconscious ones.

Treatment of Fetuses and Children

Maltreatment of fetuses, infants, and young children is a common means of lowering reproductivity.

Parental investment begins during pregnancy and includes a range of behaviors, from full support to indifference, passive neglect, and active attempts to promote fetal death. Full support begins with caring for pregnant women, supplementing their diets, and reducing their workloads (MacCormack 1982:8). Indifference or neglect begins when heavy workloads and meager diets are imposed on pregnant women. Direct abortion involves trauma such as applying pressure to the mother's abdomen, jumping on her, or having her ingest toxic substances (Riddle and Estes 1992). In a study of 350 preindustrial societies, George Devereux (1967:98) found that direct abortion occurred in all 350. Modern medical abortion differs from more traditional methods that endanger the mother almost as much as the fetus. For example, medical abortion today is the principal form of fertility control in Japan (Jitsukawa and Djerassi 1994).

Infanticide is widely practiced in preindustrial societies because abortion is dangerous to the mother.

A subtle gradation leads from indirect to direct methods of infanticide. Full support of the life of a newborn infant requires that it be fed to gain weight rapidly and that it be protected against extremes of temperature and from falls, burns, and other accidents.

 Indirect infanticide begins with neglect and under-investment—inadequate feeding, withholding emotional support, and careless and indifferent handling, especially when the infant is sick.

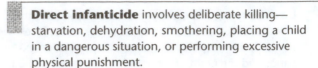 **Direct infanticide** involves deliberate killing—starvation, dehydration, smothering, placing a child in a dangerous situation, or performing excessive physical punishment.

Often no sharp emic distinction exists between abortion and infanticide. Where infanticide occurs, it usually happens early in life, before the child is regarded as a real person in the society. In this connection, it should be pointed out that many cultures do not consider children to be human until certain ceremonies, such as naming or hair cutting, are performed. Infanticide and the induced death of small children seldom take place after such ceremonies have been performed (Minturn and Stashak 1982). Hence, in the emic perspective, such deaths are rarely seen as homicides.

Treatment of Women

The treatment of women can raise or lower the age at which women begin to be capable of bearing children and the age at which they can no longer conceive. It can also affect the total number of pregnancies women are capable of sustaining.

Women who are nutritionally deprived are not as fertile as women whose diets are adequate, although considerable controversy exists over how severe the deprivation must be before a significant decline in fertility occurs.

Still, periods of severe, famine-level nutritional deprivation can reduce fertility by 50 percent (Bongaarts 1980:568). Rose Frisch (1984:184), however, maintains that even a 10 to 15 percent weight loss is sufficient to delay menarche and to disrupt the menstrual cycle. Others assign less significance to the role of body fat in fertility (Wood 1990:234).

Other effects of malnutrition on the mother, fetus, and infant are well established. Poor maternal nutrition increases the risk of premature births and of low birthweights, both of which increase fetal and infant mortality; poor maternal nutrition also diminishes the quantity if not the quality of breast milk, thus lowering the chances of infant survival still further (Frisancho et al. 1983; Hamilton et al. 1984:388). In turn, women who become pregnant and breastfeed from a nutritionally depleted body have an elevated mortality rate (Adair and Popkin 1992; Kusin et al. 1993; Lunn 1988).

Extreme malnutrition and physical and mental stress can affect male **fecundity** by reducing **libido** (sexual desire) and sperm count. The abundance of sperm, however, as compared with the small number of ova and a woman's limited capacity for birthing and nursing, means that the treatment of women is far more important than the treatment of men in regulating reproduction. High sickness and mortality rates among men are readily counterbalanced by the widespread practice of **polygyny** (one husband with several wives) and by the fact that one man can impregnate dozens of women.

Lactation

Lactation amenorrhea (disruption of the menstrual cycle) is a typical accompaniment of breastfeeding and serves as another form of birth control.

The effect of lactation amenorrhea is associated with the production of prolactin, a hormone that regulates mammary activity. When an infant suckles at the breast, prolactin is activated, which in turn inhibits the production of the hormones that regulate the ovulatory cycle. Lactating women therefore are less likely to ovulate and conceive.

Several biocultural factors appear to control the duration of lactation amenorrhea. To begin with, there is the state of the mother's health and her diet, which

Breastfeeding Older Children
San women breastfeed their children for four or five years.

affect her ability to breastfeed. Additional variables include the intensity of suckling (more intense suckling produces more prolactin in the body), the age at which the infant is fed supplemental foods, the amount of time the infant spends at the breast, and how often suckling episodes take place.

Under favorable conditions, prolonged nursing itself can clearly result in birth-spacing intervals of three or more years, with a degree of reliability comparable to that of modern mechanical and chemical contraceptives. But one must be on guard against the notion that any social group is free to adjust its fertility rate upward or downward merely by intensifying and prolonging lactation. Prolonged lactation cannot take place without suitably nourished mothers. Moreover, because human breast milk is deficient in iron, its use as the sole source of nourishment much beyond the age of 6 months will cause anemia in the infant.

Coital Frequency and Scheduling

Various forms of nonreproductive sex can influence fertility rates.

Homosexuality, masturbation, coitus interruptus (withdrawal before ejaculation), and noncoital heterosexual techniques for achieving orgasm can all play a role in regulating fertility. Age of marriage is another important population-regulating variable, but its significance depends on the existence of taboos on extramarital sex and unwed motherhood.

Type of marriage is also relevant to fertility. Polygyny, for example, assures that almost all females will marry and engage in reproductive sex (in the absence of contraception). In addition, polygyny probably results in lower rates of coital intercourse per wife as husbands grow older (Bongaarts and Odile 1984: 521–522; Hern 1992).

Clearly, preindustrial societies have never lacked means—conscious or unconscious—for regulating their reproductive rates in response to the limits and possibilities of their modes of production.

The Influence of Disease and Other Natural Factors

Most of the great lethal epidemic diseases—smallpox, typhoid fever, influenza, bubonic plague, and cholera—are primarily associated with dense urbanized populations, rather than with dispersed hunter-gatherers or small village cultures. Even such diseases as malaria and yellow fever were probably less important among low-density populations that could avoid swampy mosquito-breeding grounds.

Among many preindustrial societies, the role of disease as a long-term regulator of human population is to some extent a consequence of the success or failure of other population-regulating mechanisms, such as infanticide, lactation amenorrhea, and nonreproductive sex.

Only if other mechanisms of population control are ineffective—resulting in a rise in population density, a drop in food production, and a deterioration of diet—will some diseases figure as important checks on preindustrial population growth (Post 1985).

Obviously, a component in human birth and death rates reflects natural causes over which cultural practices have little influence. In addition to lethal diseases, natural catastrophes such as droughts, floods, and earthquakes may raise death rates and lower birthrates in a manner that leaves little room for cultural intervention.

The Costs and Benefits of Rearing Children

At the family level, parental perceptions of the costs and values of rearing children influence their reproductive decision making. Rearing children includes these costs:

- Extra food consumed during pregnancy
- Work not done by pregnant women
- Expenses involved in providing mother's milk and other foods during infancy and childhood
- Burden of carrying infants and children from one place to another
- In more complex societies, expenditures for clothing, housing, medical care, and education

In addition, the birth process itself is dangerous and often places the life of the mother at risk. The benefits that affect the demand for children include the following:

- Emotional satisfaction children can bring
- Contributions that children make to food production and to family income in general
- Care and economic security children give their parents
- Role of children in marital exchanges and intergroup alliances
- Protection that large families may provide against outsiders

In many cultures, groups exchange sons and daughters in order to obtain husbands and wives. These exchanges are used to arrange alliances against aggressors. Hence, where chronic warfare exists, larger groups are safer than smaller ones; they have more alliances as well as greater military strength.

All this, of course, is not to deny that people have children for sentimental reasons as well (see Box 6.2). Humans may have a genetically controlled propensity, shared with other primates, to find infants emotionally appealing and to derive emotional satisfaction from holding and fondling them and from watching and helping them play and learn. As children grow older, their respect and love for their parents may also be highly valued.

Much recent evidence suggests that the rate at which the parental generation has children is largely determined by the extent to which having each ad-

---

BOX 6.2   The Economy of Parental Love

Children fulfill a need for close, affectionate, and emotional relationships with supportive, concerned, trustworthy, and approving beings. We need children because we need to be loved. In the support parents lavish on children, there is a culturally instructed expectation that a balance will be struck with the love and affection that children can be so good at giving in return. Even in their least giving mood, babies respond with warm, wet sucking and mouthing; they grasp your fingers and try to put their arms around you. Already you can anticipate the ardent hugs and kisses of early childhood: the tot who clings to your neck; the 4-year-old tucked in bed, whispering "I love you"; the 6-year-old breathless at the door or running down the path as you come home from work. And with a little more imagination, you can see all the way to a grateful son or daughter, dressed in cap and gown, saying, "Thanks, Mom and Dad. I owe it all to you."

The fact that many of the sentimental rewards of parenthood are delayed does not mean that dreams rule the economy of love. As in every other kind of exchange, mere expectation of a return flow will not sustain the bonds indefinitely. The family sanctuary is a fragile temple. People will not forever marry and have children if the actual experience departs far from the expectation.

Source: Adapted from M. Harris 1989:230ff.

ditional child results in a net gain of benefits over costs for the average couple (Caldwell 1982; M. Harris and Ross 1987; Nardi 1983). According to Richard Lee (1979, 1993), !Kung San mothers try to avoid having one child right after another in order to escape the burden of carrying two children at once. The benefits of having additional children are further reduced among hunter-gatherers by the vulnerability of wild species of plants and animals to depletion. As band size increases, per capita food production tends to decline because hunter-gatherers have no effective way of increasing the population of the wild plants and animals they use for food. Finally, the children of hunter-gatherers do not produce more food than they consume until relatively late in childhood because young children cannot forage in the hot desert sun without water. For these reasons, population densities among simple hunter-gatherers seldom rise above one person per square mile.

If contemporary hunter-gatherers are at all representative of prehistoric times, *Homo sapiens* must have been a very rare creature during the early Stone Age. Perhaps as few as 5 to 15 million people lived in the entire world in those times (M. N. Cohen 1977:54; Dumond 1975; Hassan 1978:78), compared with over 6 billion today. For tens of thousands of years, the rate of growth of the human population was undoubtedly very slow.

Fertility is generally highest among agriculturalists. Farm families tend to be *pronatalist,* an ideology that values large families and equates having many children with wealth and success. Among agriculturalists, children no longer have to be carried about over long distances; they can perform many useful economic chores at an early age; and because the rate of reproduction of domesticated plants and animals can be controlled, a considerable amount of intensification and hence population growth can be achieved without a decline in per capita output. In many agricultural societies, older children rapidly begin to pay for themselves. They contribute to the production of their own food, clothing, and housing, and under favorable conditions, they may begin to produce surpluses above their own subsistence needs as early as 6 years of age. This transition is hastened with successive births, because older siblings and other children assume much of the cost of grooming and caring for their juniors.

Measuring the Costs and Benefits of Rearing Children

A number of attempts have been made to measure the economic value of children in contemporary peasant communities. For example, in village Java, boys of 12 to 14 years contribute 33 hours of economically valuable work per week, and girls 9 to 11 contribute about 38 hours a week of the same. Altogether, children contribute about half of all work performed by household members. Much household labor involves making handicrafts, working in petty trades, and processing various foods for sale. Similar findings are reported for Nepal (Nag et al. 1978; B. White 1982).

Costs are more difficult to measure, but Javanese children themselves do most of the work needed to rear and maintain their siblings, freeing mothers for income-producing tasks.

Large households are more efficient income-producing units than small households in rural Java because in large households, a smaller proportion of each individual's total labor time is required for non–income producing household tasks (such as cooking and cleaning).

Javanese women have about five births and four surviving children. This adds up to an alarming 2 percent per annum increase in population (B. White 1982:605). Meade Cain (1977:225) quantified both

Nyinba Girl Carries Mud Home for Construction
Children perform a variety of tasks that make them useful to families in nonindustrial societies.

benefits and costs for male children in a rural Bangladesh village:

> Male children become net producers at the latest by the age of 12. Furthermore, by age 15, male children work long enough hours at high enough rates of productivity to compensate for consumption. . . . Therefore, in general parents realize a net economic return on male children for the period when they are subordinate members of the parental household.

Thus, the popular perception that people in less developed countries have large numbers of children simply because they do not know how to avoid conception does not hold up.

Much evidence tells us that in agricultural societies, having more children and larger households means a higher, not a lower, standard of living in the short run.

In explaining why they did not wish to join any family-planning programs, the men of Manipur village in the Punjab explained, "Why pay 2,500 rupees for an extra hand? Why not have a son?" (Mamdani 1973:77). High fertility may simply mean that large families have a more favorable standard of living relative to that of smaller families in a situation where the farming sector is stagnant or even deteriorating (Weil 1986). As we will see next, the opposite is true in communities where new income opportunities do not support child labor.

With the expansion of urban, industrial, technical, and white-collar employment opportunities, the net return from childrearing can be increased by investing in fewer but better-educated offspring.

In Rampur village, close to the Indian capital of New Delhi, the number of children per woman declined as wage opportunities increased outside the village (Dasgupta 1978). Tractors, tube wells, and pumps reduced the demand for child labor. In addition, parents wanted their children to get more education to prepare for higher-quality jobs in New Delhi. Furthermore, white-collar jobs were becoming available for which children were unsuited because they had not achieved the required levels of literacy and mathematical skills.

In Indian villages located near the city of Bangalore, three factors accounted for the trend against child labor:

- Land holdings had become fragmented and too small to absorb the labor of additional children in agriculture.
- New nonfarm employment opportunities requiring arithmetic skills and literacy had opened up.
- Educational facilities had been introduced or improved within the villages (Caldwell et al. 1983).

Similarly, on returning to the village of Manipur in the Punjab, Nag and Kak (1984) found a sharp increase in the number of couples practicing contraception and a sharp reduction in the number of sons regarded as desirable.

Changes resulting from shifts in the mode of production may lower the demand for child labor and lead to a reduction in family size.

The loss of cattle and the increased reliance on petrochemical fuels and fertilizers have also done away with the childhood task of collecting cow dung to be used for fertilizer and fuel. With the introduction of industrial herbicides, children are no longer needed

Manipur, Punjab, India
Collection of cow dung by children to make dung cakes for use as cooking fuel is becoming less important as families become more prosperous and the land is farmed more intensively.

for weeding. Meanwhile, the mechanization of farm operations, the expanded use of credit, and the need to keep account books have made Manipur parents consciously eager to expand their children's educational horizons. Secondary school enrollment increased in a decade from 63 to 81 percent for boys and from 29 to 63 percent for girls. Parents now want at least one son to have a white-collar job so that the family will not be entirely dependent on agriculture; many parents want both sons and daughters to attend college.

The Poverty Trap

The *persistence of poverty* in many developing countries can be explained by population pressure, the costs and benefits of children, and local environmental depletions.

As presented by economist Partha Dasgupta (1995), these features form a vicious circle. In many poor countries, as resources are depleted, children must search for firewood and water over longer distances. This increases the demand for children, encourages parents to have additional babies, expands the population, and further exacerbates the depletion of resources. Finally, when they can find no more water or firewood, the families flee to the cities to join the homeless beggars and laborers who sleep on the sidewalks of Bombay and Calcutta.

Fertility rates in developing countries are affected by whether individuals gain economically from increasing or restricting fertility.

John Caldwell (1982) proposes that changes in fertility rates can be accounted for by "wealth flows," which include labor services, goods, money, and present and future securities. Higher rates of fertility are likely to be found where wealth flows upward, from younger to older members, and where parents rely on children to actively contribute to the economic well-being of the family. This is characteristic of most "poor" subsistence-based societies, where children's labor benefits the family. Stable market economies and education reverse this process; wealth begins to flow downward when parents become more economically secure and invest more in their children than they receive in return.

The Contraception, Abortion, and Infanticide Debate

Human reproduction is much more than an act that takes place at a specific instant. It implies that hu-

man reproduction is a social process that begins long before conception.

The decision to rear children is heavily influenced by the balance of costs and benefits confronting prospective parents.

This means that when the balance is adverse, some form of birth or death control will be activated at some point in the reproductive process. When and how life or death control measures will be taken varies from one culture to another. It may be shocking to Western sensibilities that many preindustrial societies employ reproduction-regulating measures that achieve their effect after children are born. That is, they practice some form of direct or indirect infanticide.

In many parts of the world, infanticide occurs when the mother is overburdened and cannot care for the child, the child is weak and unlikely to survive, or the child's paternity is inappropriate.

We must keep in mind that the options for parents in traditional societies are very different from those in our own. !Kung women maximize reproductive success by wide birth spacing, achieved in part by infanticide; poor and malnourished women may not be physically able to nurse nor have the resources to raise a child that is unlikely to survive (Dickman 1984; Scrimshaw 1984). Infanticide was common in the ancient cultures of Greece, Rome, and China and was practiced in Europe until the late nineteenth century. In Europe the practice of "overlaying" (smothering) an infant sharing a bed with its parents and abandonment of unwanted infants were common practices.

Much evidence exists that if reproduction is not limited before or during pregnancy, then it will be limited after pregnancy by direct or indirect infanticide or pedicide (the killing of young children). In nineteenth-century Japan, farmers in the countryside were at one time the world's most efficient managers of human reproduction. Japanese farm couples precisely fitted the size and sexual composition of their offspring to the size and fertility of their land holdings. The smallholder's ideal was two children, one boy and one girl; people with larger holdings aimed for two boys and one or two girls. But the Japanese did not stop there! As expressed in a still-popular saying "First a girl, then a boy," they tried to rear a daughter first and a son second. According to G. William Skinner, this ideal reflected the practice of assigning much of the task of rearing firstborn sons to an older sister. It also reflected the expectation that the firstborn son would replace his father as the farm's manager at an age when the father was ready to retire and the son was not yet so old as to have grown surly while waiting to take over. A further complexity was the age at which a couple got married. An older man would not dare to delay having a son, and so if the firstborn was a male, he would count himself fortunate. Since the parents had no way of telling the sex of a child before birth, they were able to achieve these precise reproductive goals only by practicing systematic infanticide (Skinner 1993).

Attempts to discourage contraception, medical abortion, and other forms of modern reproductive controls may inadvertently increase reliance on indirect infanticide when mothers are incapable of caring for numerous children, as seen in the shantytowns of northeast Brazil (see Profile 6.1).

We must also guard against the impression that high rates of infanticide occur only in Brazil. Selective neglect of female infants accounts for the lopsided sex ratios found in many societies, including India and China (George et al. 1992). Both indirect and direct infanticide have also been widely practiced in Europe in previous centuries (Kertzer 1993). In Japan, perhaps more than elsewhere, direct infanticide was used as a conscious means of family planning during the nineteenth century.

Today, in postindustrial societies, women give birth to few children and invest heavily in each one, whereas in some preindustrial societies, women give birth to many children and invest selectively according to culturally favored characteristics.

Industrial Modes of Reproduction

Shifts in the costs and benefits of rearing children may explain the *demographic transition* that took place in Europe, the United States, and Japan during the nineteenth century. This transition involved a drop in both birthrates and death rates and a slowing of the rate of population growth (Figure 6.1).

With industrialization, the cost of rearing children rose rapidly, especially after the introduction of child labor laws and compulsory education statutes. The skills required to earn a living took longer to acquire; hence parents had to wait longer before they could receive any economic benefits from their children. At the same time, the whole pattern of how people earned their livings changed. Work ceased to be something done by family members on the family farm or in the family shop; rather, people earned wages as individuals in factories and offices. What the family did together was to consume; its only product was chil-

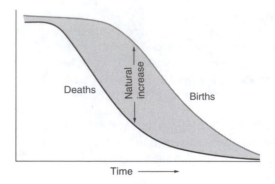

Figure 6.1 Demographic Transition
A rapid fall in the death rate followed by a slower fall in the birthrate causes a temporary increase in population growth until demographic transition is completed.

dren. The return flow of benefits from rearing children came to hinge more and more on their willingness to help out in the medical and financial crises that beset older people. But longer life spans and spiraling medical costs make it increasingly unrealistic for parents to expect such help from their children. Thus, the industrial nations have been obliged to substitute old-age and medical insurance and old-age homes for the preindustrial system in which children took care of their aged parents.

To meet the rise in the cost of rearing children in industrial societies, wives as well as husbands must participate in the wage-earning labor force. As long as this situation continues, more and more men and women will decide to have only one child or none, and more and more individuals will find that the traditional forms of marriage, family, sex, and emotional togetherness are incompatible with the maintenance of middle-class status.

Changes in the mode of production and thus reproduction can be seen in China. During the 1950s and 1960s, when China was largely preindustrial, the government promoted a pronatalist ideology, urging people to raise large families to "make China stronger." During this time, the population nearly doubled, making China the most populous nation in the world. But despite China's vast terrain, only one-tenth of its territory was suitable for agriculture, and if left unchecked, its population growth would spiral out of control. To slow population growth, China introduced a *one-child policy*, limiting urban couples to one child and allowing rural families to have two children, if the first child was a daughter.

Beginning in 1973, the Chinese government implemented an education program to encourage family planning. Initially, almost all rural families rejected the birth control policy because it threatened their short-

Northeast Brazil is a region subjected to periodic drought, chronic malnutrition, and widespread poverty. It is an area where people live in shantytowns and work as landless laborers on sugarcane plantations for insufficient wages. A large segment of the population suffers from chronic malnutrition that leaves them in a weakened state, prone to infection and disease. Life expectancy in northeast Brazil is only 40 years, and the rate of infant mortality is about 200 deaths per 1,000 births in the first year of life (compared with a rate of fewer than 10 in developed countries).

According to Nancy Scheper-Hughs (1984), who carried out a study in the town of Alto do Cruzeiro, of a total of 688 pregnancies (an average of 9.5 per woman!), there were 579 live births. Only 308 of these infants survived to age 5, an average of 3.6 infant and child deaths per woman. From circumstantial evidence, it is clear that many of these deaths are best described as forms of indirect infanticide.

In Alto do Cruzeiro, mothers spoke of children who "wanted to die," whose will and drive toward life were not "sufficiently strong or developed." Mothers regard some childhood diseases as incurable, but the diagnostic symptoms of these diseases are so broad that almost any childhood disorder can be interpreted as a sign that the child is doomed to die: fits and convulsions, lethargy and passivity, retarded verbal or motor function, or a "ghost-like" or "animal-like" appearance.

When a child marked with one of these fatal diseases dies, mothers do not display grief. They say there is no remedy, that even if you treat the disease, the child "will never be right," that it is "best to leave them to die," and that no one wants to take care of such a child. "It was a blessing that God decided to take them in their infancy." Scheper-Hughes (1984) estimates that 43 percent of child deaths are attributable to the withdrawal of support from infants and children.

An important source of motivation for indirect infanticide is the belief that after babies and infants die, they become angels. The little corpses are placed in cardboard coffins and escorted to shallow graves by a smiling and laughing throng of children. Mothers do not weep when one of their babies becomes an angel.

To the extent that mothers practice indirect infanticide through neglect, they are reacting to life-threatening conditions that are not of their own making: severe shortage of food, contaminated water supplies, unchecked infectious diseases, lack of day care, and absence of affordable medical care. These are the penalties of extreme poverty. Mothers must concede to a certain passivity toward conditions that are in many respects beyond their control. "Letting go" is all they can do. But if a child is perceived as ill fated for life, it is difficult to enlist a mother in the rescue of a child. Their patterns of nurturing differentiate those infants thought of as "thrivers" and as "keepers" from those thought of as born "already wanting to die."

While recognizing that mothers hasten the deaths of their unwanted children by rationing infant and child care, we must not fall into the trap of "blaming the victims." These women do not have access to modern forms of contraception or to medical abortion, and they are themselves too poorly nourished to limit their pregnancies by prolonging lactation. Moreover, sexual abstinence is difficult for these women because of their need to attract male support and companionship. In Scheper-Hughs's words, because of the indignities and inhumanities forced on them, these women must at times "make choices and decisions that no woman and mother should have to make" (1984:541). And so a good part of learning how to mother on the Alto includes knowing when to let go of a child who shows he or she wants to die. The other part is knowing just when it is safe to let oneself go enough to love a child, to trust that a child will remain in this life on earth.

Doomed Infant in Northeast Brazil

This baby has anemia and is listless and malnourished. The mother says she is conforming to God's will that the child will soon be an angel.

term economic security. It wasn't until the 1990s, when villagers became more affluent, that their attitudes toward having children began to change. The cost of raising children was on the rise. Parents incurred incidental expenses to show affection for their children and to provide for their education. The expensive cost of marriage was another factor. (The custom of providing a generous bride wealth and dowry flourished, and the average cost of marriage for a son increased more than tenfold from 1949 to 1999.) As families became more affluent, the perceived utility of children began to decline. Today, villagers voluntarily accept the new fertility culture and voluntarily agree to have only one child. Children no longer serve as family laborers, and their support of the elderly is rapidly declining (see Profile 6.2).

Women's Status, Education, and Fertility

Demographers agree that a number of factors are responsible for fertility rates. Classic models of demographic change assume that in nation-states, high fertility will not decline until one of the following conditions exist:

- *There is a low infant mortality rate.* Couples will continue to have large numbers of children as long as they are not confident that children will survive and be there to care for them when they are old.

- *Couples benefit economically from restricting fertility.* Parents will weigh the costs and benefits of adding additional children to the household.

PROFILE 6.2 | Raising Children in Rural China

According to Yunxiang Yan (2003), it was not until 1983 that villagers in the northeast rural community of Xiajia experienced the powerful impact of China's state-sponsored fertility program. All women of fertility age who had had a son were required to be sterilized, and all women whose first child was a girl were required to get an IUD and could later petition to have a second child. To implement the policy, China developed a system that rewarded couples who were willing to restrict family size and that penalized those who did not comply.

Fertility worship and the desire for a large family was deeply rooted in Chinese cultural tradition. Children, especially male offspring who will perpetuate the family line, invoke an almost religious feeling of fulfillment, as expressed in the saying "More sons, more happiness." Despite the provision of strong incentives for abiding by the new policy—such as free education, medical care, and monetary grants—some families continued to have multiple births. Heavy fines were subsequently imposed, and villagers with too many unpaid fines had their land confiscated as further punishment.

By the 1990s, a shortage of land and a surplus of laborers created a serious change in the Chinese economy. Children born after 1983 did not have access to land because collective land had already been distributed, and younger-generation couples were forced to establish households outside the village. This meant that the elderly parents of multiple sons often ended up living alone, as their married sons shifted responsibility for their care. Elderly parents with only daughters cultivated closer relations with their children. Villagers began to question the notion of raising sons for old age, and many started personal savings to increase old-age security.

By the 1990s, young people had also developed a much stronger desire than their parents to pursue personal happiness. This included the pursuit of material comforts, such as fashionable clothing and better housing, and followed the national trend of consumerism This also meant experiencing the rising costs of children, who now required incidental costs for such things as toys and snacks.

By the late 1990s, few Chinese violated family-planning policies. Villagers today speak of "following the big trend," as a new generation of parents are making individual choices increasingly shaped by changing costs and benefits associated with raising children in the new market economy. In fact, in contrast to the past, when the richest Chinese had large, extended families, today, Chinese families with three or more children are among the poorest. After 1993, parents with single sons no longer tried to have an additional child, and an increasing number of families with daughters did not try to have a second child. When asked how they felt about not having a son, the most common answer from these parents of only daughters was "It is unimportant whether the child is a son or daughter; the key is to have a child." The women seemed to be open minded, and several provided detailed stories about sons who had failed to support their elderly parents. Although most villagers still perceive the continuation of the family line only through sons, the pressure to produce a son for the family has begun to wane. Third births among parents of two daughters are rare, and only-daughter households are no longer exceptional.

BOX 6.3 | Population Growth Is a Global Problem

The environmental and social impacts of population growth know no national boundaries and affect us all. Population growth anywhere in the world ultimately has an impact on the entire planet's environment. Many environmental problems, such as air and water pollution and global climate change, transcend national boundaries. As our population grows, demands for resources increase, adding to pollution and waste. More energy is used, escalating the problems of global warming, acid rain, oil spills, and nuclear waste. More land is required for agriculture, leading to deforestation and soil erosion. More homes, factories, and roads must be built, reducing agricultural land and the habitats of other species, leading increasingly to their extinction.

One example of the interconnectedness of our planet's environment is the depletion of tropical rain forests. Rain forest destruction is not only causing a loss of biodiversity, but it is also upsetting the atmosphere's climate control capabilities. Sometimes called the "lungs of the Earth," rain forests are vital to all of us.

The world's current population is estimated to be 6.3 billion, with an annual growth rate of 1.5 percent (see Figure 6.2). At this rate, 88 million people (more than the population of Germany) will be added to the population this year alone. That's nearly a quarter of a million additional people to feed every 24 hours!

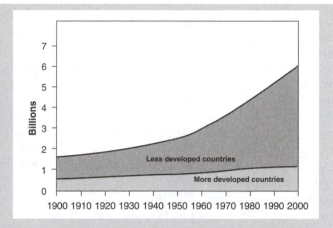

Figure 6.2 Population Growth in More Developed and Less Developed Countries, 1900 to 2000

Different demographic conditions are found in developed and less developed countries.

Note: Developed countries include Australia, Canada, Japan, New Zealand, the United States, and all of Europe. All other countries are included in less developed.

Source: Population Reference Bureau. 2004. "Transitions in World Population." *Population Bulletin,* 59(1):5. Retrieved from www.prb.org.

One of the highest fertility rates in the developing world—6.0 children per woman—occurs in sub-Saharan Africa. According to demographers John and Pat Caldwell (1993), mortality rates—more than half of which are caused by infectious and parasitic diseases—have begun to decline, but fertility rates are declining at a slower pace than in other developing regions (see Box 6.3). Poverty and rural conditions provide limited opportunities for women to work outside agriculture. Women do not inherit land, even though they are the main contributors to agricultural production. Thus, land is passed from fathers to sons, leaving women dependent on their male children to provide for them in old age. Without sons, a woman loses her right to use land after her husband's death. Women are encouraged to have children because it is an important way for them to gain status. Involuntary infertility is regarded with disdain and is considered punishment for transgressions (Goliber 1997).

There is a worldwide correlation between education and fertility decline. Women with no education have an average of two more children than women with a secondary education (Goliber 1997). Education empowers women to act in their own right. Moreover, women who are educated are more likely to be receptive to family planning (Bradley 1997; Caldwell 1982). Women opt for fewer children when they have opportunities other than childrearing. Finally, as we have seen, education makes children more expensive and less of a short-term benefit. By seeking higher education or jobs in the city, young families find they can no longer afford to raise as many children as their parents, especially if they plan on sending them all to school (Bradley 1997).

Fertility and the World's Most Expensive Children

After World War II, the fertility rate in the United States rose rapidly, producing the phenomenon of the "baby boom." But after peaking in 1957, the fertility rate fell a full 50 percent from 3.69 to 1.81 (Newitt 1985; U.S. Bureau of the Census 1994; Westoff 1986).

A common misunderstanding of this decline is that it was caused by the introduction of birth control pills. This is incorrect because the decline began in 1957, and it was not until 1963 to 1964 that the pill was widely adopted. Beyond that, many contraceptive devices and practices were available in the 1930s, as demonstrated by the fact that the fertility rate in the 1930s was much lower than immediately after World War II. Moreover, as we have seen, even preindustrial populations have effective means of limiting family size.

The key to understanding the fall in fertility rate in the United States (and in other hyperindustrial societies) lies in the increased costs and lowered benefits of raising children. In 2005, the U.S. Department of Agriculture calculated that the cost of raising a child from birth to 18 was about $160,140 for a middle income family. And that doesn't count college tuition. This translates into $8,896.66 a year, or $741.38 a month. Add between $50,000 and $100,000 for four years of college, and the cost of raising an upper-middle-class child to adulthood will easily reach half a million dollars. And the more the economy shifts toward services, information, and high-tech jobs, the greater the amount of schooling that will be needed to achieve or maintain middle-class status. In other words, "higher-quality" children cost more.

The average U.S. family cannot rear more than one or two costly high-quality children without a second income, and women are generally incapable of providing that second income if they have to raise more than one or two children (given the absence of adequate subsidized day care facilities). There are positive feedback effects among working in the labor force, staying in it, and paying the cost of rearing children. The more a woman puts into a job, the more she earns, and the more it costs her in the form of *forgone income* to give it up. As forgone income increases, so does the cost of staying home to rear children—and the likelihood that fewer children will be born.

At the same time, children in hyperindustrial societies provide fewer benefits for parents. The counterflow of economic benefits from children to parents has steadily decreased. Children now work apart from parents, establish separate households, and are no longer capable of paying the medical and housing costs of their aged fathers and mothers.

Thus, the current balance of the costs and benefits of rearing children represents the climax of the long-term shift from agricultural to industrial modes of production and from rural to urban ways of life associated with the demographic transition.

Reproductive Technologies, Embryos, and Designer Babies

An increasing number of working couples in the United States are encountering difficulties conceiving a child. One factor in this increase is the postponement of childbearing for the years it takes to establish a career and gain earning power. At age 40, a woman's chances of conceiving decline on an average of 30 percent and drop off sharply in the following years. Many couples in this situation (sometimes labeled DINKS—"Double Income, No Kids") are able to pay for expensive reproductive procedures. With in vitro fertilization, conception is brought about by combining an egg and sperm in a Petri dish. Once fertilization occurs, the resulting embryo can be implanted either inside the natural mother's womb or in a "host" womb to complete the pregnancy. These technologies, once considered radical and experimental, are now routine and so successful that many reproductive medical specialists offer refunds if the procedure fails.

A woman who is infertile or unable to carry a child to term must resort to a third party. Unlike male sperm donors, whose physical involvement is minimal, third parties brought in to carry a child for an infertile couple have long-term involvement. This practice, known as *surrogacy* or *substitute birth mothering,* remains controversial. A number of well-publicized legal cases over parental responsibilities and rights have resulted. As described by anthropologist Helena Ragone, surrogate motherhood consists of a contractual arrangement, usually brokered and supervised by a private agency specializing in surrogate mother programs. The prospective surrogate, who in some cases is married and has her own children, agrees to three or four months of attempted conception via artificial insemination and nine months of pregnancy. When the child is born, custody is immediately given to the commissioning couple, who have paid for the service, for associated legal charges, and all the medical costs. On average, surrogate mothers receive $10,000 to $15,000. The cost to the couple is close to $45,000. The average family income of an unmarried surrogate is $16,000 to $24,000; married surrogates average about $38,700. The commissioning parents are usually educated professionals, with an average family income over $100,000 a year. Despite the etic implications of the disparity in their respective incomes, most surrogate mothers—while not dismissing the importance of the monetary benefits—say their primary motivation is to help the infertile couple. For surrogate mothers, "It's the ultimate gift of love" (Ragone 1994).

SUMMARY
and *Questions to Think About*

1. Production sets limits to reproduction. Contrary to the position advocated by Thomas Malthus, populations do not normally rise to the maximum limit of production, nor are they usually checked by starvation and other catastrophes.

2. Populations are usually maintained well below carrying capacity. Reproduction, however, leads to population pressure, which leads to intensification, depletions, and changes in the modes of production. This can be seen in the sequence leading from big-game hunting to agriculture.

3. Variations in reproductive rates cannot be explained by the universal desire to have children. Rather, reproductive rates reflect the variable costs and benefits of rearing children under different modes of production.

4. Band-organized hunter-gatherer reproduction rates are influenced by the need for women to avoid carrying more than one infant at a time over long distances, as well as by the limited intensifiability of the hunter-gatherer mode of production.

5. Sedentary agriculturalists rear more children because agriculture can be intensified, the burden of carrying infants and toddlers is reduced, children more rapidly "pay for themselves," and senior children can take care of juniors.

6. Findings from contemporary peasant societies lend support to the cost–benefit approach to reproductive rates. In Java, children contribute about half of all the wealth of household members. In Bangladesh, male children by age 12 produce more than they consume and in three more years make up for all previous expenses incurred on their behalf. Moreover, contrary to the popular impression that the poorest peasant households have the most children, we often see a positive correlation between large numbers of children and family wealth.

7. With the expansion of urban, industrial, technical, and white-collar employment, the benefits of raising fewer but costlier children outweigh the advantages of rearing many but "cheaper" children. In China, India, and Sri Lanka, the number of children per woman has declined as children cease to have important roles in agriculture and as the offspring of peasants find advancement through white-collar jobs and business opportunities that require high levels of education. These shifts in the costs of rearing children in relation to new modes of production are similar to the shifts that brought about the demographic transition in nineteenth-century Europe and the United States.

8. Contrary to Malthusian theory, preindustrial cultures regulated the sizes of their families so as to minimize the costs and maximize the benefits of reproduction. Although they lacked a modern technology of contraception or abortion, they were nonetheless never at a loss for means of controlling birthrates and death rates.

9. Four principal categories of practices were used: care and treatment of fetuses, infants, and children; care and treatment of girls and women; intensity and duration of lactation; and variations in the frequency of heterosexual coitus. Subtle gradations exist from abortion to infanticide to induced child mortality. Family planning in nineteenth-century rural Japan is an example of how direct infanticide was used to maximize the benefits provided by children to farm households.

10. Much controversy surrounds the question of whether poor nutrition reduces the ability of women to conceive, but poor nutrition clearly jeopardizes the lives of the mother, fetus, and child. The amenorrhea associated with lactation is a more benign form of fertility regulation widely practiced by preindustrial people. Finally, various forms of nonreproductive sex and the degree of sexual abstinence can raise or lower reproductive rates.

11. A vivid example of cultural response to extremely adverse conditions can be seen in northeast Brazil: Impoverished mothers who lack access to modern contraception and medical abortion contribute to the extremely high rates of infant and child mortality through the selective neglect and indirect infanticide of their unwanted offspring.

Questions to Think About

1. What is the relationship between production and reproduction? How do you evaluate the views of Malthus and Boserup on population growth?

2. What are some conscious versus unconscious efforts to control population growth?

3. What are the costs and benefits of rearing children in preindustrial and industrial societies?

4. What is meant by *indirect infanticide?* What economic and health conditions explain child neglect in northeast Brazil?

5. Under what conditions are women in developing countries more likely to have fewer children?

6. What accounts for the decline in the fertility rate in the United States? How would you explain the increasing use of in vitro fertilization and surrogate motherhood?

THROUGH THE LENS
of Cultural Materialism

Conformity and Conflict • Reading Sixteen

Mother's Love: Death without Weeping

Nancy Scheper-Hughes

Mothers who live in shantytowns in northeast Brazil often withdraw support from particular infants they perceive as lacking in "readiness or fitness for life." Mothers express a preference for "quick, sharp, active, verbal, and developmentally precocious children." Children with the opposite traits are not given medical assistance when they become ill, and they are not fed as well as their siblings. Mothers speak of children who "wanted to die," whose will and drive for life was not "sufficiently strong or developed."

Emic Interpretation

- Mothers believe that sickly babies that lack "life force" are better off as angels in heaven.
- The Catholic Church provides ideological support for this practice by allowing mothers to believe their dead babies are safe in heaven yet disallows the practices of birth control, abortion, or sterilization.

Etic Interpretation

- Infant and child mortality rates are high in the shantytowns of northeast Brazil.
- Poverty forces mothers to unconsciously neglect those babies who appear too sick or weak and to allow them to die.

Infrastructure

Mode of Production

- Northeast Brazil is a farming region subjected to periodic drought and widespread poverty. Over several decades, rural workers were forced off their land as large plantation owners bought up their small subsistence plots.
- Most of the migrants ended up in shantytowns and now work as landless laborers on sugar plantations for insufficient wages.
- A large segment of the population experiences extreme poverty, chronic hunger, and malnutrition, which leaves

them in a weakened state and prone to infection and disease.

Mode of Reproduction

- Life expectancy in northeast Brazil is only 40 years, and the rate of infant mortality is about 200 deaths per 1,000 births in the first year of life (compared with a rate of less than 10 in developed countries).
- In 1965, more than 350 babies died from a population of about 5,000.
- Mothers differentiate between infants perceived as thrivers and survivors and those perceived as "wanting to die."
- Selective neglect, or indirect infanticide, is practiced as mothers allow nature to take its course when a child is unable to fight off common illness such as diarrhea, respiratory infections, and tropical fever.
- Women have sex to gain male companionship and support but are directed by the Catholic Church not to use contraceptives.

Structure

- Marriages in shantytowns are fragile, as men leave home to seek employment elsewhere.
- Most women are single parents who are forced to work as domestics or laborers on sugar plantations, where they earn insufficient wages.
- Unable to pay for child care, women often leave their babies at home alone for several hours when they go to work.

Superstructure

- Mothers believe that infant death is often fated and inevitable.
- Mothers believe it is best to let a sickly child die.
- The Catholic Church teaches resignation to domestic tragedy and that infants who die become "angels in the service of their heavenly patron."

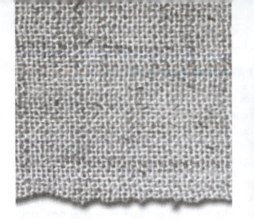

CHAPTER 7

ECONOMIC

ORGANIZATION

Goods of all kinds are bought and sold on market day in this Colombian market.

I n this chapter, our concern is not with types of production processes—such as hunting and gathering, pastoralism, and industrial manufacturing—but with the way in which people organize labor and regulate or control access to resources, goods, and services. At this point, in other words, our focus will shift from the infrastructural to the structural aspects of society and culture. This will enable us to study the extent to which the organizational features of production can be explained by the evolution of particular kinds of infrastructures.

Economies differ according to their characteristic modes of control over production and exchange. We will identify the principal kinds of exchange and explore their relationship to infrastructural conditions. We will see that many societies organize their economic activities without the use of money and that money itself comes in many specialized forms in addition to the all-purpose money with which we are familiar. The subject of money leads to the question of whether capitalist economies can be found among nonstate societies. The chapter also takes up the question of whether people work harder in industrial than in hunter-gatherer societies.

Definition of Economy

In one sense, the term *economy* refers to the kinds of decisions people make when they have only limited resources or wealth and there are unlimited goods and services they would like to acquire or use. Most professional economists hold that in making such decisions, people tend to economize.

 Economizing refers to the choices people make that they believe will provide the greatest benefit to them.

This approach views people as active strategists, as economizing actors who select the opportunities that yield the maximal good (or maximize benefits while minimizing costs; Plattner 1989:8). Unlike Western economic systems, which emphasize profit motivation, many people around the world place other goals above material wealth acquisition. People may define maximal good in terms of prestige, risk aversion, or increased leisure time, depending on how a culture defines *self-interest*. For most anthropologists, however, an economy refers to the activities people engage in to produce and obtain goods and services (setting aside the question of whether they are economizing).

Economics is embedded in the social process; production is carried out in families and communities, and distribution, exchange, and consumption have social and political functions.

In this second sense, an "economy is a set of institutionalized activities which combine natural resources, human labor, and technology to acquire, produce, and distribute material goods and specialist services in a structured, repetitive fashion" (Dalton 1969:97).

These two definitions of economy are not incompatible. Anthropologists stress the fact that cultural traditions shape the specific motivations for producing, exchanging, and consuming goods and services. Different cultures value different goods and services and tolerate or prohibit different kinds of relationships among the people who produce, exchange, and consume. Some cultures emphasize economic cooperation; others emphasize competition. Some emphasize increased consumption as a means of increasing social status, whereas others value generosity and giving away goods as a means of achieving prestige.

To understand the economies of different cultures, anthropologists must consider the goals and motivations behind the decision-making process as well as the institutionalized activities and relationships that result from production and distribution.

Exchange

For the most part, humans either directly consume the products of their labor, or they distribute it by means of exchange. **Exchange** is the practice of giving and receiving valued objects and services. This practice is more highly developed in our species than in any other. Human beings could not survive infancy without receiving basic resources and services from their parents. However, patterns of exchange differ markedly from one culture to another. Following the work of the economist Karl Polanyi, anthropologists have come to distinguish three main types of exchange: reciprocal, redistributive, and market.

Generalized Reciprocity

One of the most striking features of the economic life of simple hunter-gatherers and small-scale agricultural societies is the prominence of exchanges conducted according to the principle known as **generalized reciprocity.**

Reciprocity
Hunter-gatherers of the Kalahari Desert exchange the day's catch.

Generalized reciprocity involves mutual giving and receiving among people of equal status in which there is (1) no need for immediate return, (2) no systematic calculation of the value of the services and products exchanged, and (3) an overt denial that a balance is being calculated or that the balance must come out even.

Richard Lee has written a succinct description of reciprocity as it occurs among the !Kung: In the morning, anywhere from one to 16 of the 20 adults in the !Kung band leave camp to spend the day collecting or hunting. They return in the evening with whatever food they have managed to find. Everything brought back to camp is shared equally, regardless of whether the recipients have spent the day sleeping or hunting. Eventually all the adults will have gathered or hunted and given as well as received food. But wide discrepancies in the balance of giving and receiving may exist among individuals over a long period without becoming the subject of any special talk or action.

Some form of generalized reciprocity occurs in all cultures, especially among relatives and friends. In many parts of the world, for example, husbands and wives, friends, sisters and brothers, and other kin maintain informal, uncalculated, give-and-take transactions that are economic in nature. Teenagers do not pay cash for their meals at home or for use of the family car. Wives do not bill their husbands for cooking a meal. Friends give each other birthday gifts and Christmas presents. These exchanges, however, constitute only a small portion of the total acts of ex-

change. The great majority of exchanges in modern cultures involves rigidly defined counterflows that must take place by a certain time (as anyone who has forgotten to pay their credit card bill can tell you).

Reciprocity and the Freeloader

As we know from the experience of taking from parents or from giving a birthday or holiday gift and not receiving one in return, the failure of an individual to reciprocate in some degree will eventually lead to bad feelings, even between close relatives and friends or spouses. No one likes a "freeloader" ("moocher" or "sponge").

In economies dominated by reciprocity, a grossly asymmetrical exchange does not go unnoticed. Some individuals will come to enjoy reputations as diligent gatherers or outstanding hunters, whereas others will acquire reputations as shirkers or malingerers. No specific mechanisms exist for obliging the debtors to even up the score, yet subtle sanctions discourage one from becoming a complete freeloader. Such behavior generates a steady undercurrent of disapproval. Eventually freeloaders may meet with violence because they are suspected of being bewitched or bewitching others through the practice of sorcery.

Generalized reciprocity, therefore, does not mean that products and services are simply given away without any thought or expectation of return. No culture can rely exclusively on purely altruistic sentiments to get its goods and services produced and distributed. But in simple band and prestate village societies, people produce and reciprocally exchange goods in such a way as to avoid the notion of material balance, debt, or obligation. This system works because reciprocal exchanges are expressed as kinship obligations. These kinship obligations establish reciprocal expectations with respect to food, clothing, shelter, and other goods.

Kinship-embedded reciprocal exchanges constitute only a small portion of modern exchange systems, whereas among hunter-gatherers and small-scale agriculturalists, almost all exchanges take place among kin, for whom the giving, taking, and using of goods have sentimental and personal meaning.

Balanced Reciprocity

Balanced reciprocity involves the expectation that goods or services of equivalent value will be returned within a specified period of time.

People have an obligation to reciprocate in equal value in order for the relationship to continue. Examples include buying a round of drinks for friends, borrowing a cup of sugar from a neighbor, or giving a birthday present to a friend. **Balanced reciprocity** involves a more formal relationship in contrast to generalized reciprocity among family members. The motivation for balanced reciprocity is that it forges and maintains relationships that can be utilized in times of need and enables people to gain access to goods or services that are either regionally or periodically in short supply.

In hunter-gatherer and horticultural societies, people may want valuables such as salt, flint, obsidian, red ochre, reeds, and honey that are produced or controlled by groups with whom they have no kinship ties. Economic dealings among nonkin are based on the assumption that every "stranger" will try to get the best of an exchange through cheating or stealing. As a result, trading expeditions are likely to be full of distrust and may bear a resemblance to enemy encounters.

One interesting mechanism for facilitating trade between distant groups is known as **silent trade.** The objects to be exchanged are set out in a clearing, and the first group retreats out of sight. The other group comes out of hiding, inspects the wares, lays down what it regards as a fair exchange of its own products, and retreats again. The first group returns and, if satisfied, removes the traded objects. If not, it leaves the wares untouched as a signal that the balance is not yet even. In this fashion, the Mbuti of the Ituri Forest used to trade meat for bananas with Bantu agriculturalists, and the Vedda of Sri Lanka traded honey for iron tools with the Sinhalese.

Exchange relations become more personal when communities have more contact. Trade, for example, plays an important role in establishing alliances. Among the Yanomami, hostile villages may initiate alliances beginning with trade, then feasting, and eventually intermarriage, which solidifies relationships through kinship. Mutual exchange does not, however, guarantee mutually peaceful relationships. Groups such as the Yanomami can fall out of an alliance when personal hostilities intensify. One village may invite another to a "treacherous feast" in which the hosts attack their guests when they are least suspecting, and declare war (see Chapter 10).

More extensive trade relations occur between agricultural villages. Conditions for the development of trade markets are especially favorable in Melanesia, where villages in varied ecological niches produce different products for exchange. In New Guinea, for example, people regularly trade fish for pigs and vegetables. Among the Kapauku of western New Guinea (today, West Irian, Indonesia), full-fledged price markets involving shell and limited-purpose bead money

New Guinea Market

The man on the right is giving fish in exchange for yams, which are offered by the man on the left.

may have existed before the arrival of European or Indonesian merchants. Generally speaking, however, trade based on marketing and all-purpose money is associated with the evolution of the state (see Chapter 10) and with the use of soldiers and market police to enforce peaceful relations between buyers and sellers.

Perhaps the most common solution to the problem of trading with strangers in the absence of state-supervised markets is the establishment of special trade partnerships. In this arrangement, members of different communities regard one another as metaphorical or fictive kin. The members of trading expeditions deal exclusively with their trade partners, who greet them as brothers and give them food and shelter. Trade partners try to deal with one another in conformity with the principle of reciprocity. They deny an interest in getting the best of the bargain and offer wares as if they were gifts.

Trade in the Kula Ring

A classic example of **balanced reciprocity** is described in Bronislaw Malinowski's *Argonauts of the Western Pacific.* The Argonauts referred to here are the Trobriand Islanders, who trade with people on neighboring islands by means of daring canoe voyages across the open sea.

> The **kula ring** is a system of exchange in the Trobriand Islands, where trading partners from different islands take risky voyages to exchange shell ornaments around the ring of islands; white cowrie shell armbands are traded in a counterclockwise direction, and red shell necklaces are traded clockwise.

According to the men who take these risky voyages, the purpose of the kula trade is to exchange shell ornaments with their trade partners. The ornaments, known to the Trobrianders as *vaygu'a*, consist of white shell armbands and red shell necklaces. Armbands and necklaces are traded around the ring of islands in opposite directions, each eventually returning to the point of origin (see Figure 7.1).

Participation in the kula trade is a major ambition of youth and a consuming passion of senior men. The vaygu'a have been compared with heirlooms or crown jewels. They vary in value, depending on their history. The older they are and the more admired their previous owners, the more valuable they become in the eyes of the Trobrianders. Like many other examples of special-purpose exchange media (see the discussion of money later in this chapter), kula valuables are seldom used to buy anything. They are, however, given as gifts in marriage and as rewards to canoe builders (Scoditti 1983). Most of the time, the ornaments are simply used for the purpose of obtaining other armbands and

necklaces. To trade vaygu'a, men establish more or less permanent partnerships with each other on distant islands. These partnerships are usually handed down from one kinsman to another, and young men are given a start in the kula trade by inheriting or receiving an armband or a necklace from a relative.

When the expedition reaches shore, the trade partners greet one another and exchange preliminary gifts. Later the Trobrianders deliver the precious ornaments, accompanied by ritual speeches and formal acts concerned with establishing the honorable, gift-like character of the exchange. As in the case of reciprocal transactions within the family, the trade partner may not immediately be able to provide a shell whose value is equivalent to the one just received. He does not complain because he expects his trade partner to work hard to make up for the delay by presenting him with even more valuable shells at their next meeting.

Why all this effort in order to obtain a few baubles of sentimental or aesthetic value? As is often the case, the etic aspects of the kula are different from the emic aspects.

> The kula ring entails more than a ceremonial exchange of valued shell ornaments. Utilitarian items are traded at the same time, so that people from different islands are able to exchange locally specialized food and craft products.

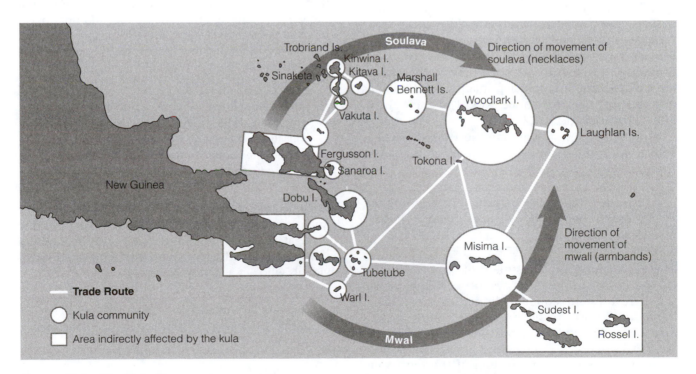

Figure 7.1   The Kula Ring

The ceremonial trading of necklaces and armbands in the kula ring encourages trade throughout Melanesia.

Kula Canoe
These large canoes are used by the Trobrianders for long-distance voyages.

The boats that take part in the kula expedition carry trade items of great practical value in the life of the island people who participate in the kula ring. While the trade partners fondle and admire their priceless heirlooms, members of the expedition trade for practical items: coconuts, sago palm flour, fish, yams, baskets, mats, wooden swords and clubs, green stone for tools, mussel shells for knives, creepers and lianas for lashings. These items can be bargained over with impunity. Although Trobrianders deny it, the vaygu'a are valuable not only for their qualities as heirlooms but also for their truly priceless gift of trade (Irwin 1983:71ff; Scoditti 1983:265).

More recent research among the Trobrianders has revealed a more complicated system of exchanges that goes beyond reciprocity.

Kula is better understood as part of the Trobriand and the neighboring islands' system of achieving and validating political rank.

There is a continued adjustment of political and social position. Trade and possession of highly valued shells creates status and rank. Important men can enhance their status by acquiring particularly famous kula ornaments and by establishing a network of kula partnerships that extends throughout the islands. Those who come into possession of the most valuable shells are usually extremely able leaders who are accomplished navigators and, in former times, bold warriors (Campbell 1983:203). Thus in modern times, kula has persisted even though fewer practical items are traded.

Redistributive Exchange

As we will see in Chapter 11, the evolution of economic and political systems is in large degree a consequence of the development of coercive forms of exchange that supplement or almost entirely replace reciprocal exchange. Coercive forms of exchange did not appear in sudden full-blown opposition to reciprocal forms. Rather, they probably first arose through what seemed to be merely an extension of familiar reciprocal forms.

 Redistribution involves the accumulation of large amounts of labor products produced by different individuals in a central place where they are sorted and counted and then given away to producers and nonproducers alike.

Considerable organizational effort is required if large quantities of goods are to be brought to the same place at the same time and given away in definite shares. This coordination is usually achieved by individuals who act as redistributors.

Typically, redistributors consciously attempt to increase and intensify production, for which they gain prestige in the eyes of their peers.

Nonstratified and stratified forms of *redistribution* must be distinguished from each other. As a nonstratified system of exchange, redistribution is carried out by a redistributor who (1) works harder than anyone else producing the items to be given away, (2) takes nonstratified form, therefore, redistribution appears to be merely an extreme example of reciprocity; the generous provider gives everything away and for the moment gets nothing in return, except the admiration of those who benefit from the transaction. In the future, however, he will be able to call on the recipients for favors, which puts him in an advantageous position. In the stratified form, however, the redistributor (1) lets others do most of the work, (2) retains the largest share, and (3) ends up with more material wealth than anyone else.

Redistributive exchange, like reciprocal exchange, is usually embedded in a complex set of kinship relations and rituals that may obscure the etic significance of the exchange behavior. Redistribution often involves a ceremonial feast held to celebrate some important event, such as a harvest, the end of a ritual taboo, the construction of a house, a death, a birth, or a marriage. A common feature of redistributive feasting is the boastful and competitive attitude of the redistributors and their kin with respect to other individuals or groups who have given feasts. This contrasts markedly with reciprocal exchange. Let us take a closer look at this contrast (see Table 7.1).

Trobriander Yam House

Yams are collected by a centralized authority, who retains a share for himself and redistributes the rest at feasts.

the smallest portion or none at all, and (3) is left with no greater material wealth than anyone else. In its

Table 7.1

Reciprocity versus Redistribution in Egalitarian and Stratified Societies

Egalitarian Societies	Stratified Societies
Members enjoy equal access to basic resources. No individual or group has appreciably more wealth, power, or prestige. There are as many positions of prestige as there are persons capable of filling them (Fried 1967).	Members have differential access to basic resources, which are converted to private property. There is inequality in power, wealth, and prestige, and such inequality is permanent and formally recognized (Fried 1967).
Voluntary form of exchange based on reciprocity. Contributions given freely.	Coercive forms of exchange such as taxation. Members make obligatory payments to a central agency, which later reallocates goods or services.
Redistributor works harder than anyone else yet ends up with no more than everyone else.	Redistributor oversees but does not work harder; he or she retains the largest share and ends up with considerable wealth.
People get back all that they put into the pool or else they get back comparable value.	People may not get back everything they give to the redistributor.
Leaders have no power to coerce. They lead by example. Their prestige lasts as long as people agree with them.	The leader (chief or emperor) has considerable power over the labor force. He or she holds an inherited office and has regional control.
Ecological conditions: Intensification would rapidly lead to the point of diminishing returns.	Ecological conditions: If people work harder, they can increase their standard of consumption without immediately depleting their habitat's resources.
Reciprocity is maintained within and between communities. Intercommunity reciprocity solidifies alliances and helps maintain temporary peace.	Production surplus makes regional distribution possible. Regional peace is maintained through a system of political ranking and through centralized administrative control.

Source: Morton H. Fried. 1967. *The Evolution of Political Society.* Copyright © 1967, reprinted with the permission of the McGraw-Hill Companies.

Redistribution is more likely to be associated with economies where intensification is possible without depleting the environment. Redistributive feasts are adaptive because they encourage people to work harder to produce more than they need in order to protect them from the possibility of crises caused by crop failures or other shortages caused by unforeseen factors. Groups that give away food at redistributive feasts store up social credit with other villages, who will reciprocate by preparing feasts for them in the future. In hunter-gatherer societies, on the other hand, inducements to collect more than is needed may be disadvantageous because overcollecting or overhunting might deplete area resources and lead to diminishing returns.

Contrary to the prescriptions for modesty in reciprocal exchanges, *redistribution* exchange systems involve public proclamations that the host is a generous person and a great provider.

Potlatches

Boasting is one of the most conspicuous features of the **potlatches**, or redistributive feasts, that were once engaged in by the Native Americans who inhabit the northwest coast of the United States and Canada. In descriptions made famous by Ruth Benedict in *Patterns of Culture* (1934), the Kwakiutl redistributor seems like a virtual megalomaniac. In the potlatch, the guests behaved somewhat like Lee's !Kung. They grumbled and complained and never appeared satisfied or impressed. Nonetheless, in public, they carefully counted all the gifts displayed and distributed. Both hosts and guests believed that the only way to throw off the obligations incurred in accepting these gifts was to hold a counter potlatch in which the tables were reversed (Jonaitas 1991).

Reciprocity and Distribution

Why do the !Kung esteem hunters who never draw attention to their own generosity, whereas the Kwakiutl and other redistributor societies esteem leaders who boast about how much they gave away? One theory is that reciprocity is a way of controlling intensification that would eventually lead to diminishing returns and environmental depletions.

Simple hunters and gatherers seldom have an opportunity to intensify production without rapidly reaching the point of diminishing returns. Intensification poses a grave threat in the form of faunal overkills.

To encourage the !Kung hunter to be boastful is to endanger the group's survival. In addition, *reciprocity* is advantageous for most hunter-gatherers because individuals and families experience a great deal of variation in their success from one day to the next. "The greater the degree of risk, the greater the extent of sharing" (Gould 1982:76). Sharing spreads the risk over many hunters, like commercial insurance policies spread the risk over many subscribers (Cashdan 1989:37). In contrast, the Kwakiutl (see Profile 7.1) had a seasonal abundance of natural resources which could be stored for lean winter months.

The Kwakiutl mode of production is highly intensifiable and requires a coordinated effort in gathering and storing food for the winter months.

Despite the overall abundance of resources, the Northwest Coast nevertheless experienced alternating periods of abundance and shortage. A village enjoying a good year would have a surplus of food that they could give away to a less fortunate village. The reward was increased prestige. When an impoverished and unprestigious group no longer had enough wealth to distribute and could not hold its own potlatches, the people abandoned their defeated redistributor–chief and took up residence among relatives in more productive villages. Thus the boasting and the giving away and displaying of wealth led to the recruitment of additional labor power for a particularly effective redistributor.

This system also helps explain why Northwest Coast peoples lavished so much effort on the production of their world-famous totem poles. These poles bore the redistributor–chief's "crests" in the guise of carved mythic figures; title to the crests was claimed on the basis of outstanding potlatch achievements. The larger the pole, the greater the potlatch power, and the more the members of poor villages would be tempted to change their residence and gather around another chief.

The Origin of Destructive Potlatches

Potlatching came under scientific scrutiny long after the people of the Pacific Northwest had entered into trade and wage labor relations with Russian, English, Canadian, and U.S. nationals. Declining populations and a sudden influx of wealth had combined to make the potlatches increasingly competitive and destructive by the time Franz Boas began to study them in the 1880s. At this period, the entire tribe was in residence at the Fort Rupert trading station of the Hudson Bay Company, and the attempt on the part of

Location: British Columbia, Canada

Subsistence: Nomadic fishing, hunting, gathering

Population Density: two to four persons per square mile

Time of Research: The late 1800s

The native societies of the Northwest Coast possessed an elaborate technology, an intensified mode of production, and a complex political organization that is considered atypical of hunter-gatherer groups. A century ago, the Kwakiutl inhabited the dense forests along the western coast of Canada, which was abundant in large game animals and bird life, berry patches, and a wide variety of marine life—most notably, salmon and candlefish, which provide abundant catches during their seasonal runs. Yet despite the high productivity of the natural ecosystem, the people expected and feared food scarcity. While huge surpluses occurred seasonably and in good years, there were unpredictable regional fluctuations in distribution. Food scarcity and even famine threatened survival during the winter months, when people lived off the food they stored during the summer and fall.

The subsistence cycle was organized around the seasonal availability of resources. During the cold winter months, the Kwakiutl aggregated in large villages, where they lived mainly on the dried and smoked provisions accumulated during the summer and fall. Winter was a time for manufacturing and repairing canoes, tools, and clothing and for ceremonial feasting.

In March and April, people from separate local groups gathered for the great candlefish runs. Using aboriginal dip nets, the Kwakiutl and their neighbors were able to fish freely without affecting the overall rate of reproduction of this species because enough fish managed to make it upriver to spawn. Candlefish are rich in oil (it is said that if you stick a wick in a dried candlefish, it will burn like a candle), and they provided a valuable preservative and additive for dried foods. The Kwakiutl invested intense labor in harvesting candlefish and rendering its oil, which was stored for home consumption and trade. Being storable, oil played an important part in the political economy.

In August and September, the Kwakiutl collected berries and the salmon runs began. Both activities required a heavy labor investment, both in collecting and storing food. The greater the labor invested, the larger the harvest, and there was little or no decline in marginal productivity (A. Johnson and Earle 2000). In good years, large amounts of salmon were harvested without declining marginal productivity because for a short period, there were more fish than could be harvested, as the salmon swam upriver to spawn. The fish then had to be processed—gutted, split lengthwise, and the backbone removed—and then they were hung to dry or smoked. Households were able to store large quantities of oil, berries, and dried and smoked fish and game for the winter months. Storage led to differences in wealth, however, between both individuals and communities, which was a precondition to social stratification, fierce warfare, and slavery (Donald 1997; Kelly 1995). Thus, it was ecologically feasible for the Kwakiutl to intensify production by using prestige and the privilege of boasting to reward those who worked harder or who got others to work harder (Ames 1994; Hayden 1992:534; Isaac 1988; Mitchell and Donald 1988).

Universal Pattern • The Kwakiutl

Infrastructure	Structure	Superstructure
Dense forests abundant in game and seasonal berry patches. Large population concentrated in villages along coast that disperses during late spring and summer months to collect wild foods.	Leadership is necessary to ensure that enough food is collected and preserved for winter months. The "big man" (known as chief) requires a share of his followers' production, which is used to pay manufacturing specialists and for feasts.	People aspire to give away large amounts of surplus to increase prestige of group. Wealth is accumulated not for consumption but for redistribution.
Seasonal availability of food resources: in spring, candlefish are harvested; summer is time for foraging; in August and September, berries are harvested and salmon runs begin; and winter is time for living off preserved food and for hunting.	Local big man organizes and regulates fishing cycles and storage. Big man maintains large storage facilities. Substantial amounts of food are stored, creating vast differences in wealth between groups in different regions.	Generosity of potlatch host is rewarded through right to boast and humiliate subordinate groups.
Annual variation in resource availability, with alternating years of abundance and scarcity. Food requirements of large population make famine threat during winter months.	Potlatch redistributes food and other valuables to neighboring villages to ensure against local food shortages. Repayment by hosting future potlatch erases debt and reinstates prestige of subordinate group.	Large totem poles symbolize outstanding potlatch power.

Kwakiutl of the Pacific Northwest

The signs over the doors read "Boston. He is the Head chief of Arweete. He is true Indian. Honest.
He don't owe no trouble to white man" and "Cheap. He is one of the head chiefs of all tribes in this
country. White man can get information." This photo was taken about 1901 or 1902.

Redistribution in China

Meat is being divided into equal portions for the members of the group.

one potlatch giver to outdo another had become an all-consuming passion. Blankets, boxes of fish oil, and other valuables were deliberately being destroyed by burning or by throwing them into the sea. On one occasion, a house almost burned to the ground when the roof caught fire from too much fish oil poured on the fire (Benedict 1960:177). Potlatches that ended in this fashion were regarded as great victories for the potlatch givers.

Before the coming of the Europeans, Kwakiutl potlatch feasts were probably less destructive and more like Melanesian competitive feasts (see Chapter 11, discussion of big man feasts).

> With the coming of the Europeans, there was a shift toward more destructive forms of redistribution. Contact led to epidemics that decimated the population and intensified competition for manpower.

The impact of European diseases reduced the population of the Kwakiutl from about 10,000 in 1836 to about 2,000 by the end of the century. At the same time, the trading companies, canneries, lumber mills, and gold-mining camps pumped an unprecedented amount of wealth into the aboriginal economy. The percentage of people available to celebrate the glory of the potlatch dropped. Many villages were abandoned; rivalry intensified for the allegiance of the survivors.

A final and perhaps the most important factor in the development of destructive potlatches was the change in the technology and intensity of warfare.

A.

B.

Kwakiutl Chiefs

A. A spokesman for a Kwakiutl chief is making a speech next to a pile of blankets about to be given away at a potlatch.   B. The height of the pole, the skill of the carvings, and the animal ancestors shown validate the claim of chiefly rank.

The earliest contacts in the late-eighteenth century between the Europeans and the Native Americans of the Northwest Pacific Coast centered on the fur trade. In return for sea otter skins, the Europeans gave guns to the Kwakiutl and to the Kwakiutl's traditional enemies. This trade had a double effect. On the one hand, warfare became more deadly; on the other hand, it forced local groups to fight one another for control of trade to get the ammunition on which success in warfare now depended. Small wonder, therefore, that as the population declined, the potlatch chiefs were willing to destroy wealth that was militarily unimportant. They ordered the destruction of property in the vain hope that such spectacular demonstrations would enhance their prestige and bring people back to the empty villages so they would have the manpower for warfare and fur trade (Ferguson 1984).

Stratified Redistribution

A subtle line separates egalitarian from forms of **stratified redistribution.** In the egalitarian form, contribu-

tions to the central pool are voluntary, and the workers either get back all or most of what they put into it or they receive items of comparable value.

In *stratified redistribution,* the workers must contribute to the central pool or suffer penalties, and they may not get back anything.

Again, in the egalitarian form, the redistributor lacks the power to coerce his or her followers to intensify production and must depend on their goodwill; in the stratified form, the redistributor has that power, and the workers must depend on that person's goodwill. The processes responsible for the evolution of one form of redistribution to another will be discussed in Chapter 11. Here, we will note only that fully developed forms of *stratified redistribution* imply the existence of a class of rulers who have the power to compel others to do their bidding. The expression of this power in the realm of production and exchange results in the political subordination of the labor force and in its partial or total loss of control over access to natural resources, technology, and the place, time, and hours of work.

Price Market Exchange: Buying and Selling

Marketplaces occur in rudimentary forms wherever groups of strangers assemble and trade one item for another. Among hunter-gatherers and simple agriculturalists, marketplace trading usually involves the barter of one valuable consumable item for another: fish for yams, coconuts for axes, and so forth. In this type of market, before the development of all-purpose money (see the next section), only a limited range of goods and services is exchanged. The great bulk of exchange transactions take place outside the marketplace and continue to involve various forms of reciprocity and redistribution. With the development of all-purpose money, however, **price market exchanges** came to dominate all other forms of exchange.

In a price market, the price of the goods and services exchanged is determined by buyers competing with buyers and sellers competing with sellers. Virtually everything that is produced or consumed soon comes to have a price, and buying and selling becomes a major cultural preoccupation or even an obsession.

One can engage in reciprocal exchange using money, as when a friend gives you a loan and does not specify when it must be repaid. Redistributive exchange can also be carried out with money, as in the collection of taxes and the disbursement of welfare payments. Or moneyless transactions, based on barter, can take place in an underground market

economy, where people directly exchange goods and services as a way of avoiding paying taxes. But these types of exchanges differ from market exchanges in several important ways.

Buying and selling in a price market is a distinctive mode of exchange; the exchange involves specification of a precise time, quantity, and type of payment, and the participants' main concern is maximizing financial gain.

Price market exchanges are noteworthy for the anonymity and impersonality of the exchange process. Unlike either reciprocity or redistribution, once the money payment is concluded, no further obligation or responsibility need exist between buyer and seller.

Money

  Money is a medium of exchange that has standard value. It is used as a means of payment for goods and services in a wide range of transactions where trade is well developed and economizing is a guiding principle.

The use of certain objects to symbolize and measure the social value of other objects occurs almost universally. Throughout much of East Africa, for example, cattle are a standard of value that can be used in exchange for a wife (see Chapter 8). In many parts of Melanesia, assorted shells, salt, and pigs are exchanged for stone implements, pottery, and other valuable artifacts.

Foraging for Food in Supermarkets
We try to maximize the benefits in supermarket shopping and are seldom concerned with the social process.

These objects, however, do not possess all the characteristics of money associated with price market economies. Like modern coins and paper currency, money has the following characteristics:

- *Portability.* It comes in sizes and shapes that make it convenient for being carried about from one transaction to the next.
- *Divisibility.* Its various forms and values are explicit multiples of each other.
- *Generality.* Virtually all goods and services can be measured by a single common monetary value.
- *Anonymity.* For most purchases, anyone with enough money to pay the market price can conclude a transaction.
- *Legality.* The money supply is controlled by a government and can't be duplicated or counterfeited.

By these criteria, cattle exchanged for wives are not money. Being neither very portable nor readily divisible, cattle would not be welcome at the supermarket checkout counter. As employed in bridewealth (see Chapter 8), cattle are frequently not convertible; that is, a large, beautiful, fat bull with a local reputation cannot readily be substituted for by two small and undistinguished animals. Furthermore, cattle lack generality because only wives can be "purchased" with them, and they lack anonymity because any stranger who shows up with the right amount of cattle will find he cannot simply leave the animals and take off with the bride. Cattle are exchanged for women only between kinship groups who have an interest in establishing or reinforcing preexisting social relationships. Finally, cattle are put into circulation by each individual household as a result of productive effort that is unregulated by any central authority.

Capitalism

The development of price markets accompanied the evolution of the first states, and they reach their highest development as part of the political economy known as **capitalism**. In capitalist societies, buying and selling by means of all-purpose money extends to land, resources, and housing. Labor has a price called *wages*, and money itself has a price called *interest*. In many cases, buyers and sellers don't even have face-to-face interaction.

A.

B.

Wealth and Money

A. The woman on the left is wearing a traditional skirt, which represents "women's wealth." **B.** *Cowrie and rongo shells are used as money in the Solomon Islands.*

Capitalism is associated with a change from production for use value to production for profit value.

Whereas production for use is aimed at satisfying specific material needs of individuals in households, capitalist production is aimed at accumulating wealth in order to purchase commodities for consumption. And because there is no end to the number of commodities one can purchase, efforts are invariably made to increase production.

By comparison with other forms of political economy, capitalism is aptly described as a system in which money can buy anything. This being so, everyone tries to acquire as much money as possible, and the object of production itself is not merely to provide valuable goods and services but to increase one's possession of money—that is, to make a profit, accumulate capital, and increase consumption for personal gain (see Profile 7.2).

The rate of capitalist production depends on the rate at which profits can be made, and this in turn depends on the rate at which people purchase, use, wear out, and destroy goods and services. Hence, an enormous effort is expended on extolling the virtues and benefits of products in order to convince consumers that they should make additional purchases.

> Prestige is awarded not to the person who works hardest or gives away the greatest amount of wealth but rather to the person who has the most possessions and who consumes at the highest rate. Capitalism inevitably leads to marked inequalities in wealth based on differential access to capital, technology, and resources.

As in all stratified political–economic systems, the rich use soldiers and police forces to safeguard their property and prevent the poor from confiscating their wealth and privileges. Without the protection of the army and police (which are paid for with the "surplus" collected by stratified redistributors), the accumulation of private wealth would not be possible.

Property Ownership

Ownership of land and resources is one of the most important aspects of political control. It is as much political as economic because unequal access to the environment implies some form of coercion applied by political superiors against political inferiors.

Ownership of garden land in *nonstratified* societies is usually claimed by kin groups in village communities, but everybody belongs to such kin groups, and hence adults cannot be prevented from using the resources they need to make a living.

Ownership of garden land in *stratified* societies is claimed and managed by the chief, who allocates land to individuals for their use in exchange for rent in labor and staples for institutional support.

As we will see in Chapter 10, ownership of land and resources results from infrastructural processes that select for more dense and more productive populations. Land ownership stimulates production because it forces food producers to work longer and harder than they would if they had free access to resources.

> Land ownership raises production because tenant food producers must work harder in order to pay the rent or tribute required for the opportunity to live or work on the owner's land.

This payment automatically compels tenants to increase their work input in order to produce for the landlord as well as for themselves. By raising or lowering rents, the landlord exercises a fairly direct measure of control over work input and production. Land ownership also means that individuals who lack title or tenure may be barred from using land, even if it leads to starvation.

Because the extraction of rent is evolutionarily associated with an increase in food production, some anthropologists regard the payment of rent as indicative of the existence of **surplus**.

 Surplus is an amount greater than what is needed for immediate consumption by the producers.

The producers, however, can very well use the full amount of their output to ease the costs of rearing children or to raise their own standard of living. If they surrender their produce, it is usually because they lack the power to withhold it. In this sense, all rent is an aspect of politics, because without the power to enforce property titles, rent would seldom be paid. Thus, there is a close resemblance between rent and taxation: Both depend on the existence of coercive power in the form of police and weapons that can be called into action if the taxpayer or tenant refuses to pay.

PROFILE 7.2 | Primitive Capitalism? The Kapauku Case

In general, band and village societies lack the essential features of capitalism because, as we have seen, their exchange systems are based on reciprocal and redistributive exchanges, rather than on price market exchanges. In some cases, however, nonstratified systems may have certain features strongly reminiscent of contemporary capitalism. The Kapauku Papuans of West Irian, in western New Guinea, are a case in point. According to Leopold Pospisil (1963), the Kapauku have an economy that is best described as "primitive capitalism." The economy is organized around individual accumulation of wealth, and there are important wealth differences within the society. All Kapauku agricultural land is said to be owned individually, money in the form of shells and glass beads can be used to buy food, domesticated animals, crops, and land; money can also be used as payment for labor.

A closer look at the land ownership, however, reveals fundamental differences. To begin with, access to land is controlled by kinship groups known as sublineages (see Chapter 10, section titled "Unilineal Descent Groups"). No individual is without membership in such a group, and therefore no one is denied access to land. These sublineages control communal tracts of land, but the economic significance of land titles is minimal, on several counts:

1. The price of land is so cheap that all the gardens under production have a market value in shell money less than the value of 10 female pigs.

2. Prohibition against trespass does not apply to sublineage kin.

3. Although even brothers will ask each other for land payments, credit is freely extended among all sublineage members, including giving land on loan.

4. Each sublineage is under the leadership of a headman (see Chapter 9), whose authority depends on his generosity, especially toward the members of his own sublineage. A rich headman does not refuse to lend his kinsmen whatever they need to gain access to the environment, because "a selfish individual who hoards money and fails to be generous never sees the time when his word is taken seriously and his advice and decisions followed, no matter how rich he may become" (Pospisil 1963:49).

Obviously, therefore, the wealth of the headman does not bestow the power associated with capitalist ownership. In Brazil or India, landlords can bar their tenants or sharecroppers from access to land and water, regardless of the landlord's reputation. In the United States, under the rules of capitalist land ownership, it is of no significance to the sheriff and the police officers when they evict farmers that the bank is being "selfish."

Pospisil states that although there are differences in wealth between sublineages and sickness and misfortune of various sorts frequently lead to inequalities in physical well-being among kinship units, such misfortunes do not lead to poverty as they do under capitalism. Without central political controls, marked economic inequalities cannot be perpetuated for long because the rich cannot defend themselves against the demands of the poor. Because wealth is displayed by generosity, a wealthy individual can retain his influence only if he distributes his wealth fairly among his fellow villagers. Thus, poverty, where it exists, does not result from a lack of access to land or credit. A stingy egalitarian redistributor is a contradiction in terms, for the simple reason that no police exist to protect such people from the murderous intentions of those whom they refuse to help. As Pospisil tells it, selfish and greedy individuals who have amassed huge personal properties but who have failed to comply with the Kapauku requirement of generosity toward their less fortunate tribesmen may be put to death. In other regions, where execution is not a penalty for greediness, a nongenerous wealthy man is ostracized, reprimanded, and thereby finally induced to change his ways (1963:49).

▪ Universal Pattern • The Kapauku of New Guinea

Infrastructure	Structure	Superstructure
People live in tropical rain forest, where there is little seasonal change in climate. Basic food staple is sweet potato, and pig is principal domestic animal.	Lineage is the largest kin group that is politically and legally unified. Law and order within lineage are maintained by headman, who has political and economic functions.	Wealth is displayed through generosity, not hoarding.
Land is controlled by kin groups that allocate farmland to lineage members. No one is denied access to land; land is given on loan, when needed.	Authority of headman depends on his generosity. Accumulation of wealth does not bestow power.	Wealthy individuals can retain influence only if they distribute wealth fairly among villagers.
Individuals can accumulate wealth and there are wealth differences within society, but no one is prevented from using land to make a living.	Differences in wealth do not result from lack of access to land or credit. Generosity is essential because rich cannot defend themselves against poor.	Nongenerous individuals are punished; may be put to death, ostracized, or reprimanded.

> The surplus food the landowner takes away as rent is not necessarily a superfluous quantity from the producers' standpoint: They have no choice but to grow crops beyond their families' basic needs so as to be able to afford to pay taxes and rent.

Two forms of property ownership existed in early agricultural states: one in which the governing elites claimed ownership over all landholdings and appointed officials to oversee and collect tribute in the form of taxes, rent, or labor services; and a second type in which land was owned privately by a class of landlords who inherited the land and maintained a class of peasants to produce surpluses. Agricultural states thus developed major inequalities between those who owned land and those who did not. As we will see in Chapter 10, these forms of extracting wealth from food producers arose as a consequence of intensification and population pressure, as chiefdoms and later states established a regional peace and regularized rules of property that allowed for the development of larger scale specialized production (Earle 2000).

Patterns of Work

Among hunter-gatherer and simple agricultural societies, one finds very little specialization. Each man does the same kind of work as other men; each woman does the same kind of work as other women. But each adult performs many different tasks from day to day, in contrast to the standardized routines of contemporary factory or office employees. Moreover, the decision to switch from one task to another—from setting traps to making arrows or collecting honey, for example—is largely voluntary and arrived at either individually or by group consensus. Therefore, people in small-scale, nonstate societies probably do not experience work as a tedious aspect of life. Indeed, recent experimental reforms of factory work patterns are designed to let industrial workers work at varied jobs and to include them in "quality circles" that make decisions about how tasks are performed. These experiments represent attempts to recapture some of the enviable characteristics of work in small-scale, unspecialized economies.

In societies with hunter–gatherer and simple agricultural infrastructures, people do not spend as much

Labor-Saving Devices That Don't Save Work
The era of mass production began in 1913 with the first assembly line at Ford's Highland Park, Michigan, magneto plant. It saved 15 minutes per unit, but the workers worked harder than ever.

time at work as they do in intensive agricultural or industrial societies. The !Kung San, for example, put in an average of only about 20 hours per week in hunting. The basic reason for this is that their mode of production is not intensifiable. Rather than run the risk of depleting the animal population below the point of recovery, the !Kung San move from one territory to another. They enjoy a good diet and don't have to work very hard to get it. In fact, the !Kung are able to work less than intensive agriculturalists or modern factory workers. When labor leaders and employers boast about how much progress has been made in obtaining leisure for today's working class, they have in mind a standard established in nineteenth-century Europe, when factory workers used to put in 12 hours a day or more. Before we enthusiastically endorse the progress that has been made through technological advances, we should keep in mind the work standards observed by foragers and horticulturalists.

Table 7.2 summarizes the average time spent in total production and housework according to society type. Based on a sample of 102 studies of time allocation, Ross Sackett (1996) shows an overall increase in total labor expenditure (production and housework) as societies move from simple to more advanced technology. In less intensive systems, the average number of hours per day (h/d) spent at work ranges from 5.7 to 7.6 hours per day (h/d), whereas in agricultural societies, the average work time is

Table 7.2

Comparison of Average Daily Adult Labor in Hours per Day*

Society Type	Men	Women
A. Production		
Foraging societies	4.2 h/d*	3.2 h/d
Horticultural societies	4.5	3.9
Agricultural societies	7.3	3.9
Industrial societies	7.5	3.6
B. Housework		
Foraging societies	1.9	3.7
Horticultural societies	1.6	3.6
Agricultural societies	1.1	5.7
Industrial societies	1.0	5.2
C. Total labor		
Foraging societies	5.7	6.1
Horticultural societies	6.1	7.6
Agricultural societies	8.4	9.9
Industrial societies	8.6	8.8

*h/d: hours per day refer to a seven-day week.
Source: Sackett 1996.

8.4 for men and 9.9 h/d for women. The reason is that in agricultural societies, labor is intensified to

A.

B.

Life in a Capitalist Economy

A. The public sale and purchase of shares in companies and corporations is a fundamental feature of capitalist economies. Buyers and sellers have no face-to-face interaction. Markets like this, the Tokyo Stock Exchange, function exclusively to maximize profits.   B. In the United States and elsewhere, many people work long hours so that work becomes a surrogate home.

produce food for both domestic consumption and to pay for taxes, rent, and other costs associated with a price market economy. Despite the many advantages of labor-saving devices and technological improvements, labor demands are similarly high in industrial society. Men average 8.6 and women 8.8 h/d, calculated on a seven-day work week so that weekends do not count as days of rest (see Box 7.1).

In terms of total labor (production and housework), men and women in industrial societies spend nearly 50 percent more time working than foragers and horticulturalists.

Work occupies an ever greater part of daily life among industrial wage earners. To the basic 8.6- and 8.8-hour day, add time for commuting and shopping and if there are children in the family, add time for chauffeuring children to and from after school activities, helping them with homework, and participating in their school events.

More recently a new and perhaps surpassing trend in work patterns has been described for corporate Americans. Arlie Russell Hochschild (1998) says people work long hours because they want to, not because they have to; people are escaping home by going to work. Although most people say that work is too demanding and the hours are too long, Hochschild found that male and female management-level workers in a Midwest Fortune 500 company regularly work 10- to 11-hour workdays (8 A.M. to 6 or 7 P.M.) because they find work to be more satisfying and they have more support at work than they do at home. Work is a way of fleeing from the stresses of home life, where they encounter high labor costs in rearing "high-quality" children and parents and spouses feel less in control and less equipped to handle problems. It is not surprising that as the corporate workplace becomes more creative and more interesting, it becomes more like a surrogate home, while the family home becomes an arena of stress that offers less support or satisfaction.

Emergent Varieties of Capitalism

Although Americans think of the United States as being a capitalist country, its political economy is actually best characterized as a mixture of capitalism and democratic state socialism—the same mixture that, to varying degrees, constitutes the political economies of Western Europe and Japan. Some 19.5 million people are directly employed by federal, state, and local governments. Approximately 1.4 million people are in the active military. Another 43 million depend

largely on government social security payments of one form or another. Other forms of state, local, and federal pensions support at least 5.8 million people.

The federal government disburses forms of financial assistance through many programs in a number of major categories. There are various types of medical aid disbursements, cash aid disbursements, food assistance programs, and types of housing allowances, as well as various jobs and job-training programs. In fact, the total number of individual disbursements is staggering. When added up, the total number of disbursements comes to over 190 million. This is not the end of the picture, as there are at least 1 million farm families that receive government agricultural subsidies. To a significant degree, U.S. citizens do depend on the redistribution of tax money rather than on sharing in the profits made from capitalist free enterprise.

The United States has other political–economic features that depart from a pure capitalist model. The essence of capitalist enterprise is the freedom to buy and sell in competitive price-making markets. Price-making markets exist where there are enough buyers and sellers to enable buyers to compete with buyers, buyers to compete with sellers, and sellers to compete with sellers for the prices that best suit their respective interests. It has long been recognized that to preserve the free enterprise system, limitations must be placed on the ability of small groups of powerful buyers or sellers to gain control over a market to the extent that the prices they offer effectively determine the price that must be paid by anyone who wants a particular product or service.

Early in this century, the U.S. Congress passed laws against the formation of monopolies and actively pursued the breakup of companies that then dominated the railroad, meat-packing, and petroleum industries. The antimonopoly laws stopped short, however, of prohibiting the formation of semimonopolies or oligopolies—that is, companies that control not all but a major share of the market for a particular product. The trend toward oligopoly was already well advanced in the earlier part of this century. But after the end of World War II, the pace of acquisitions and expansions quickened. As a result, by 1980, the 50 largest U.S. manufacturing corporations owned 42 percent of all assets used in manufacturing, whereas the top 500 owned 72 percent of these assets (Silk 1985).

The most important trend in capitalism in the 1990s was the emergence of *multinational, transnational,* and *supranational* corporations. Multinationals have their headquarters and do most of their business in one country but have markets and facilities around the globe. Transnationals also have headquarters in one country but depend on their international divisions for the bulk of their production and sales.

BOX 7.1 | Production, Consumption, and Free Time in Affluent Societies

Does modern affluence bring greater leisure and satisfy our basic needs better than previous less advanced economic systems? This question can be answered by comparing data on time allocation (based on production, consumption, and free time) among the horticultural Machiguenga of Peru and the industrial French middle class. Time use data show that the French clearly spend more time in production and consumption activities than the Machiguenga; the Machiguenga have over 50 percent (14.8 versus 9.6 hours per day) more free time than the French. This situation reflects the increasing scarcity of time felt by most members of "more affluent" societies, who produce more and consume more. In the context of perceived time scarcity, we convert free time into consumption time because we do not want to "waste time."

This brings up the question of whether consumer goods are needed in themselves or whether demand for them has been created by the producers. We cannot simply assume that goods are produced to meet people's real needs. The billions of dollars spent each year on advertising indicate that not all consumer wants arise from basic needs of the individual but that some of these needs are created in consumers by the producers themselves. This turns things around. Instead of arguing, as economists usually do, that our economic system serves us well, we are forced to consider that it may be we who serve the system by somehow agreeing to want the things it seems bent on producing.

To most economists, there is no justification for criticizing the purchasing habits of modern consumers. Purchases simply reflect personal preferences, and it would be arrogant to judge the individual decisions of free men and women. Economists assume that if people had more satisfying pathways of consumption, they would choose them. But the role of advertising in creating wants leaves open the question of whether consumption is aimed at the fulfillment of people's needs or whether mass consumption is imposed from above to increase corporate profits. How else can we explain that in modern industrial society, no matter what the level of income, people's consumer spending is up to it.

Source: From *Human Nature Magazine,* "In Search of Affluent Society," 1(9), September 1978, pp. 50–59, by Human Nature Magazine/Allen Johnson. Copyright © 1978. Reprinted with permission of Wadsworth, a division of Thomson Learning: www.thomsonlearning.com. Fax 800-730-2215.

Machiguenga at Work

As in most slash-and-burn economies, Machiguenga men fell trees and clear forests for new plantings. Here, a Machiguenga uses the felled trees to build a house.

Corporate Office Workers

Men in industrial society work 8.6 hours per day, compared to 5.7 hours for hunters and gatherers and 6.1 hours for men in simple agricultural societies. Women work even longer hours.

When threatened by unions or government regulators, they move their operations from one country to another. Supranationals have multiple or mobile headquarters. Their managers are multiethnic and multilingual and feel no particular need to identify with a particular government or labor force. It seems likely that early in the next century, the power of the transnationals—some of which already have budgets equal to those of large countries—will expand at the expense of the power of national states.

SUMMARY
and *Questions to Think About*

1. Each society has an economy—a set of institutions that combines technology, labor, and natural resources to produce and distribute goods and services. The organizational aspects of an economy are distinguished from its infrastructural aspects in order to explore the relationship between infrastructure and structure. Selection for different modes of exchange reflects differing degrees of intensifiability and population growth.

2. Exchange is an integral part of every economy, but the flow of goods and services from producers to consumers can be organized in several ways. Modern-day price markets and buying and selling are not universal. The idea that money can buy everything (or almost everything) has been alien to most of the human beings who have ever lived. Two other modes of exchange—reciprocity and redistribution—once played a more important economic role than price markets.

3. In reciprocal exchange, the time and quantity of the counterflow is not specified. This kind of exchange can be effective only when it is embedded in kinship or close personal relationships. Daily food distribution among the !Kung San is an example of reciprocal exchange. Control over the counterflow in reciprocal exchange is achieved by communal pressure against freeloaders and shirkers.

4. Reciprocity lingers on in price market societies within kinship groups and is familiar to many of us as gift giving to relatives and friends. In the absence of price markets and police or military supervision, trade poses a special problem to people accustomed to reciprocal exchange. Silent barter is one solution. Another is to create trading partners who treat each other as kin.

5. The kula is a classic example of how barter for necessities is carried out under the cloak of reciprocal exchange. Redistributive exchange involves the collection of goods in a central place and its disbursement by a redistributor to the producers. In the transition from egalitarian to stratified forms of redistribution, production and exchange cross the line separating voluntary from coerced forms of economic behavior. In its egalitarian form, the redistributor depends on the goodwill of the producers; in the stratified form, the producers depend on the goodwill of the redistributor.

6. Redistribution is characterized by the counting of shares contributed and shares disbursed. Unlike reciprocity, redistribution leads to boasting and overt competition for the prestigious status of being a great provider.

7. The Kwakiutl potlatch is a classic example of the relationships between redistribution and bragging behavior. The predominance of redistribution over reciprocity is related to the intensifiability of various modes of production. Where production can be intensified without depletions, rivalrous redistributions may serve adaptive ecological functions, such as providing an extra margin of safety in lean years and equalizing regional production.

8. The development of destructive potlatches among the Kwakiutl may have been caused by factors stemming from contact with Europeans, such as the intensification of warfare, trade for guns and ammunition, and depopulation.

9. Price market exchange depends on the development of all-purpose money, as defined by the criteria of portability, divisibility, generality, anonymity, and legality. Although some of these features are possessed by limited-purpose standards of value, all-purpose money and price markets imply the existence of state forms of control.

10. The greatest development of the price market mode of exchange is associated with the political economy of capitalism, in which virtually all goods and services can be bought and sold. Because capitalist production depends on consumerism, prestige is awarded to those who own or consume the greatest amount of goods and services. Price market exchanges are embedded in a political economy of control made necessary by the inequalities in access to resources and the conflict between the poor and the wealthy.

11. The Kapauku illustrate why price market institutions and capitalism cannot exist in the absence of a developed political form of control.

12. Land ownership becomes the focus of the mode of production and exchange in societies where there are political forms of control. Differential access to land leads to the exaction of rent and taxation; both compel tenants to increase their work input and production.

13. Paradoxically, advanced agriculturalists and factory and office workers labor longer hours than hunters and gatherers and simple agriculturalists. In the postindustrial corporate workplace, people choose to spend more time at work than at home, as home life has become more stressful.

Questions to Think About

1. What are the differences between redistribution in egalitarian versus stratified societies?

2. What is the difference between reciprocity and market exchange? What role does each play in U.S. society?

3. What infrastructural conditions help explain the Kwakiutl potlatch? What historical changes led to excess and destruction?

4. What effect does land ownership (or lack of land ownership) have on food production and distribution?

THROUGH THE LENS
of Cultural Materialism

Conformity and Conflict • Reading Two
Eating Christmas in the Kalahari
Richard Borshay Lee

When anthropologist Richard Lee decided to purchase a fat ox for a Christmas feast with the !Kung, he was unexpectedly met with criticism and mockery. He thought his ox was a great specimen, with more than enough meat to feed everyone, yet the !Kung told him that it was a mere "sack of guts and bones." Although the criticism ruined his mood for the holiday, he soon discovered that the remarks needed to be understood in terms of the !Kung political economy, which maintains that everyone is equal and that no one can claim authority by providing an abundant amount of meat.

Emic Interpretation

- Although the !Kung highly value meat, the intent of their response was to diminish the value of the gift.

- A !Kung woman's response to Lee's ox was, "Do you expect us to eat that bag of bones?"

Etic Interpretation

- By claiming the ox is worthless, the !Kung enforce humility and effectively neutralize a provider's feelings of pride and arrogance.

- The environment of the !Kung adequately supports small mobile groups. Meat is highly valued, but if hunting is intensified for the purpose of gaining authority, the !Kung would rapidly deplete available game through overhunting.

Structure
Emic

- "When a young man kills much meat he comes to think of himself as a chief or a big man, and he thinks of the rest as his servants or inferiors. We can't accept this. We refuse one who boasts, for someday his pride will make him kill somebody."

Etic

- The structure of !Kung culture is a subsistence economy, in which there is equal access to basic resources and no ownership of property. No one holds formal power, and all members have equal rights.

- The livelihood of !Kung society relies on their system of reciprocal exchange. Their mode of production is based on the practice of reciprocity, in which food is shared and dispersed among all members so that no one ever goes hungry.

Superstructure
Emic

- The !Kung believe that "there are no totally generous acts. All 'acts' have an element of calculation. One black ox slaughtered at Christmas does not wipe out a year of careful manipulation of gifts given to serve your own ends."

- The !Kung value humility and despise boastfulness.

Etic

- Skepticism toward gifts is well suited in a subsistence economy with egalitarian political organization. It allows people to resist intensification through the development of a prestige economy and to avoid domination by anyone who tries to be arrogant.

THROUGH THE LENS
of Cultural Materialism

Conformity and Conflict • Reading Thirteen
Reciprocity and the Power of Giving
Lee Cronk

Gifts can be used to strengthen relationships or form new ones, or they can be used to gain a position of prestige or power through generosity. While a gift usually has "strings attached" that affect the relationship between the parties involved, the nature of loyalty and obligation is determined by infrastructure (availability of resources) that impacts structure (the political economy) by creating egalitarian or stratified relationships between individuals. "In some societies, gift giving is a tie between friends, a way of maintaining good relationships, whereas in others gift giving has developed into an elaborate, expensive, and antagonistic ritual designed to humiliate rivals by showering them with wealth and obligating them to either give more in return or acknowledge their subordinate position" (p. 148). Even in Western societies, where people think "gifts ought to be offered freely without strings attached," they are used to nurture long-term relationships of mutual obligation, as well as to foster feelings of indebtedness.

Emic Perspective

- Gift giving and reciprocity are expressions of generosity. They demonstrate ties between friends and provide a way of reinforcing good relationships.

Etic Perspective

- Gift giving can vary, depending on how resources are allocated and controlled. Gift giving can be used either as a social security mechanism to ensure that everyone's needs are met, or it can be used to reinforce stratification when wealthy individuals give large gifts that obligate recipients to assume a subordinate position unless they can reciprocate.

Examples of Stratified Political Economies

- In some societies, the power of a gift is used to embarrass the recipient and to force repayment. During the nineteenth century in British Columbia, the Kwakiutl used gifts as symbolic weapons to resolve disputes concerning status and regional authority. At large feasts called *potlatches,* rivals competed for the honor and prestige of giving away the greatest amount of property. In the 1880s, after the Canadian government began to suppress physical warfare, potlatching became a substitute for battle among the chiefs in the region to attract followers.

- Gift giving can be used as a method of political control. In Iran, under the Shah, the government generously sponsored an irrigation project. Before development, each village managed its own internal affairs and determined its own relations with outsiders. However, after irrigation was introduced, people were forced to relocate. According to the anthropologist, the purpose behind the irrigation project was the dismantling of local institutions to enhance central government control of the oil-laden region. The "gift" of irrigation effectively crushed the autonomy of the local population because after the development, decisions were made by government bureaucrats, not local townsmen.

- "Third World leaders also have complained that too much Japanese aid is targeted at countries in which Japan has an economic stake and that such aid is tied to the purchase of Japanese goods—that Japan's generosity has less to do with addressing the problems of underdeveloped countries than with exploiting those problems to its own advantage."

Examples of Egalitarian Domestic or Political Economies

- Although repayment of gifts is expected, it is crucial that it be deferred. To reciprocate at once indicates a desire to end the relationship, to cut the strings; delayed repayment "makes the strings longer and longer." Some exchange customs are designed solely to preserve the relationship, such as the *hxaro* system of the !Kung, in which little attention is paid to whether the items exchanged are equivalent.

- Within the domestic economy of the Mukogodo of Kenya, parents teach children that "gifts carry obligations" by reminding them that the White people are the ones who gave them candy and that "gifts are meant to circulate" by asking them to part with the candies even after the candies were in their mouths.

- Anthropologist Carol Stack discovered a tradition of "benevolent exchange" in an Illinois ghetto called the Flats that consists of "swapping" between poor Blacks. "Among residents of the Flats, wealth comes in spurts; hard times are frequent and unpredictable. Swapping, of clothes, food, furniture, and the like, is a way of guaranteeing security, of making sure that someone will be there to help out when one is in need and that one will get a share of any windfalls that come along."

- The !Kung do not focus on the economic value of gifts and depreciate the value of all so-called gifts for fear of generating power hierarchies and stratification within their egalitarian society.

- In Mount Hagen, New Guinea, the system of gift giving is used to rank individuals, but no real power is associated with becoming a "big man." One donor who was pleased with himself described the symbolic meaning of gift giving by telling his recipient, "I have won. I have knocked you down by giving so much." Here, people compete for prestige but do not gain control by virtue of their generosity.

CHAPTER 8

A Japanese nuclear family at home.

DOMESTIC

LIFE

In this chapter, we continue the comparative study of structural features, focusing on the variety of family groups and their relation to aspects of infrastructure. We begin by looking at the astonishing variety of human family forms and mating arrangements: monogamy, polygyny, and polyandry and secondary marriages and preferred-cousin marriages, to mention only a few. Although this chapter is primarily descriptive, it takes up some perennially interesting questions: Is the nuclear family universal? Is marriage? Can marriage take place between partners of the same sex? Do husbands and wives have to live together for their relationship to qualify as marriage? Why do some types of marriages require a gift to the bride's family, whereas others require a gift to the groom's family? Why does every culture have a taboo against incest? Is the taboo based on instinctual sexual aversions, or is it a cultural adaptation? We can draw one important conclusion: There is no single, natural way to organize domestic life.

The Household and the Domestic Sphere of Culture

All societies have a domestic sphere of life. The focus of the domestic sphere is a dwelling space, shelter, residence, or household, in which certain universally recurrent activities take place. It is not possible to give a simple checklist of what these activities are because there is so much variety (Netting et al. 1984). In many cultures, domestic activities include preparation and consumption of food; cleaning, grooming, teaching, and disciplining the young; sleeping; and adult sexual intercourse. However, in no culture are these activities carried out exclusively within domestic household settings.

In the case of modern industrial cultures, this pattern is evident with respect to enculturation and education, which are increasingly carried out in special nondomestic buildings (schools or day care centers) under the auspices of specialists (teachers), who often spend more time with children than do the parents. Many village and band societies also separate their adolescent male children from the domestic scene to prepare them for adulthood, in the same way some parents send their children away to boarding school. In many parts of East Africa, adolescent boys are separated from the community to form a residential age set, where they are trained to assume duties and responsibilities associated with cattle herding and raiding. Their mothers and sisters cook and keep house for them until they take wives. They remain together until they establish their own households and

continue to be closely associated throughout their lives.

In many societies, married men spend a good deal of time in special men's houses. Food is handed in to them by wives and children, who are themselves forbidden to enter. One of the most interesting cases of the separation of cooking and eating occurs among the Ashanti of West Africa. Ashanti men eat their meals with their sisters, mothers, and maternal nephews and nieces, not with their wives and children. But it is the wives who do the cooking. Every evening in Ashanti land, one sees a steady traffic of children taking their mothers' cooking to their fathers' sisters' houses (see Barnes 1960; Bender 1967).

Households change over time, as their members go through the stages of the cycle of birth, marriage, aging, and death. Among the Zumbagua peasants of the Ecuadorian Andes, households undergo a gradual transition, as young couples establish themselves, in stages, as separate households. During courtship, couples have sex in the fields, away from the house where they eat and sleep. When they get married, they build a small hut that lacks a hearth for heating or cooking. This hut adjoins the house of the groom's or bride's parents. Now they sleep and have sex together under one roof, but they continue to cook and eat in their parents' kitchen. Their first children are brought up and cared for by the couple's parents. Only when a couple has several children will they finally build their own kitchen and begin to sleep, cook, eat, have sex, and nurture their offspring around their new hearth in their own household (Weismantel 1989).

 The **household** is a domestic group whose members live together and cooperate on a daily basis in production and share the proceeds of labor and other resources held in common.

Household members organize and carry out a range of activities related to production, consumption, child rearing, inheritance, and reproductive activities. Household inhabitants are usually kin but may include nonkin as well. Similarly, households may contain nonresident members, who live and work elsewhere but contribute to the household economy (Blanton 1994; Netting 1989; Yanagisako 1979). In this regard, the household is an etic behavioral unit that is defined in terms of the activities of the domestic economy. Members share food, labor, and material resources based on the requirements of the subsistence economy and the personnel available in the household. Resources are managed according to consensus and cooperation. The need to maintain enduring relationships over time results in explicit ideologies of family obligation and mutual support to sustain solidarity and cohesion between household members.

Family Groups and the Mode of Production and Reproduction

Family structure consists of the primary groups present in every society that satisfy basic human biopsychological needs and drives and sustain the health and well-being of its members. The focus of these groups is on kinship and family relations that provide food, shelter, and emotional, sexual, and reproductive needs. Anthropologists are concerned with understanding the functional roles of families and how they are transformed in relation to changes in infrastructure. These include traditional modes of production as well as global trends such as industrialization and urbanization that lead to patterns of employment, housing, demographics, and income distribution.

The Nuclear Family

Many anthropologists believe that at the center of all domestic organization is a group known as the **nuclear family.**

 The **nuclear family** consists of husband, wife, and children.

Anthropologist Ralph Linton held the view that the unit of father, mother, and child is the "bedrock underlying all other family structures," and he predicted that "the last man will spend his last hours searching for his wife and child" (1959:52). George Peter Murdock (1949, 1967) found the nuclear family in every one of a sample of 250 societies. He concluded that it occurs universally because it fulfills vital functions that cannot be fulfilled as efficiently by other groups:

- The regulation of sexual activity
- Support in reproduction during pregnancy and nursing
- Socialization of children by members of both sexes
- Cooperation in subsistence because of the sexual division of labor

Most anthropologists believe that the nuclear family is not the only group that can fulfill these functions. Other social units, including alternative institutions that may lie entirely outside the domestic sphere, can assume these functions as efficiently.

Peasants of the Peruvian Andes
This mother and father and their two children comprise a nuclear family.

Nuclear families are prevalent in small-scale hunting-gathering societies, where a high degree of mobility is required due to seasonal variations in resource availability. These smaller nuclear families move on their own in search of food but unite with several other family groups when resources are abundant. Flexibility enables nuclear family members to move in and out of camps and maintain ties across a wide regional network. Nuclear families are also adapted to the requirements of an industrial economy, particularly the middle class, where there is a high degree of geographic mobility, as people move to places where jobs and career opportunities are available. Unemployment insurance, savings, and health insurance sustain them when they are ill or between jobs. Similarly, the social security system and the growth of retirement plans relieve nuclear family members of financial responsibility for their elderly parents and increase their independence and ability to move as needed.

Polygamous Families

Historically, most cultures around the world have not followed the rule of **monogamy.**

Monogamy is the marriage of one man to one woman at a time.

Serial monogamy is marriage to two or more spouses one after another, rather than at the same time.

In some societies that prescribe monogamy, it may be acceptable for a man or a woman to maintain a lover in a separate household as long as they are reasonably discreet. In other societies, including our own, serial monogamy (remarriage after death or divorce) is an acceptable alternative to lifelong marriage to one person. But in the overwhelming majority of world cultures, plural marriage, or **polygamy**, is permitted.

 Polygamy refers to a marriage to more than one spouse at a time.

Polygyny refers to marriage in which several wives share a husband.

Polyandry is a less common form of marriage in which several husbands share a wife.

Polygyny. Polygyny occurs in over 80 percent of the societies in Murdock's (1967) sample societies. We must, however, bear in mind that where it is practiced, polygyny is the preferred form of marriage, rather than the norm. Only 20 to 45 percent of the men actually have two or more wives. In some societies, only men of high rank can seek more than one wife, and in stratified societies, only men of wealth can afford to do so.

Polygyny is common in horticultural societies where women are responsible for production. Under these conditions, women are valued for their labor as well as their role as childbearers. As long as land is readily available, additional women in the household increase both the labor supply and the productive yield (D. White 1988).

In societies where women are the main food producers, polygyny increases domestic production and there is less conflict between co-wives.

Among the horticultural Machiguenga of lowland South America, co-wives share the same dwelling and a woman must give her permission before her husband brings a co-wife, who will be like a sister, into the household. Women in fact welcome the additional labor of a co-wife, who will be like a sister, as long as they are compatible.

 Sororal polygyny is a marriage pattern in which a man marries two or more sisters.

Sororal polygyny is preferred among the Machiguenga because close kinship encourages cooperation. Sisters usually get along and are more likely to create close bonds than women who are strangers. Machiguenga co-wives each maintain their own gardens and have their own hearths but cooperate in a variety of tasks. Senior wives usually enjoy superior status and authority over younger wives, and the rights and obligations among wives are clearly defined. This pattern is typical in cultures where land is still abundant and there is little rank or stratification among males.

Dissension and jealousy among co-wives is more likely in societies where women are economically dependent on men and are valued more as childbearers than as food producers.

Where men are responsible for most of the productive work, wealthy men will take secondary wives to demonstrate their status in society. In highly stratified societies, having many wives and concubines is one of the privileges of royalty. In other societies, polygyny is a symbol of prestige. Among the Gusii of Kenya, it is thought that having many wives shows that a man is important in the clan, that he has control over people, and that he is equipped to solve disputes in the community (Hakansson and LeVine 1997). A

African Polygyny

Co-wives live in separate dwellings and often are in competition with one another.

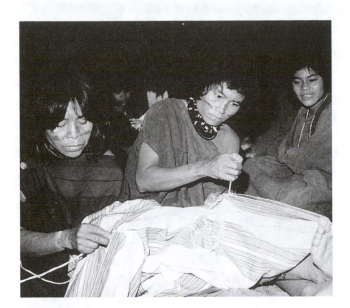

Machiguenga Co-Wives
Co-wives are like "sisters" and tend to form close bonds.

polygynously married man also has more offspring and more alliances through marriage. His co-wives, however, may not benefit equally from his status. They are likely to live in separate households and to see each other as competitors for their husband's wealth. Among the Gusii, as well as in other parts of West Africa, land and livestock are inherited through males. Co-wives differ considerably in status and wealth. Although each woman has her allotted fields and livestock, the husband controls the property and it is passed on to his sons. If a man marries more than one wife, his land is divided. The first wife gets the largest share, and subsequent wives are allocated land according to their rank (Sennyonga 1997).

Polyandry.   Polyandry is a rare family form in which a woman marries two or more men at a time. It is found in less than 1 percent of societies and is most common in Nepal, Tibet, and India. The most common form is **fraternal polyandry.** All brothers in a family, including those who have not yet been born, are married to one woman. The wife and her husbands live together in a single household on the family estate. Sexual privileges rotate among the brothers. According to Nancy Levine, the Nyinba of Nepal place little value on sexual exclusivity, and there is little overt sexual jealousy or competition (see Profile 8.1). Given polyandry and the fact that women have extramarital affairs, there is always uncertainty about paternity. Yet Nyinba men do attempt to determine the paternity of children born in polyandrous marriages because real fathers and children have special relationships. Men place emphasis on having "sons

of their own" so they will have biological children to look after them in their old age (Levine 1988:168).

Polyandry is an alternative form of family in which a woman marries and resides with two or more husbands, either brothers or men who are unrelated. Polyandry avoids subdividing the family estate and reduces population growth.

The infrastructural basis of polyandry rests on the fact that it supports low population growth because each husband will have fewer offspring than if he was married to a wife he did not have to share. While polyandry prevents some women from marrying, single women do have children, but they have fewer children than married women. Second, it prevents the partition of family land by keeping the household with its resources undivided from one generation to the next (Goldstein 1987).

Subdivision of family landholdings would leave the parcels too small to cultivate efficiently. The more men a household includes, the greater its chances for economic success.

It is clear that polyandry is not the only way to organize and manage the domestic economy in harsh, high-altitude environments. In fact, many nonpolyandrous groups live in the region, but what stands out is that polyandrous villagers such as the Nyinba are much wealthier and enjoy greater prosperity, undoubtedly because wealth is maintained intact over generations and population growth is inhibited.

Nancy Levine points out that ideologically, the importance of polyandry extends beyond economics. The Nyinba have elaborate legends that portray the ancestors in harmonious polyandrous families, and they idealize the solidarity of brothers as one of the core kinship ideals, equivalent to the obligation to support parents in their old age (Levine 1988:159). Nevertheless, there are disadvantages within the sibling group, particularly for younger men with much older wives, who have much lower chances of siring their own children. Men who have fathered few children are the most prone to initiate partition of the family estate (Levine and Silk 1997).

The Extended Family

In a majority of the societies studied by anthropologists, domestic life is dominated by groupings larger than simple nuclear or polygamous families. Some form of extended family is especially common.

PROFILE 8.1 | The Nyinba—A Polyandrous Society

The Nyinba are a Tibetan-speaking minority that live in Nepal. They are devout Buddhists in an area surrounded by Hindus. Polyandry is a part of Buddhist Tibetan culture, which values reserved emotional attachments. Passion and sexual involvement are condoned, as long as they are not excessive. Young people are expected to have sex before marriage, and extramarital affairs are tolerated as long as they are not socially disruptive.

When a woman marries, she normally moves in with a group of brothers. She is expected to treat all her husbands with equal consideration and affection. Exclusive attachment is discouraged, as it risks alienating the others and threatens to break up the family. Occasionally, more than one woman is involved in a Nyinba marriage; for example, a group of sisters may marry a group of brothers. In fact, the Nyinba tolerate various marriage arrangements. Polyandry is preferred, but polygyny is permitted.

There are also cases of *conjoint marriage,* where a man in a polyandrous marriage marries another woman and brings her into the household as his second wife. This tends to occur when there is a large sibling set and a man's needs are poorly met by his marriage. Marriages with four or more brothers are the most difficult to sustain. It becomes problematic for wives to meet each man's expectation of having a son and to satisfy the domestic labor obligations for so many men. Another factor is the brothers' parentage. The Nyinba say that the most successful polyandrous marriages involve brothers that have the same mother and father; those with different parents, especially different mothers, are more likely to experience failures in fraternal commitments that result in conjoint marriage.

Yet there are inconveniences from conjoint marriage as well. Continual dissention threatens the risk of dividing the household estate. Unless a household lacks sufficient land to undergo partition, conjoint marriages are likely to split in terms of property and persons. Men form new households around the wife or wives with whom they

Nyinban Family
This polyandrous family includes a group of brothers and their children, who share a single wife and mother.

PROFILE 8.1 | The Nyinba—A Polyandrous Society *(continued)*

are closest and the children they have fathered. The eldest brother and his family get the largest room, while the younger brother or brothers move into the storage quarters. The land is divided up among the brothers; the sons of brothers who lived in the joint family are entitled to shares from their fathers only.

Source: Adapted from Nancy E. Levine. 1988. *The Dynamics of Polyandry: Kinship, Domesticity, and Population on the Tibetan Border.* Copyright © 1988, reprinted by permission of the University of Chicago Press.

Universal Pattern • The Nyinba

Infrastructure	Structure	Superstructure
Plow agriculture with terracing, irrigation, and fertilization in rugged mountain area.	Patrilineal, patrilocal extended households, in which woman moves in with group of brothers. Sometimes second wife joins household.	Polyandry extends beyond economics; legends portray polyandrous families living in harmony.
Fixed land base with compact settlements, densely populated villages, and diversified land use, combining agriculture and herding.	All brothers are full partners in marriage and share time with wife in rotation. Satisfactory marriage is essential for avoiding division or portioning of household.	Solidarity of brothers is core kinship ideal, equivalent to supporting parents in old age.
Fraternal polyandry results in low population growth because each husband has fewer children than he would if married to a wife he did not share.	Large households are more economically successful; subdivision would leave parcels too small to cultivate efficiently.	Subdivision is seen as unfortunate failure to live up to cultural ideals.

 An **extended family** is a domestic group consisting of several related nuclear families and may include siblings, their spouses, and their children or parents and married children.

Extended families may also be polygynous or polyandrous. Depending on the rules of residence, an extended family may center around an older married couple, their sons, and their sons' wives and children. Or an extended family may center around a core of related women, with husbands marrying into the family to live with their wives' parents and sisters. Each household structure is different in its dynamics. Depending on the composition of household members, extended families provide different opportunities for family interaction and patterns of authority.

In traditional Chinese extended families, the senior couple manages the household (see Profile 8.2). The family is a corporate enterprise characterized by a common budget, shared properties, and a strict pooling of income. The senior couple arranges marriages. Women brought into the household as wives for the senior couple's sons are placed under the direct control

of their mother-in-law. Wives remain outsiders and are treated with suspicion and even hostility. A farm family goes to considerable trouble and expense to acquire a daughter-in-law, and the household members expect more from the bargain than the young girl can provide (A. Wolf 1995). She gradually learns to adjust to her status, but her only source of security comes from forming her own family, through her own children and grandchildren (M. Wolf 1972). The father–son relationship is based on paternal dominance. The son continues to turn his income over to his father and to follow his father's wishes in all business dealings.

When a family has several daughters-in-law, cooking chores are often rotated so that on any given day, a maximum contingent of the domestic labor force can be sent to work in the family's fields (M. Cohen 1976). The degree to which the nuclear family is submerged and effaced by these arrangements is brought out by a *sim pua* marriage, a custom formerly found in certain Taiwanese households: "Adopt a daughter, marry a sister." To obtain control over their son's wife, the senior couple adopts a daughter, usually someone whose parents are very poor. They bring the girl into the household at a very early age and train her to be

Throughout China, larger extended families tend to be wealthier and to have higher social standing (M. Cohen 1976). Large families are able to gain more wealth than small families for two reasons. One is that frugality is imposed on all members by strict parents in order to save as much as they can. The second advantage is that a large family allows for a division of labor. Additional sons can earn income outside the farm, and the father can invest their income in additional parcels of land to increase the family's landholdings. Extended families thus provide a larger labor pool and can carry out a greater variety of simultaneous activities, with the proceeds contributing to the family's wealth.

Taiwanese Marriage
The groom's extended family is assembled for this wedding ceremony.

Large extended families make sacrifices to become wealthy, but not all families can hold up under the pressures and partition is often inevitable. It is said that families cannot stay wealthy for too long because sooner or later, problems arise when some individuals refuse to contribute their labor or there is outright embezzlement of family funds (M. Cohen 1976:204; Pasternak et al. 1997:238).

In China today, the extended family still remains more functional than the nuclear family, but young couples are increasingly demanding independence. According to Yunxiang Yan (1997), the decollectivization of farmland in the 1980s led to an increase in both commercialism and family wealth. As a result, there is an accelerated trend toward the establishment of conjugal "husband–wife families," even before a couple has children.

A number of factors contribute to the growing trend toward conjugal families. First, young couples want their privacy and want to manage on their own, without parental intervention. According to one young woman, in an extended family, "you always feel as though you are being watched—there are eyes around the house all the time." Second, young couples are more prosperous and consume more now than in the past. Older parents, accustomed to saving, are uncomfortable with their adult children's spending patterns. The older parents prefer to have them leave if they can no longer control their purchases. Third, when couples get married, they now receive substantial gifts, including cash funds, which they are entitled to keep. These funds, which have become more substantial in recent years, make it possible for couples to leave the groom's parents' home and take advantage of new economic opportunities outside the old household (Yan 1996).

Universal Pattern • Traditional China

Infrastructure	Structure	Superstructure
Intensive plow agriculture, intensive irrigation, and fertilization.	Patrilineal, patrilocal extended families are ideal, yet large families are likely to splinter. Scarce land is passed on from father to son.	Strong patrilineal and patrilocal ties are valued. Families with same surname are seen as *clans* that are obligated to help less fortunate members.
Multiple cropping with winter and summer harvests; make maximum use of land.	Upon marriage, new wife moves into husband's parents' house, where she initially comes under economic direction of mother-in-law.	Frugality is imposed by parents to save as much as possible.
Settlements are compact, densely populated villages.	Son's loyalty to parents erodes as he becomes devoted to wife and children. After daughter-in-law has sons of her own, influence increases.	Sacrifice by extended family members often leads to family tension and pressures lead to family partition.

Nineteenth-Century Extended Family in the United States

The demand for labor was high on this Minnesota farm in 1895 and so necessitated the participation of an extended family.

hard working and obedient. Later they oblige their son to marry his stepsister. The couple remains economically dependent on the extended family within their midst but is resistant to the marriage arrangement because of their intimate childhood association and socially imposed incest prohibitions (see p. 137).

One-Parent Domestic Groups

Millions of children throughout the world are reared in domestic groups in which only one parent is present. This arrangement may result from divorce or death of one of the parents. But it also may result from inability or unwillingness to marry. In the most common form of one-parent domestic arrangement, the mother is present and the father is absent. Such households are called *matrifocal*.

 A **matrifocal household** is a domestic group comprising one or more adult women with their offspring, within which husbands/fathers are not permanent residents.

The mother has a series of men as mates, usually one at a time but sometimes several at a time. The man and woman usually reside together for brief periods, but over the years, the mother may spend long intervals without a resident mate.

Matrifocal families form under a variety of conditions. For example, early marriage of girls to men considerably older than themselves leads to high rates of widowhood while children are still young. Remarriage may be difficult or prohibited, as among upper caste Hindus in India. High rates of young widowhood and matrifocality may also be the result of warfare and political unrest. Other conditions underlying matrifocality are as follow:

1. The mother has greater access to sources of income than the biological father.
2. The father's access to sources of wealth and income depends on migration or absence from home for extended periods.
3. The mother has greater access to housing.
4. Migration or higher mortality of males leads to a shortage of males available for marriage.

At one extreme, one-parent families are associated with well-paid, employed single women (and to a much lesser extent, men), who live alone with their children and manage to hire household help in lieu of kin and family. At the other extreme, matrifocal households are common in situations of insecurity and vulnerability, such as urban poverty and high male labor migration. Matrifocality refers to situations where a poor mother and her children may live together with her sisters and her mother, constituting

Extended Family in Wenjiang, China
Guests bring wedding gifts in baskets for the young people.

a large extended family in which adult males play only temporary roles as visitors or lovers (see Profile 8.3).

Matrifocal households are best known from studies carried out in the West Indies, Latin America, and U.S. inner cities (Stack 1974; Safa 1986). But this form of household occurs throughout the world. Its incidence has been obscured by the tendency to regard such domestic units as aberrant or pathological (Moynihan 1965). Mother–child domestic groups often result from poverty and hence are associated with many social ills and regarded as undesirable. But we have no evidence that such domestic arrangements are inherently any more or less pathological, unstable, or contrary to human nature than the nuclear family.

Marriage

 Marriage is an institution that transforms the status of two or more individuals in relation to sexual access and parenthood, and establishes connections between the kin of the spouses.

Is Marriage Universal?

Although anthropologists are convinced that marriage occurs in every culture, we encounter great difficulty in coming up with a definition that can be applied universally. Evelyn Blackwood (2005a) suggests that rather than look for a universal model of relatedness and affiliation, anthropologists should look at all patterns of meaningful relationships and identify the Eurocentric conjugal couple as only one form of relatedness among many. Rather than assume that marriage is a focal relationship in domestic life, it is important to examine all forms of intimacy and interconnectedness, whether they are socially sanctioned or not.

A famous definition proposed by Kathleen Gough (1968) can serve as a starting point for our discussion: "Marriage is a relationship established between a woman and one or more other persons. This relationship assures that the child born to the woman is accorded full birth rights common to members of his or her society, provided that the child is conceived and born under certain approved circumstances." According to Gough, for most if not all societies, this definition identifies a relationship "distinguished by the people themselves from all other kinds of relationships." Yet Gough's definition seems oddly at variance with Western emic notions of marriage because it makes no reference to rights and duties of sexual access or to sexual performance.

In biological terms, sexuality and reproduction are not dependent on marriage; instead, marriage is a means of assigning social identity to children.

In omitting reference to sex as a necessary part of matrimonial relationships, Gough was influenced by historical research she used to supplement her fieldwork among the Nayar, a precolonial warrior caste of southern India that dates back to before the British conquest.

Nayar Marriage. The Nayar had an unusual marriage system, which can be best understood in the context of the traditional caste system, in which the Nayar were warriors and feudal landholders. Nayar households were matrilineal (see Chapter 9) extended families in which the men specialized in military service and were away from their villages for many months at a time. Female sexuality was allowed free reign within certain rules. In order to bear children in a socially acceptable way, pubescent Nayar girls had to go through a four-day ceremony that linked them with a "ritual husband." Sexual relations were not a necessary component of this ceremony, and after it was over, the ritual husband and his wife did not live together or have sex together. The ceremony merely legitimized her as a reproducer. The woman continued to live with her sisters, her mother, and her mother's brother

PROFILE 8.3 | The Flats

In her study of the Flats, a Black ghetto in a Midwestern U.S. city, anthropologist Carol Stack (1974) provides an account of the strategies that poverty-level families follow in attempting to maximize their security and well-being in the face of the inadequate wages of the unskilled male. Nuclear families do not exist in the Flats because the material conditions necessary for such families do not exist. Instead, the people of the Flats are organized into large female-centered networks of relatives and neighbors. The members of these networks engage in reciprocal economic exchanges, take care of one another's children, provide emergency shelter, and help one another in many ways not characteristic of middle-class domestic groups.

In the Flats, the most important factors that affect interpersonal relationships between men and women are unemployment and the difficulty that men have in finding secure jobs. Losing a job or being unemployed month after month debilitates one's self-importance and independence and for men necessitates that they sacrifice their role in the economic support of their families. Then they become unable to assume the traditional father role, as defined by U.S. society. Ironically, as Stack points out, attempts by women on welfare to form nuclear families are efficiently discouraged by welfare policy. "Women come to realize that welfare benefits and ties with kin networks provide greater security for them and their children" (Stack 1974:113).

Economic forces and successive generations of poverty make it impossible to break out of their dependence on these domestic groupings. Due to poverty, young females, with or without children, do not perceive any choice but living with their mothers or other adult relatives. Their resources go further when they share living arrangements and services. Similarly, jobless males or males who work part-time or seasonal jobs often remain living at home with their mothers, sisters, or brothers. This continues long after they become fathers.

Yet in fact, these households always have men around. These men are often intermittent members of the household, and the children have constant contact with them, especially those who are male relatives. Even when someone temporarily moves out of the household, he or she has the option to return to the relative's residence if needed. Those who live in poverty have little chance to escape the economic uncertainty into which they are born. "In times of need, the only predictable resources that can be drawn upon are their own children and parents, and the fund of kin and friends obligated to them" (Stack 2005:372).

Universal Pattern • The Flats (United States)

Infrastructure	Structure	Superstructure
Poverty-level existence due to uncertain job prospects for males.	Kin-based network is responsible for providing shelter, food, and child care over several households.	Matrifocal households are defined by absence of husband, but groups of kin do include men who are not necessarily fathers of children in the household.
No cash reserves. Unexpected expenses pose constant threat of eviction.	Family and friends are only resources that can be relied on in time of need.	*Kin* are defined as those individuals who help one another.
Security provided by kin who live close by. Pooling of resources goes farther when living arrangements are shared.	Unlike middle-class members, who are encouraged to save, people living in the Flats are unable to save because they are responsible for needs of fellow kin.	Poor people have same values as those in middle class but are unable to attain their goals because they cannot save enough to help them succeed.

and had sex with a series of visiting "husbands" of her own caste or of a higher one, who would spend the night with her at her home and would leave early the next morning. If two men showed up on the same night, the visiting "husband" who arrived first would place his weapons outside the door to let others know they should come back another time. These arrangements do not reflect casual sex; there were strict rules governing who a woman could accept as a visiting "husband." Paternity was established by having one of the visiting "husbands" bestow gifts on the woman and bearing certain expenses associated with the birth of their child. A father had to be acknowledged in order for the child to have full birth rights. Otherwise the father incurred no further obligations because the child belonged to the mother's kin group. Gough (1968) regarded the existence of the ritual husbands and approved visiting "husbands" as proof of the universality of marriage because only ritually married Nayar women could have sexual relations and full birth rights were accorded only when fathers acknowledged their children.

Besides lacking any reference to sexual access, Gough's definition of marriage is also remarkable in another way. It does not necessarily involve a relationship between males and females, because it merely refers to a woman and "one or more" other persons of unspecified sex. What can be the reason for defining *marriage* as a relationship between a woman and "persons" rather than between "women and men"? Part of the answer is that in a number of African cultures, women "marry" women.

Dahomey Marriage. Among the Dahomey, a woman, who herself is usually already married to a man, pays *bridewealth* (see p. 131) for a bride. The female *bridewealth* payer becomes a "female husband." She starts a family of her own by letting her "wife" become pregnant through relationship with designated males. The offspring of these unions fall under the control of the "female father," rather than the biological genitors. Note that this is another case of marriage that does not involve sexual relations.

Nandi Marriage. Another example is the Nandi, a pastoral agricultural society in Kenya in which female–female marriage makes up about 3 percent of all marriages. This arrangement is related to patrilineal inheritance. Each married woman holds a separate fund of property (land and cattle), which is managed by her husband and inherited only by her sons and the sons of her co-wives. If the woman has no male heirs, her share of the property will be transmitted to other legal heirs (her co-wives' sons or the sons of the husband's brother). But a barren Nandi woman can obtain a male heir by becoming the "female husband" of a younger woman. The female husband chooses the consort for her wife and becomes the legal "father" of her wife's children. According to Oboler (1988:77), "Except for the absence of the sex act, the relationship between the female husband and her wife is no different from that between a male husband and his wife." The "female husband" behaves in accordance with male role behavior; she discontinues sexual relations with men, including her male husband, she pays bride price for her wife, she manages the family estate, and she has legitimate authority for

her wife and children. In turn, she is able to pass on her share of the estate to her legal heirs, even if she herself is barren or without sons.

The Na. Recent research among the Na (also known as the Mosuo) of southwestern China shows there is at least one contemporary society where marriage is absent. The Na are a matrilineal group, where women take male lovers who visit at night but return to their mothers' houses in the morning. Matrilineally related kin—which include women, their brothers, and the women's children—live in extended families and work together to produce food and raise the children. Even though a man recognizes his biological offspring, his responsibilities are to his sisters and their children. According to Na culture, those who originate from the same female ancestor have the same "bone." In terms of reproduction, "the man is the waterer in mating." The child has no physical bond to the biological father, and it is not essential that his identity be known (Hua 2001:459)

Marriage, as it is known in other cultures, is uncommon among the Na; they prefer a visiting relationship between lovers—an arrangement they sometimes refer to as "walking marriage" or "friend marriage." Children born from such a relationship live with their mother and her male relatives; many times, the relationship between father and child is quite close but involves no social or economic obligation.

Each evening, young men depart from their mothers' homes and then return the next day to help their mothers and sisters. Sex among the Na is practiced furtively. Men secretly visit women, sometimes from great distances (which serves as a measure of a man's love for his mate). Women never visit men, for fear of losing their good name. Lovers can end their relationship at any time; a woman may signal her change of heart by simply not opening the door. While young, both men and women have several lovers, but once a child is born, they start to have a stable relationship. They say their relationships are based on love. If a couple is content, they stay together. If they feel unhappy, they can go their separate ways. As a result, there is little fighting. According to one man, " 'Friend marriage' is very good. First, we are all our mother's children, making money for her; therefore there is no conflict between the brothers and sisters" (Yuan and Mitchell 2003:237).

It not uncommon for Na women to stop having sexual relationships with their partners (usually the fathers of their children) around the age of 40. Some women stop in their thirties, usually after a relationship has ended and they have children to care for. One 83-year-old woman who had had the most lovers expressed her annoyance with men. She said that in her early thirties, after giving birth to three children, she disliked men so much that she decided it wasn't worth having sex with the fathers of her children just to get them to help out.

In recent years, the Na have become known as the last matriarchal society in the world. Tourists assume the women are promiscuous and come for the purpose of sexual entertainment. They are told that if they desire someone, all they need to do is stroke the palm of that person at a bonfire dance, and if the person strokes back, that is a sign of consent. But according to Na culture, one doesn't stroke another person's palm unless one has developed feelings for him or her. Many tourists leave disappointed, but women tourists have a better chance of success than men. In other words, Na women are not as promiscuous as Na men (Yamashita 2005).

Legitimacy

The essence of the marital relationship, according to some anthropologists, is embodied in that portion of Gough's definition dealing with the assignment of "birth rights" over children. As Bronislaw Malinowski put it, "Marriage is the licensing of parenthood."

Legitimacy involves the following:

1. It assigns birth status to the child.
2. It legally entitles the child and/or the mother to the husband's property upon his death.
3. It determines who is responsible for the child and who controls the child's future.

It is true that women are universally discouraged from attempting to rear or dispose of their newborn infants according to their own whims, but most societies have several sets of rules defining permissible modes of conception and childrearing. For example, among the people who live in the small Brazilian towns that Marvin Harris studied, four kinds of relationships occur between a man and a woman, all of which provide children with full birth rights: church marriage, civil marriage, simultaneous church and civil marriage, and consensual marriage.

For a Brazilian woman, the most esteemed way to have children is through simultaneous church and civil marriage. This mode legally entitles her to a portion of her husband's property on his death. It also provides the added security of knowing that her husband cannot desert her and enter into a civil or religious marriage elsewhere. The least desirable mode is the consensual marriage because the woman cannot make any property claims against her consort or

readily prevent him from deserting her. Yet as long as the father acknowledges paternity, the children of a consensual arrangement can make property claims against both father and mother.

Every society has rules that define the conditions under which sexual relations, pregnancy, birth, and childrearing may take place, and that allocate privileges and duties in connection with these conditions. And every society has its own, sometimes unique, combination of rules and rules for breaking rules in this domain. It would be futile to define marriage by any one ingredient in these rules—such as legitimization of children—even if such an ingredient could be shown to be universal. See Profile 8.4 to learn about marriage trends in the United States.

Economic Aspects of Marriage

Families collectively maintain an interest in the productive, reproductive, and sexual functions of their members. Individuals serve the interests of the group, and marriage must be seen primarily in the context of group interests. If a member of one extended family goes to live in the spouse's family, the spouse-givers expect something in return. The simplest form of such transactions is sister exchange, in which the groom's sister is given in marriage to her brother-in-law. Other forms of marital compensation are bridewealth, bride service, and dowry.

Bridewealth. In a sample of 1,267 societies (Gaulin and Boster 1990:994), more than half were found to participate in the institution known as **bridewealth**. Bridewealth (also known as **bride price**) is especially common where land is plentiful and the labor of additional women and children contributes to the wealth and well-being of the corporate group (Goody 1976). In bridewealth, the wife-receivers give valuable items to the wife-givers and thereby establish or reinforce alliances between the two families.

Bridewealth is the transfer of valued goods from the family of the groom to the family of the bride when a couple marries. It represents compensation to the bride's family for the loss of her labor and her childbearing capacities.

As stated earlier in the chapter, bridewealth is not equivalent to the selling and buying of commodities in capitalist price market societies. The wife-receivers do not own their woman in any total sense; they must take good care of her, or her family will demand that she be returned to them.

Since 1970, the composition of households, living arrangements, and marital status in the United States have undergone dramatic changes (U.S. Bureau of the Census 2000):

1970	2000
Married couple family households with children were 40%.	Married couple family households with children dropped to 24%.
Family households with five or more people constituted 21% of all households.	Family households with five or more people constituted only 10% of all households.
Nonfamily households (people not living with relatives) were 1.7%.	Nonfamily households (people not living with relatives) increased to 5.7%.
Single-mother family households were 12%.	Single-mother households increased to 26%.
Single-father households were 1%.	Single-father households increased to 5%.
Households containing one person were 17%.	Households containing one person were 26%.

Female-Headed Households

The majority of matrifocal households are headed by poor, nonprofessional women who are unable to find permanent spouses because of high rates of unemployment, incarceration, and mortality among inner-city marriage-age males.

The most noticeable trend has been the decline in the proportion of married couple households with children (from 40 percent to 24 percent) and an increase in the proportion of single-mother households (from 12 percent to 26 percent).

- Single-parent families maintained by women are more likely than those maintained by men to have incomes below the poverty level (34 percent compared to 16 percent).

- Women maintaining one-parent families are more likely than men in similar situations to have never married (46 percent compared to 34 percent).

What accounts for the decline in marriage and increase in female-headed households? Setting aside the relatively small number of single, middle-class, professional women who choose to become single mothers, the majority of single-parent families in the United States are headed by low-income women who would prefer to marry if they could find an appropriate spouse. In many communities, there are far fewer males than females and many have poor economic prospects. Furthermore, poverty-class women in the United States do have greater access to sources of income than poverty-class men. Unemployment among poor minority males exceeds unemployment among poor minority women. More important, poor women have access to welfare support for themselves and their children, whereas poor males are seldom favored with aid for dependent children. At the same time, it is women who have access to public housing and to housing subsidies. Poor women thus have little incentive to marry men who would be an economic burden to them. Lacking steady employment or job training, males

gravitate toward making money in illegal enterprises. Many spend time in prison, a situation that is scarcely conducive to the formation of nuclear family households. Higher rates of mortality among marriage-age males further reduce the pool of potential mates for poor women.

In her study of the Flats, a Black ghetto in a Midwestern U.S. city, anthropologist Carol Stack (1974) provides an account of the strategies that poverty-level families follow in attempting to maximize their security and well-being in the face of the inadequate wages of unskilled males. Nuclear families do not exist in the Flats because the material conditions necessary for such families do not exist. Instead, the people of the Flats are organized into large female-centered networks of relatives and neighbors. The members of these networks engage in reciprocal economic exchanges, take care of one another's children, provide emergency shelter, and help one another in many ways not characteristic of middle-class domestic groups.

In the Flats, the most important factor that affects interpersonal relationships between men and women is unemployment and the difficulty that men have in finding secure jobs. Losing a job or being unemployed month after month debilitates one's self-importance and independence and for men necessitates that they sacrifice their role in the economic support of their families. Then they become unable to assume the traditional father role, as defined by U.S. society. Ironically, as Stack points out, attempts by women on welfare to form nuclear families are efficiently discouraged by welfare policy. "Women come to realize that welfare benefits and ties with kin networks provide greater security for them and their children" (Stack 1974:113).

African Bridewealth

Cattle are commonly used as bridewealth in parts of Africa. They represent compensation to the bride's family for the loss of her labor and the children she will have.

Bridewealth is found in societies with these qualities:

- Women contribute a great deal to subsistence.
- Women are valued as childbearers.
- Land is readily available and there is sufficient work for all women.

The amount of bridewealth is not fixed; it fluctuates within a certain range from one marriage to another. (In much of Africa, the traditional measure of bridewealth has been cattle, although other valuables such as iron tools also have been used. Nowadays, cash payments are the rule.) Among the Bathonga, a family that had many daughter–sisters was in a favorable position. The family would receive many cattle when the daughter–sisters got married. These cattle would then be used as bridewealth for the women's brothers: the more cattle, the more mother–wives; the more mother–wives, the larger the reproductive and productive labor force, and the greater the material welfare and influence of the family.

Sometimes the transfer of wealth from one group to another is carried out in installments: so much on initial agreement, more when the woman goes to live with her husband, and another, usually final, payment when she has her first child. Failure to have a child often voids the marriage; the woman goes home to her brothers and father, and the husband's family gets its bridewealth back.

When a man does not have the bridewealth requirement for marriage, he may be forced to post-pone marriage well into his thirties. A man may also compete with his own father, who may prefer to marry another wife rather than give his livestock for his son's marriage. It is reported that among the Turkana of Kenya, if a man gets a woman pregnant without paying bridewealth, he must make a substantial payment but this lower "pregnancy" payment gives him no rights to either the woman or her children. The children remain with their mother and become members of her father's clan (Dyson-Hudson and Meekers 1996).

Bride Service.   In **bride service**, a common alternative to bride price, the groom or husband compensates his in-laws by working for them for several months or years before taking his bride away to live and work with him and his extended family. Bride service is found in 14 percent of societies, mostly where there is little material wealth that can be transferred. In some cases, bride service substitutes for bridewealth or reduces the amount of bridewealth.

 Bride service compensates the bride's family for the loss of a daughter. The groom moves in with the bride's family and works in exchange for his marital rights.

Dowry.   Where women's productive and reproductive roles are less valued, wives may be regarded as an economic burden. Instead of paying bridewealth to the family of the bride, the groom's family may demand a reverse payment called *dowry.*

 Dowry is a transfer of goods or money from the bride's family to the groom. It represents compensation for the future support of the woman and her future children and is found in societies where women contribute relatively little to subsistence.

Dowry is found in societies with these qualities:

- Land is in short supply.
- Women's labor cannot be used to intensify production.
- Families do not want too many children because there is not enough land to pass on to heirs.
- Females do not inherit land; instead, they are given a dowry as a share of their parents' estate.

Dowry is much rarer than bridewealth, occurring in only 3 percent of a sample of 1,267 societies (Gaulin and Boster 1990:994). The societies that have dowry are concentrated in the extremely populous states of Mediterranean Europe and Southern Asia.

An Arranged Marriage in India
The personal interests of a married couple are subordinate to those of the couple's family.

placements for in-marrying women who die prematurely. To maintain reciprocity or to fulfill a marriage contract for which bridewealth has been paid, the brother of a deceased woman may permit the widower to marry one or more of the deceased wife's sisters. This custom is known as the **sororate**.

> The **sororate** is a custom by which a wife is replaced in marriage by her sister.

Closely related to this practice is the preferential marriage known as the **levirate**.

> The **levirate** is a custom in which a widow marries her husband's brother.

The services of a man's widow are thus retained within the domestic unit by having her marry one of his brothers. (A deceased husband is replaced in marriage by his brother.) If the widow is old, the services rendered by the remarried widow may be minimal, and the levirate then functions to provide security

Throughout this region, land is scarce and there is intensive agriculture involving animal-drawn plows guided by men; women's work is largely confined to the domestic sphere. Whenever dowry payment consists of money or movable property instead of land, it tends to be associated with a low or oppressed status for women (Schlegel and Barry 1986:145; Bossen 1988; Schlegel and Eloul 1988).

An important feature of dowry is that it can be used to support social ranking. In some societies, large dowry payments are used to attract a wealthy bridegroom from an upper-status family. This system is known as **hypergamy**.

> **Hypergamy** is the use of dowry payments to improve a daughter's chance of "marrying up" and assure a better future for grandchildren.

It is also presumed that a dowry will increase the likelihood that the woman and her children will be well treated. However, in some cases, hypergamy is associated with female infanticide. In northern India, for example, high dowry costs and a strong preference for males result in high rates of female infant mortality. It is financially more advantageous for families to raise sons whose brides will bring in large dowries than to have daughters whose marriages will require a large expenditure of wealth (Miller 1981).

Another common expression of collective familial interest in marriage is the practice of supplying re-

Dowry
Dowry is provided to the groom or the groom's family as compensation for support for the woman and her future children. Sometimes it is also given to the bride in lieu of a share of her parents' estate.

for a woman who would otherwise not be able to re-marry and support herself.

Thus the organization of domestic life everywhere reflects the fact that husbands and wives usually originate in different domestic groups that continue to maintain a sentimental and practical interest in the marriage partners and their children.

Domestic Groups and the Avoidance of Incest

Marriage exchanges entail preference rules concerning whom one should or should not marry.

 Exogamy is the rule that forbids an individual from taking a spouse from within a prescribed local group in which they are both members.

Endogamy is the rule that requires an individual to take a spouse from a group in which he or she is a member.

Groups that practice *exogamy* require members to "marry out," whereas others that practice *endogamy* require members to "marry in," or within a defined group. Incest avoidance results in an almost universal rule of *exogamy* within the primary nuclear family.

 The **incest taboo** refers to cultural beliefs prohibiting sexual relations or marriage with a close relative.

Although universally unacceptable, not all cultures have explicit rules on nuclear family sexual relations. In some cultures it is considered simply unthinkable, whereas in others it is morally outrageous and punishable through supernatural retribution.

 Inbreeding avoidance refers to behavioral patterns in which individuals avoid sexual contact with people who could be sexual partners were it not for their relatedness.

It appears that in the vast majority of societies, sexual relations between members of the nuclear family are rare.

Many different explanations for incest avoidance have been given, yet there is a lack of coherence among the various theories and the taboo still presents a challenge to anthropological explanation. Two explanations are required: How did the taboo originate, and what motivates people to maintain the avoidance behavior over time?

The most universal prohibition is against sexual relations and marriage between parents and their chil-dren. In most cultures brother–sister sexual relations and marriage are also forbidden, but we know of several important exceptions, such as the ruling classes of the Incas, ancient Egypt, ancient China, and Hawaii (Bixler 1982). Most of these marriages were between half-siblings, but some were between full siblings.

The reasons for sister–brother marriage seem to have been religious and economic; a member of the royal family, who was partly a god, could not marry an ordinary human. Moreover, marriage within the family kept the royal wealth and property undivided.

Cleopatra
Eleven generations of brother–sister marriage preserved the purity of the royal Egyptian lineage and kept the property of the royals intact.

In Egypt during Roman times (approximately from 30 B.C. to A.D. 600), not only elites but also commoners practiced brother–sister marriage. Such marriages, according to historian Keith Hopkins (1980), were regarded as perfectly normal relationships, openly mentioned in documents concerning inheritance, business affairs, lawsuits, and petitions to officials. Census data from that era show that between 15 and 20 percent of marriages were between full brothers and sisters and were not just within royal families, as it is commonly believed (Scheidel 1996).

Advantages of Exogamy

If the incest taboo didn't exist and people regularly married close biological kin, then families would incestuously "grow on their own." They would not recruit new members and would be isolated from neighbors. Exogamy, by contrast, helps foster cooperation and peaceful relationships and extends the likelihood for creating and maintaining alliances. Incest avoidance and other forms of exogamy can thus be explained in terms of demographic, economic, and ecological advantages (Leavitt 1989).

The advantages of incest avoidance are not necessarily the same for all societies. For example, band societies rely on marriage exchanges to establish long-distance networks of kinspeople. Bands that form a completely closed breeding unit will be denied the mobility and territorial flexibility essential to their subsistence strategy. Territorially restricted, endogamous bands of 20 to 30 people will also run a high risk of extinction as a result of gender imbalances caused by an unlucky run of male births and adult female deaths, which will place the burden for the group's reproduction on one or two aging females. Exogamy is thus essential if a small population is to effectively utilize its productive and reproductive potential. Once a band begins to obtain mates from other bands, the prevalence of reciprocal exchange demands a counterflow of mates and other valuables.

> Incest avoidance has positive social advantages because it extends cooperation and peaceful relations to a wider network of communities by forcing people to marry outside their immediate family.

This view, known as "marry out or die out," assumes the incest taboo creates ties through intermarriage (Tylor 1871). The taboo can therefore be interpreted as a defense of reciprocal exchange relationships against the ever-present temptation for parents to keep their children for themselves or for brothers and sisters to keep each other for themselves.

After the evolution of the state, exogamic alliances between domestic groups continued to have important infrastructural consequences. Among peasants, exogamy increases the total productive and reproductive strength of the intermarried groups because it permits the exploitation of resources over a larger area than the nuclear or extended family could manage on an individual basis. Exogamy also facilitates trade and raises the upper limit of the size of groups that can be formed to carry out seasonal activities requiring large labor inputs (communal game drives, harvests, and so on). Furthermore, in prestate societies, where intergroup warfare poses a threat to group survival, the ability to mobilize large numbers of warriors is decisive. Hence, in militaristic, highly male-centered village cultures, sisters and daughters are frequently used as pawns in the establishment of alliances. These alliances do not necessarily eliminate warfare between intermarrying groups, but they make it less common, as might be expected from the presence of sisters and daughters in the enemy's ranks (Tefft 1975; Kang 1979; Podolefsky 1984).

Another factor favoring nuclear family exogamy is the institution of marriage itself. Most marriages (despite the exceptions previously discussed, such as the Nayar) limit the sexual freedom of the marriage partners. Thus the great majority of societies prohibit one or both spouses from having extramarital sex—that is, from committing adultery.

> The incest taboo thus guards against sexual impulses within the family that would lead to sexual competition and the disruption of the stability of the family.

The family could not function as an effective unit if there were sexual competition and rivalry. Illicit sexual encounters between father and daughter and mother and son constitute a form of adultery. Mother–son incest is an especially threatening variety of adultery in the many societies that have strong male supremacist institutions. Not only is the wife "double-dealing" against her husband, but the son is also "double-dealing" against his father. This may explain why the least common and emically most feared and abhorred form of incest is that between mother and son. It follows that father–daughter incest will be somewhat more common since husbands enjoy double standards of sexual behavior more often than wives and are less vulnerable to punishment for adultery. Finally, the same consideration suggests an explanation for the relatively high frequency of brother–sister matings and their legitimizations as marriages in elite classes. They do not conflict with the adultery rules for fathers and mothers.

Natural Aversion

A number of investigators have argued that incest prohibitions defend against the biological costs of "marrying in." Close inbreeding increases the likelihood that offspring will suffer from congenital deformities. Relatives who carry defective genes and mate with each other will give birth to children who suffer from pathological conditions that lower their rate of reproduction. This observationalist theory, according to Daniel Fessler (1999), assumes that people in the past observed that repeated kinds of unions have harmful effects.

From a biological perspective, inbreeding avoidance prevents people from mating with close relatives, which may have harmful biological results.

Another argument asserts that inbreeding, simply by lowering the amount of genetic diversity in a population, might adversely affect the population's ability to adapt to new diseases or other novel environmental hazards (Leavitt 1990, 1992; cf. Uhlman 1992; Schields 1993).

Motivations for Incest Avoidance

Many scholars believe that incest avoidance developed preculturally. This view has received support from field studies of monkey and ape mating behavior. As among humans, father–daughter, mother–son, and brother–sister matings are uncommon among our nearest animal relatives, although they do occur. In most nonhuman primates, males routinely leave their natal group at puberty to seek mating opportunities elsewhere (Boyd and Silk 1997:614; Pusey and Wolf 1996). Moreover, females will resist solicitations from related males more frequently than males resist approaches from related females, suggesting that females are more averse to inbreeding than males. Given the fact that females have a greater investment in reproduction (see discussion of female sexuality in Chapter 14), female disfavor of male relatives as sexual partners can be seen as evidence of female mate selectivity to avoid the risk of nonviable offspring.

Advocates of genetic theories of incest avoidance nevertheless recognize that genes are not likely to contain definite instructions for shutting down sex drives in the presence of siblings, children, and parents. Following the lead of Edward Westermark (1894), they proposed instead that members of the opposite sex have an innate tendency to experience a distinct feeling of aversion if they have been brought up in close physical proximity to each other during infancy and childhood (Shepher 1983).

 The **Westermark theory** proposes that persons raised together or persons living closely together during early childhood develop a natural aversion to having sexual relations with one another.

Westermark's theory, however, does not explain how the aversion mechanism functions, only that incest aversion is instinctive.

Sigmund Freud, in contrast, explains incest aversion as an intrapsychic process. As we discuss in Chapter 15, psychoanalytic theory assumes the desire for sexual relations within the family is strong, but such impulses are repressed into the unconscious, where they find expression in dreams and folklore.

 Freud's theory is that the incest taboo is a conscious attempt to suppress naturally occurring unconscious erotic feelings between family members.

Humor, myth, and folklore provide ample ethnographic evidence of shared unconscious incestuous wishes. However, contrary to Freud's claim that children long for sex with opposite-sex parents, the most common stories of incest are those in which fathers are attracted to their daughters and brothers are attracted to their sisters (A. Johnson and Price-Williams 1996). The attraction is thus held in check through socialization, which universally punishes individuals who engage in sex with close kin.

Evidence of Incest Avoidance

The most frequently cited cases in support of the Westermark theory—Chinese *sim pua* marriage and the kibbutz—are inconclusive and several key questions remain.

"Adopt a Daughter, Marry a Sister."

To test the Westermark theory, one cannot point to the mere occurrence of incest avoidance. Evidence must show that sexual ardor cools when people grow up together, independent of any existing norms that call for incest avoidance. Since this cannot be done experimentally without controlling the lives of human subjects, advocates of the theory lean heavily on two famous case studies that allegedly demonstrate the predicted loss of sexual ardor. The first of these concerns Taiwanese **sim pua marriage.**

 Sim pua marriage, known as "adopt a daughter, marry a sister," involves the adoption of a young girl into a family, in which she later marries one of the sons.

The husband and wife grow up together at close quarters from an early age. Studies show that such marriages lead to fewer children, greater adultery, and higher divorce rates than normal marriages, in which future wives and husbands grow up in separate households (Wolf and Huang 1980). But do these observations confirm Westermark's theory? The Taiwanese explicitly recognize that "adopt a daughter, marry a sister" is an inferior, even humiliating form of marriage. This difference makes it difficult to prove that sexual disinterest, rather than chagrin and disappointment over being treated like second-class citizens, is the source of the couple's relative infertility.

Wolf (1995) has countered such criticism by presenting data to show that girls who are adopted after age 3 do not have depressed fertility rates. The problem with this rejoinder, however, is that a 2-year-old infant taken from her mother is likely to have different experiences than a child whose adoption takes place at a later phase of childhood. Clearly, we need to know more about the experiences of infant and child adoptees and how they are treated while growing up in the homes of their future husbands.

Children on Israeli Kibbutz Celebrating the Harvest
Until recently, kibbutz children were raised together in collective dormitories like brothers and sisters. None of them later became sexually interested in one another.

Westermark in the Kibbutz.   The second case used to confirm Westermark's theory concerns an alleged lack of sexual interest displayed by boys and girls who were raised with each other from infancy through adolescence in the Israeli cooperative community known as a kibbutz.

Kibbutz children who are reared together during infancy become sexually disinterested in one another. They are so thoroughly "turned off" that among marriages contracted by people in the kibbutz, not one involved a man or woman who had been reared together during infancy.

Joseph Shepher argued that such aversion is a "genetically determined predisposition imprinted against those with whom one has been cosocialized" (Shepher 1983:114). This evidence is impressive, but anthropologist John Hartung discovered a flaw in the statistics. Out of a total of 2,516 marriages, Shepher found 200 in which both partners were reared in the same kibbutz although they were not all together in the same age group during the entire period from birth to age 6. Upon reviewing the data, Hartung (1985) pointed out that five marriages did occur between boys and girls who had been reared together for part of the first six years of their lives. Because Westermark's theory does not predict how long it

takes for reared-together boys and girls to lose their interest in each other, Hartung suggested these five marriages actually disconfirm the theory (Hartung 1985). Unfortunately, Joseph Shepher died before he had a chance to respond to Hartung, and we will have to wait for additional studies before reaching a decision on this issue.

Avoidance within the Family.   The proposal that an instinctual sexual aversion occurs within the nuclear family is challenged by the growing evidence for the actual occurrence of incest within the family. Social workers estimate that tens of thousands of cases of incest occur in the United States annually, of which the great majority involve fathers imposing on young daughters (Glaser and Frosh 1988; Cicchetti and Carlson 1989):

> Studies of fathers who seduced their daughters or step daughters suggest that fathers who commit incest did not participate in childcare or spend time with their daughters while they were young.

Williams and Finklehor (1995) compared 118 incestuous biological fathers with 116 closely mated controls. Fathers who were not involved in child care were much more likely to be incestuous than other fathers. Even though high–child care, nonincestuous fathers reported having sexual feelings toward their daughters, the researchers concluded that taking care of a child may evoke feelings of nurturance and identification with the child that deter acting on sexual feelings (see also H. Parker and Parker 1986).

Because naturally occurring cases of incest are difficult to study, Fessler and Navarrete (2002) resorted to a new method of testing the Westermark theory that looks at people's tolerance versus disgust of others' incestuous behavior (see Box 8.1). They found the following:

- Individuals who were cosocialized with siblings of the opposite sex are more disgusted by a story in which a brother and sister pose as husband and wife than those who were not raised with opposite-sex siblings.

- Females showed more overall aversion to the incest scenario than males.

- Males who were closer in age to their sisters showed greater incest aversion than males with a greater age disparity between themselves and their sisters. Because female aversion was already high, there was no significant difference for females due to the age of a sibling.

BOX 8.1 Testing the Westermark Hypothesis

College students were given a questionnaire containing a story about two adult siblings. The story says that in order to save money, the brother and sister initially decided to live together but over time began experimenting with consensual incestuous sex and ultimately decide to pose as husband and wife. The neighbors are aware that the couple is sexually involved and eventually discover the true nature of their relationship.

The study participants were asked about the number of siblings they have, their ages, and the length of time they lived together with their siblings (i.e., were cosocialized). They were then asked about their reactions to the story and eventually to respond to the following questions, which would reflect on their avoidance, disgust, and punitive feelings:

- How comfortable would they be living near, working with, and interacting with the couple?

- To what degree did they find the behavior disgusting?

- What kind of jail sentence or fine should be given the couple who were subsequently arrested because their behavior was illegal?

Source: Fessler and Navarrete 2002.

SUMMARY
and *Questions to Think About*

1. The structural level of sociocultural systems is made up in part of interrelated domestic groups. Such groups can usually be identified by their attachment to a living space or domicile in which activities such as eating, sleeping, marital sex, and the nurturance and discipline of the young take place.

2. There is no single or minimal pattern of domestic activities. Similarly, the nuclear family cannot be regarded as the minimal building block of all domestic groups. Although nuclear families occur in almost every society, they are not always the dominant domestic group, and their sexual, reproductive, and productive functions can readily be satisfied by alternative domestic and nondomestic institutions.

3. In polygamous and extended families, the father–mother–child unit may not be separate from the other sets of other relatives and their multiple spouses. And there are many instances of domestic groups that lack a coresident husband–father. Although children need to be nurtured and protected, no one has defined the limits within which human domestic arrangements must be confined in order to satisfy human nature. One of the most important facts about human domestic arrangements is that no single pattern can be shown to be more natural than any other.

4. Family structure is closely related to the domestic mode of production. The nuclear family is associated with a high degree of mobility and economic autonomy; the extended family prevails where a large labor pool is advantageous in carrying out a variety of simultaneous economic activities. Polygyny is associated with female contribution to production and may serve as a means of enhancing a man's position in the community; polyandry avoids subdividing the family estate and occurs

in only a few societies where farming and grazing land is limited.

5. Marriage practices also exhibit an enormous degree of variation. Although something similar to what is called *marriage* occurs all over the world, it is difficult to specify the mental and behavioral essence of the marital relationship. Man–man, woman–woman, female–father, and childless marriages make it difficult to give a minimal definition of marriage without offending someone. Even coresidence may not be essential, as the Nayar and other single-parent households demonstrate. And if we restrict the definition of marriage to coresident heterosexual matings that result in reproduction, we still find a staggering variety of rights and duties associated with the sexual and reproductive functions of the marriage partners and their offspring.

6. To understand coresident heterosexual reproductive marriage in extended families, marriage must be seen as a relationship between corporate family groups as much as between cohabitating mates. The divergent interests of these corporate groups are reconciled by means of reciprocal exchanges that take the forms of sister exchange, bridewealth, suitor service, dowry, and groom price. Except for dowry, the common principle underlying these exchanges is that in giving a man or woman away to another extended family, the family of origin does not renounce its interest in the offspring but expects compensation for the loss of a productively and reproductively valuable person.

7. A range of preferred and prohibited marriages reflect the pervasive corporate interests of domestic groups. Preferences for certain kinds of marriage exchanges create circulating connubia, in which reciprocity between domestic groups may be direct or indirect. Such preferences may be expressed as a rule requiring marriage with a particular kind of cousin. Preferential marriage rules such as the levirate and sororate also exemplify the corporate nature of the marriage bond.

8. Most domestic groups are exogamous. This can be seen as a result of either instinctual programming or social and cultural adaptation. The discussion of exogamy necessarily centers on the incest prohibitions within the nuclear family. Father–daughter, sister–brother, and mother–son matings and mar-

riages are almost universally forbidden. The chief exception is brother–sister marriages, which occurred in several highly stratified societies among the ruling elites among the Incas, Egyptians, and Hawaiians and among Egyptian commoners in Roman times.

9. A purely cultural theory of incest avoidance can be understood in terms of the need for marriage exogamy to establish alliances through reciprocal marriage exchanges. The perpetuation of the incest taboo may be related exclusively to the increasing genetic dangers associated with close inbreeding in populations carrying harmful genes. Motivation for incest avoidance is explained by Westermark (in terms of instinctual aversion) and Freud (as social control because of unconscious attraction). Evidence from Taiwan and Israel suggests that children reared together develop a sexual aversion to each other, but the evidence is inconclusive. Other evidence is seen in studies of father incest and students' reactions to a hypothetical incest scenario.

Questions to Think About

1. How does infrastructure influence the household composition? What are the social and economic ramifications of nuclear versus extended family households?

2. What is meant by "Marriage is the licensing of parenthood"? Does this statement apply in U.S. society today? What other rights are transmitted in marriage?

3. What is the difference between polygyny in Africa and polygyny in the Amazon basin?

4. What are the differences between polygyny and polyandry in terms of economics and household dynamics?

5. What do anthropologists mean by *cultural advantages of exogamy*?

6. Evaluate the following evidence used to explain the incest taboo:
   - *Sim pua* marriage
   - Evidence from the kibbutz
   - Evidence of people's tolerance or disgust toward others' incestuous behavior

THROUGH THE LENS
of Cultural Materialism

Conformity and Conflict • Reading Seventeen

Family and Kinship in Village India

David W. McCurdy

In the Indian village of Ratakote, the kin group is the basic unit of production; local groups of related male relatives form corporate kin networks that pool economic resources. Today, involvement in modern cash labor enterprises outside the village has the potential to break up the kinship network. But instead, the kin network has been "stretched out," meaning kin ties have been expanded to include family members who have moved to work in nearby cities, as well as those who have migrated to other countries around the world.

Emic Interpretation

- Ratakote is a patrilineal society, in which primary kin ties are based on patrilineal descent and residence. It is believed that men "plant the seeds" that grow into children, while women provide the fields in which the seeds germinate and grow.

- Arranged early marriage is preferred because parents believe young people are likely to become sexually active and may fall in love and elope, preempting the arrangement process altogether. Indians believe that marriage is too important to be decided upon by inexperienced and impressionable young people.

- Marriage represents the transfer of a woman to her husband's household as well as the acquisition of her loyalty, her labor, and her future children.

- Today, as people move away to find work on the outside, kin ties remain strong. People maintain loyalty and continue their obligation to share with family members.

Etic Interpretation

- Patrilineally related males share economic resources and import wives from other neighboring villages.

- Villagers maintain strong kinship ties of loyalty and cooperation, which works well in an agrarian society based on family-centered land holding and small-scale farming.

- Marrying a daughter outside the local village establishes an exchange network that includes ritual gift exchange and future marriage arrangements.

Infrastructure

- Ratatoke is an agrarian society that practices small-scale farming. The patrilineage cooperatively plows and sows fields and shares livestock. In the past, large families provided the necessary farm labor, but as the population grew, land was subdivided into smaller and smaller plots that could no longer sustain the family without cash input from outside sources.

- Today, men from the village work in the city as day laborers to supplement their family incomes.

Structure

- Arranged marriage is the norm, and most people, young and old, accept this custom. Marriage forms alliances between families and works to create networks between villages.

- The steps in finding a suitable marriage partner consist of first consulting lineage members and then finding eligible prospective spouses in other villages.

- One's reputation depends on the quality and number of allied kin.

- Lineage members are an essential part of the marriage process. They spread word to other villages regarding the eligibility of one of their members, loan money for wedding expenses, and provide the labor needed to prepare food and help arrange the ceremony.

- Only sons inherit from their fathers, and the children of divorced parents stay with the father's family by law. Through marriage, females join their husbands' families.

- Because new brides are at a disadvantage when they move to their husbands' villages, tension is eased through gift exchange. Bride price is paid by the groom's father to the bride's parents as a means of compensation for the loss of the bride's services to her family, and the bride's family tries to pick a groom from a village where the bride will have kin.

- Cash labor is a threat to the kinship system of India because it frees men and women from economic dependence on the family and takes time away from family-related activities. However, kinship still remains exceptionally strong. Children visit their families even though they may live far away, and they continue the arranged marriage process for their own children.

Superstructure

- The patrilineal system of India reinforces the authority of men over women and children.

- Wedding rituals help dramatize the bride's shift in family membership. For example, the bride must cry to symbolize that she is leaving her home, and the groom heroically storms the bride's house at the beginning of the final ceremony. At the end of the wedding, the groom engages in a "mock battle" with the bride's brother and other young men and symbolically abducts her.

- Kinship sentiment remains strong, despite recent changes to cash labor. The values of respecting elders are still strong, especially because elders can no longer support their families through subsistence farming alone and rely on male relatives to augment their incomes.

CHAPTER 9

DESCENT, LOCALITY, AND KINSHIP

In a Machiguenga nuclear family, couples reside matrilocally when they marry but after that residence alternates between the wife's and husband's kin.

We continue with domestic organization. We examine the principal mental and emic components of domestic groups—namely, the concept of kinship through marriage and descent. Then we relate different varieties of kinship concepts to particular kinds of domestic groups and to the influence of infrastructural conditions. To top this off, we briefly explore different kinship terminologies—systems for classifying relatives.

Like language, kinship studies demonstrate the power of culture to form systems of thought and behavior on the level of groups, rather than on the level of individuals. We will see how kinship, as a social construction, classifies members of a society into groups that structure marriage, residence, political obligations, and property rights.

Kinship

Kinship should not be confused with biological mating or biological descent. Kinship is an emic, culturally constructed concept; biologic mating and biological descent are etic concepts.

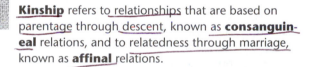

> **Kinship** refers to relationships that are based on parentage through descent, known as **consanguineal** relations, and to relatedness through marriage, known as **affinal** relations.

As discussed previously, marriage may emically establish *parentage* with respect to children who are biologically unrelated to their culturally defined *father*. Even where a culture insists that descent must be based on actual biological fatherhood, domestic arrangements may make it difficult to identify the biological father. For these reasons, anthropologists distinguish between the culturally defined father and the **genitor, the actual biological father.** A similar distinction is necessary in the case of mother. Although the culturally defined mother is usually the **genetrix,** or biological mother, the widespread practice of adoption also creates many discrepancies between emic and etic motherhood.

Every society has a kinship system consisting of the following:

- Terms used to classify various categories of consanguineal and affinal kin
- Terms used to identify kin that are more socially significant than others
- Expected rights and obligations that different categories of kin have toward one another

Descent

Descent is the belief that certain persons play an important role in the creation, birth, and nurturance of certain children. Theories of descent vary from culture to culture, but so far as we know, no human society is without such a theory (Scheffler 1973:749). Descent implies the preservation of some aspect of the substance or spirit of people in future generations and thus is a symbolic form of immortality (Craig 1979). Perhaps that is why every society believes in one form or another of descent.

In Western folk traditions, parents are linked to children by the belief that children have the same kind of "blood" as their parents. Each child's veins are thought of as being filled with blood obtained from mother and father in equal amounts. As a result of this imagery, "blood relatives" are distinguished from relatives who are linked only through marriage. This imagery led nineteenth-century anthropologists to use the ethnocentric term *consanguine* (of the same blood) to denote relations of descent. Westerners (including college professors) persist in talking about blood relatives even though we know that closely related individuals may have different blood types, that distantly related or unrelated individuals may have the same blood type, and that the closeness of a relationship is measured by the proportion of shared DNA, not by shared blood.

Descent need not depend on the idea of blood inheritance, nor need it involve equal contributions from both father and mother:

- The Ashanti of West Africa believe that blood is contributed only by the mother and that it determines only a child's physical characteristics, whereas a child's spiritual disposition and temperament are the product of the father's semen.

- The Trobrianders contend that semen does not play a procreative role. Here a woman becomes pregnant when a spirit of a deceased member of the matrilineage enters a woman's body and causes her to become pregnant. The fetus is formed by the combination of the woman's blood and the ancestral spirit. The only procreative function of the Trobriand "father" is to help develop the fetus through frequent sexual intercourse. The mother's husband nourishes the fetus with his matrilineal essence, and after the child is born, he continues to nurture the child by working hard to provide it with food and wealth. Although the Trobrianders practice premarital sex, girls usually are married by the time they are capable of becoming pregnant, so they have no evidence to refute the belief that conception is caused by the spirit of a matrilineal

American Kindred

Thanksgiving is an occasion for both siblings and cousins to get together.

ancestor and does not require a man's semen (Weiner 1987).

A number of societies in lowland South America believe that it is possible to have several biological fathers:

- The Bari of Venezuela believe that men who have intercourse with a woman during her pregnancy share the biological fatherhood of her child. The woman's cohabitating husband is considered the primary biological father, whereas the woman's lovers are secondary fathers. The husband is usually aware of the lovers. When a woman gives birth, she typically names all the men she had intercourse with during her pregnancy. These secondary fathers are obligated to provide gifts of fish and game to the child, which is likely to contribute to the child's increased chances of survival (Beckerman et al. 1998).

- Among the Mehinacu of Brazil, it is believed that the fetus is built up in the course of repeated acts of sex. A man's semen contains the seed, which is planted in the woman's body. Fathering a child does not occur in a single act; rather repeated acts of sexual relations are required during which the father and any other men who have intercourse with the mother gradually "make" the baby together. The woman's role is less active; she simply shelters the fetus in her womb (Gregor 1977:261).

Despite the many theories about the nature of procreative roles, all cultures affirm the existence of some special contribution made by both male and female to the reproductive process, although they may contribute quite unevenly and with vastly different expectations concerning rights and obligations.

The principal function of rules of descent and postmarital residence is the establishment and maintenance of networks of cooperative and interdependent kinspeople aggregated into ecologically effective and militarily secure domestic production and reproduction units.

For domestic units to act effectively and reliably, they must share an organizational ideology that interprets and validates the structure of the group and the behavior of its members. Kinship is that shared organizational ideology that prescribes who to marry, where to live after marriage, and to whom a person is obligated.

Kinship Diagrams

People in different societies may label biological connections differently and may have different expectations toward relatives. To simplify kinship systems, anthropologists use kinship diagrams that provide a standardized notation system.

Kinship symbols

◯	Represents a female
△	Represents a male
◯ = △	Represents a marriage
◯ ⊤ △ ◯	Represents descent or parentage
◯⌐△	Represents a sibling bond
◯ ≠ △	Represents a divorce
∅	Represents a person is deceased
◉	Represents a male or female ego whose genealogy is being shown

Fa	Father
Mo	Mother
So	Son
Da	Daughter
Br	Brother
Si	Sister
C	Child
Hu	Husband
Wi	Wife

Figure 9.1   How to Read Kinship Diagrams

Kinship diagrams are all viewed from the reference point of an individual called *ego* and use symbols to show how relatives are connected to ego (see Figure 9.1). A kinship diagram is different from a genealogy. A genealogy is not ego centered; it is constructed by beginning with the earliest ancestor that can be traced and including all those up to the present.

Cognatic and Unilineal Descent

By reckoning their descent relationships, individuals are apportioned different duties, rights, and privileges in regard to many different aspects of social life. Descent may be used to determine a person's name, family, residence, rank, property, ethnicity, nationality, and many other statuses.

Anthropologists distinguish two major classes of descent rules: **unilineal** and **cognatic** (nonunilineal) descent.

  Unilineal descent rules restrict parental links exclusively to males or to females.

Cognatic descent rules use both male and female parentage to establish any of the previously mentioned duties, rights, and privileges.

The most common form of cognatic rule is **bilateral descent**.

  Bilateral descent is the reckoning of kinship evenly and symmetrically along maternal and paternal links in ascending and descending generations through individuals of both sexes (Figure 9.2).

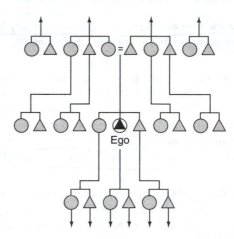

Figure 9.2   Bilateral Descent
Everyone on the diagram has a descent relationship with ego.

The second, less common variety of cognatic rule is called **ambilineal descent**.

Ambilineal descent is the reckoning of kinship through either maternal or paternal links, depending on which kin group provides greater opportunities.

Unlike bilateral descent, with ambilineal descent, ego can choose to affiliate with either the mother's or father's kin group but cannot choose both. Each generation can choose from which parent to trace descent so that a family line may be patrilineal in one generation and matrilineal in the next (Figure 9.3).

The least common variety of cognatic descent is **double descent**.

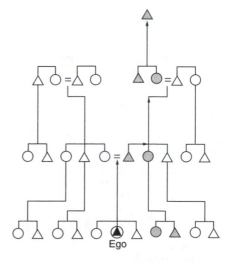

Figure 9.3   Ambilineal Descent
Ego traces descent through either males or females, depending on which kinship provides the best resources. Individuals in each generation can choose their kin group. Here ego traces kinship through his father, whereas ego's father traces kinship through his mother.

> **Double descent** traces descent matrilineally for some purposes and patrilineally for others.

Where double descent is used, the two descent lines have different functions. People may inherit livestock or ritual privileges in the maternal line and rights to land and residence in the patrilineal line.

Moving on now to **unilineal descent**, we find two main varieties: **patrilineality** and **matrilineality**.

> **Patrilineal descent** requires ego to follow the ascending and descending genealogical links through males only (Figure 9.4). Note that this does not mean that the descent-related individuals are only males; in each generation, ego has relatives of both genders.

In the passage from one generation to another, only the male links are relevant; children of females are dropped from the descent reckoning.

> **Matrilineal descent** requires ego to follow the ascending and descending links through females only. Once again, note that males as well as females can be related matrilineally; only in the passage from one generation to another are the children of males dropped from the descent reckoning because they become affiliated with their mother's kin group (Figure 9.5).

One of the most important logical consequences of unilineal descent is that it segregates the children of siblings of the opposite sex into distinct categories. This effect is especially important in the way cousins are defined. With patrilineal descent, ego's father's

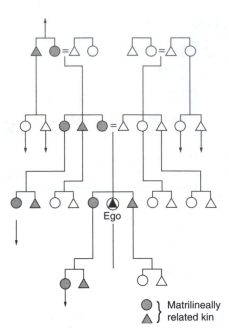

Figure 9.5   Matrilineal Descent
Descent is traced exclusively through females but includes relatives of both genders.

sister's son and daughter (FaSiSo and FaSiDa) do not share common descent with ego, whereas ego's father's brother's son and daughter (FaBrSo and FaBrDa) do share common descent with ego (Figure 9.6).

> **Parallel cousins** are the children of ego's father's brother or mother's sister and are regarded as brothers and sisters.

> **Cross-cousins** are the children of ego's father's sister or mother's brother and are regarded as affines, or potential marriage mates.

Each of these descent rules provides the logical basis for mentally aligning people into emic kinship groups. These groups exert great influence on the way people

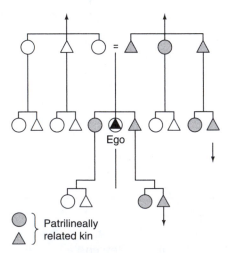

Figure 9.4   Patrilineal Descent
Descent is traced exclusively through males but includes relatives of both genders.

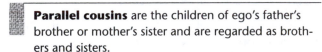
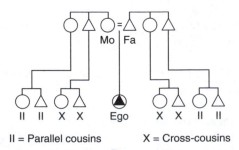

II = Parallel cousins   X = Cross-cousins

Figure 9.6   Cross-Cousins and Parallel Cousins

think and behave in both domestic and extradomestic situations.

An important point to bear in mind about kinship groups is that they need not consist of coresident relatives; members of the same lineages and clans, for example, may be found in different households and different villages. We proceed now to a description of the principal varieties of kinship groups.

Kindreds versus Cognatic Lineages

In societies that practice bilateral descent, such as our own, a person is related equally to both the mother's and father's sides of the family. Bilateral descent applied to a wide span of kin and across a number of generations may lead to the concept of groups known as **kindreds** (Figure 9.7).

  A **kindred** consists of ego's close bilateral relatives, who form a group that comes together for such occasions as when ego is born, marries, gives a feast, and so on.

When modern-day Americans and Europeans use the word *relatives*, they are referring to their *kindreds*. The main characteristic of the kindred is that the span and depth of bilateral reckoning are open ended. Relatives within a kindred can be judged as "near" or "far," depending on the number of genealogical links that separate them, but there is no definite or uniform principle for making such judgments or for terminating the extension of the kinship circle. An important consequence of this feature is that kindreds are *ego*

centered: Egos and their siblings have a kindred whose membership is different from that of everyone else. As a result, everyone in a kindred-based society belongs to different overlapping kin groups. Because a kindred is not a socially defined group, it is impossible for coresident domestic groups to consist of kindreds and very difficult for kindreds to maintain corporate interests in land and people.

The open-ended, ego-centered characteristics of the bilateral kindred can be overcome by specifying one or more apical (topmost) ancestors from whom descent is traced through the mother's or father's kinship group. In some societies, individuals must choose either the paternal or maternal line; in others, individuals can move back and forth from one descent group to another.

Ambilineal descent thus provides for more flexibility and choice than a unilineal system. Individuals can choose in accordance with the relative advantages offered by affiliating with one or another set of relatives. For example, if a man has older brothers who are already farming the family land, he may choose to affiliate with his wife's kin group if she has no brothers laying claim to the land. The resultant ambilineal descent group logically has a membership that is the same regardless of which ego carries out the reckoning. This is called the **cognatic lineage** (Figure 9.8).

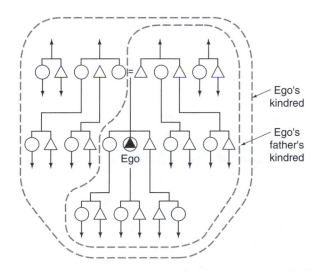

Figure 9.7 Kindreds
Children have kindreds that are different from those of either parent. Kindreds include relatives on both sides and are ego centered.

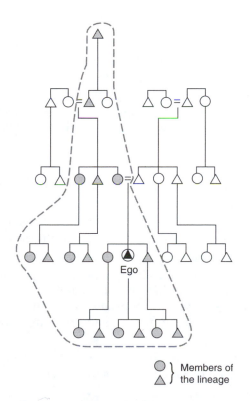

Figure 9.8 Cognatic Lineage
Descent is traced to an apical ancestor through males and/or females.

A **cognatic lineage** consists of all the descendents of an apical ancestor or ancestress who reckon descent through any combination of male or female links.

Members of cognatic lineages may not be able to demonstrate the precise genealogical links relating them to the apical lineage founder. Also, because of its flexibility and loose membership rules, a cognatic lineage is less cohesive and loyalties tend to be weaker than in a unilineal descent group. For example, people who share the same name as the apical ancestor can claim membership in the cognatic lineages of Scotland (misnamed "clans"; see Neville 1979).

Unilineal Descent Groups

All the people who trace descent patrilineally from a particular male ancestor form a *patrilineage*, whereas all the people who trace descent matrilineally from a particular female ancestress form a *matrilineage*. Each of these unilineal kin groups contains the same set of people from any ego's viewpoint.

 Unilineal descent groups have a clearly defined membership that delineates lineage members from nonmembers.

Membership in a unilineal descent group comes through a direct line from father or mother to child. As a result, the descent group is a discrete group with no overlapping membership. It is a permanent enduring unit that acts as a **corporate group.** It is a unified entity, it holds common property, and it lives on even though some of the members die out. These features make unilineal descent groups ideally suited for the following etic functions:

- *Residence.* A coresident domestic group is formed, containing members of the lineage, their spouses, and their children.

- *Regulating marriage.* Individuals are usually not permitted to marry within their unilineal descent group (exogamy).

- *Economic functions.* Lineage membership creates a corporate group that owns land and allocates it to members. Descent groups also cooperate in clearing land, building houses, and providing food for feasts.

- *Political functions.* Lineage elders settle disputes and lineage members join forces for attacking enemies for defense.

- *Religious functions.* Lineages may worship their own ancestral spirits. Ancestors can display their displeasure by causing mishaps or their pleasure by bringing good fortune.

In addition, unilineal descent groups provide a source of political unity through the belief in shared ancestry and the importance of kinship.

 Lineage segmentation allows closely related lineages to unite to oppose a threat from more distantly related lineage segments.

Some societies go through a process of segmentation that enables lineages to integrate members in different localities. Some large lineages, known as *maximal lineages,* consist of smaller lineages known as *sublineages.* Sublineages that consist of only three generations are known as *minimal.* They consist of close matrilineal or patrilineal kin who support each other against more distant minimal lineages but will join forces with these same kin in the event of a dispute with a more distant lineage segment (see Figure 9.9). Such a system provides an organizational advantage that enables groups to mobilize both larger raiding parties and larger defensive forces.

When unilineal descent from a specific ancestor is not based on demonstrated genealogical links, the group that results is known as either a *patriclan* or a *matriclan.* **Clan** members believe they are related to one another through links that go back to the beginning of time; sometimes they believe their common ancestor is a mythic animal. In many cases, however, it is difficult to decide whether a culture has unilineal lineages or unilineal clans.

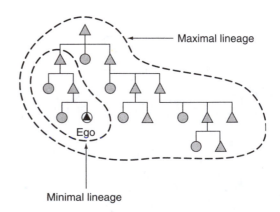

Figure 9.9 Patrilineages

Everyone on the diagram belongs to the same maximal lineage. Members of a maximal lineage will support each other against more distant maximal lineages.

Postmarital Residence Patterns

To understand the processes responsible for the evolution of different varieties of domestic groups and different ideologies of descent, we must discuss one additional aspect of domestic organization: *postmarital residence* (where a newly married couple goes to live). Table 9.1 describes the principal postmarital residence practices.

Postmarital residence rules govern with whom or near whom a couple will reside after marriage and determine whether a couple will be surrounded by the husband's or wife's kin and what kind of support each can expect to have.

Postmarital residence practices influence descent rules because they determine who will enter, leave, or stay in a domestic group (Murdock 1949; Naroll 1973). They thus provide domestic groups with distinctive cores of people related by descent and marriage.

But what determines a culture's residence rules? In many cases, residence rules reflect a society's basic patterns of production and reproduction because they are a means of organizing and justifying the structure of domestic groups in relation to particular infrastructural constraints and opportunities.

Bilocality means that a married couple elects to stay for short intervals between shifts of residence between the wife's kin and husband's kin.

Neolocality differs from bilocality in not establishing residence with kin groups at all.

Bilocality and neolocality are both associated with bilateral descent. These locality practices usually reflect a high degree of mobility and flexibility among nuclear families. Mobility and flexibility, as we have seen

Table 9.1

Principal Varieties of Postmarital Residence

Name of Pattern	Place Where Married Couple Resides
Neolocality	Apart from either husband's or wife's kin
Bilocality	Alternately shifting from husband's kin to wife's kin
Patrilocality	With husband's father
Matrilocality	With wife's mother
Avunculocality	With mother's brother

(pp. 65–67), are useful for simple hunters and gatherers and are an intrinsic feature of band organization. The !Kung San, for example, are primarily bilateral, and this reflects in turn a predominantly bilocal postmarital residence pattern. !Kung San camps contain a core of adult siblings of both sexes, plus their spouses and children and an assortment of more distant bilateral and affinal kin. Each year, in addition to much short-time visiting, about 13 percent of the population makes a more or less permanent residential shift from one camp to another, and about 35 percent divide their time equally among two or three different camps (Lee 1979:54).

In industrial societies, bilaterality is associated with a similar flexibility and mobility of nuclear families. (In the United States, about 20 percent of domestic groups change their residence each year.) Bilaterality in this case reflects a neolocal pattern that is advantageous with respect to wage labor opportunities and the substitution of price market money exchanges for kinship-mediated forms of exchange. Whereas the !Kung San always live with relatives and depend on kindreds and extended families for their subsistence, industrial age nuclear families often live far away from any relatives and interact with their kindred primarily at holidays, weddings, and funerals.

Unilocal Residence

Simple hunting-and-gathering societies tend to have cognatic descent groups and bilocal residences because their basic ecological adjustment demands that local groups remain open, flexible, and nonterritorial. With the development of horticulture and more settled village life, the identification between domestic groups or villages and definite territories increased and became more exclusive. Population density increased and warfare became more intense, for reasons to be discussed in Chapter 10, contributing to the need for group unity and solidarity (C. Ember et al. 1974). Under these conditions, unilineal descent groups with well-defined localized membership cores, a heightened sense of solidarity, and an ideology of exclusive rights over resources and people became the predominant form of kinship group.

With increased reliance on agriculture, as opposed to hunting and gathering, cognatic descent groups are replaced by unilineal descent groups. Horticultural village societies that are organized unilineally outnumber those that are organized cognatically. Moreover, almost all the unilineal societies display signs of increased population pressure, as indicated by the depletion of wild plant and food resources.

Unilineal descent groups are closely associated with unilocal residence—that is, patrilineality with patrilocality and matrilineality with matrilocality. In addition, there is a close correlation between avunculocality and matrilineality. The way in which avunculocality works and the reason for its association with matrilineality will become clearer in a moment, as we examine the infrastructural causes of matrilocality and patrilocality.

Causes of Patrilocality

The overwhelming majority of known societies has male-centered residence and descent patterns. Seventy-one percent of 1,179 societies classified by George Murdock (1967) were either patrilocal or virilocal (Table 9.1); in the same sample, societies that had patrilineal kin groups outnumbered societies that had matrilineal kin groups 588 to 164. Patrilocality and patrilineality are thus the most common modes of domestic organization. They predominate in societies that have plows and draft animals and that practice pastoral nomadism, as well as in simple horticultural societies.

Patrilocal residence is associated with internal warfare.

The type of warfare that periodically breaks out between neighboring communities is called *internal* because fighting occurs locally and there is concern for keeping the sons close to home for purposes of defense.

When there is a threat of warfare, cooperation among males is more often crucial than cooperation among females. Specifically, men are more effective in hand-to-hand combat than women, and women are less mobile than men during pregnancy and when nursing infants. As a consequence, men generally monopolize the weapons of war and the hunt, leading to male control over trade and politics.

Among patrilocal, patrilineal villages, the belligerent territorial teams consist of patrilineally related kin who constitute competitive "fraternal interest groups." These groups live in villages about half a day from each other, make shifting alliances with neighboring villages, exchange sisters, and raid each other when hostilities intensify.

Causes of Matrilocality

The question we must ask concerning the origin of matrilocality is this: Under what conditions would a community benefit from a shift to matrilocality? The most likely answer is that when men engage in long-distance trade or warfare changes from quick, short-distance forays to long-distance expeditions lasting several months, matrilocality is more advantageous than patrilocality.

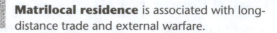 **Matrilocal residence** is associated with long-distance trade and external warfare.

When patrilocal males leave a village for extended periods, they leave behind their patrilineal kin group's corporate interests in property and people to be looked after solely by their wives. The allegiance of their wives, however, lies with another patrilineal kin group, so they have little incentive to cooperate among themselves in the absence of the men into whose corporate group they married.

Matrilocality solves this problem because it structures the domestic unit around a permanent core of resident mothers, daughters, and sisters who have been trained to cooperate with each other from birth and who identify the "minding of the store" with their own material and personal interests. Thus, matrilocal domestic groups are less likely to be disrupted by the prolonged absence of their adult males.

Furthermore, the ability to launch and successfully complete long-distance expeditions implies that neighboring villages will not attack each other when the men are away. Because men from different domestic groups marry into matrilocal communities, fathers and brothers are scattered into several different households in different villages, which prevents the formation of competitive and disruptive fraternal interest groups.

Causes of Avunculocality

Matrilocal, matrilineal societies generally favor marriage between members of the same village (village endogomy) or at least the same neighborhood, so that male members of the matrilineage do not have to be dispersed. Otherwise, males must move into their wives' residential groups at marriage and must relinquish control over their sons to the members of their wives' kin groups. One way to solve this problem is to loosen the male's marital obligations (already weak in matrilocal societies) to the point where he need not live with his wife at all.

At marriage, a male goes to live with his mother's brothers in their matrilineal domestic unit and his wife joins him there. At maturity, a male ego's son will in turn depart for ego's wife's brother's domestic unit. Thus, the male core of an avunculocal domestic unit consists of a group of brothers and their sisters' sons.

 Avunculocal residence maintains a male fraternal interest group in the residential core of the matrilineal descent group. Avunculocality thus provides the best of two worlds for males who aspire to military and political leadership.

This is the path followed by the Nayar. Nayar men, you may recall (p. 128), had no home other than their natal domestic unit; they were not responsible for their children (whom they were scarcely able to identify), but they had no difficulty keeping their sisters and their nephews and nieces under fraternal and avuncular control. But a more common solution to the tension between male interests and matrilineality is the development of avunculocal patterns of residence. Avunculocality is thus suited to maintaining the corporate interests of lineage and is correlated with the emergence of bellicose chiefdoms (Keegan and MacLachlan 1989).

Kinship Terminologies

Another aspect of domestic ideology that participates in the same strain toward functional consistency is *kinship terminology*. Every culture has a special set of terms (such as *father, mother, cousin*) for designating types of kin. The terms plus the rules for using them constitute a culture's kin terminological system.

Lewis Henry Morgan (1877) was the first anthropologist to realize that despite the thousands of languages on earth and despite the immense number of kinship terms in these languages, there are only a handful of basic types of kin terminological systems. These systems can best be defined by the way terms are applied to a small set of kin on ego's own and ego's parent generation. Here we will examine three well-known systems in order to illustrate the nature of the causal and functional relationships that link alternative kinship terminologies to the other aspects of domestic organizations. (These are basic terminological types; actual instances often vary in details.)

Inuit Terminology

The kin terminological system with which most North Americans are familiar is known as *Inuit,* shown in Figure 9.10. This system has two important features: First, none of the terms applied to ego's nuclear relatives—1, 2, 6, 5—is applied outside the nuclear family, and second, there is no distinction between maternal and paternal links. This means that the system makes no distinction between cross- and parallel cousins or between cross- and parallel aunts or uncles.

Societies that use **Inuit terminology** generally lack corporate descent groups. The nuclear family stands out as a separate and functionally dominant productive and reproductive unit. Separate kin terms are used for nuclear family members that are not extended to any other kin type.

Each nuclear family member is given a terminological identity separate from all other kin types (such as *mother, father, sister, brother*). Beyond the nuclear family, all cousins are lumped under a single term (7). This is also true for aunts and uncles from the mother's and the father's side and reflects the strength of bilateral as opposed to unilineal descent.

As the name implies, Inuit is frequently found among simple hunters and gatherers. As we have seen, simple hunting-and-gathering groups must remain mobile to cope with the movements of game and the seasonal fluctuations in the availability of plant foods. In industrial societies, the same terminological pattern reflects the high level of wage-induced social and geographic mobility.

Hawaiian Terminology

Another common kin terminological system is known as *Hawaiian*. This system is easiest to portray, since it has the fewest number of terms (Figure 9.11). In some versions, even the distinction between the sexes is dropped, leaving one term for the members of ego's generation and another for the members of ego's parents' generation.

In **Hawaiian terminology,** the same term is applied to people inside and outside the nuclear family; a single term is used for all relatives of the same sex and generation.

For example, a person's mother, mother's sister, and father's sister are all referred to as *mother*. Hawaiian terminology is thus compatible with situations where the nuclear family is submerged within a domestic

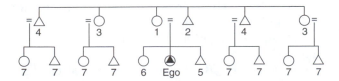

Figure 9.10   Inuit Terminology

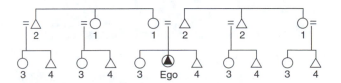

Figure 9.11   Hawaiian Terminology

context dominated by extended families and other corporate descent groups.

Theoretically, most of these descent groups should be cognatic rather than unilineal. The reason for this prediction is that the merging of relatives on the maternal side with those on the paternal side indicates an indifference toward unilineality, and an indifference toward unilineality is logically consistent with ambilineal or bilateral descent. However, data from Murdock's (1967) ethnographic sample only partially support this prediction. Indeed, many more Hawaiian terminology societies have cognatic as opposed to unilineal descent, but there are also many exceptions for which as yet no generally accepted explanation is available.

Iroquois Terminology

In the presence of unilineal kin groups, we find a worldwide tendency to distinguish parallel from cross-cousins, as previously noted. This pattern is widely associated with a similar distinction in the first ascending generation, whereby father's brothers are distinguished from mother's brothers and father's sisters are distinguished from mother's sisters.

 Iroquois terminology distinguishes between cross- and parallel cousins and cross- and parallel aunts and uncles. This pattern of merging occurs as a result of the shared membership of siblings in corporate unilineal descent groups and marriage alliances based on cross-cousin marriage between such groups.

Cross-Cousin Marriage

The Machiguenga use Iroquois kin terminology. They marry classificatory cross-cousins who are "spouses" and "in-laws," whereas parallel cousins are "brothers" and "sisters."

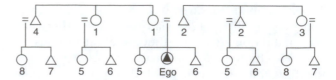

Figure 9.12 Iroquois Terminology

Mother's sister is called by the same term as mother, and father's brother is called by the same term as father. Parallel cousins are given the same term as ego's brothers and sisters, and cross-cousins are regarded either as potential spouses or in-laws (Figure 9.12).

Kin Terms Are Negotiated, Not Written in Stone

Anthropologists recognize that while kinship terminologies are internally logical, there are contradictions in the actual usage and application of kin terms. Kinship is one of the central organizing principles of human social life, but there is always room for negotiation of kinship status. As Richard Lee learned among the !Kung, "The principles of kinship do not constitute an invariant code of laws written in stone, but instead a whole series of codes, consistent enough to provide structure but open enough to be flexible" (1993:62). The flexibility of kinship systems makes it possible to transform relationships through reclassification in order to invoke a desired role relationship.

Biological descent and marriage ties are often inadequate to fulfill certain social requirements. If genealogical connections are lacking, people may have recourse to "fictive" kin ties—that is, relations that are socially constructed, rather than biologically based.

 Fictive kin ties may be established through the negotiation of kinship when genealogical connections are lacking. People invoke relations that are defined by kinship role requirements, and these ties can be extended to others who become kin according to kinship rules.

Many anthropologists have found themselves "incorporated" into a community by way of fictive kin ties. All it takes is one kin tie to become fully connected to an extended family group and to be granted affective ties and social obligations modeled on those appropriate to blood relatives.

Negation of kin ties is another means of redefining relationships. Often there are overlapping kin ties and more than one way to reckon genealogy. This results in double relationships that can be manipulated to suit individual needs or to adjust to changing social circumstances. Among the Mehinacu of Brazil, double relationships arise when people extend kinship beyond their circle of true kin. A person's kinship term for more distant kin relatives is based on his or her parents' position within the network of relationships. Because the system is bilateral and kin ties are traced equally through both parents, people often have overlapping relationships. The ambiguity can become problematic when a person tries to invoke a specific relationship, such as a sexual relationship with a distant cross-cousin. According to Thomas Gregor, Mehinacu girls will sometimes respond by saying, "No! I am like your true sister. When I get married my husband and you will be brothers-in-law" (1977:291). Sometimes, a man will argue to show how they can legitimately be considered cross-cousins, but if the girl is not interested, she will base her rejection on the ambiguity of their kin ties. Kinship is continually redefined to make or break alliances and rationalized to fit the circumstances at hand. Careful genealogical accounts are kept when wealth or succession are at stake. Otherwise, a certain amount of individual discretion is exercised in defining the outer limits of individual kin groups.

The Changing Family in North America

Because of rapidly changing economic and technological developments, nowhere can these flexible boundaries be better observed than by examining the changes in the North American family over the past decades.

At the beginning of the century, most marriages were entered into for life, and families were headed by male breadwinners. Each couple had an average of three or more children, and the children were brought up by their natural parents unless the marriage was terminated by death. Today, single-parent domestic groups are the fastest-growing form of family, up 80 percent since 1960. Largely as a result of divorce, separation, and the growth of female-headed households, families have had to devise novel ways of coping with life under changing conditions. Carol Stack (1974) and Jagna Sharff (1998) have shown how urban poor use extended kinship ties as a strategy for sustaining life as people go through economy-driven changes.

Whether or not the traditional family with full-time domesticity was ever a reality, it certainly is not today. There has been a virtual explosion of new family forms in the last half-century: surrogate motherhood, new reproductive technologies, a major increase in single mothers and matrifocal households, blended families, open adoption, and gay and lesbian families. No longer is there a single, culturally dominant family pattern; instead, Americans have crafted a multiplicity of family and household arrangements. Another point also seems to be clear: that poor families are not the only ones who seek new kinship arrangements as creative responses to changing economic and social conditions.

Other trends that can be seen as directly linked to these alternative family practices are an increase in the number of intergenerational households and households composed of nonbiological families. Now we can identify a new middle class with "crowded," rather than "empty nests," filled with "incompletely launched young adults," a pattern that has long been associated with less privileged families (Stacy 1990:254). Families are reorganizing and diversifying, adopting a kinship arrangement that has been "long familiar to the less privileged," similar to the innovative arrangements of the urban poor described by Stack and Sharff.

Along with the shift in infrastructural conditions in the last half-century, from a heavily industrialized, production-oriented economy to a highly technological service and information economy, have come many superstructural changes. What was perceived as odd, not "respectable," or even deviant is now commonplace and frequently accepted by the society at large. A willingness to experiment and the formation of families by conscious choice can be seen as supporting factors in the emergence of new family forms. A Yale University study showed that by a ratio of 3 to 1, people defined the *family* as "a group of people who love and care for each other," rather than just those biologically or legally connected in marriage

Blended Family

Although the traditional nuclear family is still a cultural ideal, many people remarry and bring their children into newly formed households.

Lesbian Mothers

People are redefining kinship and family.

(Stacey 1990:270). A study of counterculture families, who came of age in the 1960s, shows that many did not sustain their unconventional lifestyle over time. But their conscious desire to adopt new family forms set the foundation for the reorganization of middle-class family forms that later followed. Their family experiments were examples of many of the practices that later diffused into the wider society. Today, many Americans no longer recall a time when single parenthood by choice or an unmarried couple raising children was a rare or stigmatizing path to take (Weisner and Bernheimer 1998:252).

Other examples of culturally evolved kinship ties are those that have been forged by gay and lesbian men and women. Kath Weston, who studied lesbian and gay families in the San Francisco area, found that in response to anticipated or actual exclusion by their natural families, gays and lesbians have forged a new ideological basis for kinship by proclaiming "Love makes a family." Many see a relationship's ability to weather conflict as itself a sign of kinship. They say family members are people who "are there for you"; people you can count on (1991:113). These "chosen families" have flexible boundaries and are often inclusive of former lovers who make the transition from lover to friend without disrupting the relationship. Most importantly, these chosen family members provide material and emotional support within and across households. They include people who not only share enduring solidarity but who also provide services for one another out of strong bonds of affection. Thus, the "chosen families" of lesbians and gays are both responses to the perceived or actual loss of traditional kin support and products of conscious choice.

As we have learned, who is defined as *family* does not necessarily reflect biological connections or even marriage relationships. Many different forms of family have always existed as cultural responses that enable people to adapt to their circumstances. In North America now, families are once again adapting to the material, economic, and emotional requirements of our complex, ever-changing times. The diversity of family forms seen today is evidence that the boundaries of kinship are flexible and expand (or contract) to allow people to cope more effectively with their changing circumstances.

SUMMARY
and *Questions to Think About*

1. To study kinship is to study the ideologies that justify and normalize the corporate structure of domestic groups. The basis of kinship is the tracing of relationships through marriage and descent. Descent is the belief that certain persons play special roles in the conception, birth, or nurturance of certain children. Many folk theories of descent exist, none of which corresponds precisely to modern scientific understandings of procreation and reproduction.

2. The principal varieties of cognatic descent rules are the bilateral and the ambilineal; these are associated, respectively, with kindreds, on the one hand, and with cognatic lineages and clans, on the other. The principal varieties of unilineal descent are matrilineality and patrilineality. These are associated, respectively, with patri- and matrilineages or patri- and matriclans.

3. An important key to understanding alternative modes of descent and domestic organization is the pattern of postmarital residence. Bilateral descent and bilateral descent groups are associated with neolocality, bilocality, and ambilocality. More specifically, the flexible and mobile forms of band organization are facilitated by bilocality, whereas the greater isolation of nuclear families in price market economies gives rise to neolocality. Cognatic lineages, on the other hand, give functional

expression to ambilocality, whereby a person can affiliate with either the mother's or the father's kinship group.

4. Unilineal domestic groups reflect unilocal patterns of residence. These patterns in turn imply well-defined membership cores and an emphasis on exclusive rights over resources and people. A strong correlation exists between patrilocality and patrilineality, on the one hand, and among matrilineality, matrilocality, and avunculocality, on the other. Patrilocal and patrilineal groups are far more common than matrilocal, matrilineal, and avunculocal groups. A reason for this is that warfare, hunting, and trading activities among village societies are monopolized by males. These activities, in turn, are facilitated by stressing the coresidence of fathers, brothers, and sons and the formation of fraternal interest groups.

5. Under conditions of increasing population density and pressure on resources, local groups may find it adaptive to engage in long-distance expeditions for war, trade, and hunting. Such expeditions are facilitated by breaking up the fraternal interest groups and structuring domestic life around a residential core of mothers, sisters, and daughters—or, in other words, by developing a matrilocal, matrilineal organization. Because males in matrilineal, matrilocal societies continue to dominate military and political institutions, they are inclined to keep their male relatives close to home after marriage. This tendency accounts for the fact that as many matrilineal societies are avunculocal as are matrilocal.

6. Thus, the principal function of alternative rules of descent and postmarital residence may be described as the establishment and maintenance of networks of cooperative and interdependent kinspeople aggregated into ecologically effective and militarily secure domestic production and reproduction units. For such units to act effectively and reliably, they must share an organizational ideology that interprets and validates the structure of the group and the behavior of its members. Kinship is that shared organizational ideology.

7. This interpretation of descent and postmarital residence rules can also be applied to the principal varieties of kin terminological systems. Such systems tend to classify relatives in conformity with the major features of domestic organization, locality practices, and descent rules. Inuit terminology, for example, is functionally associated with domestic organizations in which nuclear families tend to be mobile and isolated. Hawaiian terminology is functionally associated with cognatic lineages and cognatic clans. And Iroquois terminology, with its emphasis on the distinction between cross- and parallel cousins, is functionally associated with unilinear descent groups.

8. Although kinship terminologies are consistently applied in every culture, kinship structures are open and flexible. Nonrelatives are incorporated by way of fictive kinship, whereby social obligations and affective content is modeled on those of appropriate blood relatives. Social relationships can also be manipulated to suit individual needs or to adjust to changing circumstances through the negotiation of kin ties.

Questions to Think About

1. Describe the infrastructural conditions that help explain why foraging and industrial societies both have cognatic descent groups.

2. What role does consanguineal and affinal kinship have in arranging marriage and controlling competition between groups?

3. How does internal versus external warfare influence locality and descent?

4. Why is kinship so important to anthropologists? What do real and fictive kinship tell us about the beliefs and expectations people hold toward one another?

THROUGH THE LENS
of Cultural Materialism

Conformity and Conflict • Reading Nineteen
Uterine Families and the Women's Community
Margery Wolf

In rural Taiwan villages, kinship is reckoned through patrilineal descent, leaving women without strong family ties. Women are able to create their own "uterine families,"

however, through their children and grandchildren and also establish networks of support through ties with women from other households.

Emic View

• Despite the belief that family is the source of security, women do not have a sense of belonging to their fathers' or husbands' families because of their temporary status prior to marriage and their subordinate position as a new bride in the husband's family.

- From a male perspective, the family is based on patrilineal ties from father to son to grandson. From a female perspective, the family is a group that comes into existence through a woman's connection to other women in the village and later through her own sons, her own children, and her own grandchildren.

Etic View

- A "women's community" helps women cope with the insecurity of their structural position. It exists below the level of consciousness and does not have a public presence.

- To be successful, women appear to abide by male rules yet know how to manipulate them so they can look after their own interests.

Infrastructure

- Taiwanese villages practice irrigation agriculture. Sons are preferred over daughters because sons cooperate to support the family. Wives are outsiders who provide heirs.

Structure

- Kinship is based on patrilineal descent; land is inherited through the male line, and men become permanent members of an unbroken line of descendents.

- For women, the patrilineal family is temporary; women are born into one family and married into another, where the mother-in-law has authority.

- After marriage and upon entering the household of her husband, a woman is not considered a member of the family because her mother-in-law views her with ambivalence. A new bride's family is formed when she creates her own uterine family, consisting of her children and grandchildren.

- Women's informal ties to women outside their own households provide sufficient backing to maintain some independence and even assume indirect control over men. Women perform activities out of the house—washing clothes on the riverbank, cleaning and paring vegetables at a communal pump, mending under a tree—and it is through these activities that they develop ties and use their network to wield power.

Superstructure

- Chinese children are taught by proverb, by example, and by experience that the family is the source of their security and that relatives are the only people who can be depended on.

- The uterine family has "no ideology, no formal structure, and no public existence." It is based on sentiment and loyalty.

- A women's informal network is a powerful means of curbing male offensive behavior by giving or taking away "face" from a man. It is said, "When no one is talking about a family, you can say it has face." However, if a man behaves badly, the women will talk about him. He will lose face, and if he continues, he may bring shame to the family of his ancestors and descendents.

- Taiwanese woman are expected to learn the rules, but if they are to be a successful, they must learn not to manipulate them without appearing to do so. A truly successful woman is an individualist who has learned to depend largely on herself while appearing to lean on her father, husband, and sons.

- Although females are regarded as subordinate to men within the kinship structure, their uterine family and network of women outside the home provide them with a sense of solidarity and influence over domestic affairs.

CHAPTER 10

LAW, ORDER, AND WAR IN NONSTATE SOCIETIES

The fiercest Cheyenne warriors were young men who were indifferent to the risks of battle.

A s we continue with the structural aspect of sociocultural systems, the focus shifts to the maintenance of political cohesion and law and order within and between band and village societies. These societies enjoy a high degree of personal security without having written laws, police officers, jails, or any of the other parts of modern criminal justice systems. How do they do it? This is not to say that band and village societies have no violence. On the contrary, feuds and armed combat do occur, even among hunter-gatherers and small village societies that have very low population densities. Some anthropologists argue that the propensity to engage in armed combat is part of human nature. Others, however, point out that even low-density populations may have scarce resources worth fighting over. In one important case, at least, a scarce resource seems to be game animals. War, as we will see, springs no more from human nature than does peace.

Law and Order in Band and Village Societies

In every society, people have conflicting interests. Even in band-level societies, old and young, sick and healthy, men and women do not want the same thing at the same time. Moreover, in every society, people want something that others possess and are reluctant to give away. Every culture, therefore, must have structural provisions for resolving conflicts of interest in an orderly fashion and for preventing conflicts from escalating into disruptive confrontations. Band and village societies, however, have distinctive conflicting interests and distinctive methods for preventing disruptive confrontations.

> Despite the presence of conflict, simple hunter-gatherer societies enjoy a high degree of personal security without having any rulers or law-and-order specialists.

These societies have no kings, queens, dictators, presidents, governors, or mayors; police forces, soldiers, sailors, or marines; CIA, FBI, treasury agents, or federal marshals. They have no written law codes and no formal law courts; no lawyers, bailiffs, judges, district attorneys, juries, or court clerks; and no patrol cars, paddy wagons, jails, or penitentiaries. This is also true of many village societies. How do people in band and village societies get along without law enforcement specialists and facilities, while modern societies are so dependent on them?

The Subsistence Economy versus the Political Economy

The reason for these differences is that band and village societies are primarily embedded in the **subsistence economy** and have the following characteristics:

- Communities are small in size.
- Domestic groups and kinship are of central importance.
- There is relative equity in access to resources and technology.
- Each household is similar and self-sufficient.
- Households produce all their needs by means of a division of labor by age and sex.

Small size means that everyone knows everyone else personally; therefore, the group can identify stingy, aggressive, and disruptive individuals and expose them to the pressure of public opinion. The centrality of domestic group and kinship relations means that reciprocity can be the chief mode of exchange and that members of the domestic group have personal incentives to uphold collective interests. Prestige is accorded to those who appear generous, whereas confrontation results in the loss of a person's good name. Finally, equality of access to technology and natural resources means the society is **egalitarian**—that food and other forms of wealth cannot be withheld by a wealthy few while others endure shortages and hardships.

> An **egalitarian society** lacks formalized differentiation in access to and power over basic resources among its members.

Yanomami Club Fight
Egalitarian societies are not without problems of law and order.

158

In small-scale societies with scattered populations, communities are largely self-sufficient and the production of basic needs is governed by the **subsistence economy**. "Theoretically, no surplus is produced beyond a security margin—what may be needed if things turn bad. The overriding goal is to fulfill the household's needs at the lowest cost that affords security" (A. Johnson and Earle 2000:23).

> The **subsistence economy** is essentially the household economy. It is organized at the household level to meet basic needs, such as food, clothing, housing, defense, and technology.

Consistent with evolutionary change, the feedback between population growth and technological development results in the growth of the subsistence economy through intensification. The usual outcome is that people become bound to their land, production requires more careful management, and the subsistence economy is increasingly transformed into the **political economy**.

> The **political economy** regulates the flow of goods in large multifamily settings and supports existing power relationships.

In band and village societies, exchanges and disputes are handled informally. As territories become more crowded, there is constant potential for competition over resources. Unlike the subsistence economy, where kinship upholds collective interests, an economy geared toward intensification and maximization of production requires greater managerial oversight and leadership. As problem solvers, leaders manage the economy to the advantage of the growing community. But as communities grow and the landscape becomes more crowded, the political economy expands and so does the power of its leaders.

Primitive Communism?

Among small band and village societies, all adults usually have access to the rivers, lakes, beaches, and oceans; to all the plants and animals; and to the soil and the subsoil. Insofar as these are basic to the extraction of life-sustaining energy and materials, they are communal property (Lee 1990). Among the !Kung San, waterholes and hunting-and-gathering territories are said to be "owned" by the residential core of particular bands. But neighbors who ask for permission to visit and exploit the resources of a particular camp are seldom refused.

> Neighboring bands contain many intermarried kin and therefore commonly share access to resources as a result of mutual visiting.

Even people who come from distant bands and who lack close kin ties with the hosts are usually given permission to stay, especially for short periods, because all parties understand that the hosts may return the visit at some future date (Lee 1979:337). !Kung elderly are cared for by relatives and nonrelatives alike. No one, not even a childless person, is denied support in their old age (Lee 1990:175).

> Everyone among the !Kung is recognized as entitled to the necessities of life by right of being a member of society.

The prevalence of communal ownership of land, however, does not mean that simple hunter-gatherers lack private property altogether. There is little support for the theory that "primitive communism" is a universal stage in the development of culture marked by the complete absence of private property. Many material objects are effectively controlled ("owned") by specific individuals in band-level societies, especially items the user has produced. The members of even the most egalitarian societies usually believe that weapons, clothing, containers, ornaments, tools, and other personal effects should not be taken away or used without the consent of the "owner." However, the chance is remote that theft or misappropriation of such objects will lead to serious conflict (Woodburn 1982). Why not?

First, the accumulation of material possessions is rigidly limited by the recurrent need to break camp and travel long distances on foot. In addition, most utilitarian items may be borrowed without difficulty when the owner is not using them. If there are not enough such items to go around (arrows, projectile points, nets, bark or gourd containers), easy access to the raw materials and mastery of the requisite skills provide the have-nots with the chance of making their own. Moreover, among societies having no more than a few hundred people, thieves cannot be anonymous. If stealing becomes habitual, a coalition of the injured parties will eventually take action. If you want something, better to ask for it openly. Most such requests are readily obliged, because reciprocity is the prevailing mode of exchange. Finally, contrary to the experience of the successful modern bank robber, no one can make a living from stealing bows and arrows or feather headdresses, because band-level societies have no regular market at which such items can be exchanged for food (see Chapter 7).

The existence of private property does not lead to inequalities in wealth and power because, according to the rules of reciprocity, people can openly ask for possessions and such requests cannot be denied.

Mobilizing Public Opinion

When disputes occur in small egalitarian societies, the disputants rely on the backing of their kin groups for support.

In the absence of law-and-order institutions such as the police and courts, people seek the support of kinfolk as they press their claims against other members of the community. As long as the disputants feel they have the backing of their kin groups, they will continue to press their claims and counterclaims. The members of their kin groups, however, are not eager to be caught in a situation in which they are opposed by a majority of people. Public opinion influences the support disputants can expect from their kin. Often what matters is not so much who is morally right or wrong or who is lying or telling the truth; the important thing is to mobilize public opinion on one side or the other decisively enough to prevent the outbreak of large-scale feuding.

The Inuit song duel is a classic example of how public opinion influences the support that disputants can expect from their respective kin groups.

Among the central and eastern Inuit, mobilization of public support can be achieved independently of abstract principles of justice or even reference to the events that led to the dispute. Here, it is common for a man involved in a dispute to claim that the other has stolen his wife. The counterclaim is that she was not stolen but left voluntarily because her husband "was not man enough" to take good care of her. The issue is settled at a large public meeting. Unlike a court, no testimony is taken in support of either of the two versions of why the wife has left her husband. Instead, the disputants take turns singing insulting songs, each accusing his opponent of sexual excess or impotence. The "court" of public opinion responds to each performance with different degrees of laughter. Eventually one of the singers gets flustered, and the hooting and hollering raised against him become total; even his relatives have a hard time not laughing (Box 10.1).

The Inuit have no police or military specialists to see to it that the decision is enforced. Yet chances are that the man who has lost the song duel will give in because he can no longer count on anyone to back him up if he chooses to escalate the dispute. Nonetheless, the defeated man may decide to go it alone, and wife stealing does occasionally lead to murder. When this happens, the man who has lost public support may survive on the strength of his own vigilance and fighting skill. He will probably have to kill again, however, and with each transgression, the coalition against him becomes larger and more determined, until finally they may kill him in an ambush.

Song Contest
Inuit disputants in "court" in eastern Greenland.

Kuikuru Shaman

The shaman is leaving the village with his assistants on the way to a nearby lake to recover the lost soul of a patient lying ill. The shaman intends to dive to the bottom of the lake and wrest the soul away from the evil spirit who stole it from the patient, and then implant it back into the patient's body.

Shamans and Public Opinion

In small, egalitarian societies, shamans play an important role in mobilizing public opinion and in eliminating persistent sources of conflict.

 Shamans are part-time practitioners of magico-religious rites of divination and curing, skilled in slight of hand, and the techniques of trance and possession.

Most cultures reject the idea that misfortune results from natural causes. If animals suddenly become scarce or if several people fall sick, it is assumed that somebody is practicing witchcraft by using psychic powers to harm others through supernatural means. It is the shaman's job to identify the culprit. Normally this is done through the art of *divination,* or clairvoyance. Putting himself into a trance with the aid of drugs, tobacco smoke, or monotonous drumming (see Chapter 16, the section titled "Shamanistic Cults"), the shaman discovers the name of the witch. The people demand vengeance, and the culprit is ambushed and murdered.

Chances are that the accused individual never attempted to carry out any witchcraft at all! In other words, the witches are probably wholly innocent of the crimes with which they are charged. Nonetheless, the shaman's witchcraft accusations usually conserve rather than destroy the group's feeling of unity because the person identified as the perpetrator is regarded as a troublemaker and lacks support from his or her kin (Box 10.2). This system, however, is not "fail-safe." Many cases are known of witchcraft systems that seem to have broken down because witchcraft accusations have led to a series of destructive retaliations and murders.

Headmanship

To the extent that political leadership can be said to exist at all among small societies, it is exercised by *headmen* or, less commonly, headwomen.

A headman, unlike such a specialist as a king, president, or dictator, is a relatively powerless figure, incapable of compelling obedience.

When the headman gives a command, he is never certain of being able to punish physically those who

BOX 10.2 | How to Choose a Witch

Gertrude Dole (1966) reported the following events among the Kuikuru—an egalitarian Brazilian Indian society:

Lightning had set fire to two houses. The shaman went into a trance and discovered that the lightning had been sent by a man who had left the village some years previously and never returned. This man had only one male relative, who was also no longer living in the village. Before the accused witch had departed, he had tried unsuccessfully to court a girl whom the shaman's brother wanted to marry. During his trance, the shaman carried out a dialogue with various members of the vil-

lage. When he finally disclosed the identity of the culprit, he was readily believed. As the excitement grew, the shaman's brother and several companions left the village to kill the man suspected of witchcraft (1966:761).

Among the Kuikuru, a change of residence from one village to another usually indicates that there is trouble brewing and that, in effect, the individual has been ostracized. Thus, the witch was not a randomly chosen figure but one who fulfilled several well-defined criteria: a history of disputes and quarrels within the village, a motivation for continuing to do harm (the unsuccessful courtship), and weak backing from kin.

disobey. (Hence, if he wants to stay in "office," he gives few direct commands.) Among the Inuit, leadership is especially diffuse, being closely related to success in hunting. A group will follow an outstanding hunter and defer to his opinion with respect to choice of hunting spots. But in all other matters, the leader's opinion carries no more weight than that of any other adult. In contrast, the political power of genuine rulers depends on their ability to expel or exterminate any readily foreseeable combination of nonconforming individuals and groups. Genuine rulers control access to basic resources and to the tools and weapons for hurting or killing people, whereas a

headman has an achieved status that requires him to lead by example and persuasion.

An **achieved status** is acquired through talents, efforts, and accomplishments, rather than ascription.

Among the !Kung San, each band has its recognized leaders. Such leaders may speak out more than others and are listened to with a bit more deference than is usual, but they "have no formal authority" and "can only persuade, but never enforce their will on others" (Lee 1979:333–334; 1982). When Richard Lee asked the !Kung San whether they had headmen in the

Mehinacu Headmanship
In front of the men's house, the headman is redistributing presents given to him by the ethnographer.

sense of powerful chiefs, he was told, "Of course we have headmen! In fact we are all headmen. Each one of us is headman over himself" (1979:348).

There are no mechanisms for forcing people in band and village societies to do what they do not want to do because they can simply move to another location.

A similar pattern of leadership is reported for the Semai of Malaya. Despite attempts by the Malayan government to bolster the power of Semai leaders, the headman is merely the most prestigious figure among a group of peers. In the words of Robert Dentan, who carried out fieldwork among these egalitarian shifting horticulturalists, "[The headman] keeps the peace by conciliation rather than coercion. He must be personally respected. Otherwise people will drift away from him or gradually stop paying attention to him" (1968:681).

The Semai recognize only a few occasions on which he can assert his authority:

- Dealing as a representative of his people with non-Semai
- Mediating a quarrel, if invited by the quarreling parties to do so
- Selecting and apportioning land for fields

Most of the time, a good headman gauges the general feeling about an issue and bases his decision on that, so that he is more a spokesman for public opinion than a molder of it.

The headman among Brazilian Indian groups, such as the Mehinacu of Brazil's Xingu National Park, performs a thankless and frustrating job. The first one up in the morning, the headman tries to rouse his companions by standing in the middle of the village plaza and shouting. If a task needs to be done, it is the headman who starts doing it, and it is the headman who works at it harder than anyone else (see Profile 10.1).

The headman must set an example not only for hard work but also for generosity.

After a fishing or hunting expedition, he is expected to give away more of the catch than anyone else; if trade goods are obtained, he must be careful not to keep the best pieces for himself.

The headman motivates individuals to avoid conflict and restrain violence.

Without political authority to enforce rules against violence, the headman must rely on interpersonal skills to motivate people to avoid confrontations. When malicious gossip and accusations break out, he uses his oratory skills to diffuse the hostility by eloquently reminding people of the dangerous consequences of expressing anger.

The Leopard Skin Chief

As we have seen, the ever-present danger confronting societies that lack genuine rulers is that their kinship groups tend to react as units to real or alleged aggression against one of their members. In this way, disputes involving individuals may escalate. The worst danger arises from disputes that lead to homicide. The members of most simple band and village societies believe that the only proper reaction to a murder is to kill the murderer or any convenient member of the murderer's kin group. Yet the absence of centralized

Leopard Skin Chief

The leopard skin chief is an outside mediator who is believed to have supernatural powers.

Location: Tropical forest along the headwaters of the Xingu River in Central Brazil.

Density: The Mehinacu, who number nearly 150 people, are one of nine separate villages in the Xingu National Park; the overall density is less than one person per square mile.

Production: Slash-and-burn horticulture with an extraordinarily abundant supply of fish.

Time of Study: 1967 to 1989.

The Mehinacu are part of a wider Xingu cultural system under government protection, beyond the reach of missionaries, ranchers, and farmers. The Mehinacu and their neighbors are refugees from larger more aggressive native groups that were decimated in the late 1800s through contact with Western disease. Present-day Xingu communities are autonomous villages representing four major language groups that trade, intermarry, and participate in one another's rituals.

The Mehinacu recognize some members as being of chiefly descent. Although referred to as "chief," the leader is in fact a headman, who unlike a chief in more politically complex societies does not have the power to coerce, nor does he live significantly better than anyone else (see Chapter 11). The most significant qualifications for Mehinacu leadership are learned skills and personal attributes. The chief, for example, is expected to excel at public speaking. Each evening he should stand in the center of the plaza and exhort his fellow tribespeople to be good citizens. He must call on them to work hard in their gardens, to take frequent baths, not to sleep during the day, not to be angry with each other, and to honor sexual taboos. In addition to being a skilled orator, the chief is expected to be a generous man. This means that when he returns from a successful fishing trip, he will bring most of his catch out to the men's houses, where it will be cooked and shared by the men of the village. His wife must be generous, bringing manioc cakes and pepper to the men

whenever they call for it. Further, the chief must be willing to part with possessions. When one of the men catches a harpy eagle (whose feathers are used for headdresses), for example, the chief must buy it from him with a valuable shell belt in the name of the entire village. A chief should also be a man who never becomes angry in public. In his public speeches he should never criticize any of his fellow tribespeople, no matter how badly they may have affronted the chief or the village as a whole (Gregor 1977).

Within the village, allegations of witchcraft are common, as deaths from natural causes are usually attributed to witches. The fear of witches makes people conduct themselves with restraint and avoid confrontations. The same fear also applies to the headman, who continually worries that his leadership might provoke a disgruntled witch. Because no one can be sure who is a witch, a policy of appeasement and courtesy is generally followed. Villagers honor requests for food and possessions, not only because of the rules of reciprocity and mutual cooperation but because otherwise they might become the victims of sorcery. If conflict escalates, families leave the community for extended periods by moving off to nearby campsites or staying with kinspeople in neighboring communities.

Peace between villages is sustained by bringing villagers together to exchange goods and partake in ceremonial events and ritual wrestling matches, but these are sporadic events and people need constant reminders of the need to maintain peace. Besides intertribal and local ceremonies, the Mehinacu readily talk about the dangers of not being peaceful, the horrors of warfare, and the ugliness of violence. They despise and fear the conduct of non-Xingu communities, who in the past have raided their villages. No prestige is given to a warrior. Displays of anger and aggression are seen as vivid reminders of the failure to exercise restraint. Violent outsiders are cast as negative role models, and nonviolence is a symbolic ethnic boundary marker that sets the "civilized" Mehinacu apart from other "savage" animal-like people (Gregor 1994).

Universal Pattern • The Mehinacu

Infrastructure	Structure	Superstructure
Tropical forest horticulture with abundant fishing.	Egalitarian political organization, with few differences in wealth or power.	Peace and nonviolence are emphasized in ideology; danger is associated with violence and projected on outsiders, who are cast as negative role models.
Sufficient territory available for community, with no restrictions on access to land.	Leadership based on personal attributes that include oratory skills and ability to set example of hard work and generosity.	Prosocial behavior is promoted through fear of witchcraft accusation. If conflict emerges, people leave community to live alone or with kin in nearby communities.
Community is protected from intrusion by outsiders (by national government).	Peaceful relations between neighboring communities are maintained through trade, ritual, and intermarriage.	Nonviolence sets members of culture apart from others who are believed to be less civilized and animal-like.

political authority does not mean that blood feuds cannot be brought under control.

Mechanisms for preventing a homicide from flaring into a protracted feud include the transfer of substantial amounts of prized possessions from the slayer's kin group to the victim's kin group.

This practice is especially common and effective among pastoral peoples, whose animals are a concentrated form of material wealth and for whom bride price is a regular aspect of kin group exogamy. For example, the Nuer, a pastoral and farming people who live near the Upper Nile in the Sudan, have no centralized political leadership (Box 10.3). The Nuer settle their feuds (or at least deescalate them) by transferring 40 or more head of cattle to the victim's relatives. If a man has been killed, these animals will be used to buy a wife whose sons will fill the void left by the man's death. The dead man's closest kin are obliged to resist the offer of cattle, demanding instead a life for a life. However, more distant kin do their best to convince the others to accept the compensation. In this effort, they are aided by certain semisacred arbitration specialists. The latter, known as *leopard skin chiefs,* are usually men whose kin groups are not represented locally and who can hence act more readily as neutral intermediaries.

The **leopard skin chief** is an outside mediator, believed to have supernatural powers, who is called on to resolve disputes between kin groups and prevent the escalation of hostilities.

The leopard skin chief is the only one who can ritually cleanse a murderer. If a homicide takes place, the killer flees at once to the leopard skin chief's house, which is a sanctuary respected by all Nuer. Nonetheless, the leopard skin chief lacks even the rudiments of political power; the most he can do to the reluctant members of the slain man's relatives is to threaten them with various supernatural curses. Yet the desire to prevent a feud is so great that the injured relatives eventually accept the cattle as compensation.

Nonkin Associations: Sodalities

Although relations of affinity and descent dominate the political life of headman-type societies, nonkin relations and groups also occur to a limited extent. Such groups, known as sodalities, are special purpose groups.

Sodalities are non–kinship based groups that span several villages and serve widely different functions.

Their special purpose activities include economic, military, religious, and recreational functions, such as coordinated large-scale seasonal hunting and military mobilization. A common form of sodality is the exclusive men's or women's association or club. These usually involve men or women who partake in public or sectet performances that reinforce regional solidarity through ritual.

Age-grade associations, or age-sets, are another common form of sodality, already mentioned with respect to the East African warrior camps (see Chapter 8, "The Household and the Domestic Sphere of Culture" section). Among the Samburu, another group of East African pastoralists, all men initiated into manhood over a span of about 12 to 14 years composed an age-set whose members had a special feeling of solidarity that cut across domestic and lineage kin groups. The age-set members advanced as a group from junior to senior status or grade. As juniors they were responsible for military combat, and as seniors they were responsible for initiating and training the upcoming age-sets (Bernardi 1985; Spencer 1965).

BOX 10.3 | Ordered Anarchy

The lack of governmental institutions among the Nuer and the absence of developed leadership and organized political life is remarkable. The ordered anarchy in which they live accords well with their character, for it is impossible to live among the Nuer and conceive of rulers ruling over them.

The Nuer are a product of hard and egalitarian upbringing. They are deeply democratic yet easily roused to violence. No man recognizes a superior, and wealth makes no difference. A man with many cattle is envied but not treated differently from a man with few cattle. There is no master or servant in their society but only equals who regard themselves as God's noblest creation. Any suspicion of an attempt to control riles a man; he will not submit to any authority that clashes with his own interest, and he does not consider himself bound to anyone.

Source: Adapted from Edward E. Evans-Pritchard. 1940. *The Nuer: A Description of the Modes of Livelihood and Political Institutions of a Nilotic People.* Copyright © 1940, reprinted by permission of Oxford University Press.

A classic case of sodality is the native North American military associations that developed on the Great Plains after the introduction of the horse. Among the Crow and the Cheyenne, these associations tried to outdo one another in acts of daring during combat and in horse-stealing expeditions. Although the members of each club did not fight as a unit, they met in their teepees to reminisce and sing about their exploits, and they wore distinctive insignia and clothing.

Gretel and Pertti Pelto (1976:324) have aptly compared these organizations to the Veterans of Foreign Wars and the American Legion because their main function was to celebrate military exploits and to uphold the honor and prestige of the tribe. However, in prestate societies, military sodalities would take turns supervising and policing the general population during large-scale group activities, such as collective hunts and long migrations to new territories. For example, sodalities prevented overeager hunters from stampeding the buffalo herds, and they suppressed rowdy behavior at ceremonials by fining or banishing disruptive individuals. But these were only seasonal functions, because only during the spring and summer, when food was abundant, could large numbers of unrelated people congregate (John Moore 1987:201ff).

Warfare among Hunters and Gatherers

We turn now to the subject of warfare as an aspect of the maintenance of law and order between nonstate societies.

 War is armed combat between groups of people who constitute separate territorial teams or political communities.

By this definition, feuds, "grudge fights," and "raiding" constitute warfare (Otterbein 1994). Some anthropologists hold that warfare is universally practiced and that it occurred as far back in time as the early Stone Age (Lizot 1979:151; Keeley 1996). By excluding feuds and raids from their definitions of warfare, however, others hold that warfare was absent or uncommon until the advent of chiefdoms and states (Ferguson 1989a:197; Reyna 1989).

Several hunter-gatherer societies—the Andaman Islanders, the Shoshoni, the Yahgan, the Mission Indians of California (Lesser 1968; MacLeish 1972), and the Greenland Eskimo (Weyer 1932:109–110)—have been offered as exceptions to the claim that warfare is a universal feature of human social life. Bonta (1993)

lists some 50 societies that are classified as nonviolent. But the peacefulness of some of these groups may result from having been defeated and forced into more marginal territories when warfare was practiced in earlier times. William Divale (1972) lists 37 hunting-and-gathering societies in which warfare (feuds and raids included) is known to have been practiced. But some anthropologists attribute these cases to the shocks of contact with state societies (Ferguson and Whitehead 1992).

Archeologists who have studied the patterns of dented, broken, and perforated bones suggest that warfare occurred among simple hunter-gatherers during periods of population increase and environmental stress. For example, in the Channel Islands off the coast of California, skull fractures attributable to clubs and projectiles increase in tandem with the growth of population during the prehistoric period. A similar increase on the mainland, where populations could disperse over a larger territory, was not observed (Walker 1988). Similarly, violence appears to be the cause of death among young and mature adult males during periods of resource deprivation, as seen in the high rate of projectile injuries in skeletal remains exhibiting poor health (Lambert 1997).

There is a fine line between warfare and personal retribution among hunters and gatherers. This is well illustrated in the example of armed conflict among the Tiwi of Bathurst and Melville Islands in Northern Australia. As recounted by C. W. Hart and Arnold Pilling (1960), a number of men from the Tiklauila and Rangwila bands developed personal grievances against a number of men who were residing with the Mandiimbula band. The aggrieved individuals, together with their relatives, put on the white paint of war, armed themselves, and set off, some 30 strong, to do battle with the Mandiimbula at a predetermined clearing. Both sides then exchanged a few insults and agreed to meet formally in the morning.

During the night, individuals from both groups visited each other, renewing acquaintances. In the morning, the two armies lined up at the opposite sides of the battlefield. Hostilities were begun by elders shouting insults and accusations at particular individuals in the enemy ranks. Although some of the old men urged that a general attack be launched, their grievances turned out to be directed not at the Mandiimbula band but at specific individuals: "Hence when spears began to be thrown, they were thrown by individuals for reasons based on individual disputes" (Hart and Pilling 1960:84). Marksmanship was poor because it was the old men who did most of the spear throwing. "Not infrequently the person hit was an old woman . . . whose reflexes for dodging spears were not as fast as those of the men. . . . As soon as somebody was wounded . . . fighting stopped immediately until the implications of this new incident could be assessed" (p. 84).

Hunters and gatherers seldom try to annihilate each other. They often retire from the field after one or two casualties have occurred, yet the cumulative effect may be quite considerable.

Overall, foragers have less warfare than nonforagers. Most foragers described in the ethnographic record have small populations, and many are surrounded by more powerful societies so that going to war would not be cost effective or feasible (Ember and Ember 1997). Remember that the average !Kung San band has only about 30 people. If such a band engages in war only twice in a generation, each time with the loss of only one adult male, casualties due to warfare would account for more than 10 percent of all adult male deaths. This is an extremely high figure when one realizes that less than 1 percent of all male deaths in Europe and the United States during the twentieth century were battlefield casualties.

Warfare among Sedentary Village Societies

Although village peoples, including complex hunter-gatherers and small agricultural societies, were not the first to practice warfare, they did expand the scale and ferocity of military engagements. Village peoples have more possessions to defend, such as storehouses filled with food, garden lands with crops growing on them, and prime fishing locations.

The more people invest in improving their environment, the more likely they will defend their territory and take land or other resources from the defeated group.

They cannot resolve disputes with other villages by simply moving off to a more remote territory. Thus warfare among village societies is likely to be more costly in terms of battle casualties than among non-sedentary hunters and gatherers.

The Nyangatom, of southwestern Ethiopia, have a mixed economy of pastoralism with agriculture that requires large stretches of land. They number about 5,000 and are surrounded by neighboring groups who they call "strangers" or "enemies." Between 1970 and 1976 they clashed with their neighbors eight times and lost about 400 lives (Tornay 1979).

"In emergencies, there is spontaneous mobilization of individuals . . . there being no need to refer to any authority before taking action" (1979:114). This flexibility is effective in defensive wars, but without military leadership, there is risk of anarchy. Elders are sometimes unable to hold back the young warriors, who are eager to distinguish themselves by killing an enemy, for this brings high status. "Anyone who has killed an enemy is proud to be addressed by this 'enemy's name'" (Tornay 1979:114).

Why War?

Anthropologists have offered a number of explanations for warfare in nonstate societies: (1) war as instinct, (2) war as sport and entertainment, (3) war as revenge, (4) war as a struggle for reproductive success, and (5) war as a struggle for material benefits.

1. *War as instinct:* This explanation proposes that we humans have innate aggressive tendencies that make us hate other people and want to kill them. Warfare is just one of the ways by which this tendency expresses itself (Wrangham and Peterson 1996).

   Comment: As a species, we are certainly capable of aggression on an unparalleled scale. But the capacity for collective violence does not explain the occurrence of war, because even warlike societies fight only occasionally, and some societies have no war at all. Thus, this peacetime–wartime cycle cannot be explained by the constants of human nature. Rather, the explanation for warfare must be sought in the variable conditions of society and culture that evoke violence, instead of reciprocity and cooperation (Knauft 1987, 1994).

2. *War as sport:* People enjoy the thrill of using martial arts, testing their courage, and risking their lives in combat.

   Comment: Combat is seldom entered into light-heartedly; the warriors need to "psych themselves up" with ritual dancing and singing and often set out only after they have subdued their fears by taking psychotropic drugs. Furthermore, warfare violently disrupts people's lives; it brings casualties and a general decline in the quality of life. Health deteriorates, people are afraid to leave the village, they bicker, and they are in constant fear of attack.

3. *War as revenge:* This is the most common explanation for going to war given by nonstate combatants. It is frequently accompanied by the belief that the spirits of the ancestors who have been killed in previous battles will not rest unless a relative of the

culprit is killed in turn. The desire for revenge keeps wars going generation after generation, whether the combatants win or lose.

Comment: Vengeance is undoubtedly a powerful motivation. But it does not have an unlimited power to keep wars going. As Brian Ferguson (1992:223) points out with respect to the Yanomami, combatants can declare that their ancestors have been avenged and stop fighting. Why do some societies manage isolated homicides without further vengeance, whereas others do not? Vengeance is thus an emic rationalization for continuing hostilities, but it does not explain why the hostilities got started or why old hostilities give way to new ones. As Ferguson explains,

> In my view, the Yanomami control revenge; they are not controlled by it. For people other than the victim's very closest kin, revenge is a real but highly malleable motivating factor. There are frequently many dormant reasons for seeking revenge, and if none exists, some can be made up. Vengeance is "good to think" and good to persuade. But a focus on vengeance will not elucidate why wars happen. (1995:354)

4. *War as a struggle for reproductive success:* Biological anthropologists explain nonstate warfare as a means of obtaining higher rates of reproductive success: Fierce warriors are more attractive as mates. They gain marital and reproductive benefits, and they have more wives and a greater number of surviving children. Napoleon Chagnon (1989, 1990) has attempted to show how this theory applies to warfare among the Yanomami, where men who have killed have more wives and children, on the average, than men who have not killed.

Comment: One of the problems is that those who "live by the spear" are more likely to "die by the spear." In fact, the man with the greatest number of kills among the Yanomami (22) died without leaving any descendents. This theory has also been shown to be inapplicable to the Cheyenne, one of the most warlike of the Indian peoples who lived in the region of the Great Plains. The fiercest Cheyenne warriors were young men who were indifferent to the risks of battle. Not only did they die young, but many also took vows of chastity in order to concentrate all their energies on war and so died without heirs (Moore 1990).

5. *War as a struggle for material benefits:* War is fought only to the extent that it provides material advantages for some of the combatants.

Comment: Among nonstate societies, warfare provides the winners with access to valuable resources, such as game animals and garden lands.

Of course, warfare also has its costs, principally in the form of combat deaths. Evidence suggests that nonstate warfare results in substantial immediate material gains related to the relief of population pressure. In his study of warfare among the Mae Enga of the western highlands of Papua New Guinea (Profile 10.3 on p. 173), Mervyn Meggitt estimates that aggressor groups succeeded in gaining significant amounts of enemy land in 75 percent of their wars. "Given that the initiation of warfare usually pays off for the aggressors, it is not surprising that the Mae count warfare as well worth the cost in human casualties" (1977:14–15). More general confirmation of this point has been supplied by Carol and Melvin Ember (1992, 1997), who have found in a study of 186 societies that preindustrial people mostly go to war to cushion or moderate the impact of unpredictable (rather than chronic) food shortages and that the victorious side almost always takes land or other resources from the losers. This is the point of view held by cultural materialists and the one that we consider to be the most useful explanation (Balee 1984; Biolsi 1984; Ferguson 1984, 1989a, 1989b, 1995; A. Johnson and Earle 1987; Keeley 1996; Shankman 1991; but see Knauft 1990 for a contrary view).

Band and village people go to war because they lack alternative solutions to problems of securing resources in response to subsistence needs and environmental depletion.

Yanomami Resource Scarcity

The theory relating meat to warfare among the Yanomami is this: As Yanomami villages grow, intensive hunting diminishes the availability of game nearby. Meat from large animals grows scarce, and people eat more small animals, insects, and larvae. The point of diminishing returns draws near. Increased tensions within and between villages lead to the breaking apart of villages before they permanently deplete the animal resources. Tensions also lead to the escalation of raiding, which disperses the Yanomami villages over a wide territory and also protects vital resources by creating "no man's lands," which function as game preserves (Harris 1984) (see Profile 10.2).

Outbreaks of violence are fueled by tensions resulting from scarcity of key resources.

Opponents of this theory point to the fact that the Yanomami show no clinical signs of protein deficiency. Moreover, they have shown that Yanomami villages with low levels of protein intake (36 grams) seem to engage in warfare just as frequently as those with high protein intake (75 grams) per adult. Finally, they point out that the other groups in the Amazon enjoy as much as 107 grams of animal protein per capita and still go to war frequently (Chagnon and Hames 1979; Lizot 1977, 1979).

Kenneth Good (1987, 1989), however, maintains that obtaining adequate supplies of meat is a constant preoccupation among the Yanomami and that meat is actually consumed only once or twice a week on the average. Because of fluctuations in the number and size of animals captured, many days actually pass during which the village has little or no available meat. On days when a large animal such as a tapir is caught, the consumption rate may rise to 250 or more grams per adult, but for weeks at a time, the consumption rate may not rise above 30 grams per adult per day.

Yanomami Trekking

The desire to maintain or increase their level of meat consumption explains trekking, an important feature of Yanomami life. Three or four times a year, the Yanomami move out of their village as a group and go on a prolonged trek through the deep forest that lasts a month or more. Indeed, counting the time that the villagers also spend at distant campsites, where they prepare new gardens, the Yanomami spend almost half the year away from their communal house. The desire for plant foods cannot provide the motive for going on a trek or planting new gardens, because the Yanomami could easily increase the size of their existing gardens and have enough bananas and plantains to feed themselves by staying at home. Although they gather wild fruits while trekking, meat remains their main preoccupation. Good (1989, 1995) has shown that while on the trek, the efficiency of hunting improves considerably and the hunters find more meat. Were it not for these long sojourns away from the village, game near the village would soon be completely wiped out. While on their treks (or shorter hunting trips), the villagers are constantly on the lookout for places to plant their new gardens. Once these gardens begin to bear bananas and plantains, the old communal house is abandoned and a new one is built near the new gardens.

Kenneth Good makes two crucial points regarding this move. First, plenty of forested land suitable for expanding the old gardens remains available near the old communal house. Second, the new communal house and gardens are not located near the old house and gardens but several kilometers away. Clearly,

then, the gardens are not moved in order to increase the efficiency of plant production, nor is the site of the house moved because it has become insect infested, decayed, or surrounded by human excrement (cf. Ferguson 1989b:250). (Why not simply build the new house on the other side of the old gardens?)

> Moving improves the accessibility of game animals that have been hunted out or frightened away from the old sites. Warfare among the Yanomami and other tropical forest peoples therefore can be readily understood as a form of competition between autonomous villages for access to the best hunting territories.

After all, we have no difficulty in understanding why modern nations go to war to maintain access to oil. Why, then, should we find it unlikely that the Yanomami go to war to maintain or increase access to game?

Warfare and Female Infanticide

It is generally accepted that slightly more boys than girls are born on a worldwide basis and that the average sex ratio at birth is about 105 males to 100 females. This imbalance, however, is much smaller than that found among the Yanomami, whose sex ratios between boys and girls averages about 132:100. What accounts for this large imbalance? High junior-age sex ratios favoring males are characteristic of societies with high levels of warfare (Table 10.1), and it probably reflects direct and indirect infanticide practiced against females more often than against males. (See Chapter 6 for a discussion of indirect infanticide.) There is a strong correlation between societies that admit to practicing infanticide and those that were actively engaged in warfare when a census was first made of them. In these societies, at least, female infanticide was more common than male infanticide (Divale and Harris 1976).

Table 10.1

Sex Ratios and Warfare

Young Males per 100 Females	
Warfare present	128
Stopped 5 to 25 years before census	113
Stopped over 25 years before census	109

Sources: Divale and Harris 1976; Divale et al. 1978; cf. Hirschfeld et al. 1978.

PROFILE 10.2   The Yanomami—Warfare and Game Animals

Location: Amazon rain forest of southern Venezuela and northern Brazil. Most of the population lives in the high-lands, away from the major rivers, except for about 5 percent who live in Venezuela along the Orinoco River.

Production: Slash-and-burn horticulture, mostly bananas and plantains along with frequent trekking to hunt and collect wild foods away from the communal house.

Population density: Villages ranging in size from 30 to 100 persons; sometimes growing to 200 before fission-ing; approximately one person per square mile.

Time of study: A number of researchers have worked with the Yanomami from 1964 to the present.

The Yanomami provide an important test of the theory that warfare has an infrastructural basis even among band and village groups that have very low population densities. The Yanomami, with a population density of less than one person per square mile, derive their main source of food calories, with little effort, from the plan-tains and banana trees that grow in their forest gardens.

The Yanomami burn the forest to get these gardens started, but bananas and plantains are perennials that provide high yields per unit of labor input for many consecutive years. Because the Yanomami live amid the world's greatest tropical forest, the little burning they do scarcely threatens to "eat up the trees." A typical Ya-nomami village has fewer than 100 people in it, a popula-tion that could easily grow enough bananas or plantains in nearby garden sites without ever having to move. Yet the Yanomami villages constantly break up into factions that move off into new territories.

Despite the apparent abundance of resources, the high level of warfare in some Yanomami territories is probably related to population pressure arising from re-source depletion. The resource in question is meat. The Yanomami lack domesticated sources of meat and must obtain their animal foods from hunting and collecting. Moreover, unlike many other inhabitants of the Amazon basin, the Yanomami traditionally have not had access to big-river fish and other aquatic animals that elsewhere in

Yanomami Warriors
Preparations for battle include body painting and "line-ups."

PROFILE 10.2 | The Yanomami—Warfare and Game Animals *(continued)*

Yanomami Grievances

Grievances between villages can be resolved with a chest-pounding duel like this one. This event is more like a sporting contest and results in no further animosity, unless someone is severely injured. Then, emotions will flare and more serious fights may ensue.

the Amazon region provide high-quality animal foods sufficient to supply villages inhabited by over 1,000 people. Of course, human beings can remain healthy on diets that lack animal foods; however, meat, fish, and other animal products contain compact packages of proteins, fats, minerals, and vitamins that have made them extremely appealing and efficient sources of nutrients throughout most of history and prehistory (Eaton et al. 1988).

According to Napoleon Chagnon (1997), the frequency and intensity of conflict in Yanomami villages increases in relation to village size. Chagnon attributes this to the failure of the political organization to effectively govern a large population; the political system—

with its powerless headman—cannot control the factions that occur in large villages. Chagnon attributes conflict to intense competition among men for wives; men attempt to acquire more than one wife to increase their status. Some men succeed in obtaining several wives, whereas others have none. (The shortage of women is compounded by female infanticide, described later.) The Yanomami say they fight to capture women and to take revenge for past killings, but these "reasons for fighting" do not explain the ecological context in which warfare takes place. The Yanomami are an expanding population in a restricted environment with resources that are rapidly depleting.

▨ Universal Pattern • Warfare among the Yanomami

Infrastructure	Structure	Superstructure
Increased population pressure and imbalance in sex ratios due to infanticide. Competition over faunal resources. Competition over access to steel tools.	Weak leadership ("powerless headman") unable to contain factions in large communities. Polygyny (intensifying shortage of women). Marriage exchange and ceremonial feasting to cement alliances between groups.	Male supremacist complex: • Preference for male babies • Preference for fierce warriors Rewarding warriors with mates and sex. Endo-cannibalism (ingesting ashes of the deceased) to revenge the dead.

A plausible reason for the killing and neglect of female children is that success in nonindustrial warfare depends on the size of male combat teams; having more males is desirable because it increases the group's ability to protect its women and children from raids by neighboring villages.

Where weapons are muscle-powered clubs, spears, and bows and arrows, victory will belong to the group that has the largest number of aggressive males. Because infrastructure limits the number of people who can be reared by band and village societies, war-making band and village societies are compelled to rear more males than females. As we have seen, this culturally induced scarcity of women accounts for the frequency of fights over women—which the Yanomami identify as the prime cause of war. Unless the depletion of game animals is stabilized or reversed, warfare and female infanticide will continue to be practiced.

Warfare and Trade Goods

The Yanomami have long been misrepresented as a people whose culture remained virtually free of Western influences and who had remained outside the orbit of the capitalist world system until the 1960s. For some interior groups, this isolation was said to have lasted even into the 1980s. A study carried out by R. Brian Ferguson (1995) has demonstrated that in fact the Yanomami have a long history of contact with gold miners, missionaries, travelers, and traders. Ferguson accepts the general principle that nonstate warfare is a means of competing for scarce resources, but in his view, what the Yanomami are competing for is not game but Western trade goods, specifically what is known as "steel": machetes, axes, pots, and fishhooks.

The Yanomami villages strive to monopolize access to providers of Western goods; they use pleas, threats, and deceptions to control the flow of "steel." Western manufactures are passed along from village to village through networks of kinship. An incomplete listing of goods distributed by the Catholic mission at Iye-wei-teri for 1960 to 1972 includes 3,850 machetes, 620 axes, 2,850 pots, 759,000 fishhooks, and large quantities of other items. Most of these goods were traded to more remote villages (Ferguson 1992:209).

An important point in the theory that relates warfare to trade goods is that when Yanomami villages split and move, it is generally in the direction that gets them closer to the sources of "steel."

Ferguson accepts that game depletions are responsible for village fissioning, but he believes that the desire for steel is also a driving force in warfare. A struggle for hunting territories and a struggle for Western trade goods may be going on at the same time.

It is quite possible that the level of warfare among the Yanomami was much lower before they had Western trade goods as well as hunting territories to fight over.

Warfare, the Politics of Prestige, and the "Big Man" System

Throughout Melanesia and the South Pacific, high population density gives rise to a new pattern of leadership known as the "big man" system. Most of the prime land is under continuous cultivation, and people have to grow their crops on small, intensely utilized plots of land. The survival of each local descent group depends directly on its ability to keep neighboring groups from seizing its land at the first sign of weakness. To increase their defensive posture, local descent groups establish alliances through marriage exchanges, feasting, and a system of debt and credit. A big man, who stands at the head of each local descent group, is in a ranked position of prestige relative to other powerful big men in the society.

A **rank society** has equal access to economic resources and power, but social groups have unequal access to status positions and prestige.

The leader's position is based on his ability to extend his influence in advancing alliances with other descent groups and in settling disputes.

A **"big man"** is a local entrepreneur who successfully mobilizes and manipulates wealth on behalf of his group in order to host large feasts that enhance his status and rank relative to other big men in the region. He is a man of prestige and renown but has no formal authority or power nor more wealth.

Melanesian groups such as the Mae Enga of Papua New Guinea (Profile 10.3), who live in a densely populated environment with frequent warfare, attempt to neutralize the external threat from other Enga lineage groups by doing the following:

- Maintaining a large unified group that shows strength in numbers, which makes others afraid to attack them
- Collaborating in accumulating food and wealth that is given away at ceremonies to increase their prestige and obligate other groups to reciprocate

Location: The Western Highlands of New Guinea

Production: Year-round sweet potato cultivation and pigs, with up to 49 percent of agriculture produce going to feed pigs

Population Density: 85 to 250 persons per square mile

Time of Research: The 1950s and 1960s

The Mae Enga are similar to the Tsembaga Maring, except that Enga population density is double that of the Tsembaga; land is more scarce and warfare is more frequent and oriented to seizing prime land from defeated groups (Meggitt 1977). Each household is responsible for its own subsistence but is part of a larger patrilineal subclan consisting of about 90 members, which has ceremonial and political functions. Households have heavy demands placed on them for contributions for bridewealth payments and mortuary payments to honor ancestors. These payments are used to host feasts that reflect back on the subclan and its "big man," who competes with other big men for recognition at the clan level. The clan, which averages 350 people (Meggitt 1965), is a corporate group with rights to land. It owns an ancestral dance ground, where ceremonial exchanges are made with other clans.

According to Mervyn Meggitt, when the population density of a growing clan exceeds 250 persons per square mile, people become increasingly land hungry (1977:31). When disputes arise about garden boundaries, the big men from neighboring clans meet to work

Melanesian Pig Redistribution

Leaders, known as "big men," show their generosity and thereby gain prestige by mobilizing resources for lavish feasts.

out the details to attack a third more vulnerable group and take over their land. A group's ability to defend its territory and seize new territory depends on how large a fighting force it can organize, based on the number of allies it can recruit. This in turn depends on the prestige and success of the clan's big man in amassing pigs to be given away at ceremonial exchanges, which puts him in a position to negotiate with neighboring clans on matters of war and peace.

Universal Pattern • The Mae Enga

Infrastructure	Structure	Superstructure
Increased population pressure and intensification of production. Population density of 85 to 250 per square mile. Environment has become degraded by intensive agriculture.	A big man represents the clan in the local political economy by hosting ceremonial events. A big man acts as entrepreneur who accumulates wealth through exchange that brings prestige to group. A big man has influence but lacks power to coerce.	Strong patrilineal patrilocal ties are valued for defense.
Faunal resources have been depleted. Domesticated pigs provide only source of protein for humans. Root crops are grown in permanent fertilized gardens to feed both humans and pigs. Land is kept in constant production.	Permanent settlements based on patrilineal descent are defensive units that protect members from outsiders. Patrilineal clan members pay for ceremonial events that both unify the group and elevate group prestige to attract allies.	Generosity is basis for acquiring prestige.
Land scarcity creates competition that leads to warfare.	Local clans are potential enemies. Conflict is diffused through negotiation, exchange, and ceremony. Losers in war must relocate to less desirable territory.	Successful big men are intense competitors for prestige and regional influence but are unable to gain economic control beyond their own clans.

■ Being strong and wealthy so that they will be attractive as allies for defensive purposes, turning neighboring groups into either friends or outnumbered enemies who will be afraid to attack (A. Johnson 1989).

To achieve and maintain alliances to protect their boundaries, local descent groups must be willing to comply with their big man's requests for food and wealth so that he can gain prestige and advertise his group's attractiveness as an ally.

The Melanesian big man system is similar to that of the Kwakiutl (see Chapter 7) in that leaders compete to achieve a high rank by hosting elaborate feasts and giveaways. For the Kwakiutl, the big man manages stored goods and hosts feasts to gain prestige in order to secure resources during times of regional scarcity. In Melanesia, where there are no storageable resources and land is scarce, the big man hosts feasts to gain prestige, build alliances, and increase the group's military strength to deter neighboring groups from attacking.

SUMMARY
and *Questions to Think About*

1. Orderly relationships among the individuals and domestic groups in band and village societies are maintained without governments and law enforcement specialists. This is possible because of small size, predominance of kinship and reciprocity, and egalitarian access to vital resources. Public opinion is the chief source of law and order in these societies.

2. Individual or nuclear family ownership of land is absent among hunting-and-gathering bands and most village peoples. However, even in the most egalitarian societies, people privately own some items. Still, the prevalence of the reciprocal mode of exchange and the absence of anonymous price markets render theft unnecessary and impractical.

3. The major threat to law and order among band and village societies stems from the tendency of domestic and kinship groups to escalate conflicts in support of real or imagined injuries to one of their members. Such support does not depend on abstract principles of right and wrong but on the probable outcome of a particular course of action in the face of public opinion. The Inuit song duel illustrates how public opinion can be tested and used to end conflicts between individuals who belong to different domestic and kinship groups.

4. Witchcraft accusations also give public opinion an opportunity to identify and punish persistent violators of the rules of reciprocity and other troublemakers. The shamans acts as the mouthpiece of the community. Under stressful conditions, witchcraft accusations may build to epidemic proportions and become a threat to the maintenance of law and order.

5. Headmanship reflects the egalitarian nature of the institutions of law and order in band and village societies. Headmen can do little more than

harangue and plead with people for support. They lack physical and material means of enforcing their decisions. Their success rests on their ability to intuit public opinion. As exemplified by the Nuer, avoidance of blood feud can be facilitated by the payment of compensation and by appealing to ritual chiefs, who have even less political power than headmen.

6. Other instances of nonkin political organization take the form of voluntary associations or sodalities such as men's and women's clubs, secret societies, and age-grade sets. However, all these nonkin modes of political organization remain rather rudimentary and are overshadowed by the pervasive networks of kinship alliances based on marriage and descent, which constitute the "glue" of band and village societies.

7. Warfare concerns the maintenance of law and order between separate societies and cultures. Although simple hunter-gatherers engage in warfare, warfare is usually more intense among sedentary societies.

8. Warfare cannot be explained solely as a consequence of innate aggression, an enjoyable sport, a thirst for revenge, or a struggle for reproductive success. Warfare is a particular form of organized activity and only one of the many ways in which cultures handle aggression.

9. The causes of war in band and village societies are rooted in problems associated with production and reproduction and almost always involve attempts to protect or improve standards of living.

10. Even where population densities are very low, as among the Yanomami, problems of depletion and declining efficiency may exist. Thus warfare

11. Among patrilocal band and village societies, warfare could have the effect of controlling population growth through the encouragement of direct and indirect female infanticide. Evidence for population pressure as a cause of nonstate warfare consists of cross-cultural studies that correlate unbalanced sex ratios with active warfare.

12. Warfare among the Yanomami appears to be primarily a struggle for access to game and hunting territories. The importance of game can be gauged by the fact that the Yanomami frequently split up their villages and move to new and distant garden sites even though they still have plenty of additional garden land nearby. The prominence of trekking by the Yanomami also indicates the importance of game in their lives.

13. New data, however, show that besides access to hunting territories, trade for Western manufactures may account for the special intensity and high frequency of Yanomami warfare, especially in recent decades.

14. The "big man" system found throughout Melanesia is a political system based on rank, feasting, and alliance that regulates relations between local descent groups in an area of high population density and intense warfare.

Questions to Think About

1. What role does public opinion play in mediating disputes in prestate societies? How is this forum different from our own legal system?

2. What are the functions of a headman, and what are the limitations on his power?

3. What accounts for the relatively peaceful nature of the Mehinacu?

4. What explanations do anthropologists give for Yanomami warfare?

5. What are the functions of a "big man"? What is his role in maintaining regional relations of war and peace?

THROUGH THE LENS
of Cultural Materialism

Conformity and Conflict • Reading Twenty-Six

Life without Chiefs

Marvin Harris

During nearly all of human prehistory, our ancestors lived in small, largely nomadic hunting-and-gathering bands containing about 30 to 50 people. It was in this social context that human nature evolved. It has been only in the last 2,000 years that people have lived in societies with formal political institutions and social inequities.

- *Headmen* are associated with hunting-and-gathering societies marked by social equality and reciprocal exchange.

- *"Big men"* are associated with slightly larger horticultural societies that employ regional redistributive exchange. They are compensated purely with admiration in proportion to their success in hosting large feasts.

- *Chiefs* are associated with concentrated agriculture, production of surplus, and regional management and redistribution of resources, which leads to opportunities for political control. They receive donations and control large storehouses to be used in times of scarcity and to fund large communal projects, such as war and long-distance trade. This enables a chief to rule over a large political community, and his control over abundant har-

vests elevates his status to a hereditary position, complete with an insignia of high rank, respect, and a more lavish lifestyle that sets him apart from his followers.

Infrastructure

- In small-scale societies, low population density facilitates freedom of access to natural resources and reciprocity to meet basic survival needs.

- Horticulture emerged within the last several thousand years of human existence. Higher yields were sufficient to support larger settlements and political regulation was required to oversee production and redistribution beyond the domestic unit. "Big men" and later chiefs emerged to regulate the ceremonial flow of goods to and from a central office.

Structure

- Our ancestors got along quite well for the greater part of prehistory without a paramount chief. With 50 people in a band or 150 in a village, people knew one another intimately and shared freely.

- Traditionally, individuals who were lucky in collecting food one day needed a handout the next. So the best way to secure against a "rainy day" was to be generous. "The greater the risk, the greater the extent of sharing."

- Leadership positions in band and village societies are assumed by headmen. When something needs to be done, the headman initiates and works harder than anyone else. He sets an example not only for hard work but also for generosity. Headmen, however, lack the power to compel others to obey their orders. They have no formal authority and can only persuade, not command.

- When conditions permit, several would-be headmen vie with each other to hold the most lavish feast and to redistribute the most food and valuables. When this occurs, leaders are referred to as *big men*.

- The more abundant the harvest and the less perishable the crop, the greater the potential for endowing a leader with power. In times of scarcity, people come to him expecting to be fed; in return, he can call on those with special skills to make cloth, pots, canoes, or a fine house for his own use.

- Eventually, the redistributor no longer needs to work harder than everyone else to maintain his big man status. Management of harvest surplus and large giveaways are sufficient to validate his status. His dominion is no longer a small, autonomous village but a large political community. At this point, the big man becomes a chief.

- Trobrianders had hereditary chiefs who held sway over more than a dozen villages containing several thousand people. Only chiefs could wear certain shell ornaments as the insignia of high rank, and commoners were forbidden to stand or sit in a position that put a chief's head at a lower elevation. The chiefs validated their status by storing and redistributing large quantities of yams acquired through donations from their brothers-in-law at harvest time. Supported by voluntary donations, chiefs enjoyed a lifestyles that increasingly set them apart from their followers. They could build bigger and finer houses for themselves, eat and dress more sumptuously, and enjoy the sexual favors and personal services of several wives.

- The emergence of hierarchical groups is not part of our human nature. Increasingly stratified forms of leadership result from modes of economic exchange. Cultural conditions such as population density, production of storable surplus, and management of food distribution led to the emergence of increasingly stratified leadership.

Superstructure

- Generosity is taken for granted in small-scale societies. Saying "thank you" is considered rude because it suggests that one has calculated the amount of a gift and that one did not expect the donor to be generous.

- Egalitarian redistributors are compensated with admiration in proportion to their success in giving feasts. They personally contribute more than anybody else, and ask little or nothing for their effort.

- Chiefs are not only admired but also control strategic resources that give them advantages in wealth and lifestyle.

CHAPTER 11

ORIGINS OF CHIEFDOMS AND THE STATE

Liliuokalani was the last reigning queen of the Hawaiian islands (1891 to 1893).

I n this chapter, we contrast the forms of political life characteristic of band and village societies with those of chiefdoms and states. How did the relatively egalitarian societies that once prevailed throughout the world give way to class-structured societies that rank people high and low and divide them into rulers and ruled? In seeking the answer to the origin of states, we will take account of both structural and infrastructural factors, such as risk management, technology, warfare, and trade, that present political leaders with opportunities for control.

The Evolution of Political Systems

As we have seen in other chapters, there is a strong positive relationship between population growth and socioeconomic complexity. Population growth has two key consequences for the *subsistence economy:*

- As resources are depleted, people turn to more costly alternatives that modify the environment and improve productivity through technology and resource management.

- As landscapes become crowded, there is constant potential for food shortages and aggressive competition over the most desired resources. To overcome these threats, careful management of food redistribution and defense is required.

As the *political economy* evolves, a *surplus* (or tax) is mobilized from the subsistence economy in order to finance economic, military, and religious institutions that in their more elaborated forms are run by non-food producers. These institutions are used in turn to support and justify elite ownership of the region's productive resources, especially improved agricultural land.

As outlined in Johnson and Earle (2000), growth in the political economy results in three interrelated evolutionary processes:

- Intensification
- Political integration
- Social stratification

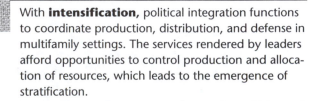

With **intensification,** political integration functions to coordinate production, distribution, and defense in multifamily settings. The services rendered by leaders afford opportunities to control production and allocation of resources, which leads to the emergence of stratification.

Solomon Island Chiefs
They prefer to be called chiefs *rather than* mumis, *as of old.*

From "Big Man" Systems into Chiefdoms

As noted in the last chapter, headmen often function as intensifiers of production and as redistributors. They get their relatives to work harder, and they collect and then give away the extra product. A village may have several headmen, each with his own group of kin-based followers. So-called big men emerge where technological and ecological conditions encourage intensification, and leaders living in the same village become rivals. They vie with one another to hold the most lavish feasts and to redistribute the greatest amount of valuables. The most successful redistributors earn the reputation of being "big men" and gain prestige for themselves and their kin group (Hayden 1993a, 1995) (see Profile 11.1).

Where big man systems evolve into **chiefdoms,** changes take place in these areas:

- *Size of the population*—Chiefdoms are associated with larger communities.

- *Leadership*—Chiefdoms are based on stratification, with a hierarchy of offices at the regional and community level.

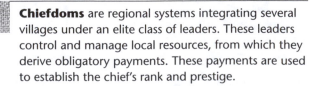

Chiefdoms are regional systems integrating several villages under an elite class of leaders. These leaders control and manage local resources, from which they derive obligatory payments. These payments are used to establish the chief's rank and prestige.

The sizes of chiefdoms can vary greatly. At the lower end, chiefdoms such as the Trobrianders are very similar to big man systems; at the upper end, chiefdoms such

PROFILE 11.1 | The Suiai—"Big Men" and Warfare

Location: Bougainville in the Solomon Islands, Papua New Guinea

Production: Horticulture, primarily sweet potatoes and yams

Density: 34 persons per square mile

Time of Study: 1938 to 1939

Among the Siuai, a big man is called a *mumi,* and to achieve mumi status is every youth's highest ambition. A young man proves himself capable of becoming a mumi by working hard and by carefully restricting his consumption of meat and coconuts. Eventually, he impresses his wife, children, and near relatives with the seriousness of his intentions, and they vow to help him prepare for his first feast. If the feast is a success, his circle of supporters widens and he sets to work readying an even greater display of generosity.

He aims next at the construction of a men's clubhouse, in which his male followers can lounge about and in which guests can be entertained and fed. Another feast is held at the consecration of the clubhouse, and if this is also a success, the circle of people willing to work for him grows still larger, and he will begin to be spoken of as a mumi. Larger and larger feasts mean that the mumi's demands on his supporters become more irksome. Although they grumble about how hard they have to work, they remain loyal as long as their mumi maintains or increases his renown as a "great provider."

Finally, the time comes for the new mumi to challenge the others who have risen before him. He does this at a *muminai* feast, where a tally is kept of all the pigs, coconut pies, and sago-almond puddings given away by the host mumi and his followers to the guest mumi and his followers. If the guest mumi cannot reciprocate in a year or so with a feast at least as lavish as that of his challenger, he suffers a great social humiliation, and his fall from mumihood is immediate. In deciding on whom to challenge, a mumi must be very careful. He tries to choose a guest whose downfall will increase his own reputation, but he must avoid one whose capacity to retaliate exceeds his own.

At the end of a successful feast, the greatest of mumis still faces a lifetime of personal toil and dependence on the moods and inclinations of his followers. Mumihood does not confer the power to coerce others into doing one's bidding, nor does it elevate one's standard of living above anyone else's. In fact, because giving things away is the essence of mumihood, great mumis

may even consume less meat and other delicacies than an ordinary, undistinguished Siuai. The Kaoka, another Solomon Island group reported on by H. Ian Hogbin (1964:66), have this saying: "The giver of the feast takes the bones and the stale cakes; the meat and the fat go to the others."

At one great feast attended by 1,100 people, the host mumi, whose name was Soni, gave away 32 pigs plus a large quantity of sago-almond puddings. Soni and his closest followers, however, went hungry. "We shall eat Soni's renown," his followers said.

Formerly, the mumis were as famous for their ability to get men to fight for them as they were for their ability to get men to work for them. Warfare had been suppressed by the colonial authorities long before Douglas Oliver carried out his extensive study, but the memory of mumi war leaders was still vivid among the Siuai. As one old man put it, "In the olden times there were greater mumi than there are today. Then they were fierce and relentless war leaders. They laid waste to the countryside and their clubhouses were lined with the skulls of people they had slain" (Oliver 1955:411). In singing praises of their mumis, the generation of pacified Siuai call them "warriors" and "killers of men and pigs."

Oliver's informants told him that mumis had more authority in the days when warfare was still practiced. Some mumi war leaders even kept one or two prisoners, who were treated like slaves and forced to work in the mumi's family gardens, and people could not talk "loud and slanderously against their mumis without fear of punishment." This fits theoretical expectations, because the ability to redistribute meat and other valuables goes hand in hand with the ability to attract a following of warriors, equip them for combat, and reward them with spoils of battle.

Rivalry among Bougainville's war-making mumis appeared to have been leading toward an islandwide political organization when the first European voyagers arrived. According to Oliver (1955:420), "For certain periods of time many neighboring villages fought together so consistently that there emerged a pattern of war-making regions, each more or less internally peaceful and each containing one outstanding mumi whose war activities provided internal social cohesion." These mumis enjoyed regional fame, but their prerogatives remained rudimentary. For example, the mumis had to provide their warriors with women brought into the clubhouses and with gifts of pork and other delicacies. Said one old warrior, "If the mumi didn't furnish us with women we were angry. All night long we would copulate and still want more. It

(continued)

PROFILE 11.1 **The Suiai—"Big Men" and Warfare** *(continued)*

was the same with eating. The clubhouse used to be filled with food, and we ate and ate and never had enough. Those were wonderful times" (Oliver 1955:415). Furthermore, the mumi who wanted to lead a war party had to

be prepared personally to pay an indemnity for any of his men who were killed in battle and to furnish a pig for each man's funeral feast.

Universal Pattern • The Suiai

Infrastructure	Structure	Superstructure
Slash-and-burn horticulture with pigs used as domestic animals.	Regional network of alliances to secure peace and gain allies in case of war.	Successful big men enjoy regional fame.
Crowded landscape comprised of villages.	A big man lacks power to coerce others and does not have higher standard of living. He gains regional prestige and rank when his supporters are willing to work for him to host elaborate feasts.	A big man owns prestige goods that signify his status.
Competition among villages for most desirable land.	A big man gives wealth away at feasts to gain rank and attract following of warriors for combat.	A big man who cannot reciprocate by hosting feasts suffers humiliation and downfall.

as Hawaii approximate states. As the size increases, the distinctions between leaders and followers widen; big men have to build up power by attracting personal followers (see Box 11.1), whereas a chief comes to power that is vested in an inherited office. Big men who are successful redistributors are hard to distinguish from the leaders of small chiefdoms. Whereas big men must

achieve and constantly validate their status by recurrent feasts, chiefs have **ascribed status** and hold their offices even if they are temporarily unable to provide their followers with generous redistributions.

 Ascribed status is determined for a person at birth.

BOX 11.1 **"Big Man" versus Chief**

"Big Man"

The big man's status is achieved through his ability to attract followers. His position is ranked among other big men according to prestige.

A big man's followers provide him with wealth that he in turn redistributes through feasts and a system of debt and credit. He must maintain the loyalty of his followers because he can be replaced if he is unable to continue to affirm his status through redistribution.

A big man does not have an improved standard of living. He may even end up with less, because of the importance of generosity. He wears shell ornaments during a feast, but once it is over, he reverts to living like everyone else.

In the past, big men were fierce war leaders who rewarded their warriors with the spoils of battle and compensated the families of those who died in battle.

Chief

A chief holds an inherited office determined by virtue of his membership in a high-ranking lineage.

A chief's position is relatively permanent; he maintains his office even if he is unable to temporarily provide generously for his followers, but he can be deposed by a more powerful chief through defeat in war.

A chief lives better than commoners. He has more access to resources than anyone else. He is allowed to have many wives, he stores surplus yams, and he owns prestige valuables that are used as political currency to compensate people for their services.

In the past, the chief used his storage facilities to support warriors on long-distance expeditions, expanding the territories under the chiefdom's control.

Chiefs tend to live better than commoners; unlike headmen, they do not always keep only "the bones and the stale cakes" for themselves. Yet in the long run, chiefs too must validate their titles by waging successful war, obtaining trade goods, and giving away food and other valuables to their followers (Earle 1991, 1997; Hayden 1995).

Infrastructural and Structural Aspects of Political Control

The evolution of chiefdoms—and later states—depends on the leader's ability to control production and exchange and to mobilize resources to finance various institutions. These resources consist of food staples and wealth in the form of precious artifacts (Johnson and Earle 2000; Earle 1997).

A chief takes advantage of the opportunity to control resources by monopolizing the management of production and exchange and extracting a surplus that becomes the basis of his power. Four kinds of opportunities for control can be identified:

- *Risk management.* As we saw with the Kwakiutl, there is always a danger of regional food scarcity when there is high population density. Production of a food surplus provides a safeguard against starvation.

- *Capital investment.* As people produce more food, technology helps offset the rising labor costs of increased agricultural output. Irrigation, as we saw in the case of Luts'un, permits intensified production through the management of water, which provides an opportunity to produce surpluses that support local chiefs.

- *Warfare.* For regional integration, warfare has to be brought under control. Although warfare alone does not necessarily lead to stratification, it enables chiefdoms to expand by incorporating and controlling populations that provide surplus production.

- *Large-scale trade.* Long-distance trade requires political coordination and management to construct roads or sea-going canoes. Trade provides access to valuable raw materials and storable food resources (to reduce the risk of food shortages), and it builds alliances that manage regional relations of war and peace.

Chiefdoms similar to the Trobrianders are found throughout the world (see Profile 11.2). For example, the political organization of the Cherokee of Tennessee (and of other southeastern woodland American Indi-

Trobriand Islanders Reenact War Dance
In the past, Trobriand armies conquered people from faraway islands.

ans) bears a striking resemblance to the Trobrianders' redistribution–warfare–trade–chief complex. The Cherokee, like the Trobrianders, were matrilineal, and they waged external warfare over long distances. At the center of the principal settlements was a large, circular *council house*, where the council of chiefs discussed issues involving several villages and where redistributive feasts were held. The council of chiefs had a supreme chief who was the central figure in the Cherokee redistributive network. At harvest time, a large crib, identified as the *chief's granary*, was erected in each field. "To this each family carries and deposits a certain quantity according to his ability or inclination, or none at all if he so chooses." The chief's granaries functioned as "a public treasury to fly to for succor" in the case of crop failure, as a source of food "to accommodate strangers, or travellers," and as a military store "when they go forth on hostile expeditions." Although every citizen enjoyed "the right of free and public access," commoners had to acknowledge that the store really belonged to the supreme chief, who had "an exclusive right and ability to distribute comfort and blessings to the necessitous" (Bartram 1958:326).

Location: A group of small coral islands about 120 miles north of the western tip of New Guinea

Production: Intensive agriculture (yams and taro) and fishing, with regional specialization in fishing, agriculture, and craft production

Density: Ranging from 60 to 100 persons per square mile; mostly scattered along shallow coastal lagoons and the interior

Time of Study: Early 1900s and 1960s

The difference between big men and chiefs can be illustrated with the case of the Trobriand Islanders (also discussed in Chapter 7). Trobrianders have a pervasive concept of rank; the society is divided into elite and commoner matrilineal clans and subclans, through which collective title to garden land is inherited. The chiefs of high-ranking subclans compete among themselves to improve their regional position through the accumulation of wealth. The chief of the most powerful subclan assumes the position of "paramount chief." Unlike the Siuai mumis, the Trobriand chiefs occupy a hereditary office and can be deposed only through defeat in war. Bronislaw Malinowski (1920) describes a paramount chief who had control over more than a dozen villages, containing several thousand people. Only chiefs can wear certain shell ornaments as the insignia of high rank, and no commoner can stand or sit in a position that puts a chief's head at a lower elevation than anyone else's. Malinowski tells of seeing all the people present in the village of Bwoytalu drop from their verandas as if blown down by a hurricane at the sound of a drawn-out cry announcing the arrival of an important chief.

The Trobrianders attribute the distinctions of rank in their society to wars of conquest carried out long ago. Malinowski (1920) reports that the Trobrianders are keen on fighting and conduct systematic and relentless wars, venturing across the open ocean in their canoes to trade—or, if need be, to fight—with the people of islands over 100 miles away. But the Trobriand chief's power rests ultimately on his ability to play the role of "great provider." Chiefs acquire up to a dozen or more wives and are entitled to obligatory gifts of yams—which, along with kula valuables (see Chapter 7, "Trade in the Kula Ring"), represent prestige and political currency—from each of his wives' brothers. These yams are delivered to the chief's village and displayed on special yam racks. Some of the yams are then distributed in elaborate feasts, at which the chief validates his position as a great provider; the remainder are used to feed canoe-building specialists, artisans, magicians, and family servants who thereby become partially dependent on the chief's power. In former times, the yam stores also furnished the food for launching long-distance kula trading expeditions among friendly groups and raids against enemies (Brunton 1975; Malinowski 1935).

Even though the Trobrianders fear and respect their chiefs, they are still a long way from being a state society. Living on islands, the Trobrianders are not free to spread out; their population density has risen, but there are few opportunities for control. For example, the chiefs cannot monopolize enough of the production system to acquire great wealth and power. Perhaps one reason for this is that Trobriand agriculture lacks cereal grains. Because yams rot after four or five months (unlike rice or maize), the Trobriand great provider cannot manipulate people through dispensing food year-round, nor can he support a permanent police military garrison out of his stores. Another important factor is the open resources of the lagoons and ocean from which the Trobrianders derive their protein supply. The Trobriand chief cannot cut off access to these resources and hence can not exercise permanent coercive political control over subordinates.

Universal Pattern • The Trobriand Islanders

Infrastructure	Structure	Superstructure
Group of islands that specialize in agriculture and have abundant supply of fish.	Elite and commoner matrilineal clans and subclans provide collective title to garden land.	Chiefs wear shell ornaments as insignia of high rank.
Land is controlled by kin groups that allocate farmland to lineage members. No one is denied access to land; land is given on loan, when needed.	Chiefs of most powerful subclans compete for status through accumulation of wealth.	Chief's power is symbolized by his ability to be "great provider."
	Chiefs occupy hereditary office and can be deposed only through defeat in war.	Chief's power lacks permanence because of his inability to dispense food year-round or deprive people of access to marine resources.

The Origins of States

Under certain conditions, large chiefdoms evolved into states. The state is a form of politically centralized and **stratified society**, whose governing elite have the power to compel subordinates to pay taxes, render services, and obey the law (Carneiro 1981:69).

 A **stratified society** arranges statuses or subgroups according to socially superior and inferior ranks that reproduce inequality.

The transformation of chiefdoms into states first occurred when dense populations came to subsist on intensifiable forms of agriculture, especially on the cultivation of staple grains such as rice, wheat, barley, and maize, which could be stored for a year or more without becoming inedible. In addition, early state formation generally occurred when the dissatisfied factions of stratified chiefdoms who sought to flee from the growing power of paramount chiefs found themselves blocked by similarly stratified chiefdoms in adjacent territories or by features of the environment that required them to adopt a new and less efficient mode of production and to suffer a drastic decline in their standard of living. This condition is known as circumscription.

The significance of circumscription is that factions of discontented members of a chiefdom cannot escape from their elite overlords without suffering a sharp decline in their standard of living.

Many of the earliest states were circumscribed by their dependence on modes of production that required irrigation and were associated with fertile river valleys surrounded by arid or semiarid plains or mountains. But circumscription can also be caused by the transformation of low-yielding habitats into higher-yielding ones as a result of a long-term investment in the mounding, ditching, draining, and irrigating of a chiefdom's territory (Dickson 1987).

Three infrastructural conditions are instrumental in the transformation of a chiefdom to a state:

- Population increase
- Intensive agriculture with storable staples
- Circumscription that restricts migration

Given these infrastructural conditions, certain changes in a chiefdom's political and economic structure become likely:

1. The larger and denser the population and the greater the surplus harvested, the greater the ability of the elites to support craft specialists, palace guards, and a standing professional army.

2. The more powerful the elite, the greater its ability to engage in long-distance warfare and trade and to conquer, incorporate, and exploit new populations and territories.

3. The more powerful the elite, the more stratified its redistribution of trade wealth and harvest surplus.

4. The wider the territorial scope of political control and the larger the society's investment in the mode of production, the less opportunity a person has to flee and the less a person gains by fleeing.

Soon, contributions to the central store cease to be voluntary—they become taxes. Access to the farmlands and natural resources cease to be rights—they become dispensations. Food producers cease being the chief's followers—they become peasants who labor on their lands far from the ruler's palaces. Redistributors cease being chiefs but become kings, and chiefdoms turn into states (Box 11.2).

As the governing elite compels subordinates to pay taxes and tribute, provide military or labor services, and obey laws, the entire process of intensification, expansion, conquest, stratification, and centralization is amplified.

Control is continuously increased, or *amplified*, through a form of change known as *positive feedback* (Box 11.3). Where certain modes of production could sustain sufficient numbers of peasant farmers and warriors, this feedback process recurrently resulted in states conquering other states and in the emergence of preindustrial empires involving vast territories inhabited by millions of people (Carneiro

BOX 11.2 | Warning!

The transition from egalitarean village to chiefdom to state presented here is a "model" of how these political and economic systems might have evolved from each other. All transitions leading to the first states did not necessarily follow the same sequence. But it seems likely that some of them did. Thus the model should be regarded as hypothetical, awaiting the test of more empirical evidence.

BOX 11.3 | Two Kinds of Feedback

Negative: Changes are checked when certain limits are reached. Initial conditions tend to be restored.
Example: Household temperature stays slightly above or slightly below the level set on a thermostat.

Positive: Changes are not checked. Each successive change increases or amplifies the tendency to change.
Example: A microphone picks up the sound of its own loudspeaker and sends the signal back through its amplifier, which sends a stronger signal to the loudspeaker, resulting in a louder and louder squeal.

1981; R. Cohen 1984a; Feinman and Neitzel 1984; Fried 1978).

Once the first states came into existence, they themselves constituted barriers against the flight of people who sought to preserve egalitarian systems.

With states as neighbors, egalitarian peoples found themselves increasingly drawn into warfare and compelled to increase production and give their redistributor war chiefs more and more power in order to prevail against the expansionist tendencies of their neighbors.

Thus, most states of the world were produced by a great diversity of specific historical and ecological conditions (Fried 1967). Once states come into existence, they tend to spread, engulf, and overwhelm nonstate peoples (Carneiro 1970; R. Cohen 1984a; Haas 1982; Hommon 1986; Kirch 1984; MacNeish 1981; Service 1975; Upham 1990).

Would the Hawaiian *polities* (i.e., political organizations) have achieved a more stable and centralized state if their political history had not been interrupted by the landings of Europeans on their shores? According to the theory presented, the answer is no (see Profile 11.3). It was only as a result of that contact that a unified Hawaiian kingdom was established in 1810.

All the conditions for state formation were present with one exception: The Hawaiian chiefs had no storable staples that could be used during times of drought or warfare. They did have storehouses for root crops such as taro and yams, which they used to sustain their followers during emergencies. But unlike grains, these root crops cannot be stored for a whole year or more.

Hawaiian Chief Brings Gifts to Captain Cook
Hawaiian chiefs were able to amass large quantities of wealth and control a sizable labor force. They, however, lacked food resources that could be stored for long periods of time.

David Malo, a nineteenth-century Hawaiian chief, noted that the storehouses of the Hawaiian kings were designed as a means of keeping people contented so that they would not desert them: "As the rat will not desert the pantry, so the people will not desert the king while they think there is food in his storehouse" (D'Altroy and Earle 1985:192). Lacking staple grains that provided the nutritional and energetic basis for the emergence of states elsewhere, the Hawaiian chiefs were unable to sustain large numbers of followers, especially during times of food shortage. Thus, no ali'i nui was able to achieve an enduring advantage over his rivals.

Ideology as a Source of Power

Large populations, anonymity, and vast differences in wealth make the maintenance of law and order in state societies more difficult to achieve than in bands, villages, and chiefdoms. This accounts for the great elaboration of police and paramilitary forces and the other state-level institutions and specialists concerned with crime and punishment. Although every state ultimately stands prepared to crush criminals and political subversives by imprisoning, maiming, or killing them, most of the daily burdens of maintaining law and order against discontented individuals and groups are borne by institutions that seek to confuse, distract, and demoralize potential troublemakers before they have to be subdued by physical force.

PROFILE 11.3   Hawaii—On the Threshold of the State

Location: The north central part of the Pacific Ocean.

Production: Irrigation and terracing, mainly yams, sweet potatoes, taro, and pigs.

Density: Approximately 39 persons per square mile in a landscape of steep terrain and varied rainfall. Populations are concentrated along the coast and in valleys, with densities over 300 persons per square mile.

Time period: Before contact with Europeans, during the 1700s.

When visited by Captain James Cook in A.D. 1778, the Hawaiian Islands were divided into four markedly hierarchical polities, each containing between 10,000 and 100,000 persons and each on the threshold (if not past it) of becoming a full-fledged state. Each polity was divided into named districts containing populations that ranged from about 4,000 to 25,000 people. The districts were in turn divided into many elongated territorial units called *ahupua'a,* which extended inland from the coast to the higher elevations of the island's interior, and were each inhabited by an average of 200 persons. These inhabitants were of the commoner class, the *maka'ainana*—fishermen, farmers, and craftsworkers.

Each ahupua'a was administered by officials called *konohiki,* the local land managers who oversaw production for the powerful district chiefs, called *ali'i* (see Figure 11.1). These ali'i based their claims to high chiefly status on genealogies that extended upward for ten generations. (Such genealogies, however, were constantly ad-

justed and negotiated.) District chiefs who provided the most political and military support were rewarded with grants of land. The chiefly class was topped off by a paramount figure called the *ali'i nui,* who was the owner of all lands and responsible for assigning privileges and administrative posts to the ali'i, in return for a portion of the local goods produced. In practice, the ali'i were in ceaseless turmoil over their relative rank, and the issue was decided by wars of conquest rather than genealogical reckoning. Competition for high office was intense. Following the death of a paramount chief, warfare followed, as district chiefs competed for succession and control. Until the time of European contact, no ali'i nui had managed to gain firm control over all the districts on an island.

Chiefs had legitimate managerial functions, such as allocating land, organizing community rebuilding after periodic flooding, and most importantly, managing intensified agriculture. Hierarchical, taxlike forms of redistribution siphoned both food and craft items from the maka'ainana commoners to the ali'i. It was the konohiki's main responsibility to see to it that the commoners in his charge produced enough to satisfy the demands of the ali'i. The ali'i in turn used these "gifts" to pay the non-food-producing craft specialists; to reward his warriors, priests, allies, and konohiki; and of course, to make payments to the paramount chief.

Recent archeological research demonstrates that the Hawaiian polities evolved out of more egalitarian chiefdoms as a result of the positive feedback among population increase, environmental depletions (deforestation and soil erosion), intensification of production (irrigation and pig husbandry), increased trade, escalating warfare, and competition for elite status. The process took place in three gradual stages (Earle 1989; Hommon 1986; Kirch 1984):

Phase I: A.D. 500–1200. Initial colonization and population growth. Settlements are on best coastal sites. No irrigation is needed. Settlements are egalitarian and kinship organized.

Phase II: A.D. 1200–1500. Expansion into less desirable interior island sites. As population grows rapidly, production increases through the use of floodwater irrigation, mulching, and reduction of fallow periods.

Phase III: A.D. 1500–1778. Expansion of irrigation systems. Intensification and expansion of agricultural production through terracing and expanded irrigation; greater stratification as yields and surpluses increase. Rivalry and warfare between chiefs, as they compete to gain access to land, taxes, and political power.

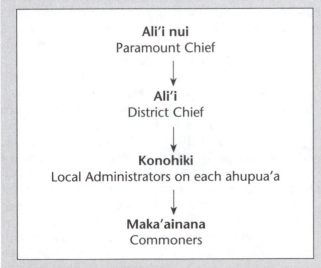

Figure 11.1   Hawaiian Political Hierarchy
Source: Adapted from Earle 1978. Used by permission.

(continued)

PROFILE 11.3 Hawaii—On the Threshold of the State (continued)

Universal Pattern • Hawaii

Infrastructure	Structure	Superstructure
Population density concentrated in coastal areas and valleys.	Four polities, each divided into territorial units (ahupua'a) of about 200 persons each.	Storehouses of root crops symbolize security and keep people content because they promise to sustain population in emergency.
Intensive irrigation agriculture, with terracing and production of surplus root crops.	Each ahupua'a is administered by a district chief (ali'i), who reports to the chief. Ali'i use taxes to pay clergy, craftsworkers, and military and payment to district and paramount chief.	Commoners are invited to identify with governing elite and are thereby willing to pay taxes.
Abundant marine resources available to everyone.	Paramount chief is unable to achieve enduring advantage over rivals, due to lack of storable surplus.	

Every state, ancient and modern, has specialists who perform ideological services in support of the status quo.

These services are often rendered in a manner and in contexts that seem unrelated to economic or political issues, yet they serve to direct thoughts and actions. The main ideological apparatus of preindustrial states consists of magico-religious institutions (see Chapter 16, "Ecclesiastical Cults" section) that legitimize power relations within society. Religious ideology imparts an understanding of what is right and what is natural. It is based on real experiences that people have in common, that lie outside the mind. These experiences are derived from material objects such as large public monuments, ceremonial facilities, and special regalia (such as fine clothes, a crown, or jewels) that represent the power of the dominant classes.

Timothy Earle (1997) calls this the **process of materialization**, meaning that ideology becomes transformed from abstract ideas and values into material objects that become public symbols (DeMarrais et al. 1996). These public symbols create shared experiences that state rulers can manipulate and use to mold individuals' beliefs about the nature of power dynamics in the universe. Monuments—especially tombs of past rulers—and their adjoining ceremonial plazas are part of the elaborate religions of the Inca, Aztecs, ancient Egyptians, and other nonindustrial civilizations that remind the populace of the great-

ness of the state. These symbols of power give permanence to the powers and privileges of the ruling elite by providing a place where people can come together to witness the exalted status of their rulers.

Ceremonial events and imposing monuments transform the ruling ideology from abstract ideas into concrete, shared experiences.

These powerful ideologies legitimize and uphold the doctrine of the divine descent of their rulers by sanctifying the belief that the continuity of the universe requires the subordination of commoners to persons of noble and divine birth (see Profile 11.4).

In many states, religion has been used to condition large masses of people to accept relative deprivation as necessity, to look forward to material rewards in the afterlife rather than in the present one, and to be grateful for small favors from superiors, lest ingratitude call down a fiery retribution in this life or in a hell to come. (Religion, of course, has other functions, as we will see in Chapter 16.) Yet it is important to remember that it is not ideology (emic perceptions in people's heads) that keeps subordinate segments of society where they are. Nor is their belief in the legitimacy of ruling-class privilege responsible for their political and economic subordination. As we have seen, it is the monopolization of production and exchange and the extraction of surplus that become the basis of power for the ruling elite.

Pomp and Ceremony
The crowning of Queen Elizabeth II in England in 1952 was a mass spectacle viewed by millions.

Thought Control in the United States
Saluting the flag instills national loyalty in children.

Ideology is a source of political power. It directs thoughts that legitimize the actions of the ruling elite, and it motivates people to work for the interests of the ruling segment of society.

A considerable amount of conformity is achieved not by frightening or threatening people but by inviting them to identify with the governing elite and to enjoy vicariously the pomp of state occasions. Public spectacles such as religious processions, coronations, and victory parades work against the alienating effects of poverty and exploitation.

Today, movies, television, and radio provide states with far more powerful means of thought control. Through modern media, the consciousness of millions of listeners, readers, and watchers is often manipulated along rather precisely determined paths by censors and propaganda specialists. However, thought control via the mass media need not take the form of government-directed propaganda and censorship. More subtle forms of control arise from the voluntary filtering of news by reporters and commentators, whose career advancements depend on avoiding objective coverage (Chomsky 1989; Herman and Chomsky 1988). "Entertainment" delivered through the air or by cable directly into the shantytown house or tenement apartment is another form of thought control, perhaps the most effective "Roman circus" yet devised (Kottak 1990; Parenti 1986).

Compulsory universal education is another powerful modern means of thought control. Teachers and schools serve the instrumental needs of complex industrial civilizations by training each generation to provide the skills and services necessary for survival and well-being. But schools also teach civics, history, citizenship, and social studies. These subjects are loaded with implicit and explicit assumptions about culture, people, and nature that favor the status quo. All modern states use universal education to instill loyalty through mass rituals. These include saluting the flag; pronouncing oaths of allegiance; singing patriotic songs; and staging patriotic assemblies, plays, and pageants (Bowles and Gintis 1976; Ramirez and Meyer 1980).

In modern industrial states, as in ancient ones, acceptance of extreme social and economic inequality depends on thought control more than on the exercise of naked repressive force. Children from economically deprived families are taught to believe that the main obstacle to achievement of wealth and power is their own intellectual merit, physical endurance, and will to compete. The poor are taught to blame themselves for being poor, and their resentment is directed primarily against themselves or against those with whom they must compete and who stand on the same rung of the ladder of upward mobility (De-Mott 1990; Kleugel and Smith 1981).

The State and Physical Coercion

Although thought control can be an effective supplementary means of maintaining political control, there are limits to the lies and deceptions that governments can get away with. If people are experiencing stagnant or declining standards of living, no amount

PROFILE 11.4 | The Inca—A Native American Empire

Location: The Andean regions of present-day Ecuador, Peru, Bolivia, Chile, and Argentina.

Production: Hoe agriculture, with potatoes, corn, and quinoa as staples; alpaca, llama, and guinea pigs.

Density: 40 people per square mile. (Density is low because much of the terrain is arid and rocky.)

Time period: The Inca Empire reached its peak between 1476 and 1532.

In both the Old and New Worlds, state systems arose in which scores of former small chiefdoms were incorporated into highly centralized superstates or empires. In the New World, the largest and most powerful of these systems was the Inca Empire. At its prime, the Inca Empire stretched 1,500 miles from northern Chile to southern Colombia and contained possibly as many as 6 million inhabitants. Because of government intervention in the basic mode of production, agriculture was organized in terms of villages, districts, and provinces. Each such unit was supervised by appointed government administrators, known as *curacas,* responsible for planning public works and for delivering government-established quotas of laborers, food, and other material.

The village, or *ayllu,* was a corporate kin group similar to the Hawaiian *ahupua'a.* The ayllu ranged in size from a few hundred people to perhaps a thousand. It operated a highly productive, intensive system of agropastoralism that required terracing, canal irrigation and management of crop rotation, and alpaca and llama herds. Ayllu lands were divided into three parts,

the largest of which was used to support the peasants. Harvests from the second and third parts were stored in granaries and turned over to support religious and state agents (D'Altroy and Earle 1985; D'Altroy 1992). The distribution of staples such as maize, potatoes, and quinoa was entirely under the control of the curacas, who transported the food to administrative centers and to regional warehouses where staple reserves were kept for times of need—in case of food shortage. The warehouses were positioned to impress people and reassure subjects that the state could adequately manage the risks and uncertainties of agropastoralism (Moseley 2001).

Likewise, when military service and labor power were needed to build roads, bridges, canals, fortresses, and other public works, curacas recruited people directly from the villages. Community lands remained under state ownership, and the right to use them was granted in exchange for *mit'a,* or obligatory labor. Peasant communities were also obligated to produce craft goods for state use, particularly llama wool woven into cloth. Careful records of labor and storable wealth produced for the state were kept by *khipu,* mnemonic devices made of rows of knotted string.

The size of the administrative network and the density of population permitted a large labor force to be placed at the disposal of the Inca engineers to construct a vast road system and monumental building projects. Thousands of miles of roads were built, along with bridges and stairways carved into hillsides, to connect the vast regions of the empire. In the construction of Cuzco's fortress of Sacsahuaman, probably the

Sacsahuaman
The principal fortress of the Inca Empire, near Cuzco, Peru.

PROFILE 11.4 | The Inca—A Native American Empire *(continued)*

greatest masonry structure in the New World, 30,000 people were employed in cutting, quarrying, hauling, and erecting huge monoliths, some weighing as much as 200 tons. Labor contingents of this size were rare in medieval Europe but common in ancient states such as Egypt, the Middle East, and China.

The Inca state expanded its power by conquering and integrating many of the warring ethnic chiefdoms into the empire. Instead of conquering land and expelling defeated populations, the Inca incorporated the defeated populations into the empire. After conquering a new region, the state took ownership of the land and appointed curacas to manage and expand local production, regulate the mit'a service, and deliver the goods stockpiled in storehouses. Tired of the war, the people welcomed the opportunity for regional peace and the functional advantage of food storage to secure against shortages in food production because of climate fluctuations. In the event of local hostility toward the empire, entire communities were relocated forcibly through a strategy of divide and rule. This ensured loyalty to the state because access to land came from state assignment (Johnson and Earle 2000).

Control over the entire empire was concentrated in the hands of the Inca. He was the firstborn of the firstborn, a descendant of the god of the sun and a celestial being of unparalleled holiness. This god-on-Earth enjoyed power and luxury undreamed of by the poor Mehinacu chief in his plaintive daily quest for respect and obedience. Ordinary people could not approach the Inca face to face. His private audiences were conducted from behind a screen, and all who approached him did so with a burden of wood or stone on their backs. When traveling, he reclined on an ornate palanquin carried by special crews of bearers. A small army of sweepers, water carriers, woodcutters, cooks, wardrobe men, treasurers, gardeners, and hunters attended the domestic needs of the Inca in his palace in Cuzco, the capital of the empire.

The Inca ate his meals from gold and silver dishes in rooms whose walls were covered with precious metals. His clothing was made of the softest vicuna wool, and he gave away each change of clothing to members of the royal family, never wearing the same garment twice. The Inca enjoyed the services of a large number of concubines who were methodically culled from the empire's most beautiful young women. However, to conserve the holy line of descent from the god of the sun, his wife had to be his own full or half sister. When the Inca died, his wife, concubines, and many other retainers were strangled during a great drunken dance in order that he suffer no loss of comfort in the afterlife. Each Inca's body was eviscerated, wrapped in cloth, and mummified. Women with fans stood in constant attendance on these mummies, ready to drive away flies and to take care of the other things mummies needed to stay happy.

Universal Pattern • The Inca Empire

Infrastructure	Structure	Superstructure
Large diverse landscape, filled with rocky mountains and fertile valleys. Agropastoralism with llamas and alpacas as sources of protein. Canal irrigation used to intensify agriculture. Storable staple crops such as corn, potatoes, and quinoa. Circumscription through investment in irrigation and other capital investments.	Land was cultivated by local kin-based communities that cooperated in management of land and herds. Complex system of surplus storage of staple reserves and taxation was managed by local administrators (curacas): • Mit'a labor for construction and military • Share of agricultural produce • Textiles System of recolonization of entire communities was used to quell unrest.	State religion was worship of the sun, divine ancestor of Inca emperor. Gods of local communities ranked below supreme deity. Imposing monuments provided public symbols and shared experiences that reinforced beliefs about nature of state power. Public celebrations coinciding with agricultural cycle were financed through staple reserves; display of surplus reassured subjects of state's ability to manage risk. Festivities also reinforced belief that curacas were obligated to be generous toward their subjects.

Law and Disorder

When discontent with the political economy mounts, people become restless and there is danger of a breakdown in law and order.

of propaganda and false promises can prevent them from becoming restless and dissatisfied. As discontent mounts, the ruling elite must either increase the use of direct force or make way for a restructuring of political economy.

Maintaining law and order is on ongoing challenge in the United States, which has one of the highest rates of violent crime found among industrial nations.

Actually, the violent crime rate declined in the mid-1990s. This was achieved through a massive prison-building spree and long mandatory sentences aimed at locking up young offenders. Nationwide there are over 1 million prisoners in state and federal facilities (Butterfield 1996).

One reason for the high rate of violent crime in the United States is that U.S. citizens own far more pistols and rifles per capita than the citizens of other countries. (Switzerland is a notable exception: All men are part of the militia and *must* bear arms.) The right to bear arms is guaranteed by the U.S. Constitution. But the failure to pass stricter gun control laws itself reflects, in part at least, the pervasive, realistic fear of being robbed or attacked and the consequent desire

to defend person and property. Hence, the cause of the high incidence of violent crimes must be sought at deeper levels of U.S. culture.

Much evidence links the unusually high rate of crime in the United States to the long-term, grinding poverty and economic hopelessness of the nation's inner-city minorities, especially of African Americans and Latinos. Although suburban crime has also risen, the principal locus of violent crime remains the inner cities. African Americans constitute 12 percent of the population but account for 59.5 percent of arrests for robbery and 54.4 percent of arrests for murder and manslaughter (*Statistical Abstract of the United States* 1997; No. 328). One should note, however, that proportionately, African Americans themselves suffer more from violent crimes than do Whites. According to the U.S. Bureau of Justice (2006), most homicides are intraracial. From 1976 to 2002,

- Eighty-six percent of White victims were killed by Whites.

- Ninety-four percent of Black victims were killed by Blacks.

Homicide is the ranking killer of African American males between 15 and 24 years of age. More Black males die from homicide than from motor vehicle accidents, diabetes, emphysema, and pneumonia. (Two out of five Black male children born in a U.S. city in 1990 will not reach age 25.) Over half of all Black teenagers are unemployed; further, in ghettos such as Harlem in New York City, the unemployment rate among Black youth may be as high as 86 percent (R. Brown 1978; National Urban League 1990).

Has the United States turned the corner on crime? What explains the reduction in reported crime? One reason is the dramatic increase in the U.S. prisoner population. Predictably, African Americans are over-represented; 47.3 percent of state prison inmates are African American.

The dominant classes of Western democracies rely more on thought control than on physical coercion to maintain law and order, but in the final analysis, they too depend on jails to protect their privileges. Disasters such as Hurricane Andrew in 1992 and the Los Angeles riots in 1994 quickly led to extensive looting and widespread disorder, proving that thought control is not enough and that large numbers of ordinary citizens do not believe in the system and are held in check only by the threat of physical punishment.

SUMMARY
and *Questions to Think About*

1. Headmen, "big men," chiefs, and kings are found in different forms of political organization: autonomous bands and villages, chiefdoms, and states, respectively.

2. The "big man" is a rivalrous form of leadership marked by competitive redistributions that expand and intensify production. As illustrated by the mumis of the Solomon Islands, being a big man is a temporary status requiring constant validation through displays of generosity that leave the big man poor in possessions but rich in prestige and authority. Because they are highly respected, big men are well suited to act as leaders of war parties, long-distance trading expeditions, and other collective activities that require leadership among egalitarian peoples.

3. The evolution from big man society to chiefdom is marked by infrastructural and structural opportunities for control in four areas—risk management, control of technology that intensifies production, warfare, and trade—that enable leaders to mobilize resources and increase their power.

4. Chiefdoms consist of several more or less permanently allied communities. Like big men, chiefs also play the role of great provider, expand and intensify production, give feasts, and organize long-distance warfare and trading expeditions. However, as illustrated by the Trobriand and Cherokee chiefdoms, chiefs enjoy hereditary status, tend to live somewhat better than the average commoner, and can be deposed only through defeat in warfare.

5. The power of chiefs is limited by their ability to support a permanent group of police military specialists and to deprive significant numbers of their followers of access to the means of making a living. In the transition from band and village organizations through chiefdoms to states, a continuous series of cumulative changes occurs in the balance of power between elites and commoners. The subtle gradations along this continuum make it difficult to say at exactly what point in the process we have chiefdoms rather than an alliance of villages or states rather than a powerful chiefdom.

6. Dense populations, intensifiable modes of production, trade, storable grains, circumscription, and intense warfare provide the basic conditions for state formation. Hawaii is an example of a chiefdom whose lack of storable grains may have inhibited the transition to a state form of polity. The difference between chiefdoms and states is illustrated by the case of the Bunyoro (whose staple was the grain millet). The Mukama was a great provider for himself and his closest supporters but not for the majority of the Bunyoro peasants. Unlike the Trobriand chief, the Mukama maintained a permanent court of personal retainers and a palace guard.

7. The most developed and highly stratified form of statehood is that of empire. As illustrated by the Inca of Peru, the leaders of ancient empires possessed vast amounts of power and could not be approached by ordinary citizens. Production was supervised by a whole army of administrators and tax collectors. Although the Inca was concerned with the welfare of his people, they viewed him as a god to whom they owed everything, rather than as a headman or chief who owed everything to them.

8. Because all state societies are based on marked inequalities between rich and poor, rulers and ruled, the maintenance of law and order presents a critical challenge. In the final analysis, it is the military, with its control over the means of physical coercion, that keeps the poor and exploited in line. However, all states find it more expedient to maintain law and order by controlling people's thoughts. This is done in a variety of ways, ranging from universal education and state religions to public monuments and ceremonies that symbolically represent the power of the state.

Questions to Think About

1. What are the characteristics of a "big man"? What are the limitations on his power?

2. What are the opportunities for control that enable leaders in chiefdoms (and later states) to increase the basis of their power? How does the opportunity to produce a surplus enable the chiefdom to expand?

3. What role do the following infrastructural conditions have on the transformation of chiefdoms to states: population growth, intensive agriculture, and circumscription?

4. What is the infrastructural and structural (administrative) basis of the Inca Empire? How did the empire manage to incorporate such a vast territory into its control? What did the empire offer the people in return?

5. What is the role of ideology in reinforcing the power of state rulers? What importance do material objects have in transforming ideology into shared experiences that support the status quo?

CHAPTER 12

CLASS AND
CASTE

This poor family sorts through the trash in an alley in São Paulo, Brazil.

Now we examine the principal varieties of stratified groups found in state societies. We begin with groups known as *classes*. We will see that people who live in state societies think and behave in ways that are determined to a great extent by their membership in stratified groups and by their position in a stratification hierarchy. The values and behaviors of such groups are in turn often related to a struggle for access to the structural and infrastructural sources of wealth and power. In this regard, to what extent can subordinated classes be seen as the authors of their own fates? Do the poor have cultural traditions that keep them down? Should we blame the unemployed for being unemployed? Next, we move on to the hierarchical groups known as *castes*, comparing them, especially castes in Hindu India, with classes and other hierarchical groups.

Two other hierarchical groups associated with the rise of the state—*ethnic groups* and *social races*—are also subjects of this chapter. How ethnic groups and social races differ from classes and castes is one of the questions to be considered. We address the worldwide confusion concerning the relationship of biological races to social races and ethnic groups and explore the dynamic processes that lead to more or less successful outcomes of the competition among social races and ethnic groups.

Class and Power

All state societies are organized into a hierarchy of groups known as *classes*.

A **class** is a group whose members possess similar amounts of power within a stratified society.

Power is the ability to force other people to obey one's requests or demands.

In practice, power depends on the ability to provide or take away essential goods and services, and this ability in turn ultimately depends on who controls access to energy, resources, technology, and the means of physical and psychological coercion.

The beginnings of class hierarchies can be traced to chiefdom societies. As we saw in Chapter 11, while everyone gave to the chiefs, the chiefs gave to their relatives and paid specialists to manufacture prestige goods. Chiefdoms often kept war captives as slaves and drew further distinctions of rank between commoners and a ruling elite. But the fullest elaboration of class systems occurs in state societies.

All state societies necessarily have at least two classes arranged hierarchically: the rulers and the ruled.

Where more than two classes exist, they are not necessarily all arranged hierarchically with respect to each other. For example, fishermen and neighboring farmers are usually regarded as two separate classes because they relate to the ruling class in distinctive ways; have different patterns of ownership, rent, and taxation; and exploit entirely different sectors of the environment. Yet neither has a clear-cut power advantage or disadvantage with respect to the other. Similarly, anthropologists often speak of an urban as opposed to a rural lower class, although the quantitative power differentials between the two may be minimal.

One other feature of classes should be noted: They come in relatively closed and open systems.

In **open-class systems**, people can move up or down the hierarchy, as in modern Western democracies.

In **closed-class systems**, there is little mobility up or down.

In medieval Europe, for example, serfs remained serfs for life. At their extreme, closed-class systems strongly resemble castes and ethnic groups.

Emics, Etics, and Class Consciousness

Class is an aspect of culture in which emic and etic points of view often differ sharply (Berreman 1981:18). Many social scientists accept class distinction as real and important only when the members of the class are aware of their class identity and act in unison. For a group to be considered a class, its members must be conscious of having common interests and a common identity. Other social scientists believe that classes exist only when people with similar forms and quantities of social power organize into interest groups, such as political parties and labor unions. The position we favor is that classes exist if there are actual concentrations of power in certain groups, regardless of any shared awareness of class identity among the people concerned (such as the U.S. corporate elite) and regardless of whether the groups are represented by political parties, unions, or other organizations.

From an etic and behavioral viewpoint, classes can exist even when the members of the class deny that they constitute a class.

Classes can exist even when, instead of collective organizations, they have organizations that compete, such as rival business corporations or rival unions (DeMott, 1990). Subordinate classes lacking class consciousness are obviously not exempt from the domination

A.

Poverty and Power

These people are both impoverished and disempowered. **A.** *This inner-city man will most likely spend his entire life in poverty.* **B.** *This homeless person lives on the streets of Washington, D.C., the capital of the richest country in the world.*

B.

of ruling classes. Similarly, ruling classes containing antagonistic and competitive elements nonetheless dominate those who lack power. Of course, there is no disputing the importance of a people's belief about the shape and origin of their stratification hierarchy. Consciousness of a common plight among the members of a downtrodden and exploited class may very well lead to the outbreak of organized class warfare.

Consciousness is thus an element in the struggle between classes, but it is not essential for the existence of class differences.

Class and Lifestyle

Classes differ from one another not only in amount of power per capita but also in broad areas of culture and lifestyle. Peasants, urban industrial wage workers, middle-class suburbanites, and upper-class chief executive officers of large corporations differ in their lifestyles. The contrasts among them is as great as the contrast between life in an Inuit igloo and life in a Mbuti camp in the Ituri forest.

Classes have their own subcultures, made up of distinctive work patterns, architecture, home furnish-

ings, diet, dress, domestic routines, sex and mating practices, magico-religious rituals, art, and ideology. In many instances, different classes even have different dialects. Moreover, because their body parts may be exposed to sun, wind, and callus-producing friction, working-class people tend to look different from those of higher socioeconomic levels. Further distinctions result from dietary specialties. The fat and the rich were once synonymous, as the expression "fat cats" reminds us. (Today, in advanced capitalist societies, fatness is a sign of a diet overloaded with fats and sugars, together with a lack of exercise, and is associated with poverty rather than with wealth.)

Throughout almost the entire evolutionary career of stratified societies, class identity has been at least as explicit as the distinction between male and female genders. The Chinese Han dynasty peasant, the Inca commoner, or the Russian serf could not survive without knowing how to recognize members of the "superior" classes. Any lingering doubts were removed by state-enforced standards of dress: Only the Chinese nobility could wear silk clothing, only the European feudal overlords could carry daggers and swords, and only the Inca rulers could wear gold ornaments. Violators were put to death. In the presence of these elite, commoners still perform definite rituals of subordination, among which lowering the

A.

B.

Class and Lifestyle
Compare the lifestyle in this East Harlem neighborhood to that of Hampton Beach, New Hampshire.

head, removing the hat, averting the eyes, kneeling, bowing, crawling, or maintaining silence unless spoken to occur almost universally.

> Throughout much of the world, class identity, signified by standards of dress, deference, and sometimes dialect, continues to be sharp and unambiguous.

Among most contemporary nations, differences in class-linked lifestyles show little prospect of diminishing or disappearing. Indeed, given the convergence in former communist countries toward market economies, extremes of poverty and wealth may be on the rise. The contrast between the lifestyles of the rich and powerful and those of people living in peasant villages and urban shantytowns may be greater than ever before.

During the recent period of industrial advance, governing classes throughout the world have gone from horse-drawn carriages to Rolls Royces to private jets, whereas their subordinates still find themselves without even a donkey or a pair of oxen. The elite now jet to the world's best medical centers to be treated with the most advanced medical technology, whereas vast numbers of less fortunate people have never heard of the germ theory of disease and can't even afford penicillin. The elite attend the best universities, whereas over 1.4 billion of the world's adults remain illiterate (L. Brown et al. 1993:122).

Caracas Shantytown
So-called squatters in Latin American cities often enjoy the best views, since apartment houses for wealthy tenants are not built on hilltops because of lack of water. But the squatters have to carry their water up the hill in cans.

Peasant Classes

About 40 percent of the people in the world make a living from farming and are members of one kind of peasant class or another.

 Peasants are people who use nonindustrial technologies to cultivate land in state societies and pay rent and/or taxes in the form of cash, crops, or services to elite groups for use of the land.

All peasants produce a surplus that flows into the urban centers. In archaic states, the agricultural labor of peasants fed the craftworkers, the merchants, the

Mexican Peasants

This peasant makes a meager living from a small plot of land near Oaxaca.

priesthood, the military, and the political elite. The peasantry of medieval Europe, for example, paid half of their annual harvest to their lords.

Today, peasants grow crops as small landowners or agricultural laborers. The basic unit of production is the family or household, and total production is not much larger than what is needed for the family, taxes, and rent. Two major types of peasant class can be distinguished:

1. *Landless peasants* are subject to the control of wealthy landowners, who provide access to land use in exchange for rent or a share of the harvest. Rent may also take the form of labor service in the landlord's kitchens or fields.

   Landless peasants are fast disappearing from the world but are still an important component in the underdevelopment of many Third World countries. This heritage remains strong in several Central and South American countries, especially in Guatemala, El Salvador, Ecuador, and Peru. In these countries, land ownership continues to be concentrated in huge estates owned by small numbers of politically powerful families. The peasants who live on or near these estates depend on the big landowners for access to land, water, loans, and emergency assistance. The extreme disparity in landholdings and the semifeudal relationships between the estate owners and the peasants lie behind the guerrilla movements that are found throughout this region (Stern 1988). The states in these countries are all powerful, setting production quotas, controlling prices, and extracting taxes in kind and in labor.

2. *Capitalist peasants* are found in Africa, Latin America, India, and Southeast Asia. Landless peasant-

ries have been replaced by peasants who enjoy increased opportunities to buy and sell land, labor, and food in competitive price markets. Most of the world's remaining peasants belong to this category. The varieties of structured inferiority within this group defy any simple definition.

Capitalist peasants own land, but most are in debt to large landowners; others are subordinate to banks that hold mortgages and promissory notes. In more isolated and unproductive regions, holdings may be very small, giving rise to the phenomenon known as "penny capitalism" (i.e., they are market oriented, buying and selling food, handicrafts, tools, etc. for cash).

The Image of Limited Good

A recurrent question concerning the plight of contemporary peasant communities is the extent to which they are victims of their own values. It has often been noted, for example, that peasants distrust innovations and cling to their old ways of doing things. Based on his study of the village of Tzintzuntzan, in Mexico, George Foster (1967) developed a general theory of peasant life based on a concept called the **image of limited good:** the peasant worldview in which all desired things are considered finite, so that if one person takes a lot, everyone else will be deprived. According to Foster, the people of Tzintzuntzan, like many peasants throughout the world, believe that life is a dreary struggle and that very few people achieve success.

Image of Limited Good

Peasant women of Tzintzuntzan sell their homemade pottery in the local market.

According to the **image of limited good,** everything is perceived as finite: land, wealth, health, love, friendship, honor, respect, status, power, influence, safety, and security. Everything is scarce; successful individuals take more than their fair share from a common pool, thereby succeeding at the expense of other people.

Peasants can accept individuals who manage to increase their wealth if it comes from outside the village. However, if wealth comes from local activity, public opinion acts as a leveling mechanism. For example, wealthy individuals may be forced to sponsor ceremonies, which reduce differential wealth. Successful peasants may also be the targets of gossip, envy, physical violence, and hostility. Accordingly, peasants try to hide their good fortune and are reluctant to even attempt to change their way of life (see Box 12.1).

Because peasants are fearful that someone else might get the best of them, they are reluctant to cooperate or agree to leadership from within the community. This theory assumes that peasants are so risk averse that they also avoid economic progress. Peasant conservatism, however, is based on a rational attitude of maximizing security.

Although an image of limited good exists in many peasant villages in Mexico and elsewhere, it is not the cause of underdevelopment.

In Tzintzuntzan, people were, if anything, overeager to accept community development projects sponsored by the United Nations. These projects ended in disasters that had more to do with inept aid policies than with the values held by the villagers. Further,

BOX 12.1 | A World of Limited Good

The fundamental truth is that in an economy like Tzintzuntzan's, hard work and thrift are moral qualities of only the slightest functional value. Because of the limitations on land and technology, additional hard work does not produce a significant increase in income. It is pointless to talk of thrift in a subsistence economy because usually there is no surplus with which to be thrifty. Foresight, with careful planning for the future, is also a virtue of dubious value in a world in which the best-laid plans must rest on a foundation of chance and capriciousness.

Source: Foster 1967:150–151.

most of the community's cash income came from jobs as migrant laborers in the United States. To get across the border, the migrants had to bribe, scheme, and suffer great hardships. Yet 50 percent of them had succeeded in getting through, "many of them ten times or more" (Foster 1967:277).

Foster suggests that the image of limited good is not a crippling illusion but rather a realistic appraisal of the facts of life in a society where economic success or failure is capricious and hinged to forces wholly beyond one's control or comprehension.

James Acheson, who studied a community near Tzintzuntzan, has argued that without realistic economic opportunities, development would not occur.

If opportunities present themselves, some individuals will always take advantage of them, regardless of the image of limited good.

"It is one thing to say that Tarascans [the people of the region of Tzintzuntzan] are suspicious, distrustful, and uncooperative; it is another to assume that this lack of cooperation precludes all possibility for positive economic change" (Acheson 1972:1165; see also Acheson 1974; Foster 1974). The primary task in development is not only to change the peasants' view of their social and economic universe but to provide expanding opportunities in an open system so peasants can feel safe in displaying initiative.

Poverty

Poverty in the developed world is different from that in developing countries. In developed countries, people earn over 200 times the per capita income of people in the poorest developing countries. Developed countries usually measure poverty in terms of income level—as an amount below which a person or family cannot afford basic needs, including housing. The United States has a higher rate of poverty than most developed countries. In 2000 the Census Bureau reported that about 11.8 percent of the population lived below the poverty level, which was $15,911 for a family of four. Some 24.7 percent of single mothers lived in poverty, compared to 4.7 percent of married couples (U.S. Bureau of the Census 2000).

Between 1960 and the early 1970s, poverty in the United States dropped substantially as the Johnson administration declared the War on Poverty, adopting a series of programs geared to helping poor people. Those programs (plus a strong economy) succeeded

Ecuadorian Peasants
These peasants farm "postage-stamp" plots of land on steep hillsides.

in dramatically reducing poverty from 22.2 percent in 1960 to 11.3 percent in 1973. The incidence of poverty among African Americans and Hispanics, however, is more than twice the poverty rate among Whites. Table 12.1 shows that among Whites, the poverty rate was 7.5 percent in 2000. In sharp contrast, African Americans and Hispanics had poverty rates of 22.1 percent and 21.2 percent, respectively (U.S. Bureau of the Census 2000). Note, however, that because Whites are the largest ethnic group, overall there are far more poor among Whites than among other groups.

A "Culture of Poverty"?

In studying the problems of people living in urban slums, Oscar Lewis thought he had found evidence

Table 12.1

Persons in Poverty in 2000 by Ethnicity

Groups	Poverty Rate (within each ethnic group)
Whites	7.5%
Blacks	22.1%
Hispanics	21.2%

Source: Data from U.S. Bureau of the Census 2000.

for a distinct set of values and practices that he called the **culture of poverty.**

> According to Oscar Lewis, some groups remain poor because they are crippled by certain cultural features that perpetuate poverty and that are passed down from one generation to the next.

Although not exactly comparable point by point, the concepts of the culture of poverty and the image of limited good resemble each other in many respects and represent similar attempts to explain the perpetuation of poverty by focusing on the traditions and values of subordinate classes (see Box 12.2).

Lewis (1966) pictured the poor in cities such as Mexico City, New York, and Lima as tending to be fearful, suspicious, and apathetic toward the major institutions of the larger society; as hating the police and being mistrustful of government; and as "inclined to be cynical of the church." They also have "a strong present-time orientation with relatively little disposition to defer gratification and plan for the future." This statement implies that poor people are less willing to save money and are more interested in "getting mine now" in the form of cellular phones, big-screen televisions, the latest-style clothing, and sporty automobiles. It also implies that the poor "blow" their earnings by getting drunk or going on buying sprees.

Like George Foster, Lewis recognized that in some measure, the culture of poverty was partly a rational response to the objective conditions of powerlessness and poverty: "an adaptation and a reaction of

The Poor in Lima
How did these Peruvians end up living on a garbage heap?

BOX 12.2 | The Causes of Poverty and Homelessness

The immediate cause of poverty and homelessness in advanced industrial countries, such as Italy and the United States, is the lack of jobs. But what determines the number of jobs available? Is it the amount of effort that the unemployed expend in trying to find employment?

Many people seem to think that if only the poor and homeless would try harder, they would be able to find decent jobs. Government policies that seek to solve the problems of the poor and homeless by enrolling them in job-training programs are based on the same premise. If the poor try harder, they will find employment. But this way of looking at poverty and homelessness involves a lot of misinformation and even hypocrisy, for it is the government (through the Federal Reserve System) that mandates what the rate of unemployment will be. It does so by raising and lowering interest rates in order to prevent or lower inflation. (Raising interest rates slows down the rate of business expansion, which in turn means fewer new jobs.) If the government were to create an abundance of jobs, working people would demand higher wages. In turn, the price of goods would go up and inflation would take over.

The system, as presently constructed, demands that a certain percentage of people (at least 4 percent in the current estimates) must be losers in the competition for jobs that can raise people above the poverty line. Is it fair to blame the losers for their loss and to deny them the help they need?

Source: Adapted from Dehavenon 1995. Reprinted with permission of the University Press of Florida.

---

the poor to their marginal position in a class-stratified society" (1966:21). But he also stated that once the culture of poverty comes into existence, it tends to perpetuate itself: "By the time slum children are six or seven they have usually absorbed the basic attitudes and values of their subculture. Thereafter they are psychologically unready to take full advantage of changing conditions or improving opportunities that may develop in their lifetime" (Lewis 1966:21). Lewis proposed that only 20 percent of the urban poor actually have the culture of poverty, implying that 80 percent fall into the category of those whose poverty results from infrastructural and structural conditions, rather than from the traditions and values of a culture of poverty (Leeds 1970).

The concept of the culture of poverty has been criticized on the grounds that the poor have many values other than those stressed in the culture of poverty—values they share with other classes. Furthermore, values said to be distinctive of the urban poor are actually shared equally by the middle class. For example, being suspicious of government, politicians, and organized religion is not an exclusive poverty-class trait, nor is the tendency to spend above one's means. There is little evidence that the middle class as a whole lives within its income more effectively than poor people do. But when the poor, who live from paycheck to paycheck, mismanage their incomes, the consequences are much more serious. If the male head of a poor family yields to the temptation to buy nonessential items, his children may go hungry or his wife may be deprived of medical attention.

The consequences of poverty result from being poor, not from an inability to defer gratification or live up to the norms of the dominant culture.

Poverty in Naples

Thomas Belmonte lived for a year in a slum neighborhood of Naples, Italy, a city that is known as the "Calcutta of Europe." Belmonte (1979) described the neighborhood, Fontana del Re, as being inhabited by

The Poor in Naples
The infamous one-room hovels of the Bassi—usually without ventilation, running water, separate toilets, and heating—are home for tens of thousands of Neapolitan families.

a subproletariat, or underclass, who lacked steady employment and who produced so little that they could not even be said to be exploited because they had nothing to be taken away from them. Gabriele, for example, collected metal junk and broke it into pieces with the help of his four children but also ran a little store during the day and drove a taxi for prostitutes at night. Others were part-time sailors, food servers, bartenders, dockworkers, and movers. Some groomed dogs, and others were jacks-of-all-trades.

According to Belmonte, "The poor hesitate to plan for the future because they are hard put to stay afloat in the present." Their avoidance of banks relates to a realistic fear of inflation and a realistic mistrust of official literate institutions. They do not shop at department stores because they prefer to cultivate their own, more personalized networks of local credit, marketing, and exchange. In direct contradiction to Lewis's formulation, the poor of Naples purchase vital supplies wisely and in bulk. They place numerous cultural controls on consumption, wasting nothing. They are habituated to delaying gratifications in terms of clothing, housing, plumbing, heating, travel, transportation, and entertainment. Confronted by a scarcity of opportunities, they become resigned to preserve their sanity and do not think to transcend their condition so long as they remain in underdeveloped Naples. They have a culture that is simultaneously against poverty, adapted to the stresses of poverty, and mangled by poverty (Belmonte 1979:144).

The people of Naples have many of Oscar Lewis's culture of poverty traits. But most of these traits are attributed to being penniless and lacking steady employment, not to being a member of a particular subculture.

Causes of Income Inequality

Income inequality in the United States has risen over the past two decades. Substantial numbers of poor people work full time year round while others worked full time for over six months of the year. Because of low wages relative to inflation and because of difficulties in finding year-round jobs, the income of most poor workers is not enough to take them out of poverty (see Profile 12.1). As of February 2006, the federal minimum wage was still $5.15 an hour. It has remained unchanged since 1996 when Congress raised it by 90 cents. The "working poor," who work at the minimum wage, earn $10,300 a year, which is not enough to support a family of three. In 1997, the poverty line was $12,802 for a family of three, leaving a gap between income earned and income needed to

get to the poverty level. This came at a time when *Business Week* magazine declared that corporate profits were "taking an ever rising share of national income, the highest since 1968 . . . [while] the share of workers' compensation has decreased to the lowest proportion since 1968" (cited in Ginsburg 1999).

A number of factors are responsible for why wages of non–college graduates have not kept up with inflation:

- The decline of unions and collective bargaining
- The high cost of employee compensation going for benefits
- An overall sharp decline in manufacturing jobs
- An increase in part-time and minimum-wage jobs staffed by students and immigrants

Castes in India

Castes bear many resemblances to closed classes, ethnic groups, and social races. No sharp line can be drawn between the castes of India and such groups as the Amish or African Americans in the United States or the Inca elite. However, some features of the Indian caste hierarchy are unique and deserve special attention.

 Castes are closed, endogamous, and stratified descent groups.

The unique features of Indian castes have to do with the fact that the caste hierarchy is an integral part of Hinduism, the religion of most people in India. (This does not mean that one must be a Hindu in order to belong to a caste. Muslim and Christian castes also exist in India.)

It is a matter of religious conviction in India that all people are not spiritually equal and that the gods have established a hierarchy of groups.

This hierarchy consists of the four major **varnas**, or grades of being. According to the earliest traditions (for example, the Hymns of Rigveda), the four varnas correspond to the physical parts of Manu, who gave rise to the human race through dismemberment:

- His head became the Brahmans (priests)
- His arms the Kshatriyas (warriors)
- His thighs the Vaishyas (merchants and craftsmen)
- His feet the Shudras (menial workers)

PROFILE 12.1 | The Effect of Poverty on Achievement in the United States

If you are a lower-class adolescent—whether White or Black—the odds are stacked against you that you won't make it out of poverty. This is the conclusion reached by Jay MacLeod in *Ain't No Makin' It*. MacLeod followed two groups of lower-class males during the 1980s who attended the same high school and lived in the same housing project: the White teens are known as *the Hallway Hangers* and Black teens call themselves the *Brothers*.

The Hallway Hangers are self-professed "bad boys." They are part of a tightly knit peer group that prides itself for its street smarts and dismisses school as irrelevant. The Hallway Hangers reject the achievement ideology because, in their experience, there is no clear connection between effort and reward. Their depressed aspirations are grounded in the fact that the possibilities open to them are limited from the outset. Given that their parents share the same ideology, there is no one to counter their rejection of the American dream. The establishment of a peer group that rejects what society values provides the only alternative for generating self-esteem.

In stark contrast, the Brothers are Black teenagers who actively pursue mainstream ideals. They attend school regularly, avoid breaking the law, avoid fights, and refrain from drinking and drug use. They believe that racial injustice has been curbed in the last 20 years and that they will not have to confront the same barriers to success as their parents. This optimism is also reinforced by their parents, who support their sons' positive orientation toward school. It would seem that the Brothers' validation of the achievement ideology would secure their success.

When the neighborhood was revisited eight years later, it was no surprise that the Hallway Hangers had not fared well. All still lived in the surrounding area, and many were in jail. The Brothers also lived nearby, and although all of them had graduated from high school and several attended college, overall they fared only slightly better than the Hallway Hangers. Most had failed to move out of low-wage, high-turnover jobs. One of the Brothers even turned to "crack capitalism"—"a career that was catalyzed by the anger and betrayal he felt when the police planted marijuana on him" (MacLeod 1995:207). The only member who met the criteria of success, ironically, advanced to his position by doctoring his credentials.

The possibilities available to lower-class youth are limited from the outset because there are not enough good jobs to go around. Dutifully playing by the rules hardly guarantees success. Layoffs, seasonal cutbacks, and factory closings are widespread. Stable employment is crucial for settling down, marrying, and establishing an independent household. Holding a subordinate position in the class structure reinforces the feelings of personal failure that working-class students are likely to bear.

MacLeod concludes that rather than assume a lack of ambition is the barrier to lower-class achievement, schools should recognize the existence of a class structure and teach students how to overcome the barriers to social mobility. Poverty itself is not a barrier to lower-class advancement. Disappointment and lack of aspiration is a direct result of the impermeability of the class structure and presumed cultural deficiencies of the lower class are the consequences, rather than the causes, of poverty.

Source: Adapted from MacLeod 1995.

Ranked below the lowest caste are people of no caste, the *untouchables,* who perform tasks considered "polluting."

According to Hindu scripture, an individual's varna is determined by a descent rule; that is, it corresponds to the varna of one's parents and is unalterable during one's lifetime.

 Dharma, or "path of duty," is the basis of Hindu morality; it is the idea that each varna has its appropriate rules of behavior.

At the death of the body, the soul meets its fate in the form of a transmigration into a higher or lower be-ing (**karma**). Those who follow their **dharma** will be rewarded with a higher point on Manu's body during their next life. Deviation from the dharma will result in reincarnation in the body of an outcaste or even a wild animal (Long 1987). One of the most important aspects of the dharma is the practice of certain taboos regarding marriage, eating, and physical proximity. Marriage below one's varna is generally regarded as a defilement and pollution. Acceptance of food cooked or handled by persons below one's varna is also a defilement and pollution, and any bodily contact between Brahman and Shudra is forbidden.

In parts of India, the untouchables were also unseeable—even their shadows were thought to pollute a superior group—and therefore these people could come out only at night. The worst of these restrictions became illegal after India gained its independence in 1950, although untouchables continue to face discrimination in getting work and housing.

Although the general outlines of this system are agreed on throughout Hindu India (Long 1987; Maloney 1987a, 1987b), enormous regional and local differences occur in the finer details of the ideology and practice of caste relationships. The principal source of these differences is the fact that it is not the varna but thousands of internally stratified subdivisions known as *jatis* (or subcastes) that constitute the real functional endogamous units. Moreover, even jatis of the same name ("washermen," "shoemakers," "herders," and so on) further divide into local endogamous subgroups and exogamous lineages (Klass 1979).

Today, India's legal system discourages discrimination based on caste identity. Yet caste still plays an important part in people's everyday lives. Hindu religion continues to have powerful sanctions against those who violate caste prescriptions.

The people of India vary widely in skin color. In general people in the north tend to be lighter than those in the south. But unlike the racialized situation of Blacks and Whites (often also called castes) in the United States, physical appearance does not indicate jati identity so that dark skin and high-caste status can occur together (Sanjek 1994a).

Untouchables
The caste system in India must be seen from the bottom up to be understood.

Caste from the Top Down and Bottom Up

There are two very different views of the Hindu caste system. The view that predominates among Westerners is top down. It conforms largely to the emics of the top-ranking Brahman caste.

Each caste and subcaste has a hereditary occupation that guarantees its members basic subsistence and job security.

The lower castes render vital services to the upper castes. Hence, the upper castes know they cannot get along without the lower castes and do not abuse them. In times of crisis, the upper castes will extend emergency assistance in the form of food or loans. Moreover, because the Hindu religion gives everyone a convincing explanation of why some are inferior and others superior, members of lower castes allegedly do not resent being regarded as a source of pollution and defilement and have no interest in changing the status of their caste in the local or regional hierarchy (Dumont 1970).

The other view—the view from the bottom up— makes the Indian caste system hard to distinguish from other kinds of hierarchical groups such as classes and ethnic groups with which Westerners are familiar. Critics of the top-down view point out that Whites in the United States once insisted that the Bible justified slavery and that the slaves were well treated, contented with their lot in life, and not interested in changing their status. According to Joan Mencher (1974), who has worked and lived among the untouchable castes of southern India, the error in the top-down view is just as great in India as in the United States.

The lower castes are not satisfied with their station in life and do not believe they are treated fairly by their caste superiors.

As for the security allegedly provided by the monopoly over such professions as smiths, washermen, barbers, and potters, such occupations taken together never engaged more than 10 to 15 percent of the total Hindu population. Thus caste professions never provided basic subsistence for the majority of the members of most castes. Among the Chamars, for example, who are known as leatherworkers, only a small portion of the caste engages in leatherwork. In the countryside, almost all Chamars provide a source of cheap agricultural labor. When questioned about their low station in life, many of Mencher's low-caste informants explained that they had to depend on the other castes because they had no land of their own.

Anthropological studies of actual village life in India have yielded a picture of caste relationships drastically opposed to the ideals posited in Hindu theology (Carroll 1977). One of the most important discoveries is that local jatis recurrently try to raise their ritual status. Such attempts usually take place as part of a general process by which local ritual status is adjusted to actual local economic and political power. Some low-ranking subcastes may passively accept their lot in life as a result of their karma assignment; such groups, however, tend to be wholly lacking in the potential for economic and political mobility. "But let opportunities for political and economic advance appear barely possible and such resignation is likely to vanish more quickly than one might imagine" (Orans 1968:878).

The propensity for jatis to redefine their spiritual level is seen in the widespread lack of agreement over the shape of local ritual hierarchies, as seen by inhabitants of the same village, town, or region. Even the lowest untouchables may reject the position others assign to them (Khare 1984).

Different individuals and families in the same caste give different versions of the rank order of their group in an attempt to redefine their status.

Elsewhere, even the claims of Brahman subcastes to ritual superiority are openly contested (Srinivas 1955). The conflict among jatis concerning their ritual position may involve prolonged litigation in the local courts and, if not resolved, may lead to violence and bloodshed (see Berreman 1997 [1972]; Cohn 1955). While lower castes may pursue upward mobility in an effort to raise their status, castes already at the top of the hierarchy try to raise their status through Westernization: the adoption of Western culture and Western patterns of material consumption.

The stratification system of India is noteworthy not merely for the presence of endogamous descent groups possessing real or imagined racial and cultural differences. Every state-level society has such groups.

It is, rather, that India has an extraordinary profusion of such groups. Nonetheless, the caste system of India is fundamentally similar to the systems of other countries that have closed classes and numerous ethnic and racial minorities.

Is There a Ruling Class in the United States?

Most Americans do not think of themselves as being members of a class, and class has always been downplayed as a factor in U.S. history. Thus, according to former president George H. W. Bush, "Class is for European democracies or something else—it isn't for the United States of America. We are not going to be divided by class" (DeMott 1990:11). But like all state-organized societies, the United States is a stratified society and has a complex system of class, ethnicity, and race.

There is no doubt that the United States is a highly stratified society. This is evident from the distribution of wealth. According to the Congressional Budget Office (which uses both census data and IRS data—which includes after tax income and income from capital gains), wealth disparities are much greater than income disparities. In fact, wealth has become more concentrated in recent years than at any other time since the Great Depression (Shapiro and Greenstein 1999). According to the same study, in 1995:

- The wealthiest 1 percent of households owned 39 percent of the nation's wealth and received about 13 percent of the nation's after-tax income.
- The wealthiest 20 percent of households owned 84 percent of the nation's wealth and received a little more than 50 percent of the national after-tax income.
- The bottom 80 percent of households owned only 16 percent of the nation's wealth, significantly less than half the wealth the wealthiest 1 percent of the population possessed.

The most important question that can be asked about class in the United States is whether there is a *ruling class*. Paradoxically, this is a subject about which relatively little is known. The existence of a ruling class in the United States seems to be negated by the ability of the people as a whole to vote political office holders in or out by secret ballot. Yet the fact that less than half of the voting-age population votes in presidential elections suggests that the majority of citizens distrust the candidates' promises or doubt that one candidate can do anything more than any other to make life significantly better. The actual selection of political candidates and the financing and conduct of election campaigns are controlled through special interest groups and political action committees. Small coalitions of powerful individuals working through lobbyists, lawfirms, legislatures, the courts, executive and administrative agencies, and the mass media can decisively influence the course of elections and national affairs. The majority of the decision-making process consists of responses to pressures exerted by special interest groups (Drew 1983; Sabato 1989). In campaigns for Congress, the candidate who spends the most money usually wins.

Wealth is related to political power because people who have large amounts of wealth can make political contributions or can use their money to run for office.

Those who claim that the United States has no ruling class argue that power is dispersed among many different contending blocs, lobbies, associations, clubs, industries, regions, income groups, ethnic groups, states, cities, age groups, legislatures, courts, and unions and that no coalition powerful enough to dominate all the others can form (Dahl 1981). But the crucial question is this: Is there a class of people who share a set of underlying interests in the perpetuation of the status quo and who by virtue of their extreme wealth are able to set limits to the kinds of laws and executive policies that are enacted and followed out?

The evidence for the existence of such a category of people consists largely of studies of the extent of interlocking memberships on corporate boards of directors and the concentration of ownership and wealth in giant corporations and well-to-do families. This kind of data alone cannot prove the existence of a ruling class, since the problem remains of how boards of directors and wealthy families actually influence decisions on crucial matters such as the rate of inflation, unemployment, national health service, and the tax structure.

The concentration of wealth and economic power in the United States shows at least that there is a real potential for such influence to be exerted (Roberts and Brintnall 1982:259). According to the Federal Reserve Board (Kennickell and Woodburn 1992; Kennickell et al. 2000), the richest 1 percent of U.S. families owned the following types of wealth.

45 percent of all nonresidential real estate

49 percent of all publicly held stock

78 percent of all trusts

62 percent of all business assets

A rough idea of the trend toward greater concentration of economic power can be derived from changes in family income. Between 1977 and 1989, the average pretax income of the top 1 percent of American families rose 77 percent while the pretax income of the bottom 40 percent of families fell by between 1 and 9 percent. The United States has greater extremes of rich and poor than any other industrial nation (Bradsher 1995).

Another revealing statistic is the growing disparity between the incomes of chief executive officers (CEOs) and ordinary employees. In the 1970s, CEOs made 35 times what employees made; in 1990, they made 120 times more (Noah 1991), and by 1995, they made close to 200 times what the average worker made (Weinstein 1995).

It is entirely possible, therefore, that a small group of individuals and families could exert a decisive influence over the policies of a small but immensely powerful group of corporations. Anthropologists have been remiss in not studying the patterns of thoughts and actions of the superrich.

SUMMARY
and *Questions to Think About*

1. Class differences involve both differential access to power and profound differences in lifestyles.

2. The understanding of class and all other forms of social stratification is made difficult by the failure to separate emic and etic versions of stratification hierarchies. From an etic and behavioral point of view, classes can exist even if the members show no emic recognition of their existence and even if segments of the same class compete.

3. In open hierarchies, ruling-class membership can change rapidly from one generation to the next. Similarly, subordinate classes need not be conscious of their identity and may exist only in an etic and behavioral sense.

4. Peasants are structured inferiors who farm with preindustrial technologies and pay rent or taxes. Their structured inferiority depends on either their inability to acquire land or on the existence

of a price market in land and labor controlled by big landlords, corporations, and banks.

5. Among peasant classes, an image of limited good is widespread. However, their conservative values and attitudes do allow for innovations and risk taking under appropriate structural and infra-structural conditions.

6. The counterpart of the image of limited good for subordinate urban classes is the culture of poverty. This concept focuses on the values and traditions of the urban poor as an explanation for poverty. However, many of the values in the culture of poverty, such as distrust of authority, consumerism, and improvidence, are also found in the middle classes.

7. Much of the behavior of the underclass, as in the case of Naples, Italy, can be understood as a con-sequence of chronic unemployment.

8. Opportunities for upward mobility are extremely limited, despite the belief that the United States has an open class system. Poor youth experience the pervasive power of social class, where ambi-tion is not enough to overcome one's marginal status.

9. Castes are closed endogamous groups that resem-ble classes and ethnic groups. Traditional views of Indian castes have been dominated by top-down idealizations, in which the lower castes are repre-sented as voluntarily accepting their subordinate status. Bottom-up studies show that lower Indian castes struggle for upward mobility and attempt to bring their castes' ranking in line with their economic status.

10. Although class is downplayed in the United States, there is no doubt that this society is highly stratified. There is a strong wealth disparity in the United States, and money plays a major role in the political process.

Questions to Think About

1. What is power, and under what conditions is it more likely to be enforced?

2. Why does Foster believe that the image of lim-ited good hinders development in Mexico?

3. What is the culture of poverty, and why has the concept been criticized?

4. What are the features of caste stratification? How is caste hierarchy challenged?

5. How does the caste system compare with so-cial class in the United States?

6. Why is it so difficult to achieve the "American dream," or even succeed to work full time?

7. What changes in the U.S. economy contribute to income disparity?

THROUGH THE LENS
of Cultural Materialism

Conformity and Conflict • Reading Fifteen
Office Work and the Crack Alternative
Philippe Bourgois

The underground drug economy in New York City supports many Puerto Rican inner-city males who are unable to find stable legitimate jobs that afford them a sense of dignity. Instead of blaming these men for their failure to find main-stream employment, it is important to understand the con-ditions that motivate them to become drug dealers.

Etic Perspective

- The loss of manufacturing jobs in New York City during the 1960s, 1970s, and 1980s left only low-level, mini-mum-paying jobs in the service sector of the economy.

- These jobs are not suited to the behavior that inner-city males learn on the streets and create class, ethnic, and gender conflicts that force them to become drug dealers.

Emic Perspective

- The street identity of undereducated Puerto Rican males makes them resist work in the service sector.

- This makes them feel intimidated and that they do not fit in because they lack the skills and demeanor ex-pected by White, middle-class culture.

Infrastructure

- New York is one of the most expensive cities to live in and has a high rate of poverty as well as great afflu-ence.

- During the 1980s, the real value of the minimum wage declined by one-third, social services were cut back, and an influx of immigrants arrived who were willing to work hard for low income.

- Factory work, which provided the previous genera-tion of Spanish-speaking, native-born workers with stable unionized jobs, is no longer available. It has been replaced by jobs in the service economy, which require a more educated, homogeneous workforce.

Structure

- Many adolescents initially drop out of school to work at service jobs in the inner city, which provide them with basic necessities. As they get older, their lack of education and failure to acclimate to the mainstream culture limits their opportunities for advancement.

- The contemporary service sector requires work skills and social skills, that Puerto Rican males are not accustomed to, such as the ability to follow specific instructions and to take orders from women.

- Unlike Mexican immigrants—many of whom are illegal, speak only Spanish, and are willing to work hard for minimum pay—Puerto Rican inner-city males are proficient in English and do not require work permits. They are therefore unwilling to make the same sacrifices as other unskilled workers.

Superstructure

- Young Puerto Rican males are unable to gain a satisfying identity by working in mainstream jobs and so turn to a street identity. Doing so enables them to maintain their dignity and sense of masculinity.

- Legal office work requires bicultural interactional skills that inner-city males lack.

- They experience the dominant culture as disrespecting them and feel insulted when they have to subordinate themselves across gender lines.

- Rather than feel disrespected in entry-level service jobs, Puerto Rican males refuse to assume bicultural skills and instead join the drug culture, which is lucrative and does not affront their dignity and masculinity.

CHAPTER 13

ETHNICITY, RACE, AND RACISM

Germans participate in an antiracism protest march at Dachau, the site of a World War II concentration camp.

T wo other hierarchical groups associated with the rise of the state—ethnic groups and social races—are the subject of this chapter. How *ethnic groups* and *social races* differ from *classes* and *castes* is one of the questions to be considered. We will also address the worldwide confusion concerning the relationship of biological races to social races and ethnic groups. Then we will explore the dynamic processes that lead to more or less successful outcomes of the competition among social races and ethnic groups. We will pay special attention to the alternatives of assimilation and pluralism in the United States, where White racism against African Americans and other non-Whites continues to flourish. This leads to a critique of the key evidence for White superiority. Ethnic and racial chauvinists of any ilk may have a hard time setting aside beliefs, often unconsciously held, about how Europeans came to dominate other cultures.

Ethnicity

Ethnic groups appeared as a consequence of the rise of the state. States achieved prominence in political evolution precisely because of their ability to extend boundaries to include near and distant polities such as chiefdoms and other states. Ethnic groups first formed when conquered populations retained distinctive linguistic and cultural features associated with their preconquest status. In modern times, ethnic groups have formed as much through migration as through conquest.

> An **ethnic group** is a group that has been incorporated into a state through conquest or migration, that maintains distinctive cultural and/or linguistic traditions, and that has a sense of a separate, shared, and age-old identity.

Members of ethnic groups often believe that they have a distinctive appearance, that they are descended from common ancestors, and that they share distinctive traditions and customs. Some ethnic groups, such as the White ethnics (Irish Americans, Italian Americans, Polish Americans, Jewish Americans, Greek Americans, and so forth) in the United States, see themselves as divisions or branches of a single racial group. But other ethnic groups (such as Cubans in Miami, Haitians in New York) may themselves recognize that they are not racially homogeneous (see Profile 13.1).

Ethnicity is believed to be associated with distinctive cuisines, holidays, religious beliefs, dances, folklore, dress, and other traditions, but the single most powerful cultural source of ethnic identity is the possession of a common language or dialect. Use of a common language or dialect instills a sense of community that is powerful enough to override regional differences, differences of class, and the absence of other kinds of common cultural traditions.

Throughout history, individuals and groups moved to new areas or changed their identities by acquiring memberships in different groups. Many ethnic groups intermarried frequently and exchanged spouses to form political and economic alliances. There are also examples of individuals who changed their ethnic identities for personal reasons and those who maintained multiple ethnicities and spoke several languages (Smedley 1993).

As in the case of class identity, emic and etic versions of ethnicity may bear little resemblance to each other. Ethnics do not necessarily speak the language of their ancestors. Moreover, their ancestral customs are not necessarily the heritage of remote ancestors; some are actually the inventions of recent generations. Some ethnic groups may neither speak the language of their ethnic ancestors nor preserve ancestral customs, old or new (Roosens 1989). Preservation of ethnic identity may merely result from marrying endogamously and using family names indicative of ethnic descent. Even high rates of intermarriage do not necessarily impede the continuity of an ethnic group: Various rules of descent can be used to retain the children of mixed marriages within the ethnic group of one of the parents.

Ethnic Empowerment

In a democracy, only those who speak up are heard, and outsiders never achieve a secure power base. Translated into the terms of ethnic politics, this means that for empowerment, nondominant ethnic groups need both to learn to speak loudly in their own voice and to rely primarily on their own material and ideological resources.

Wars and migration have been the major sources of the ethnic diversity we see around us. Captured and enslaved African peoples were transported against their will across the ocean, and Native Americans, defeated in their attempt to safeguard their homelands, were forced to move to distant reservations. Conquest also lies at the root of the Hispanic ethnic group in the Southwest and in California. Meanwhile, White ethnics, especially those from Ireland and from Eastern and Southern Europe, migrated under various degrees of compulsion in search of relief from religious or political persecution, military impressment, or the threat of outright starvation. Although each ethnic group has its distinctive history, they all share many experiences and have evolved

PROFILE 13.1 | Diversity among Hispanic Americans

Hispanic groups in the United States (also called *Latinos*) are heterogeneous because of historical and local conditions, which have led to the creation of distinct cultural adaptations to U.S. culture. According to the 1990 U.S. Census, approximately 60 percent of Hispanic Americans are of Mexican origin, 12 percent are of Puerto Rican origin, 5 percent are of Cuban origin, and 23 percent are "other Hispanic," mostly from Central and South America and the Dominican Republic. According to the U.S. Bureau of the Census (2001), the Hispanic population increased by almost 58 percent between 1990 and 2000. Approximately 58.5 percent of Hispanic Americans are of Mexican origin; 9.6 percent are of Puerto Rican origin; 3.5 percent are of Cuban origin; and 28.4 percent are "other Hispanic," mostly from Central and South America and the Dominican Republic.

A Mexican American Extended Family in Texas
Some families date back several generations.

Differences in economic success and family structure distinguish Hispanic groups. For example, mainland Puerto Ricans, more than any other group, are economically disadvantaged. They have more families headed by single females and have the highest rate of welfare dependency. Despite the advantage of U.S. citizenship, Puerto Ricans are concentrated in urban areas of the Northeast with declining manufacturing jobs. Between 1950 and 1970, population growth and a decline in subsistence agriculture in Puerto Rico resulted in high rates of labor expulsion and migration. In the United States, Puerto Ricans faced discrimination in the highly unionized labor force. Because they were not subject to deportation, they would not work for low wages and were effectively excluded from the workforce. Employers instead opted to hire other undocumented immigrant groups, such as East Indians and Dominicans, who were willing to work for less.

Cuban Americans, on the other hand, are exceptionally successful, especially the first wave of refugees that arrived in 1959 and received government assistance. Many are political refugees who are concentrated in Miami, where they have created an enclave economy with entrepreneurial activities and small businesses that create jobs for new arrivals and opportunities for economic mobility. Cuban Americans have also managed to preserve their culture. A section of Miami known as "Little Havana" has become a cultural center where artists, actors, and musicians preserve some Cuban traditions more than in Cuba itself.

Mexican Americans are by far the largest and oldest Hispanic group. Many have lived in the United States for several generations, as part of a Northern Mexican colonial population that dates back some 400 years. Two-thirds of Mexican Americans are concentrated in California, Texas, and New Mexico; other states with more recent Mexican American populations include Illinois, Colorado, Arizona, and New Jersey. In the Southwest, Mexicans have traditionally been a reliable source of agricultural wage labor. They have maintained close ties with relatives across the border and identify with Mexican culture. However, as the younger generation gains more education and economic power, the competitive individualistic norms of U.S. culture are adopted. Other children of Mexican American immigrants may experience intense culture conflict due to what Diego Vigil (1988, 1997) terms *multiple marginalities*—confusion over identity, parents with limited education, and a lack of well paying jobs. In most cases, the transition is achieved through identification with the mainstream, but in others, these identity issues propel some Mexican American youths into gangs.

Hispanic populations are at different levels of integration into U.S. society. Most American-born Hispanics speak better English than Spanish. Only a few call themselves *Latino* or *Hispanic,* and many want to be called American. Many take on the attitudes and voting patterns of European Americans and believe there are

(continued)

PROFILE 13.1 | Diversity among Hispanic Americans *(continued)*

too many immigrants in the United States and that continued immigration depresses wages. Up to 60 percent of second-generation Hispanics favor legal sanctions against employers who hire undocumented workers.

Except for those who have very dark skin and are poor, most Hispanics are blending into the general population at least as fast as earlier White ethnic groups did. Many are moving into the suburbs, while immigrant newcomers find themselves working as undocumented workers in communities with segregated schools and with salaries that are 30 percent less than those of their legal counterparts.

Source: Adapted from "Latino Legacies: Crossing National and Creating Cultural Boundaries" and "The Culture of Latinos in the United States" by Thomas Weaver and reprinted with permission from the publisher of *Handbook of Hispanic Cultures in the United States: Anthropology* (Houston: Arte Publico Press, University of Houston, copyright © 1994).

along similar lines in response to similar pressures. Some groups, however, have been better prepared by their own cultural traditions to cope with the challenges of their new conditions of life.

> Those ethnic groups with a strong literate tradition and a history of individualized competition for upward mobility are preadapted for competing in the rapidly changing world of an urban industrial society.

There is an ongoing effort to continue to promote ethnic pride and to revitalize old ethnic traditions or to invent new ones. Young people, in unprecedented numbers, have taken up the study of languages spoken by their grandparents, promoted public festivals and parades to celebrate their cultural traditions, established various single-group ethnic social clubs, and vigorously campaigned to block or reverse affirmative action policies designed to help non-Whites.

Some ethnic groups have become unified for the rational goal of gaining political and economic power. In the past, Latinos saw themselves as separate ethnicities based on their countries of origin. More recently, there has been a feeling of shared cultural identity that has been fostered by Latino leaders to reinforce Latino unity.

Confronting Ethnocentrism

In the course of ethnic politics, each group tends to pay far more attention to its own origins, history, heroism, suffering, and achievements than to those of other ethnic groups. In this context, ethnicity turns out to mean an especially aggressive and virulent form of **ethnocentrism,** the sense that one's own ethnic group is superior to others.

> The origins of ethnocentrism are linked to the concept of descent, the principle whereby individuals and groups establish their identities and consider themselves distinctive.

Although theories of **descent** vary from culture to culture, the basic idea occurs universally—namely, that individuals acknowledge a special relatedness to parents and to children that endures after death. Descent implies the preservation of some aspect of the substance or spirit of people in past and future generations and thus is a symbolic form of immortality. Descent lies at the heart of the formation of social races and ethnic groups. Various systems for identifying ethnic groups are in use throughout the world.

Whenever one large group interacts with another, a sense of unified opposition, whether it is based on religious, ethnic, national, or racial affiliation, can act as a dividing force. Individuals are not usually preoccupied with group identity until they are threatened. When a group is in conflict or at war with another group, members become acutely aware of their group identity—even to the point where it may outweigh concern for individual needs or survival. The preconditions for such conflicts usually consist of infrastructural deficiencies (resource shortages derived from population pressure) and differences in the distribution of wealth and quality of life. The more stressful the environment, the more likely neighboring groups will become preoccupied with one another.

The process of dehumanizing a perceived ethnic enemy may occur in stages—starting with intense prejudice toward an unwanted group and escalating to physical struggle through forced assimilation, resettlement, and genocide under the label of "ethnic cleansing." After the Holocaust, many believed that systematized atrocities could never occur again. But according to the Carter Center in Atlanta, ethnic terrorism is on the rise, with most conflicts taking place between ethnic groups within the boundaries of single countries: Protestants and Catholics in Ireland; Jews and Palestinians in Israel; Hutus and Tutsis in Burundi; and ethnic Albanians and Serbs in Kosovo, just to name a few (Volkan 1997).

Each ethnic group is the product of shared historical experiences that serve to unite and distinguish the group from others and give it a distinct identity.

The terms *chosen trauma* and *chosen glory* have been used to describe the collective memory of a past calamity or a heroic event, respectively, that befell a group. These feelings about the past are brought into the present, and that serves as a collective origin myth for defining a distinctive ethnic identity. Inclusion in the origin myth legitimates a people's status as members of a group. Adopting a chosen trauma enhances a sense of victimization that unifies the group and justifies ethnic aggression to reverse misfortune into triumph, whereas reactivating a chosen glory (such as a war of independence) is a legendary event that bolsters a group's self-esteem (Volkan 1997).

Biological Races versus Social Races versus Ethnic Groups

The popular conception of **biological race** is flawed because differences between populations are largely superficial, resulting from adaptations to local climatic conditions during the most recent period of human evolution. Genetic analysis, which provides a deeper and more reliable measure of biological differences between people, reveals that overall, people are remarkably similar in their genetic makeup.

 Biological races are etic populations in which several genes occur together with distinctive frequencies over many generations.

Of the genetic differences that do exist, more variation occurs within so-called racial groups than between them. That is, two people from the same race are, on average, almost as biologically different from each other as any two people in the world chosen at random (see Box 13.1). This lack of genetic continuity results from the fact that human populations exchange genes through mating, creating ever-changing patterns of genetic variations (Armelagos and Goodman 1994).

Humans are much more alike than they are different.

Despite the lack of genetic boundaries, undeniable physical differences between populations are used to classify people. These classifications are more appropriately called **social races**, or groups that are assumed to be biologically different from each other but are in fact classified according to culturally defined categories, such as common descent, skin tone, and facial features. Moreover, children of mixed marriages automatically get their racial identity from the minority parent, which is a culturally defined practice rather than one with any biological justification.

 Social races are assumed to have a biological basis but are in fact culturally constructed.

Human populations have always engaged in so much interbreeding that it would be meaningless to speak of fixed boundaries between races. Also, the distribution of hereditary physical traits does not follow clear boundaries; there is often greater variation within one racial group than between different groups.

Social races differ from ethnic groups only as a matter of degree. Social races claim common ancestry based on the practice of endogamy and rules of descent. They or others believe that they can be picked out in a crowd simply on the basis of their looks. The resemblance between social races and ethnic groups is so close that many people use the terms *ethnic group* and *race* interchangeably. Others, however, claim that racial differences are more permanent and visible than the differences in dress or language found among ethnics (see Wolf 1994).

Social race is an emic construct that can be used politically to justify prejudice and stratification.

Some African Americans, for example, claim that racial markers become the focus for discrimination by dominant ethnic and racial groups because they are indelible. As a result, racially different individuals have no chance to escape from the persecution and discrimination of the dominant group. The argument is only valid, however, because of culturally constructed principles such as descent and physical characterizations that are employed to give individuals a racial identity.

BOX 13.1 Racial Classification Schemes Explain Very Little about Genetic Variation

The biological fact of human variation is that there are no traits that are inevitably associated with one another. Morphological features do vary from region to region, but they do so independently, not in packaged sets. For example, we could divide the world into two groups of blondes and brunettes, but if we start adding other traits—like skin color, eye color, stature, blood type, and so on—it won't take long before we have a race with only one person in it. Despite the obvious physical differences between people from different regions, the vast majority of human genetic variation occurs within populations, not between them.

The American Anthropological Association position on race (1998) states that human populations are not clearly demarcated, biologically distinct groups. Evidence from the analysis of genetics (e.g., DNA) shows that geographic "racial" groupings differ from one another only in about 6 percent of their genes. Throughout history whenever different groups have come into contact, they have interbred and the continued sharing of genetic materials has maintained all of humankind as a single species.

While most anthropologists believe that race is no longer a useful concept for describing human variation, medical researchers find racial categories useful for organizing health-related data; each year dozens of reports in health journals show purported differences between the races in susceptibility to disease, infant mortality rates, life expectancy, and other markers of public health. In the United States, African American infants are almost 2.5 times more likely to die within the first 11 months of life than non–African American infants. African Americans are almost twice as likely as Euro-Americans to suffer from hypertension, or high blood pressure—a condition that carries with it an increased risk of heart failure and other cardiovascular diseases. And it's been shown that Native Americans are far more likely than other ethnic groups to carry an enzyme that makes it harder to metabolize alcohol; this would leave them genetically more vulnerable to alcoholism.

Are these studies pointing at genetic differences between the races, or are they using race as a convenient scapegoat for health deficiencies whose causes might better be explained by a person's socioeconomic status and environment? The higher incidence of hypertension in African Americans could be attributed to higher dietary sodium levels, increased exposure to psychological stress, and limited access to health care. The hope is for the medical community to treat hypertension in African Americans more aggressively, but whether the findings really say anything about the role of race in disease is another matter altogether.

Source: Adapted from Shreve 1994.

The One-Drop Rule

Various systems for identifying social races are in use throughout the world today. In the United States, African Americans are not identified as a distinct social race solely on the basis of their skin color. Reliance on skin color alone would leave the identity of millions of people in doubt because skin color (and other supposedly African and Caucasian traits) varies across a broad spectrum of nuanced differences, from very dark to brown to very light, as a result of recent and remote interracial matings and marriages (Root 1992). In the context of slavery and its aftermath, when it was U.S. official policy to discriminate against Blacks, Whites needed some rule or principle to categorize people as either Black or White so that the discriminatory measures could be applied to Blacks who looked like Whites but not to Whites who looked like Blacks. To solve this quandary, Whites constructed the one-drop rule.

According to the one-drop rule, a Black person was anyone who had the slightest amount of Black "blood," as attested to by having even one ancestor who was known to have been identified as Black (whether or not this ancestor was also a child of a mixed marriage or mating).

By the one-drop rule still in force today, children of a mixed marriage between one biologically White and one biologically Black parent are socially black (Root 1992; Spickard 1992:16). Louisiana law declares anyone with at least 1:32 "Negro blood" to be legally Black. But scientifically, we know that all of us inherit half of our cell nucleus genes from mother and half from father, so it is clear that the rule is arbitrary and race is culturally constructed.

A very different construction of social race prevails in Latin America and the Caribbean Islands.

Racial Identity in Brazil

Brazilians have a great number of racial categories for facial features, skin color, and hair texture. They recognize the physical variation that exits in their population, which suggests it is futile to think of human beings in terms of a small number of fixed and sharply distinct races.

In Brazil, for example, racial categorizations depend mainly on the perceptions that people have of each other's appearance, with equal emphasis on skin tone and hair form. But a person's racial identity may also be influenced by his or her wealth and profession. Brazilians use many more terms for identifying any individual's particular combination of traits. In one study (M. Harris 1970), 492 terms were encountered. Thus, two people of the same color can be classified in different categories depending on their profession and economic status. The one-drop rule doesn't exist in Brazil; ancestry or descent is not important for racial identity. This means that children can have a racial identity that is different from that of their parents and further that one child can be identified as the equivalent of White whereas his or her full brother or sister can be identified as the equivalent of Black (M. Harris et al. 1993). Although Brazil prides itself on its racial harmony, most darker-skinned Brazilians tend to be poorer and less educated. Brazilians of African descent, who are descendents of slaves, are poor because they have lacked access to land or commercial wealth, and upward social mobility is difficult. Poor darker-skinned Brazilians therefore face discrimination despite so much diversity (Kottak 1994).

Biological Race and Culture

The relationship between biological race and culture is a source of much confusion the world over. One of the most important tasks of anthropology is to clarify the difference between them.

Etically, a *biological race* is a population—an interbreeding group of people defined by a set of distinctive gene frequencies. A *culture* is a way of life.

A large-scale biological race does not have just one culture; it has hundreds of cultures. And these cultures cover the whole spectrum of cultural types, from bands and villages to states and empires. Thus people who belong to different biological races may possess very similar or even identical cultures, and people who possess very different cultures may belong to the same biological race.

In the United States, millions of racially diverse children and grandchildren of Asians and Africans have a way of life that is essentially similar to the way of life of the Caucasian majority. These biological and anthropological facts, however, are often ignored in the construction of social races. As we will see momentarily, the sense of having a distinctive culture is important for the mobilization of resistance within disadvantaged social races and ethnic groups. However, the view that race and culture are rigidly linked is a form of racism that runs counter to all that is scientifically known about the transmissibility of cultures across racial and ethnic boundaries. It bears repeating that at birth, every healthy human infant, regardless of race, has the capacity to acquire the traditions, practices, values, and languages found in any of the world's 5,000 or so different cultures.

The Competitive Dynamics of Ethnic and Racial Groups

The most important point to bear in mind about ethnic groups and social races is that they are invariably locked into more or less open and conscious forms of political, social, and economic struggle to protect or raise their positions in the stratification system. To a surprising degree, the class struggle predicted by Karl Marx has been overshadowed by race and ethnic struggles, creating a hierarchy of group inequality in which race, not class, became the central stratifying variable. While class differences have rarely led to class consciousness and class solidarity, racial and ethnic groups the world over have been at the forefront of conscious and often violent struggles aimed at changing the stratification hierarchy.

Ethnic and racial groups rise or fall in the hierarchy depending on their numbers, their special cultural strengths and weaknesses, and their initial advantages or disadvantages during the formation of the stratification system. Thus, although many ethnic groups and social races are subject to severe forms of discrimination, segregation, and exploitation, others—such as the Chinese living in Indonesia—may actually enjoy fairly high, though not dominant, status positions.

An emphasis on differences in language, religion, and other aspects of lifestyle increases a group's sense of solidarity, and this solidarity may help its members compete, especially in impersonalized, class-structured, capitalist societies.

Ethnic merchants and businesspeople frequently enjoy important commercial advantages as a result of sharing information and obtaining loans and credit from their ethnic associates. Many Americans continue to use their ethnic networks actively when looking for jobs or spouses. Many prefer to live in neighborhoods dominated by people with the same origins as themselves, and they continue to regard themselves as Italians, Poles, and so on, in addition to being Americans—two generations or more after their ancestors left the country of origin. Moreover, racial and ethnic consciousness is a necessary condition for mobilizing the mental and physical resources of groups to defend or improve their position in the hierarchy. Thus, all ethnic and racial groups find themselves under pressure to cast their history and their achievements in the most favorable light.

The problem is that strong ethnic and racial solidarity carries with it the danger of backlash. In maintaining and increasing their own solidarity, social races and ethnic groups run the risk of increasing the dominant group's resentment and hence of becoming the scapegoats of discriminatory and even genocidal policies. The persecution of the Jews in Germany and Poland, the Hindu Indians in East and Southern Africa, the Chinese in Indonesia, and the Muslims and Sikhs in India are some of the better-known examples of "successful" adaptations that were followed by mass slaughter or forced migrations.

Ethnic Chauvinism

Although members of many ethnic groups in the United States have moved toward assimilation, there is also a growing concern with preserving ethnicity identity. Glazer and Moynihan (1963) have stated that the most important point to be made about the American "melting pot" is that it never occurred. They argue that rather than eradicating ethnic differences, modern U.S. society has actually created a new awareness in people, a concern about roots and origins. Even though ethnic groups may adopt the language of the majority and become culturally similar to the dominant majority, they nevertheless maintain cultural traditions of their common ancestry.

The intensity of racial and ethnic struggles in the United States presents a counterpoint to the generally unconscious and confused nature of class relations. Every racial and ethnic group has a sense of its own identity and collective purpose, yet it exists within a larger, class-based system of stratification. Definition of ethnicity has political importance in the United States today. Those ethnic groups that have high public visibility generally have political clout, whereas others do not. Instead of uniting to improve schools, neighborhoods, jobs, and health services, minority ethnic and racial groups often seek to achieve their own advancement at one another's expense. The prejudice that ethnic minorities feel toward one another is part of the political and economic struggle that preserves the overall pattern of class stratification (see Box 13.2). Ethnic chauvinism thus pits "have nots" against "have littles" and thereby allows the "haves" to maintain their wealth and power. Once again, the emic–etic distinction is vital to the comprehension of this situation.

Class-consciousness among minority ethnic groups has not developed in many cases because in the short run, it has been disadvantageous for the White working class.

A.

B.

C.

D.

Ethnic Festivals

A. An Irish parade in New York.   B. An Italian festival in Boston.   C. Fiesta Day in Ybor City, Florida.   D. A Japanese festival in Los Angeles.

BOX 13.2 | **Ethnic Intolerance**

After a massive earthquake in Soviet Armenia in 1988, the Soviets collected blood for Armenian victims from Armenia's neighbors, the Azerbaijanis. But the Armenians refused to accept it, even as the casualties rose to over 20,000. The long-standing hatred between the two groups had been suppressed during Soviet rule, but as Soviet republics gained independence, old ethnic conflicts over disputed territory reemerged. By the time of the earthquake, the Armenians would rather have died than accept Azerbaijani blood—a symbolic contamination of Armenian identity—into their veins (Volkan 1997). From a medical and biological point of view, there was, of course, no significant difference between Armenian and Azerbaijani blood.

With the possibility for relatively high upward mobility, working-class Whites were disinclined to make an alliance with non-White members of the working class. European immigrants stopped defining themselves by their countries of origin to protect their privileged group position. By abandoning other racial and ethnic groups, they increased their own chances of rising to middle-class status. Thus, European immigrants became middle class by heading toward suburbia, while segregation kept African Americans out of the suburbs, and redlining made sure banks would not loan them money to buy homes in White neighborhoods (Brodkin 1994). However, it can be argued that working-class Whites have had to pay an enormous penalty for failing to unite with non-White poor and working classes. For example, in a 1970s study of a working-class neighborhood in Brooklyn, New York, Ida Susser (1982) found that racial divisions debilitated collective action and allowed elected officials and commercial developers a free hand that benefited middle- and upper-class Whites. "So long as racial issues kept white voters loyal, elected officials could ignore the needs of a poor white working-class constituency" (1982:208).

One reason for the limited success of ethnically based political activism in the United States is that it provoked a reactive increase in the solidarity sentiments and activities of majority White ethnic groups.

In response to real or imagined threats to their schools, neighborhoods, and jobs, European ethnics resisted the attempts of non-Whites at gaining political power. They mounted antibusing campaigns and created new private and public school systems based on segregated suburban residence patterns.

With time, however, both White and non-White minorities found they had to rethink the consequences of ethnic chauvinism. As European ethnics left the cities for suburbia, cities became transformed from the solidly White neighborhoods of the 1960s to some of the most ethnically mixed communities in the world. The early stages of this transformation entailed a downgrading or disinvestment in local neighborhoods. As poorer people started moving in, deliberate downgrading took place; jobs were eliminated, landlords deferred maintenance, and government resources for neighborhoods declined.

One such neighborhood is Elmhurst–Corona in New York, where the neighborhood White population fell from 98 percent in 1960 to 18 percent in 1990. Finally, in 1993, when the quality of life deteriorated in terms of school overcrowding, lack of youth recreational facilities, housing code violations and drug sales, and lack of police response, civic activism across ethnic lines became important (see Profile 13.2).

Assaults on the quality of life, brought on by the erosion of community resources in multiethnic neighborhoods, have finally prompted residents to cross the lines of race and ethnicity to bring about political change.

In Roger Sanjek's words, "Politics is more than attitudes. It is also about interpersonal connections and group action. . . . The struggles, defeats, and victories that constitute neighborhood politics occur, not because attitudes somehow change but because [people take action]" (1998:368–369).

In multicultural Los Angeles, the deep recession of the early 1990s led to interethnic resentment instead of collaboration. How can we understand the deep rift between Blacks and Korean Americans in South Central Los Angeles that culminated in widespread destruction of Korean-owned businesses in the 1992 uprising? As we saw in Chapter 4, cultural misunderstandings may account for perceptions of the others as outright rude and generate passionate feelings of prejudice. But the cause of the conflict is not ideological; it stems from conditions at the infrastructural and structural levels (see Profile 13.3). Black resentment toward Koreans can best be understood in terms of dwindling economic prospects in the community and the deep recession of the 1990s. At the time, middle-class Blacks were doing well in terms of increased income, home ownership, and education, but Blacks with low capital were hard hit by the recession of the early 1990s and additionally faced competion for jobs, housing, and political power from the influx of Latinos from Mexico and Central America. This formed the background for the three-day uprising against the White power structure.

Defining Racism

Racism as a cultural construct emerged out of historical circumstances. Many contemporary scholars believe that race is a relatively recent concept in human history and that its use coincides with colonial conquest and exploitation by Western European nations during the past 500 years. Even though slavery existed prior to colonialism, they say, it never took the form of racial slavery. People of all physical and ethnic variations were subject to enslavement, but their bondage was never rationalized by denying that they were fully human (Smedley 1993).

PROFILE 13.2   Elmhurst–Corona—Joining Forces across Ethnic and Racial Lines

At no one's request and by no one's design, Elmhurst–Corona, Queens, a New York City neighborhood, was transformed from a solidly White community to a heterogeneous ethnically mixed community. By 1990, Elmhurst–Corona was 45 percent Latin American, 26 percent Asian, and 10 percent African American.

When African Americans and other other non-White immigrants first moved into the area, the shift to a multi-ethnic community produced racial and social tensions. As Whites noticed the changes, they voiced discontent. The new tenants were labeled as "welfare recipients" and were blamed for the overall deterioration of the community. Also, the growing immigrant newcomers of Elmhurst–Corona were misidentified as "illegal aliens." One local community board chairman referred to immigrant newcomers as "people pollution."

Finally, residents turned to one another for support in solving problems. Racial and class lines slowly began to blur. An Italian American woman began petitioning to keep a police precinct house in the neighborhood by going door to door and setting up networks and block associations that included all ethnicities. Latin and Asian American groups became politically active for the first time. In 1980, an organization was formed to help members of the Hispanic community become part of the American political process by providing immigration assistance and registering voters. Korean merchants established ties with non-Koreans to enforce city sanitation collection for storeowners.

As members of different ethnic groups began to work together, leadership shifted to females. This occurred in

Bridging Ethnic and Racial Boundaries

Anthropologist Kyeyoung Park (front row, second from left) led a group of African Americans and Latinos to Korea to promote better understanding of Korean history and culture.

part because of women's concern for their children's safety. Also, many of Elmhurst–Corona's female leaders were accustomed to working in formal organizations, where interpersonal skills and improvisation were more important than structured or titled positions. Women used their personal ties to lobby across racial and ethnic lines for various quality-of-life issues such as obtaining a security guard for the local library; petitioning for traffic signs, parking enforcement, and park cleanup; and organizing neighborhood safety patrols. As one resident commented, "We have to live with one another, or we won't survive."

Racism is the belief that the cultural and intellectual characteristics of a population are linked to its biological racial character, with the notion that some races are inherently superior to others.

Today, the term *racism* also refers to a social system in which certain groups are oppressed and exploited with the rationalization that they are racially (biologically) inferior. Racism implies a belief in a biologically determined hierarchy of human groups (see Box 13.3).

Racialism is a relatively benign form of making racial distinctions, such as skin color and facial characteristics, intended for reference purposes.

Racialism is the recognition that differences between people exist, but that one group is not superior to the others. The term was defined by Kwame Anthony Appiah (1992) to identify heritable characteristics which allow us to divide people in such a way that all the members of these groups share certain traits and tendencies with each other that they do not share with members of other groups.

Feelings about race are so sensitive in U.S. society that elaborate linguistic codes have developed to permit the indirect expression of racist views. Current codes of expressions for the exclusion of minorities from social equality include the need to "protect property values" (to keep minorities out of all-White neighborhoods) and "no busing of schoolchildren" (to keep school systems segregated).

Most White people presume that being White is normal. White people don't have to think about race

PROFILE 13.3   Black/Korean Tension in South Central Los Angeles

Unlike Elmhurst–Corona, the predominantly Black neighborhood of South Central Los Angeles experienced intense racial conflict associated with economic downturn. During the 1980s, the neighborhood bore the brunt of the nation's decline in manufacturing employment as factories closed and capital flowed out of the community. More than 300 plants and industries closed down, and approximately one in three households had incomes below the poverty line. There was a definite decline in the quality of life; there were few full-service grocery stores and small Mom-and-Pop stores charged considerably more than bigger retailers. This is when a new wave of entrepreneurial Korean immigrants began buying up struggling businesses in South Central, in hope of fulfilling the American capitalist dream.

Korean immigrants had access to outside sources of capital and used local rotating credit associations to obtain loans for investments. They showed a willingness to work long hours and used family members to cut labor costs. Most Korean immigrants operate successful small family businesses, such as grocery stores and gas stations, with few or no local employees. They do not reside in the neighborhood in which they work and remain separate from the community at large. They live in ethnic enclaves and strive to fulfill middle-class dreams of home-ownership, a good education for their children, and a comfortable life in their old age. Consequently, the Black community came to view Korean merchants as surrogate Whites—as people who take from the community without giving anything back (Park 1995, 1996).

Racial tension escalated and culminated in the 1992 uprising following the initial acquittal of four White police officers accused of police brutality in the beating of Black motorist Rodney King. Many people associated the King verdict with economic injustice in their own lives. The protest resulted in a three-day turbulent uprising. Although Blacks, Whites, and Latinos all took part in the looting, Korean American businesses suffered disproportionate damage. Some Koreans defended their property with automatic weapons as the looting and burning progressed, yet hundreds of Korean businesses were damaged or destroyed. Nearly half of the city's $1 billion in damages was suffered by Korean American small business owners.

or what it means to be a White person. They are not cognizant of the privileges U.S. society confers on people who have White skin. The privileges of being White entail advantages received simply by being born with features that are highly valued by society.

The Wages of Racism

Many people remain convinced that some racial groups are naturally smarter, more musical, more athletic, or more spiritual than others. These stereotypes

BOX 13.3   Racism on Campus

During the 1980s and 1990s, tensions between whites and blacks and other minorities increased all across the United States. A wave of racially motivated hostility affected not only urban neighborhoods but college campuses as well. This resurgence of overt racism results in part from conservative policies that foster racial polarization by cutting back on critical social programs. But a deeper level of sociocultural causation needs to be considered. One must ask why conservative political programs became attractive. The answer may be that the electoral success of political leaders who were indifferent about the plight of minorities was related to the marked deterioration in the economic prospects of the White majority. Polls reveal that many working- and middle-class Whites have grown apprehensive about being able to improve or even maintain their level of socioeconomic well-being. For the first time in U.S. history, many young people are convinced that they will not be able to live as comfortably as their parents. These are not groundless fears. While unemployment remains relatively low, there is a growing scarcity of secure white-collar jobs. It is understandable, therefore, why Whites should increasingly regard any form of affirmative action as "reverse discrimination." Coming from segregated neighborhoods and segregated schools, African Americans and Whites seldom form friendships in their youth. They grow up as if they came from entirely different societies. It is no wonder, then, that when African Americans and Whites are thrown together in predominantly White high schools and colleges, African Americans mass together for security against insensitive or hostile treatment.

arise from a common methodological problem: the failure to control for the effects of historical and cultural influences on the behavior of the groups in question. In the nineteenth century, the failure of Blacks and other "races" to compete successfully against "White nations" in manufacturing, commerce, and war was taken as incontrovertible evidence that Whites were a superior race. Had not Whites from Europe and their descendents in North America gained political and economic control over almost the entire human species?

Eager to justify their imperial expansion, Europeans and North Americans failed to see the hollowness of this argument. They conveniently forgot that history is full of tales of empires brought to their knees by peoples who were at one time considered to be unalterably backward, such as the "barbarians" who conquered Rome and China. It was not intellectual superiority that enabled Europeans to invent new technology and develop political complexity; their advantage was derived from differences in environment that contained animals and grains suitable for domestication and that enabled them to generate food surpluses to support large populations and political complexity. This advantage was largely accidental and unintended, yet it gave European cultures a tremendous long-term advantage over other populations (Diamond 1997).

Why Africa Lags

Why do vast regions of Africa lag behind in terms of technological and political development? These deficits are well marked in the lands south of the Sahara, where the highest concentration of people with dark skin occur. And this region is also the homeland of most of the slaves who were brought to the Americas. To understand why racial differences do not merit serious consideration as an explanation of Black Africa's predicament, we must explore the historical reasons for Black Africa's lagging pace of development.

In A.D. 500, West Africa had feudal kingdoms— Ghana, Mali, Sanghay—which strongly resembled the feudal kingdoms of Europe except for the fact that the Africans were cut off by the Sahara from the heritage of technology and engineering that Rome had bequeathed to Europe. Subsequently, the great desert also inhibited the southward flow of Arabic influences that did so much to revitalize European science and commerce. The presence of the tsetse fly in the forested regions of Africa south of the Sahara meant that cattle could not be used as a source of traction power and milk products. Without traction animals, hoes rather than plows became the main agricultural implements. Horses, which became the chief engines of war in medieval Europe, were scarce if not absent completely in tropical Africa.

Although the people who lived in the Mediterranean basin carried out their trade and warfare on ships and became maritime powers, their dark-skinned counterparts south of the Sahara lacked the means of naval defense. So when the first Portuguese ships arrived off the Guinea coast in the fifteenth century, the Europeans were able to seize control of the ports and seal the fate of Africa for the next 500 years.

After the Portuguese exhausted the gold mines, the Africans concentrated on hunting slaves to exchange for European cloth and firearms. The slave trade led to increased amounts of warfare and rebellion and the breakup of the indigenous feudal states, cutting short the trajectory of Africa's political development and turning vast portions of the interior into a no-man's-land whose chief product was a human crop bred for export to the sugar, cotton, and tobacco plantations on the other side of the Atlantic.

When the slave trade ended, the Europeans tightened their control and forced the Africans to farm and mine for them. Meanwhile, colonial authorities tried to keep Africa subservient and backward by encouraging tribal wars, by limiting African education to the most rudimentary level possible, and above all, by preventing colonies from developing an industrial infrastructure that might have allowed them to compete in the world market after they achieved political independence.

Multiethnicity in the United States

Many Americans of mixed ancestry do not fully identify with one single ethnic or racial category. Also, in the absence of rigid rules of descent, the ethnic identity of children and grandchildren of ethnically mixed marriages tends to grow weaker and become more a matter of choice than of ascription (Leo 1993; Sanjek 1994b). In the 2000 U.S. census, nearly 7 million Americans reported that they have mixed ancestry.

Intermarriage has been an important social mechanism for reworking White ethnic distinctions, but relatively little intermarriage has occurred between Whites and African Americans (see Box 13.4). Moreover, intermarriage does not modify the social identities of African Americans. Today intermarriage remains subject to criticism from both Whites and African Americans. Rates of interracial marriage involving African Americans, although increasing, remain far lower than those of other racial minorities. Under these circumstances, African Americans have understandably turned their attention away from assimilation and have redoubled their efforts to instill

BOX 13.4 | Intermarriage

Fears of ethnic divide in the United States are being challenged by the rate at which couples of different races and ethnicities are marrying one another.

Since 1970, the number of interracial marriages in the United States increased more than ten-fold, from less than 1 percent to more than 5 percent of the estimated 57 million couples recorded in the 2000 census. This reflects both population growth and an increased tendency to marry across racial lines. At the same time, there have been dramatic improvements in American attitudes toward race. A Gallup poll conducted at the end of 2003 shows that 66 percent of White respondents said they would accept a child or grandchild marrying someone of a different race.

Based on the 2000 census, interracial marriage has increased across most racial groups and is generating a growing population of multiracial Americans.

- The typical interracial couple is a White person with a non-White spouse. Intermarriage between two people from minority racial groups is relatively infrequent.

- About one-fourth of Hispanic couples are inter-Hispanic, a rate that has been fairly stable since 1980.

- Whites and Blacks have the lowest intermarriage rates while American Indians, Hawaiians, and multiple-race individuals have the highest.

- Black men are more likely to intermarry than Black women, while Asian women are more likely to intermarry than Asian men. Men and women from other racial groups are equally likely to intermarry.

- Younger and better-educated Americans are more likely to intermarry than older and less-educated Americans.

Intermarriage and the resulting mixed-race children they produce are gradually blurring the racial boundar-

Interracial Marriage
People are calling into question widely held concepts of race and are now identifying themselves according to their own categories.

ies that have long divided the nation. Potentially, race could lose much of its meaning in this country much like ethnicity has for Whites.

Some demographers note that race could eventually lose much of its meaning in the United States, much as ethnicity has lost its meaning among many Anglo Americans. Interracial tolerance is increasing as the nation's Hispanic and Asian populations continue to grow. Moreover, many new immigrants come from countries with mixed-race traditions, which may make them more open to interracial marriage.

Source: Adapted from Lee and Edmonston 2005.

---

pride in being Black by emphasizing African American cultural achievements.

Race, Poverty, Crime, Drugs, and Welfare in the United States

Unlike the European immigrants of previous generations, Blacks have with the passage of time become more, not less, concentrated inside their ghettos. To those who lack realistic chances to escape from the ghettos, the benefits of criminal behavior may seem to outweigh the risks of getting caught and being sent to jail. John Conyers, a member of the Black Congressional Caucus, writes, "When survival is at stake, it should not be surprising that criminal activity begins to resemble an opportunity rather than a cost, work rather than deviance, and a possibly profitable undertaking that is superior to a coerced existence directed by welfare bureaucrats" (1978:678).

The high odds against attaining economic success by going to school and acquiring the skills neces-

Effects of Drugs and Crime

Despite the shortage of low-cost housing, the Pruitt–Igoe public housing complex in St. Louis was dynamited into rubble. It had become drug and crime infested and had been vandalized beyond repair.

sary to compete with Whites for the better jobs lies behind the decision of many African American, Hispanic, and other minority youth to traffic in illicit drugs (Liebow 1967). A week spent selling crack can bring more wealth than a year of working as a dishwasher or fast-food server. Ironically, the most successful drug businesses are run by young men who refrain from taking drugs themselves and who display many of the characteristics associated with entrepreneurship in legitimate businesses. They break into the trade with a small investment, hire employees, keep careful accounts, strive to establish good relationships with their regular customers, encourage the consumption of their product, adjust prices to market conditions, and keep careful tabs on what their competitors are doing. Of course, the use of crack and other addictive substances has a devastating effect on the consumers, who use drugs to escape from a squalid reality. The people of the United States pay an enormous price for the drug trade in the form of increased crime rates, overburdened courts and jails, and drug-related health problems such as AIDS (Bourgois 1995; Massing 1989, 1996; T. Williams 1989).

Anthropologist Jagna Sharff (1980) found that all the women on welfare in a group of 24 Hispanic families living in New York City's Lower East Side had sons who made substantial contributions to their household's economic balance through their involvement in street crime and dope peddling. In addition, they conferred an important benefit on their moth-

ers in the form of protection against the risk of rape, mugging, and various kinds of ripoffs to which the ghetto families are perpetually exposed. Sharff found that mothers valued their sons for streetwise "macho" qualities, especially their ability to use knives or guns, which is needed to protect the family against unruly or predatory neighbors. Although the mothers did not actively encourage their sons to enter the drug trade,

New York City's Lower East Side

In this neighborhood, the vicinity of Jagna Sharff's study, incarceration is the likely future of many young men.

everyone recognized that a successful drug dealer could become a very rich man.

To get ahead in the drug business, one needs the same macho qualities that are useful in defending one's family. When a young man brings home his first drug profits, his mother has mixed feelings of pride and apprehension. In her sample of families on welfare, Sharff compiled a record of 10 male homicides in three years (see Table 13.1). Because young ghetto males have a 40 percent chance of dying by age 25, a ghetto mother must have more than one son if she hopes to enjoy the protection of a street-wise male.

Sharff (1995) kept in touch with the people of the neighborhood for over 20 years. During that time, practically every male she knew eventually became involved with the criminal justice system. Indeed, a 1996 study showed that about one of every three Black men in their twenties was in prison or on probation or parole in New York State (Butterfield 1996). Sharff presented data in support of the view that the prison population grows larger when economic conditions for the working and middle classes grow more adverse. Thus, the prisons are a mechanism not merely for controlling crime but also for controlling the poor and for preventing them from trying to get a share of the nation's wealth.

Table 13.1

Male Homicides in 24 Welfare Families, 1976–1979

Victim's Age	Immediate Cause of Death
25	Shot in drug-related incident
19	Shot in dispute in grocery store
21	Shot in drug-related incident
28	Stabbed in drug-related incident
32	"Suicide" in a police precinct house
30	Stabbed in drug-related incident
28	Poisoned by adulterated heroin
30	Arson victim
24	Shot in drug-related incident
19	Tortured and stabbed in drug-related incident

Source: Sharff 1980. Reprinted with permission of the Department of Anthropology, Columbia University.

SUMMARY
and *Questions to Think About*

1. Ethnic groups are present in virtually all state societies. These groups differ from classes in having been formed through conquest or migration. They have internal class differences of their own and have high levels of group consciousness.

2. Ethnic groups differ from social races only in the degree to which ethnic groups stress cultural differences (actual or invented) over physical appearance.

3. Social race differs from biological race in that social race is unrelated to scientific understanding of heredity—as illustrated in the one-drop-of-blood rule and in the contrasting example of the Brazilian system for identifying the children of mixed matings.

4. Failure to understand the difference between biological race and culture is a common feature of the dynamics of social races and ethnic groups.

5. The term *race* denotes a population with a distinctive set of gene frequencies; *culture* denotes a way of life. A rigid linking of race and culture is a form of racism that runs counter to all that is scientifically known about the transmissibility of culture across racial and ethnic boundaries.

6. The most important point about the dynamics of racial and ethnic groups is that they almost always compete with other racial and ethnic groups, both dominant and subordinate, to defend and improve their standard of living.

7. Although class struggle has been consistently difficult to identify and raise to conscious levels, race and ethnic struggle and race and ethnic consciousness are ubiquitous features of the contemporary world.

8. As part of an attempt to improve their position in the social and economic hierarchy, racial and ethnic groups seek to mobilize their resources and instill a conscious pride in their identities. Thus, all racial and ethnic groups that seek to survive and improve their condition tend to recast their historical achievements in the most favorable light and to emphasize their cultural separateness. When they do so, the threat of backlash is ever present.

9. The United States provides a picture of how ethnic and racial dynamics operate in a complex multicultural society. Despite a high degree of homogenization of their cultures and much invention

of tradition, White ethnic groups are maintaining their identities. By invoking ambilineal forms of descent, White European ethnics continue to identify with ancestral ethnic groups as a matter of choice.

10. The situation is less benign among African Americans, who are largely blocked by the one-drop rule from choosing their social race. Racism remains a salient feature of the relations between Whites of European origin and African Americans (and other non-White groups).

11. In the nineteenth century, the dominant political position of the European powers was interpreted as proof of the superiority of the White race. But efforts to rank human races as inferior or superior based on technological, commercial, or military prowess are negated by the many historical examples of "underdogs" becoming "top dogs," as in ancient Rome and China and in modern Japan. Racial explanations of Black Africa's underdevelopment must be rejected in favor of explanations that take into account the effects of sub-Saharan ecology, colonialism, and the slave trade.

12. A disproportionate share of violent urban crime in the United States is committed by Black and Hispanic juveniles who live in families with below-poverty-level incomes. Crime and drugs provide an opportunity that often results in prison or death.

Questions to Think About

1. What is the difference between biological race and social race?

2. Is race a useful concept in the social sciences?

3. What obstacles have kept ethnic groups from joining forces to improve their economic position in society?

4. What concessions made it possible for residents of Elmhurst–Corona to join forces in becoming politically active in their community?

5. In what ways have the experiences of African Americans been different from those of Euro-American immigrants?

6. Why are Korean immigrants able to run small businesses in Black neighborhoods successfully, and what are some of the reasons for ethnic tension in these neighborhoods?

THROUGH THE LENS
of Cultural Materialism

Conformity and Conflict • Reading Twenty-Three

Mixed Blood

Jeffrey M. Fish

Americans determine race based on heritage, rather than physical appearance. Brazilians, on the other hand, classify people according to *tipos,* or based on physical features that include skin color, nose shape, hair, and lips.

Emic Interpretation

- Some Americans believe that races are subgroups of the human species and that biological differences exist between races.

Etic Interpretation

- In an attempt to classify superficial differences between people, Americans and Brazilians have come up with culture-specific constructions of race that are essentially folk taxonomies.

- Scientific evidence shows that biological race does not exist and that all humans are genetically similar.

Infrastructure

- Folk taxonomies of race vary in relation to conquests by European powers, different local ecologies, and differing patterns of slavery.

- Mutation, natural selection, and genetic drift account for the physical differences among human beings. A number of differences in physical appearance among populations are adaptive to specific environments. For instance, dark skin serves as protection against the sun and a round body provides heat retention in a cold environment.

Structure

- Differences in IQ scores between social races can be attributed to social environment and social advantages or disadvantages. The social advantages of U.S. Whites as a group compared to the social disadvantages of U.S. Blacks as a group account for differences in average test scores.

Superstructure

- In every culture, people classify things along culture-specific dimensions of meaning—folk taxonomies.

Americans believe blood is the quality inherited by members of so-called races.

- Racial categories arbitrarily include certain dimensions (light versus dark skin) and exclude others (rounded versus elongated bodies). These are folk taxonomies that vary from one place to another, not biologically significant factors.

- In the United States, the rule of *hypo-descent* states that offspring, regardless of physical appearance, always inherit the less prestigious racial category of mixed parentage.

- More recently, immigration from around the world has brought people to the United States that do not fit into White and Black categories.

- Intermarriage has resulted in even greater diversity among children, requiring new ways of identifying people—for instance, using terms such as *multiracial* and *other.*

CHAPTER **14**

SEXUALITY AND GENDER STRATIFICATION

The story of Adam and Eve is thematically similar to other myths that justify gender stratification.

T here is no single pattern of human sexuality and thus no absolute gender roles. As in all other domains of human life, the definition of what is normal varies from one culture to another. We will discuss the qualities that males and females look for in choosing a mate; the diversity of sexual desire, including homosexuality; and the relevance of evolutionary mechanisms for understanding gender roles.

Here are some of the questions this chapter addresses: Do men and women interpret gender differences from the same perspective, or do they have different versions of which gender is dominant? What positions of authority can women achieve and under what circumstances? How does the mode of production and reproduction affect the position of women? Why are gender relations more egalitarian in some agricultural societies than in others? Is there a relationship between warfare and male domination? Why is low female status so closely associated with the use of the plow? And finally, what kinds of changes in gender roles can we expect as the industrial nations continue to develop high-tech infrastructures and service and information economies? In answering these questions, we will see that gender relations, even in industrial societies, have a long way to go before reaching equality.

Sex versus Gender

The etic sexual identity of human beings can be established by examining an individual's chromosomes, interior and exterior sex organs, and secondary sexual characteristics such as body build, size of breasts, and fat deposits (see Box 14.1). Although all societies recognize a distinction between male and female based on some of these features, the emic definition of being male or female, or some other gender, varies considerably from one society to another.

Sex refers to anatomical and physiological attributes.

Gender refers to learned cultural and psychological attributes.

Anthropologists use the term *gender* to denote the variable emic meanings associated with culturally defined, sex-based identities (Errington and Gewertz 1987; Gilmore 1990; Jacobs and Roberts 1989; Ortner and Whitehead 1981). *Gender identity* thus refers to a fundamental sense of how a person feels and his or her identity, whether male, female, or blended.

Male and Female Sexual Strategies

The quest for sexual pleasure motivates much of human behavior and should be seen as an aspect of infrastructure affecting the mode of reproduction. Needless to say, reproduction depends very much on the biological givens of human sexuality. Human mating strategies evolved through natural selection to solve problems associated with the need to reproduce and rear dependent offspring to reproductive age. Understanding why these strategies developed and what problems they were designed to solve provides insight for understanding how culture may impact our future course of behavior (Buss 1994:209).

BOX 14.1 | How Many Biological Sexes Are There?

According to Anne Fausto-Sterling (1993:24), there are at least five biological sexes:

1. *Hermaphrodites:* Individuals born with one testis and one ovary and a mixture of male and female genitalia

2. *Male pseudohermaphrodites:* Individuals who have two testes and a mixture of male and female genitalia but no ovaries

3. *Female pseudohermaphrodites:* Individuals who have two ovaries and a mixture of male and female genitalia but no testes

4. *Females:* Individuals born with two ovaries and female genitalia

5. *Males:* Individuals born with two testes and male genitalia

Some hermaphrodites have a large penis and a vagina and enjoy sex with either a male or a female partner. Fausto-Sterling questions the practice of using surgery and hormones to "correct" hermaphroditic conditions: "Why should we care if there are people whose biological equipment enables them to have sex 'naturally' with both men and women? . . . Society mandates the control of intersexual bodies because they blur and bridge the great divide: they challenge traditional beliefs about sexual difference."

According to Meredith Small (1992, 1995), research on attitudes toward sex in Western society shows that men and women want very different things:

- More men than women approve of casual sex.
- When having sex, more men than women report orgasms.
- Men seek out sex more often; they start having sex at an earlier age and have a higher number of partners over a lifetime than women.
- Men like sex for its own sake, whereas women express a need for emotional intimacy and are more selective in choosing a mate.

And according to Buss (1994), men and women differ in the weight given to cues that trigger sexual jealousy. Men are more distressed by imagining their partner having "passionate sex with another person," whereas women are more distressed by emotional infidelity—their partner forming a "deep emotional attachment" to someone else.

In sum, males want to maximize their reproductive success by having sex with many different females and invest in their offspring only when they have to, whereas females have a different agenda. Unlike males, they have a limited number of eggs and must invest heavily in their infants.

Males are interested in spreading their genes around, whereas women are more selective because they incur a much greater investment due to the high maintenance required to ensure that each child will survive on its own.

Women choose to mate with men who are most likely to contribute to the rearing of children; they want mates who have good genes, have sufficient resources, and are willing to commit to the rearing and protection of their children.

Unlike nonhuman primates, who mate with males during a restricted period of the year, human females mate at all phases of the hormonal cycle and ovulate regardless of whether they have intercourse. Women thus have the capacity to be continuously ready for sex and can use their readiness to their advantage. Because fertilization occurs internally, men are always less than certain that a woman's child is genetically their own. Men therefore want women who are sexually loyal and are willing to make a commitment to secure fidelity and increase certainty of their paternity.

The absence of estrus in human females can be seen as an adaptation that allows females to be always available for sex, increases the likelihood of a pair bond, and keeps men close at hand to help with the raising of children. Men, on the other hand, want exclusive sexual access to women to be assured of their paternity.

In discussing the importance of biological strategies in human sexuality, we should not lose sight of the ability of culture to override such strategies. Despite the fact that in a study of 186 cultures, 77 percent considered the male and female sex drives to be equally strong (Whyte 1978), female sexuality is often suppressed and denigrated. As we will see later, this suppression of female sexuality occurs most frequently in stratified societies, where questions about

Maximizing Reproductive Success
This Kenyan man has 40 wives and 349 children. Men have historically tried to win and inseminate as many females as possible so they can pass along more genes.

inheritance of land and other forms of wealth reduce the freedom of women to mate as they wish.

Notice, however, that all interspecific comparisons of sexual performance can be expressed only as potentials. Because of the pervasive effects of culture, humans can be the least, instead of the most, sexy of primates, as is the case when celibacy is practiced. Nor is it the case that men everywhere cannot tolerate sharing a wife with other men. As we saw in Chapter 8, polyandrous Nyinba women have several husbands who take turns having sex with their shared wife. Also, Profile 14.1 shows that promiscuity is tolerated among the Mehinacu, as long as it is done discreetly.

Under postindustrial conditions, the long-range trend toward decreased fertility and women's growing economic status undoubtedly will impact mating strategies. Women are pregnant on average less than 5 percent of their adult lives and are slowly but surely gaining parity with men in the workforce. In all probability, these infrastructural conditions will continue to change domestic organization and gender ideology. Women do not have to be the ones to stay home and care for children and be sexually dependent on males. As underlying demographic, technological, and economic conditions change, so do new cultural definitions of gender roles.

PROFILE 14.1   Mehinacu Extramarital Affairs

In the central Brazil village of the Mehinacu (see Profile 10.1), extramarital liaisons make up a large part of Mehinacu sexual activity. According to Thomas Gregor (1973, 1985), young men report having sex with other adulterous women four to five times more often than with their spouses. Sex with a mistress is said to be more pleasurable than with a spouse.

Affairs are typically initiated by men. A man wants to be fairly certain he will not be rejected before approaching a woman outside the village, or he may use an intermediary to set up the relationship for him. Once the affair is established, the lovers arrange to meet in the forest in a secluded spot, invisible from the main path. When the couple meet, they may exchange small gifts and then have sex, often with a minimum of foreplay, especially if they are concerned about being observed. Afterward, they may talk for a while to assure one another that they enjoyed the experience. There is no word for a woman's sexual climax, and it appears that women do not have orgasms from intercourse (Gregor 1985:34). Women seem to take pleasure in sex, but their interest is lower than that of men. Men often begrudge the fact that women are "stingy with their genitals." Nonetheless, extramarital relationships are highly valued. When they are new, they are often emotionally intense, and they may actually last a lifetime. Upon the death of a partner, the survivor may go through an attenuated and discreet mourning process, being sure that his or her spouse is not offended.

The Mehinacu do not believe that pregnancy results from a single sexual encounter. According to Gregor, "They believe that a newborn is literally composed of accumulated ejaculate from repeated instances of sexual intercourse" (1973:246). This theory of conception and paternity is incorporated into the kinship system so that if a woman has sexual relations with several lovers during pregnancy, they are all considered to have jointly produced the child along with the woman's husband. When her children mature, a woman identifies a lover who was close to her so that her children can recognize him as a kind of father and honor the incest taboo in their relationships to his other children.

In a village of 37 adults, at the time of Gregor's initial study, there were approximately 88 affairs (out of 150 theoretically possible pairings after eliminating incestuous relations). The average man engaged in 4.4 affairs at a time, and most men were close to that average. Women, in contrast, had a much greater range: "The three most sexually active women in the village account[ed] for almost forty percent of the total number of liaisons, while the three least active women account[ed] for none of the community's extramarital relationships" (Gregor 1985:36).

The villagers' overt enthusiasm about sex is tempered with anxiety about the consequences of their sexuality. These anxieties are expressed in myth, dreams, and ritual. Men express a great deal of ambivalence toward women. The men claim, for example, that female sexuality, menstruation, and female genitalia are unattractive and can cause loss of strength, stunted growth, and, in myth, even castration. Moreover, some men fear sexual dysfunction. Sexual function is a critical part of masculine identity, and if a man's failure becomes common knowledge, his reputation as a lover will be hurt by gossip. Also, because of the imbalance in male and female sexual interest, men's libido is always greater than the opportunity for sexual affairs. Thus, even in this permissive setting, sex is scarce relative to male demand, and the men experience sexual frustration and dissatisfaction.

Sex in Mangaia versus Sex in Inis Beag

All aspects of sexual relationships, from infantile experiences through courtship and marriage, exhibit an immense amount of cultural variation (Frayser 1985; Gregersen 1994; Suggs and Miracle 1993). For example, consider the modes of sexuality found among the Mangaians of Polynesia as compared with those of the Irish of Inis Beag.

According to Donald Marshall (1971), the people of the Pacific Islands of Mangaia never hold hands or embrace in public. Mothers and daughters and fathers and sons do not discuss sexual matters with one another. Yet both sexes are enthusiastic participants in intercourse well before puberty. After puberty, both sexes enjoy an intense premarital sex life. Girls receive varied nightly suitors in the parents' houses, and boys compete with their rivals to see how many orgasms they can achieve. The average girl will have three or four sexual partners between the ages 13 to 20, whereas a boy may have an average of 10 or more sexual partners. Sexual intimacy is not achieved by first demonstrating personal affection; the reverse is true. For the Mangaian girl, demonstration of sexual virility and masculinity is the first test of her partner's desire for her and a reflection of her own desirability. Personal affection may or may not result from acts of sexual intimacy.

According to a consensus of Marshall's informants, young men are expected to have as many as three or four orgasms per night. Sexual activities were described as a national pastime, in which both males and females participate enthusiastically. Marshall concluded there was no indication of anything like romantic love, only sexual attraction.

How much confidence can we place in this account? Helen Harris (1995) has called Marshall's study into question on the grounds that his data were collected primarily from discussions with young men, who might have been prone to exaggerate their sexual prowess. She contends that Marshall was the victim of some "good-natured lying" (1995:108).

Nonetheless, there are certain important points of agreement between the two accounts. As in many South Sea Polynesian societies, Mangaians have a relatively permissive attitude toward sexual behavior. Romantic love was not absent but was deemphasized in comparison with contemporary patterns of courtship and marriage in other parts of the world. Thus Harris (1995:123) writes of two distinct patterns of heterosexual interaction created by dissimilar emphasis placed on romantic love versus sexual attraction:

> The Polynesian pattern emphasizes sexual expression to the point that researchers like Marshall actually overlook other (romantic) features of

heterosexual relationships while the American pattern minimizes sex to such an extent that our own social scientists fail to consider it when discussing romantic love.

The extreme opposite of sex in Mangaia is practiced in Inis Beag, an island off the coast of Ireland. Here, sex is shrouded in guilt and sin; it is regarded as a duty women must perform for their husbands. Women remain entirely passive during coitus. They engage in a minimum of foreplay; there is rough fondling of the buttocks and some kissing. Husbands always initiate sex and reach orgasm as quickly as they can, on the assumption that women have no interest in prolonging intercourse. Husband and wife keep their underwear on during intercourse and turn off the lights, even though they are not visible to anyone but themselves (Messenger 1971).

Female orgasm is unheard of. Sex is never discussed among friends or family; parents are so embarrassed that they cannot bring themselves to discuss sex with their children. Instead, they believe that nature will take its course after marriage. Sex is also thought of as being injurious to one's health. Therefore, a man will refrain from having sex the night before he is to perform a strenuous activity.

Restrictive versus Permissive Cultures

Despite a high level of curiosity, little is known about the actual forms of sexual behavior in different societies. The major reason is that in virtually every society that has ever been studied, sex is performed in private. Anthropologists, therefore, have had to rely on accounts of sexual behavior elicited from informants rather than on actual observation. (Ethical issues inhibit discussion of participatory sexual observations, if any, by anthropologists during fieldwork.)

Why do some societies restrict heterosexual sex whereas others are more permissive? George Murdock notes that sexual behavior is more likely to be regulated where it serves the interests of society.

Greater restrictions on premarital sex occur in societies stratified by class, where inheritance and property rights belong to men.

Restrictions fall primarily on females and are largely a precaution against childbearing out of wedlock (Murdock 1949:265). Stratified societies with differential wealth are concerned with preventing their children from marrying beneath them. Premarital sexual restrictions thus ensure that daughters will be chaste and in a position to marry well.

Control over female sexuality is a way of controlling paternity.

Widespread disapproval of adultery is based on the special sexual privilege associated with marriage. Yet some societies are more lax about extramarital affairs than others. Adultery can be disruptive to social bonds and create uncertainty regarding paternity. Societies with patrilineal inheritance—particularly where there is land scarcity—are more likely to place restrictions on sexuality to ensure that a man's estate is passed on to his biological sons and not those of a lineage rival. This is the case in most parts of India, China, the Mediterranean, and the Middle East, where inheritance and property rights belong to men and women's sexuality is oriented to reproduction and safeguarded through chastity vows. In Naples, Italy, for example, religious ideology reinforces sexual control by making female purity sacred. Virginity and chastity are essential to female purity. Motherhood is regarded with reverence, and a woman's identity is bound to her role as a caring mother. Women are expected to guard their sexuality to preserve their family honor. A woman who engages in sex outside marriage jeopardizes her position within her family and society (Goddard 1996).

Sexually permissive societies tend to be kin-based societies, with corporate ownership of land and minimal property inheritance. Here sexuality is enjoyable and can be explored by both men and women. Women can also increase their well-being by having sex with several men who assume possible paternity and provide food and protection for her and her offspring. Nisa, a !Kung woman, describes the rewards of multiple sex partners:

> One man can give you very little. One man gives you only one kind of food to eat. But when you have lovers, one brings you something and another brings you something else. One comes at night with meat, another with money, another with beads. Your husband also does things and gives them to you. (Shostak 1981:271)

Homosexuality

Male Homosexuality

Attitudes toward homosexuality range from horror to chauvinistic enthusiasm. Given the many ways in which humans separate sexual pleasure from unwanted reproduction, the widespread occurrence of homosexual behavior should come as no surprise (see Box 14.2). Most societies—between 64 and 69 percent (Gregersen 1994:341), according to one survey—tolerate or actually encourage some degree of same-sex along with opposite-sex erotic behavior.

BOX 14.2 | Is Homosexuality Genetic?

There is some evidence that homosexuality is linked to genes, but this does not mean a "gay" gene has been found nor is it likely that one will be. There is, however, an area of the X chromosome that often looks the same in brothers who are gay. A study carried out by Dean Hammer and associates at the National Cancer Institute (Hammer et al. 1993) found that when families of homosexuals were traced, there were more homosexual males on the mother's side than on the father's side, specifically among the maternal uncles and sons of maternal uncles. Since men inherit their only X chromosome from their mother, the researchers compared 40 pairs of gay brothers and found that 33 shared an identical pattern of five DNA markers at the lower tip of the X chromosome.

In another study of sibling sets, Bailey and Pillard (cited in Small 1999:174) found the following:*

- Among 56 gay men who had identical twins, 52 percent of the co-twins were themselves gay.
- Among 54 gay men who had fraternal twins, 22 percent of the co-twins were gay.
- Among gay men who had adoptive brothers, only 11 percent of the adoptive siblings were gay.
- Among 71 lesbians who had identical twins, 48 percent of the co-twins were also lesbian.
- Among 37 lesbians who had fraternal twins, 16 percent of the co-twins were lesbian.
- Among lesbians who had adoptive sisters, only 6 percent of the adoptive siblings were lesbian.

As with all human behavioral traits, sexual preference must be considered an outcome of both genetic tendencies and environment.

*Most often, a figure of 4 to 7 percent of the total population is given for male homosexuality and about half that range for female homosexuality.

If one includes clandestine and noninstitutionalized practices, then it is safe to say that homosexual behavior occurs to some extent in every human population.

Homosexual behavior in different cultural contexts is as variegated as heterosexual behavior (Weston 1993). For example, in many cultures there is a sharp contrast between male and female roles, which makes it difficult to accept effeminate males. Moreover, in many Latin and Mediterranean countries, there is a widely occurring distinction between active and passive homosexual roles. A man is never dishonored if he takes the active role, but the male partner who takes the passive role jeopardizes his masculinity. In Brazil, household surveys reveal that a high proportion of heterosexual men engage in anal sex to avoid unwanted pregnancies. Others do so for the pleasure and excitement associated with the nonconforming practice (Herdt 1997:143).

Several cultures studied by anthropologists incorporate male homosexuality into their systems for developing masculine male personalities but do not have a concept for *homosexual* or *gay*. Among the Azande of the Sudan, also renowned for their prowess in warfare, the unmarried warrior-age males, who lived apart from women for several years, had homosexual relations with the boys of the age grade of warrior apprentices. After their experiences with "boy-wives," the warriors graduated to the next age status, got married, and had children (Evans-Pritchard 1970). Although the Azande allow for age-structured

Azande Warriors

Azande men were known for their prowess in warfare. Unmarried warrior males had homosexual relations with younger apprentices and then went on to marry and have many children.

relations between boys and men, they penalize any other form of homosexual relations that does not conform with the accepted pattern.

Male homosexuality was highly ritualized in many New Guinea and Melanesian societies. It was ideologically justified in a manner that has no equivalent in Western notions of sexuality (see Profile 14.2).

Ritualized homosexuality was not viewed as a matter of individual preference but as a social obligation.

Men were not classifiable as homosexual, heterosexual, or bisexual. All men were obliged to partake in homoerotic acts as a matter of sacred duty and practical necessity. The Etoro believe that each man has only a limited supply of semen. When the supply is exhausted, a man dies. Although coitus with their wives is necessary to prevent the population from becoming too small, husbands stay away from wives most of the time. Indeed, sex is taboo between husband and wife for over 200 days of the year. The Etoro males regard wives who want to break this taboo as witches. To complicate matters, the supply of semen is not something that a man is born with. Semen can be acquired only from another male. Etoro boys get their supplies by having oral intercourse with older men. But it is forbidden for young boys to have intercourse with each other, and like the oversexed wife, the oversexed adolescent boy is regarded as a witch and condemned for robbing his age-mates of their semen supply. Such wayward youths can be identified by the fact that they grow faster than ordinary boys (Kelly 1976).

Herdt (1997:183) argues that the ancient Greeks, the Azande warriors, and the New Guinea villagers, are not homosexual, because they do not identify themselves as such. Same-gender relations have a different meaning in these cultures and should not be confused with what Americans call *gay* or *lesbian*.

"Two-Spirit" People

Among North American native peoples, gender roles are not defined by mere sexual preference or conduct. Gender is defined by personality traits and occupational preferences. Such individuals were referred to as *berdaches* [sic] by early White settlers, who ridiculed them and considered them to be "failed" or cowardly men. Today most people prefer the term *two-spirit* to signify the complexity of the spiritual and sexual that is contained in this culturally sanctioned role.

PROFILE 14.2 | Sambia Boy-Inseminating Rituals

Among the Sambia of the southeastern highlands of New Guinea, boys are allowed to play with girls only until age 4 or 5. Thereafter, they are strictly regulated, and all heterosexual play is forcefully punished. Late in childhood, boys undergo a series of inseminating rituals, which are not primarily intended to give pleasure but to help the younger males grow and become masculine. This gift of semen from their seniors is intended to prepare the young boys for warfare and to enhance their reproductive ability. Males must then continue to avoid any heterosexual contact until they are married (Herdt 1987).

Boy-inseminating rituals have several distinct features (Herdt 1997:84):

- They are implemented through initiation or puberty rites that are collective rather than individualized.
- The rites have religious sanctification, in which the ancestral spirits bless the proceedings.
- The erotic relations are associated with graded social roles that enable the boy to advance to a higher status.
- These sexual relations do not preclude marriage and passion with women, which offers a different form of social achievement and sexual desire.

Ritualized insemination and semen beliefs in New Guinea and Melanesia are closely associated with a heightened level of male–female sexual antagonism, fear of menstrual blood, and exclusive male rituals and dwellings. Obligatory same-gender sexual relations and intense warfare in New Guinea are also strongly associated with each other. Warfare justified and rationalized an ethos of masculine prowess that placed men above women as desirable sexual partners (Herdt 1984a:169). Finally, as in other patrilocal warlike village societies (see Chapter 10, section "Warfare and Female Infanticide"), their juvenile sex ratios show a marked imbalance favoring males over females, attaining ratios as high as 140:100 (Herdt 1984b:57).

Today, both warfare and boy-inseminating rituals have died out, yet a small number of men report voluntarily having had anal sex at the age of 16, without the support of traditional customs. Herdt suggests that within a generation, same-gender relations may more closely resemble the kind of homosexual roles known elsewhere.

Two-spirits are individuals who take on aspects of a culturally defined gender role that combines feminine and masculine traits and is seen as a "third gender." Sexuality in itself is not a defining gender characteristic of the two-spirit.

Two-spirit males and females are a combination of the masculine and feminine and are often seen as a gender of their own. There are many variations of two-spirit roles in native North American cultures, yet there are several common features:

- Transvestitism
- Cross-gender occupation
- Cultural process of recruitment
- Ritual roles and spiritual powers

In some cultures, two-spirits act on a spiritual calling—a powerful vision or dream—that causes them to adopt the behavior, identity, and clothing of the opposite sex. A two-spirit may also be identified as a child who shows interest in the work activities of the opposite sex (S. Lang 1997). Two-spirits are often thought to have extraordinary powers, demon-strated by their ability to heal and foretell the future. In many native cultures, two-spirits were defined by characteristics unconnected to sexuality. These include spirituality, medicine, self-identity, ritual performance, or power (Herdt 1997).

Two-spirits never married or had sex with other two-spirits, and when marriages between two-spirits and their mates ended, partners typically did not marry another person of their own gender. The former wife of a female two-spirit would marry a man and the former husband of a two-spirit would marry a woman (Bonvillain 1998:191).

Today traditional gender roles for two-spirit individuals have disappeared. Young people who grow up to be "different" can only identify themselves as gay. Reservation communities often reject gays, and so most leave to join gay and lesbian communities in the cities and return only periodically to visit their families (Lang 1997).

Female Homosexuality

Less is known about female homosexuality than about male homosexuality because of the predominance of flexible and context specific than those found in the United States and Europe (Blackwood 1986).

Several reported cases of institutionalized lesbianism are related to the migration of males in search of work. On the Caribbean island of Carriacou, where migrant husbands stay away from home for most of the year, older married women bring younger single women into their households and share the absent husband's remittances in exchange for sexual favors and emotional support. A similar pattern exists in South Africa, where it is known as the "mummy–baby relationship"—an institutionalized long-term friendship between girls and women regarded as an affair or erotic romance that coexists with heterosexual marriage (Gay 1986). The older ("mummy") arranges the rendezvous and is the one to give gifts to her "baby" and advice on sex and protection from men's aggressive courtship. Among the !Kung San, adolescents go through a phase of sexual experimentation that includes both same-sex and opposite-sex partners as part of a learning period that precedes heterosexual marriage (Shostak 1981:114).

One of the most interesting forms of institutionalized lesbianism occurred in midnineteenth-century to early twentieth-century China in several of the silk-growing districts of the Pearl River delta region in southern Kwangtung. There, single women provided virtually all the labor for the silkworm factories. Although poorly paid, they were better off than they would have been had they married their prospective husbands. Rather than accept the subordinate status that marriage imposed on Chinese women, the silk workers formed antimarriage sisterhoods that provided economic and emotional support. Although not all the 100,000 sisters formed lesbian relationships, enduring lesbian marriages involving two and sometimes three women were common (Sankar 1986). These sisterhoods were both a resistance to marriage and a way to resolve the threat that unmarried women pose to men's control of their wives.

Even when allowance is made for blind spots in the ethnographic reports of male observers, there appear to be fewer forms of institutionalized female than of male homosexuality. Does this mean that females engage in homosexual behavior less often than males? Probably not. More likely, most female same-sex sexuality has simply been driven underground or has been expressed in noninstitutionalized contexts that fall outside Western categories and therefore escape observation (Blackwood 2005b). Polygynous marriage, for example (see Chapter 8), is another context in which lesbian relationships probably flourish. The practice seems to have been common in West Africa among the Nupe, Hausa, and Dahomey and among the Azande and Nyakyusa in East Africa. In

Native American "Two-Spirits"
Finds-Them-and-Kills-Them is a Crow "man–woman" or "two-spirit."

male-biased ethnographies. Unlike males, females seldom seem to be subjected to initiation rituals that entail homosexual relationships. It is reported, however, that among the Dahomey of West Africa, adolescent girls prepared for marriage by attending all-female initiation schools, where they learned how to "thicken their genitalia" and engaged in sexual intercourse (Blackwood 1986).

With the exception of the Dahomey, women seldom bear the brunt of military combat and thus have little opportunity to use same-sex erotic apprenticeships to form close-knit teams of warriors. Similarly, enforced absence from the classical Greek academies precluded women's participation in homosexual philosophical apprenticeships, and because men in most stratified societies controlled women's sexual behavior, the incidence of overt lesbian behavior between women of high rank and slave girls or other social inferiors was probably never very high.

Nevertheless, cross-cultural evidence shows a diversity of women's sexualities and the importance of socioeconomic factors in the construction of sexuality. Women's sexual feelings take on many forms that include desires, longings, and practices that are more

Middle Eastern harems, where co-wives seldom saw their husbands, many women entered into lesbian relationships despite the dire punishment such male-defying behavior could bring (Blackwood 1986; Lockard 1986).

Gender Ideologies

Each culture has **gender scripts** that <u>define what it means to be male and female and how men and women should interact in a variety of social settings</u>.

 Gender scripts are ideals that guide conventional masculinity and femininity and that become a basis for self-perception for most individuals.

These scripts are learned through enculturation and are legitimized and sanctioned through gender-related ideologies contained in creation myths and by rituals that validate gender role authority and dominance (Sanday 1981).

In many Amazonian and Melanesian cultures, males believe they are spiritually superior to females and that females are dangerous, polluting, and weak. It is common for men to claim a monopoly over secret rituals; to maintain residence in a separate men's house, from which women and children are excluded; and to impersonate spiritual beings to frighten the women and uninitiated boys. Any woman who admits to knowing the secrets of the cult is threatened with rape or execution (Gregor 1985:94ff; Gregor and Tuzin 2001; Hays 1988).

Another feature of male-dominant societies is the myth of primordial matriarchy. On the surface, these myths—set in a time when women held most positions of authority—appear as a shared historical reality that depicts a reverse mirror image of patriarchy. Such myths, however, are not about history but ideology. Rather than pay tribute to women, the myths address the symbolic insecurity of male status. This insecurity is reflected in the reality of men's early years, in which they are largely raised by women, and the fact that the foundation of their ideological dominance is shaky. The myths represent universal gender psychology, in which men are intimately raised by their mothers and then must learn to identify with their more distant fathers and become outcasts from closely knit female domestic units.

Rather than replicate a historical reality, myths of former rule by women provide ideological justification for why women cannot rule.

The myth of matriarchy invariably highlights women's failure as rulers (i.e., women were incapable of handling power) and reaffirms the inferiority of their present position (Bamberger 1974). Women are ambivalently conceived as destructive because men are afraid they may take over. The myth protects the men from experiencing insecurity and provides a justification of their superiority.

In the case of the Mundurucu of the Brazilian Amazon (see Box 14.3), the myth describes a reversal in the social order from a time when women controlled the sacred instruments. The women did not know how to protect the instruments, however, so the men took control of them and became the dominant sex. By the same token, men must actively assert their superiority because there is always the possibility that their dominance can be taken away. As Margaret Mead has said, "If the men were all that powerful, they wouldn't need such rigmarole" (quoted in Murphy and Murphy 2004:252).

The Relativity of Gender Ideologies

How much of the male claim to spiritual superiority do women believe? To begin with, we must be skeptical that any subjugated group really accepts the reasons the subjugators give to justify their claims to superior status.

Much new evidence suggests that women have their own gender ideologies, which have not been properly recorded because earlier generations of ethnographers were primarily male and neglected or were unable to obtain the woman's point of view.

For example, male ethnographers have consistently interpreted the seclusion of menstruating women among the Yurok Indians of northern California as a demonstration of the need to protect men from the pollution of menstrual blood. Only in the 1980s did it become clear that Yurok women had a completely different sense of what they were doing (Buckley 1982; Child and Child 1985). A menstruating woman should isolate herself because this is the time when she is at the height of her powers. Thus, the time should not be wasted in mundane tasks and social distractions, nor should one's concentration be broken by concerns with the opposite sex. Rather, all of one's energies should be applied in concentrated meditation on the nature of one's life, "to find out the purpose of your life," and toward the "accumulation" of spiritual energy. The menstrual shelter, or room, is "like the men's sweathouse," a place where

BOX 14.3   The Mundurucu Myth of the Sacred Instruments and Male Ascendancy

The sacred trumpets of the Mundurucu, called the *karoko,* are taboo to the sight of women, but the women once owned them. In fact, it was the women who first discovered the trumpets.

Three women named Yanyonbori, Tuembiru, and Parawaro would frequently hear music from some unknown source whenever they went to collect firewood. One day, they became thirsty and went to search for water. Deep in the forest, they found a shallow lake of which they had no previous knowledge. Another day, they heard the music again, coming from the direction of the lake. At the lake, they found only fish in the water, which they were unable to catch.

Back in the village, one of the women had the idea of catching the fish with hand nets rubbed with a nut that made fish sleepy. Back at the lake, each woman caught one fish. These fish turned into hollow cylindrical trumpets. That is why each men's house now has a set of only three instruments. The women hid the trumpets in the forest and secretly played them every day.

The women, as possessors of the trumpets, gained ascendancy over men. The men had to carry firewood and fetch water and also had to make the manioc cakes. The men were forced to enter the dwelling houses for a night, and the women marched around the village playing the trumpets. They then entered (what is now) the men's house and installed the instruments there. Then each woman went to the dwelling houses and forced the men into coitus. The men could not refuse, just as women today cannot refuse the desires of men. The next day the men took the trumpets from the women and forced them to go back to the dwelling house. The women wept at their loss.

Source: Adapted from Yolanda Murphy and Robert F. Murphy. *Women of the Forest.* Copyright © 1985 Columbia University Press. Reprinted with permission of the publisher.

---

you "go into yourself and make yourself stronger" (Buckley 1982:48–49). Rather than feeling that they were being confined for the benefit of Yurok men, they felt that they were enjoying a privileged opportunity to get away from the chores of everyday life,

Interior of Men's House, New Guinea
The men use masks to frighten the women and children.

to meditate on their life goals, and to gather spiritual strength.

Women do not necessarily resent being excluded from male-centered rituals because they do not attach much importance to what the men are doing with their bull roarers and masked dancing. Dorothy Counts (1985) tells how an old blind woman among the Kaliai of Papua New Guinea turned down the "honor" of being invited to remain in the village while the men performed their secret ceremonies. She left with the other women, as she had always done, to feast and make lewd fun of the men's "secrets" (1985:61).

Why don't the women have myths and rituals of their own to validate their position and express their opposition to men? The following observation is made for the Mundurucu of the Brazilian Amazon:

Perhaps it is that the women have fewer anxieties, less of a feeling that they have a vested interest which can be lost. . . . They knew all about (the men's) ritual paraphernalia . . . and they were neither mystified or cowed. It is as if they investigated the secret sources of men's power—and found absolutely nothing. (Murphy and Murphy 1985:166–176)

Societies with explicit expressions of male dominance tend to assert male superiority as a defense against female dominance in the domestic domain.

While gender scripts vary from culture to culture, there are certain underlying cross-cultural similarities. Gilmore (1990) suggests that manhood is almost universally seen as problematic. Manhood is not a natural condition that comes with maturation but presents "a critical threshold that boys must pass through." While women may be judged on their physical attributes or their morality, their right to gender identity is a biological given and women's right to their gender is never publically questioned. Men, on the other hand, have to earn and validate their manhood through personal achievement, whether as a skilled hunter, fierce warrior, or good provider. Boys have to be encouraged—sometimes actually forced by social sanctions—to undertake the efforts to achieve culturally defined manhood.

Gender Stratification

The status of women is difficult to define because it contains multidimensional emic and etic viewpoints. Gender behavior is affected by public versus private setting, the life cycle, kin dynamics, and other systems of inequality related to rank, class, and race that produce other dimensions of power or oppression apart from gender. In other words, men and women have multiple identities and perceptions of relative gender status and power relations that are cross-cut by other hierarchies and ideologies.

The complexity of these features makes it difficult to determine whether women have high or low status. Westerners must be careful not to impose their cultural bias in evaluating gender behavior. Westerners, for example, might mistake public displays of politeness as displays of gender stratification. When a Machiguenga woman walks behind her husband in the forest, she is not kowtowing to a man but is being protected by her husband. In the United States, the deference that men show to women by holding doors and walking curbside is an indication of good manners and reflects more on the man than on the status of the woman. To Westerners, giving bridewealth at marriage may appear as though women are treated as a commodity—bought and sold by male kinfolk—yet in the African context, a woman would not be respected without it.

Variations in Gender Stratification

It is recognized that the status of women varies from one society to another. In some societies, such as the !Kung, relationships among men and women are more egalitarian, whereas in others, such as in northern India, women are clearly in a subordinate posi-

tion. Upon reviewing a sample of 93 societies, Martin Whyte (1978) showed that no single variable is correlated with high or low female status. In some cases, women have rights equal to or superior to men's in property inheritance and in access to religious roles, such as that of shaman. However, women rarely have political leadership roles equal to those of men. Headmen, rather than headwomen, dominate both egalitarian and stratified forms of trade and redistribution. The same male preeminence is evidenced by the Semai and Mehinacu headmen, the Solomon Island mumis, the New Guinea "big men," the Nuer leopard skin chief, the Kwakiutl and Trobriand chiefs, the Inca, and the emperors of China and Japan. If queens reigned, they generally did so as temporary holders of power that belonged to the males of the lineage.

In the majority of societies, males are assigned more aggressive and violent roles than females, and with the evolution of political organization, males often preempt the major centers of public power and control. The strongest correlation in Whyte's study was between societal complexity and low status for women. As we have seen, political complexity is the result of population growth, competition for resources, and increased stratification. Women in complex societies have fewer property rights, more unequal authority in the household, and greater sexual restrictions. The mode of production is associated with intensive agriculture and private property. Men do most of the agricultural labor, which usually involves the use of the plow and draft animals; women's work increasingly involves food processing of storable grains (wheat, rice, corn, millet, barley) inside the household, and with intensive agriculture, women have higher fertility and more child care responsibility. The intensification of male-controlled production deprives women of access to productive means and undermines their status by eroding the economic and political integrity of women's kin groups. By comparison, women in prestate societies have in general fared better in peaceful, noncompetitive environments, suggesting that male dominance may be a response to stress associated with endemic warfare and competition over resources.

For those interested in directing social change and working for greater gender equality in the future, being aware of past systems of gender stratification can help in understanding what must be done to reduce gender inequalities.

Women among Hunter-Gatherers.
In the words of Eleanor Leacock (1978:247), we cannot go from the proposition that "women are subordinate as regards political authority in most societies" to "women are subordinate in all respects in all societies." The very

notion of equality and inequality may represent an ethnocentric misunderstanding of the kinds of gender roles that exist in many societies. Leacock (1978:225) does not dispute the fact that when "unequal control over resources and subjugation by class and by sex developed," it was women who in general became subjugated to men (recognizing, of course, that the degree of subjugation varied depending on local ecological, economic, and political conditions). In the absence of class and the state, Leacock argues that gender roles were merely different, not unequal.

In his study of the forest-dwelling Mbuti of Zaire, Colin Turnbull (1968 [1961]) also found a high level of cooperation and mutual understanding between the men and women, with considerable authority and power vested in women. Despite his skills with bow and arrow, the Mbuti male does not see himself as superior to his wife. He "sees himself as the hunter, but then he could not hunt without a wife, and although hunting is more exciting than being a beater or a gatherer, he knows that the bulk of his diet comes from the foods prepared by the women" (1982:153).

Generally, women hunt and collect only those animal species that do not require the use of spears, spear throwers, heavy clubs, or bows and arrows (Murdock 1967). The Agta of northeastern Luzon in the Philippines are an exception; there, women hunt deer and wild pigs with knives and bows and arrows. They traverse difficult terrain over considerable distances, using dogs to corner and hold their prey as they get ready for the kill. More recently, Agta women have become entrepreneurial in other ways; they earn income from working for neighboring farmers and purchase market goods for use and resale at a profit (Estioko-Griffin 1986; Estioko-Griffin and Griffin 1997).

Women among the Matrilineal Iroquois.   As we have seen, a high correlation exists between matrilineal–matrilocal chiefdoms and intense external warfare (see Chapter 9, "Causes of Matrilocality" section). Although these societies should not be confused with matriarchies, women in matrilineal–matrilocal societies often dominated domestic life and exercised important prerogatives in political affairs. The Iroquois can serve as an example.

The Iroquois were skillful warriors who subdued other Native American groups throughout the region. From their palisaded villages in upstate New York, they dispatched armies of up to 500 men to raid targets as far away as Quebec and Illinois. On returning to his native land, the Iroquois warrior joined his wife and children at their hearth in a village longhouse. The affairs of this communal dwelling were directed by a senior woman, who was a close maternal relative

of the warrior's wife. Because the women remained in their natal homes after marrying men from other villages, local kin groups revolved around mothers and sisters. Iroquois matrons—the elderly heads of households and work groups—organized the work that the women of the longhouse performed at home and in the fields. In turn, Iroquois agriculture yielded bountiful harvests that the matrons owned and distributed.

Because men engaged in external warfare against non-Iroquois villages, the women exercised control over the food supply.

When husbands returned from their expeditions—absences of a year or more were common—they slept and ate in the female-headed longhouses but had virtually no control over how their wives lived and worked. If a husband was bossy or uncooperative, the matron might at any time order him to pick up his blanket and get out, leaving his children behind to be taken care of by his wife and the other women of the longhouse.

Turning to public life, the formal apex of political power among the Iroquois was the council of elders, consisting of elected male chiefs from different villages. The longhouse matrons nominated the members of this council and could prevent the seating of the men they opposed. But they did not serve on the council itself.

Iroquois women influenced the council decisions by exercising control over the distribution of food.

If a proposed action was not to their liking, the longhouse matrons could withhold the stored foods, wampum belts, feather work, moccasins, skins, and furs under their control. Warriors could not embark on foreign ventures unless the women filled their bearskin pouches with the mixture of dried corn and honey for the men to eat while on the trail. Religious festivals could not take place, either, unless the women agreed to provide the necessary stored food. Even the council of elders did not convene if the women decided to withhold food for the occasion (Brown 1975; Gramby 1977).

Women in West Africa.   Women have relatively favorable gender statuses in the precolonial chiefdoms and kingdoms of the forested areas of West Africa. The region, which traditionally had low population densities and root crop agriculture, is known as an area of female farming, where men felled the trees and women performed the subsequent operations using a hand-held hoe. Among the Yoruba, Ibo (also called

African Elite
Women were able to command considerable wealth in regions of Africa with traditional low population density and female farming.

Igbo), and Dahomey, for example, women had their own fields and grew their own crops. They dominated the local markets and acquired considerable wealth from trade. To get married, West African men had to pay bridewealth—iron hoes, goats, cloth, and in more recent times, cash. This transaction in itself indicated that the groom and his family and the bride and her family agreed that the bride was a very valuable person and that her parents and relatives would not "give her away" without being compensated for her economic and reproductive capabilities (Bossen 1988; Schlegel and Eloul 1988). West African men and women believed that to have many daughters was to be rich.

Although men practiced polygyny, they could do so only if they consulted their senior wives and obtained their permission. Women, for their part, had considerable freedom of movement to travel to market towns, where they often had extramarital affairs. Furthermore, in many West African chiefdoms and states, women themselves could pay bride price and marry other women.

Like big men, women in West Africa could command labor and wealth and were able to build a following by redistributing wealth and doing favors for others.

In West African kingdoms, women could mobilize other women through personal initiative and success in accumulating wealth.

West African women not only dominated the local markets but also belonged to female clubs and secret societies, participated in village councils, and mobilized en masse to seek redress against mistreatment by men.

The supreme rulers of these West African chiefdoms and states were almost always males. However, their mothers, sisters, and other female relatives occupied offices that gave them considerable power over both men and women. In some Yoruba kingdoms, the king's female relatives directed the principal religious cults and managed the royal compounds. Anyone wanting to arrange rituals, hold festivals, or call up communal labor brigades had to deal with these powerful women first, before gaining access to the king. Among the Yoruba, women occupied an office known as "mother of all women," a kind of queen over females, who coordinated the voice of women in government, held court, settled quarrels, and decided what positions women should take on the opening and maintenance of markets, levying of taxes and tolls, declarations of war, and other important public issues.

Women in India. As we have seen (Chapter 2, "Emics, Etics, and Sacred Cows" section), Indian culture exhibits a distinct regional pattern with grain agriculture in the north and wet rice cultivation in the south. Unlike parents in West Africa, parents in northern India express a strong preference for sons over daughters. As Barbara Miller (1981, 1987a, 1987b, 1992) has shown, the women of India are an "endangered sex" as a result of the high rate of female infant and child death caused by parental neglect. A north Indian man who has many daughters regards them as an economic calamity, rather than an economic bonanza. Instead of receiving bridewealth, the north Indian father pays each daughter's husband a dowry (see Chapter 8, "Economic Aspects of Marriage" section) consisting of jewelry, cloth, or cash. Unlike southern India—where daughters are seen as economically more valuable—a north Indian woman's dowry goes to the groom and his family and is used to finance a dowry for the groom's sister.

Discrimination against daughters affects women in a number of ways (Malhotra et al. 1995):

- Women are denied access to education.
- Women marry earlier.
- Chastity is emphasized.
- Women start childbearing sooner and have higher rates of fertility.

- Child mortality rates are higher.
- Women marry exogomously, which deprives them of support from their natal kin.

In recent years, disgruntled or merely avaricious husbands have taken to demanding supplementary dowries. This has led to a spate of "bride burnings," in which wives who fail to supply additional compensation are doused with kerosene and set on fire by husbands who pretend the women died in cooking accidents (Crossette 1989; Sakar 1993). In a case cited in Stone and James (2001:311), the husband accused of burning his younger wife claimed she committed suicide because she could not forget her "murky past" involving previous sexual activity. Moreover, wife beating seems to be widespread in India, again, especially in the northern states (Miller 1992).

North Indian culture has always been extremely unfriendly to widows. In the past, a widow was given the opportunity of joining her dead husband on his funeral pyre. Facing a life of seclusion with no hope of remarrying, subject to food taboos that brought them close to starvation, and urged on by the family priest and their husbands' relatives, many women chose this fiery death rather than widowhood.

By contrast, in southern India—which has wet rice agriculture—there is much less discrimination against women. Women have a substantial productive role because labor-intensive wet rice cultivation involves more input from women than the cultivation of wheat or other crops. Women in southern India therefore have better access to such key resources as education and employment and other opportunities. Participation in agriculture and the paid labor force is the basis for greater autonomy. As a result,

- Women marry later.
- Fertility is lower.
- Child mortality rates are lower.
- Women's literacy rates are higher.

However, despite these important gains by women, men still have better access to job training and employment (Malhotra et al. 1995).

Causes of Variation in Gender Stratification

Many factors affect gender stratification, and none has thus far been shown to be a primary determinant at all times and in all places.

In general, women's material contributions and their ability to control distribution of resources enables them to achieve influence in both domestic and public affairs.

But no matter how much control women achieve, male dominance of some sort characterizes most human societies. In searching for key factors related to women's secondary status, we have argued that physical differences do not alone dictate or explain gender inequality. Physiological differences do not preclude women from participating in activities that require physical strength, but culture assigns tasks so that members of each sex do what they are physically able to do best. Males are trained to hunt and become warriors because hand-held weapons depend on muscle power, and most men have a small edge over women, particularly in life-and-death situations such as warfare.

Warfare and Gender Stratification. Warfare is a major factor influencing the status of women in band and village societies. Males on average have a physical advantage over females, especially in upper-body strength. Because males constitute the main fighting force in band and village societies, they are trained to be fierce and aggressive and to kill with weapons far more often than women are. The training, combat experience, and monopoly that men possess over the weapons of war empowers them to dominate women. Thus, the gender-equal !Kung and Machiguenga seldom if ever engage in warfare, whereas the Yanomami, Sambia, and other bands and village societies with marked gender hierarchies engage in frequent warfare.

Brian Hayden (Hayden et al. 1986) has tested the theory that wherever conditions favor the development of warfare among hunter-gatherers, the political and domestic subordination of women increases. Using a sample of 33 hunter-gatherer societies, he found that the correlation between low status for females and deaths due to armed combat was "unexpectedly high." Local groups under lethal threat may lose over one-fourth of the male population due to homicide, and defeat would result in the capture of women and the displacement of the whole group from its ancestral land.

The practice of warfare is cross-culturally associated with male supremacist behavior patterns. It is evident in the military service and is activated in such male-centered social groups as fraternities and athletic teams. Male supremacist behavior patterns are not human universals but are found in situations of intense competition, where men engage in activities from which women are excluded.

> The **male supremacist complex** is a by-product of male monopoly over weapons, training of males for combat, bravery, and other male-centered institutions. The reason for such overwhelming male dominance is that where there is warfare, the lives of group members depend on male bravery.

Male supremacy, in its fullest form, is brought about through warfare, where people's lives are in danger and defeat is costly. Warriors have to be brave, stand up to challenges, show physical strength, take courageous action, and not be afraid of danger. Such heroic behavior does not come naturally. It is instilled through socialization and requires a good deal of shoring up and repression of inner insecurity. As Gilmore notes, "Real men do not simply emerge naturally over time. . . . They must be assiduously coaxed, . . . shaped and nurtured, counseled and prodded into manhood" (1990:106). Outside combat, male groups engage in ritual activities, sports, and other collective endeavors to shore up their masculine identity. During this time, boys need to find reassurance in their achievement and gain certainty that they will be able achieve full status as men. The only clear indicator of masculine selfhood is that men are superior to females, and participating in rituals and sports symbolizing masculine power will help them overcome the fears and anxieties associated with fulfilling their masculine role.

Male Supremacy
Aggressive sports such as football activate the male supremacist complex.

We must remember, however, that the correlation between intense warfare and female subordination does not hold in the case of matrilocal and matrilineal societies. In these societies, warfare is practiced against distant foes and therefore forestalls, rather than encourages, male control over production and domestic life (see earlier example of the Iroquois).

> When the men are engaged in long-distance warfare and are away from their villages for several months at a time, the women are left in charge of the family economic holdings and exercise a great deal of control over decision making.

The correlation between frequency and intensity of warfare and male dominance also does not hold for advanced chiefdoms and states. Although stratified societies have bigger armies and wage war on a much grander scale than classless societies, the effect of warfare on women is less direct and generally less severe than in bands and villages (but not as favorable as in matrilineal societies).

> In advanced chiefdoms and state societies, soldiering is reserved for professionals.

Most males no longer train from infancy to be killers of men or even killers of animals (because few large animals are left to hunt, except in royal preserves). Instead, they themselves become unarmed peasants and are no less terrified of professional warriors than are their wives and children. Warfare does create a demand for suitably "macho" men to be trained as warriors, but in state societies most women do not have to deal with husbands whose capacity for violence has been honed in battle. Nor does women's survival depend on training their sons to be cruel and aggressive (except perhaps in preparation for the drug trade warfare, described in Chapter 12). In advanced chiefdoms and states, therefore, female status depends less on the intensity, frequency, and scale of warfare than on whether the anatomical differences between men and women endow males or females with a decisive advantage in carrying out some crucial phase of production.

The fact that thousands of women served as combat troops in the Russian Revolution and in World War II on the Russian front, as well as with the Viet Cong and other nineteenth- and twentieth-century guerrilla movements, and that they serve today as terrorists, soldiers, police officers, and prison guards, does not alter the importance of warfare in shaping gender hierarchies among band and village peoples.

The weapons used by women in the modern context are firearms, not muscle-powered weapons.

Hoes, Plows, and Gender Stratification

The contrasting gender hierarchies of West Africa and northern India are associated with two very different forms of agriculture. In West Africa, the main agricultural implement is not an ox-drawn plow, as in the plains of northern India, but a short-handled hoe (Goody 1976). The West Africans do not use plows because in their humid, shady habitat, the tsetse fly (see p. 219) makes it difficult to rear plow animals. Besides, West African soils do not dry out and become hard packed as in the arid plains of northern India, so that West African women using nothing but hoes are as capable as men of preparing fields and have no need for men to grow, harvest, or market their crops.

In northern India, on the other hand, men maintain a monopoly over the use of ox-drawn plows, which are indispensable for breaking the long dry season's hard-packed soils. Men achieved this monopoly for essentially the same reasons that they achieved a monopoly over the weapons of hunting and warfare: Their greater bodily strength enables them to be 15 to 20 percent more efficient than women. This advantage often means the difference between a family's survival and starvation, especially during prolonged dry spells, when every fraction of an inch to which a plowshare penetrates beneath the surface and every minute less it takes a pair of oxen to complete a furrow are crucial for retaining moisture. As Morgan MacLachlan (1983) found in a study of the sexual division of labor in India, the question is not whether

Man and Beast
An Indian farmer plowing with a pair of oxen.

Gender Roles and Agriculture
Women and children typically perform the work of transplanting rice.

peasant women could be trained to manage a plow and a pair of oxen but whether, in most families, training men to do it leads to larger and more secure harvests.

Further support for this theory can be found in the more female-favorable gender roles that characterize southern India and much of Southeast Asia and Indonesia (Peletz 1987). In these regions, noted for their strong matrifocal and complementary gender relationships, rice rather than wheat is the principal crop. Rice cultivation involves the operation known as *transplanting,* during which the rice seedlings are pulled up and replanted in a more dispersed pattern. Women and children typically perform this crucial "stoop" labor.

Is a factor as simple as male control over plowing sufficient to explain such phenomena as female infanticide, dowry, and widows throwing themselves onto their husbands' funeral pyres? Not if one thinks only of the direct effects of animal-drawn implements on agriculture itself. However, in evolutionary perspective, this male specialty was linked to a chain of additional specializations that together can plausibly explain many features of the depressed status of women in northern India as well as in other agrarian state societies with similar forms of agriculture in Europe, Southwestern Asia, and Northern China.

Wherever men gained control over the plow, they became the master of large traction animals. Wherever they yoked these animals to the plow, they also yoked them to all sorts of carts and vehicles. Therefore, with the invention of the wheel and its diffusion across Eurasia, men yoked animals to the principal means of land transport.

Control over the plow gave men control over the transportation of crops to market, and from there it was a short step to dominating long-distance trade and commerce and other professions.

Because men already dominated trade, they became the first merchants with the invention of money. As trade and commerce increased in importance, it was to men—already accustomed to keeping track of profits and losses—that the task fell of keeping records. Therefore, with the invention of writing and arithmetic, men came to the fore as the first scribes and accountants. By extension, men became the literate sex; they did reading, writing, and arithmetic. Therefore, men, not women, were the first historically known philosophers, theologians, and mathematicians in the early agrarian states of Europe, Southwestern Asia, India, and China.

All these indirect effects of male control over traction animals acted in concert with the continuing gender role effects of warfare. By dominating the armed forces, men gained control over the highest administrative branches of government, including state religions. And the continuing need to recruit male warriors made the social construction of aggressive manhood a focus of national policy in every known state and empire. It is therefore no wonder that at the dawn of industrial times, men dominated politics, religion, art, science, law, industry, and commerce, as well as the armed forces, wherever animal-drawn plows had been the basic means of agricultural production.

Gender and Exploitation

As economic development proceeds, women tend to lose ground relative to men. Whenever modern technology is introduced, it benefits men more than women because women are relegated to sex-specific, low-technology work at marginal wages. Also, as societies move from a subsistence economy to a monetary system, women's status suffers because their nonmonetary productive roles are not recognized, and the value of their unpaid work is much lower than that of men. When development projects are introduced, Western experts choose to deal with men, thereby depriving women of access to new sources of income. And in an economic downturn, women are hit much harder then men because they were earning less to begin with. Thus, the ratio of women to men is greater in the poorest income groups. This trend is known as the **feminization of poverty.**

 The **feminization of poverty** refers to the growing number of female heads of households and the greater impact that poverty has on women.

The percentage of households headed by women increased worldwide in the 1980s. In addition to their lower wages and lack of access to land and finance, women constitute a disempowered class of workers that feed the service sector of the new economy, where jobs are abundant but women's work is undervalued. Women are also harder hit by poverty because rearing children is seen as women's responsibility and men who father children may abandon them. The rearing of children then becomes the sole responsibility of women, especially when migration to urban centers provides men with new economic opportunities. In the United States, the majority of female-headed households lives below the poverty line because women earn less than men and many fathers fail to pay child support. According to the U.S. Department of Health and Human Services (2005), women in female-headed households with no spouse experienced higher rates of poverty (24.4 percent) than women in married-couple families (5.2 percent) and men in male-headed households (8.8 percent).

Often women are denied the same rights as men. In patriarchal societies, basic rights violations against women are treated as a women's issue, rather than a human rights issue. From a legal standpoint, women in some cultures are denied the right to obtain a divorce and are more severely punished than men for adultery. They lack political rights such as the right to vote and hold political office and to make economic decisions, and they are often denied the right to an education. Moreover, violence and physical abuse against women by their partners is growing worldwide. We saw that in India, wife burnings have become more common, especially in lower-caste families, because the husband can acquire another dowry when he remarries. Also, women more often than men are forced into prostitution or subjected to rape.

Gender and Hyperindustrialism

During the smokestack phase of industrialism, women had little opportunity to overthrow the patriarchal heritage of the classic Eurasian gender hierarchy.

 Patriarchy, or rule by father or a male authority, assumes that women are naturally subservient to their fathers and husbands. Although widespread, patriarchy exists in different forms and degrees.

Matriarchy refers to a hypothetical social system in which domestic and political authority is wielded solely by women.

After an initial period of intense exploitation in factory employment in the early part of the century, American women were excluded from industrial work and confined to domestic tasks in order to assure the reproduction of the working class. Factory-employed male breadwinners collaborated in this effort in order to preserve their privileges and fend off the lowering of male wages. Indeed, most Americans during the 1950s didn't think that women should have equal wages, especially if they had men to support them. A decisive break came in the 1960s, with the shift in infrastructure toward the information and service economy. This shift led to a call-up of literate women into low-paid, nonunionized information and service jobs, the feminization of the labor force, a fall in fertility rates to historic lows, and the destruction of the male breadwinner family (see following section).

The anatomical and physiological differences between men and women (except to the extent that women still may wish to have children) have lost their relevance in today's **hyperindustrial** world.

 The term **hyperindustrial** refers to the fact that the world has now become more (not less) industrial, extending mass production into new areas.

It is no accident that women's rights in hyperindustrial societies are rising as the strategic value of masculine brawn declines. Who needs extra muscle power when the decisive processes of production take place in automated factories or while people sit at desks in computerized offices? Men continue to fight for the retention of their old privileges, but they have been routed from one bastion after another, as women fill the need for service and information workers by offering competent performance at lower wage rates than males. Even more than the market women of West Africa, women in today's advanced industrial societies have moved toward gender parity based on their ability to earn a living without being dependent on husbands or other males.

A serious barrier to equality is the conflict between women's new roles in the workplace and the demands of the family and children. A sexual double standard still persists when it comes to housework. Many women have traded in their domestic roles for a double day in the paid workforce and the unpaid household. Although it is true that income dispari-

ties between men and women have been closing, 80 percent of women who choose to have children are forced to choose occupations where job flexibility compensates for lower pay in order to accommodate childrearing. Yet more women than ever before are taking advantage of new opportunities in the information and service economy. Women-owned businesses are showing tremendous momentum in growth. Over the last decade, the number of all women-owned firms has increased up to two times the rate of the national economy (Center for Women's Business Research 2005). As one female business owner says, "Nothing levels a playing field like money" (Vrana 1997) (see Box 14.4).

A Theory of Gender Stratification Change

All the recent trends toward parity in gender roles can be related to the hyperindustrial mode of production. The trend away from manufacturing and factory employment required and facilitated the call-up of female labor that had been previously absorbed by child and home care. The emerging hyperindustrial economy required an educated workforce to fill the new jobs in service and information processing. Concurrently the increase in the so-called opportunity costs of pregnancy and parenting (that is, the amount of income forgone when women stop working to bear and raise children) inflated the costs of rearing children, weakened the marriage bond, depressed the fertility rate, and furthered the separation of the reproductive from the recreational components of sexuality. The principal change that has occurred in the labor force is not merely an increase in the proportion of women who are employed but a growth in the proportion of employed women who are married and have children. Before World War II, only 15 percent of women living with husbands worked outside the home. By the late 1990s, this proportion had risen to 70 percent.

The link between feminization and the information and service economy is reciprocal: Women, especially married women, formerly were barred from unionized, male-dominated manufacturing jobs, in which they were seen by husbands and unions as a threat to the wage scale. The nonunionized and traditionally feminine information and service occupations—secretaries, schoolteachers, health workers, saleswomen, and so on—were high-growth sectors that offered less resistance. Seen from the perspective of capital investment, the housewives constituted a source of cheap, docile labor that made the processing

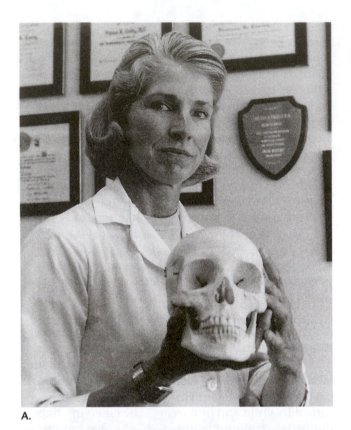

A.

B.

C.

D.

E.

Breaking the Gender Barrier

A. Neurosurgeon Francis Conley.   *B. Executive.*   *C. Construction engineer.*   *D. Soldier.*
E. Pregnant worker.

BOX 14.4 | American Women Are Becoming a Formidable Force in Business

The rapidly growing number of women-run businesses is proof that women are not only successfully carving a niche in the corporate world but creating an important economic force. The number of women-owned businesses grew 20 percent between 1997 and 2002, twice the national rate for all private companies. In 2002, women owned about 28 percent of all private companies (Forbes 2006).

Because women are becoming a prominent business force, major corporations are rushing to meet the needs of women employers. Moreover, marketing divisions recognize that women represent a potentially lucrative market sector. Thus, they have created strategies to target women business owners and are hiring women to lead them.

Studies have shown that women have different business styles from their male counterparts, and corporations are training their salespeople to understand these differences. For example, women tend to be consensus builders and often take more time and require more information before making key purchasing decisions. Thus, when a woman business owner says she'll think about it, she literally means it; for a man, on the other hand, it is a way of saying no. In addition, women place greater priority on establishing long-term relationships with suppliers, and once they contract with a supplier, they remain loyal. Third, because women value personal relationships, they tend to buy major items from a person rather than a catalog. Also, when purchasing technology, women place greater value on service, such as a 24-hour toll-free hotline and a long-term warranty. One of the largest financial institutions in the United States has identified three priorities for women in business: being taken seriously, establishing a relationship with a financial institution, and having information presented clearly. Men want these things also, but they give them lower priority.

Source: Vrana 1997.

of information and people a profitable alternative to investment in factories devoted to goods production.

Thus the feminization of the labor force and the decline of goods manufacturing are closely related phenomena, although as we have seen, this relationship has nothing to do with the inherent capacities of the sexes for physical labor and factory work. Why did U.S. women respond in such large numbers to the service and information call-up? Ironically, their primary motivation was to strengthen the traditional multichild, male breadwinner family in the face of rising costs of food, housing, and education. Despite their lower rate of remuneration, married women's wages became critical for maintaining or achieving middle-class status.

As we have seen in Chapters 8 and 9, family structure is closely correlated with infrastructural conditions. It is impossible in the present case to mistake the direction of causality. Although multiple and complex feedback has operated at all stages of the process, the main thrust emanated from changes occurring at the infrastructural level—the shift from goods production to service and information production. Alterations at the structural level—marriage and the organization of the family—did not show up until a substantial commitment to the new mode of production had taken place. For example, the number of women who had husbands present and who were participating in the workforce had already risen from 15 to 30 percent by 1958. Yet it was not until 1970 that the feminist movement attained a level of national consciousness, when women marched down New York's Fifth Avenue shouting slogans like "Starve a rat tonight; don't feed your husband." These antics expressed the pent-up frustration of wives who were already in the labor force and experiencing the contradictions of the old and new gender roles. As noted by Maxine Margolis in her book *True to Her Nature,*

> Women's consciousness was raised . . . by the material conditions of their lives, by the disjunctions between ideology and reality, the very disjunctions that led to the feminist revival. Viewed from this perspective, the women's movement is ultimately the result rather than the cause of women's discontent. (2000:156)

Changes in sex role attitudes lagged behind behavioral changes, indicating that changes in behavior gradually have brought about changes in sex role norms rather than the reverse. Moreover, the start of the rapid changes in women's labor force behavior greatly preceded the rebirth of the feminist movement.

This is not to say that more equalitarian sex role attitudes and a feminist ideological perspective are not major motivating forces, but as Oppenheimer says, "These attitudes reinforce or provide an ideological rationale (or normative justification)" (1982:30).

To identify the infrastructural conditions of a social movement and to assign them a causal priority over values and ideas is not to diminish the role of values and ideas—or of volition—in the dynamism of history. Nonetheless, it is essential in this case, as well as in other controversial social movements, that both those who favor and those who oppose a particular change comprehend that some outcomes are more probable than others. In the present instance, for example, it seems highly improbable that women in the United States can be restored to their former situation as housewives. In order to resurrect the male breadwinner family and put women "back behind the sink," the nation would have to revert to a more primitive phase of capitalism and industrialization, a course that even the most conservative antifeminists do not propose to take.

Given the high cost of living and women's commitment to the job market, it is unlikely that women will revert to full time in the domestic realm. The prevailing productive and reproductive conditions have led most people to accept that a wife may pursue a career, but some people feel that a mother should not. While women today no longer have to choose between a career and marriage, many are still being pressured to choose between a career and motherhood (Stone and McKee 2002:167). It is, therefore, no surprise that both men and women are delaying marriage and women are having children much later in life.

SUMMARY
and *Questions to Think About*

1. Humans have evolved adaptive mating strategies based on the need to reproduce and rear dependent offspring. Cross-cultural variations in sexual behavior, however, prevent any single culture from serving as the model for what is natural in the realm of sex.

2. Mangaian heterosexual standards and practices contrast sharply with those of Inis Beag.

3. Restrictions on sexuality are related to increased stratification and the need to control property and social status.

4. Homosexuality also defies neat stereotyping, as can be seen in the examples of the Crow and the Azande. Ritual male homosexuality, as among the Etoro, Sambia, and other New Guinea and Melanesian societies, is an elaborate, compulsory form of sexuality that has no equivalent in Western societies. It was probably associated with the need to rear male warriors under conditions of environmental stress and intense intersocietal competition.

5. While genes may contribute to homosexual activities and preferences, it is clear from these examples and the worldwide variability of such activities and preferences that the way homosexuality is expressed is largely under the control of culture.

6. Among native North Americans, male and female "two-spirits" were known for spiritual powers associated with gender variance.

7. Female homosexuality is less frequently reported, possibly as a result of male bias among ethnographers and the suppression of female liberties by dominant males. Nevertheless, there are various reported cases of intimate female friendships.

8. Gender groups are subject to the same kinds of hierarchical distinctions, advantages, and disabilities as classes, castes, ethnic groups, and social races.

9. In many cultures, males believe that they are spiritually superior to females and that women are a source of pollution. These beliefs are present in the male-centered cultures, which hold that women once dominated but lost their power because of inappropriate conduct.

10. Women often do not accept these male versions of gender roles, as illustrated by the examples of the Yurok and Mundurucu. Moreover, as demonstrated in the restudy of the Trobriand Islanders, male ethnographers have often underestimated the etic power of women.

11. Nonetheless, men have more frequently dominated women politically, and the mirror image of patriarchy—matriarchy—is unknown. However, men in societies with explicit expressions of male dominance are required to earn and validate their manhood through personal achievement, whether as a skilled hunter, fierce warrior, or good provider, and tend to assert male

superiority as a defense against female dominance in the domestic domain.

12. Gender roles among hunter-gatherers are often egalitarian, as among the !Kung, Naskapi, Mbuti, and Agta.

13. Female-favorable gender roles are found in many matrilineal societies, such as the Iroquois, but perhaps the most powerful women in preindustrial societies lived in West Africa among the Yoruba, Ibo, and Dahomey.

14. In contrast, the male-dominant gender roles of northern India endanger the survival and well-being of females, especially very young or very old females.

15. Variations in gender hierarchies among hunter-gatherers and village societies are closely correlated with the frequency and intensity of warfare carried out against nearby groups.

16. By contrast, long-distance warfare between village groups tends to promote matrilocality and a higher status for women.

17. At the advanced chiefdom and state levels, only specialist warriors receive training for armed combat; consequently, variations in gender hierarchies depend less on the frequency and intensity of warfare than on the significance of the anatomical differences of men and women for carrying out certain crucial agricultural tasks.

18. Underlying the contrast between West African gender relations and those of northern India are two contrasting modes of agricultural production: hoe agriculture and plow agriculture, respectively.

19. Women can use hoes as effectively as men, which leads to their controlling their own food supply, being involved in trade and markets, having an equal say in the management of household affairs, and wielding considerable political power.

20. In northern India, men outperform women in the critical task of preparing hard-packed soils for planting by means of ox-drawn plows, leading to the preference for sons, female infanticide, dowry, and the mistreatment of widows, in contrast to southern India and West Africa, where daughters are valued.

21. Further consequences of the Eurasian animal-drawn plow complex include male control over trade, accounting, mathematics, literacy, and church and state bureaucracies, as well as continued control over the army. Women's massive entry into the labor force during the 1950s and 1960s was the result of high inflation, falling male wages, and an increase on the demand for female labor. Material conditions, such as low wages and primary responsibility for child care and housework, were at the root of female discontent and the birth of feminism. Despite women's growing integration into the hyperindustrial economy, women are still responsible for the greater burden of household chores at home. However, as women become more successful in the workplace, they are able to achieve greater parity with men.

Questions to Think About

1. What are the differences between male and female mate selection?

2. Under what conditions is female sexuality most likely to be suppressed by society?

3. Under what conditions do males tolerate female infidelity? What do they gain in the arrangement?

4. Why are male inseminating rituals not considered homosexual behavior?

5. How are "two-spirit" people different from gays and lesbians?

6. Under what circumstances might women adopt homosexual social roles?

7. In what ways are women believed to be spiritually inferior to men, and how can this phenomena be explained?

8. What is the basis of women's dominant status in West African chiefdoms?

9. What accounts for the strong preference for males over females in northern India?

10. How does warfare affect the position of women in band and village societies as opposed to chiefdom and state societies?

11. What new challenges and opportunities for gender equality do women have in industrial and hyperindustrial societies?

THROUGH THE LENS
of Cultural Materialism

Conformity and Conflict • Reading Twenty

Symbolizing Roles: Behind the Veil

Elizabeth W. Fernea and Robert A. Fernea

The veil is symbolic of cultural differences between the Western and Middle Eastern worlds. Westerners see the veil as oppressive to women, but for Middle Easterners, the veil has other meaning. Rather than reinforcing the asymmetrical differences between men and women, Middle Eastern women use the veil to redefine their traditional values and their opposition to Western modernity.

Emic Interpretation

- In Islamic culture, women are seen as needing protection because they are unable to control their sexuality. They must be restrained so that men will not give way to the desire that they inspire.
- In the face of modernity, Middle Eastern women also use the veil to show their opposition to Western standards.

Etic Interpretation

- The veil is a cultural construction that signifies honor. Women wear the veil as a symbol of morality.
- It secludes women from men and makes women responsible for maintaining their honor by not evoking men's desire.

Infrastructure

- The mode of production in the Middle East is male dominated; women engage mostly in food preparation, rather than food production.

- Only poor women engage in manual labor in the fields, where they are unable to wear a veil. The veil therefore signifies a middle- or upper-class lifestyle and becomes an object of envy, rather than resentment.

Structure

- Patrilineal inheritance gives men economic and political control. An emphasis on female chastity and seclusion, before and after marriage, ensures the husband's paternity of his children.
- The family is of extreme importance in Middle Eastern society. Family life is hidden away from strangers, and great effort is made to avoid family shame.
- Veiling and seclusion maintain social status and the asymmetrical relationship between men and women.
- Since abolishment of the floor-length cotton veil in 1935, Iran's women have themselves chosen to wear veils.

Superstructure

- Among the first true followers of Islam, veils did not conceal but rather announced the religious status of women, drawing attention to the fact that they were Muslims and therefore should be treated with respect.
- Today, women choose to wear veils to be part of the time-honored notion of feminine decorum. They would think badly of a husband who "permitted them to be exposed to the public gaze."
- The veil is symbolic of modesty, respectability, and religious piety in modern Middle Eastern urban life. It allows women to go outside their homes while remaining pious and respectable.

THROUGH THE LENS
of Cultural Materialism

Conformity and Conflict • Reading Twenty-One

Society and Sex Roles

Ernestine Friedl

A complex relationship exists among technology, social organization, environment, and sex roles. In any society, status goes to those who control the distribution of valued goods and services outside the family. Control over valued resources enables women to achieve prestige, power, and equality.

Emic Perspective

- Because women are subordinate to men in many societies, some people conclude that it is natural for men to dominate.

Etic Perspective

- Relations between men and women are shaped by a culturally defined division of labor based on sex.
- Sex roles are not fixed and tend to vary according to the degree to which women control the dis-

tribution of food and other valuables beyond the household.

Infrastructure

- Hunter-gatherers subsist on wild plants collected by hand; they hunt large land animals and sea mammals and catch fish with hooks and nets.

- For most of human history, humans have relied on hunting and gathering. This mode of production has endured for about 2 million years and was replaced by farming and animal husbandry only 10,000 years ago.

- Hunting and gathering societies vary in the degree to which they rely on animal protein versus vegetable foods:

  - The Washo people of northern California collect large quantities of fish in the spring. Everyone—men, women, and children—participate. In the fall, some men hunt deer, but the most important source of animal protein is the jackrabbit, which is captured in communal hunts where men and women together drive rabbits into nets. To provide food for the winter, husbands and wives work as teams in the late fall to collect pine nuts.

  - Among the Hadza of Tanzania, men and women work alone to feed themselves. They live in an area rich in edible berries, roots, and small game that can be obtained by men and women alike.

  - The Tiwi of Melville and Bathurst Islands are representative of the most common form of foraging society, in which the men supply large quantities of meat. Yet meat represents less than half the food consumed by the group.

  - The Eskimo are representative of the rarest type of forager society, in which men provide all the meat by hunting large game. Inland Eskimo men hunt caribou throughout the year to provide for the entire society, and maritime Eskimo men depend on whaling, fishing, and some hunting to feed their extended families.

Structure

- The source of male power among hunter-gatherers lies in their control of a scarce, hard-to-acquire but necessary nutrient—animal protein.

- Patriarchies are strongest in societies in which men control significant goods that are exchanged with people outside the family. Regardless of who produces food, the person who gives it to others creates the obligations and alliances that are at the center of all political relations. The greater the male monopoly on the distribution of scarce items, the stronger their control of women seems to be.

- Among the !Kung San of Africa, after the meat is distributed to all the men in the hunting party, each hunter distributes his share to his blood relatives and his in-laws, who in turn share it with others. The meat distributed by the men is a public gift. Its source is widely known, and the donor expects a reciprocal gift when other men return from a successful hunt. A man gains honor as a supplier of a scarce item and simultaneously obligates others to him.

- Vegetable foods, in contrast, are not distributed beyond the immediate household. No one outside the family regularly eats any of the wild fruits and vegetables that are gathered by women.

- The division of labor in hunting and gathering societies varies according to the type and quantity of game that is available. Because women are usually pregnant or caring for young children, they do not hunt large animals, especially when it requires them to go far from home. Women do, however, hunt small game and fish and partake in communal hunts.

  - The Washo are among the most egalitarian of hunter-gatherers. Everyone participates in most food-gathering activities, there are no individual distributors of food, and there is relatively little difference in male and female rights. Men and women are not segregated in daily activities. Both are free to take lovers after marriage, both have the right to separate whenever they choose, and menstruating women are not isolated from the rest of the group.

  - Among the Hadza, the sexes are relatively equal due to the abundance of food. Because Hadza men distribute little meat, their status is only slightly higher than that of the women. People flock to the camp of a good hunter, and the camp might take on his name because of his popularity, but he is in no sense a leader of the group. A Hadza man and woman have an equal right to divorce, and each can repudiate their marriage simply by living apart for a few weeks.

  - Among the Tiwi of Melville and Bathurst Islands, males dominate females. A woman must always be married; female infants are betrothed at birth, and widows are remarried at the gravesides of their late husbands. Men form alliances by exchanging daughters, sisters, and mothers in marriage, and some have been known to have as many as 25 wives.

  - Among the Eskimo, men hunt and women process the carcasses, sew skins to make clothing, cook the food, and care for the young. Women collect no food on their own and depend on the men to supply all the raw materials. Eskimo women are treated almost exclusively as objects to be used, abused, and traded by men. After puberty, each Eskimo girl is fair game for any interested male. A man shows his intentions by grabbing the belt of a woman, and if she protests, he may cut off her trousers and force himself upon her.

- In contemporary industrial society, women who provide services without pay are vulnerable to dominance.

Women can obtain social recognition only if they control valued resources and are able to exchange them outside the household. By giving to others, women, like men, are able to create obligations and form alliances that are essential to political relations.

THROUGH THE LENS
of Cultural Materialism

Conformity and Conflict • Reading Twenty-Two

A Woman's Curse?

Meredith F. Small

Among the Dogon, men pay close attention to when women are in menstrual huts to infer the paternity of their children. Paternity is important in this patrilineal society because inheritance is reckoned through males. If a woman goes to the menstrual hut, it is clear she is not pregnant or lactating. Therefore, the hut signals important information about a woman's fertility that would otherwise be hidden.

Emic Perspective

- Menstrual taboos set women apart from the rest of society because menstruating women are seen as impure and polluting.
- Women themselves believe that their condition is a danger to the gods and that disaster may befall their village if they fail to abide by the taboo.

Etic Perspective

- The taboo requires menstruating women to be segregated from the rest of society, enabling men to acquire knowledge that helps them assess their paternity.
- In doing so, they are better able to channel resources to their biological sons and avoid cuckoldry.

Infrastructure

Mode of Production

- The Dogon are an African society of millet and onion farmers for whom land is scarce.

Mode of Reproduction

- Nonmenstrual women may be either pregnant, lactating, or menopausal. Timing of intercourse and timing of menstruation provides men with information for assessing paternity.
- Dogon women menstruate about 110 times during their fertile lives; Western women do so about 350 times. Dogon women menstruate less because they are pregnant more often and because they nurse their babies for at least 20 months, spending most of their reproductive years in lactation amenorrhea.

Structure

- Dogon descent is through the male line; land is passed down from fathers to sons, so information about paternity is crucial to a man's entire lineage.
- The Dogon endorse polygyny; each man may have as many as four wives, making it difficult to keep track of women's reproductive cycles.
- The menstrual hut is a round structure set apart from the rectangular dwellings of the rest of the village. It is situated outside the walled compounds of the village but is in full view of the men's thatched-roof shelters, so that men can readily see who leaves the hut in the morning and returns in the evening.
- Women cooperate in marking their menstrual cycles because they depend on men to support their children. Nonetheless, women follow the taboo reluctantly and cease visiting the hut if their husbands convert from the traditional religion to Islam or Christianity, which does not impose menstrual taboos.

Superstructure

- Menstrual taboos prohibit a woman from having sex with her husband and from cooking for him. Women are also forbidden from visiting sacred places and taking part in sacred activities. These taboos also forbid women from touching items used by men, such as hunting gear and weapons, and from eating certain foods and bathing at certain times of day.
- Menstruating women are believed to be a threat to the sanctity of religious alters, and their aura of pollution may bring calamity upon the village. This belief is ingrained in women, who have internalized the taboo and feel guilty if it is violated.

CHAPTER 15

PSYCHOLOGICAL

ANTHROPOLOGY

This Laotian father is bathing his son. Anthropologists study how child rearing practices affect personality.

E arlier in this century, psychologically oriented anthropologists began to study the
relationship between culture and personality. Did cultures shape people's personalities, or did
their personalities shape their cultures? According
to the followers of Sigmund Freud, some personality
complexes occur universally and affect cultures everywhere. We will see to what extent this is true. Others
follow Freud in contending that culturally prescribed
differences in childhood training greatly influence
adult personality. But can it be said that all adults
brought up in a particular culture, under a given
mode of production, have the same personality? Do
the Japanese, for example, have a distinctive national
character, or are there different components to the
self that express themselves in different contexts? And
what of the relationship between culture and cognition: Are there cultural differences in perception and
how do people make decisions? What about mental
health? Do certain forms of mental illness occur in
only one culture?

Culture and Personality

Personality, as defined by Victor Barnouw (1985:8),
"is a more or less enduring organization of forces
within the individual associated with a complex of
fairly consistent attitudes, values, and modes of perception which account, in part, for the individual's
consistency of behavior." More simply, "Personality
is the tendency to behave in certain ways regardless of the specific setting" (Whiting and Whiting
1978:57).

 Culture refers to the patterned ways in which the
members of a society think, feel, and behave.

Personality also refers to patterned ways of thinking, feeling, and behaving, but the focus is on the
individual.

The concepts employed in describing the thinking, feeling, and behavior of personality types differ
from those employed in describing infrastructure,
structure, and superstructure, yet psychological processes are highly relevant for understanding social
life. Psychologists talk about motives, values, and
emotions, whereas anthropologists see these concepts as derived from cultural traditions and ideologies that set forth standards and expectations
for how people should feel and behave in given
contexts.

Freud's Influence

Sigmund Freud, who developed the theory of **psychoanalysis**, had a major influence on early culture
and personality research.

 Psychoanalysis emphasizes the importance of
thought and unconscious fantasies in determining
personality and behavior.

Today most psychological theories accept three important elements of Freudian theory:

- Adult personality is shaped by early experiences
  during infancy and childhood.
- Psychological development occurs in stages, during
  which certain mental events regularly take place.
- Certain thoughts and feelings are under the influence of the unconscious, which follows laws different than those that govern conscious experience.

The Oedipus Complex

One of the most important stages in a child's development is the stage of sexual awareness between the
ages of 3 and 6, when the child, according to Freud,
unconsciously wishes to possess the parent of the opposite sex and get rid of the parent of the same sex.
Freud called this the **Oedipus complex.** Oedipus, according to ancient Greek legend, killed his father and
married his mother.

 The **Oedipus complex** refers to the emotional attachment and desire that boys have for their mothers
and feelings of rivalry and guilt that they feel toward
their fathers. The female counterpart is the **Electra
complex,** which refers to a similar attraction of a
daughter to her father and rivalry toward her mother.

According to Freud, boys and girls go through the Oedipal stage differently. The boy wishes for exclusive
intimacy with his mother, similar to what he experienced as an infant, nursing at his mother's breast. This
happens around age 3, as the boy separates from his
mother yet is drawn by strong instinctual erotic impulses to be close to her. He views his father as a rival
and wishes to replace him. These feelings arouse fear
and guilt in the young boy because in his fantasies,
the boy will be punished for wanting to replace his
father and feels guilty for his hostility.

The fantasies of the early Oedipal period cause
the child to react to the conflicting feelings of love,
fear, and guilt by suppressing them into the unconscious. Resolution of this conflict is believed to

occur though identification with the parent of the same sex and renunciation with the parent of the opposite sex. In learning to control and reject these unacceptable wishes, the growing boy acquires and learns to direct his aggression away from his father and toward socially constructive activities. While acknowledging the significance of Oedipal relations, some psychologists ascribe the child's antagonism toward the father not necessarily to sexual rivalry but to resentment of the father's authoritarian power.

Freud admitted that he did not quite know what to make of girls. He envisioned a parallel but fundamentally different trauma. A girl's sexuality is also initially directed toward her father, but she soon makes a fateful discovery that she lacks a penis. Her love for the father and for other men is mixed with a feeling of envy, for they possess something she lacks. Freud believed that women would have a lingering sense of *penis envy* all of their lives.

Clearly, Freud's notions about gender roles were projections of his own experiences as a male in highly male-centered, late–nineteenth century Vienna, where he lived and formulated his ideas. Sexual politics aimed at perpetuating the gender hierarchy, not science, provided the basis for his idea that women necessarily envied men and were destined always to be the second sex. If women feel inferior to men, it is not because they are dissatisfied with their anatomy; they are dissatisfied because of the disadvantages of their second-class status in patriarchal society (Horney [1939] 1967).

The Oedipal theme takes many forms in folktales around the world (see Box 15.1). Allen Johnson and Douglass Price-Williams (1996) surveyed 164 "family romance" folktales that describe incest and

BOX 15.1 | Oedipal Myths

Father–Daughter Incest: Navajo, Native North American Myth

A man named Crow had many children. His oldest daughter was the prettiest, and Crow decided to make her his wife. He pretended he was ill and told his wife to make him a bed in a tree. He put a piece of liver under the bed and told his wife that if worms started falling out of it, she would know he was dead and must move away. Then she must give the oldest daughter in marriage to the first person she saw carrying four prairie dogs.

Crow did this so he could have intercourse with his daughter. But he had a big scar on the side of his head. After the worms fell out of the tree and his family moved away, he disguised himself and met his family with four prairie dogs in hand. No one recognized him, and his daughter was given to him as a wife.

One night he told his daughter to clean his head of lice. He knew she would recognize him by his scar, so he told her not to touch the other side of his head. The girl became curious and at night, while he was asleep, she looked to see if he had lice on the other side. She saw the big scar and knew it was her father.

She sneaked out and ran to her mother. She and her mother returned while her father was still asleep. When the mother saw it was her husband, she threw a rock at his head and that is how he was killed.

Source: Adapted from A. Johnson and Price-Williams 1996:241–243.

Mother–Son Incest: Yamana, Native South American Myth

Although Little Woodpecker was very young, he had fallen in love with his mother. She carried him in a bag and never took him out or left him alone. When she went to the forest to collect mushrooms, she set the bag down and her little son became a grown man. He climbed up the tree and picked many mushrooms, which he threw to the ground. He told his mother to lie down and part her legs so that he could see her vagina. He then threw the mushrooms at her vagina, which was a great pleasure for both of them. He then lay down on his mother and she received him with great pleasure, for his penis was extremely large. When they got up, the son got back into the bag and became an infant again.

They continued to go to the forest to gather mushrooms and have intercourse. The other women wondered how she collected so many mushrooms in such a short time. They followed her unnoticed and watched as her son became a man, threw the mushrooms at her vagina, and lay down on her. The women were horrified and rushed back to tell her husband what they had seen.

When his wife returned, the husband waited until evening. When they were asleep, he took his knife and cut down the bag. The boy fell out and the father could see the boy's large penis. With horror, he seized the knife and cut off his son's penis. The boy turned into a woodpecker, flew off into the forest, and never returned to his parents' hut.

Source: Adapted from A. Johnson and Price-Williams 1996: 293–295.

family violence. Where boys are concerned, such stories depict a struggle between a young man and a father figure and an inappropriately close, often erotic relationship between a young man and a mother figure. But stories about girls suggest that female Oedipality differs from the Freudian version. A common theme is that the father is sexually attracted to the daughter, but the daughter does not reciprocate his feelings. Nor does the daughter view the mother as a competitor for the father; instead she joins in an alliance with the mother to resist the father's advances. Nancy Chodorow (1974, 1978) supports the view that the girl's attachment to her father is not as intense as that of the boy's for his mother. Unlike the boy, who must turn away from the mother to achieve masculine independence, the daughter experiences continuity in her relationship with her mother, which gives her a sense of interpersonal connection with the primary parent.

We can conclude that Oedipal concerns appear to be universal to the extent that children grow up in families where there is emotional ambivalence and children have fantasies of an exclusive relationship with the parent of the opposite sex. The content and severity of the Oedipus complex, however, varies from one society to another in relation to the structure of the domestic group.

Most societies have Oedipal stories about incest and violence, but the content of these "family romance" stories vary in relation to societal structure.

In patriarchal societies, the rivalry between father and son is structurally embedded in family organization. Horney ([1939] 1967) argues that the Oedipal intergenerational antagonism is further intensified in class-structured, commercially competitive societies, where parents stimulate hostility in children through critical and domineering behavior. Similarly, tribal warfare, where the emphasis is on fierce competitive males, creates a male supremacy complex. When the objective of childrearing is to produce aggressive, dominant males, young men will feel insecure about their manliness and there will be competition between males in adjacent generations.

How Culture Constructs Personality

Many anthropologists have examined psychological concepts cross-culturally. Ruth Benedict, for example, showed that cultures mold personalities in distinctive ways, according to **cultural configurations.**

 Cultural configuration refers to the unique social patterns that a culture has standardized.

In her famous book *Patterns of Culture* (1934), Benedict described cultures as learned solutions to problems confronted by every society. Each culture is a uniquely integrated whole with a distinctive configuration of customs and values that influence individual psychology.

Benedict believed that each society develops a unique pattern, or cultural configuration, elaborating certain aspects of human experience and ignoring others.

Benedict described these societies:

- The Kwakiutl are "Megalomaniac" because their potlatches are dominated by fantasies of wealth and power with an uninhibited will to be superior.

- The Zuni Pueblo people are "Appollonian," given to moderation and the "middle of the road" in all things. She saw them as emphasizing cooperation and communal activities and avoiding all strong emotions, such as anger and jealousy.

- The Dobu are suspicious and hostile, consisting of nasty and paranoid individuals who enjoy trickery and deceit.

Most anthropologists have rejected such attempts to use one or two psychological terms to describe whole cultures. Even the smallest hunter-gatherer societies have too many personalities to be summed up and depicted in terms of single labels.

Margaret Mead expanded on the idea that culture shapes human development in her research on adolescent Samoan girls.

Mead set the stage for future research into the relationship among culture, childhood training, and adult personality by showing how children grow up under varied cultural conditions.

Her goal was to show that human nature was not "rigid and unyielding." In *Coming of Age in Samoa* (1928 [1961]), she suggested that adolescence is not necessarily a turbulent emotional period for Samoan girls, as it is in Western societies. The crisis of adolescence is relative to the demands a culture places on young people. Thus, the lesson proposed by Mead is similar to that of Ruth Benedict: The world's cultures do not adhere to the same cultural patterns. In *Sex and Temperament in Three Primitive Societies* (1935 [1963]), Mead used three New Guinea societies to challenge Western gender ideologies. She showed that men and women display different temperaments in terms of appropriate masculine and feminine characteristics:

- The Tchambuli—Men are preoccupied with art and their appearance; they prepare elaborate costumes for ceremonial events. The women are the breadwinners; they do all the fishing and have real positions of power.

- The Mundugamor—Both men and women are violent, aggressive, and masculine.

- The Arapesh—Both men and women are peaceful, caring, and feminine according to Western standards.

Mead emphasized that human nature is highly malleable and that even sex roles are not biologically determined.

The assignment of temperament in each society fits the cultural configuration but is one among several possibilities. Although there are patterns of gender difference (see Chapter 14), Mead urges that we recognize the diversity of human potentials and make room for those who cannot conform to conventional standards.

National Character

When the population involved is an entire nation, the modal personality is often called **national character.** A common theme in national character studies, as elsewhere, is that childrearing customs have a major impact on adult personality traits. Several studies of national character were made during World War II, to understand the psychology of the combatants. Because direct fieldwork was not possible, anthropologists did their research by studying "culture at a distance," through the analysis of books and newspapers and through interviews with expatriates aimed at gathering material on memories of childhood and cultural attitudes.

Japanese national character was the most puzzling to U.S. policymakers and the general public. In *The Chrysanthemum and the Sword* (1946), Ruth Benedict tried to explain the seemingly incomprehensible contradiction between (1) Japanese restrained aestheticism, expressed in Japanese flower arranging, and (2) fanatical militarism, expressed in the cult of the sword and samurai warrior. Benedict noted that these contradictions are grounded in socialization practices that induce shame in children. Japanese children learn to subordinate personal desires to family and group demands. She explained that childhood shame is transformed into adult concern with saving face to avoid disgrace to themselves and family. Serious

---

BOX 15.2 | The Japanese at Home

"People are relaxed and do not worry about formalities. They can talk and joke about their innermost concerns. Even the most formal of women may be informal with close friends. They even tease each other about the formalities which they notice on other occasions. With close friends, one can argue, criticize, and be stubborn without endangering the relationship. There is inevitably a great deal of laughter mixed with mutual support and respect. It is partly the sharp contrast between seeing a close friend and a mere acquaintance that makes contacts with outsiders seem so stiff. The visitor to Japan who does not appreciate the difference in behavior toward friends and acquaintances is likely to consider the Japanese as more formal than they actually are."

Source: Quoted in Sugimoto and Mouer 1983.

---

disgrace can be overcome only by honorable death in battle or by suicide.

These theories about Japanese national character changed after World War II, when the Japanese adapted to their defeat and took the lead in the peace movement in Asia, hardly confirming the portrait of wartime brutality. Moreover, it is now believed that subordination to the group does not necessarily entail the loss of individuality.

The Japanese concept of self can be understood in the broader context of East Asian, collectively oriented cultures, which emphasize the need to accommodate to others. East Asian notions of self are antithetical to those of North Americans. Unlike the individualized concept of self that promotes self-expression and independence, East Asians start with the Confucian assumption that a person exists in relationship to others (Suh 2000). Personal well-being is derived from avoiding confrontation.

The Japanese sense of self is more interdependent. An important source of personal satisfaction is achieved by maintaining harmonious relations with others.

Based on self-reported psychological tests, the Japanese experience their emotions as less intense than those of Americans and are more intuitive about the needs of others (Markus and Kitayama 1991). But does this mean that the Japanese do not have feelings of anger and other strong emotions? By accommodating themselves to others and controlling their public performance, the Japanese—like many other East Asians who live in high-density, kinship-oriented, socially immobile communities—are exercising the functional restraint necessary to get along in restricted environments. In China, "individuals do not have the choice to just change or cancel out their relationships with those individuals in their social world. Therefore their primary concern would be how to live with each other's differences and 'get along' " (quoted in Lindholm 2001:214). A strong effort must be made to monitor emotions so as not to offend others.

The interdependent self can be seen as governed by an inner overseer capable of adapting behavior to conform to social demands and maintaining control to meet the cultural demand for self-effacement (Lindholm 2001). Consequently, the Japanese have been described as having "faces" for different situations; group activities require public behaviors appropriate in particular contexts (see Profile 15.1). Different faces are reflected in different speech forms used on different occasions (Hendry 1995:54). According to Takie Lebra (1992), the **public (interactional) self** is the surface layer of self that is exposed to appraisal by others. It varies according to its reference group—whether one stands with family, neighbors, or colleagues. The **private (inner) self** is more stable and authentic. It is immune to social relativity and provides a fixed core for self-identity. The private self is seen as morally superior and thus accounts for

PROFILE 15.1 | Japanese National Character

Valid interpretations of personality configurations in alien cultures require great familiarity with the language and deep immersion in the context of everyday life. The experience of being a member of another society often cannot be adequately represented by simple contrasts and conventional categories. For example, the Japanese are stereotyped by Westerners as a people who are deferential, shy, self-effacing, conformist, and dependent on group approval. "Few Japanese," writes one anthropologist, "achieve a sense of self that is independent of the attitude of others" (cited in Kumagai and Kumagai 1986:314; cf. Plath 1983).

Examples of exaggerated deference are found in the frequent bowing and elaborate courtesy of Japanese business conferences and the readiness with which Japanese identify themselves as a work team or a corporation, rather than as individuals. Indeed, self-effacement has been linked by many observers to the secret of Japan's industrial success. Japanese management style plays down the difference between executives and workers. Everyone eats in the same company cafeteria, and groups of workers regularly join with management to solve problems of mutual interest in a cooperative rather than adversarial manner. However, another side of the Japanese personality is reserved for private and intimate occasions. If you are not a member of a Japanese family group and do not interact with family members when there are no guests or outside observers present, you would not see the strength of individual ego assertion that is also part of Japanese daily life.

Most Japanese are brought up to be adept at changing back and forth between the private assertive self and the deferential public self. The significance of these different modes of presenting one's self has little if anything to do with the inner psychological strength of the Japanese ego. Because Westerners have no real equivalent of a public formal mode of self-effacement, they have often incorrectly and unfavorably perceived Japanese personality. Lacking a Western equivalent, Westerners interpret the posture of self-effacement as indicative of hypocrisy and deviousness.

On the other side, the Japanese are equally befuddled by the failure of Westerners to make a distinction between expressions of one's ego in public formal versus intimate private situations. As recounted by a Japanese social scientist, being a dinner guest in a U.S. home can be especially perplexing: "Another thing that made me nervous was the custom whereby an American host will ask a guest, before the meal, whether he would prefer a strong or a soft drink [and after dinner] whether [he takes] coffee or tea, and—in even greater detail—whether one wants it with sugar, and milk, and so on" (Kumagai and Kumagai 1986:12). Although the visitor soon realized that the hosts were trying to be polite, he felt extremely uncomfortable with having to say what he would like, because in the self-effacing and deferential posture appropriate to being a guest in a Japanese home, one avoids expressions of personal preference with respect to what is being served. Guests are dependent on hosts and surrender all vestiges of personal preference. The hosts in turn must avoid embarrassing their guests by asking them to choose their own food. Unlike North Americans, Japanese hosts do not discuss how they prepared the main dish. They say, "This may not suit your taste, but it is the best we could do." The guests are not supposed to be interested in knowing any of the details of this effort.

Japanese Men in a Public Setting
The public interactional self is exposed to appraisal by others.

the ambivalence a Japanese person holds for the self-conscious, self-effacing self that is presented in public settings (1992:106–112).

The concept of national character cannot be reconciled with the fact that every society includes a great range of personalities and that the more populous, complex, and stratified the society, the greater the variability. Despite cultural stereotypes (see Figure 15.1), in every society, many individuals have personalities that deviate widely from the statistical mode (most frequent type), and the range of individual personalities produces wide overlaps between different cultures.

So, how does the cultural context influence personality, and how do we explain intracultural variability? It has been suggested that differences in the types of experiences provided to individuals by different culture groups, including their structural positions within the cultures (occupational role, status, and other socially relevant groupings), produce behavioral regularities in given settings (Bock 1988).

Anthony Wallace (1952) was the first to attend to the problem of interpersonal variability. In working with the Tuscarora people of North America, Wallace used Rorschach tests to show that even homogeneous societies accommodate a great deal of variability. By scrupulously attending to individual variability, he demonstrated a central personality tendency and then charted variability in relation to the central type. His research on the Tuscarora demonstrated that only about one-third of the people in his sample could be said to share a common personality. In place of the assumption that personality is uniform and directly reflects culture, Wallace proposed that culture is characterized by "kaleidoscopic variety," by diversity of individuals and groups that are in competition and active cooperation at different times (1961:24). Wallace saw culture as "organized diversity," a cognitive and moral framework within which individuals could solve problems and try to predict the outcome of behavior.

Socialization Practices and the Mode of Production

Parents in a particular culture tend to follow similar childhood training practices involving the feeding, cleaning, and handling of infants and children. These practices vary widely from one society to another and are probably responsible for some cross-cultural

A.   B.   C.

Figure 15.1   National Character Stereotypes
Allen Funt's popular TV show Candid Camera *frequently explored national character differences by means of informal cross-cultural experiments. The three scenes represented here show the same young woman in three different countries, standing at a curb with a suitcase filled with 100 pounds of bricks. In each scene, she solicits a male passerby to help her get her suitcase across the street. In Country A, the man tugs and pulls at the suitcase with all of his might, finally managing to get it across the street. In Country B, the man tries to move the suitcase, but when he finds it unexpectedly heavy, he gives up and goes on his way. In Country C, on finding the bag too heavy for one person to pick up, the man enlists the aid of another male passerby, and the two of them carry it across with no difficulty. Can you guess which country each scene depicts? In view of the recent changes in gender roles, what other scenarios might be likely to occur today?*

Answers: (A) England   (B) France   (C) United States

A.

B.

Care of Children

*Cultures vary greatly in the amount of body contact between mother and infant.   **A.** This Swazi mother carries her child on her back to keep her hands free.   **B.** This Arunta mother has an all-purpose carrying dish on her head and digging stick in her hand, yet she carries her child with her free arm.*

differences in adult personalities. In some cultures, for example, nursing may be on demand at the first cry of hunger; in others, feeding occurs at regular intervals at the convenience of the mother. Nursing at the mother's breast may last for a few months or several years or may not take place at all. Weaning may take place abruptly, as when the mother puts a bitter substance on her nipples, or it may be gradual. In some cultures, infants are kept next to their mother's skin and carried wherever the mother goes; elsewhere, they may be left behind with relatives or other caretakers. In some cultures, infants are fondled, hugged, kissed, and fussed over by large groups of adoring children and adults; in others, they are kept relatively isolated and touched infrequently.

Another series of variables relevant to personality formation consists of later childhood and adolescent experiences: the importance of the mother versus other caretakers, responsibilities for sibling caretaking and other work that children are expected to

do, the composition of children's play groups, and opportunities for formal schooling and literacy at home (Weisner and Gallimore 1977; B. Whiting and Edwards 1988). As we will see, children's experience with caretaking and sibling interaction impacts social skills such as nurturance, responsibility, and independence training.

Today, most anthropologists believe that childrearing practices are adaptive in the context of the economic requirements of society—that society produces personalities that are suited best to the performance of survival activities. John Whiting and colleagues developed a model for psychocultural research that proposed a causal relationship between parts of culture designated as "antecedents" and parts seen as "consequences," with childrearing and the development of personality as crucial connecting links. According to Whiting and Child (1953), the antecedent elements consist of infrastructural and structural aspects of culture that comprise the **maintenance system.**

Learning Nurturance and Responsibility
Machiguenga infants and toddlers are constantly held by their mothers or older siblings.

 The **maintenance system** consists of the "basic customs surrounding the nourishment, sheltering, and protection of its members" (Whiting and Child 1953). It includes the mode of production and the organization of domestic and political life, as it affects how adults raise their children.

Different modes of production require different daily life routines, which impel parents to interact with their children in certain ways, to assign different tasks, and to reward and punish different types of behavior. The maintenance system influences the child's learning environment, including task assignment, the people with whom the child interacts, the nature of those interactions, and the methods of teaching skills and emotional expression. These experiences, in turn, affect adult modal personality.

The psychocultural model states that economic, social, and political factors outside the control of parents and other caretakers have universal influence on how parents rear their children.

The model also suggests that modal personality influences culture. The assumption is that if people have similar experiences and similar personalities, they will be more likely to find the same beliefs more plausible than others. These cultural beliefs, which include religious beliefs, rituals, and concepts of the self, are part of superstructure.

Male Initiation Rites

Following Freud's theory of Oedipal attachment, John Whiting reasoned that boys who had intense early attachments to their mothers would have to go through a difficult separation process and would have hostility toward their fathers. Male Oedipal dependency is strongest in situations where boys sleep exclusively with their mothers past early infancy, identify with their mothers, and develop a *cross-sex identity*. Cross-cultural research shows the following:

- Exclusive mother–child sleeping arrangements are correlated with patrilocality and postpartum sex taboos that forbid the father from having intercourse with the mother for a year or more after she has given birth.

- Long postpartum sex taboos are mostly found in tropical areas, where infant diets are deficient in protein. Long-term nursing ensures the child's health, so men are forbidden from having sex with their wives to guard against early pregnancy.

Male initiation rites tend to occur in patrilocal societies where young boys initially sleep exclusively with their mothers and and then must reject such intimacy in order to join the world of men.

A boy's primary identification with his mother creates a special problem in patrilineal and patrilocal societies, where adult males must make a strong identification with their fathers and other males. The conflicting roles are reconciled at the cultural level through **severe male initiation rites**, involving circumcision and other forms of mutilation and trials of courage and stamina that mark the transition from boyhood to manhood and strengthen his masculine identification (Burton and Whiting 1961; Harrington and Whiting 1972:491).

Socialization of Children

Parents and other caretakers try to reward certain behaviors and ignore or punish others to communicate what kind of people they want their children to become. **Socialization** starts with infant care—how babies are held, how quickly they are responded to, and the degree to which they are indulged or frustrated.

 Socialization refers to the process of transmitting appropriate behaviors and values to produce socially and culturally competent individuals capable of functioning successfully in society.

Parental Acceptance versus Rejection. Cross-cultural research shows that when children are neglected or are not treated affectionately, they tend to be hostile and aggressive as adults. Parental rejection is more likely to occur in more complex societies with intensive agriculture, where mothers have to work long hours and there is greater economic uncertainty (Rohner 1975). In a classic study on the small Melanesian island of Alor, Cora Du Bois (1944) describes Alorese children as having a tenuous relationship to their mothers and as they grow up, they develop a pervasive sense of suspicion and resentment (see Profile 15.2). This personality is produced by infant neglect, which results from the conditions of subsistence farming. Farmland suitable for cultivation is far from home, and women are required to leave their children alone for long hours while they tend their gardens. This leaves children "nurturance deprived," an attitude that is reflected in myths of trickery, tales of animosity, and apathy toward ancestors.

Task Assignment. In technologically simple societies with subsistence agriculture, children as young as

3 and 4 years are expected to help prepare food, fetch water and firewood, and clean the house. Around the age of 6 to 8, children are also expected to take care of their younger siblings while the mother is engaged in other work. Results from the Six Cultures Study show that where mothers have a heavy workload, children are required to do domestic chores and child caretaking (see Box 15.3). They spend much of their time around adults and younger children and show more nurturance and responsibility. In technologically complex societies, mothers expect their children to do well in school and be competitive and achievement oriented. Here children perform fewer chores, spend more time with children their own age, and display more dependence and dominance behavior.

Social Structure. Whether the family is nuclear or extended influences how children are reared and how children relate to one another. In nuclear families, husbands and wives are more likely to have a more intimate relationship, with little overt aggression, and fathers tend to be close to their children. Observations show that children in nuclear families display

PROFILE 15.2 | Childhood in Alor

The people of Alor have a very low level of esteem for their ancestors. Like many other people, the Alorese make wooden effigies of the deceased, which they use for ritual purposes. But Alorese effigies are singularly ill-fashioned and, once used, are immediately discarded. Unlike other Oceanian cultures, the Alorese do not provide the ancestral spirits with housing nor do they worry about feeding them. According to Emil Oberholzer, the psychoanalyst who worked with the data provided by Du Bois, Alorese religion becomes more intelligible when it is viewed as a projection of basic personality. Based on his examination of Rorschach tests administered by Du Bois, Oberholzer characterized the Alorese basic personality as follows:

> They are indifferent and listless; they let things slide and get dilapidated. . . . Conscience and its dynamic expression is not developed. . . . Outlets offered by a capacity for long-lasting enthusiasm and self-sacrifice, for sublimation, contemplation, and creative power—all of these are ruled out. There must be emotional outbursts and tempers, anger and rage. . . . The Alorese must be lacking in individual personal contact, living beside one another but not with one another. . . . Either there are no

friendships . . . or there are none that are deeply rooted. (Quoted in Barnouw 1973:158)

Another aspect of Alorese basic personality that is relevant to their indifference toward the ancestral spirits is their failure to idealize their parents. What is responsible for this personality syndrome? Turning to the childhood training experiences, Du Bois found that Alorese infants are frustrated by inadequate and irregular nursing. About 10 days after giving birth, the Alorese mother resumes work in her food gardens. Instead of taking her infant with her to the fields, as is common among many horticulturalists, the Alorese mother leaves her baby with its father, grandparents, siblings, or any other kinfolk who happen to be available. Nursing is often postponed for several hours until the mother's return.

Alorese children are notable for the length and intensity of their temper tantrums. Thus, as adults, the Alorese are suspicious and distrustful, display slovenly workmanship, and seem to have little interest in the outside world. It has been suggested that the infant pattern of frustration instills hostility toward the mother and that this in turn is responsible for the apathetic and emotionally stunted adult personality that in turn is responsible for an apathetic and uncreative conception of the ancestor spirits.

BOX 15.3   Studying Childhood: The Six Cultures Study

John and Beatrice Whiting sent research teams to observe children's behavior in Kenya, Mexico, India, the Philippines, Okinawa, and the United States. A standard set of protocols was used in all the field studies; children were observed at specified times and places for five minutes, and their behaviors were recorded in narrative form by trained observers. These behavioral records were later used to extract a category system of 12 social acts dealing with dominance, aggression, nurturance, and prosocial action. It should be noted that all the behaviors described were found in all communities, but there were cultural differences in both the frequency of behaviors and their emphasis in expressed norms.

more *sociable intimate behavior*. In larger extended family situations, where the family lives with or near the husband's parents and (as is typical in patrilineal kinship systems) relationships are hierarchical, there is increased tension between husbands and wives because a man's loyalties are divided between his parents, siblings, uncles, and his wife. These fathers tend to be more distant from their children, and children display more *authoritarian–aggressive behavior*.

In analyzing the results of the study, John and Beatrice Whiting (1975) used two dimensions for comparing children's social behaviors:

- *Dimension A,* differentiating nurturance and responsibility from dependence and dominance
- *Dimension B,* differentiating sociable and intimate from authoritarian and aggressive behavior

Dimension A was found to be related to differences in *technological complexity* (children stay home versus attend school):

Nurturance and Responsibility	Dependence and Dominance
Simpler, lacking super-ordinate authority	Complex, with class stratification
Require high degree of cooperation within family and community	Train children to be competitive and achievement oriented
Mothers have heavy workload; children required to do domestic chores and child caretaking	Children expected to do well in school; their domestic chores are more arbitrary

Dimension B was found to be related to differences in *social organization* (nuclear versus extended households):

Children's Behavior Is More Sociable and Intimate	Children's Behavior Is More Authoritarian and Aggressive
Organized around nuclear families	Organized around extended families
Husband and wife sleep together	Husband and wife sleep apart
Low overt husband–wife aggression; couple likely to have intimate relationship	High husband–wife aggression; man's loyalties are divided between his parents, siblings, uncles, and his wife
Father–child relations are closer	Father–child relations are more distant

Effects of Social Environment on Children

To understand how culture influences the lives of families and children, psychological anthropologists look at the range of variation in children's behaviors in terms of the **social ecology of childhood.**

 The **social ecology of childhood** refers to the environment of children's experiences that is most likely to affect their development.

Features that affect the behavior of parents and children include the following:

- The community and physical space where behavior takes place
- The personnel (cast of characters) with whom people interact
- The activities (daily routines) that are customarily performed

Thomas Weisner (1979) describes the environmental effects of urban versus rural households on children's social behavior. He studied a group of Kenyan mothers and children who spend time in the countryside and in the city. Because of migration and wage labor opportunities in towns, men work in the city and their wives periodically visit with their preschool children. Weisner found that in the city, children are more socially disruptive than they are in the countryside. In the city, families live in crowded neighborhoods and are confined to cramped quarters. Because older siblings stay behind to attend school, there is no one present to help care for younger children. Compared with their rural counterparts, urban children lack opportunities to spend time with older siblings while they engage in tasks and chores. Consequently, they seek to dominate and act more aggressively toward each another and are more severely punished for fighting.

Socialization is also affected by the learning environment. Anthropologists expect to find adults teaching children how to do things and explaining the reasons, but in fact, very little of this takes place. Children learn their culture on their own initiative, without explanations. At first, children perform tasks with supervision, perhaps working alongside an older sibling. Children are highly motivated to observe and imitate people they respect. As they observe the behavior being modeled, they spontaneously imitate the action and receive corrective feedback if they do something wrong. They are never given an explanation of the nature of the deficiency but are expected to figure it out for themselves.

Thus, if people acquire their culture in large part by observation, imitation, and incremental participation, then researchers must do the same—not by asking people to explain the rules or perceptual constructs but by observing their behavior and learning about culture the same way that native participants acquire cultural skills and experiences (Fiske 1999).

Acquiring Cultural Skills
Children work alongside older individuals and learn by imitating their behavior.

Adult Personality and Subsistence

Some of the most powerful influences on adult personality also emanate from socioeconomic conditions. Adults respond to the stresses and opportunities of their domestic systems and political economies. For example, reciprocal exchange patterns of the !Kung San as contrasted with redistributive exchange patterns among the Kwakiutl lead to patterns of modesty and self-deprecation on the one hand and boastfulness and self-glorification on the other (see Chapter 5). Highly generalized forms of approval and disapproval from peers, parents, siblings, and strangers actively experienced or passively observed throughout an individual's life account for the attitudes and behaviors appropriate to reciprocal as opposed to redistributive exchange systems. Similarly, wherever hunting constitutes an important subsistence technique, special emphasis is placed upon rearing self-reliant and persevering males with high frustration thresholds.

Walter Goldschmidt (1965) designed a comparative study of four communities in East Africa, known as the Culture and Ecology Research Project, to show a direct relationship between subsistence activities and adult personality. Four tribal groups were selected—the Kamba, Hehe, Sebei, and Pokot—which each have groups that live primarily as pastoralists and others as horticulturalists. Robert Edgerton (1971) used a battery of questionnaires and TAT tests (see Figure 15.2) to elicit cultural values and attitudes of adult members in eight communities (four tribal groups with two subsistence modes in each tribe) and to compare the effects of cultural membership versus mode of production on personality attributes.

The results showed that both culture (tribal affiliation) and subsistence modes account for differences among the groups. For example, the researchers

Western Socialization Process
Western culture is primarily concerned with stimulating children's cognitive and social development.

Figure 15.2   Thematic Apperception Test (TAT)

This is one of many methods used by psychological anthropologists. These pictures, developed specifically for East Africa, present situations for expressing values about aggression. Respondents are asked to tell a story about "What is happening in the picture?" and "What ought to happen?" (from Edgerton 1971).

found uniformity within each tribal group so that a Pokot pastoralist is more like a Pokot farmer than he is like a pastoralist from another tribal group. At the same time, there were also clear differences between pastoralists and farmers that are consistent with the kinds of subsistence activities in which they engage.

The most significant differences were these:

Farmers	Pastoralists
Farmers favor conflict avoidance and show indirect aggression.	Pastoralists more openly express both positive and negative feelings.
Farmers resort to secrecy and emotional restraint.	Pastoralists are more direct in their actions and believe people should be allowed to fight.
Farmers more often talk about witchcraft and magic, which is sign of covert aggression.	Pastoralists believe that sorcery occurs when anger is not dispelled.

Farmers live under conditions of high population density because of a shortage of suitable farmland. They must cooperate with a fixed set of neighbors and, despite differences in wealth, must contain hostile feelings because they are tied to the land and cannot easily move away in times of conflict. **Pastoralists** maintain a high degree of mobility and can move when hostility surfaces. They need to be self-reliant, able to make quick decisions, and be ready to protect their herds from theft and predatory animals.

Schemas and Cognition

Psychological anthropologists have long been interested in the relationship between culture and cognitive processes (how people think). The concept of **schema**, borrowed from cognitive psychology, reveals how thoughts about culture are organized in the minds of individuals (D'Andrade 1992, 1995).

 Schemas provide people with simplified cultural models of what the world is like and how they should act, feel, and think.

A classic example of a schema is what one can normally expect to happen if one goes to a restaurant (Strauss 1992:198):

Sit at a table.

Look at a menu.

Tell a waiter or waitress what we want.

Eat.

Wait for a check.

Pay it.

Go out.

Such a sequence, sometimes called a *script,* is never exactly what happens in any particular instance, but the knowledge of such a schema organizes our perceptions of ongoing restaurant experiences or our understanding of stories of what happens when other people go to restaurants.

> Schemas represent knowledge developed from prior experiences; they are abstract representations (not carbon copies) of perceived regularities that help us comprehend new events and experiences.

Cultures differ in their repertoire of schemas. One that is found in Samoa, for example, is organized around the concept of *alofa,* loosely equivalent to our "love." It is associated with the following scenario: an old person is carrying a heavy burden, walking along the road on a hot day. Just as a New Yorker knows the script for a restaurant, so a Samoan knows what to do if such an encounter takes place (Strauss 1992:198):

Offer to carry the burden.

Bring the old person into the shade.

Serve a cooling drink.

According to Roy D'Andrade (1992:30–31), cultural schemas help us understand people's motivations—what leads them to act as they do.

> Schemas not only determine how we act and interpret the world but also serve as goals and models that motivate our behavior.

Schemas are culturally adaptive in that they organize motivation as well as knowledge. They use a small amount of information that provide cues to set goals (both conscious and unconscious) for specific cultural contexts, define what certain events mean, and elicit culturally appropriate behavioral and affective responses.

According to Claudia Strauss (1992), schemas have different kinds of motivational force, based on a person's experience. In fact, goals embedded in a schema may be contradictory, and while people adhere to these goals, they cannot always follow them. For example, based on her research on career choices of five factory workers in Rhode Island, Strauss identified two main schemas that have different motivational effects: *the success model,* associated with initiative for "getting ahead," and the *breadwinner model,* which focuses on the interests of the family and the need for a steady paycheck.

Four of the five men she interviewed endorsed the success model, agreeing that hard work will bring success. But only one of the four made career moves that were strategically consistent with the goal for success. The other three shared the values but did not feel they applied to them personally. The role of breadwinner, in contrast, was seen as unavoidable reality. All five

felt they had to bring home the paycheck. The breadwinner role is not just an ideal but a way of life that is class and gender specific. They felt their obligation was to support their families and keep a steady paycheck coming. This forced them to subordinate their own goals for success. For these men, "it is not a question of striving for wealth above all, but of avoiding near-poverty" (Strauss 1992:208).

The one man who rejected the success model turned out to be the one who worked harder than anyone else in the group. He had a large family to support and worked two jobs, including overtime. His rejection of the success model was based on his identification with the poor and his distaste for businesspeople, whom he saw as greedy and overly concerned with making money.

This research suggests that motivation is not automatically acquired through cultural schemas. Schemas organize alternative goals that are often in competition with one another. For example, Naomi Quinn (1996) showed that American women's notions of marriage involve contradictory schemas of equity, obligation to the role, and personal integrity:

- Women feel that their role should be based on equality and fairness. They want to have the same opportunities as their husbands.

- Women want to fulfill their wifely duties to their husbands.

- Women feel they should be able to reach their potential and not be held back.

These incompatible cultural schemas may lead to moral conflicts and resistance. They are useful for understanding how emic models are organized but do not tell us what choices people will make and how they will act. Only etic knowledge, based on behavioral outcomes, can reveal which cultural messages are incorporated and which ones are ignored. Therefore, schema theory is useful for understanding how emic models are organized, but etic knowledge is needed to explain why some cultural messages are incorporated and others are ignored.

Culture and Mental Illness

Medical research has shown that such classic mental disorders as *schizophrenia* and *bipolar disorder* (previously called *manic depression*) probably have important viral–genetic and chemical–neurological bases.

This accords with the evidence that the rates of these diseases are similar among groups as diverse as Swedes, the Inuit, the Yoruba of West Africa, and modern Canadians (Murphy 1976; Warner 1985).

However, there is no doubt that while broad symptoms of the same mental diseases can be found cross-culturally, specific symptoms and the way they are perceived in different cultures vary considerably. In fact, striking cultural and social class differences in both symptoms and outcome of mental disorders have been found (Jenkins et al. 1991).

Schizophrenia

Medical research has shown that classic mental disorders such as schizophrenia probably have important genetic and chemical–neurological bases. The same core signs of **schizophrenia** appear in cultures around the world: hallucinations, delusions, inappropriate behaviors, and disturbances of thought. Despite biological vulnerability to the disease and similar broad symptoms, it appears that specific symptoms of schizophrenia vary cross-culturally and that social environment may affect the course of the illness.

 Schizophrenia refers to a group of mental disorders that involve a complex set of disturbances of thinking, perception, affect, and social behavior.

Because there are no biological markers, diagnosis of schizophrenia relies on clinical interviews and observation of behavior. The World Health Organization (1968, 1979) conducted a nine-country study of schizophrenia that showed the incidence of core symptoms was similar worldwide (between 1.5 and 4.2 per 100,000). There were, however, differences in the frequency of subtypes of schizophrenia. The catatonic type was observed mainly in developing countries, whereas the paranoid type was more prevalent in developed counties. Moreover, the study found that patients in the least developed countries were likely to have a better outcome than patients in the most developed countries. Patients in less developed countries sought treatment earlier, were discharged sooner, and their recovery was more complete (Jenkins and Karno 1992). It is speculated that communities in developing countries are more accommodating (i.e., there is less stigma) and that families are more supportive.

In developing countries, the extended family is an important resource for the treatment of schizophrenia and other disorders.

Relatives in less developed countries render emotional and physical support, while the community may blame the schizophrenic's bizarre behavior on some pesky spirit. In contrast, schizophrenics in industrial societies are often expelled from both family and community, deprived of emotional and physical support, isolated, and made to feel worthless and guilty. These culturally constructed conditions make the prospect for recovery much poorer in industrial societies, despite the availability of modern medical therapies.

Family emotional climate affects the course of mental illness.

Families that respond with tolerance and acceptance toward schizophrenic family members contribute to improved outcome. Research in England, India, and the United States found that *expressed emotion* (EE)—a measure of criticism and hostility on the part of family members—is associated with poor outcome. Among high EE Anglo American relatives, there is often doubt or disbelief in the legitimacy of the illness (Jenkins et al. 1991).

A comparative study of Mexican American and Anglo American families with schizophrenic family members showed that Mexican American families are typically lower in EE than Anglo Americans. Janis Jenkins points out that the concept of *nervios* (nerves)—which describes a wide range of mental conditions—is also used to account for schizophrenic illness. The term reduces the stigma associated with mental illness and reinforces tolerant inclusion. Many relatives report that they feel more affection for the patient and that they would never abandon their ill relative (Jenkins et al. 1986:45). This contrasts sharply with both Irish and Irish American families, who often adopt the heavily stigmatized term *mental*, which virtually leads to complete family rejection and abandonment (see Profile 15.3).

Depression

Feeling sad, "down" or "blue" at times is a normal emotion. Psychologists, however, consider **depression** to be a disorder when it goes beyond normal sadness into a state of constant and excessive sadness, despair, and isolation.

 Depression exhibits primary symptoms such as depressive mood, insomnia, and lack of interest in one's social environment. The illness may be accompanied by secondary symptoms that are culturally shaped.

PROFILE 15.3 | Schizophrenia in Rural Ireland

According to the World Health Organization *Statistics Report* (1968), the psychiatric hospitalization rate for Ireland is 7.37 people per 1,000, the highest recorded for any country in the world. Approximately half the Irish psychiatric hospital population is diagnosed as schizophrenic. According to Nancy Scheper-Hughes (1979), the highest rates of the illness are among middle-aged bachelors from economically depressed areas in Ireland's conservative western counties.

Male patients in the 35 to 45 age range outnumber female patients by two to one.

> Stress resulting from the breakdown of traditional patterns of social organization, in combination with worsening economic conditions result in elevated rates of schizophrenia in western Ireland.

Traditionally, Irish countrymen managed the family farm by keeping landholdings intact. Children did not marry until late in life, when the father was ready to abdicate his control over the farm. The most capable son was chosen to inherit the farm, and the parents moved into the "west room," where they lived out the remainder of their lives. One or more daughters might marry; otherwise the siblings either remained on the farm or took jobs in town (Arensberg 1968). Since the midnineteenth-century "Great Famine," celibacy and late marriage have tended to increase. These can be seen as adaptations to the high rural birthrates and land shortages.

The Irish family farmer cannot keep up with the forces of industrialization that have impacted the region. Large-scale industrialized agriculture contradicts the basic values of the local small-scale farmer. Older villagers refuse to hire tractors or pay people to increase productivity. The dissatisfaction with life on small farms is greatest among girls and their mothers. Over 80 percent of the unmarried women reject the roles of wife and mother on the small farms. There is a steady migration of young women, as well as men, to England and other urban centers at a younger age than ever before.

The result is a large male bachelor population with little hope of marriage. Only one in three adult males in Ballybran is married; there are 64 bachelors in the parish over age 35 but only 27 unmarried women in their age group. The youngest son, who is usually the last one to escape, is apt to get stuck with the marginal farm and a life of celibacy and service to his elderly parents. The one "stuck" is often ridiculed by parents and friends. Even before the fact, he is labeled the "dummy" and in other ways made to feel inadequate.

Traditional patterns of child care have also been altered as a result of the breakdown of the extended farm family. Parents are ambivalent toward infants and children; children are seemingly greatly desired—the source of envy and jealousy among adult villagers who have none—yet often resented by those who do have them. Small children are both overprotected and frequently ignored (Scheper-Hughes 1979:133). Child care is regarded as low-status work, suitable for old women, who were responsible for it in the past. Mothers say that the heavy workload is responsible for their not breastfeeding or singing lullabies to their children. Mothers do not cuddle infants, and there is low tolerance for crying. Passivity is rewarded; babies are left to "cry it out" or are tranquilized with brandy to keep them quiet. A child who questions an order or does not do what he or she is told is subjected to a beating, so that fear becomes a strong sentiment among children toward their parents. Children learn to deal with disappointment and other emotional hurts with silent resentment. As adults, it is particularly bad for males to show signs of "weakness," such as tenderness or love. This early conditioning interferes with marital and sexual intimacy; it creates problems between men and women expressed in a lack of sexual vitality and reluctance for men to court and marry. As one man put it, "I missed a lot in never marrying. But if, by mistake, I'd taken the wrong woman, I would have got stuck for good" (Scheper-Hughes 1979:104).

Marriages used to be arranged by parents. Today young people want to base marriage on romantic love, and women particularly expect sexual and emotional fulfillment. Sex, however, remains a conflict-ridden area; husbands and wives are unable to communicate about such matters and retreat into silent resentment.

Men express fears of impotence and have low self-esteem. They accept the burden of responsibility laid upon them and suffer most from trying to reconcile conflicting role demands. They are more passive and conforming to authority than women and show suppressed rage in anti-authoritarian fantasies. Women, on the other hand, show more open rebellious tendencies against parental control and a greater sense of autonomy, which prepares females for early emigration from the village and allows them to feel less guilt about leaving elderly family behind.

The connection between bachelorhood and mental illness is associated with the economic changes that have led to the demise of the rural economy. The men who inherit the land experience emotional isolation, loss of self-esteem, and frustration by their inability to marry and continue the family farm. Scheper-Hughes concludes that the high rate of schizophrenia in rural Ireland results from the demise of the rural economy.

The cultural conception of the problem of depression varies cross-culturally. In Latin America, it is associated with a profound sense of tragedy that is part of a tradition of working through oppressive life circumstances, whereas among Anglo Americans, suffering is not an expectable or acceptable state; it is something that must be overcome in order to pursue happiness. In some cultural contexts, people are willing to endure suffering associated with expressed sadness, whereas Americans more commonly voice anger and frustration.

A number of studies have reported a significantly higher rate of depression among women than men. For married women, depression is associated with the conflicts generated by the traditional female role. For women, the predominant symptoms are more likely to be depressive episodes and phobias, whereas for men, antisocial personality and alcohol abuse are more likely (Robins et al. 1984). Low socioeconomic status is also linked to vulnerability and depression. Thus, sociopolitical aspects of emotion clearly go beyond biological and psychological states of mind and must be viewed in terms of power relations and social inequalities.

Culture-Specific Psychoses

Evidence for more powerful effects of culture on mental illness can be found in **culture-specific psychoses**—disorders that have a distinctive set of symptoms limited to only one or a few cultures (Simmons and Hughes 1985). There are several well-known examples of these culture-specific psychoses that are experienced and communicated in culturally specific forms in non-Western societies.

> **Culture-specific psychoses** refer to mental disorders that have a distinctive set of symptoms limited to a specific culture.

- *Amok* is a hysterical reaction in which young men attack other people and destroy their property. It is found primarily in New Guinea, only among men between ages 25 and 35. After a period of initial depression, the victim emerges in a burst of energy and runs amok. He appears delirious. This is what the Gururumba of New Guinea describe as "being a wild pig," attacking people, bursting into houses, and stealing things. Philip Newman describes an event that lasted three days:

    > His actions had all the classic signs of anxiety hysteria: his speech and hearing were partially blocked. . . . He behaved irrationally, and when he did speak it was either in the form

of commands or blatant false statements. . . . When it was over, he claimed no memory of it. (1965:96)

The victim left the village for several days, and while he was gone people talked about what had happened. They believed the young man was susceptible to the disorder because of his inability to deal with mounting economic pressures. On his return, people left him alone to function at a less intense level of community involvement, which allowed him to readjust to the demands of society.

- *Susto,* traditionally translated as "soul loss" or fright, is similar in some ways to depression. It appears in many regions of the Spanish-speaking New World, in Indian and non-Indian populations, among rich and poor, and among urban and rural dwellers. Victims feel tired and listless, lose their appetites, have trouble sleeping, and don't care about their appearance. A healing specialist must visit the victim to coax the spirits to release the soul. The healer engages in medicinal "sweeping" to remove the internalized illness through the

Spirit Possession
By being possessed (or "mounted") by spirits, a person can achieve emotional release and other psychological benefits that compensate for the frustrations of everyday life.

patient's recollection of the event precipitating the trauma. The healer then removes the illness so that the soul can return to the body. Susto is likely to occur when a person is under stress or has difficulty meeting social demands. The illness communicates an inability to adequately fulfill cultural expectations. Susto thereby provides an adaptive mechanism to self-perceived social inadequacies (Rubel 1998).

■ **Spirit possession** is a disorder in which a person behaves as if possessed by a spirit. The entity that possesses the person may be a deceased family member or a local spirit. Spirit possession is rare in developed countries but is frequently observed in lower-class segments of stratified societies. According to Ericka Bourguignon (1978), the hierarchical arrangements of spirits in Haitian vodoun mirror the racial and linguistic distinctions in the society. Here the concept of possession is that a person is voluntarily "mounted" by a spirit. This is a culture-bound term, which from an etic psychological perspective would best be described as *dissociation;* a split-off part of the personality takes over the person's field of consciousness. The Haitian emic explanation is that the individual is the "vehicle" whose behavior is transformed by the spirit. This state of possession trance is induced through suggestion, dance, drumming, or group atmosphere. By impersonating the spirits, a person can obtain a broader scope of action to achieve emotional release and other psychological benefits that compensate for the frustrations of everyday life. In this regard, dissociation provides the individual with an alternate set of roles by which unfulfilled desires get a second chance at fulfillment through ritually sanctioned behavior (1978:487).

■ **Anorexia nervosa** is an obsessive–compulsive disorder characterized by an unrealistic appraisal of one's body as overweight, resulting in self-starvation to achieve a more slender look. Eating disorders are most prevalent among young females in Western Europe and North America. The cultural ideal of a slim body is associated with an expectation that perfection can be achieved through control and mastery of one's body. Victims of the disorder are "model children" who commonly feel inadequate in their social roles. They use their bodies as instruments of competition to gain mastery and fulfillment. When other things in life are not working, not eating is the one thing they feel they can control.

SUMMARY
and *Questions to Think About*

1. Culture and personality are closely related concepts concerned with the patterning of thoughts, feelings, and behaviors. Personality is primarily a characteristic of individuals; culture is primarily a characteristic of groups.

2. Anthropologists who studied personality during the 1940s and 1950s generally accepted the Freudian premise that personality is molded by childhood experiences. This premise has led to an interest in both universal and culture-specific aspects of early childhood experiences and personality formation. Freud's theories, however, have been modified. Today most anthropologists acknowledge that Oedipal conflicts may result from the emotional ambivalence of family relationships but emphasize that emotional content varies in relation to structural aspects of culture.

3. Early approaches to culture and personality attempted to characterize whole cultures in terms of central themes or patterns. Ruth Benedict believed each culture is organized around a distinctive configuration of customs and values that influence individual personality.

4. Margaret Mead emphasized that human nature is malleable. Knowledge of the range of variation of cultural patterns and the spectrum of enculturation practices should contribute to our understanding of alternatives to Euro-American culture.

5. To understand cross-cultural variation in psychological characteristics, researchers have focused on childrearing customs. The Whitings showed that a culture's maintenance system (the means of production, settlement patterns, social structure, etc.), which influences parental acceptance or rejection, task assignment, and domestic organization, affects children's social behavior.

6. In the case of the Alor, infant neglect, which was the consequence of subsistence farming, resulted in conflicted adulthood, characterized by suspicion and resentment.

7. The means of production also directly influences adult personality. Members of farming and pastoral communities show personality differences related to resource ownership, mobility, and defense.

8. The concept of schemas has been used to identify the cognitive organization of cultures. Schemas organize motivation and elicit culturally appropriate responses. Schemas, however, do not completely predict behavior; they provide a range of possibilities rather than a blueprint for behavior. Cultural schemas may also express conflicting desires and ambivalence, as seen in American women's notions of marriage.

9. A wide range of personality types is found in any large population. This is not to deny that profound differences exist between personality patterns in different cultures. The Japanese, for example, have a distinctive disposition to separate ego-effacing from ego-asserting situations. This disposition, however, cannot be reduced to the stereotype that Japanese are hypocritical or devious; the Japanese have different presentations of self in public and private settings.

10. Classic mental disorders such as schizophrenia and depression are modified by cultural influences, yet they occur in many societies and probably result from interactions among cultural, biochemical, and genetic variables. Culture influences family response to mental illness and can affect the patient's prospects for recovery.

11. The high rate of mental illness in western Ireland suggests that family conditions may be pathogenic. The economic decline of the rural farm presents a burden for the youngest sons, who are left on the homestead to take care of their elderly parents. They are left with a worthless farm and no prospect of marrying.

12. Culture-specific psychoses such as amok, susto, spirit possession, and anorexia nervosa indicate that cultural factors may powerfully influence the state of mental health.

Questions to Think About

1. What modifications have anthropologists made to Freud's definition of the Oedipal complex?

2. How do Ruth Benedict and Margaret Mead demonstrate that culture determines personality differences?

3. What role does the maintenance system have in forming cultural patterns of behavior?

4. What are the strengths and weaknesses of national character studies?

5. How does social complexity and household structure influence children's behavior in the Six Cultures Study?

6. What are cultural schemas, and how do they influence behavior?

7. How does culture influence mental illness?

CHAPTER **16**

RELIGION

A Buddhist monk worships in a shrine in Rangoon, Myanmar.

ow we are entering the inner sanctum of **superstructure**: the domain of religion, myth, magic, ritual, and all the other aspects of cultures that are intended to mediate between ordinary beings and forces, on the one hand, and extraordinary beings and forces, on the other. First some basic definitions will be needed. Then we will try to classify the basic types of religious organizations and rituals. Finally, we will range over the vast variety of religious behaviors, from puberty rites to messianic cults, from prayer to cannibal feasts, and from abominable pigs to sacred cows.

Can aspects of religion be explained in terms of structure and infrastructure? To a considerable degree. Yet religion can frequently become a powerful force in its own right. Although infrastructural and structural conditions provide means for understanding the origin of many specific beliefs and rituals, religion frequently plays a crucial role in strengthening the impulses leading toward major transformations in social life.

Animism

The earliest anthropological attempt to define religion was that of E. B. Tylor (1871). In his book *Primitive Culture,* he demonstrated that members of every society believe that inside the ordinary, visible, tangible body of a human or other life form, there is a normally invisible, normally intangible being: the soul. He named this belief **animism.**

> **Animism** is the belief that humans share the world with a population of extraordinary, mostly invisible beings.

Animism is spiritual belief originated from the experience of dreaming in which a phantom version appears. Sleep, fainting, madness, and death all lead to the notion of a world of spirits who enter and leave human bodies at will. Once imagined, this world of spirits can explain anything: The power of this impersonal power increases in the human mind to the point where humans find themselves captive in an imaginary world and become the vassal of the spiritual forces that they created.

Why is animism universal? Tylor reasoned that if a belief recurred again and again in virtually all times and places, it could not be a product of mere fantasy. Rather, it must have grounding in evidence and in experiences that were equally recurrent and universal. What were these experiences? Tylor pointed to dreams, trances, visions, shadows, reflections, and death. During dreams, our body stays in bed, yet an-

other part of us gets up, talks to people, and travels to distant lands. Trances and drug-induced visions also bring vivid evidence of another self, distinct and separate from one's body. Shadows and mirror images reflected in still water point to the same conclusion, even in the full light of normal wakefulness.

The concept of an inner being—a soul—makes sense of all this. It is the soul that wanders off when we sleep, that lies in the shadows, and that peers back at us from the surface of the pond. Most of all, the soul explains the mystery of death: A lifeless body is a body permanently deprived of its soul.

Tylor has been criticized by twentieth-century anthropologists for his suggestion that animism arose merely as a result of the attempt to understand puzzling human and natural phenomena. Today, we know that religion is much more than an attempt to explain puzzling phenomena. Like other aspects of superstructure, religion serves a multitude of economic, political, and psychological functions.

Another important criticism of Tylor's stress on the puzzle-solving function of religion concerns the role of hallucinations in shaping religious beliefs. During drug-induced trances and other forms of hallucinatory experience, people "see" and "hear" extraordinary things that seem even more real than ordinary people and animals. One can argue, therefore, that animistic theories are not intellectual attempts to explain trances and dreams but direct expressions of extraordinary psychological experiences. Nonetheless, it cannot be denied that religion and the doctrine of souls also provides people with answers to fundamental questions about the meaning of life and death and the causes of events (Pandian 1992:88).

Although certain animistic beliefs are universal, each culture has its own distinctive animistic beings and its own specific elaboration of the soul concept. Even the number of a person's souls varies cross-culturally:

- The ancient Egyptians had two and so do many West African cultures: one from the mother's ancestors and one from the father's.

- The J'varo of Ecuador (Harner 1984) have three souls. The first soul—the *mekas*—gives life to the body. The second soul—the *arutam*—has to be captured through a drug-induced visionary experience at a sacred waterfall. It confers bravery in battle to the possessor. The third soul—the *musiak*—forms inside the head of a dying warrior and attempts to avenge his death. It is to gain control over the musiak soul that the J'varo cut off the fallen warrior's head, "shrink" it, and bring it back to their village, where it is the focus of rituals designed to transfer its powers to its captor.

J'varo Shrunken Head
The shrunken head of a dead warrior is used in rituals that seek to capture his power.

- The Dahomey say that women have three souls and that men have four. Both sexes have an ancestor soul, a personal soul, and a *mawn* soul. The ancestor soul gives protection during life, the personal soul is accountable for what people do with their lives, and the mawn soul is a bit of the creator god, Mawn, who supplies divine guidance. The exclusively male fourth soul guides men to positions of leadership in their households and lineages.

- The Fang of Gabon have seven: a brain soul, a heart soul, a name soul, a life force soul, a body soul, a shadow soul, and a ghost soul (Riviere 1987).

Animatism and Mana

Robert Marett (1914) complained that Tylor's definition of religion as animism was too narrow. When people attribute lifelike properties to rocks, pots, storms, and volcanoes, they do not necessarily believe that souls cause the lifelike behavior of these objects. Hence, Marett introduced the term **animatism** to designate a supernatural force that does not derive its effect from souls.

> **Animatism** is the belief in diffuse impersonal power that people can control under certain conditions.

Marett uses the Melanesian word **mana** to refer to a concentrated form of animatistic force.

> **Mana** is the possession of a concentrated animatistic force that gives certain objects, animals, and people extraordinary powers independent of the power derived from souls and gods.

An adze that makes intricate carvings, a fishhook that catches large fish, a club that kills many enemies, and a horseshoe that brings good luck all have large amounts of mana. People, too, may be spoken of as having more or less mana. A woodcarver whose work is especially intricate and beautiful possesses mana, whereas a warrior captured by the enemy has obviously lost his mana.

In its broadest range of meaning, mana simply indicates belief in a powerful force. In Western cultures, the concepts of luck and charisma closely resemble the idea of mana. A horseshoe posesses a concentrated power that brings good luck. Vitamin pills are consumed by many millions of people in the expectation that they will exert a powerful effect on health and well-being. Soaps and detergents are said to clean because of "cleaning power," gasolines provide engines with "starting power" or "go-power," salespeople are prized for their "selling power," and politicians are said to have charisma or "vote-getting power." Many people fervently believe that they are "lucky" or "unlucky," which can be interpreted as a belief that they control varying quantities of mana.

Natural and Supernatural

Marett's idea that religion involves a belief in mana is problematic because the distinction between natural and supernatural is culturally defined. If a belief in a powerful supernatural force constitutes religion, then what prevents a belief in the natural force of gravity, electricity, or other concepts of physics from being regarded as religious beliefs? Saying that mana is a supernatural force outside the realm of the observable world, whereas electricity is a natural force because it can be scientifically tested, does not solve this problem.

> Most cultures do not distinguish between natural and supernatural realms.

In a society where people believe ghosts are always present, it is not necessarily either natural or supernatural to provide dead ancestors with food and drink. The culture may simply lack emic categories for natural and supernatural. Similarly, when a shaman blows smoke over a patient and triumphantly removes a sliver of bone allegedly inserted by the patient's enemy, the question of whether the performance is natural or supernatural may have no emic meaning.

Writing of the Gururumba of the highlands of western New Guinea, Philip Newman noted that they "have a series of beliefs postulating the existence of entities and forces we would call supernatural." Yet the contrast between natural and supernatural is not emically relevant to the Gururumba themselves:

> It should be mentioned that our use of the notion "supernatural" does not correspond to any Gururumba concept: they do not divide the world into natural and supernatural parts. Certain entities, forces, and processes must be controlled partially through lusu, a term denoting rituals relating to growth, curing, or the stimulation of strength, while others need only rarely be controlled in this way. However, lusu does not contrast with any term denoting a realm of control where the nature of controls differ from lusu. Consequently lusu is simply part of all control techniques and what it controls is simply part of all things requiring human control. (1965:83)

Magic and Religion

In his famous book *The Golden Bough* (1911–1915), Sir James Frazer attempted to define religion. For Frazer, the question of whether a belief was religious or not centered on the extent to which the participants felt they could make an entity or force do their bidding. If the participants felt insecure and humble and were inclined to supplicate and request favors and dispensations, their beliefs and actions were essentially religious. If they thought they were in control of the entities and forces governing events, felt no uncertainty about the outcome, and experienced no need for humble supplication, their beliefs and practices were examples of **magic**, rather than of religion.

Religion refers to beliefs and actions that are based on the assumption that the world is under the control of supernatural forces that humans must please.

Magic refers to a practice intended to manipulate supernatural forces to achieve a specific result. Magic is less spiritual and less ethical than religion.

Frazer regarded prayer as the essence of religious ritual and magic as a more primitive form that preceded religion. But prayers are not always rendered in a mood of supplication, and magic is still prominent in a wide range of modern-day pursuits. Thus, the line between prayers and magical spells is actually hard to draw.

Not all cultures approach their gods as supplicants. In many cultures, people try to intimidate, bribe, and lie to their gods. The Tsimshian of the Canadian Pacific Coast stamp their feet and shake their fists at the heavens and call their gods "slaves" as a term of reproach. The Manus of the Bismarck Archipelago keep the skulls of their ancestors in a corner of the house and try their best to please "Sir Ghost." However, if someone gets sick, the Manus may angrily threaten to throw Sir Ghost out of the house. This is what they tell Sir Ghost: "This man dies and you rest in no house. You will but wander about the edges of the island [used for excretory functions]" (Fortune 1965:216).

Religion and magic are both symbolic systems that help people cope with the ambiguities and anxieties of everyday life. Religion, however, emphasizes explanation and is practiced regularly, whereas magic is a means of manipulation that targets specific, immediate problems. When people face danger or uncertainty, they turn to magic. According to Malinowski (1935), magic provides psychological safety, allowing people to perform tasks without being distracted by fears.

One can find an analogous use of magic in the little rituals and routines that baseball players engage in as they come up to bat, such as touching their caps, spitting in the dirt, and rubbing their hands. Other rituals include eating the same food at the same time of day, taking the same route to the ballpark, wearing the same clothes, and carrying certain good luck charms in order to keep a winning streak going (Gmelch 1971). None of this has any real connection with getting a hit, but constant repetition reduces anxiety and can improve a player's performance.

The Organization of Religious Beliefs and Practices

Anthropologist Anthony Wallace (1966) distinguished four principal varieties of religious *cults*— that is, forms of organization of religious doctrines and activities—that have broad evolutionary implications. The passage of time has not brought forth a better classification. Wallace's four principal forms are (1) individualistic cults, (2) shamanistic cults, (3) communal cults, and (4) ecclesiastical cults (see Table 16.1).

Table 16.1

Principal Types of Cults

Cult Type	Role Specialization	Political Complexity	Examples
Individualistic	No role specialization. Most basic form of religious life. Each person enters into relationship with animistic being when in need of control or protection.	Egalitarian band and village societies	Inuit hunters, Crow warrior vision quest
Shamanistic	Part-time specialization. Shamans work in direct communication with supernatural as diviners, curers, spirit mediums, and magicians. They serve people in need in exchange for gifts, fees, prestige, or power.	Egalitarian band and village societies	!Kung, J'varo, and Tapirapé
Communal	Groups of nonspecialists perform rites for community, deemed vital to well-being of individuals and society.	Lineage-based societies	Rites of solidarity; rites of passage among Ndembu
Ecclesiastical	Full-time professional clergy who work as intermediaries between society and supernatural in hierarchical organization under control of centralized church.	State societies	Aztec, Incas (also Egyptians, Christianity, Judaism, Buddhism, and Islam)

Source: Based on Wallace 1966.

Individualistic Cults

Individualistic cults do not make distinctions between specialists and laypeople. One might call this "do-it-yourself" religion.

 In **individualistic cults,** all people are their own specialists.

As is common among native North and South Americans, individuals acquire a personal guardian spirit or supernatural protector—typically by means of a visionary experience induced by fasting, self-inflicted torture, or hallucinogenic drugs.

The Inuit. The individualism of much of Inuit belief and ritual parallels the individualism of the Inuit mode of production. Hunters alone or in small groups constantly match their wits against the cunning and strength of animal prey and confront the dangers of travel over the ice and the threats of storms and month-long nights. The Inuit hunter is equipped with an ingenious array of technological devices that make life possible in the Arctic, but the outcome of the daily struggle remains in doubt. From the Inuit's point of view, it is imperative to be well equipped to handle both the danger of the harsh physical elements and the danger of offending or not properly warding off unseen spirits and forces.

Vigilant individual effort is needed to deal with wandering human and animal souls, place spirits, Sedna (the Keeper of the Sea Animals), the Sun, the Moon, and the Spirit of the Air. Part of each hunter's equipment is his hunting song, a combination of chant, prayer, and magic formula that he inherits from his father or father's brothers or purchases from some famous hunter or shaman. In return for protection and hunting success given by his spirit helpers, the hunter has to observe certain taboos, refrain from hunting or eating certain species, or avoid trespassing in a particular locale. Moreover, a hunter should never sleep out on the ice edge. Note that some of these superstitions may alleviate psychological stress or have a practical value for hunting or some other aspect of Inuit life. Not sleeping out on the ice, for example, is a safety precaution.

The Crow. For many native North Americans, a hallucinatory vision is the central experience of life. Young men need this hallucinatory experience to be successful in love, warfare, horsestealing, trading, and all other important endeavors. In keeping with their code of personal bravery and endurance, they seek these visions primarily through self-inflicted torture.

Among the Crow, a youth who craves the visionary experience of his elders goes alone into the mountains, strips off his clothes, and abstains from food and drink. If this is not sufficient, he chops off part of the fourth finger of his left hand. Coached from childhood to expect that a vision would come, most Crow vision-seekers are successful. A buffalo, snake, chicken hawk, thunderbird, dwarf, or mysterious stranger appears; miraculous events unfold; and then these strange beings "adopt" the vision-seeker and disappear.

Scratches-Face, who was one of Robert Lowie's informants, prayed to the morning star: "Old woman's grandson, I give you this (finger joint). Give me something good in exchange. . . . A good horse . . . a good-natured woman . . . a tent of my own to live in" (Lowie 1948 [1924]:6). Lowie reported that after cutting off his finger, Scratches-Face saw six men riding horses. One of them said, "You have been poor, so I'll give you what you want." Suddenly the trees around them turned into enemy warriors, who began to shoot at the six horsemen. The horsemen rode away but returned unscathed. The spokesman then said to Scratches-Face, "If you want to fight all the people on the earth, do as I do, and you will be able to fight for three days or four days and yet not be shot." The enemy attacked again, but Scratches-Face's benefactor knocked them down with a spear. According to Lowie (1948 [1924]:6), "In consequence of his blessing Scratches-Face struck and killed an enemy without ever getting wounded. He also obtained horses and married a good-tempered and industrious woman."

Although each Crow's vision had some unique elements, they were usually similar in the following regards:

- Some revelation of future success in warfare, horse-raiding, or other acts of bravery was involved.
- The visions usually occurred at the end of the fourth day—four being a sacred number.
- Practically every vision was accompanied by the acquisition of a sacred song.
- The friendly spirits in the vision adopted the youth.
- Trees or rocks often turned into enemies who vainly shot at the invulnerable spirit being.

Lowie concluded:

He sees and hears not merely what any faster, say in British Columbia or South Africa would see and hear under like conditions of physiological exhaustion and under the urge of generally human desires, but what the social tradition of the Crow tribe imperatively suggests. (1948 [1924]:14)

Shamanistic Cults

To become a **shaman**, an individual must undergo a difficult apprenticeship to acquire the ability of entering into trance states. In trance, the shaman's powers increase. He or she can then heal the sick.

 Shamans are women and men who are socially recognized as having special abilities for entering into contact with spirit beings and for controlling supernatural forces.

There are broad similarities in the techniques used by shamans to cure their patients. The shaman goes into a trance by smoking tobacco, taking drugs, beating on a drum, dancing monotonously, or simply by closing his or her eyes and concentrating. The trance begins with rigidity of the body, sweating, and heavy breathing. While in the trance, the shaman may act as a medium, transmitting messages from the ancestors. With the help of friendly spirits, shamans predict future events, locate lost objects, identify the

Female Shaman
Piegan "medicine woman." Female shamans are as common as male shamans.

cause of illness, battle with spirits on behalf of the patient, prescribe cures, and give advice on how clients can protect themselves against the evil intentions of enemies.

There is a close relationship between shamanistic cults and individualistic vision quests. Shamans are usually personalities who are psychologically predisposed toward hallucinatory experiences. In cultures that use hallucinogenic substances freely in order to penetrate the mysteries of the other world, many people may claim shamanistic status. Among the J'varo, one out of every four men is a shaman because the use of hallucinogenic vines makes it possible for almost everyone to achieve the trance states essential for the practice of shamanism (Harner 1972:154). Elsewhere, becoming a shaman may be restricted to people who are prone to having auditory and visual hallucinations.

An important part of shamanistic performance in many regions of the world consists of simple tricks of ventriloquism, sleight of hand, and illusion. Siberian shamans, for example, signaled the arrival of the possessing spirit by secretly shaking the walls of a darkened tent. Throughout South America, the standard shamanistic curing ceremony involves the sleight-of-hand removal of slivers of bone, pebbles, bugs, and other foreign objects from the patient's body.

The practice of these tricks should not be regarded as evidence that the shaman has a cynical or disbelieving attitude toward the rest of the performance. Michael Harner (1980), a modern proponent of shamanic rituals, insists there is nothing fraudulent about the sucking cure. It is not the object itself that is in the patient's body and causing the trouble; rather, it is the object's spiritual counterpart.

Shamans put the material object in their mouth during the sucking cure because this helps withdraw its spiritual counterpart.

Although trance is part of the shamanistic repertory in hundreds of cultures, it is not universal. Many cultures have part-time specialists who do not make use of trance but who diagnose and cure disease, find lost objects, foretell the future, and confer immunity in war and success in love. Such persons may be referred to variously as magicians, seers, sorcerers, witch doctors, medicine men or medicine women, and curers. The full shamanistic complex embodies all these roles (Atkinson 1992; but see Winkelman 1990).

The !Kung. The !Kung use a method of healing based on the principle of **n/um**, which is the heal-

!Kung San Curing
!Kung healers enter a trance called a kia, *which brings them to "near death."*

ing energy that originates from the gods. N/um is accessed during an all-night dance. As dancing intensifies, the n/um of the healers is activated in the healers through the *kia* (trance)—an enhanced state of consciousness that is both painful and feared. Healing is a routine cultural event among the !Kung, open to everyone. But to become a healer, a person must undergo intense training. By the time they reach adulthood, about half the men and 10 percent of the women have become healers.

The kia, or activated n/um, is said to boil fiercely within the healer (Katz 1982). Those who learn to heal are called the "masters" or "owners" of n/um. Healers are able to access the realm where the gods and spirits of dead ancestors live. These are the spirits that try to carry off the sick into their own realm by bringing misfortune and death. In the kia, healers express the wishes of the living by entering into a struggle with the spirits to rescue the souls of the sick.

Healers who are in kia lay their hands on a person to pull out the sickness. They shriek and howl, expressing the pain and difficulty of healing work.

Then they shake their hands toward the outside of the dance circle to cast away the sickness they have taken from the person being treated. Such healing may go on for several hours. Healers plead and argue with the gods to save the people from illness, demanding that the spirits of their dead ancestors spare the sick person. They plead and yell at the spirits to leave the sick person alone, saying that he or she is not ready to go and wants to remain with loved ones. If the healer's *n/um* is strong, the spirits will retreat and the sick person will live.

The Tapirapé.   Among the Tapirapé, a village people of central Brazil (Wagley 1977), shamans derive their powers from dreams in which they encounter spirits who become their helpers. Dreams are caused by the soul leaving the body and going on a journey. Frequent dreaming is a sign of shamanistic talent. Mature shamans, with the help of the spirit familiars, can turn into birds or launch themselves through the air in gourd "canoes," visit with ghosts and demons, or travel to distant villages forward and backward through time.

Tapirapé Shaman
The shaman has fallen into a tobacco-induced trance and cannot walk unaided.

Tapirapé shamans are frequently called on to cure illness. This they do with sleight of hand and the help of their spirit familiars while in a semitrance condition induced by gulping huge quantities of tobacco, which makes them vomit. It is interesting to note in conjunction with the discussion of the widespread use of tobacco in Native American rituals that tobacco contains hallucinogenic alkaloids and may induce visions when consumed in large quantities.

Charles Wagley (1943:73–74) provided the following description of a Tapirapé shaman:

A shaman comes to his patient, and squats near the patient's hammock; his first act is always to light his pipe. When the patient has a fever or has fallen unconscious from the sight of a ghost, the principal method of treatment is by massage. The shaman blows smoke over the entire body of the patient; then he blows smoke over his own hands, spits into them, and massages the patient slowly and firmly, always toward the extremities of the body. He shows that he is removing a foreign substance by quick movement of his hands as he reaches the end of an arm or leg.

The more frequent method of curing, however, is by the extraction of a malignant object by sucking. The shaman squats alongside the hammock of his patient and begins to "eat smoke"—swallow large gulps of tobacco smoke from his pipe. He forces the smoke with great intakes of breath deep down into his stomach. Soon he becomes intoxicated and nauseated; he vomits violently and smoke spews from his stomach. He groans and clears his throat in the manner of a person gagging with nausea but unable to vomit. By sucking back what he vomits, he accumulates saliva in his mouth.

In the midst of this process he stops several times to suck on the body of his patient and finally, with one awful heave, he spews all the accumulated material on the ground. He then searches in this mess for the intrusive object that has been causing the illness.

Wagley reports that

Never once did I see a shaman show the intrusive object to observers. At one treatment a Tapirapé [shaman] usually repeats this process of "eating smoke," sucking, and vomiting several times. Sometimes, when a man of prestige is ill, two or even three shamans will cure side by side in this manner and the noise of violent vomiting resounds throughout the village. (1943:73–74)

Communal Cults

No society is completely without communally organized religious beliefs and practices. Even the Inuit have group rites. Under the cross-examinations of shamans, frightened and sick individuals publicly confess violations of taboos that have made them ill and that have endangered the rest of the community.

> **Communal cults** use rituals to strengthen group continuity by communicating socially constructed meaning signifying the continuity of the group.

Communal rites fall into two major categories: (1) rites of solidarity and (2) rites of passage. In **rites of solidarity**, participation in dramatic public rituals enhances the sense of group identity, coordinates the actions of the individual members of the group, and prepares the group for immediate or future cooperative action. **Rites of passage** celebrate the social movement of individuals into and out of groups or into or out of statuses of critical importance to the individual and to the community. Reproduction, the achievement of manhood and womanhood, marriage, and death are the principal worldwide occasions for rites of passage.

The performance of **rituals** is an integral part of religion.

> **Rituals** are formal, stylized, and repetitive acts that are performed in special, sacred places at set times.

Most rituals are performed in special places under specific conditions removed from the ordinary world. Rituals convey information that is repeated time after time and convey messages and sentiments and translate them into action. As such, rituals are social acts. They are powerful forces that bring participants to accept a common social and moral order that transcends their status as individuals. By reinforcing group norms, they bring about homogeneity. A uniformity of beliefs helps bind people together and reinforces group identity.

Communal Rites of Solidarity.

Rites of solidarity are common among clans and other descent groups.

> **Rites of solidarity** are directed toward the welfare of the community, rather than the individual. They reaffirm the power of the group, which transcends individuals.

Such groups usually have names and emblems that identify group members and set one group off from

another. Animal names and emblems predominate, but insects, plants, and natural phenomena such as rain and clouds also occur. These group-identifying objects are known as **totems**.

> **Totems** are objects, such as animals and plants, that serve as the emblems or symbols of a kinship group or a person.

Members of each totemic group believe they were descendents of their totem. They view their totem with awe and refrain from harming or eating their totem. Each group sees their totem as their companion and protector. Though it is generally agreed that totemism is not a religion, totemism contains religous elements—the cult of ancestors, ideas of the soul, beliefs in spirits—in varying degrees. The specific forms of totemic belief, however, vary greatly, and no single totemic complex can be said to exist.

The Arunta of Australia provide one of the classic cases of totemic ritual. Here, an individual identifies with the totem of the sacred place near which one's mother passed shortly before becoming pregnant. These places contain the stone objects known as **churinga**, which are the visible manifestations of each person's spirit. The churinga are believed to have been left behind by the totemic ancestors as they traveled about the countryside at the beginning of the world. The ancestors later turned into animals, objects, and other entities. The sacred places of each totem are visited annually.

These totemic rituals have many meanings and functions. The participants are earnestly concerned with protecting their totems and ensuring their reproduction. But the exclusive membership of the ritual group also indicates that they are acting out the mythological dogma of their common ancestry.

> The totem ceremonies reaffirm and intensify the sense of common identity of the members of a regional community.

The handling of the churinga confirms the fact that the totemic group has "stones" or, in a more familiar metaphor, "roots" in a particular land.

In contemporary U.S. society, rites of solidarity are mostly secular events, such as the Fourth of July parades and football games. Groups meet for traditional barbecues or watch college and professional games. These events become unifying cultural traditions that symbolize key features of American life. On Super Bowl Sunday, for example, millions of Americans from diverse cultural backgrounds come together to watch televised football. Although the symbolism of football—teamwork and reward for consistency—are important, it is the common experience of participating in a national event that reinforces group solidarity.

Communal Rites of Passage. The most common occasions for rites of passage are birth, puberty, marriage, and death.

 Rites of passage are ceremonies that mark changes in a person's social position that are of general public concern.

The individual who is born, who reaches adulthood, who takes a spouse, or who dies is not the only one implicated in these events. Many other people must adjust to these momentous changes. Being born not only defines a new life but also brings into existence or modifies the position of parent, grandparent, sibling, heir, age-mate, and many other domestic and political relationships. Rites of passage are important public rituals that recognize a wider set of altered social relationships. Contemporary passage rites include confirmations, baptisms, bar and bat mitzvahs, and fraternity hazings (see Box 16.1).

Rites of passage conform to a remarkably similar pattern among widely dispersed cultures (Eliade 1958; Schlegel and Barry 1979).

The three phases of rites of passage are separation, transition, and incorporation.

Passing a Driver's Test
Getting a driver's license marks a much anticipated change in status for a U.S. teen.

BOX 16.1 | No Rites Hurt, Too

Westerners are likely to be shocked and dismayed by examples of painful puberty rituals, but the system that has been substituted for such rituals may not have any clear advantage as far as eliminating pain and suffering. The passage from child to adult in advanced industrial societies is not marked by any rituals at all. No one is quite sure when adulthood begins. As a result, the young girl or boy must pass through a prolonged period of stress, known as *adolescence*, which is marked by high rates of accidents, suicides, and antisocial behavior. Which system is more cruel?

The Jewish bar mitzvah and bat mitzvah, held at age 13 for boys and girls, respectively, creates boy–men and girl–women for whom adult status lies many years ahead. Similarly, the Christian rite of confirmation, also performed in the teen years, is only vaguely associated with the passage to adulthood.

First, the principal performers are separated from the routines associated with their earlier life and prepare to move from one place or status to another. Second, decisive physical and symbolic steps are taken to extinguish the old status. Often, depersonalization accompanies separation; a person may leave his or her group and experience a symbolic death. Army boot camp is a good example of this process. Inductees are stripped of their former identity; they are issued numbers, dressed in identical uniforms, and given short hair cuts. All ties are severed during their confinement. Often, these steps include the notion of killing the old personality. To promote "death and transfiguration," old clothing and ornaments are exchanged for new, and the body is painted or mutilated.

The second phase, known as the **liminal phase**, is a period of ambiguity during a person's transition between one status and another.

 The **liminal phase** is a temporary ritual state, during which the individual is cut off from normal social contacts to demarcate a contrast from regular social life.

According to Victor Turner (1967), liminality involves the suspension of social norms; a person's past and future positions in society are ignored and he or she is subjected to experiences that are different or even reversed from what they are in the ordinary world.

Sometimes passage rites are collective. Collective liminality, called **communitas**, creates a community spirit and feeling of togetherness.

> **Communitas** is an intense community spirit, a feeling of social solidarity, equality, and togetherness that is achieved through liminality.

People who experience communitas form a community of equals that is symbolically marked by reversals of ordinary behavior, such as fasting and seclusion. Permanent liminal groups, such as cults and sects, are found in complex societies. They are set apart from other religious groups and from society as a whole. Members become submerged in the collective group and abide by such liminal features as sexual abstinence, poverty, and silence.

Ecclesiastical Cults

Ecclesiastical cults or groups have a professional clergy or priesthood organized into a bureaucracy. This bureaucracy is usually associated with and under the control of a central temple. At secondary or provincial temple centers, the clergy may exercise a considerable amount of independence.

> **Ecclesiastical** religion is found in highly centralized political systems.

The ecclesiastic specialists differ from both the Tapirapé shamans and the Ndembu circumcisers and guardians (see Profile 16.1). They are formally designated persons who are elected or appointed to devote themselves to conducting rituals at regular intervals. These rituals usually include a wide variety of techniques for reinforcing support for the supremacy of the ruling class.

> Throughout history, the ecclesiastical specialists have generally lived much better than the population at large.

In many cases, it has been common for them to be part of the ruling class; material support for these full-time specialists is usually closely related to the power of taxation. It is therefore no surprise that in class societies, religion reflects the ideology of the dominant class. Among the Inca (see Profile 11.4, p. 188), the state and the priesthood were both supported by the rent and tribute extracted from the peasants (see Profile 16.2). Under feudalism, feudal lords received rights to land from the king, who was granted the right to rule by God. The priests of that time supported feudalism by endorsing the God-given rights of the nobility. The peasants had to work the land in exchange for the right to cultivate for themselves, while the priesthood preached humility and acceptance of one's station in life. In modern ecclesiastical religions such as Christianity, Judaism, and Buddhism, a

A.

B.

Ecclesiastical Cult

A. Celebration of high mass is a Roman Catholic ritual.   B. The local congregation celebrates Good Friday in Chichicastenango, Mexico.

PROFILE 16.1 Ndembu Communal Rites of Circumcision

Communitas can be seen in the male initiation ceremonies of the Ndembu of northern Zambia. Here, as in many African and Middle Eastern cultures, the transition from boyhood to manhood involves the rite of circumcision. Young boys are taken from their separate villages and placed in a special bush "school." They are circumcised by their own kinsmen or neighbors, and after their wounds heal, they are returned to normal life. Among the Ndembu, the process of publicly transforming boys to men takes four months and is known as *mukanda*.

Victor Turner (1967) gave a detailed account of a mukanda that he was permitted to witness in 1953. It began with the storage of food and beer. Then a clearing was made in the bush and a camp established. This camp included a hearth, at which the mothers of the boys undergoing circumcision cooked for them. On the day preceding the circumcision, the circumcisers danced and sang songs in which they expressed antagonism to the boys' mothers and made reference to the "killing" that was about to take place. The boys and their families assembled at the campsite, fires were lit, and a night of dancing and sexual license was begun.

According to Turner, "Suddenly the circumcisers entered in procession, carrying their apparatus. . . . All the rest of the gathering followed them as they danced crouching, holding up different items of apparatus, and chanting hoarsely. In the firelight and moonlight the dance got wilder and wilder" (1967:205). Meanwhile, "those who were about to die" sat in a line attended by their mothers and fathers. During the night, they were repeatedly awakened and carried about by their male relatives. The next morning, they were given a "Last Supper" (a last breakfast) by their mothers, "each mother feeding her son by hand as though he were an infant." The boys tried not to look terrified, as after breakfast, the circumcisers, their brows and foreheads daubed with red clay, danced about brandishing their knives.

The actual circumcision took place in another clearing some distance away from the cooking camp. The boys remained in seclusion at this site, which was known as the "place of dying." They slept in a brush lodge, watched over and ordered about by a group of male "guardians." After their "last breakfast," the boys were marched down the trail toward the "place of dying." The guardians came rushing out, seized them, and tore off their clothes. The mothers were chased back to the cooking camp, where they began to wail as at the announcement of a death. The boys were held by the guardians while circumcisers "stretch out the prepuce, make a slight nick on top and another underneath as guides, then cut through the dorsal section with a single movement and follow this by slitting the ventral section, then removing sufficient amount of the prepuce to leave the glans well exposed" (Turner 1967:216).

A.

B.

Ndembu Rites
A. Although the women are supposed to be terrified of the "monster," they are actually amused and skeptical.   B. The circumcision camp is known as the "place of dying."

PROFILE 16.2 | The Religion of the Aztecs

The Aztecs of Mexico had an ecclesiastical religion whose priests were held responsible for the maintenance and renewal of the entire universe. By performing annual rituals, priests could obtain the blessing of the Aztec gods, ensure the well-being of the Aztec people, and guard the world against collapse into chaos and darkness. According to Aztec theology, the world had already passed through four ages, each of which ended in cataclysmic destruction. The fifth age was in progress, ruled over by the sun god and doomed to destruction sooner or later by earthquakes.

The principal function of the 5,000 priests living in the Aztec capital was to ensure that the gods governing the world were sufficiently pleased so that the end of the world would come later, rather than sooner. The best way to please the gods was to give them gifts, the most precious being fresh human hearts—especially the hearts of war captives, because they were won only at great expense and risk.

Aztec ceremonial centers were dominated by large pyramidal platforms topped by temples. These structures were vast stages on which the drama of human sacrifice was enacted at least once a day throughout the year. First the victim would ascend to the top of the pyramid, where four priests would seize the victim and place him or her over the sacrificial stone. A fifth priest cut the victim's chest open with an obsidian knife and wrenched out the beating heart. The heart was smeared over the statue of the god and later burned. During a four-day dedication ceremony of the main Aztec temple in Tenochtitlán, some 20,000 prisoners of war were sacrificed in this manner.

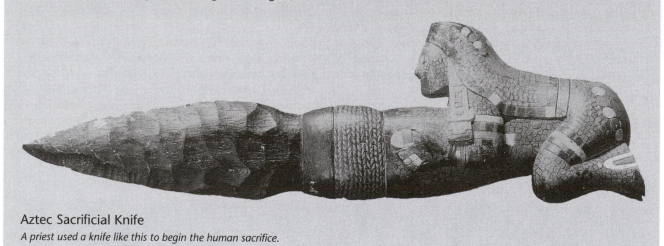

Aztec Sacrificial Knife

A priest used a knife like this to begin the human sacrifice.

full-time professional clergy is supported through dues, donations, and gifts.

It must be stressed, however, that the congregation does not altogether abandon individualistic shamanistic and communal beliefs and rituals. These practices are all continued, sometimes secretly, in neighborhoods, villages, and households, side by side with the higher rituals, despite efforts by state-sanctioned religions to stamp out what it often calls superstitious, pagan, or heathen beliefs and performances.

Although it is considered controversial, Michael Harner's (1977) explanation of the Aztec state's unique ecclesiastical cannibalism is a viable theory. Harner starts from the fact that as a result of millennia of intensification and population growth, the Central Mexican highlands had lost their best domes-

ticable animal species. Unlike the Inca, who obtained animal foods from llama, alpaca, and guinea pigs—or the Old World states that had sheep, goats, pigs, and cattle—the Aztec had only semidomesticated ducks and turkeys and hairless dogs. Wild fauna, such as deer and migrating waterfowl, were not abundant enough to provide the Aztecs with more than 1 or 2 grams of animal protein per capita per day (compared with over 60 grams in the United States). The depleted condition of the natural fauna is shown by the prominence in the Aztec diet of bugs, worms, and "scum cakes," which were made out of algae skimmed off the surface of Lake Texcoco (see M. Harris 1979b; Sahlins 1978).

According to Harner, the severe depletion of animal resources made it uniquely difficult for the

PROFILE 16.2 | The Religion of the Aztecs (continued)

It is estimated that nearly 15,000 people were sent to death annually to placate the blood-thirsty gods. Most of these victims were prisoners of war, although local youths, maidens, and children were also sacrificed from time to time (Coe 1977; Berdan 1982; Vaillant 1966 [1941]). After being killed, the bodies of most of those who were sacrificed were dismembered and probably cooked and eaten (Harner 1977; see also Box 16.2 for evidence of Aztec cannibalism).

Prior to the emergence of states, many societies, especially chiefdoms, practiced human sacrifice and ritually consumed all or parts of the bodies of prisoners of war (M. Harris 1985, 1989). Lacking the political–military means to tax and conscript large populations, chiefdoms had little interest in preserving the lives of their defeated enemies. With the advent of the state, however, cannibalism and human sacrifice tended to disappear. As we have seen in Chapter 11, conquered territories were incorporated into the state, and the labor power of defeated populations was tapped through taxation, conscription, and tribute. Thus, preserving the lives of defeated peoples became an essential part of the process of state expansion.

The Aztecs, however, were an exception to this general trend. Instead of making human sacrifice and cannibalism taboo, the Aztec state made them the main focus of ecclesiastical beliefs and rituals. As the Aztecs became more powerful, they sacrificed increasing numbers of prisoners of war and became more rather than less cannibalistic (see also E. Wolf 1998).

The Aztec Practice of Human Sacrifice Is Well Documented
Anthropologists still debate the reasons for such ritual sacrifice.

Aztec state to prohibit the consumption of human flesh. Human flesh, rather than animal flesh, was redistributed as a means of rewarding loyalty to the throne and bravery in combat.

According to Tim White (1997), there is no doubt that cannibalism was a common practice. At archeological digs all over the globe, researchers have found evidence of cannibalism. Human bones were broken open for their marrow and smaller fragments were boiled to extract fatty residues. White concludes that it used to be thought that the Spanish made up (as propaganda, to justify their own cruelty) the stories of the Aztecs eating their prisoners. But now excavations in Mexico City are finding evidence, such as carefully splintered bones, that the Aztecs really were cannibals (see Box 16.2).

BOX 16.2 | The Evidence for Aztec Cannibalism

Bernadino de Sahagun, who started collecting data on the Aztecs in the 1540s, is generally considered to be the most honest and reliable historian and ethnographer of Aztec culture. In his *General History of the Things of New Spain*, he repeatedly describes the fate of the Aztec's sacrificial victims as follows:

"After they had slain them and torn out their hearts, they took them away gently, rolling them down the steps. . . . They carried the bodies to the houses . . . where they divided them up in order to eat them" (Sahagun 1951:24).

Skull Rack

This photo shows one of the smaller racks in the Aztec capital. The skulls are sculpted in stone; during Aztec times, real skulls were exhibited on wooden structures, as found in the ongoing excavations in Mexico City.

Religion and Political Economy: High Gods

Full-time specialists, monumental temples, dramatic processions, and elaborate rites performed for spectator congregations are incompatible with the infrastructure and political economy of hunters and gatherers. Similarly, the complex astronomical and mathematical basis of ecclesiastical beliefs and rituals is never found among band and village peoples.

The level of political economy also influences the way in which gods are thought to relate to each other and to human beings. For example, the idea of a single high god who created the universe is found among cultures at all levels of economic and political development. These high gods, however, play different kinds of roles in running the universe after they have brought it into existence. Among hunter-gatherers and other nonstate peoples, the high gods tend to become inactive after their creation task is done (Sullivan 1987). To obtain assistance, one must turn to a host of lesser gods, demons, and ancestor souls (see Hayden 1987). In stratified societies, the high god bosses the lesser gods and tends to be a more active figure, to whom priests and commoners address their prayers (Swanson 1960), although ordinary people may still revere the lesser gods more actively.

Societies whose rulers rely on religious indoctrination to secure and legitimize their position of power have a different reward system than secular societies. In such societies, conformity is reinforced through the promise of spiritual rewards, especially promises of rewards in the afterlife or martyrdom in exchange for deprivation in this world or sacrifice in battle.

A plausible explanation for this difference is that nonstate cultures have no need for the idea of a central or supreme authority. Just as centralized control over people and strategic resources is absent in life, so in religious belief the inhabitants of the spirit world lack decisive control over each other. They form a more or less egalitarian group.

> The belief that superordination and subordination characterize relationships among the gods helps obtain the cooperation and submission of the commoner classes in stratified societies.

One way to achieve conformity in complex stratified societies is to convince commoners that the gods demand obedience to the state. Myths and rituals express the commoners' dependence on the rulers' well-being. To challenge the ruler would be like challenging the very order of the universe. The priesthood dazzles, mystifies, and intimidates the commoners through the performance of highly intricate rituals and the construction of grandiose temples in order to discourage the commoners from opposing their rulers. Disobedience and nonconformity result not only in retribution administered through the state's police military apparatus but also in punishments in the present or future life, administered by the high gods themselves. In nonstate societies (for reasons discussed in Chapter 18), law and order are rooted in common interest. Consequently, there is little need for high gods to administer punishments to those who have been "bad" and rewards to those who have been "good."

Revitalization Movements

The relationship of religion to structure and infrastructure can also be seen in the process known as *revitalization*.

> **Revitalization movements** occur during times of change, in which religious leaders emerge to bring forth positive change.

Anthony Wallace (1970) defines **revitalization movements** as "deliberate and organized attempts by some members of a society to construct a more satisfying culture through rapid acceptance of a pattern of multiple innovations." Most revitalization movements follow a fairly uniform process:

- A society is in the state of equilibrium.
- A society is pushed out of equilibrium by various forces, such as climatic or biotic change, epidemic disease, war and conquest, and so forth.
- The society becomes disillusioned and disorganized.
- Social deterioration sets the stage for a revitalization movement to appear in an effort to bring about a more satisfying society.
- An individual or group constructs a new, idealistic image of culture that forms the basis for social action.

Under the severe stresses associated with colonial conquest and intense class or minority exploitation, religions tend to become movements concerned with achieving drastic improvements in the immediate conditions of life or in the prospects for an afterlife. These movements are sometimes referred to as *nativistic, revivalistic, millennarian,* and *messianic.* The concept of revitalization is intended to embrace all the specific cognitive and ritual variants implied by these terms (Wallace 1966).

> Revitalization occurs during times of cultural stress brought about by rapid change, foreign domination, and perceived deprivation.

Revitalization is a process of political and religious interaction among a depressed caste, class, ethnicity, or other subordinate social group and a superordinate group. Some revitalization movements emphasize passive attitudes, the adoption of old rather than new cultural practices, or salvation through rewards after death; others advocate more or less open resistance or aggressive political or military action (see Profile 16.3). These differences largely reflect the extent to which the subordinate groups are prepared to cope with the challenge to their power and authority. Revitalizations that take place under conditions of massive suffering and exploitation sooner or later result in political and even military confrontations, even though both sides may overtly desire to avoid conflict (Worsley 1968).

Native American Revitalizations

Widespread revitalizations were provoked by the European invasion of the New World, the conquest and expulsion of the Native American peoples, and the destruction of their natural resources. The native peoples of the American West had been mostly confined to reservations by the 1870s; their economic base was ruined with the destruction of buffalo herds and occupation of their lands. The coercive authority imposed on them brought an atmosphere of total defeat and discouragement, which provided the conditions for numerous revitalization movements.

The most famous of the nineteenth-century revitalization movements was the **Ghost Dance** that began among the Piute Indians and then spread across the Plains. The main phase of the Ghost Dance began in 1889 under the inspiration of a prophet named Wovoka. Wovoka and his followers envisioned a day when all their ancestors would return to life. Songs and dances revealed to Wovoka would make this happen. The Ghost Dance prophecy was in the tradition of myths about the dead returning to life and the beginning of a life of plenty.

> The **Ghost Dance,** Native Americans believed, would place dancers in contact with the spirit world and hasten the time when people would be reunited with their dead ancestors. This meant that they would outnumber the Whites and hence be more powerful.

Wovoka
This Piute prophet was leader of the Ghost Dance.

PROFILE 16.3 | Melanesian Cargo Cults

In New Guinea and Melanesia, revitalization is associated with the concept of cargo. The typical vision of the leaders of Melanesian revitalization movements is that of a ship bringing back the ancestors and a cargo of European goods. Over the years, airplanes and spaceships have become the favorite means of delivering the cargo.

Inspired by the abundance of goods U.S. military forces displayed during the Pacific Island campaigns of World War II, Melanesians developed the belief that they too would become wealthy. Some revitalizations stressed the return of the Americans. In 1944, a local leader named Tsek urged his people to destroy all trade goods and throw away their clothes in preparation for the return of the mysteriously departed Americans. Some of the U.S.-oriented revitalizations had placed specific U.S. soldiers in the role of cargo deliverers. On the island of Tana in the New Hebrides, the John Frumm cult cherished an old GI jacket as the relic of one John Frumm, whose identity is not otherwise known. The followers of John Frumm built landing strips, bamboo control towers, and grass-thatched cargo sheds. In some cases, beacons were kept ablaze at night and radio operators stood ready with tin-can microphones and earphones to guide the cargo planes to a safe landing. The natives were waiting for a total upgrading of their lives. They believed the phantom ships and planes would mark the beginning of a whole new era.

The Melanesians had several revitalization scenarios. Some believed that the cargo planes and ships had been successfully loaded by their ancestors at U.S. ports and were on their way but that the local authorities had refused to permit the cargo to be landed. In another version, the cargo planes had been tricked into landing at the wrong airport. In a metaphorical sense, these sentiments applied to the actual conditions under colonialism. The peoples of the South Seas were indeed often tricked out of their lands and resources.

The confusion of the Melanesian revitalization prophets stemmed from naiveté about the workings of cultural systems. The prophets did not understand how modern industrial wage labor societies were organized, nor could they comprehend how law and order were maintained among state-level peoples. Their leaders dismissed the standard European explanation of hard work equaling wealth as a calculated deception. Anyone could see that the European "big men," unlike their native prototypes, scarcely worked at all. The natives insisted that the material wealth of the industrial age was really created in some distant place, not by humans but by supernatural means. To the Melanesians, the material abundance of the industrial nations and the

A.

B.

Followers of John Frumm

A. Some members of the John Frumm cargo cult perform a ritual march. They await the day that John Frumm, their messiah, will return, bringing freedom and wealth. This movement has been in existence for more than 60 years.   B. This cult is active on the South Seas Island of Tana in the New Hebrides.

PROFILE 16.3 | Melanesian Cargo Cults *(continued)*

poverty of others constituted an irrational flaw, a massive contradiction in the structure of the world.

The belief system of the cargo cults vividly demonstrates why we can't assume that all people distinguish between natural and supernatural categories. Cargo leaders who had been taken to see modern Australian stores and factories, in the hope that they would give up their beliefs, returned home more convinced than ever that they were following the best prescription for obtaining cargo. With their own eyes, they had observed the fantastic abundance the authorities refused to let them have (Lawrence 1964).

Westerners were impressed by the natives' inability to understand European economic lifestyles. The impli-

cation was that the natives were too backward or superstitious to grasp the principles of civilization. However, it was not that these natives could not grasp the principles in question; rather, it was that they found them unacceptable. When their leaders learned more about how Europeans produced wealth, they were less prepared to accept their explanation of why their people were unable to share in it. Without the cheapness of native labor and the expropriation of native lands, the colonial powers would never have gotten so rich. In one sense, the natives were entitled to the products of the industrialized nations, even though they couldn't pay for them. The cargo cult was their way of saying this.

Ostensibly, Wovoka's teachings lacked political content, and as the Ghost Dance spread eastward across the Rockies, its political implications remained ambiguous.

The Sioux interpreted the vision differently and initiated a version of the Ghost Dance that included the return of all the bison and the extermination of the Whites under a huge landslide. The Sioux led pure lives and believed that violence was no longer necessary because the world would change by itself. They put on Ghost Dance shirts, believing they would make them invulnerable to bullets. Nevertheless, the Ghost Dance frightened settlers, who feared

that the movement would spark a political uprising. After the Sioux leader Sitting Bull was arrested and killed, the U.S. Army ended the Ghost Dance movement by massacring 200 members of the Lakota Sioux—mainly women and children—at Wounded Knee, South Dakota, on December 29, 1890 (Mooney 1965).

After all chance of military resistance was crushed, the Native American revitalization movement became more introverted and passive. Visions in which all the Whites were wiped out ceased to be experienced, confirming once again the responsiveness of religion to political reality.

A.

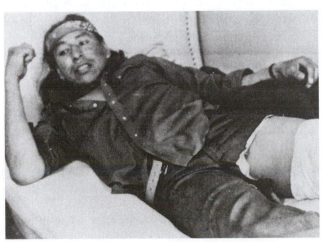

B.

Wounded Knee

*A. In the first battle, in 1890, 200 Lakota Sioux Indians were killed by the U.S. Army.   **B.** In the second battle, in 1973, militant Indians occupied the village of Wounded Knee, South Dakota, and exchanged gunfire with U.S. marshals.*

Peyote Ceremony

Delaware Indians of Oklahoma spend the night in prayer and meditation. At right, they emerge to greet the dawn.

The development and spread of beliefs and rituals centering on peyote, mescal, and other hallucinogenic drugs is characteristic of many current Native American revitalizations. Peyote ritual, as practiced in the Native American Church, involves a night of praying, singing, peyote eating, and ecstatic contemplation followed by a communal breakfast. Peyote, which is a small cactus that grows in northern Texas, produces vivid hallucinations. The peyote eaters are not interested in bringing back the buffalo or making themselves invulnerable to bullets; they seek self-knowledge, personal moral strength, and physical health (Stewart 1987).

Religion and Society

Emile Durkheim believed the essence of religion is a moral system that enables individuals to function as coordinated units. Religion originates in the experience by which people feel a moral force exterior to themselves—a state of consciousness affected by social conditions of which the individual remains unaware. Religion is a unified system of beliefs and practices relative to sacred things that unite those who adhere to them into a moral community (Durkheim 1995 [1912]:76–77).

Durkheim saw the fundamental psychological aspect of religion as the elimination of the self and the denial of individuality for the purpose of the social group, which is greater than the self.

Religion is a symbolic representation of society.

When people come together in social assemblies, a social effervescence is created, out of which religious ideas are confirmed and given greater emotional meaning.

Religion emerges through the distinction between *sacred* and *profane*. Human actions take on special meaning through the realm of the *sacred*—that which pertains to the transcendental and extraordinary. Sacred objects may look like *profane* ones; the distinction between sacred and profane does not reside in the intrinsic properties of the object but in its symbolic representation and meaning.

The **sacred** is the realm of human experience that evokes an attitude of awe and reverence.

The **profane** is the realm of the secular. It is the world of everyday domestic duties that are essentially utilitarian.

For example, sacramental wine symbolizing the blood of Christ may not differ from ordinary table wine, yet it is defined as holy and treated in a reverential manner. Religious beliefs and social behaviors are guided by what a culture deems sacred. Sacred propositions are taken to be unquestionably true because their sacred meanings elicit a sense of certainty in the validity of the propositions that is beyond question. A sanctified message is certified, so there is no need to prove it.

Sanctity is the quality of unquestionable truthfulness credited by the faithful to unverifiable propositions.

Sanctity ensures that participants will fulfill their commitments and greatly increases the likelihood of conformity. Religion reinforces group norms by defining what is proper and improper behavior. If individuals do the proper things in life, they will earn approval of the gods. Otherwise, they will suffer supernatural retribution. Religion has been used to affect action and mobilize people to support certain views or policies. Similarly, religion has been used to persuade people that groups who hold different views are threatening and dangerous. This is why throughout history, political leaders have used religion to instill fear and hatred for political purposes. This is evident in the case of Holy Wars such as the Crusades, aimed at recapturing Jerusalem from Islam, and jihad, a duty imposed on Muslims to spread Islam by waging war.

Witchcraft accusations are another means of instilling social control through fear. As we saw in Chapter 10, antisocial or otherwise deviant behavior can result in an individual being labeled as a witch. Since witches are feared, they are often ostracized or killed. During the sixteenth and seventeenth centuries in Germany, the witch craze was directly aimed at demobilizing protests by the poor and deflecting their demands for redistribution of wealth (Harris 1974:239).

Roy Rappaport (1975, 1979) has shown that sacred propositions also provide a means of expression for ecological adaptation by maintaining the predominance of certain conventions against the challenge of alternatives. The conventions through which societies are regulated are sanctified, but they themselves are not sacred. "To sanctify statements is to certify them" (1973:69). If people are more likely to accept sanctified messages as unquestionable, then their response will be be more predictable. Sancity, as we will see, takes behavior out of the hands of individual decision makers and increases the likelihood of compliance.

Incest Taboo

If religious sanctions evoke a sense of the sacred, it follows that an appeal to the sacred nature of a rule governing interpersonal relations will resolve the uncertainties about what people should do or how they should behave. For example, the prohibition on incest is widely regarded as a sacred obligation. One plausible explanation is that people are strongly tempted to commit incest but that the short-run satisfactions would have long-term negative consequences for them and for the community (see Chapter 8, "Domestic Groups and the Avoidance of Incest" section). By surrounding incest prohibitions with the aura of sacredness, the long-term individual and collective interest comes to prevail, and the ambiguities and doubts that the individual feels about renouncing the prohibited relationship are resolved more decisively than would otherwise be possible. This does not mean that incest does not occur or that all psychological doubts are removed but that such doubts are brought under effective social control.

Taboos against Eating Pork

Anthropologists have debated the issue of whether strongly held religious beliefs are ecologically adaptive. Do various religiously sanctioned taboos on the consumption of certain foods, for example, have negative nutritional consequences? Do such taboos sometimes actually contribute to a more efficient use of a society's infrastructural potential? In answering these questions, both the costs and benefits of not eating a particular food and the availability of more efficient alternatives must be considered.

A tension between short-run and long-run costs and benefits may also explain the origin of certain food taboos that are regarded as sacred obligations. Consider, for example, the ancient Israelite prohibition on the consumption of pork. Pigs require shade and moisture to regulate their body temperature. Moreover, unlike the domesticated ruminants, such as cattle, sheep, and goats, pigs don't give milk. They also can't pull carts or plows, nor can they subsist on grass. With the progressive deforestation and desertification of the Middle East caused by the spread and intensification of agriculture and stock raising and by population growth, habitat zones suitable for pig rearing became scarce. Hence, an animal that was at one time reared and consumed as a relatively inexpensive source of fat and protein could no longer be reared and consumed by large numbers of people without reducing the efficiency of the main system of food production (M. Harris 1985). The temptation to continue the practice of pig raising persisted, however—hence, the invocation of sacred commandments in the ancient Hebrew religion.

Note that the explanation of the ancient origins of this taboo does not account for its perpetuation into the present. Once in existence, the taboo against pork (and other foods) acquired the function of demarcating or bounding Jewish ethnic minorities from other groups and of increasing their sense of identity and solidarity. Outside the Middle East, the taboo no longer served an ecological function, but it continued to be useful on the level of structural relationships.

The Sacred Cow

The case of the sacred cattle of India conforms to the general theory that the flesh of certain animals is made taboo when it becomes very expensive as a result of ecological changes. Like pigs in the Middle East, cattle were sacrificed and eaten quite freely in India during the Neolithic period. With the rise of the state and of dense rural and urban populations, however, cattle could no longer be raised in sufficient numbers to be used both as a source of meat and as the principal source of traction power for pulling plows. But as the taboo on cattle use developed, it took a form quite different from the Israelite taboo on the pig.

Whereas the pig was valued almost exclusively for its flesh, cattle were also valued for their milk and especially for their traction power. When pigs became too costly to be raised for meat, the whole animal became taboo and an abomination. But as cattle in India became too costly to be raised for meat, their value as a source of traction power increased. (The land had to be plowed more intensively as population grew.) Therefore, they had to be protected and so the Hindu religion came to emphasize everyone's sacred duty to refrain from killing cattle or eating beef. The Hindu doctrine of *ahimsa* puts the full power of religion in support of the command not to kill cattle or eat beef, even in times of extreme food scarcity. Interestingly, the Brahmans (see Chapter 12, "Castes in India" section), who at one time were the caste responsible for ritually slaughtering cattle, later became the caste most concerned with their protection and most opposed to the development of a beef-slaughtering industry in India (M. Harris 1977, 1979a, 1985; cf. Simoons 1979).

What about sacred cattle today? Are the religious ban on the slaughter of cows (female cattle) and oxen (castrated male cattle) and the taboo against the consumption of beef functionally useful features of modern Hinduism? Everyone agrees that the human population of India needs more calories and proteins, yet the Hindu religion still bans the slaughter of cattle and taboos the eating of beef. These taboos are often held responsible for allowing large numbers of aged, decrepit, barren, and useless cattle. Such animals are depicted as roaming aimlessly across the Indian countryside, clogging the roads, stopping the trains, stealing food from the marketplace, and blocking city streets. A closer look at some of the details of the ecol-

Sacred Cows
The cows of Calcutta, India, safely roam the streets, and their owners can reclaim them when they are needed.

ogy and economy of the Indian subcontinent, however, suggests that the taboo in question does not decrease the capacity of the present Indian system of food production to support human life.

The basis of traditional Indian agriculture is the ox-drawn plow. Each peasant farmer needs at least two oxen to plow the fields at the proper time of the year. Despite the impression of surplus cattle, there is in fact a shortage of oxen, because one-third of the peasant households own less than the minimum pair. It is true that many cows are too old, decrepit, and sick and the Hindu farmer is depicted as ritually obsessed with preserving the life of each sacred beast, rather than killing dry, barren, and weak cattle, no matter how useless it may become. But from the point of view of the poor farmer, these creatures may be quite useful. The farmer would prefer to have more vigorous cows but is prevented from achieving this goal not by the taboos against slaughter but by the shortage of land and pasture (Chakravarti 1985a, 1985b; George 1990).

Even barren and weak cattle are by no means a total loss. Their dung makes an essential contribution to the energy system as fertilizer and as cooking fuel. Millions of tons of artificial fertilizer, at prices beyond the reach of the small farmer, would be required to make up for the loss of dung if substantial numbers of cattle were sent to slaughter. Because cattle dung is also a major source of cooking fuel, the slaughter of substantial numbers of animals would require the purchase of expensive dung substitutes, such as wood, coal, or kerosene. Cattle dung is relatively cheap because the cattle do not eat foods that can be eaten by people. Instead, they eat the stubble left in the fields and the marginal patches of grass on steep hillsides, roadside ditches, railroad embankments, and other nonarable lands. This constant scavenging gives the impression that cows are roaming around aimlessly, devouring everything in sight. But most cattle have an owner, and in the cities, after poking about in the market refuse and nibbling on neighbors' lawns, each animal returns to its stall at the end of the day.

In a study of the bioenergetic balances involved in the cattle complex of villages in West Bengal, Stuart Odend'hal (1972) found that "basically, the cattle convert items of little direct human value into products of immediate human utility." Their gross energetic efficiency in supplying useful products was several times greater than that characteristic of agroindustrial beef production. He concluded that "judging the productive value of Indian cattle based on Western standards is inappropriate."

Another crucial question is whether the taboo on slaughter accounts for the ratio of cows to oxen. Despite the ban on slaughter, Hindu farmers cull their herds and adjust sex ratios according to regional needs. The cattle are killed by various indirect means of neglect. As discussed in Chapter 2, culling unwanted female calves results in having over 200 oxen for every 100 cows in the Gangetic plain in northern India, where oxen are needed for traction, despite the fact that the region is one of the most religiously orthodox in India (Vaidyanathan et al. 1982).

There are additional reasons for concluding that the Hindu taboo has a positive effect on the carrying capacity of the ecosystem. Cows seldom go to waste because animals that die a natural death are consumed by the untouchables, who are not obligated by the beef-eating taboos, and their skin is preserved as leather. Moreover, the function of the ban on slaughter is critical during famines. When hunger strikes the Indian countryside, the taboo on slaughter helps the peasants resist the temptation to eat their cattle.

If the temptation to eat their cattle were to win out over their religious scruples, the Indian peasants would be unable to plant new crops when the rains begin again. Thus, the intense resistence among Hindu saints to the slaughter and consumption of beef takes on a new meaning in the context of the Indian infrastructure. In the words of Mohandas Gandhi: "Why the cow was selected for apotheosis is obvious to me. The cow was in India the best companion. She was the giver of plenty. Not only did she give milk but she also made agriculture possible" (1954:3).

SUMMARY
and *Questions to Think About*

1. E. B. Tylor defined religion as animism or the doctrine of souls. According to Tylor, from the idea of the soul arose the idea of all godlike beings, and the idea of the soul itself arose as an attempt to explain phenomena such as trances, dreams, shadows, and reflections.

2. Tylor's definition has been criticized for failing to consider the multifunctional nature of religion and for overlooking the compelling reality of direct hallucinatory contact with extraordinary beings. And as the J'varo belief in three souls demonstrates, each culture uses the basic concepts of animism in its own distinctive fashion.

3. Marett sought to supplement Tylor's definition of religion with the concepts of animatism and mana. Animatism is the belief in an impersonal

life force in people, animals, and objects. The concentration of this force gives people, animals, and objects mana, or the capacity to be extraordinarily powerful and successful. This concept does not readily separate mana from such forces as electricity or gravity.

4. The Western distinction between natural and supernatural is of limited utility for defining religion. As the case of the Gururumba indicates, in many cultures, there are no supernatural versus natural controls, only controls.

5. Frazer tried to cope with the enormous variety of religious experience by separating religion from magic. Humility, supplication, and doubt characterize religion; routine cause and effect characterize magic. This distinction is difficult to maintain in view of the routine and coercive fashion in which animistic beings are often manipulated.

6. The principal varieties of belief and ritual show broad correlations with levels of political economic organization. Four levels of religious organizations or cults can be distinguished: individualistic, shamanistic, communal, and ecclesiastical.

7. Inuit and Crow religions illustrate the individualistic or do-it-yourself level. Each individual carries out a series of rituals and observes a series of taboos that are deemed essential for survival and well-being, without the help of any part-time or full-time specialist.

8. No culture is devoid of shamanistic cults, the next level, which are defined by the presence of part-time magico-religious experts, or shamans, who have special talents and knowledge, usually involving sleights of hand, trances, and possession. As the cases of the !Kung and Tapirapé shamanism indicate, shamans are frequently employed to cure sick people; often they identify and destroy evildoers as well.

9. Communal cults, involving public rituals deemed essential for the welfare or survival of the entire social group, also occur to some extent at all political economic levels. Two principal types of communal rituals can be distinguished: rites of solidarity and rites of passage. As illustrated by the Arunta totemic rituals, rites of solidarity reaffirm and intensify a group's sense of common identity and express in symbolic form the group's claims to territory and resources. As illustrated in the Ndembu circumcision rituals, rites of passage symbolically and publicly denote the extinction or "death" of an individual's or group's socially significant status and the ac-

quisition or "birth" of a new socially significant status.

10. Finally, ecclesiastical cults are those dominated by a hierarchy of full-time specialists or priests, whose knowledge and skills are usually commanded by a state-level ruling class. To preserve and enhance the well-being of the state and of the universe, historical, astronomical, and ritual information must be acquired by the ecclesiastical specialists. Ecclesiastical cults are also characterized by huge investments in buildings, monuments, and personnel and by a thoroughgoing split between the specialist performers of ritual and the great mass of more or less passive spectators, who constitute the congregation.

11. With the development of the state, the objective of warfare shifted from that of routing enemy populations to incorporating them within imperial systems. This brought an end to the practice of sacrificing and eating prisoners of war. However, it was difficult for the Aztec state to refrain from rewarding its armies with the flesh of enemy soldiers in its effort to justify, expand, and consolidate ruling-class power. The Aztecs' consumption of human flesh may have been an adaptive strategy because alternative sources of animal foods had been depleted.

12. Revitalization movements, such as those of Native Americans and Melanesians, constitute another category of religious phenomena that cannot be understood apart from political–economic conditions. Under political–economic stress, subordinate castes, classes, minorities, and ethnic groups develop beliefs and rituals concerned with achieving a drastic improvement in their immediate well-being or their well-being in a life after death.

13. Religions can be powerful, dynamic forces in society that reinforce group norms. They also play an important role in social control by defining what is right and wrong and can be used to mobilize people for war or control antisocial behavior by labeling people as witches.

14. Religious beliefs and rituals also exhibit adaptive relationships in the form of sanctified messages. The ancient Israelite pig taboo, for example, can be understood as an adaptation to the changing costs and benefits of pig rearing brought about by population increase, deforestation, and desertification.

15. The sacred cow of India serves as a final example of the way in which religious beliefs adapt to changing political, economic, and ecological contexts.

Questions to Think About

1. What are some of the psychological and social functions of religion?

2. How would you explain the efficacy of shamanic curing?

3. What are rites of passage, and what is their function for the individual and the group?

4. In what ways are revitalization movements both religious and political in nature? Give examples that show how the attempts of local prophets try to affect a more satisfied society.

5. How do taboos help resolve the conflict between short-term benefits and long-term costs?

6. How can sacred injunctions have economic and ecological consequences? Give examples.

THROUGH THE LENS
of Cultural Materialism

Conformity and Conflict • Reading Twenty-Seven
Taraka's Ghost
Stanley A. Freed and Ruth S. Freed

Ghost possession is related to anxieties that are caused by stressful and seemingly unmanageable aspects of life. Sita was stressed by the need to have sex with her husband and the lack of support she would encounter as a new bride in her husband's household. This occurred in the context of the deaths of three friends and several brothers and sisters. The claim of ghost possession ultimately provided an acceptable reason. Sita's family should give her support to help her cope with stresses of her new life and her duties as a married woman.

Emic Perspective

- Sita was possessed with the ghost of Taraka, a childhood friend who committed suicide. Taraka's ghost declared that she would not leave Sita.

- Sita's family used various curing techniques—engaging the ghost in conversation, identifying it, trying to satisfy its wishes or demands so that it would leave voluntarily, attempting to drive it away with verbal abuse, and finally, if necessary, using physically painful or unpleasant measures.

Etic Perspective

- The social and psychological vulnerability of a bride makes her a prime candidate for attack by ghosts.

- Under the stress of mental or physical pain, the body produces morphinelike substances called *endorphins*, which relieve the pain but may trigger mental states called *alternate, altered,* or *dissociative*.

- Ghost possession is one such dissociative mental state.

- In this case, ghost possession reduced Sita's anxiety and gained her the support of her natal and conjugal families.

Infrastructure

- In rural North India, there is plow agriculture, and men dominate the mode of production.

- As her parent's first-born child, Sita lived through the deaths of four infant brothers and five infant sisters, who all died because they could not digest their mother's milk.

Structure

- In northern India, postmarital residence is patrilocal.

- At an early age, a female moves from her natal family, where she is loved, cherished, and indulged, to her marital family, where she is chaperoned and required to restrict her movements. She must adjust to her husband and his often large family.

- A married woman and her kin are regarded as social inferiors to her husband's kin. A new bride is expected to shoulder harder and more onerous household chores and farmwork than the daughters in her husband's family. A new bride also is generally uninformed about the relations between menarche and childbirth and is apprehensive about beginning sexual relations with her husband.

- Having been raised in a one-caste village with little caste, Sita had faced little caste discrimination in her own village. Her husband's village, however, was multicaste, and Sita's caste was near the bottom of the hierarchy.

- Taraka was Sita's cousin and close friend. She was engaged to a man of another village but had an illicit affair with a boy from her own village. She became pregnant but was afraid to reveal the loss of her premarital chastity.

- When Taraka went to her husband's family to begin her marital life, her husband's parents immediately discovered she was pregnant. Renouncing all rights to her, they returned her to her father. Despite Taraka's pleas, her father was unforgiving and told her to commit suicide. Shortly thereafter, when playing with her friends, Taraka went to a nearby well, jumped in, and drowned.

- Sita lost three of her close childhood friends. A schoolmate had been raped by a schoolteacher; her father was furious and blamed her for what happened. He flew into a rage, raped and murdered her, and threw her into a well. Another of Sita's schoolmates died of typhoid and malaria shortly after beginning sexual relations with her husband.

- Sita attended school, planning on becoming a teacher. However, her mother became concerned about Sita's untrustworthy male schoolteacher and took Sita out of school. The abrupt end of her education and dream of becoming a teacher was a shock to Sita.

Superstructure

- In rural North India, almost all Hindus believe that the soul goes through a cycle of rebirths. Following a person's death, it becomes a ghost, lingering for 13 days in the village cremation grounds.

- Most villagers who follow a traditional version of Hinduism believe that the soul travels to the Land of the Dead, ruled by Yama, Lord of the Dead. There, Yama and his scribe review the soul's past actions before deciding on its future. An important element in what happens to the soul at death is its *karma*, the sum of its good and bad actions from all its past lives. After being judged, the soul may be reborn or, if the sum of its actions is unusually good, released from the cycle of rebirths to join with many other souls and the Universal Absolute, a neuter deity known as the Ultimate Reality, where all souls are joined into one.

- Many Hindus believe in an additional possibility: A soul may become a ghost that lingers, possibly for decades, haunting the places where it lived and died. These are the souls of people who died tortured or from disease,

accident, suicide, or murder; who violated norms of behavior; who died before the years allotted to them by Yama; or who never attained the satisfaction of adult life. The ghosts of persons who are murdered or commit suicide are the most malevolent and tarry the longest.

- Ghosts are feared because they are believed to attack the living to seize their souls. Many villagers, but not all, believe that being seized by a ghost can cause illness or death. Ghost possession is the most vivid form of attack, in which a ghost enters and speaks through its victim, who has fallen into semiconsciousness. After recovering, the victim does not remember what took place. Because people in a state of possession may attempt to commit suicide by drowning in a well or by jumping in front of a train, they are usually watched by relatives or neighbors.

- The virtue of daughters is crucial to family honor in North India, and a daughter's sexual misbehavior, if it becomes generally known, may force a father to induce her suicide or murder her.

- A North Indian rural woman must make an extraordinary social and psychological adjustment when she marries. In Sita's mind, the deaths of her friends were linked with mating, marriage, childbirth, and disappointed dreams of further education.

- Sita blamed herself for Taraka's suicide. She became possessed by Taraka's ghost on the fourth night of sexual relations with her husband. Taraka's ghost said that Sita's husband was her husband. The statement indicated that Taraka's ghost had been with Sita at the time of her wedding, which meant that both women were married to Sita's husband.

- Treatment for ghost possession by exorcists and amulets relieved Sita's anxiety and reduced her stress. They also brought her other advantages: support from her natal and marital families, a reduction in her workload, and permission to visit her retired father every summer.

THROUGH THE LENS
of Cultural Materialism

Conformity and Conflict • Reading Twenty-Eight
Baseball Magic
George Gmelch

Many professional baseball players believe that rituals, taboos, and fetishes give them luck in a game filled with uncertainty. Players holding positions of greatest uncertainty—namely, pitching and hitting—practice the most baseball "magic" to control the forces of chance.

Emic Perspective

- Baseball players feel they never know what might have a positive effect on their game, so when they are winning, they tend to do everything the same way. In this regard, they are similar to the Trobriand Islanders, who believe that rituals, fetishes, and taboo avoidance give them supernatural power that help them succeed during times of uncertainty.

- The psychological dynamic associated with the power of magic can be understood by B. F. Skinner's experiment with pigeons who were given food at random intervals. The birds associated the arrival of the food with a particular action, such as tucking their head under a wing or walking in a clockwise circle. About 10 seconds after the arrival of the last pellet, the bird would begin doing whatever behavior it associated with getting the food and then repeat the behavior until the next pellet would arrive.

Etic Perspective

- Magic—including use of rituals, taboos, and fetishes—is used to manage the anxiety generated by unpredictable events that challenge human control.
- Because their livelihood depends on how well they perform, many professional baseball players, like the Trobriand Islanders, use magic to control the outcomes of activities that involve a high degree of chance.
- Magical beliefs give their practitioners a sense of control; that added feeling of confidence has positive effects on behavior.

Infrastructure

- Trobriand Islanders fish in two different settings. In the inner lagoon, where fish are plentiful and there is little danger, fishing magic is not practiced. On the open sea, where fishing is dangerous and the yield varies, a great deal of magical ritual is used to ensure safety and increase the catch.
- For professional baseball players, baseball is more than a game; it is an occupation that impacts their livelihood. Players who pitch and hit have little control over their game and use magic to gain confidence.

Superstructure

- The most common way players attempt to reduce feelings of uncertainty is to develop a *routine*—a course of action that is regularly followed. "They come out here [ballpark] and everything has to be the same, they don't like anything that knocks them off their routine." Routines are comforting; they bring order to a world in which players have little control.
- Some actions, however, go beyond mere routine. Their actions become *rituals*—prescribed behaviors in which there is no empirical connection between the means (e.g., tapping home plate three times) and the desired end (e.g., getting a base hit). By repeating a behavior that is linked to good performance, the player seeks to gain control. When in a slump, most players make a deliberate effort to change their routines and rituals and thus get rid of their bad luck.
- *Taboos* are the opposite of rituals. These are things you shouldn't do. Players believe that breaking a taboo leads to undesirable consequences or bad luck. Most players observe at least a few taboos, such as never stepping on the white foul lines. Taboos usually grow out of exceptionally poor performances, which players attribute to particular behaviors.
- *Fetishes* are charms, or material objects believed to embody supernatural power, that can aid or protect the owner. Good-luck charms are standard for some ballplayers. These include a wide assortment of objects from coins, chains, and crucifixes to favorite baseball hats. The fetishized object may be a new possession or something a player found that coincided with the start of a streak and so is presumed responsible for the good fortune. Some players regard certain uniform numbers as lucky. A young player may request the number of a former star, sometimes hoping that it will bring him the same success. Or he may request a number he associates with good luck. Clothing, both the choice and the order in which it is put on, combines elements of both ritual and fetish.

THROUGH THE LENS
of Cultural Materialism

Conformity and Conflict • Reading Twenty-Nine

Run for the Wall: An American Pilgrimage

Jill Dubisch

The Run for the Wall is a pilgrimage undertaken by motorcyclists who travel for 10 days each spring from Los Angeles to Washington, D.C., to commemorate soldiers lost during the Vietnam War. Those who make it to Washington visit "the wall," their name for the Vietnam Veterans Memorial, which bears the names of all those who died in the war. The bikers participate in "rolling thunder," a parade of thousands of motorcyclists ending at the U.S. Capitol, to honor and remember soldiers who were captured, missing, and killed in the Vietnam War.

Emic Perspective

- Participants describe the aim of their pilgrimage as twofold: to heal the individual wounds of the war and to have a ride on behalf of all veterans, especially those left behind—the prisoners of war and those missing in action.

- Pilgrimages are associated with the notion that one needs to go to a different place in order to achieve transformation, to touch the sacred, or to receive an important message from the other world.

Etic Perspective

- The Run for the Wall is a ritual readily adapted to a variety of situations and to a range of human emotional needs.

- It is continually modified to give people a sense of fulfillment and personal growth.

Structure

- The people who participate in the Run for the Wall are former Vietnam veterans who feel the Vietnam War is, in some sense, not really over. Unresolved conflicts over the meaning of the war and the fact that the United States did not "win" have made it difficult to gain closure, not only for veterans but for Americans in general.

- The sense of solidarity and brotherhood that exists among the bikers is also important in the Run for the Wall. It echoes the camaraderie of warriors in combat.

Superstructure

- *Ritual* is defined as a "patterned, repetitive, and symbolic enactment of a cultural belief or value."

- A *pilgrimage* involves ritually structured travel that physically removes people from their everyday lives as they journey to a place that evokes important, often life-changing emotions. As rituals, pilgrimages are structured around repetitive acts that symbolize past events, places, stories, and meanings. Although pilgrimages are often associated with religion, they may also occur in more secular contexts but with much the same effect.

- Many of the participating veterans are making a journey into the past and their own painful memories. They are revisiting a time of personal danger, fear, and grief and of national dissension and conflict. The Vietnam War split a generation and remains a painful period of U.S. history.

- Rituals are ideological and involve sensory symbols. Rituals engage our senses; the power of Angel Fire lies in its setting—the remoteness, the beauty, the steep, winding, and somewhat hazardous mountain roads that must be traversed to get there. In Limon, Colorado, the light of the candles, the growing darkness, the open space of the looming plains ahead, and the mountains behind all create a powerful ritual atmosphere. Rituals also convey important messages about social values. The Vietnam Veterans Memorial is a simple yet profound structure, with its two black granite wings, engraved with the names of over 58,000 U.S. soldiers who died in the war.

- *Liminality* is an important feature of rites of passage, in which individuals or groups move from one stage to another. Veterans seek to transform the meaning of being a Vietnam veteran from shame to pride and to give their comrades the chance for the homecoming reception most never had. Through ritual, the riders rewrite their own history, as well as that of the war, and become heroes in what is for many "the parade they never had."

- Motorcycles symbolize important U.S. values of freedom, self-reliance, and individualism. Many bikers also see themselves as a breed apart, rebels against the norms and restrictions of conventional society. The sense of marginality that some veterans felt upon their return to civilian life and the difficulty many experienced in adapting to that life thus fit the marginality of at least some segments of motorcycle culture, especially that of outlaw bikers and similar groups. Motorcycle riding can also have important therapeutic effects, providing a space in which veterans feel that they can clear their heads and find some peace from the memories and emotional traumas that continue to haunt them.

THROUGH THE LENS
of Cultural Materialism

Conformity and Conflict • Reading Thirty

Cargo Beliefs and Religious Experience

Stephen C. Leavitt

Cargo cults in New Guinea are religious attempts to generate material wealth through what is thought to be under the control of ancestral spirits. Cult members believe that wealth will be forthcoming if they gain their ancestors' ac-

ceptance and forgiveness. Cargo cults are a means for understanding larger economic processes that are otherwise incomprehensible to native people.

Emic Perspective

- Cargo cults are religious movements that use rituals to attain vast amounts of material wealth believed to be under the control of ancestral spirits.

- Traditional religion sees ancestors as taking care of the living. Getting cargo means receiving a sign or a gift from your own parents or grandparents, which shows that they forgive you and still care about you during difficult times.

Etic Perspective

- An emphasis on ritual, reliance on visions of charismatic leaders, and hope for world transformation are common features of cults in response to colonial domination. Cargo cults provide meaning in a time of cultural crisis and a way to gain independence in the face of colonial rule.
- Through their reliance on ancestors, people translate bewildering colonial experiences into a more personal and hopeful set of concepts about love and nurturance. The belief in cargo helps the people deal with the fact they have relatively little wealth compared to outsiders and helps them integrate this concept into their personal senses of self.

Infrastructure

- The people of Papua New Guinea earn money through wage labor or cash-cropping and buy Western goods.
- Papua New Guineans witnessed the amazing amounts of wealth brought in by European colonists, which seemed to appear miraculously from an unknown place.

Structure

- Traditional culture in Papua New Guinea placed a great deal of emphasis on the exchange and giving of gifts as a basis for building relationships and achieving prestige. People cemented friendships, built alliances, and resolved disputes by mounting large-scale exchanges of food with others.
- European colonists did not share the native view of how prestige is gained. They had control over attractive material goods but refused to enter into exchange relations with the local people. Instead, they instituted colonial control and acted as superiors.
- The ancestors that people turn to for cargo are not distant and anonymous supernatural beings; they are the personal spirits of familiar relatives, such as fathers, mothers, and other close kin, who are expected to show their eternal affection.

Superstructure

- It is a common belief among the Bumbita that some Europeans are the spirits of dead relatives who have come back to help them.
- Traditional Bumbita leaders gained power and prestige by giving away pigs and yams, so to these people, it is unthinkable that powerful people would hoard their wealth.
- Most Bumbita found in Christianity the promise of a transformed world of happiness. They believed that when Jesus came, there would no longer be illness, hunger, or death. But many also hoped for the arrival of vast material wealth. In their view, Jesus would bring huge quantities of rice, meat, clothing, housing materials, and other goods. These are the kinds of goods that Europeans brought with them into the area.
- The Bumbita believe material wealth must have a magical or spiritual origin. Their own ancestors must really own the wealth, and somehow the Europeans were able to gain access to some of it. The Bumbita believe that when Jesus returns, their ancestors will pass the wealth to their living descendents and rightful heirs.
- Cargo cult rituals imitate the behaviors of Europeans, such as forming rigid lines, marching in unison, and singing hymns in church services. Cargo movements incorporate Christian ideals, even though the missionaries oppose this kind of reinterpretation of the Christian message.

Masked dancers celebrate their culture in Dogon, Mali.

CHAPTER **17**

ART

This chapter is concerned with additional aspects of superstructure—namely, the thoughts and behaviors associated with painting, music, poetry, sculpture, dance, and other media of art. What is *art?* Is art, as defined by Western art critics, a valid definition of art in other cultures? How and why do the specific forms and styles of artistic expression vary from one culture to another? Is art ever created only for art's sake? We will see that art is not an isolated sector of human experience. It is intimately connected with and embedded in religion, politics, technology, and many other components of human social life.

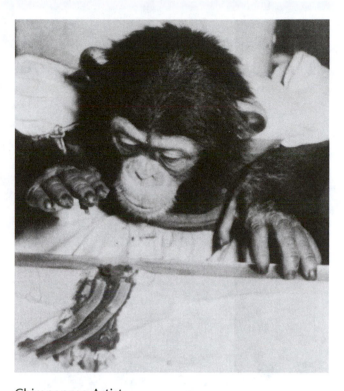

Chimpanzee Artist
This 2-year-old chimpanzee is fingerpainting at the Baltimore Zoo. Note the attempt to center the image on the paper.

What Is Art?

Alexander Alland (1977:39) defines *art* as "play with form producing some aesthetically successful transformation-representation." The key ingredients in this definition are play, form, aesthetic, and transformation:

- **Play** is an enjoyable, self-rewarding aspect of activity that cannot be accounted for simply by the utilitarian or survival functions of that activity.

- **Form** involves a set of restrictions on how the art play is to be organized in time and space—the rules of the game of art.

- **Aesthetic** refers to the existence of a universal human capacity for an emotionally charged response of appreciation and pleasure when art is successful.

- The term **transformation–representation** refers to the communicative aspect of art that conveys information through symbols and metaphors.

Art represents something that is not portrayed in its literal shape, sound, color, movement, or feeling. Art communicates information, not in its literal form or shape but in metaphors and symbols that convey ideas and emotions that carry greater meaning than the objects for which they stand (see Chapter 4, "Language and Symbolic Representation" section).

Art, expressed through music, painting, sculpture, and dance, is found in every known society, suggesting that it has important functions in human life. Art provides emotional gratification and contributes to social well-being. All people derive some level of aesthetic appreciation and enjoyment from art. For the artist, artistic expression is an outlet for emotional energy. For the nonartist, art can elicit powerful emotional responses that may or may not be shared.

Art also helps sustain, integrate, and organize social life. Through various symbols, art in all its forms reflects and shapes values, beliefs, and other ideological themes. As Alland points out, play, adherence to form, and an aesthetic sense are found in many nonhuman animals. Chimpanzees, for example, like to play with paints. Their adherence to form can be demonstrated by their placement of designs in the center of a blank space or by their balancing of designs on different parts of a page. (They don't simply paint right off the page.) An aesthetic sense can be inferred by their repeated attempts to copy simple designs such as circles and triangles accurately. Just as grammatical language remains rudimentary among apes in nature, so too does their artistry. Although the rudiments of art can be found in our primate heritage, only *Homo sapien* can justly be called the "artistic animal."

Art as a Cultural Category

Although it is possible to identify art as an etic category of thought and behavior in all human cultures, an emic distinction between art and nonart is not universal (just as the distinction between natural and supernatural is not universal). What most Westerners mean by *art* is a particular emic category of modern Euro-American civilization. Euro-American schoolchildren are enculturated to the idea that art is a category of activities and products that stands

Art Has Many Media

*Native American cultures produced these objects.   A. Gold mummy mask with green stone eyes: Chimu,
Peru.   B. Feathers of blue and yellow form the design of a Tapirapé mask: Brazil.   C. Ceramic jar:
Nazca, Peru.   D. Blanket in blue, black, and white with stripes and frets: Navajo, United States.*

opposed to the category of nonart. They learn to believe, in other words, that some paintings, carvings, songs, dances, and stories are not art.

In Western civilization, a particular performance is deemed artistic or not by a distinct group of authorities—an art establishment—who make or judge art and who control the museums, conservatories, critical journals, and other organizations and institutions devoted to art as a livelihood and style of life. However, most cultures lack any semblance of an art establishment. This does not mean they lack art or artistic standards (Anderson 1992). A painted design on a pot or a rock, a carved mask or club, or a song or chant in a puberty ordeal is subject to critical evaluation by both performers and spectators. All cultures

distinguish between less satisfactory and more satisfactory aesthetic experiences in decorative, pictorial, and expressive matters.

Basic to the modern Western idea of art and nonart is the exclusion of designs, stories, and artifacts that have a definite use in day-to-day subsistence activities and that are produced primarily for practical purposes or for commercial sale. Carpenters are distinguished from people who make wooden sculptures, bricklayers from architects, house painters from those who apply paint to canvas, and so forth.

The opposition between art and practicality is seldom found in other cultures.

In most cultures, works of art are produced and performed in harmony with utilitarian objectives. People everywhere, whether specialists or nonspecialists, derive pleasure from playfully embellishing and transforming the contours and surfaces of pots, fabrics, wood, and metal products. All cultures, however, recognize that certain individuals are more skilled than others in making utilitarian objects and in embellishing them with pleasing designs. Anthropologists generally regard skilled woodcarvers, basketmakers, potters, weavers, or sandal makers as artists.

Art and Invention

As noted earlier, *play* is a form of exploratory behavior that permits human beings to try out new and possibly useful responses in a controlled and protected context. The playful, creative urge that lies behind art, therefore, is probably closely related to the creative urge that lies behind the development of science, technology, and new institutions.

Art and technology often interact, and it is difficult to say where technology ends and art begins or where art ends and technology begins.

The beautiful symmetry of nets, baskets, and woven fabrics is essential for their proper functioning. Even the development of musical expression may have technological benefits. For example, there was probably some kind of feedback between the invention of the bow as a hunting weapon and the twanging of taut strings for musical effect. No one can say which came first, but cultures with bows and arrows usually have musical strings. Wind instruments, blowguns, pistons, and bellows are all related. Similarly, metallurgy and chemistry relate to experimentation with the ornamental shape, texture, and color of ceramic and textile products. The first fired ceramics were figurines rather than utilitarian pots (Vandiver et al. 1989). Thus, it is practical to encourage craftworkers to experiment with new techniques and materials. Small wonder that many cultures regard technical virtuosity as mana (see Chapter 16, "Animation and Mana" section). Others regard it as the gift of the gods, as in the classical Greek idea of the Muses—goddesses of oratory, dance, and music—whose assistance was needed if worthy artistic performances were to occur.

Art and Cultural Patterning

Most artwork is deliberately fashioned in the image of preexisting forms. It is the task of the artist to replicate these forms by original combinations of culturally standardized elements—familiar and pleasing sounds, colors, lines, shapes, movements, and so on. Of course, the artist must always add some playful and creative ingredient, or it will not be art. However, if the transformation–representation is to communicate something—and it must communicate something if it is to be a successful work of art—the

!Kung San Plays the Bow
The thumb plucks the string; the mouth opens and closes, moving along the string to control the tone and resonance. Which came first: the bow for hunting or the bow for making music?

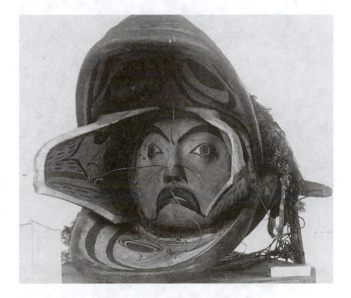

Kwakiutl Mask
This is actually a mask within a mask within a mask. The whale conceals the bird, which conceals the human face, which conceals the face of the wearer.

work cannot be the artist's own private invention. Complete originality, therefore, is not what most cultures strive after in their art.

Each culture tends to repeat traditional and familiar elements, thus generating a characteristic sound, look, or feel.

For example, Northwest Coast Native American sculpture is well known for its consistent attention to animal and human motifs rendered in such a way as to indicate internal as well as external organs. These organs are symmetrically arranged within bounded geometrical forms. Maori sculpture, in contrast, requires that wooden surfaces be broken into bold but intricate filigrees and whorls. Among the Mochica of ancient Peru, the sculptural medium was pottery, and Mochica pots are famous for their representational realism in portraiture and in depictions of domestic and sexual behavior. Hundreds of other easily recognizable and distinctive art styles of different cultures can be identified. The continuity and integrity of these styles provides the basic context for a people's understanding and liking of art.

Establishment art in modern Western culture is again unique in its emphasis on formal originality. Westerners take it as normal that art must be interpreted and explained by experts in order to be understood and appreciated. Since the end of the nineteenth century, the greatest artists of the Western art establishment have been those who break with tradition, introduce new formal rules, and at least for a time render their work incomprehensible to a large number of people. Joined to this deemphasis of tradition is the peculiar and recent Western notion of artists as lonely people, struggling in poverty against limitations set by the preexisting capability of their audience to appreciate and understand true genius.

Thus, the creative, playful, and transformational aspects of modern art have taken the upper hand over the formal and representational aspects. Contemporary Euro-American artists consciously strive to be the originators of entirely new formal rules. They compete to invent new transformations to replace the traditional ones.

Modern aesthetic standards hold that originality is more important than intelligibility.

Indeed, a work of art that is too easily understood may be condemned. Many artists take it for granted that novelty must result in a certain amount of obscurity. What accounts for this obsession with being original?

One important influence is the reaction to mass production. Mass production leads to a downgrading of technical virtuosity. It also leads to a downgrading of all artwork that closely resembles the objects or performances others have produced. Another factor to be considered is the involvement of the modern artist in a commercial market in which supply perennially exceeds demand. Artists in band and village societies are not obsessed with being original, except to the extent that it enhances the aesthetic enjoyment of their work. Their livelihood does not depend on obtaining an artistic identity and a personal following.

Another reason for the obsession with originality is the high rate of cultural change in modern societies. To some extent, the emphasis on artistic originality merely reflects and expresses this rate of change. Finally, the alienating and isolating tendencies of modern mass society may also play a role. Much modern art reflects the loneliness, puzzlement, and anxiety of the creative individual in a depersonalized and hostile urban, industrial milieu.

Art and Religion

The history and ethnography of art are inseparable from the history and ethnography of religion. The earliest paintings found on the walls of caves are generally assumed to have been painted as parts of ancient religious rituals.

Mochica Pot
A pre-Columbian portrait made by the Mochica of northern Peru.

Art is intimately associated with all four organizational levels of religion.

At the individualistic level, magical songs are often included among the revelations granted the vision seekers of the Great Plains. Even the preparation of trophy heads among the J'varo must meet aesthetic standards, and singing and chanting are widely used during shamanistic performances. On the communal level, puberty rituals, as among the Ndembu (Profile 16.1), provide occasions for dancing and myth and storytelling. Body painting is also widely practiced in communal ceremonies, as among the Arunta. Singing, dancing, and the wearing of masks are common at both puberty and funeral rituals. Furthermore, much artistic effort is expended in the preparation of religiously significant funeral equipment, such as coffins and graveposts. Many cultures include ceremonial artifacts such as pottery and clubs, points, and other weapons among a deceased person's grave

goods. Ancestors and gods are often depicted in statues and masks that are kept in men's houses or in shrines. Churingas, the Aranda's most sacred objects, are artfully incised with whorls and loops depicting the route followed by the ancestors during the dream time. Finally, on the ecclesiastical level, art and religion are fused in pyramids, monumental avenues, stone statuaries, monolithic calendar carvings, temples, altars, priestly garments, and a nearly infinite variety of ritual ornaments and sacred paraphernalia.

Clearly, art, religion, and magic satisfy many overlapping psychological needs in human beings. They are media for expressing sentiments and emotions not easily expressed in ordinary life. They impart a sense of mastery over or communion with unpredictable events and mysterious, unseen powers. They impose human meanings and values on an indifferent world—a world that has no humanly intelligible meanings and values of its own. They seek to penetrate behind the facade of ordinary appearance into the true, cosmic significance of things. And they use

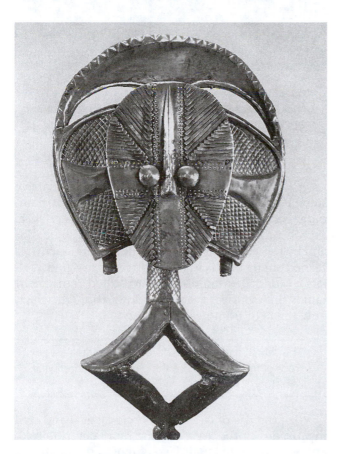

Ba Kota Funerary Figures

The Ba Kota of the Gabon Republic place the skeletal remains of dead chiefs in bark boxes or baskets surmounted by Mbulu-ngulu guardian figures of wood, faced with brass or copper sheets or strips. Although the figure expresses the creative individuality of the artist, it also conforms to stylistic pattern.

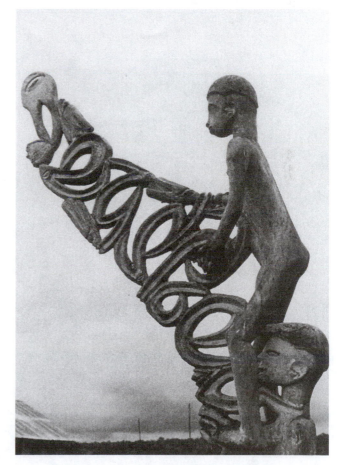

Asmat Gravepost

Around the world, much talent has been lavished on commemorating the dead, but styles and media vary enormously.

illusions, dramatic tricks, and sleights of hand to get people to believe in them.

Art and Politics

Art is also intimately related to politics. The relationship is especially clear in the context of state-sponsored art. As we have seen, in stratified societies, religion is a means of social control. To strengthen this control, the skills of the artist are harnessed by the ruling class to instill religious notions of obedience and to sanctify the status quo. State-sponsored monumental architecture was a visible representation of the power of the gods and the rulers. Contrary to the popular modern image of the artist as a free spirit disdainful of authority, most state-level art is politically conservative; artists preserved the status quo by creating magnificent works of art that represented the awesome power of the state (Paztory 1984:20).

Ecclesiastical art generally interprets the world in conformity with prevailing myths and ideologies, justifying inequities and exploitation.

Gold Death Mask of Tut
This mask is another example of the interrelationship of art, religion, and politics.

Art makes the gods visible as idols. Gazing on massive stone blocks carved as if by superhuman hands, commoners comprehend the necessity for subservience. They are awed by the immense size of the pyramids and by the processions, prayers, pomp, and sacrifices carried out by priests in dramatic settings—golden altars, colonnaded temples, great vaulted roofs, huge ramps and stairways, and windows through which only the light from heaven passes.

The church and the state have been the greatest patrons of the arts in all but the past few hundred years of history.

With the rise of capitalism, ecclesiastical and civil institutions in the West became more decentralized, and wealthy individuals largely replaced church and state as patrons of the arts. Accumulating valuable art objects served as another way to display one's power. At the same time, individualized sponsorship of artists promoted greater flexibility and freedom of expression. Politically neutral, secular, and even revo-

Art and Architecture
Brightly painted faces adorn a men's house in the Sepik River basin, New Guinea.

lutionary and sacrilegious themes became common. The arts became established as individualistic, secular forms of expression and entertainment.

To protect and preserve its newfound autonomy, the art establishment adopted the doctrine of "art for art's sake." But once they were free to express themselves as they saw fit, artists were no longer sure what they wanted to express. They devoted themselves more and more to idiosyncratic and obscure symbols organized into novel and unintelligible patterns, as noted earlier in this chapter. And the patrons of art, concerned less and less with communication, increasingly looked toward the acquisition and sponsorship of art as a prestigious commercial venture that yielded substantial profits, tax deductions, and a hedge against inflation.

The Evolution of Music and Dance

Some anthropologists hold that structural and infrastructural components directly influence the formal characteristics and aesthetic standards of different cultural styles. According to Allan Lomax and his associates (Lomax 1968; Lomax and Arensberg 1977), for example, certain broad characteristics of song, music, and dance are closely correlated with a culture's level of subsistence.

Bands and villages in general tend to have a different complex of music, song, and dance than do chiefdoms and states.

Dividing cultures into those that are low and those that are high on the scale of subsistence technology leads to the following correlations:

- *Musical intervals:* The less advanced subsistence systems employ musical scales in which notes are widely separated—that is, have intervals of a third or more. Advanced subsistence systems employ scales that are marked by more and smaller intervals.

- *Repetition in song text:* The less advanced subsistence cultures employ more repetition in their lyrics—fewer words, over and over again.

- *Complexity and type of orchestra:* Less advanced subsistence systems use only one or two kinds of instruments and small numbers of each. Advanced subsistence is correlated with musical performances involving more performers and greater variety of instruments.

- *Dance styles:* The advanced subsistence systems are correlated with dance styles in which many body parts—fingers, wrists, arms, torso, legs, feet, toes—have distinctive movements to make or roles to play.

The more advanced the subsistence system, the more the dance style tends to emphasize complex curving motions, as opposed to simple up-and-down and side-to-side steps, like hopping or shuffling.

Lomax sees these correlations as resulting from direct and indirect influence of subsistence. Large, complex orchestration, for example, reflects the structural ability of a society to form large, coordinated groups. Dance styles, in contrast, may simply express the characteristic movements employed in using such implements of production as digging sticks versus plows or complex machines. Some dances can be regarded as training for work, warfare, or self-defense, but dance obviously has many other functions (Box 17.1). Modern rock, for example, has a strong erotic component, expressed through pelvic gyrations and thrusts.

Lomax's correlations have been criticized on technical grounds relating to sampling and coding procedures (see Kaeppler 1978). But Lomax's attempt to measure and compare music and dance styles and to relate them to social structure and subsistence constitutes an important avenue of approach.

BOX 17.1   Some Social Functions of Music, Song, and Dance

1. *Emotes:* Lets people express emotion; makes them feel good.
2. *Socializes:* Teaches traditions.
3. *Educates:* Develops poise and confidence in performance.
4. *Bonds:* Creates a sense of togetherness among performers.
5. *Rallies:* Prepares for dangerous situations (for example, warfare and journeys).
6. *Aggresses:* Lets people demonstrate physical prowess harmlessly.
7. *Worships:* Brings people closer to the gods.
8. *Seduces:* Arouses sexual passions, displays charms.
9. *Coordinates:* Gets people to work or move together, as in sea chanties and military marches.
10. *Entertains:* Prevents boredom.

Verbal Arts

All societies use words as a form of creative expression. Verbal arts fall under the general heading of folklore, which includes jokes, proverbs, folksongs, limericks, prayers, myths, and folktales.

Folktales serve as a charter for how a culture expects its members to think and behave; heroes and heroines are triumphant because they possess admirable traits, whereas antagonists are punished for their character flaws.

 Folktales are traditional narratives from the deep past that reflect social situations that play on ordinary human fears and desires.

Typically, **myths** involve creation and the origins of the people who tell them and serve as the ultimate rationale for how events have unfolded. The main character is a god or culture hero who successfully brings a necessity such as fire or sun to humanity. Myths are believed to be true by the people who tell them and serve as the ultimate rationale for how events have unfolded.

 Myths are sacred tales in which deities appear to explain issues of human existence.

Myth and Binary Contrasts

Anthropologists have found considerable evidence suggesting that certain formal structures recur in widely different traditions of oral and written literature, including myths and folktales. These structures are characterized by *binary contrasts*—that is, by two elements or themes that can be viewed as standing in diametric opposition to each other.

Many examples of recurrent binary contrasts can be found in Western religion, literature, and mythology: good versus bad, up versus down, male versus female, cultural versus natural, young versus old, and so forth. According to French anthropologist Levi-Strauss, the founder of the research strategy known as **structuralism** (Chapter 2), the reason these binary contrasts recur so often is that the human brain is "wired" in such a way as to make binary contrasts appealing, or good to think.

From the structuralist point of view, the main task of the anthropological study of literature, mythology, and folklore is to identify the common, unconscious binary contrasts that lie beneath the surface of human thought and to show how these binary contrasts undergo unconscious transformation–representations.

Consider the familiar tale of Cinderella: A mother has two daughters and one stepdaughter. The two daughters are older, and the stepdaughter is younger; the older ones are ugly and mean, whereas Cinderella is beautiful and kind. The older sisters are aggressive; Cinderella is passive. Through a kind fairy godmother, as opposed to her mean stepmother, Cinderella goes to the ball, dances with the prince, and loses her magical shoe. Her sisters have big feet, and she has little feet. Cinderella wins the prince. The unconscious deep structure of this story might include the following binary oppositions:

passive	aggressive
younger	older
smaller	larger
good	evil
beautiful	ugly
culture	nature
fairy godmother	stepmother

Structuralists contend that the enjoyment people derive from tales and their durability across space and time stems from the unconscious oppositions and their familiar yet surprising representations.

Structural analyses of literature, art, myths, rituals, and religion abound in anthropology. However, they are surrounded by considerable controversy, primarily because it is not clear whether the binary oppositions discerned by the anthropologists really exist as unconscious realities in the minds of the people being studied. It is always possible to reduce complex and subtle symbols to less complex and gross symbols and then finally to emerge with such flat oppositions as culture versus nature or male versus female. But this does not mean that these categories are emically significant within the local cultural context.

The Complexity of Primitive Art: Campa Rhetoric

A common misconception about the arts of band and village societies is that they are necessarily more simple or naive than art in modern industrial societies (Titon et al. 1984). Although as we have just seen, many stylistic aspects of art have undergone an evolution from simple to more complex forms, other aspects may have been as complex among Stone Age hunter-gatherers as they are today. The case of Campa rhetoric illustrates this point.

 Rhetoric is the art of persuasive public speaking and is closely related to the theatrical arts.

As Gerald Weiss (1977) discovered, the preliterate Campa, who live in eastern Peru near the headwaters of the Amazon river, use most of the important rhetorical devices cultivated by the great philosophers and orators of ancient Greece and Rome. Their object in public discourse is not merely to inform but to persuade and convince. "Campa narration is 'a separate time,' where a spellbinding relationship between narrator and audience is developed, with powerful rhetorical devices employed to create and enhance the quality of that relationship" (1977:173).

Here are a few examples of these devices, as translated by Weiss from the Campa language, which belongs to the Native American family of languages known as *Arawak*:

- *Rhetorical questions:* The speaker makes the point that the Campa are deficient in their worship of the sky god, the sun, by asking a question that he himself will then answer: "Do we supplicate him, he here, he who lives in the sky, the sun? We do not know how to supplicate him."

- *Iterations (effect by repetition):* The speaker imparts an emphatic, graphic, cinematic quality to the point by repeating some key words: "The enemy comes out of the lake: And so they emerged in great numbers—he saw them emerge, emerge, emerge, emerge, emerge, emerge, emerge, emerge, emerge, all, all."

- *Imagery and metaphor:* Death is alluded to in the phrase "the earth will eat him." The body is described as "the clothing of the soul."

- *Appeal to evidence:* To prove that the oilbird was formerly human in shape: "Yes, he was formerly human—doesn't he have whiskers?"

- *Appeal to authority:* "They told me long ago, the elders, they who heard these words, long ago, so it was."

- *Antithesis (effect by contrast):* A hummingbird is about to raise the sky rope, which the other larger creatures have failed to do: "They are all big whereas I am small and chubby."

In addition, the Campa orator uses a wide variety of gestures, exclamations, sudden calls for attention ("Watch out, here it comes"), asides ("Imagine it, then"; "Careful that you don't believe, now"). Altogether, Weiss lists 19 formal rhetorical devices used by the Campa.

SUMMARY
and *Questions to Think About*

1. Creative play, formal structure, aesthetic feelings, and symbolic transformations are the essential ingredients in art. Although the capacity for art is foreshadowed in the behavior of nonhuman primates, only humans are capable of art involving transformation–representations.

2. The distinctive human capacity for art is thus closely related to the distinctive human capacity for the symbolic transformations that underlie the semantic universality of human language.

3. Western emic definitions of art depend on the existence of art authorities and critics who place many examples of play, structured aesthetic, and symbolic transformation into the category of nonart. The distinction between crafts and art is part of this tradition. In contrast, anthropologists regard skilled craftspersons as artists.

4. Art has adaptive functions related to creative changes in other sectors of social life. Art and technology influence each other, as in the case of instruments of music and the hunt and in the search for new shapes, colors, textures, and materials in ceramics and textiles.

5. Despite the emphasis on creative innovation, most cultures have art traditions or styles that maintain formal continuity through time. This makes it possible to identify the styles of cultures such as the Northwest Coast Native Americans, Maori, and Mochica. The continuity and integrity of such styles provide the basic context for a people's understanding of and liking for the artist's creative transformations.

6. Establishment art in modern Western culture is unique in emphasizing creativity as well as original transformations. This drive for originality results in the need to break with tradition and development of novel and obscure styles. Lack of communication between the Western artist and the rest of society may be caused by the artist's reaction to mass production, commercialization of art markets, rapid rate of cultural change, and the depersonalized milieu of urban, industrial life.

7. Art and religion are closely related. This relationship can be seen in the songs of the vision quest; preparation of shrunken heads; singing and chanting in shamanistic performances; shamanistic myths; storytelling; singing and dancing; Arunta churingas; and many other aspects of individual, shamanistic, communal, and ecclesiastical cults. Art and religion satisfy many similar psychological needs, and it is often difficult to tell them apart.

8. Art and politics are also closely related. This relationship is clear in state-sponsored ecclesiastical art, much of which functions to keep people in awe of their rulers. It is only in recent times, with the rise of decentralized capitalist states, that art has enjoyed any significant degree of freedom from direct political control.

9. To the extent that bands, villages, chiefdoms, and states represent evolutionary levels and to the extent that art is functionally related to technology, economy, politics, religion, and other aspects of the universal cultural pattern, the content of art has clearly evolved. A more controversial finding is that styles of song, music, and dance—including musical intervals, repetition in song texts, complexity and type of orchestra, body part involvement, and amount of curvilin-ear motion—have also undergone evolutionary changes.

10. The structuralist approach to art attempts to interpret myths, rituals, and other expressive performances in terms of a series of unconscious universal binary oppositions. Common binary oppositions can be found in the Cinderella myth, but these may not be emically valid categories.

11. As the example of Campa rhetoric shows, the art styles of band and village peoples can be highly sophisticated.

Questions To Think About

1. How is art distinct from other forms of communication?

2. How does art in traditional society compare with art in modern Western society?

3. What kinds of economic influences are found in artistic forms?

4. How is art a medium of both conservative and revolutionary political expression?

5. What is the relationship between art and religion? What psychological needs do both satisfy?

THROUGH THE LENS
of Cultural Materialism

Conformity and Conflict • Reading Eight

Body as Visual Language

Enid Schildkrout

Body art is a means of transmitting meaning of personal or group identity. Symbolic messages only make sense in the context of culture. Because body art is a highly personal art form, it continually challenges cultural assumptions about the ideal, the desirable, and the appropriate presentation of the body.

Emic Interpretation

• Body art takes on specific meanings in different cultures.

• It is a symbolic expression of culturally recognized life transitions, social status, and personal rebellion.

Etic Interpretation

• Body art is a visual language that communicates cultural ideals of beauty, as well as a person's individuality or group identity.

Structure

• Makeup can accentuate the differences between men and women, camouflage perceived imperfections, or signify a special occasion or ritual state.

• Hair has symbolic significance that tells people how we want to be seen; covering the head is often a sign of piety, whereas reversing the normal treatment of hair can signify rebellion or special status.

• Styles of combing, braiding, parting, and wrapping hair can signify status and gender, age, ritual status, or membership in a certain group.

• Tattooing, piercing, and scarification likely signal a person's place in society or an irreversible life passage, such as transition from childhood to adulthood. Temporary forms of body art, like clothing, ornaments, and painting, more often mark a moment or simply fashion.

• A specially shaped head may signify nobility, as was the case for the Inca of South America and the Maya of Central America.

- Piercing allows for insertion of ornaments, which can be of precious and rare materials and signify privilege and wealth.

Superstructure

- People mark their bodies to signify individuality, social status, and cultural identity. There is no culture in which people do not or did not paint, pierce, tattoo, reshape, or simply adorn their bodies. Fashions change and forms of body art come and go, but people everywhere "package" their appearance.

- Ideals of beauty vary from one culture to another. In some cultures, people see being fat as a sign of health and wealth, while in others it is the opposite. People in some cultures admire and respect signs of aging, while others do all they can to hide their gray hairs and wrinkles.

- Body art is an expression of individuality and group identity. Because it is an obvious way of signaling cultural differences, people use it to reinvent themselves and to cross boundaries of gender, national identity, and cultural stereotypes.

CHAPTER **18**

APPLIED

ANTHROPOLOGY

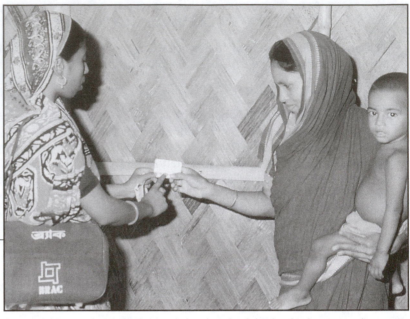

The work of applied anthropology underlies the role of this family-planning worker in Bangladesh.

U p to now, you have probably been thinking that at least some of this is pretty interesting stuff (I hope). But what good is it? Does it have any practical use? Well, a lot of people (and not only anthropologists) think it does. In this chapter, we explore some of the relationships between anthropological research and the attempt to achieve practical goals by organizations that sponsor or use such research. The sample of cases presented in this brief survey does not fairly represent the great variety of applied projects being carried out by anthropologists. This rapidly growing field is hard to keep up with.

What Is Applied Anthropology?

Since World War II, an increasing number of anthropologists have become involved in research that has immediate practical applications. Such anthropologists are said to practice **applied anthropology.**

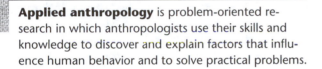

Applied anthropology is problem-oriented research in which anthropologists use their skills and knowledge to discover and explain factors that influence human behavior and to solve practical problems.

The core of applied anthropology consists of research commissioned by public and private organizations in the hope of achieving practical goals of interest to them. Such organizations include federal, state, local, and international government bureaus and agencies, such as the U.S. Department of Agriculture (USDA), U.S. Department of Defense, U.S. National Park Service, U.S. Bureau of Indian Affairs (BIA), U.S. Agency for International Development (USAID), World Bank, World Health Organization (WHO), Food and Agricultural Organization (FAO), various drug abuse agencies, education and urban planning departments of major cities, and municipal hospitals—to mention only a few. In addition, private organizations that have hired or contracted with anthropologists to carry out practical, goal-oriented research include major industrial corporations, research foundations such as Planned Parenthood and the Population Council, and various branches of the Rockefeller and Ford Foundations' International Crops Research Institutes (Chambers 1985; Willigen 1991).

Research, Theory, and Action

Although the hallmark of applied anthropology is involvement in research aimed at achieving a special practical result, the extent to which the applied anthropologist actually participates in bringing about the desired result varies from one assignment to another. At one extreme, the applied anthropologist may merely be charged with developing information the sponsoring organization needs in order to make decisions. In other instances, the applied anthropologist may be asked to evaluate the feasibility of a planned program or even to draw up a set of plans for achieving a desired goal (Husain 1976). More rarely, the anthropologist, alone or as a member of a team, may be responsible for planning, implementing, and evaluating a whole program from beginning to end. When anthropologists help implement a program, they are said to be practicing **action anthropology.**

It is often difficult to draw a line between applied and nonapplied research.

Abstract theorizing about the causes of sociocultural differences and similarities can itself be construed as applied anthropology if it provides a general set of principles to which any action program must conform if it is to achieve success. For example, general theories about the causes of underdevelopment or of urban poverty (see Chapter 12, "A 'Culture of Poverty'" section) can have considerable practical consequences, even though the research behind these theories may not have been sponsored by organizations with the expressed goal of eliminating underdevelopment and urban poverty. Similarly, a better understanding of the processes responsible for the evolution of advanced industrial societies may be of immediate relevance to organizations that advise firms and governments on investment policies. Applied anthropology premised on blatantly incorrect theory is "misapplied anthropology" (R. Cohen 1984b).

What Do Applied Anthropologists Have to Offer?

The effectiveness of applied anthropology is enhanced by three distinctive attributes of general anthropology, as discussed in Chapter 2:

- Relative freedom from ethnocentrism and Western biases
- Concern with holistic sociocultural systems
- Concern with both ordinary etic behavioral events and the emics of mental life

Detecting and Controlling Ethnocentrism

The applied anthropologist can assist sponsoring organizations by exposing the ethnocentric, culture-bound assumptions that often characterize cross-cultural contacts and that prevent change-oriented programs from achieving their goals.

By adhering to the principle of *cultural relativism,* applied anthropologists seek to understand the cultural barriers that may affect change-oriented programs.

For example, Western-trained agricultural scientists tend to dismiss peasant forms of agriculture as backward and inefficient, thereby overlooking the cumulative wisdom embodied in age-old practices handed down from generation to generation (Netting 1993). The attitude of Western experts toward the use of cattle in India is a case in point (see Chapter 16, "The Sacred Cow" section). Anthropologists are more likely to reserve judgment about a traditional practice such as using cattle to plow fields, whereas narrowly trained specialists might automatically wish to replace the animals with tractors.

Again, applied anthropologists could add a valuable perspective to the attempt to set up a health care delivery system. Simply modeling it after those with which Western-trained doctors are familiar may not be the answer. Providing expensive staffs, costly hospitals, and the latest electronic gadgetry, for example, is not necessarily the way to improve the quality of health services (Cattle 1977:38). For example, the American notion that milk is the "perfect food" has led to much grief and dismay throughout the world. Many populations in less developed countries have been sent tons of surplus milk in powdered form as nutritional supplements, yet the people have lacked the enzyme needed to digest lactose, the predominant form of sugar in milk. Finally, Western notions of hygiene automatically suggest that mothers must be persuaded not to chew food and then put it in their babies' mouths. Yet it was found that in the case of the Pijoan people of the U.S. Southwest, premastication of infant foods effectively combated the iron-deficiency anemia that afflicted infants who were fed exclusively on mother's milk (Freedman 1977:8).

A Holistic View

As industrial society becomes increasingly specialized and technocratic (that is, dominated by narrowly trained experts who have mastered techniques and machines others do not understand), the need for anthropology's holistic view of social life becomes more urgent. In diverse fields (for example, education, health, economic development), narrow sets of easily quantified variables, such as standardized tests for students and rates of productivity, are increasingly being used to simplify an organization's performance. All too often, however, the gain in verifiability is offset by a loss in *validity* (or "meaningfulness"). Easily quantified variables may represent only a small part of a much bigger system whose larger set of difficult-to-measure variables could cancel out the observed effects of the small set of variables (Bernard 1994:41).

Holism is the idea that the various components of a sociocultural system are linked; a change in one part of the system leads to changes in other parts of the system. For example, after World War II, the U.S. auto industry found it could earn more money by building heavier and more powerful cars without paying too much attention to the question of how long the cars would function without need of repairs. Other sets of variables—namely, the ecological consequences of auto emission pollution, the political and military conditions that made it possible for the United States to enjoy low oil prices, and the perception by foreign auto producers that there was a market for small, fuel-efficient, reliable, and long-lasting vehicles—were considered irrelevant to the task of maximizing the U.S. auto industry's profits. Hence, what appeared in a narrow context to be a highly objective measure of success (large profits and domination of the U.S. auto market) turned out in a longer timeframe to be devoid of validity.

Thus, in common-sense language, anthropological holism boils down to being aware of the long term as well as the short term, the distant as well as the near, parts other than the one being studied, and the whole as well as the parts. Without understanding the needs and attitudes of local communities, even a seemingly straightforward and simple project can end up as a disaster.

Etic and Emic Views of Organizations

Technification and specialization are usually accompanied by the growth of bureaucracy. An essential component of bureaucracy is an emic plan by which the units within an organization are related to each other and according to which individuals are expected to perform their tasks.

In most sociocultural systems, the etic behavioral aspects of organizations and situations differ substantially from the mental emics of the bureaucratic plan.

Anthropologists who are trained to approach social life from the ground up and who are concerned with everyday events as they actually unfold often can provide a view of organizations and situations that the bureaucracy lacks. Thus, anthropologists have studied schools, factories, corporations, and hospitals in a manner that provides both emic and etic viewpoints—to look at what is meaningful and relevant to the students, workers, and managers in the organizations as well as what is happening in terms of everyday events as they unfold.

Applied Anthropology and Development

The number of applications for applied anthropology is constantly growing. This makes it difficult to provide a complete list of these activities, let alone to provide examples of each category listed in Box 18.1. The examples that follow are intended merely to provide a sense of the broad scope of applied anthropological projects that have been carried out during the last decade.

One of the most important subfields of applied anthropology focuses on the problem of agricultural development in peasant and small farmer communities.

As mentioned previously (Chapter 12, "Peasant Classes" section), anthropologists have studied peasants more often than they have studied other kinds of groups. Their knowledge of the conditions and aspirations of peasant life makes anthropologists useful as consultants to or members of interdisciplinary projects aimed at raising Third World standards of living (Barlett and Brown 1985).

Without Holism: Merino Sheep Fiasco

International experts tried without success to get the peasant Indians of Chimborazo Province in Ecuador to substitute high-yield Australian merino sheep for the scrawny sheep the Indians owned. If the Indians would use them to breed new flocks, they could have them free of charge. Finally, one "progressive" individual accepted the offer and raised a flock of crossbred merinos that were far woollier and heavier than the traditional Indian sheep.

Unfortunately, the native people of Chimborazo compete with other ethnic and racial groups for scarce resources. Non-Indian, Spanish-speaking farmers who live in the lower valleys resented the attention being paid to the Indians; they began to fear that the Indians would be emboldened to press for additional economic and social gains, which would undermine their own positions. The merinos attracted someone's attention, and the whole flock was herded into a truck and stolen. The rustlers were well protected by public opinion, which regarded the animals as "too good for the Indians anyway."

The "progressive" innovator was left as the only one in the village without sheep. Variables such as ethnic and class antagonisms, opportunities for theft,

---

| BOX 18.1 | Domains of Applied Anthropology |

Agricultural development	Environmental protection
Alcohol and drug behavior	Gender and development
Alternative energy	Gerontology (alternative treatment of the elderly)
Appropriate and affordable housing	Government and private bureaucracies
Combating and exposing racism, sexism, and ageism	Health and medicine
Community action (helping to complete community projects)	Industrial productivity
	Land claims (Native Americans)
Criminal justice and law enforcement	Military forces
Cultural resource management (archeology)	Multinational corporations (adaptation to multicultural globalization)
Depletions and sustainable production	
Design and architecture	Nutrition and diet
Disaster research	Population regulation
Economic development	Poverty
Education and schools	Refugees and resettlement
Employment and labor	

and the political subservience of peasants are not part of the expertise of sheep breeders, but awareness of these factors nonetheless proved essential to the achievement of their goals.

The Haitian Agroforestry Project

The Haitian Agroforestry Project is a good example of how anthropology can contribute to agricultural development. Planned and directed in its initial phase by anthropologist Gerald Murray, the project has successfully induced Haitian peasants to plant millions of fast-growing trees in steep hillside farmlands threatened by erosion. Depletion of soil as a result of rapid runoff from treeless hillsides has long been recognized as one of Haiti's greatest problems. In addition, trees are needed as a source of charcoal—the principal cooking fuel in poor households—and as a source of building materials. Many other reforestation programs have been tried in Haiti, but they have met with little or no success, either because the funds for planting were squandered or diverted by government bureaucrats or because peasants refused to cooperate and protect the seedlings from hungry goats.

The Haitian Agroforestry Project was designed to avoid both pitfalls. In accepting a $4 million grant

Haitian Agroforestry Project
These trees are of the species Leucaena leucophala *and are about 2½ years old. Several other species are also being planted.*

from the U.S. Agency for International Development (USAID), Murray insisted on an unusual stipulation: No funds were to be transferred to the Haitian government or through the Haitian government. Instead, the funds were to be given to local community groups—private voluntary organizations—interested in peasant welfare. In practice, the majority of these groups were grass-roots religious associations formed by Catholic or Protestant priests, pastors, or missionaries. The project provided these groups with seedlings of fast-growing species matched to local ecological conditions and with expert advisors. The private voluntary organizations, in turn, undertook to assemble and instruct the local farmers and to distribute the seedlings to them free of charge, provided each farmer agreed to plant a minimum of 500 (G. Murray 1984).

> Unless the peasants themselves were motivated to plant the seedlings and to protect them, the project could not succeed.

Murray's analysis of why previous projects had been unable to obtain the peasants' cooperation was based on his firsthand knowledge of Haitian peasant life and on certain principles of anthropological theory. Haitian peasants are market oriented: They produce crops for cash sale. Yet previous attempts to get them to plant trees stipulated that the trees should not be sold. Instead, the peasants were told that they were an unmarketable national treasure. Thus, the trees were presented as exactly the opposite of the cash crops that the peasants planted on their own behalf. Putting himself in the peasants' shoes, Murray realized that previous reforestation projects had created an adverse balance of costs over benefits for the peasants. It was perfectly rational for the peasants to let their goats eat the seedlings instead of donating their labor and land to trees that they would be forbidden to harvest (or could only harvest 30 or 40 years in the future).

Accordingly, Murray decided to distribute the trees as a cash crop over which the peasants would have complete control. The project merely informed the peasants how to plant the trees and take care of them. They were also shown how to set the seedlings in rows, between which other crops could be planted until the trees matured. They were told, too, how fast the trees would grow and how much lumber or charcoal they could expect to get at various stages of growth. Then the peasants were left on their own to decide when it would be in their best interest to cut some or all of them (Murray 1991).

BOX 18.2 | The Theory behind the Haitian Reforestation Project

Gerald Murray predicts that cash-oriented agroforestry will become a major feature of peasant agriculture throughout the Third World. He interprets cash-oriented agroforestry as a response to a set of infrastructural conditions that are similar to the conditions associated with the rise of agricultural modes of production out of hunting and gathering: widespread depletion of a natural resource and population pressure. Peasants, having depleted the trees on which they depend for soil regen-

eration, fuel, and building material, will now find it to their advantage to plant trees as one of their basic crops. In Murray's words (personal communication), "The anthropologically most important element of the model is the diachronic (evolutionary) component in which I am positing a scarcity-and-stress-generated readiness for a repeat in the domain of fuel and wood of the transition from foraging to planting which began some 15 millennia ago in the domain of food."

Over 20 years, about 50 percent of Haiti's farm households have participated in the project, achieving an important conservation goal at very modest cost. The project offered farmers a good cash-earning opportunity on terms they decided themselves. Attitudes toward wood trees have been profoundly modified by the project, not through education or ecological preaching, but by curtailing erosion and successfully using the trees for charcoal and building purposes (Murray and Bannister 2004). (See Boxes 18.2 and 18.3.)

Archeological Knowledge and Agricultural Development

Agricultural development is not exclusively the concern of cultural anthropologists.

Archeological knowledge of the past can contribute directly to technological improvements in the present.

In Bolivia, on the marshy and barren shores of Lake Titicaca, for example, archeological studies have revealed the presence of an intricate system of canals, terraces, and raised fields constructed between 1,000 and 1,500 years ago. During this period, archeological evidence shows, potatoes and the Native American grain called *quinoa* were grown successfully in raised fields despite the freezing conditions that prevail in the high Andes. Further research demonstrated that the ancients were able to grow their crops because the water in the criss-crossing canals absorbed enough heat during the day to prevent killing frosts at night.

American and Bolivian archeologists then proceeded to test their theory by establishing experimental fields that conformed to the ancient design. These experimental fields had crop yields that were at least double those of the other fields. Moreover, severe frosts that decimated the crops grown in the standard modern manner had little effect on those grown in the ancient manner (Erickson and Chandler 1989; Ferraro et al. 1994:211–212).

BOX 18.3 | Coopting the Demon behind Deforestation

Here are Manning's own words on the subject:

"I propose that we look carefully at the 'demon' which is currently blamed for putting the final touches on the environment of Haiti—the market which currently exists for charcoal and construction materials. It is this market, many would argue, which sabotages forever any hopes of preserving the few remaining trees in Haiti.

"I would like to argue that it is precisely this market which can restore tree growth to the hills of Haiti. The demon can be 'baptized' and joined in wedlock to the ecological imperatives whose major adversary he has been up till now. With creative programming we can

turn the tables on history and utilize the awe-inspiring cash-generating energy present throughout Haitian society in a manner which plants trees in the ground faster than they are being cut down. If this is to be done, it must be the peasant who does it. But he will not do it voluntarily or spontaneously unless tree planting contributes to the flow of desperately needed cash into his home. I propose that the mechanism for achieving this is the introduction of cash-oriented agroforestry."

Source: G. Murray 1984:147.

Medical Anthropology

Medical anthropology studies the interaction among culture, disease, and health care.

Anthropologists have, for example, studied the ethnography of everyday life in hospitals, organizations that offer a rich source of jarring discrepancies between the emics of various staff specialists and the etics of patient care. From the perspective of the hospital bureaucracy, its various rules and regulations are designed to promote the health and well-being of patients. In fact, numerous studies have shown that the main effect of many rules and regulations is to shock and depersonalize the patients and to create in them a level of apprehension comparable to that observed in a Ndembu boy awaiting the rite of circumcision in the "place of death."

Unfortunately, discovering what is wrong with hospitals and health care delivery is easier than discovering how to change them for the better. Melvin Konner, an anthropologist and M.D., points out that modern medicine is not a conspiracy against patient autonomy, cultural differences, or any of the other nonmedical dimensions. Instead, physicians are required to practice "defensive medicine" aimed more at protecting themselves against lawsuits than at curing their patients and therefore must rely excessively on technology. But these defects arise from systemic forces rather than the venality of physicians as a group: It is not the fault of physicians. If society lacks compassion for the ill poor—making the doctor–patient encounter intolerably brief, stressful, and inadequate for both—it is neither fair nor productive to blame the doctor or to rail against 'bourgeois' medicine" (Konner 1991:81).

Western medical training is a powerful cultural system that emphasizes technology and an assembly-line approach to efficient medical treatment. Childbirth, for example, is treated in a highly standardized way. The vast majority of U.S. women are hooked up to an electronic fetal monitor and an IV, encouraged to take pain-relieving drugs, given an episiotomy (an incision to prevent tearing), and made to give birth lying flat on their backs, while the doctor stands in control when the baby's head is beginning to emerge. In the words of Robbie Davis-Floyd, "American obstetrical procedures can be understood as rituals . . . (that) are patterned, repetitive, and profoundly symbolic, communicating messages concerning our culture's deepest beliefs about the necessity for cultural control of natural processes" (2005:459).

Most medical practitioners recognize that the way people think and experience illness is influenced by the culture in which they reside. The biomedical paradigm is itself the product of a historical and cultural process.

Biomedicine refers to medicine based on the application of the principles of the natural sciences, especially biology and biochemistry.

Medical anthropologists explore how sickness is culturally constructed—that is, how sickness is understood, what causes ill health and misfortune, and how illness is treated.

Ethnomedicine aims to understand the health-related beliefs, knowledge, and practices of cultural groups.

Applied medical anthropologists try to put **ethnomedical** knowledge at the service of improving medical treatment and health care. This includes applied work in the following settings:

- International health, as consultants to specific programs that try to institute health services and prevention programs on a worldwide basis
- American hospitals serving ethnically diverse communities
- Medical schools to modify the curriculum to provide training to facilitate better communication between physicians and patients
- International programs that promote the cooperation of traditional practitioners within international health programs

The Humoral Theory of Medicine

Humoral medicine conceives the universe as made of opposing qualities—hot and cold, wet and dry—and sees health as a matter of balance between these opposites.

Humoral systems are found in Islamic and popular Hispanic traditions and Ayurveda and Chinese medicine. According to Byron Good (1994), the categories of *warming* and *cooling* do not translate into the English concepts of *hot* and *cold;* but after spending time in a culture that practices humoral medicine, the categories begin to make intuitive sense:

Gender, age, individual temperament and type of illness are all taken into consideration when selecting an herbal remedy for a particular illness or in deciding what foods someone who is ill should avoid. Humoral concepts also provide the basis for special diets followed at particular stages of life. In a Turkish-speaking community, for example, women are known to be weak and cool during the first forty days after delivery, and thus vulnerable to cool illnesses. A special diet of hot foods, such as pistachios and eggs, are given to post-partum women to combat coldness. (Good 1994:102)

Treatment Choice in Medically Pluralistic Settings

 Plural medical systems are characterized by alternative systems of care and multiple usage patterns. People are likely to pursue several treatment alternatives simultaneously ("dual use") or use a sequence of treatments.

In Africa, researchers report medical alternatives that include biomedicine, herbal healing, Christian and Muslim healing, and divination (Janzen 1981). In Taiwan, Kleinman (1980) reports the use of Western doctors, Chinese-style pharmacies, herbalists, and spiritual healers (see also Profile 18.1).

"Health-seeking behavior may involve several steps, such as self-care, then asking a relative, then going to a pharmacy, then going to a health care center. . . . People may go back and forth between resources or use several simultaneously" (Scrimshaw and Hurtado 1987:3). While bioscience clearly surpasses traditional medicine in the treatment of pathogenic disease caused by bacteria, viruses, parasites, or fungi, there are many forms of illness that are subjective in their content.

Medical anthropologists, therefore, use an emic interpretive approach to study the meaning that illness or symptoms have for individuals in given cultural contexts—the personal trauma, life stresses, fears and expectations about the illness, social reactions of friends and authorities, and how people feel about the therapueutic experience. An etic approach, on the other hand, would look at behavioral factors commonly associated with treatment choice, such as the quality and severity of symptoms, insurance status, and barriers to care such as deductibles and co-insurance, levels of distress, and social networks (Mechanic 1986).

AIDS

According to the Center for HIV Information, the 2005 World statistics for HIV/AIDS are as follows:

Adults age 15 to 49 with HIV/AIDS	38,000,000
New HIV infections in 2005	4,900,000
Prevalence of HIV among adults	1.1%
Women age 15 to 49 with HIV/AIDS	17,500,000
Children with HIV/AIDS	2,300,000
Deaths resulting from AIDS	3,100,000

AIDS is mainly a sexually transmitted disease that has a complex epidemiology. The risk for getting AIDS seems to be related to patterns of sexual and related behaviors as exhibited by different populations. One way to stop or slow the spread of the virus and the disease it causes is to identify and modify risk-increasing and risk-decreasing patterns of behavior. Anthropologists are making a contribution to efforts to prevent AIDS by providing detailed ethnographic studies of the behavior of high- and low-risk populations (MacQueen 1994; Merson 1993).

Young women are especially vulnerable to HIV for both biological and social reasons. They are physically more susceptible to infection than men are and they often lack the self-confidence to resist sexual advances or persuade older men to use a condom. In many countries, prevailing gender attitudes mean that male treatment needs often come first. Families are also hesitant to send women to clinics for fear of disrupting the "care economy" that these women provide through their household duties—duties that often include tending to other family members with AIDS (Lalasz 2004).

The case of AIDS among the Baganda of Uganda illustrates the need for detailed ethnographic knowledge. Uganda has one of the highest HIV infection rates in the world—and the rate is highest not among men but among women ages 20 to 30. AIDS prevention programs advise women to protect themselves by sticking to one partner. In theory, this advice corresponds to traditional mating patterns and should be readily accepted. Why then are the infection rates so high?

One problem is that the Baganda have rules for breaking the rule of monogamy. Thus, Baganda women recognize the need to seek an additional partner if they find themselves under severe economic distress. Poor African women who are more likely to have several sexual partners have significantly higher rates of infection. Clearly, therefore, a woman can follow the advice to stick with one man only if she has alternative means of supplementing her income. Moreover, though women may practice monogamy, men traditionally expect to have more than one wife plus additional sexual partners. Finally, most men and women know that condoms reduce the risk of contracting AIDS, but men are adamant in their

PROFILE 18.1   Why the Machiguenga Prefer Native Curers
to Biomedical Health Care Providers

In the Machiguenga community of Kamisea, there is a health post staffed by a Peruvian doctor and nurses who provide virtually free government subsidized biomedical health care. The health post, however, is greatly underutilized by locals because they do not have confidence in the health providers.

The medical personnel do not understand or respect Machiguenga medical beliefs and illness practices. When community members come to the health post, the nurses reprimand them for relying on local remedies and failing to seek care sooner. The Machiguenga are asked about their physical symptoms and are given medication without an explanation of why they are sick, how the treatment will alleviate their suffering, or how to properly administer the medication. A further deterrence is that mothers are met with an impassioned lecture on maternal care, implying that if they truly loved their children, they wouldn't wait so long before bringing them to the health post.

It is therefore no surprise that the Machiguenga prefer to seek medical care from native curers, even though they charge for their services, and go to the health clinic only as a last resort. Curers understand Machiguenga cultural beliefs about illness. They heal by extracting offensive objects from the patient's body, which coincides with the Machiguengan belief that the body is permeable and susceptible to outside intrusions that must be extracted to restore a person's health. Diagnostic techniques include use of steam, touching the body, and eliciting the patient's history and complaints. The curer removes the offensive material from the body, and the patient's family assists by being present and actively participating in the curing process by disposing of the extracted illness-causing substance in the river. This cathartic form of cleansing provides relief to the sufferer and the family and legitimizes the patient's complaints as well as the role of the curer.

Native Healers

A native Machiguenga healer uses steam as a diagnostic technique. He also touches the patient's body and elicits a history of complaints. Illness-causing substances are extracted from the body, and this form of cleansing brings relief to both the patient and the family.

The curer acknowledges the patient's fears and alleviates suffering by labeling the illness, thereby providing meaning as well as treatment. As long the patient's physical suffering, anxiety, and depression go unrecognized by biomedical practitioners, the Machiguenga will continue to seek local therapies that address their physical as well as their emotional needs.

Source: Izquierdo 2001.

---

refusal to use them, and Baganda women cannot refuse to have sex with their husbands (McGrath et al. 1992). Curtailing HIV transmission requires not only changes in sexual behavior but also changes in the material conditions that disempower women and put their lives at risk. Women's greatest vulnerability is their inability to negotiate strength in sexual relations (Schoepf 2001).

A particularly tragic aspect of the AIDS epidemic is that mothers can transmit the virus to their newborns during birth. This outcome is not automatic,

however; not all children of infected mothers become infected. But if they do, they have a short life expectancy. Of all HIV-positive women, intravenous drug users are the least likely to opt for terminating their pregnancies. The reason for this seems obvious: As intravenous drug users, these women have lost their sense of responsibility and are unable to think of the consequences of their behavior for their children. The full extent of their depravity seemingly is revealed by the fact that many of these women already have children for whom they are unable to care and who are being raised by relatives or adoptive parents.

But this reasoning can be stood on its head. An anthropological study carried out in the Bronx, New York, suggests a wholly different interpretation: Women who find themselves isolated by disease, poverty, and drug addiction desperately want to have children of their own to reaffirm their status as women and as human beings. It is the very fact that their children have been taken away from them that motivates them to get pregnant and have another child, despite the terrible risk that they may not be able to see the child grow to adulthood (Pivnik et al. 1991).

Cross-cultural variability in sexual preferences also poses a problem in implementing effective AIDS prevention programs. When AIDS first appeared in Brazil in 1983, it spread rapidly among urban middle-class homosexuals. The virus then continued to spread throughout the population. As we saw in Chapter 14, bisexual behavior in men is not stigmatized as long as a man maintains his masculine identity and assumes the active role. Furthermore, unmarried women are often encouraged to engage in anal sex to maintain their virginity, and married women do so to avoid pregnancy. This greatly increases the chances of viral transmission, even though heterosexual behavior is not considered to be high risk for HIV transmission. More detailed examinations of indigenous categories and classifications of sexual behavior and the social and cultural context of such behavior should enable us to gain a wider understanding of AIDS than is provided by the preconceptions of Western medical science (R. Parker 1987:170–171).

Forensics

 Forensic anthropology uses anthropology to help solve crimes.

Biological anthropologists are highly trained in human anatomy and human biology. Hence, they are often called upon to serve in a **forensic** capacity—that is, to assist the courts and law enforcement agencies in identifying corpses and in determining the circumstances surrounding the deaths of suspected victims of foul play. Careful examination of the skeletal and dental remains enables forensic specialists to identify the sex and age of a corpse and to estimate the date of death and burial and the nature of the implements used against the victim.

An example of anthropological forensics at work has been described by Douglas Ubelaker (1994). He as-

sisted in the identification of a murder victim whose skeleton was found near Rapid City, South Dakota. The police believed that the victim was a Native American man who had been missing for several months. They had a suspect but needed a positive identification of the victim in order to go to trial. Ubelaker determined that the victim was between 30 and 46 years old, that he had died from blows to the face and head from a blunt instrument, and that he was probably of Native American descent. X-rays from the missing man's health records showed healed fractures that matched healed fractures of the victim's leg and elbow. They also showed a small notch on his right shoulder blade that was present on the skeleton. The possibility remained, however, that this notch was not peculiar to the victim but was a feature that occurred quite frequently among Native American populations. To rule out this possibility, Ubelaker examined 200 skeletons in the Smithsonian Institution's collection of Native American skeletons. None of them possessed the notch. The identity of the deceased was confirmed, and the accused murderer was then brought to trial (Ferraro et al. 1994).

Business and Anthropology

Anthropologists have used their knowledge of foreign cultures to help businesses function more successfully in multicultural settings. With the globalization of trade and increase in international joint ventures, corporations have had to open foreign facilities and employ multinational labor forces. At home, U.S. companies have similarly had to hire an ever-growing multiethnic workforce. These companies have not been very adept at handling the wide range of cultural customs, assumptions, and language use that is necessary to function successfully in multicultural and international business arenas. Cultural ignorance often leads to misunderstandings that are costly in terms of lost contracts, ineffective marketing strategies, and labor problems such as low morale and lack of dedication.

Anthropologists have used participant observation and interview techniques to study organizational culture. Ferraro (1994) has observed that business organizations have cultures not unlike those studied by traditional anthropologists. Business organizations, like people in small-scale societies, have corporate myths and rituals, adhere to corporate norms and behaviors, and have socially stratified roles and statuses with conflicting interests and loyalties.

Ethnographic techniques have been used to diagnose management problems afflicting U.S. companies that must train and oversee an ethnically diverse workforce. To retain workers, managers find that they must welcome multiple perspectives. Managers must tap the talents of all employees. By involving employees in the organizational process, companies can more effectively meet their organizations' business goals.

Anthropologist Karen Stephenson applies network analysis to "map" invisible networks in the corporate workplace. She uses an etic approach to identify the communication channels—the basic building blocks of employee networks which, like DNA, all have the same underlying structure. The individuals in these networks have the working knowledge that makes the company function—procedural policies that include knowledge of how products are made or services are delivered. She asks people at each site to describe whom they communicate with the most and what is the content of their interactions. These are the relationships in the organization that show how the work is actually accomplished and who is communicating with whom on an organizational level. These patterns of interaction within a company are the same, regardless of size, industry, or nationality. They all contain people who perform the following roles:

- *Hubs* are well-connected employees who know a lot of people and hold a lot of face-to-face conversations. Hubs are centrally connected to the greatest number of people.

- *Gatekeepers* are the connectors between the hubs who channel information to other employees. For example, when information must funnel through one person on the way to another, you have a gatekeeper. If that person dislikes you, he or she can withhold information and slow down the process.

- *Pulsetakers* are workers who have the most indirect ties. They wield a lot of clout, but it tends to be subtle and beneath the surface. These are people who often operate beneath the radar of upper management.

Such mapping of invisible networks reveals "on the ground" activity not evident from a person's job title or position in the corporate hierarchy. For example, it can show where channels of communication get dammed up, if employees are unable to make simple decisions without approval from higher up, and where there are gaps in communication between groups of employees along racial, gender, or work-specific lines (de Lisser 1998; Johnson 2001).

Poverty and Health

Although the study of poverty might seem to be more appropriate for cultural anthropologists, physical anthropologists actually occupy a key position in the attempt to understand the relationship between poverty and numerous disabilities suffered by the poor, especially children who are poor.

Physical anthropologist Deborah Crooks (1995) has attempted to provide an overview of the intricate feedback that links poor health and performance to disabling cultural and biological conditions under poverty. For example, the ability of children to succeed at school is related to their diets—to the experience of hunger, overconsumption of starchy foods, and breathing and ingestion of toxic substances such as lead. Poor children are disabled by allergens emitted by cockroaches and mites. They tend to have lower birthweights as a result of their mothers' poor health and addiction to tobacco and other drugs. For reasons not completely understood, poor children also grow more slowly and have shorter stature than more affluent children.

Children who are born in poverty and who grow up in poverty may be at extreme disadvantage for cognitive functions and literacy, which again impairs scholastic achievement. Their attention span, dropout rate, school absences, grade repetition, and overall academic performance are all affected adversely.

Crooks concludes with the following comments about the role of biological applied anthropology:

> Biological anthropologists bring a unique perspective and set of skills that enables the linking of biological data to social outcome. . . . Complex multivariate analysis linked to ethnographic data provides a more thorough picture of the lives of children in [the] context of their environments. Collaboration with our cultural colleagues may further enhance our ability to unravel the complex linkages outlined in this model. . . . Continued research of this sort will provide a clearer understanding of the consequences of poverty, enhancing the success of policy implementation resulting from our research. (1995:81)

Witnessing for the Hungry and Homeless

Applied anthropologists may serve as expert witnesses concerning the violation of a group's rights.

Sociocultural anthropologist Anna Lou Dehavenon has studied the causes of urban hunger and homelessness in New York City and has served as an ex-

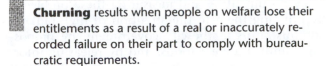

Churning results when people on welfare lose their entitlements as a result of a real or inaccurately recorded failure on their part to comply with bureaucratic requirements.

The requirements most often at issue have to do with failure to keep appointments with a caseworker as indicated in a mailed notification or failure to supply requested information or fill out a questionnaire. The most common reasons for not complying with these administrative rules stem from problems of communication. Mailboxes are frequently broken into; postal employees give up trying to find the person being contacted and mark the envelope "whereabouts unknown." And, of course, a considerable amount of correspondence sent by people in compliance to welfare offices is not routed to the proper desk. Moreover, many welfare recipients are ill and cannot keep their appointments.

Regardless of the reason, the welfare recipients lose their entitlements until their cases can be reopened pending completion of proper forms and other procedures that may take as long as two or three months. While this administrative churning is going on, an estimated 18,000 people a month who are legally entitled to assistance find themselves in a food emergency, which often means that an individual or family has been without solid food for two days or has incurred considerable weight loss over the previous month. Others find themselves without money for rent—hence, the connection between churning and the people showing up at the emergency assistance units (see Box 18.4).

Understanding the Lives of the Homeless
Anthropologists study people who are homeless to understand how agencies can better serve their needs.

pert witness in court cases designed to help the poor. Her work has focused on two problems: the situation of individuals and families who need food and shelter on an emergency basis and the situation of individuals and families whose welfare entitlements have lapsed as a result of bureaucratic apathy and ineptitude.

By doing fieldwork in the city's emergency assistance units, Dehavenon was able to document the failure of these units to find temporary shelter for homeless families until the early hours of the morning. A lawsuit brought against the city used her data to compel the city's Human Resource Administration to find suitable shelter during regular working hours, if possible, but in no case later than midnight.

Dehavenon discovered that the appearance of families seeking emergency food help was also closely connected with the administrative phenomenon known as **churning.**

BOX 18.4 | Apathy or Hostility?

As explained by Dehavenon, "Profound indifference to the plight of the poor may explain their ever-worsening condition of the past several years. Churning, however, is difficult to explain as a product of indifference alone. Rather, it is the direct and logical consequence of a government policy that places a high premium on preventing the erroneous issuance of benefits, but often seems to care much less if eligible recipients are denied the assistance they desperately need to survive. Unless our society is one consumed by hostility to the poor, it must put a stop to this perverse policy and secure for poor people the benefits to which they are entitled" (1989–1990:254).

By documenting and measuring these problems, by bringing them to the attention of high-ranking administrators in the city government, by proposing administrative reforms, and by releasing information to the news media, Dehavenon's 1989–1990 research has helped bring about a substantial reduction in the amount of churning. For example, welfare recipients are now alerted to look for mail setting up appointments. The Human Resources Administration has also made a start toward abandoning the policy of dropping people whose mail comes back "whereabouts unknown" or who fail to return questionnaires. But much remains to be done. These are some of Dehavenon's additional recommendations and goals:

- People who have medical problems or lack a fixed address should receive important notices by messenger.

- All missed appointments should be automatically rescheduled once.

- Recipients should have 60 days to comply with an administrative requirement.

- Their cases should not be closed but suspended so that as soon as they are in compliance, their payments can resume retroactively.

Anthropological Advocacy

The fact that the implementation phase of a project is often controlled by administrators or politicians who will not accept the anthropologist's analysis or suggestions has led a number of applied anthropologists to adopt the role of advocate.

 The **advocacy role** requires the anthropologist to actively support a group of people and often involves political action.

Advocacy anthropologists have fought to improve conditions in women's jails, lobbied in state legislatures for raising welfare allotments, submitted testimony before congressional committees in support of child health care programs, lobbied against the construction of dams and highways that would have an adverse effect on local communities, and engaged in many other consciousness-raising and political activities.

To Advocate or Not to Advocate: Is That the Question?

Despite her involvement with poverty problems, Dehavenon regards herself as an expert witness, rather than as an advocate for the poor. Many applied anthropologists collect relevant knowledge and construct alternative plans but prefer not to be categorized as professional advocates. Some hold the view that the only legitimate professional function of the applied anthropologist is to provide administrators, politicians, and lawyers with objective analyses of a situation or organization and that at most, action should be limited to suggesting but not implementing a plan. In this way, applied anthropologists hope to preserve the scientific standing of anthropology, because an all-out attempt to achieve a practical goal frequently involves rhetorical skills and cajolery and may increase the risk of biased presentations (D'Andrade 1995).

Against this view, advocacy anthropologists insist that the objectivity of anthropology and the other social sciences is illusory and that failure to push for the implementation of a goal represents a form of advocacy in itself. The objectivity is illusory, they argue, because political and personal biases control the commitment to study one situation rather than another (to study the poor rather than the wealthy, for example; see the last section in Chapter 12). And refraining from action is itself a form of action and therefore a form of advocacy because one's inaction assures that someone else's actions will weigh more heavily in the final outcome. Anthropologists who do not actively use their skills and knowledge to bring about what they believe to be solutions simply make it easier for others with opposite beliefs to prevail. Such anthropologists are themselves part of the problem (Scheper-Hughes 1995).

No consensus exists among anthropologists about how to resolve these views of the proper relationship between knowledge and the achievement of controversial practical goals. Perhaps the only resolution of this dilemma is the one that now exists: We must search our individual consciences and act accordingly.

In conclusion, it should be emphasized that we have looked at only a few of the many faces of applied anthropology; many other equally important and interesting cases could have been presented.

SUMMARY
and *Questions to Think About*

1. Applied anthropology is concerned with research that has practical applications. Its core consists of research sponsored by public and private organizations with an interest in achieving practical goals.

2. The role of the applied cultural anthropologist may consist merely in researching the possible means of attaining such goals; sometimes it includes drawing up plans and helping implement them, as well as evaluating the results of implementation.

3. Applied anthropologists involved in implementation are known as practitioners of action anthropology. Beyond that core, other forms of research may also be considered part of applied anthropology. For example, abstract theorizing often has important practical implications, as in the case of studying alternative theories about the causes of underdevelopment or urban poverty.

4. Applied anthropology has three major and distinctive contributions to make to the analysis and solution of urgent practical problems: (a) exposure of ethnocentric biases; (b) a holistic viewpoint stressing the long as well as the short term, the interconnectedness of the parts of a sociocultural system, and the whole of the system as well as its parts; and (c) a commitment to distinguishing etic behavioral events from emic plans and ideologies.

5. All too often, the intended effects of an organization's plans and policies differ sharply from their actual everyday etic consequences.

6. One important focus of applied cultural anthropology is the problem of underdevelopment, which requires a holistic approach to understand the political as well as economic implications of development. The Haitian Agroforestry Project is an example of anthropological research, planning, implementation, and evaluation—in this case, applied to the goal of getting peasants to plant and protect trees. Development projects use a number of methodologies, including knowledge of the archeological record, as in the case of the reconstruction of ancient raised-field agriculture in Bolivia.

7. Another focus of applied anthropology is medical anthropology. Studies of biomedical health care delivery systems and of everyday life in hospitals have attracted considerable interest among anthropologists. Medical anthropologists are also interested in health-related beliefs, knowledge, and practices of alternative and plural medical systems, where people pursue nonbiomedical treatment alternatives.

8. Applied anthropologists have also become involved in the attempt to slow the spread of HIV and AIDS. The epidemiology of AIDS presents puzzles that can be solved only by a detailed ethnographic knowledge of the sexual behavior of people who have and have not contracted the disease.

9. Another interesting domain is applied demographics. Few people realize that sociocultural anthropologists have been called on to study why minority groups are underenumerated in the U.S. Census by as much as 25 percent.

10. Applied physical anthropology also makes many contributions that the public is not aware of. Forensic anthropology provides important services to the criminal justice system.

11. Anthropologists are employed in a number of capacities in business settings. They train people to function successfully in multicultural and international business arenas, and they study the etic networks in corporate settings to improve workplace efficiency.

12. The work of applied anthropologists demonstrates the impact of poverty on health and school achievement and shows that a combination of biological and sociocultural perspectives provides the best way to approach many important social issues.

13. Finally, as brought out in the case of the "churning" of welfare recipients in a merciless bureaucratic machine, anthropologists have a legitimate role in helping people who cannot help themselves.

14. Applied anthropologists work through direct advocacy or through research that is primarily fact finding and objective. Which route to follow is a matter of individual values.

Questions to Think About

1. Why must applied anthropology assume a holistic view? How can long-term effects be different from short-term effects?

2. Why must change-oriented programs avoid ethnocentrism in achieving their goals? What might happen if they do not?

3. Why are both emic and etic approaches important for understanding how organizations work?

4. Why might a target population resist economic change? Under what circumstances is economic change more likely to be accepted?

5. How can anthropologists help corporations at home and abroad?

6. How can applied anthropologists help improve medical care and treatment of disease?

7. How can applied anthropology bring administrative reforms to problems of people who are poor and homeless?

THROUGH THE LENS
of Cultural Materialism

Conformity and Conflict • Reading Four
Fieldwork on Prostitution in the Era of AIDS
Claire E. Sterk

Ethnographic fieldwork shows the importance of gaining firsthand knowledge of people's lives to gain a better understanding of the problems they confront. Fieldwork among prostitutes reveals six themes: women's justifications for engaging in prostitution, women's identities as prostitutes versus drug users, the role of pimps, the impact of AIDS on the women's lives, violence and abuse, and escape from prostitution.

Emic Interpretation

- One of the goals of ethnographic research is to understand a culture through the eyes of its members.

- Ethnography on prostitution describes women's explanations for their work and their experiences on the job. It uses open-ended interviews that allow informants to teach the anthropologist about their lives.

Etic Interpretation

- Etic descriptions are based on criteria important to the anthropologist.

- In this case, the anthropologist asks her subjects to describe their behavior: where the prostitutes work and how they avoid the contraction of sexually transmitted diseases.

Etic Data

- Most prostitutes come from impoverished backgrounds; prostitution gives them an opportunity to make money to support themselves and sometimes to support their drug habit.

- Key individuals central to the local scene are pimps and more senior prostitutes, who function as gatekeepers that protect the prostitutes and screen outsiders.

- Prostitutes and clients include people from all walks of life.

Emic Data

- *Emic categories used by prostitutes to describe different kinds of prostitutes:* There are various kinds of prostitutes: (a) streetwalkers, who work the streets and who do not use drugs; (b) hooked prostitutes, who identify themselves as prostitutes but began using drugs soon after they started working; (c) prostitute addicts, who view themselves mainly as drug users and who became prostitutes to support their drug habit; and (d) crack prostitutes, who trade sex for crack.

- *Emic description of who helps protect prostitutes:* Pimps are entrepreneur lovers who work in prostitution for business reasons. They treat the women as their employees and view them primarily as economic commodities. The more successful a woman becomes in earning a pimp money, the more difficult it is for her to leave him.

- *Emic description of the violence experienced by prostitutes:* Women describe abuse from customers, pimps, and law enforcement.

- *Emic description of how hard it is to get out of the business and establish a new life:* Prostitution follows them like a "bad hangover."

Emic Insight

- The anthropologist spends long periods of time on the streets, where prostitutes hang out, and tries to develop relationships of trust to learn about their experiences, how they explain their situations, and how they feel about their lives.

- The women's explanations for their involvement in prostitution include traumatic past experiences (especially sexual abuse), lack of love experienced as children, pressures by friends and pimps, the need for drugs, and economic necessity.

- Most women dislike the label of *pimp* and prefer to use *old man* or *boyfriend.* Most prostituting addicts and some hooked prostitutes work for a lover pimp, a man who is their steady partner but who also lives off their earnings. Typically, such pimps employ only one woman.

- Society has blamed prostitutes for introducing and spreading sexually transmitted diseases. Similarly, it makes them scapegoats for the spread of HIV/AIDS. Yet their pimps and customers are not held accountable. Although most are knowledgeable about HIV risk behaviors and the ways to reduce them, many misconceptions exist. The women describe the complications associated with condom use. Many women have mixed feelings about HIV testing, wondering how to cope with a positive test result when no cure is available.

- The most common violence prostitutes encounter is from customers. These men often assume that because they pay for sex, they buy a woman. Casual customers pose more of a danger than regulars. The types of abuse the women encounter are emotional, physical, and sexual.

- Ex-prostitutes struggle with the stigma of their past, the challenge of developing a new identity, and the negative impact of their past profession on current intimate relationships.

- Prostitutes often feel there is no opportunity for them to escape the life of prostitution.

- Nevertheless, many women gain a sense of control over their lives; they learn how to manipulate pimps, how to control the types of services and amount of time they spend with customers, and how to select customers. While none of these tactics improves their working conditions, they make the women feel stronger and better about themselves.

THROUGH THE LENS
of Cultural Materialism

Conformity and Conflict • Reading Twelve

Forest Development the Indian Way

Richard K. Reed

The Guaraní Indians combine slash-and-burn horticulture with commercial harvesting of natural products in a manner that maintains their sustainable tropical forest environment. This strategy allows the environment to regenerate and gives the Guaraní an opportunity to develop a commercial product that gives them access to market goods without destroying the forest. However, pressure from outside forces to increase productivity is threatening to take away their sustainability and is in effect deteriorating their mode of production and the well-being of their communities.

Emic Perspective

- The Guaraní once referred to themselves as *ka'aguygua,* or "people of the forest."

- As developers took away their traditional livelihood, they increasingly called themselves *indios,* the pejorative slur used by their nonnative neighbors, because they no longer had the intimate, sustainable relationship with the environment that they once did.

Etic Perspective

- Intensive commercial development focused on short-term profit led the Guaraní to cut down forest, which

was essential for the sustainability of their traditional slash-and-burn mode of production.

- Eventually, they became solely dependent on intensive farming, which caused further environmental degradation.

- This infrastructural change brought social and political changes: The Guaraní became increasingly dependent on outside patrons, which eroded the mutual interdependence of their traditional social organization.

Infrastructure

- Traditional Guaraní farming was well suited to the tropical forest. Because their population density was low and because they practiced a mixture of slash-and-burn agriculture and foraging, they did not overexploit forest resources and allowed the forest to regenerate before it was cleared again.

- The secret to successful slash-and-burn agriculture is field shifting or rotation. Their "swidden" system relies on the cyclic use of a large area of forest, with a part under cultivation and a much larger portion lying fallow in various stages of recomposition.

- Crops flourish the first year and are plentiful the next, but the sun and rain soon take their toll on the exposed soil. By the third year, the soil is overrun with weeds and only manioc tubers can grow. Rather than replant, the Guaraní clear a new field nearby, where soils are naturally more fertile. The old field recovers and is again cleared and replanted within 10 or 15 years.

- Fish also supplied protein for the Guaraní diet and reduced their dependence on agricultural produce. In addition to using hook and line, men captured fish by using a poison extracted from the bark of the timbo vine. Floated over the surface of the water, the poison stunned the fish and allowed them to be caught by hand.

- The forest also supplied a variety of useful products for the Guaraní. They made houses from tree trunks and bamboo stalks; rhododendron vines secured thatched roofs. Villagers collected wild honey and fruit to add sweetness to their diets. If the manioc in the fields was insufficient, wild tubers provided a basic staple. The Guaraní also knew about a wide variety of medicinal plants. They processed roots, leaves, flowers, and seeds to release powerful alkaloids, making teas and poultices for the sick and injured.

- Intensive commercial development in recent years has cleared Guaraní land for fields of cotton, soybeans, and pasture. Where once the land was home for game, it now provides pasture for cattle. Without the forest to provide game, fish, and other products, the Guaraní have become solely dependent on farming and cash crops. Encroaching new settlers have claimed land titles, which has further reduced the Guaraní's terrain. They are now forced to replant without sufficient time for soil regeneration, which causes lower crop yields.

- Poor crop yields, along with the loss of game, has caused malnutrition. Health problems have been further exacerbated by new diseases brought by settlers, for which the Guaraní have little inherited resistance. Tuberculosis has quickly become the major killer in the community.

Structure

- Like most horticulturists, the Guaraní lived in small, widely scattered communities. Homesteads—which consisted of a clearing, a thatched hut, and a field— were scattered throughout the forest, often out of sight of one another. Pathways throughout the forest connected houses to each other and to a slightly larger homestead, that of the *tamoi*, the group's religious leader.

- As in many small societies, households were tied together by kinship, which wove a tapestry of relations that organized social affairs and linked Guaraní communities.

- Their small population afforded them a more personal social organization, one with an emphasis on cooperation and sharing. Although of greater size and complexity than most hunter-gatherer bands, Guaraní villages contained many of the same cultural values found in these nomadic societies.

- Sisters often shared work and child care. Brothers usually hunted together. Food was distributed among members of the extended family, including cousins, aunts, and uncles. Families distributed any surplus with compatriots who had less and expected the same treatment in return. People emphasized the general community welfare, not personal wealth.

- The tamoi, although in no sense a leader with formal authority, commanded considerable respect in the community. He settled disputes, chastised errant juniors, and led the entire community in evening religious ceremonies, where all drank kanguijy (fermented corn) and danced and chanted to the gods.

- Deforestation by commercial development disrupted social institutions. The Guaraní found themselves needing additional cash to buy food and goods. The men were forced to seek work as farmhands, planting pastures and picking cotton on land where they once hunted. The women stayed at home to tend children and till the deteriorating soils of the family farms. The search for wage labor eventually forced whole Guaraní families to move. Entire families left home for hovels they constructed on the land of their employers. From independent farmers and gatherers, they became tenants of *patrones* (landowners), who prohibited the Guaraní farmhands from planting gardens of their own. The displaced Guaraní were thus forced to buy all their food, usually from the patrones themselves.

Superstructure

- The forest is basic to indigenous cosmology. Villagers often name their children after the numerous forest songbirds, a sign of their close personal ties to the environment.

- The Guaraní traditionally relied on a complex knowledge of how the forest works and how it can be used. They distinguished among a variety of ecozones, each with a unique combination of soil, flora, and fauna. In all, the Guaraní distinguished among nine resource zones; the subtle distinctions among ecozones enabled them to use the forest to its best benefit.

- Environmental destruction caused by commercial development has taken a psychological toll on the Guaraní. They have become depressed, get drunk on cheap cane liquor, and all too often commit suicide. A number of suicides were noted among the Guaraní in Brazil in the 1990s, and subsequent research in Paraguay showed that indigenous people were killing themselves at almost 50 times the national average. The epidemic hit 15- to 24-year-olds the hardest. These young people saw little future for themselves, their families, and their people.

- As individuals and families left the Guaraní villages in search of work on surrounding farms and ranches, tamoi leaders lost influence. It became impossible to gather disparate relatives and friends for religious rituals. The distances were too great for the elders' nieces and nephews to seek counsel and medicines. The tamoi could neither control nor explain the changing world.

THROUGH THE LENS
of Cultural Materialism

Conformity and Conflict • Reading Twenty-Four

Cross-Cultural Law: The Case of the Gypsy Offender

Anne Sutherland

Differences in cultural standards can lead to conflict when members of minority ethnic groups refuse to assimilate. Gypsies residing in the United States create distance between themselves and the population within which they live and have been victimized because their traditions are different from those of the dominant culture. Gypsies exploit multiple occupational opportunities and use relatives' social security numbers with no criminal intent. This is, however, a felony in the United States, and the case of S. N. shows that a lack of cultural understanding can produce negative consequences for all parties.

Emic Interpretation

- Gypsies do not seek to become integrated into the dominant culture. They value their separateness and rely on kin support, rather than government assistance. They share resources with their kin, including social security numbers, to take advantage of business opportunities.

- When one of them used a relative's social security number to purchase a car, the government interpreted the action as criminal—namely, as an intention to steal.

Etic Interpretation

- The gypsies are a marginal cultural group that has historically been persecuted and driven away.

- They typically engage in occupations where they can be competitive by pooling resources and holding down costs.

- They often live outside the law and survive by manipulating the system to their advantage.

Infrastructure

- Gypsies are traditionally a nomadic people who exploit marginal employment opportunities.

- Gypsies remain outside the legal system; they occupy a niche that allows them to provide cheap services to other marginal populations, such as the urban poor.

Structure

- Gypsies frequently borrow each other's "American" names and social security numbers, viewing them as a kind of corporate property of their cognatic descent group, or *vitsa*. Within members of a vitsa, identification is corporate in nature. Members of the group have corporate access to property owned by other members of the group.

- The rights and statuses of individual gypsies are directly linked to their membership in a vitsa. Reciprocity between members is expected, as families share economic resources, stay in each other's homes, help each other in work and preparation of rituals, and loan each other cars, information, identification, and money.

- The U.S. government bureaucracy stresses the importance of individuality and individual identification in legal matters. This clashes with the gypsies' ideology, which considers descent and extended family ties as the defining factors for identification.

Superstructure

- American culture has derived negative stereotypes of gypsies because of their marginal position in society.

- While Gypsies use many American names, individuals have only one gypsy name because it is difficult to translate their names into English.

- The clash between S. N. and the U.S. bureaucratic system stems from gypsy reliance on corporate kinship identity versus the American belief in individual rights and responsibilities.

- Gypsy culture follows essential rules of cleanliness. Residing in a dirty prison and eating the food of nongypsies causes a gypsy to become *marime,* a condition of ritual impurity that results in being shunned by one's relatives and other gypsies and ultimately leads to physical exile from the community.

- S. N. was distressed in jail because gypsies avoid situations that require them to be in prolonged contact with nongypsies. He was worried that he would become *marime.*

THROUGH THE LENS
of Cultural Materialism

Conformity and Conflict • Reading Twenty-Five
Notes from an Expert Witness
Barbara Joans

Cross-cultural misunderstandings are bound to arise in multicultural societies. Anthropologists can shed light on alternate perspectives for understanding the motivations and behaviors of people from different cultural backgrounds. Below are three examples of situations where knowledge derived from participant observation was useful in resolving cultural conflict.

Case 1

- Social services claimed that six Shoshoni women failed to declare rental income of about $2,000 each and therefore were required to refund SSI benefits (supplemental security income) they received from the government. The women claimed that they didn't know they had to include the income in their annual statement, and the dispute ended up in court.

- The anthropologist determined that although all six women could speak and understand everyday English, only one of them could understand English nuances, and none understood the English used by the government. The women were cleared of misconduct because of cultural misunderstanding due to a lack of language proficiency.

Case 2

- A deceased Plains Indian family member who had left the reservation over 50 years earlier had died and been cremated by mistake. The family sued the funeral home for substantial damages because cremation was forbidden and believed to prevent the dead from resting in peace.

- The Indian family claimed that according to their religion, cremation was an abomination and the dead man would never be able to travel back to his homeland.

- Through her research, the anthropologist discovered that under certain unusual circumstances, cremation

had occurred in Indian society. She also learned that Indians conduct funeral ceremonies in many ways and that sometimes they are done even in the absence of physical remains. It was therefore possible to have a memorial service even though the bodily remains were in the form of ash.

- The anthropologist also pointed out that under traditional circumstances, Indian family members would not spend 50 years without seeing an important relative.

- In the end, the anthropologist's report brought an out-of-court settlement between the Plains Indian family and the funeral home.

Case 3

- A father and mother battled for custody of their 2-year-old daughter. The father wanted shared custody, whereas the mother wanted sole custody. The mother was planning a second marriage and intended to live abroad.

- The court psychologist determined the mother to be the better parent because she could offer the child a nuclear family with a stay-at-home mother and a new half-sibling.

- The anthropologist, however, pointed out that the father was also an excellent parent. He lived close to his own parents and siblings; the child had cousins to play with and grandparents who also assumed a custodial role. The anthropologist compared the father's situation to that of an extended family, "fully operational and amazingly functional."

- The court psychologist, however, favored the mother as the custodial parent because it was believed that she could provide a more favorable home environment.

- The anthropologist's report did not help the father win custody because it was stipulated that only one social science professional (the court-appointed psychologist) was permitted to submit a written evaluation.

THROUGH THE LENS
of Cultural Materialism

Conformity and Conflict • Reading Thirty-Five

Medical Anthropology: Improving Nutrition in Malawi

Sonia Patten

Medical anthropology can help identify how to improve infant and child nutrition in developing countries, where children often become undernourished when they are weaned from their mothers' breast. The goal of the project is to find appropriate ways for women in Malawi to help their children survive during periodic hunger seasons, when there is insufficient food to feed the population.

Etic Perspective

- Villagers in Malawi raise goats for meat but seldom eat them. Goats are owned by the men and serve as "bank accounts," which are cashed in when money is needed.

- Village women in Malawi breastfeed their children for two to three years, providing them with sufficient protein and calories, and then feed them corn gruel when they are weaned. Corn, however, is low in protein and nutritionally inadequate.

- A decision was made to introduce protein-rich goat's milk to rural women and to teach them how to care for the goats and safely handle the milk.

- Researchers bred several varieties of goats with the local variety and found the South African Saanes goats to be the most hardy. The goats were cross-bred and distributed to the villagers.

- Because the villagers could not afford to buy the goats, they were asked to return the first healthy kid to the collage farm, required to attend demonstrations on the care and handling of the goats, and asked to allow researchers to measure and weigh their children each week.

- Animal theft became a problem when a family from another village started to steal the goats. The women responded by taking their goats with them to the fields and into their houses at night.

- Children who received goat milk showed steady weight and other significant health gains.

Emic Perspective

- Everyone acknowledged that the children were suffering from malnutrition, and the death of a child caused great sorrow to the family.

- At first, the men in the community objected to allowing the women to own dairy goats because they were con-

cerned it would impact social relations. The men subsequently agreed because the goats were for the children, who were suffering from malnourishment.

- Overall, people's responses were positive. The only problem was that the women objected to having their children measured because it seemed as if they were being measured for coffins.

- When the children's growth reached a plateau, the village women understood why goat milk was not available (a goat had to have two kids before it produced a suitable doe) and asked researchers for help in growing soybeans, which could be ground into flour to feed the children.

Infrastructure

- Malawi has an agricultural mode of production, with many crops designated for export. Droughts, floods, and soil depletion and erosion make food production more difficult. A high rate of inflation and low prices for cash crops make it difficult to supplement the diet. The annual hungry season typically runs from December through March, although people sometimes start to run out of food as early as September.

- Three out of five children in Malawi are undernourished. After being weaned, the children have a high-carbohydrate diet and often fail to thrive. There is a 24 percent mortality rate.

- The people of Malawi depend of the International Monetary Fund for outside assistance.

Structure

- The native Chewa people of Malawi are matrilineal with matrilocal residence. Married women live in their villages of birth with related females, and men live in their brides' villages.

- Both men and women do agricultural work, although men traditionally own livestock.

- The Chewa chief is a man who inherits his position from his mother's brother. Approval from the chief is necessary to allow the women to own the goats.

Superstructure

- The people of Malawi value their children and so participated in the program, despite their reluctance to allow the women to own goats.

- Everyone supported the program because it was acceptable to the local people and they were able to have input.

THROUGH THE LENS
of Cultural Materialism

Conformity and Conflict • Reading Thirty-Six
Using Anthropology
David W. McCurdy

Anthropology can make a unique contribution to the study of organizations by viewing them as microcultures. It utilizes a *holistic* approach, which assumes that the components of a culture are interrelated and that a change in one component will affect the others, as well as participant observation and qualitative research to understand problems from the perspective of the participants (emic view). In business, holistic and qualitative research has the advantage of looking for solutions that take workers' knowledge and feelings into account. This increases workers' satisfaction and ultimately results in higher productivity.

Etic Perspective

- A manager, Susan Stranton, with a background in anthropology was hired by a division of a large corporation called UTC, which shipped educational materials to customer outlets around the United States. She was told to improve service and gain control of the warehouse inventory.

- Stranton approached the problem as stemming from a misunderstanding between two departments (or microcultures) and questioned the workers in both departments about their jobs to understand how the system worked and how they perceived the inventory problem.

Emic Perspective

- The new manager interviewed the workers in the customer outlets of the corporation to understand what poor service meant to them:

  1. It took too long for learning materials to arrive; the quantities were incorrect; and the materials arrived in poor condition (books were dented or gouged).

  2. The customer outlet department was charged for the number of materials that was ordered, not for the number that was actually sent.

  3. Employees felt that warehouse workers were to blame; they felt they were lazy and uncaring.

- The warehouse workers explained their problems:

  1. They felt rushed and overburdened.

  2. Books sent to the warehouse came in large boxes that were too heavy for the women to lift and carry.

  3. Books were improperly packed and arrived damaged from transit.

  4. Books were loosely stacked and took too long to count.

  5. There were often discrepancies between the number logged in on the computer and the actual number available for shipping.

Solution

- The discovery of the fundamental causes of the problem made it easier to devise a solution. Shrink-wrapping books in set quantities made it easier to keep track and count the inventory. Also, using smaller shipping boxes made it easier for employees to lift and carry the inventory.

Outcome

- By talking directly to the employees, the manager/anthropologist was able to address many of their concerns. This made employees feel that their opinions counted and that management cared about them.

CHAPTER **19**

GLOBALIZATION

Multinational corporations are increasingly gaining influence around the world.

U ntil now, we have presented a static view of culture, showing how cultural differences and similarities can be explained through an understanding of infrastructure and structure. We have discussed a range of cultures, using the ethnographic present without reference to time. In this chapter, we look at global culture within a broad historical context to show how the present-day global economy evolved and is responsible for the changes taking place in traditional cultures today.

What Is Globalization?

The term *globalization* was first coined in the 1980s to refer to changes in the world economic system: the fusing of national markets through the removal of protectionist barriers that stimulated free movement of capital and paved the way for the emergence of **multinational corporations.**

 Multinational corporations are not economically tied to or dependent on any single country. They have manufacturing plants in several countries and move their facilities in search of cheaper labor, lower taxes, and favorable government regulation.

The concept of globalization, however, dates back centuries to early colonialism, when European trading empires increased their power and wealth by using the labor and resources of less powerful regions. They colonized areas where people still lived directly off the land and where natural resources were plentiful. Colonizers sought to acquire new resources and productive land and to gain strategic positions against rival nations in political and military confrontations.

During the 1600s, several Western European countries—led by Portugal, the Netherlands, Spain, France, and Britain—used their colonial territories to obtain goods for consumption and trade. In the late eighteenth century, the Industrial Revolution brought mechanized production to many nations and ushered in a second period of **colonialism.**

 Colonialism is the political and economic domination of a territory and its people by a foreign power through conquest, settlement, and exploitation.

Industrialization began in Britain and soon spread to North America, much of Western Europe, and some Pacific nations, such as Japan. Industrialized countries could produce much larger quantities of goods and resources than previously had been possible. To achieve this level of production, they relied on colonies to provide raw materials for building and powering machines and for supplying their factories. The industrialized countries and many of the people living in them experienced increases in wealth and ease of access to essential resources, including clothing, building materials, and staple foods.

Interest in **postcolonial** studies rose in the 1980s. Research focused on relations between wealthy nations and their former colonies and on the lasting impact of colonialism on local cultures, particularly on how the experiences and identities of local cultures have been affected by colonization.

 Postcolonial refers to study of the interactions between European nations and the societies they colonized, both during colonialism and after. In a broader sense, *postcolonial* is used to signify a position against imperialism and Eurocentrism.

Colonialism and Underdevelopment

Most of the underdeveloped nations of today are former colonial dependents. The phenomenon of underdevelopment has not arisen because the peoples of the underdeveloped world have been lazy. If anything, they have worked too hard. But their labor has been wasted on producing tropical and semitropical plantation crops—sugar, cotton, tea, tobacco, sisal, hemp—which steadily brought lower prices per man-hour relative to the value of industrial products in international trade. Most of the regions and countries that gave themselves over to the tropical and semitropical plantation crops did so as a result of being conquered and made into colonies.

The wealth produced in these colonies was used to further the development of Europe, rather than the development of the lands where the crops were grown and the work was performed. This happened in several ways: through taxation, through interest on bank loans to buy slaves and milling machinery, and through one-sided trade relations that compelled colonies to purchase commodities above world market prices. Even when the colonists accumulated capital, they frequently were forbidden by law or by the tax structure from establishing businesses that might compete with those of the Europeans. It was to end such colonial restrictions that the 13 North American colonies took up arms against England in 1776.

The more tropical the land, the more desirable it was as a colony. The most lucrative crops were those that could not be grown at home. Moreover, tropical crops were less likely to disturb the politically powerful landed aristocracies at home. But as new colonial regions were brought into production for the world market, the prices of tropical and semitropical crops declined in relationship to manufactured goods.

One way to compensate for declining prices is to increase labor productivity through technological improvements. This is what has happened in the agricultural sectors of the industrial nations. But in the colonies, it was profitable to grow cheap crops for export for hundreds of years without raising productivity through capital improvements. Instead of investing in machinery, fertilizers, and other production facilities, colonial entrepreneurs made profits by keeping labor costs down to the barest minimum without investing in improved production facilities.

Why has underdevelopment persisted—and even grown worse—now that so many countries have won their independence? No general formula can hope to explain all the predicaments of the postcolonial era. Differences in developmental potential are associated with (1) endowments of natural resources; (2) population size and population density; (3) the degree of exploitation under colonialism; (4) the conditions under which freedom was obtained (e.g., whether through unifying wars of liberation or through hasty withdrawal of bankrupt administration); and (5) the degree of cultural, linguistic, and ethnic unity. In the case of Africa, as discussed in Chapter 13, the Europeans not only prevented Africans from developing an industrial infrastructure but also exhausted the gold mines and other raw materials

One basic problem of the former colonial countries is the handicap of having a late start: They are like the bicycle manufacturer who wants to start making automobiles or the kite manufacturer who would like to produce airplanes. After a certain level of technological and organizational competence has been reached in a particular industry, it becomes increasingly difficult for latecomers to compete. Also, after the colonial powers divested their holdings, they left a political vacuum. The international community is laden with small nation-states carved out at the last minute from former empires, unable to secure either sovereignty or economic solvency, and with large nation-states erected without a common ethnic base. Many of the world's postcolonial areas have been scenes of protracted and violent ethnic and religious conflict, such as the Arab–Israeli conflict, clashes between India and Pakistan, and wars in Rwanda, Somalia, Afghanistan, and the Balkans. The end of colonialism did not bring with it politically stable nation-states, nor did it bring a new era of peace and prosperity.

Sociocultural Evolution and Development

As we saw in Chapter 5, sociocultural evolution is the result of population growth, which depends on intensification of the food supply through technology and the organization of production (infrastructural and structural changes than enable people to produce more food per unit of land). This process, as noted in Chapters 10 and 11, involves three correlates to population growth: subsistence intensification, political integration, and social stratification. At each level of sociocultural development, there are two distinct economies: the **subsistence economy**, which is geared toward meeting basic human needs and is managed at the household level, and the **political economy**, geared to maximizing production for use by social, political, and religious institutions, which over time evolve into a ruling elite.

The Industrial Revolution

The Industrial Revolution is known as the fourth great technological leap of humankind, after the urban revolution, the domestication of plants and animals, and the dawn of culture itself. But the Industrial Revolution entailed more than just the invention of industrial technology. It also signified the rise of **commercialization** (Bodley 1996).

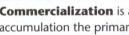 **Commercialization** is a process that makes capital accumulation the primary objective and leads to the production of great inequalities of wealth and power.

The economy is transformed through commercialization from a process that produces goods and services to meet basic human needs to an "autonomous entity whose growth is considered essential for well-being" (1999:20).

Given the late start of former colonial countries, one solution was to open underdeveloped countries to commercialization and actively to encourage foreign industrial investment. However, this process has shown little prospect of raising per capita income fast enough to outpace population growth. In many instances, such as in the contrast between the industrial and agricultural regions of Brazil, the principal effect of large-scale foreign investment has been a lopsided distribution of income within the country. The reason for this is that the type of industrial sector that is developed is limited to what is convenient to the multinational corporations with respect to their previously established enterprises. Profits of multinational corporations are withdrawn as dividends, rather than reinvested to generate further technological innovation. The amount of capital withdrawn from underdeveloped countries in the form of profits and payments on loans is generally greater than the amount invested.

The Green Revolution

All too often, development has been viewed as a narrow problem that can be solved simply by technological change. Development, however, is a problem that also requires an understanding of political, economic, and ecological processes on an anthropological scale. The so-called **Green Revolution** well illustrates the calamitous possibilities inherent in development approaches that disregard the relationships between technology and environment, on the one hand, and between politics and economy, on the other.

The Green Revolution had its origin in the late 1950s in the dwarf varieties of "wonder wheat" developed by a Nobel Prize winner, plant geneticist Norman Burling at the Rockefeller Foundation's Ciudad Obregon research center in northwest Mexico.

The **Green Revolution** was designed to increase grain yields through the use of miracle seeds as a key to ending world hunger.

Designed to double and triple yields per acre, wonder wheat was soon followed by dwarf varieties of "miracle rice" engineered at a joint Rockefeller and Ford Foundation research center in the Philippines. The significance of the dwarfed forms is that short, thick stems can bear heavy loads of ripe grain without bending over. On the basis of initial successes in Mexico and the Philippines, the new seeds were hailed as the solution to the problem of feeding the expanding population of the underdeveloped world and were soon planted in vast areas of Pakistan, India, and Indonesia (Cloud 1973) (see Profile 19.1). Although the new seeds have resulted in a definite increase in output per area, they have done so only at considerable economic and social cost.

The main problem with the miracle seeds is that they were engineered to outperform native varieties of rice and wheat only if grown in fields that have been heavily irrigated and treated with enormous inputs of chemical fertilizers, pesticides, insecticides, and fungicides. Without such inputs, the high-yield varieties perform little better, and sometimes worse, than the native varieties, especially under adverse soil and weather conditions. Irrigated croplands form only 30 percent of Asian croplands (Wade 1973) (see Profile 19.2). Most peasants in the underdeveloped world not only lack access to adequate amounts of

irrigation water, but they are unable to pay for expensive chemical fertilizers and other chemical inputs. This means that unless extraordinary support efforts are made by the governments of countries switching to the miracle seeds, the chief beneficiaries of the Green Revolution will be the richest farmers and merchants, who already occupy the irrigated lands and who are best able to pay for the chemical inputs (see Box 19.1).

While production increased, only wealthy farmers, who owned the most land, reaped the benefits of the Green Revolution. Many of the poorest farmers had to sell their land and move to the cities, where they became unskilled laborers.

Limits to Technification and Industrial Growth

During the past decades, many anthropologists and economists have become disillusioned with the possibility and desirability of achieving development by means of advanced industrial technologies and production methods. Rather than emulate the experience of the industrial nations, greater consideration is now being given to raising living standards by means of *intermediate* or *appropriate* types of technologies. Such technologies use local materials and preexisting skills, have high labor demand and low-energy budgets, and raise production efficiency without destroying the continuity of the local culture. This approach has been stimulated by the recognition that the prosperity of wealthy countries is threatened by the side effects of industrialization, such as pollution, and by the rapidly increasing costs of fossil fuels. Energy considerations alone show that U.S. agribusiness cannot be exported intact to the rest of the world.

Bullock versus Tractor

Reliance on appropriate or intermediate technology for development involves a commitment to low-energy rather than high-energy production processes, recycled rather than new materials, and renewable rather than nonrenewable resources. An example of an appropriate technology that is currently being considered as an alternative to technification in India is the use of bullock (oxen) power instead of tractors. Some 83 million bullocks are already in use. They are fed mainly on renewable agricultural by-products such as straw from grains supplemented with cotton seed or sesame seed. Unlike tractors, bullocks recycle their fuel by producing dung, which is used as fertilizer. They can be produced and maintained by

PROFILE 19.1 | The Green Revolution in Java

Richard Franke (1974, 1975) studied the Green Revolution in central Java. He describes three phases of the Indonesian government's attempt to distribute miracle rice:

- In Phase I, the government gave loans to individual peasants for purchase of the high-yield rice seeds and chemical inputs. The poorest peasants, desperately in need of cash, sold the fertilizers on the black market; others defaulted on the loans. Corruption and mismanagement among the officials who disbursed the loans and seeds created additional problems, and the program was stopped.

- Phase II began in 1969. The government, having lost faith in its own ability to distribute the miracle seeds, contracted for a number of multinational corporations to do the job. For each hectare converted to miracle rice, the corporations received $54. Peasants were again given loans by the government to pay for the seeds and chemicals, to be repaid with one-sixth of the rice harvest. The loans were to be collected by the army. To make certain that prescribed amounts of insecticides were applied on schedule, the corporations hired planes and pilots to spray a million hectares from the air, endangering the fish in the ponds and the water buffalo, not to mention the peasants themselves. At harvest time, the peasants underreported the quantity of rice they had grown in order to lower the amount they would have to hand over to the army in repayment of their loans, and the army overestimated the amount produced in order to enlarge their personal cut of the one-sixth due the government. Phase II ended when it was discovered that the corporations were getting $2 for every $1 worth of rice that the army said it was getting from the peasants. Miracle rice was costing $305 a ton to produce, when the world market price of ordinary rice was $130 a ton.

- Phase III began in 1970. The government shipped the seeds and chemicals to local warehouses, and peasants took out low-cost loans and were "free" to use the seeds and inputs as they saw fit. Despite the fact that yield increases of up to 70 percent were being obtained, in the village studied by Franke, only 20 percent of the farming households had joined the

Tending Rice Fields

Governments in Asia have encouraged farmers to cultivate new varieties of rice and use chemical fertilizers and pesticides. This has helped well-to-do farmers but brought greater poverty to small-scale farmers, who were the intended beneficiaries of the program.

program. The chief beneficiaries were the farmers who were already better off than average, owned the most land, and had adequate supplies of water. The poorest families did not adopt the new seeds. They made ends meet by working part time for well-to-do farmers who lent them money to buy food. The rich farmers prevented their part-time workers from adopting the new seeds. The rich farmers feared that they would lose their supply of cheap labor, and the poor farmers feared that if they cut themselves off from their patrons, they would have no one to turn to in case of sickness or drought.

Franke concludes that the theories behind the Green Revolution are primarily rationalizations for ruling elites who are trying to find a way to achieve economic development without the social and political transformation that their societies need.

traditional means right in the countryside, whereas tractors make farmers dependent on distant factories and urban specialists in India and abroad for maintenance and replacement.

But what about the relative efficiency of bullocks and tractors? Surprisingly enough, it is very difficult to show that if tractors replaced bullocks, the average farmer would be any better off. While a 35-horsepower

PROFILE 19.2 | Priests and Irrigation Technology in Bali

For centuries, farmers in the wet-rice terraces of Bali relied on priests of local "water temples" to coordinate irrigation among hundreds of farming communities. The Balinese agricultural tradition entailed complex processes that optimized water sharing, reduced pest infestations, and successfully produced rice and other food crops. During Asia's Green Revolution in the early 1970s, the zealous spread of new agricultural technologies that promised to radically increase rice production proved disastrous for Balinese agriculture.

According to Stephen Lansing (1991), the water temples were either ignored or misunderstood by foreign planners. Ranging from mountain lakes to seacoast, water temples were an instrumental part of a delicately balanced system of cooperation between neighboring farmers, steeped in symbolic ritual activities such as food offerings to the deities. Due to the rigorous social coordination orchestrated through the water temples, pest levels were minimized and water sharing optimized in the rice paddies.

In the fervor of the Green Revolution, the Indonesian government persuaded Balinese farmers to adopt new fertilizers, pesticides, and cultivate hardy "miracle rice" in a multimillion dollar scheme of modernization. Farmers were pressured to plant rice as frequently as possible and to disregard the traditional irrigation schedules of neighboring paddies. After a brief increase in productivity, crops dwindled drastically because of water shortages and infestation by vermin. Balinese farmers began pressing the government for a return to irrigation scheduling by the water temples but were castigated for their religious conservatism and resistance to change.

In 1987, Lansing and his collaborators produced a computer simulation using historical rainfall data to show that the traditional water temple system was far more effective than the government's current policy. Officials finally acknowledged their mistake, and development agencies encouraged Balinese rice farmers to return to the system that had served them well for over a thousand years. Clearly, these ancient traditions have wisdom we can learn from.

Source: Adapted from Lansing 1991.

---

tractor can plow a field almost 10 times faster than a pair of bullocks, the initial investment in the tractor is more than 20 times greater than the investment in the bullocks. Moreover, the cost per hour of tractors remains greater than the cost per hour of bullocks, unless the tractor is used more than 900 hours per year. This implies that tractors are cheaper than bullocks only on very large farms. But the majority of Indian farms are very small, and the use of tractors could be justified only if elaborate provisions were made to lease or rent the machines. Similar provisions, however, could also easily lower the cost of using bullock power. Hence, given the enormous initial expense in converting from bullocks to tractors, it may be more economical to concentrate on ways of improving bullock power by breeding programs, changes in cropping patterns, and land tenure, thereby increasing bullock working hours and lowering costs still further.

This example suggests that in countries poorly endowed with industrial sources of energy, much of the development process will have to be carried out by socially more efficient and more equitable management of existing means of production, rather than by the introduction of a new technological base. (See Box 19.2,

---

BOX 19.1 | Who Benefits from the Green Revolution?

Much of the enthusiasm for the Green Revolution originated in the boardrooms of multinational corporations that sell the chemical inputs and industrial hardware essential for agribusiness systems. In the Philippines, for example, Exxon (formally Esso) played a key role in the introduction and marketing of high-yield rice. This company opened 400 stores throughout the Philippines and hired a sales staff of hundreds of agent–representative–entrepreneurs, who served as extension agents to promote the rice program and train farmers (U.S. Agency for International Development 1971). The Philippine government, for its part, provided the loans with which the farmers bought the packages containing the fertilizers and other chemicals produced by Exxon at a government-subsidized factory.

BOX 19.2 | The Emergence of American "Superfarms"

The United States is the true birthplace of the Green Revolution, and its success has been largely due to the emergence of "superfarms." Improved seeds combined with chemical fertilizers and pesticides have pushed corn yields up nearly threefold since 1950, with smaller but still significant gains for wheat, rice, and soybeans. Since World War II, as larger harvests have pushed down the prices farmers get for their crops while the costs of farming have shot up, farmers' profit margins have been drastically narrowed. By the early 1990s, production costs had risen from about 50 percent to over 80 percent of gross farm income.

So who survives today? Two very different groups: those few farmers who chose not to buy into industrialized agriculture and "superfarmers" who are able to keep expanding their acreage to make up for their lower per-acre profit. Among this second group are the top 1.2 percent of farms by income, those with $500,000 or more in yearly sales. In 1969, the superfarms earned 16 percent of net farm income; by the late 1980s, they garnered nearly 40 percent.

Superfarms triumph not because they are more efficient food producers or because the Green Revolution technology itself favored them but because of advantages that accrue to wealth and size. They have the capital to invest and the volume necessary to stay afloat even if profits per unit shrink. They have the political clout to shape tax policies in their favor. Another reason superfarms have prospered is that farmland is bought and sold like any other commodity, and society allows the unlimited accumulation of farmland by corporations who come to replace family farms. Moreover, small farmers and farm workers lack bargaining power relative to suppliers of farm inputs and food marketers, so smaller-scale producers get a shrinking share of the rewards from farming.

Big-Business Farming

Superfarms have prospered because farmland is bought and sold like any other commodity. Large corporations have accumulated so much land that small farmers no longer have bargaining power and are left with a shrinking share of profits.

Source: Adapted from Lappe et al. 1998.

however, to learn about the application of technology on U.S. farms.)

Free Market versus Antimarket Forces

The real social transformation brought by industrialism is through the self-regulating ("free") market and neoliberalism. Many observers celebrate the triumph of the self-regulating market for transforming the world into one global economic system. Others,

however, argue that antimarket forces must be instituted to curb excessive exploitation.

In the United States, *economic liberalism* (not to be confused with *political liberalism*) refers to abolition of government intervention in economic matters. The theory dates back to 1776, when English economist Adam Smith published *The Wealth of Nations*, which stated that free trade was the best way for a nation's economy to develop. Economic liberalism prevailed in the United States until the Great Depression of the 1930s, when it became apparent that full employment is necessary for capitalism to grow and that the government and central banks should intervene and increase employment. This led to President Franklin D. Roosevelt's New Deal, which put people back to work through government-sponsored work programs.

During the past 30 years, liberal economics has reemerged—hence the term **neoliberalism**, or a new kind of liberalism.

 Neoliberalism refers to free enterprise, or "the rule of the market." It suggests that an unregulated market is the best way to increase economic growth, which will ultimately benefit everyone.

Neoliberalism suggests the following:

- Cutting public expenditure for social services and instituting a sense of individual responsibility, in which people are required to find solutions to their problems on their own within the framework of the free market

- Deregulation and the reduction of government regulation that would limit profits

- Privatization of state owned enterprises to private investors, including all key industries such as schools, hospitals, banks, railroads, and the like, which would be run with greater efficiency and less waste

The adaptive aspects of the self-regulating market long preceded the Industrial Revolution. This *market principle*—referring to transactions where the value of the goods and services exchanged is set by supply and demand—is found in marketplaces in nonindustrial societies where no liberal state exists. Trading posts where people exchange their specialized production, silent trade, trade in the kula ring, and barter between pastoralists and farmers all exhibit an opportunistic effort to maximize personal benefit in light of local supply and demand, even where the institutional framework of a liberal state is lacking. The market principle, in fact, is found wherever bargaining takes place and solves many problems in the subsistence economy without control or direction by elites. Individuals approach transactions as opportunities to obtain what they lack by offering what they can afford to give up. Each individual is empowered to make the best deal he or she can, given the realities of the situation.

 The **antimarket critique** is that the free market promotes an egocentric individualism that dissolves the integrity of society. The market creates and sustains class inequalities, which increases suffering for the great majority of workers while opening the door to consumption excesses for an exclusive few.

The **antimarket critique** consists of two forms:

- One recognizes that the free market dissolves social bonds, leaving individuals to stand alone against an overwhelming array of power centers that seek to exploit market opportunities to their own benefit

- The other is based on the potential damage market behavior does to ecology and the environment. It points to the role of markets in environmentally destructive activities like deforestation, fisheries depletion, pollution, and global warming.

The antimarket critique assumes that the proper role of government is to place restraints on aggrandizers in the market in order to enhance values other than greed and bring about a fair distribution of wealth (so-called distributive justice; see Plattner 1989:380).

The antimarket critique also focuses on the destruction of the health and sustainability of the environment on which people depend. The free market interest in profits tends to be a short-term goal: extract the resource, market it, pocket the income, and move on when the resource is exhausted. Strip mining, clear-cut forestry, and fisheries depletion all stand as dramatic contemporary examples of this tendency. As a moral philosophy, the political–ecological position places a premium on reaching a sustainable accommodation with the natural world. We owe it to ourselves and to future generations to consume only what we can replace and to clean up what we despoil. In this view, the well-being of the earth's ecosystem is of concern to everyone.

The Effect of Globalization on Indigenous Peoples

Many indigenous peoples and their cultures have completely disappeared as a result of contact with outsiders. Besides death and decline through contagious disease, political conflicts within indigenous peoples' territory often threaten their survival. Indigenous peoples have also suffered from intentional efforts to take over their land by force, to prevent them from practicing their traditional lifestyle, and to integrate them into the nation-state (see Box 19.3).

According to Bodley (1990:153), *indigenous peoples* are defined as follows:

Indigenous people are those who live in countries with populations composed of different ethnic groups who are descendants of the earliest populations which survive in the area, and who do not, as a group, control the national government of the countries within which they live.

BOX 19.3   A World Systems Perspective on Globalization

Although global economic integration has been a long-term trend since the seventeenth century, there are unique qualities of the new stage globalization that are producing political movements required to create a democratic global system. Advances in information technology have created a context in which one global market, rather than many national markets, is the relevant arena for economic competition. It then follows that economic competitiveness needs to be assessed in the global context, rather than in a national or local context.

Globalization is a long-term, upward trend of political and economic change that includes the following:

(1) Common Ecological Constraints

This aspect of globalization involves global threats because of the world's fragile ecosystem and the globalization of ecological risks. Ecological degradation, such as global climate change and destruction of ocean fisheries, has only recently begun to operate on a global scale, and this fact creates a set of systemic problems that require global collective action.

(2) Cultural Globalization

This aspect of globalization relates to the diffusion of two sets of cultural phenomena:

- The proliferation of individualized values, originally of Western origin, to larger parts of the world population. These values are expressed in social constitutions that recognize individual rights and international efforts to protect human rights.

- The adoption of originally Western institutional practices. Bureaucratic organization and rationality, belief in a lawlike natural universe, and the values of economic efficiency and political democracy have been spreading throughout the world.

(3) Globalization of Communication

Another meaning of globalization is connected with the new era of information technology. Global communication facilities have the power to move things visible and invisible from one part of the globe to another, whether any nation-state likes it or not. This applies not only to economic exchange but also to ideas, and these new networks of communication can create new political groups and alignments.

(4) Economic Globalization

Economic globalization means globe-spanning economic relationships, such as interrelationships between markets, finance, goods, and services. Economic globalization has been accelerated by what information technology has done to the movement of money. It is commonly claimed that the market's ability to shift money from one part of the globe to another by the push of a button has changed the rules of policy making, putting economic decisions much more at the mercy of market forces than before.

(5) Political Globalization

Since the early nineteenth century, the European interstate system has been developing an increasingly consensual international order and international political structures that regulate all sorts of interaction. This phenomenon, termed *global governance*, refers to the growth of international organizations, such as the European Union, the League of Nations, and the United Nations. The idea is that international economic competition as well as geopolitical competition are becoming increasingly important as more and more international trade and international investment occur. The ideology of globalization has also undercut the support behind institutions such as labor unions, socialist parties, and welfare programs.

Source: Adapted from Chase-Dunn 1999.

This does not mean that should indigenous peoples gain control of the government, they would no longer be indigenous. They are native to the countries they inhabit and have rights of prior occupancy to their lands but reject the authority of the state and have not adopted the culture of the mainstream population (Maybury-Lewis 1997:7).

The cultures of indigenous peoples are vulnerable to destruction from capitalist expansion partly because their way of life differs so significantly from that of the culture of capitalism. Despite their cultural differences, they share certain characteristics:

- They tend to be mobile and their territory may cross international boundaries.

- Most have subsistence economies that require low population density and large tracts of land.

- They have communal ownership of resources; their land cannot be readily sold but their territory and its valued resources are not protected from capitalist exploitation.

For example, the Urueu-Wau-Wau people of the Amazon use a bark that Merck Pharmaceuticals "discovered" and is attempting to develop as an anticoagulant to be used in heart surgery, yet almost no benefits accrue to the Urueu-Wau-Wau, who are threatened with extinction (Posey 1990). In other parts of the Amazon, native communities are fighting against the incursion of oil and gas exploration and drilling interests (see Profile 19.3), and in many areas, colonists and coca growers in search of livelihood and profit continue to encroach on native lands.

Most small-scale indigenous societies are relatively egalitarian and maintain a subsistence economy in which they produce mainly for consumption. They seldom grow cash crops and do not produce a sur-plus for the market. Their consumption needs are minimal—generally limited to steel tools, aluminum pots, cloth, and other household goods. Given that they have far less need for material possessions to mark their status, they are poor consumers and contribute little to the state-run capitalist economy.

As John Bodley (1990:4) writes,

> The struggle between tribes and states has been over conflicting systems of resources management and internal social organization. Tribes represent small-scale, classless societies, with decentralized, communal, long-term resource

PROFILE 19.3 | The Machiguenga Today

The Machiguenga (see Profiles 5.2 and 18.1) have long had contact with missionaries, explorers, and rubber patrons, but they have recently faced critical change as large international oil companies have begun to exploit gas and oil reserves in the region. Mobile Oil and Dutch Shell initiated the multimillion-dollar Kamisea Natural Gas Project in the heart of Machiguenga territory.

Barges and helicopters hauling supplies up and down the river became a common sight. The impact of the economic development created problems at the family and communal level. Males were exported as laborers to clear the forest for the intended pipeline, leaving women and children behind to subsist on inadequate food supplies. While the men were gone, relatives gave meat and fish to their families but received nothing when the men returned to the community.

The new exchange economy altered the influx of merchants in the region. The Machiguenga complained that river traders overcharged them for consumer goods and began to realize that working for wages did not afford them the quality of life they previously enjoyed. Yet some Machiguenga became wealthier and gained more influence due to their ownership of prized items such as shotguns, power tools, boats, and generators.

With the introduction of wealth inequality, people today feel greater stress and project their frustration onto others. When they become sick, they believe the illness is caused by someone who harbors feelings of resentment because of jealousy or envy, resulting in witchcraft accusations (Izquierdo 2001). Although it was traditionally believed that witchcraft could only be caused by outsiders who were non-Machiguenga, today people are suspicious of others in their own community. Even husbands and wives, who used to be close and affectionate, today have strained relations, and wife abuse is on the increase.

Kamisea Natural Gas Project

The project consists of extracting natural gas and transporting it to Lima through two pipelines. Local rivers and streams are becoming contaminated with drilling water containing metals and hydrocarbons, harming aquatic species and human communities.

management strategies, whereas states are class-based societies, with centralized management systems that extract resources for the short-term profit of special interest groups.

Attempts to incorporate indigenous peoples to the nation-state occur in stages, generally beginning with the establishment of a frontier and advancing through military presence, the extension of government control, and the gradual destruction of indigenous culture through land takeovers, cultural modification (including religious conversion), and economic development. Political control is established by various means. One is simply direct rule, in which a person from the dominant group is appointed to administer the native population. More common, and probably more effective, is the method used by the British in Africa, called *indirect rule*. The role of traditional leaders was strengthened or leaders were created when they did not exist, who were puppets and a convenient means of control for state administrators.

After imposing control over indigenous peoples, the next step for the nation-state was to modify their culture. Any native custom considered immoral, offensive, or threatening was abolished. At various times, such things as the payment of bride price, infant betrothal, polygamy, secret societies, and traditional kinship duties and obligations have been attacked or banned. The extended family was particularly criticized by economic development agents as an obstacle to economic progress (Robbins 2002).

Assimilation

One of the most successful ways of incorporating indigenous cultures is through formal education. Schooling is a prime coercive instrument of cultural modification that has proved to be highly effective in creating a sense of nationalism through the teaching of history and celebration of holidays. The first efforts at education were controlled by missionaries. It was a useful partnership for both the church and the nation-state. The missionaries educated indigenous children in the ways of the nation-state and converted them at the same time. They tried to integrate them into the national economy under the rubric of progress.

Progress is a highly ethnocentric term that that does not take the native people's quality of life into account. *Transformation* is a far more appropriate term in this context. The process of transformation begins by using Western medicine as a tool of conversion. According to Karl Heider, who worked among the Dani of New Guinea:

One missionary told me that when he gave penicillin shots (for yaws, a type of skin ulcer)

he had the patient pray with him to Jesus. Then, when the yaws were cured, he would point out that the Dani owed the cure to Jesus. (1991:13)

Missionaries were usually the first to introduce Western goods and compete for the loyalty of indigenous groups by offering trade goods. Missionaries often demeaned native religious beliefs and rituals and were eager to save their souls but not their lands and freedom.

Another common way of incorporating indigenous peoples into the capitalist economy is through forced labor. Settlers and colonial governments found that many people didn't want or need to work for wages because their consumption needs were modest and they were able to meet those needs by growing their own crops or sharing products among kinspersons or other groups. Taxation is a technique that forces indigenous peoples into the capitalist economy. Forcing people to pay taxes in cash requires them to work for wages on plantations or mines or to raise cash crops for sale. These measures are staunchly defended as necessary to "civilize the savages" in order to further economic development in the nation-state.

Resistance to Oppression

Antonio Gramsci (1971) developed the concept of **hegemony** to describe the means by which dominant social groups obtain the consent of subordinate groups without the use of force.

 Hegemony is a stratified social order in which subordinate groups internalize the ideology of the dominant group and accept the dominant ideology as natural and inevitable.

As we saw in Chapter 11, ideology and thought control are powerful means of controlling politically subordinate groups. Global culture is spreading rapidly, not as a gradual spontaneous process resulting from technological innovation and increased trade but as the result of tremendous investments of time, energy, and money by transnational corporations that use marketing techniques and advertising to associate happiness with the consumption of Western products (Janus 1991). According to Scott (1990), "Relations of domination are, at the same time, relations of resistance."

This does not mean that subordinate groups passively accept domination. Resistance comes in many forms, ranging from full-fledged rebellion to everyday forms of resistance that occur on a small scale and are disguised rather than defiant. Scott (1985) calls these "weapons of the weak." This indirect strategy includes foot-dragging, false compliance, pilfering, feigned ignorance, slander, arson, sabotage, and so forth. Such forms of class struggle require little or no coordination or planning; they often represent a form of individual expression and typically avoid any direct symbolic confrontation with authority or elite norms.

The Zapatista Rebellion

Outright rebellion, by comparison, directly challenges the power of the dominant regime. In Chiapas, Mexico, a strong resurgence of activity by indigenous peoples and groups that support them occurred during the 1990s. Native Mayans had been forced off their land, and those who remained lived in extreme poverty. On January 1, 1994, the Zapatista National Liberation Army (EZLN) launched a rebellion to demand indigenous rights and justice. Subcomendate Marcos, one of the few nonnative fighters, became internationally known for his communiqués issued in the name of EZLN. He waged a war of words through the Internet, writing essays that combined humor, storytelling, and sharp political critique of the Mexican government. Marcos continued to communicate via the Internet and won the support of students, union leaders, and human rights advocates outside Chiapas (Cleaver 1994).

The native people of Chiapas have since taken matters into their own hands. They have driven out the local government and now govern for themselves. The army has surrounded the area but is being watched by international peace observers invited by the Zapatistas to their villages to track and report on the movement of the military.

Why have the Zapatistas denounced Mexican development plans? For them, development is just another step in their cultural assimilation and economic annihilation. Based on their experience, development means they will end up at the bottom of the wage/income hierarchy; it means they will lose their land and their autonomy and be reduced to impoverished wage earners or to attractions within the tourist industry—where primitive people are viewed as curiosities.

For Mexico, the promise of free trade means that the country will develop faster, but for the people of Chiapas, free trade means that their region will export raw materials and drain the wealth from their land, while a flood of cheap food from the United States, produced by capital-intensive methods, will drive down the prices of their produce and force them to sell their land. The Chiapan residents are

Rebellion by Indigenous Peoples
These native Mayans are fighting against development because they believe it will mean losing their land and autonomy and being forced to the bottom of the wage/income hierarchy.

already suffering from the withdrawal of government support for coffee production, which resulted in low coffee prices. The government has promised to provide emergency loans but has made it clear that it will foreclose on indebted farmers.

Preserving Indigenous Cultures

While **genocide** is today universally condemned, **ethnocide** is generally accepted when it comes to indigenous peoples. It is, in fact, advocated as an appropriate policy toward people who are perceived as "backward" because it is presumed that they must become civilized and be able to coexist with others in the modern world.

Genocide is the physical extermination of a defined category of people.

Ethnocide is the destruction of a people's way of life.

Today, the cultures of indigenous peoples are threatened, even though their lives may not be at risk, and it is to their cultures that they cling to give meaning and dignity to their lives. Indigenous peoples are accused of standing in the way of development, and this is sufficient ground for dispossessing them and destroying their ways of life. If they are unable or unwilling to abandon their separate identities and become part of the mainstream, they are said to undermine the state and to impede modernization. Sometimes we are told that the disappearance of such archaic cultures may be regrettable but that it is also inevitable because they cannot survive in the modern world.

Indigenous Peoples Today

At the heart of the prejudice against indigenous societies are the twin issues of modernization and development. States feel they cannot modernize effectively if they tolerate indigenous cultures in their midst. They feel even more that they cannot exploit the resources that lie within their territories if access to them is impeded by indigenous peoples (see Profile 19.4). Modern governments in parts of Latin America, Africa, and Asia face serious economic, political, and social problems. Many governments—including those democratically elected—are under pressure to pursue policies that lead to the displacement or assimilation of the indigenous peoples whose territories lie within their national boundaries. In many countries aspiring to modernization, indigenous people living in remote, undeveloped regions are forced to move aside in the interest of what the dominant ethnic group sees as the "greater good" of their nation.

Indigenous communities are also adversely affected by the efforts of well-meaning people to promote environmental causes such as habitat preservation and animal conservation (see Profile 19.5). For some, preservation and conservation of governments of nations with large indigenous populations sometimes react to such concerns by resettling people out of areas they have lived in for centuries. (An irony is worth pointing out here: Often the areas deemed appropriate for conservation or preservation efforts are those that are recognized as relatively undisturbed—partly because it is mainly

---

PROFILE 19.4 | **The Yanomami Today**

Until the early 1970s, most of the approximately 9,000 Yanomami (Profile 10.2) were relatively isolated from outside influences. In 1974, the Brazilian government constructed a road through the southern part of Yanomami territory. Workers involved in forest clearing and road building introduced new diseases, such as influenza and measles.

In the late 1980s, the forest habitat of the Yanomami was ravaged by a gold rush. Thousands of gold seekers poured into the area in search of wealth. By early 1990, as many as 40,000 prospectors had invaded traditional Yanomami territory and extracted gold worth an esti-

mated $1 billion. The miners dug huge holes using high-power hoses. Mercury, used to separate the gold and soil from the excavations, poisoned the streams where the Yanomami fish; road and airplane traffic frightened off the game; and pools of stagnant water produced by the mining operations provided breeding conditions for malaria-bearing mosquitoes. In three years, the population of the Brazilian Yanomami fell by 20 percent as a result of malaria, other contagious diseases, and malnutrition.

Source: Turner 1991.

PROFILE 19.5   The !Kung Today

Within the Southern African nation of Botswana lies the Central Kalahari Game Reserve (CKGR), which is the second-largest game reserve in all of Africa. The reserve was established in 1961, partly to provide the !Kung San hunters and gatherers of the region with adequate resources for their subsistence (see Profile 5.1). In the 1960s and 1970s, local groups of San used the territory for subsistence foraging, sometimes on horseback. In the 1980s, some environmentalists tried to persuade the European Union to pressure Botswana officials to remove the people and declare the area game reserve. By the 1990s, the remaining San were encouraged to move outside the reserve by various methods, including failure to repair a needed well, intimidation or selective enforcement of game laws, and (allegedly) physical punishments of accused "poachers."

Then, in 1997, the government of Botswana resettled several hundred San outside the boundaries of the reserve, placing them in an environment with few trees and wild plant foods and offering them very little compensation. This action was taken partly in the name of conservation. But the San argued that increasing numbers of tourists in four-wheel-drive vehicles were destroying the land and that more cattle were on the reserve. According to an article by Robert Hitchcock (1999:54) in the journal *Cultural Survival Quarterly,* the San "expressed that the reason they were being removed was so that well-to-do private citizens could set up lucrative safari camps in the reserve."

Recently, the government decided to promote more widespread tourism. As a result, many San communities are confronted by the tourism industry whether they like it or not. Because of their extreme poverty and marginalization, communities are forced to participate in tourism activities because they are the only available source of income (‡Oma, Kxao, and Thoma 2002).

Resettlement of Indigenous Peoples
The government of Botswana resettled several hundred San, forcing them to live in houses made of corrugated aluminum and work for wages. This was done in the name of conservation so that !Kung land could be preserved as a wild animal park.

the indigenous peoples who have been using them all along!)

Vanishing Knowledge

Anthropologists are especially concerned with the rights of indigenous peoples for several reasons. First, because of our interest in cultural diversity, we are more aware of what has happened to non-Western cultures in the past several centuries than are most people. Second, we identify with indigenous peoples partly because so many of us have worked among them. Third, our professional training gives us a relativistic outlook on the many ways of being human, so we can appreciate other people's customs and beliefs as viable alternatives to our own. Finally, the fieldwork experience often affects our attitudes about our own societies. Deep immersion into other cultural traditions leaves some of us not so sure about our commitment to our own.

Ethical concerns for the human rights of indigenous peoples, combined with a respect for their cultural traditions, are the primary reasons for preserving their rights to survive as traditional communities. Beside ethical reasons, there are also compelling practical arguments for why cultural diversity should not be destroyed. Cultural diversity provides vast knowledge accumulated throughout the generations by people throughout the world. A large amount of knowledge has been widely preserved and disseminated by means of written language. Other local knowledge is orally passed down from one generation to the next. It is stored only in the minds of members of traditional cultures. Most local knowledge will disappear if cultural traditions disappear—even if the people themselves survive. How much of this local knowledge is knowledge that may (today, tomorrow, someday) prove useful to all humanity?

Certainly, we have much to learn from indigenous cultures. In fact, many people in the ecological movement have been inspired by indigenous attitudes and practices in restructuring human relationships with nature, and health practitioners have benefited from local knowledge of traditional healing practices and herbal treatments to complement biomedicine in treating illness.

SUMMARY
and *Questions to Think About*

1. Globalization refers to changes in the world economic system that stimulate free movement of capital and pave the way for the emergence of multinational corporations.

2. Colonialism preceded globalization; colonizers acquired resources and productive land from underdeveloped territories to gain strategic positions against rival nation-states in political and military confrontations.

3. Most of today's underdeveloped nations are former colonial dependents. Europeans prevented the colonies from developing an industrial infrastructure and left a political vacuum that resulted in protracted ethnic conflict.

4. Commercialism transforms the economy from one that produces goods and services to meet basic needs to an economy in which capital accumulation is the primary objective.

5. Attempts such as the Green Revolution, designed to increase the productivity of developing countries, benefited large multinational corporations and wealthy farmers; many of the poorest farmers had to sell their land and move to the cities to find work.

6. Globalization is fueled by neoliberalism which believes the market should self-regulate. Antimarket forces argue that control must be set to keep powerful forces from unduly exploiting the market and destroying the environment.

7. Globalization has had a devastating effect on indigenous peoples who want to remain in their communities and continue the ways of their ancestors. Governments, however, are intent on incorporating indigenous peoples into the capitalist economy and bringing them under the control of the state.

8. One example of indigenous resistance is seen in the case of the Zapatista rebellion in Chiapas, Mexico. The people have rejected being incorporated into the global economy because they feel it will undermine their traditional way of life and force them off their land.

9. Other indigenous groups—such as the !Kung, the Machiguenga, and the Yanomami—have been adversely affected by efforts to bring "progress" (to bring a safari reserve, drill for gas and oil, or mine for gold). Outsiders do not recognize the rights or interests of indigenous peoples when they enter their territories to exploit valued resources.

10. Besides ethical reasons, there are compelling practical reasons for preserving cultural diversity. Indigenous peoples have valuable traditions and knowledge that we can learn from.

Questions to Think About

1. Why have so many of the former colonies become underdeveloped countries in the global economy?

2. What was wrong with the way the Green Revolution was conceived of and carried out?

3. What do you think could have been done to improve the economies of developing countries in the 1960s?

4. Evaluate the strengths and weaknesses of neoliberalism and antimarket forces.

5. What is hegemony, and what influence does it have in the global market?

6. Why are the Zapatistas resisting the forces of globalization?

7. Why are indigenous peoples being forced to conform to global economic interests?

THROUGH THE LENS
of Cultural Materialism

Conformity and Conflict • Reading Thirty-Four

The Kayapo Resistance

Terence Turner

The Kayapo were able to use new media technology to have their voices heard regarding their concerns for the future of their environment and the preservation of their way of life.

Emic Perspective

- The Kayapo see the destruction of their forest and the killing of their fish as an assault on their livelihood and their society.

- They also understand they need help from environmental groups to preserve their way of life. "There is no point saving the animals if the forest is burned down; there is no point saving the forest if the people and animals who live in it are killed or driven away."

- They know they cannot win without the support of outside groups, and the groups cannot win without the support of the natives who can tell the world what is happening.

Etic Perspective

- The industrial development of the Amazon has affected the Kayapo—namely, by threatening the sustainability of their mode of production and social organization.

- They have responded by using a multidimensional approach to garner public opinion and have thus far been successful in warding off destruction of their habitat.

Infrastructure

- The Kayapo are a nation of Ge-speaking native people who inhabit the middle and lower reaches of the valley of the Xingu River. Their total population is 2,500, divided among 14 mutually independent communities.

- For the Kayapo, like most contemporary Amazonian natives, traditional subsistence is still essential. The Kayapo mode of production is a combination of slash-and-burn horticulture, hunting, fishing, and foraging.

- Kayapo gardens require extensive land; the gardens produce for about three years. Most families maintain three gardens in production at any one time. After a garden is abandoned, it takes about 25 years for reforestation and reuse. The Kayapo also go on communal, seminomadic hunting-and-gathering treks several months a year.

- Since the 1960s, there has been massive destruction of the Amazon environment, including the cutting and burning of the forest, the building of roads, and the erosion and pollution of the river caused by mining and building of giant hydroelectric dams.

- A new road brought heavy traffic from outsiders and along with them the perils of infectious disease. The discovery of gold at the huge mine of Serra Pelada led to intense prospecting and exploratory gold-mining activity.

- Rumors spread that the Brazilian government was planning to build a series of hydroelectric dams, which would flood large areas of Kayapo land and put an end to fishing in the river.

- Some Kayapo leaders gave timber companies logging concessions in exchange for sizeable money payments and the construction of modern housing and other facilities in Kayapo villages. Most of the money went into communal accounts, but some individuals draw on these funds for personal use, giving rise to tension and resentment among community members.

Structure

- The Kayapo lack political influence to defend themselves and their forest.

- Two western Kayapo communities whose land was severed by the road started a campaign of armed attacks on all Brazilian intruders who attempted to open ranches. The leaders of these two communities meanwhile began a campaign of diplomacy, making repeated trips to Brasília to pressure the government to return the stolen land and thus end the violent standoff. The two communities subsequently joined into a single large village and have resolutely banned all Brazilian mining, timber, and agricultural interests. They have also successfully kept out settlers from their reclaimed areas.

- The leaders of the largest Kayapo village used income from miners to purchase a light plane and hired a Brazilian pilot to patrol their borders from the air to spot intruders and would-be squatters. Within a year, invasions effectively ceased.

- When the government planned to dump radioactive waste on traditional Kayapo land, the Kayapo sent 100 men to Brasília to demonstrate. Suitably painted and feathered, they staged a sit-in in the president's palace.

- In 1988, two Kayapo leaders were invited to the United States to participate in a conference on tropical forest ecology. They traveled to Washington, D.C., met with members of Congress, and spoke with World Bank officials about the negative effects of the proposed Xingu Dam on the local people and environment.

- Kayapo leaders who objected to the building of hydroelectric dams on the Xingu River attracted international public attention to their cause, which helped them gain press attention and financial support.

- In February 1989, 600 Amazonian natives and an equal number of Brazilian and international journalists, environmental advocates, and documentary filmmakers converged on the small river town of Altamira to protest construction of the dam. Within two weeks, the World Bank rescinded the loan earmarked for the dam project.

Superstructure

- The daunting threats to Kayapo existence were a catalyst for political awareness.

- The Kayapo, with cooperation from national and international environmental activists, launched a public opinion campaign that disseminated information about the disastrous effects of the proposed dam on the Xingu River and effectively put pressure on the World Bank to withdraw funding for construction.

Achieved status is acquired through talents, efforts, and accomplishments, rather than ascription.

Adaptation refers to biological and cultural traits that improve opportunities for individuals of a population to survive and reproduce.

The **advocacy role** requires the anthropologist to actively support a group of people and often involves political action.

Aesthetic designates the existence of a universal human capacity for an emotionally charged response of appreciation and pleasure when art is successful.

Affinal refers to relatedness through marriage.

Affinity refers to relatedness through marriage.

African American Vernacular English (AAVE, also known as Ebonics, derived from *ebony* and *phonics*) contains certain features that are unacceptable in White, middle-class settings.

Altruism is the act of maintaining the well-being of an individual's close relatives and their offspring to ensure their survival so that their genes will be continued in the next generation.

Ambilineal descent is the reckoning of kinship through either maternal or paternal links, depending on which kin group provides greater opportunities.

Ambilocality is postmarital residence in which a married couple elects to stay on a relatively permanent basis with either the wife's or the husband's domestic group.

Amok is a hysterical reaction in which young men attack other people and destroy their property.

Animatism is the belief in diffuse impersonal power that people can control under certain conditions.

Animism is the belief that humans share the world with a population of extraordinary, mostly invisible beings.

Anorexia nervosa is an obsessive–compulsive disorder characterized by an unrealistic appraisal of one's body as overweight, resulting in self-starvation to achieve a more slender look.

Anthropological linguistics is the study of the great variety of languages spoken by human beings.

The **antimarket critique** is that the free market promotes an egocentric individualism that dissolves the integrity of society. The market creates and sustains class inequalities that increase suffering for the great majority of workers while opening the door to consumption excesses for an exclusive few.

Applied anthropology refers to problem-oriented research in which anthropologists use their skills and knowledge to discover and explain factors that influence human behavior and solve practical problems.

Arbitrariness refers to the fact that there is seldom a connection between the abstract symbols employed by humans and the events and properties they signify.

Archeology examines the material remains of past cultures left behind on or below the surface of the earth.

Ascribed status is determined for a person at birth.

Avunculocal residence maintains a male fraternal interest group in the residential core of the matrilineal descent group. Avunculocality thus provides the best of two worlds for males who aspire to military and political leadership.

Balanced reciprocity involves the expectation that goods or services of equivalent value will be returned within a specified period of time.

A **"big man"** is a local entrepreneur who successfully mobilizes and manipulates wealth on behalf of his group in order to host large feasts that enhance his status and rank relative to other big men in the region. He is a man of prestige and renown but has no formal authority or power and no more wealth.

Bilateral descent is the reckoning of kinship evenly and symmetrically along maternal and paternal links in ascending and descending generations through individuals of both sexes.

Bilocality is postmarital residence in which a married couple elects to stay for rather short intervals between shifts of residence between the wife's kin and husband's kin.

Binary contrasts refer to two elements or themes that can be viewed as standing in diametric opposition to each other.

Biomedicine refers to medicine based on the application of the principles of the natural sciences, especially biology and biochemistry.

Bride service compensates the bride's family for the loss of a daughter. The groom moves in with the bride's family and works in exchange for his marital rights.

Bridewealth compensates the bride's group for the loss of her labor and the children she bears, who become full members of the husband's group.

Capitalism is associated with a change from production for use value to production for profit value.

Carrying capacity is the upper limit on production and population that can occur in a given environment under a given technology without degrading the resource base.

Castes are closed, endogamous, and stratified descent groups.

Churning results when people on welfare lose their entitlements as a result of a real or inaccurately recorded failure on their part to comply with bureaucratic requirements.

A **class** is a group whose members possess similar amounts of power within a stratified society.

Code switching is the practice among multilingual language speakers of selectively alternating between languages or dialects within a single conversational segment.

Cognatic descent rules are those in which both male and female parentage are used to establish any of the above-mentioned duties, rights, and privileges.

Commercialization is a process that makes capital accumulation the primary objective and leads to the production of great inequalities of wealth and power.

Communal cults use rituals to strengthen group continuity by communicating socially constructed meaning signifying the continuity of the group.

Communitas is an intense community spirit, a feeling of social solidarity, equality, and togetherness that is achieved through liminality.

Cognatic lineages are all the descendents of an apical ancestor or ancestress reckoning descent through any combination of male or female links.

Consanguineal refers to relatedness through descent.

A **corporate group** is a unified entity that holds common property and lives on even though some of the members die out.

Cross-cousins are the children of ego's father's sister or mother's brother who are regarded as potential marriage mates.

Cross-talk takes place when listeners miss or misinterpret cues in communication.

Cultural adaptation refers to the knowledge and behavior that enable people to survive and thrive in a given environment.

Cultural anthropology (sometimes called *social anthropology*) deals with the description and analysis of cultures—the socially learned traditions of past and present ages.

Cultural configuration refers to the unique social patterns that a culture has standardized.

Cultural materialism is a research strategy that holds that the primary task of cultural anthropology is to give scientific causal explanations for the differences and similarities in thought and behavior found among human groups.

Cultural relativism stipulates that behavior in a particular culture should not be judged by the standards of another. Yet it is evident that not all human customs or institutions contribute to the society's overall health and well-being, nor should they be regarded as morally or ethically worthy of respect.

Cultural "takeoff" occurred once the capacity for language and language-assisted thought developed. A vast number of cultural differences and similarities appeared independently of changes in genotype.

Culture refers to the learned, socially acquired traditions of thought and behavior found in human societies. It is a socially acquired lifestyle that includes patterned, repetitive ways of thinking, feeling, and acting.

Culture-specific psychosis refers to mental disorders that have a distinctive set of symptoms limited to a specific culture.

The **culture of poverty** depicts the poor as fearful, suspicious, apathetic toward major intuitions, and present-time oriented. It assumes that some groups remain poor because of certain cultural features that perpetuate poverty and that are passed down from one generation to the next.

Culture shock is the feeling of anxiety and disorientation that develops in an unfamiliar situation when there is confusion about how to behave or what to expect.

Cumulative cultural evolution refers to behavior or artifacts that are transmitted and modified over many generations and gain complexity as they evolve.

Depression exhibits primary symptoms such as depressive mood, insomnia, and lack of interest in one's social environment. The illness may be accompanied by secondary symptoms that are culturally shaped.

Descent refers to parentage from a common ancestor.

Diffusion takes place when culture contact leads to the borrowing and passing on of culture traits.

Diglossia refers to a pattern of language use in a bilingual community where two languages or dialects are used according to social circumstances.

Direct infanticide involves deliberate killing—starvation, dehydration, smothering, placing a child in a dangerous situation, or using excessive physical punishment.

Direct systematic behavior observations refer to the study of activity patterns that show patterns of action and interaction of the people we study.

Displacement refers to the ability to send or receive a message without direct sensory contact with the conditions or events to which the message refers.

Double descent traces descent matrilineally for some purposes and patrilineally for others.

Dowry is a transfer of goods or money from the bride's family to the bride. It represents compensation for the future support of the woman and her future children and is found in societies where women contribute relatively little to subsistence.

Early *Homo* is the hominid group from which modern humans were probably descended.

Ecclesiastical religion is found in highly centralized political systems.

Ecclesiastical art generally interprets the world in conformity with prevailing state ideologies that justify inequities and exploitation.

Ecological anthropology is concerned with cultural and biological responses that affect or are affected by the survival, reproduction, and health and spatial distribution of human populations.

Economizing refers to the choices people make they believe will provide the greatest benefit to them.

Egalitarian society lacks formalized differentiation in access to and power over basic resources among its members.

Electra complex. See **Oedipus conflict.**

Emics describe culture from the participants' viewpoint. The observer uses concepts and distinctions that are meaningful and appropriate to the participants.

Enculturation is a partially conscious and partially unconscious learning experience whereby the older generation invites, induces, and compels the younger generation to adopt traditional ways of thinking and behaving.

Endogamy is the rule that requires an individual to take a spouse from a group in which he or she is a member.

Energy-capturing technology refers to how people apply human labor and technology to natural resources.

Ester Boserup proposed an alternative view that holds that food production tends to rise to the level demanded by population growth. As population expands and the point of diminishing returns is reached, people invent or adopt new and more efficient modes of food production.

Estrus is the period in the sexual cycle of female primates, during which they are sexually receptive and likely to conceive.

Ethnocentrism is the belief that one's own patterns of behavior are always natural, good, beautiful, or important and that strangers, to the extent that they live differently, live by savage, inhuman, disgusting, or irrational standards.

Ethnocide is the destruction of a people's way of life.

Ethnography is a firsthand description of a living culture based on personal observation.

Ethnography of speaking is the study of speech interaction in different cultures and of the interrelationships between language and other aspects of culture.

Ethnology is a study of a particular topic or problem in more than one culture using a comparative perspective.

Ethnomedicine aims to understand the health-related beliefs, knowledge, and practices of cultural groups.

Etics describe culture from the observer's perspective.

Exogamy is the rule that forbids an individual from taking a spouse from within a prescribed local group in which they are both members.

Falsification entails the rejection of a theory because the prediction is not supported by the data.

Features of the environment consist of sunlight, rainfall, soil quality, forests, and mineral deposits.

The **feminization of poverty** refers to the growing number of female heads of household and the greater impact that poverty has on women.

Fieldnotes are the data collected by anthropologists.

Fieldwork refers to the firsthand experience with the people being studied. It involves integration into a community through long-term residence and knowledge of the local language and customs while maintaining the role of observer.

Folktales are traditional narratives from the deep past that reflect social situations that play on ordinary human fears and desires.

Forensic anthropology uses anthropology to help solve crimes.

Form designates a set of restrictions on how the art play is to be organized in time and space—the rules of the game of art.

Fossil fuels consist of materials such as coal, petroleum, and natural gas derived from decomposed remains of prehistoric organisms over a period of hundreds of millions of years.

Gender refers to the learned cultural and psychological attributes.

Gender scripts are ideals that guide conventional masculinity and femininity and that become a basis for self-perception for most individuals.

Generalized reciprocity involves mutual giving and receiving among people of equal status in which there is (1) no need for immediate return, (2) no systematic calculation of the value of the services and products exchanged, and (3) an overt denial that a balance is being calculated or that the balance must come out even.

Genocide is the physical extermination of a defined category of people.

The **Ghost Dance,** it was believed, would place dancers in contact with the spirit world and hasten the time when people would be reunited with their dead ancestors, which was when they would outnumber the Whites and hence be more powerful.

The **Green Revolution** was designed to increase grain yields through the use of miracle seeds as a key to ending world hunger.

In **Hawaiian terminology,** the same term is applied to people inside and outside the nuclear family; a single term is used for all relatives of the same sex and generation.

A **headman,** unlike such specialists as king, president, and dictator, is a relatively powerless figure incapable of compelling obedience.

Hegemony is a stratified social order in which subordinate groups internalize the ideology of the dominant group and accept the dominant ideology as natural and inevitable.

Heteroglossia refers to the use of multiple dialects or language styles based on the social setting (e.g., formal, casual, professional) and social context (status and role relationships) of the speakers.

Holism is an approach that assumes that any single aspect of culture is integrated with other aspects, so that no single dimension of culture can be understood in isolation.

Horticulture is the farming of domesticated plants and is practiced mainly in tropical regions.

A **humanistic approach** aims to describe and interpret each culture on its own terms; it believes comparisons distort the unique qualities of a given culture.

Humoral medicine conceives the universe as comprising opposing qualities—hot and cold, wet and dry—and sees health as a matter of balance between these opposites.

Hyperindustrial refers to the fact that the world has now become more (not less) industrial, extending mass production into new areas such as services and information processing.

A **hypothesis** is a proposition or tentative explanation of the relationship between certain phenomena that can be validated (or invalidated) by evidence collected according to explicit procedures.

In the **image of limited good,** everything is perceived as finite: land, wealth, health, love, friendship, honor, respect, status, power, influence, safety, and security. Because everything is scarce, success is viewed as a zero-sum game; successful individuals take more than their fair share from a common pool, thereby excelling at the expense of other people.

Inbreeding avoidance refers to behavioral patterns in which individuals avoid sexual contact with people who could be sexual partners were it not for their relatedness.

Incest taboo refers to cultural beliefs prohibiting sexual relations or marriage with a close relative.

Indigenous peoples are those who live in countries with populations composed of different ethnic groups who are descendents of the earliest populations that survive in the area and who do not, as a group, control the national government of the countries within which they live.

Indirect infanticide begins with neglect and underinvestment—inadequate feeding, withholding emotional support, and careless and indifferent handling, especially when the infant is sick.

In **individualistic cults,** all people are their own specialists.

Informants are people through whom the anthropologist learns about the culture through observation and by asking questions.

The **infrastructure** consists of the technologies and productive and reproductive activities that bear directly on the provision of food and shelter, protection against illness, and the satisfaction of sexual and other basic human needs and drives.

In **Inuit terminology,** the nuclear family stands out as a separate and functionally dominant productive and reproductive unit. Separate kin terms are used for nuclear family members that are not extended to any other kin type.

Intensification refers to an increase in labor output (i.e., using more people, working longer hours, or working faster) to produce greater yields without expanding the amount of land used.

Interviews rely entirely on research subjects as sources of knowledge.

Iroquois terminology distinguishes between cross- and parallel cousins and cross- and parallel aunts and uncles.

A **kindred** consists of ego's close bilateral relatives who form a group that comes together for such occasions as when ego is born, marries, gives a feast, and so on.

Kinship refers to relationships that are based on relatedness through descent and marriage.

The **kula ring** is a system of exchange in the Trobriand Islands, where trading partners from different islands take risky voyages to exchange shell ornaments around the ring of islands; white cowrie shell armbands are traded in a counterclockwise direction, and red shell necklaces are traded clockwise.

Lactation amenorrhea (disruption of the menstrual cycle) is a typical accompaniment of breastfeeding and serves as another form of birth control.

Legitimacy assigns birth status to the child, legally entitles the child and/or the mother to the husband's property upon his death, and determines who is responsible for the child and who controls the child's future.

The **leopard skin chief** is an outside mediator, believed to have supernatural powers, who is called upon to resolve disputes between kin groups and prevent the escalation of hostilities.

The **liminal phase** is a temporary ritual state during which the individual is cut off from normal social contacts to demarcate a contrast from regular social life.

According to **Liebig's law of the minimum,** a population will be limited by critical resources that are in the shortest supply.

Lineage segmentation allows closely related lineages to unite to oppose a threat from more distantly related lineage segments.

Magic refers to a practice intended to manipulate supernatural forces to achieve a specific result. Magic is less spiritual and less ethical than religion.

A **maintenance system** consists of the basic customs surrounding the nourishment, sheltering, and protection of its members. It includes the mode of production and the organization of domestic and political life, as it affects how adults raise their children.

The **male supremacist complex** is a by-product of male monopoly over weapons, training of males for combat, bravery, and other male-centered institutions.

Malthus believed that the population would always increase more rapidly than the food supply; in fact, population growth would tend to rise faster than any conceivable rise in productivity, thereby dooming a large portion of humanity to perpetual poverty, hunger, and misery.

Mana is the possession of concentrated animatistic force that gives certain objects, animals, and people extraordinary powers independent of power derived from souls and gods.

Marriage is an institution that transforms the status of two or more individuals in relation to sexual access and parenthood, and establishes connections between the kin of the spouses.

Matriarchy refers to a hypothetical social system in which domestic and political authority is wielded solely by women.

Matrilineal descent requires ego to follow the ascending and descending links through females only.

Matrilocal residence is associated with long-distance trade or external warfare.

Maximum sustainable yield is the level of production reached immediately prior to the point of diminishing return.

Medical anthropology studies the interaction among culture, disease, and health care.

Money is a medium of exchange that has standard value. It is used as a means of payment for goods and services in a wide range of transactions where trade is well developed and economizing is a guiding principle.

Monogamy is the marriage of one man to one woman at a time.

A **morpheme** is the smallest part of an utterance that has a definite meaning.

Multinational corporations are not economically tied to or dependent on any single country. They have manufacturing plants in several countries and move their facilities in search of cheaper labor, lower taxes, and favorable government regulation.

Myths are sacred tales in which deities appear to explain issues of human existence.

National character refers to the personality configuration of members of a cultural group or nation, characterized by consistent attitudes and behaviors over time.

Natural selection refers to changes in the frequencies of certain genetic traits in populations due to the differential reproductive success between individuals.

Neoliberalism refers to free enterprise, or "the rule of the market." It believes that an unregulated market is the best way to increase economic growth, which will ultimately benefit everyone.

Neolocality differs from both bilocality and ambilocality in not establishing residence with kin groups at all.

Nomadic pastoralism is often associated with migrations that follow established routes over vast distances.

The **Oedipus complex** refers to the emotional attachment and desire that a boy has for his mother and feelings of rivalry and guilt that he feels toward his father. The female counterpart is the **Electra complex,** which refers to a similar attraction of a daughter to her father and rivalry toward her mother.

In **open-class systems,** people can move up or down the hierarchy, as in modern Western democracies.

Optimal foraging theory predicts that hunters or collectors will pursue or harvest only those species that give them the maximum energy return for the time spent foraging.

Parallel cousins are the children of ego's father's brother or mother's sister and are regarded as brothers and sisters.

Participant observation places the ethnographer at the scene, where a combination of direct observation and interviews provide the evidence from which ethnographic accounts are constructed.

Patriarchy, or rule by father or male authority, assumes that women are naturally subservient to their fathers and husbands. Although widespread, patriarchy exists in different forms and degrees.

Patrilineal descent requires ego to follow the ascending and descending genealogical links through males only.

Patrilocal residence is associated with internal warfare.

Peasants are people who use nonindustrial technologies to cultivate land in state societies and pay rent and/or taxes in the form of cash, crops, or services to elite groups for the use of the land.

Personality, like culture, refers to patterned ways of thinking, feeling, and behaving, but the focus is on the individual.

Phones represent etic occurrences. They occur due to variations in the location of the tongue and lips and the stress, pitch, and tone of the sound.

Phonemic differences are derived from patterns of sounds that are meaningful to native speakers.

Phonemes are units of sound (phones) that lack meaning in themselves; they are the smallest sound *contrasts* that distinguish meaning.

Phonetic sound patterns represent etic occurrences. They occur due to variations in the location of the tongue and lips and the stress, pitch, and tone of the sound. They can be observed and identified in speech without having to question the speaker.

Phonetics is the study of the phones, or individual sounds, that native speakers make.

Physical anthropology (also called *biological anthropology*) connects the other anthropological fields to the study of animal origins and the biologically determined nature of *Homo sapiens*.

Play is an enjoyable, self-rewarding aspect of activity that cannot be accounted for simply by the utilitarian or survival functions of that activity.

Plural medical systems are characterized by alternative systems of care and multiple usage patterns. People are likely to pursue several treatment alternatives simultaneously ("dual use") or use a sequence of treatments.

Point of diminishing returns is the point at which the amount of food produced per unit of effort begins to fall.

The **political economy** regulates the flow of goods in larger communities and supports existing power relationships.

Population pressure often leads to intensification, diminishing returns, and irreversible environmental depletions. Depletions often lead, in turn, to new technologies and to new modes of production.

Postcolonial refers to the study of the interactions between European nations and the societies they colonized, both during colonialism and after. In a broader sense, postcolonial is used to signify a position against imperialism and Eurocentrism.

Postmarital residence rules govern with whom or near whom a couple will reside after marriage. They determine whether a couple will be surrounded by the husband's or wife's kin and what kind of support each can expect to have.

Poverty persistence can be explained by population pressure, the cost/benefits of children, and local environmental depletions.

Power refers to the ability to force other people to obey requests or demands.

The **principle of linguistic relativity** is the hypothesis that when two language systems differ radically, their speakers live in wholly different thought-worlds.

The **principle of primacy of infrastructure** states that infrastructural variables are more determinative of the evolution of sociocultural systems.

Productivity refers to the infinite capacity of human language to create new messages—never before uttered—to convey information about an infinite number of subjects in greater and greater detail.

The **profane** is the realm of the secular. It is the world of everyday domestic duties that are essentially utilitarian.

Psychoanalysis emphasizes the importance of thoughts, unconscious fantasies, and conflicts in determining personality and behavior.

Racialism is a relatively benign form of making racial distinctions, such as skin color and facial characteristics, intended for reference purposes.

Rainfall agriculture utilizes naturally occurring showers as a source of moisture.

A **rank society** has equal access to economic resources and power, but social groups have unequal access to status positions and prestige.

Redistribution involves the accumulation of large amounts of labor products produced by different individuals in a central place, where they are sorted and counted and then given away to producers and non-producers alike.

Religion refers to beliefs and actions that are based on the assumption that the world is under the control of supernatural forces that humans must please.

Reproductive success refers to the number of offspring an individual rears to reproductive age.

Revitalization movements occur during times of change in which religious leaders emerge to bring forth positive change.

Rhetoric is the art of persuasive public discourse and is closely related to the theatrical arts.

Rites of passage are ceremonies that mark changes in a person's social position that are of general public concern.

Rites of solidarity are directed toward the welfare of the community rather than the individual. They reaffirm the power of the group, which transcends individuals.

Rituals are formal, stylized, and repetitive acts that are performed in special sacred places at set times.

The **sacred** is the realm of human experience that evokes an attitude of awe and reverence.

The **Sapir–Whorf hypothesis** is the belief that when two language systems differ radically in their vocabularies and grammars, their speakers live in wholly different thought-worlds.

Sanctity is the quality of unquestionable truthfulness credited by the faithful to unverifiable propositions.

Schemas provide people with simplified cultural models of what the world is like and how they should act, feel, and think.

Schizophrenia refers to a group of mental disorders that involve a complex set of disturbances of thinking, perception, affect, and social behavior.

Science is a system of knowledge, one of whose most important features is that it seeks to control the influence of various biases on the conduct of research.

The **scientific approach** aims to explain cultural differences and similarities; it believes that regularities exist across cultures and can be discovered through empirical data collection and systematic comparison.

Semantic universality is a unique aspect of human communication. It refers to the communicative power of language—the fact that language provides for nearly infinite combinations that express different experiences and thought in different ways.

Serial monogamy is marriage to two or more spouses one after another, rather than at the same time.

Sex refers to anatomical and physiological attributes.

In **shamanistic cults,** shamans with supernatural powers that ordinary individuals lack are sought out for curing and divination.

Shamans are women or men who are socially recognized as having special abilities for entering into contact with spirit beings and for controlling supernatural forces.

Slash-and-burn farming (also known as *shifting agriculture*) requires large stretches of fallow land because long periods are necessary for the soil to be replenished.

The **social ecology of childhood** refers to the environment of children's experiences that is most likely to affect their development.

Socialization refers to the process of transmitting appropriate behaviors and values to produce socially and culturally competent individuals capable of functioning successfully in society.

Society refers to an organized group of people who share a homeland and who depend on each other for their survival and well-being.

Sociolinguistics is concerned with how language is used in different social contexts and what it tells us about social relationships.

Sodalities are non–kinship based groups that span several villages and serve widely different functions.

A **speech community** is a group of people who speak the same language and who share norms about the appropriate use of language.

Spirit possession is a disorder in which a person behaves as if possessed by a spirit. The entity that possesses the person may be a deceased family member or a local spirit.

A **stratified society** arranges statuses or subgroups within a society according to socially superior and inferior ranks that produce inequality.

Structure consists of the groups and organizations present in every society that allocate, regulate, and exchange goods, labor, and information.

A **subsistence economy** is essentially the household economy. It is organized at the household level to meet needs for food, clothing, housing, defense, and technology.

Superstructure consists of the behavior and thought devoted to symbolic, ideational, artistic, playful, religious, and intellectual endeavors as well as all the mental and emic aspects of a culture's infrastructure and structure.

Surplus is an amount greater than what is needed for immediate consumption by the producers.

Susto, traditionally translated as "soul loss" or "fright," is similar to depression and appears in many regions of the Spanish-speaking New World.

A **symbol** is an object or behavior that has a culturally defined meaning that does not necessarily relate to its inherent physical quality.

Symbolic thought occurs when a person simultaneously associates two or more complex ideas that evoke a reaction.

Syntax consists of the unconscious rules governing the arrangement of words in sentences and phrases.

Totems are objects such as animals and plants that serve as emblems or symbols of a kinship group or a person.

Transformation–representation refers to the communicative aspect of art that conveys information through symbols.

Transhumance is a form of pastoralism organized around the seasonal migration between mountain pastures in warm seasons and lower altitudes the rest of the year.

Unilineal descent groups have clearly defined memberships that delineate lineage members from nonmembers.

Unilineal descent rules restrict parental links exclusively to males or exclusively to females.

The **universal pattern** is a set of categories that are comprehensive enough to afford logical and classificatory organization for a range of traits and institutions that can be observed in all cultural systems.

War is armed combat between groups of people who constitute separate territorial teams or political communities.

References

In the citation system used in this text, the names in parentheses are the authors of the publications mentioned or of publications that support the description or interpretation of the matter being discussed. The year following each name or set of names is the year of the publication and should be used to identify the specific source when more than one publication is included from a given author or set of authors. The letters following a year (e.g., 1990a) distinguish different publications of the same author/authors for that year. Specific page numbers following the year are provided only for direct quotes or for controversial points.

Acheson, J. M. 1972. "Limited Good or Limited Goods: Response to Economic Opportunity in a Tarascan Pueblo." *American Anthropologist,* 74:1152–1169.

———. 1974. "Reply to George Foster." *American Anthropologist,* 76:57–62.

Adair, L., and B. Popkin. 1992. "Prolonged Lactation Contributes to Depletion of Maternal Energy Reserves in Filipino Women." *Journal of Nutrition,* 122:1643–1655.

Agar, M. 1994. *Language Shock: Understanding the Culture of Conversation.* New York: William Morrow.

Alland, A., Jr. 1977. *The Artistic Animal: An Inquiry into the Biological Roots of Art.* Garden City, NY: Doubleday/Anchor Books.

American Anthropological Association. 1998. "American Anthropological Association Statement on 'Race.'" www.aaanet.org/stmts/racepp.htm.

Ames, K. 1994. "The Northwest Coast: Complex Hunter–Gatherers, Ecology and Social Evolution." *Annual Review of Anthropology,* 23:209–229.

Anderson, R. 1992. "Do Other Cultures Have Art?" *American Anthropologist,* 94:926–929.

Appiah, A. K. 1992. *In My Father's House: Africa in the Philosophy of Culture.* New York: Oxford University Press.

Arensberg, C. 1968. *The Irish Countryman.* New York: Natural History Press. Originally published 1937.

Armelagos, G., and A. Goodman. 1994. *The Case against Race.* Paper read at the Southern Anthropological Society Meeting, Atlanta, April 28.

Atkinson, J. 1992. "Shamanisms Today." *Annual Review of Anthropology,* 21:307–330.

Bailey, B. 2001. "Communication of Respect in Interethnic Service Encounters." In *Linguistic Anthropology,* edited by A. Duranti. Malden, MA: Blackwell.

Baksh, M. 1984. *Cultural Ecology and Change of the Machiguenga Indians of the Peruvian Amazon.* Unpublished doctoral dissertation. Ann Arbor, MI: University Microfilms International.

———. 1985. "Faunal Food as a 'Limiting Factor' on Amazonian Cultural Behavior: A Machiguenga Example." *Research in Economic Anthropology,* 7:145–175.

Balee, W. 1984. "The Ecology of Ancient Tupi Warfare." In *Warfare, Culture and Environment,* edited by R. B. Ferguson (pp. 241–265). Orlando, FL: Academic Press.

Bamberger, J. 1974. "The Myth of Matriarchy: Why Men Rule in Primitive Society." In *Woman, Culture and Society,* edited by M. Z. Rosaldo and L. Lamphere (pp. 263–280). Stanford, CA: Stanford University Press.

Barfield, T. 1993. *The Nomadic Alternative.* Englewood Cliffs, NJ: Prentice-Hall.

Barlett, P., and P. Brown. 1985. "Agricultural Development and the Quality of Life: An Anthropological View." *Agriculture and Human Values,* 2:28–35.

Barnes, J. A. 1960. "Marriage and Residential Continuity." *American Anthropologist,* 62:850–866.

Barnouw, V. 1973. *Culture and Personality.* Homewood, IL: Dorsey Press.

———. 1985. *Culture and Personality,* 4th ed. Homewood, IL: Dorsey Press.

Barth, F. 1961. *Nomads of South Persia.* Boston: Little, Brown.

Bartram, W. 1958. *The Travels of William Bartram,* edited by F. Harper. New Haven, CT: Yale University Press.

Bar-Yosef, O., and B. Vandermeersch. 1993. "Modern Humans in the Levant." *Scientific American,* April, pp. 94–100.

Bates, D. 1996. *Human Adaptive Strategies: Ecology, Culture, and Politics.* Boston: Allyn & Bacon.

Bayliss-Smith, T. 1977. "Human Ecology and Island Populations: The Problems of Change." In *Subsistence and Survival: Rural Ecology in the Pacific,* edited by T. Bayliss-Smith and R. Feachem (pp. 11–20). New York: Academic Press.

Beckerman, S., et al. 1998. "The Bari Partible Paternity Project: Preliminary Results." *Current Anthropology,* 39:164–167.

Bell, D. 1973. *The Coming of Post-Industrial Society: A Venture in Social Forecasting.* New York: Basic Books.

Belmonte, T. 1979. *The Broken Fountain.* New York: Columbia University Press.

Bender, D. 1967. "A Refinement of the Concept of Household: Families, Co-Residence, Domestic Functions." *American Anthropologist,* 69:493–503.

Benedict, R. 1934. *Patterns of Culture.* Boston: Houghton Mifflin.

———. 1946. *The Chrysanthemum and the Sword.* Boston: Houghton Mifflin.

———. 1960. *Patterns of Culture.* New York: Mentor.

Berdan, F. 1982. *Aztecs of Central Mexico.* New York: Holt, Rinehart and Winston.

Berlin, B., and P. Kay. 1991. *Basic Color Terms: Their Universality and Evolution.* Berkeley: University of California Press.

Bermejo, M., G. Illera, and J. Sabater-PI. 1989. "New Observations on the Tool-Behavior of Chimpanzees from Mt. Assirik (Senegal, West Africa)." *Primates,* 30(1):65–73.

———. 1994. *Research Methods in Anthropology,* 2nd ed. Thousand Oaks, CA: Sage.

Bernardi, B. 1985. *Age Class Systems: Social Institutions and Politics Based on Age.* New York: Cambridge University Press.

Berreman, G. D. 1981. "Social Inequality: A Cross-Cultural Analysis." In *Social Inequality: Comparative and Developmental Approaches,* edited by G. D. Berreman (pp. 3–40). New York: Academic Press.

———. 1997 [1972]. *Hindus of the Himalayas,* 2nd ed. Oxford, England: Oxford University Press.

Bickerton, D. 1990. *Language and Species.* Chicago: University of Chicago Press.

Biolsi, T. 1984. "Ecological and Cultural Factors in Plains Indians Warfare." In *Warfare, Culture and Environment,* edited by R. B. Ferguson (pp. 141–168). Orlando, FL: Academic Press.

Bixler, R. 1982. "Comment on the Incidence and Purpose of Royal Sibling Incest." *American Ethnologist,* 9:580–582.

Blackwood, E. 1986. "Breaking the Mirror: The Construction of Lesbianism and the Anthropological Discourse on Homosexuality." In *Anthropology and Homosexual Behavior,* edited by E. Blackwood (pp. 1–18). New York: Haworth Press.

———. 1998. "*Tombois* in West Sumatra: Constructing Masculinity and Erotic Desire." *Cultural Anthropology,* 13(4):491–521.

———. 2005a. "Wedding Bell Blues: Marriage, Missing Men, and Matrifocal Follies." *American Ethnologist,* 32(1):3–19.

———. 2005b. "Women's Intimate Friendships and Other Affairs: An Ethnographic Overview." In *Gender in Cross Cultural Perspective,* 4th ed., edited by C. Brettell and C. Sargent (pp. 268–278). Upper Saddle River, NJ: Prentice Hall.

Blanton, R. E. 1994. *Houses and Households: A Comparative Study.* New York: Plenum Press.

Boas, F. 1948. *Race, Language, and Culture.* New York: Macmillan.

Bock, P. 1988. *Rethinking Psychological Anthropology: Continuity and Change in the Study of Human Action.* New York: W. H. Freeman.

Bodley, J. 1999. *Victims of Progress,* 4th ed. Mountain View, CA: Mayfield.

Boesch, C., and H. Boesch. 1984. "Mental Map in Wild Chimpanzees: An Analysis of Hammer Transports for Nut Cracking." *Primates,* 25(2):169–170.

———. 1991. "Dim Forest, Bright Chimps." *Natural History,* September, pp. 50–56.

Bongaarts, J. 1980. "Does Malnutrition Affect Fertility? A Summary of the Evidence." *Science,* 208:564–569.

———. 1994a. "Can the Growing Human Population Feed Itself?" *Scientific American,* March, pp. 36–42.

———. 1994b. "Population Policy Options in the Developing World." *Science,* 263:771–776.

Bongaarts, J., and F. Odile. 1984. "The Proximate Determinants of Fertility in Sub-Saharan Africa." *Population and Development Review,* 10:511–537.

Bonta, B. 1993. *Peaceful Societies: An Annotated Bibliography.* Belmont, CA: Wadsworth.

Bonvillain, N. 1997. *Language, Culture and Communication: The Meaning of the Message.* Englewood Cliffs, NJ: Prentice-Hall.

———. 1998. *Women and Men.* New Jersey: Prentice Hall.

Boserup, E. 1965. *The Condition of Agricultural Growth: The Economics of Agrarian Change under Population Pressure.* Chicago: Aldine.

Bossen, L. 1988. "Toward a Theory of Marriage: The Economic Anthropology of Marriage Transactions." *Ethnology,* 27:127–144.

Bourgois, P. 1995. *In Search of Respect: Selling Crack in the Barrio.* Cambridge, England: Cambridge University Press.

Bourguignon, E. 1978. "Spirit Possession." In *The Making of Psychological Anthropology,* edited by G. Spindler. Berkeley: University of California Press.

Bowles, S., and H. Gintis. 1976. *Schooling in Capitalist America.* New York: Basic Books.

Boyd, R., and J. Silk. 1997. *How Humans Evolved.* New York: Norton.

———. 2006. *How Humans Evolved.* New York: Norton.

Bradley, C. 1997. "Why Fertility Is Going Down in Margoli." In *African Families and the Crisis of Social Change,* edited by T. Weisner et al. Westport, CT: Bergin and Garvey.

Bradsher, K. 1995. "Gap in Wealth in U.S. Called Widest in West." *New York Times,* April 17, pp. A1ff.

Brodkin, K. 1994. "How Did Jews Become White Folks?" In *Race,* edited by S. Gregory and R. Sanjek (pp. 78–102). New Brunswick, NJ: Rutgers University Press.

Brown, J. K. 1975. "Iroquois Women: An Ethnohistoric Note." In *Toward an Anthropology of Women,* edited by R. Reiter (pp. 235–251). New York: Monthly Review Press.

Brown, L., et al. 1991. *State of the World 1991: A Worldwatch Institute Report on Progress toward a Sustainable Society.* New York: W. W. Norton.

———. 1993. *Vital Signs.* New York: W. W. Norton.

———. 1994. "Facing Food Insecurity." In *State of the World 1994,* edited by L. Brown (pp. 177–197). New York: W. W. Norton.

Brown, R. 1978. Testimony: Hearings before the Subcommittee on Crime, House of Representatives, 95th Congress, Serial No. 47. Washington, DC: U.S. Government Printing Office.

Brumberg, J. J. 1988. *Fasting Girls: The Emergence of Anorexia Nervosa as a Modern Disease.* Cambridge, MA: Harvard University Press.

Brunton, R. 1975. "Why Do the Trobriands Have Chiefs?" *Man,* 10(4):545–550.

Buckley, T. 1982. "Menstruation and the Power of Yurok Women." *American Ethnologist,* 9:47–90.

Burton, R. V., and J. Whiting. 1961. "The Absent Father and Cross-Sex Identity." *Merrill-Palmer Quarterly of Behavior and Development,* 7(2):85–95.

Buss, D. M. 1994. *The Evolution of Desire Strategies of Human Mating.* New York: Basic Books.

Butterfield, F. 1996. "Study Finds Disparity in Justice for Blacks." *New York Times,* February 13, p. 8A.

Cain, M. 1977. "The Economic Activities of Children in a Village in Bangladesh." *Population and Development* (Review) 3:201–227.

Caldwell, J. 1982. *Theory of Fertility Decline.* New York: Academic Press.

Caldwell, J., and P. Caldwell. 1993. Cultural Factors Tending to Sustain High Fertility. In *Population Growth and Reproduction in Sub-Saharan Africa,* edited by G. T. Acsadi, G. Johnson-Acsadi, and R. A. Bulatao. Washington, DC: World Bank.

Caldwell, J., et al. 1983. "The Causes of Demographic Change in Rural South India: A Micro Approach." *Population and Demographic Review,* 8:689–727.

Campbell, S. 1983. "Kula in Vakuta: The Mechanics of Keda." In *The Kula: New Perspectives on Massim Exchange,* edited by J. Leach and E. Leach (pp. 201–227). Cambridge, England: Cambridge University Press.

Carneiro, R. 1970. "A Theory of the Origin of the State." *Science,* 169:733–738.

———. 1981. "Chiefdom: Precursor of the State." In *The Transition to Statehood in the New World,* edited by G. Jones and R. Kautz (pp. 37–75). New York: Cambridge University Press.

Carroll, L. 1977. "'Sanskritization,' 'Westernization,' and 'Social Mobility': A Reappraisal of the Relevance of Anthropological Concepts to the Social Historian of Modern India." *Journal of Anthropological Research,* 33(4):355–371.

Cashdan, E. 1989. "Hunters and Gatherers: Economic Behavior in Bands." In *Economic Anthropology,* edited by S. Plattner (pp. 21–48). Stanford, CA: Stanford University Press.

Castro, L., and M. A. Toro. 2004. "The Evolution of Culture: From Primate Social Learning to Human Culture." *Proceedings of the National Academy of Sciences of the United States of America,* 101(27):10235–10240.

Cattle, D. 1977. "An Alternative to Nutritional Particularism." In *Nutrition and Anthropology in Action,* edited by T. Fitzgerald. Amsterdam, The Netherlands: Van Gorcum.

Center for HIV Information. 2005. "HIV/AIDS in the World." http://hivinsite.ucsf.edu/global?page=cr-00-01.

Center for Women's Business Research. 2005. www.cfwbr.org.

Chagnon, N. 1989. "Response to Ferguson." *American Ethnologist,* 1989:565–569.

———. 1990. "Reproductive and Somatic Conflicts of Interests in the Genesis of Violence and Warfare among Tribesmen." In *The Anthropology of War,* edited by J. Haas (pp. 77–104). Cambridge, England: Cambridge University Press.

———. 1997. *Yanomamo,* 5th ed. New York: Harcourt, Brace, Jovanovich.

Chagnon, N., and R. Hames. 1979. "Protein Deficiency and Tribal Warfare in Amazonia: New Data." *Science,* 203:910–913.

Chakravarti, A. K. 1985a. "Cattle Development Problems and Programs In India: A Regional Analysis." *Geo Journal,* 10:21–45.

———. 1985b. "The Question of Surplus Cattle in India: A Spatial View." *Geografska Annala,* 67B:121–130.

Chambers, E. 1985. *Applied Anthropology: A Professional Guide.* Englewood Cliffs, NJ: Prentice-Hall.

Chase-Dunn, C. 1999. "Globalization: A World Systems Perspective." *Journal of World-Systems Research,* 5(2):165–185.

Child, A., and J. Child. 1985. "Biology, Ethnocentrism, and Sex Differences." *American Anthropologist,* 87:125–128.

Chodorow, N. 1974. "Family Structure and Feminine Personality." In *Woman, Culture, and Society,* edited by M. Rosaldo and L. Lamphere (pp. 43–66). Stanford, CA: Stanford University Press.

———. 1978. *The Reproduction of Mothering.* Berkeley: University of California Press.

Chomsky, N. 1973. "The General Properties of Language." In *Explorations in Anthropology: Readings in Culture, Man, and Nature,* edited by M. Fried (pp. 115–123). New York: Crowell.

———. 1989. *Necessary Illusions: Thought Control in Democratic Societies.* Boston: South End Press.

Cleaver, H. 1994. "The Chiapas Uprising and the Future of Class Struggle in the New World Order." February. www. gopher://mundo.eco.utexas.edu/00.

Cloud, W. 1973. "After the Green Revolution." *The Sciences,* 13(8):6–12.

Coe, M. 1977. *Mexico,* 2nd ed. New York: Praeger.

Cohen, J. 1995. "Population Growth and the Earth's Human Carrying Capacity." *Science,* 269:341–346.

Cohen, M. 1976. *House United, House Divided.* New York: Columbia University Press.

Cohen, M. N. 1977. *The Food Crisis in Prehistory.* New Haven, CT: Yale University Press.

Cohen, R. 1984a. "Warfare and State Foundation: Wars Make States and States Make Wars." In *Warfare, Culture and Environment,* edited by R. B. Ferguson (pp. 329–355). Orlando, FL: Academic Press.

———. 1984b. "Approaches to Applied Anthropology." *Communication and Cognition,* 17:135–162.

Cohn, B. 1955. "Changing Status of a Depressed Caste." In *Village India: Studies in the Little Community,* edited by M. Marriott. *American Anthropological Association Memoirs,* 83:55–77.

Condominas, G. 1977. *We Have Eaten the Forest.* New York: Hill and Wang.

Conyers, J. 1978. "Unemployment Is Cruel and Unusual Punishment." Hearings before the House Subcommittee on Crime, House of Representatives. Ninety-Fifth Congress, Serial No. 47, pp. 647–679. Washington, DC: U.S. Government Printing Office.

Counts, D. 1985. "Tamparonga: The Big Women of Kaliai (Papua New Guinea)." In *In Her Prime: A New View of Middle-Aged Women,* edited by J. Brown and V. Kerns (pp. 49–64). South Hadley, MA: Bergin and Garvey.

Craig, D. 1979. "Immortality through Kinship: The Vertical Transmission of Substance and Symbolic Estate." *American Anthropologist,* 81:94–96.

Crooks, D. 1995. "American Children at Risk: Poverty and Its Consequences for Children's Health, Growth, and School Achievement." *Yearbook of Physical Anthropology,* 38:57–86.

Crossette, B. 1989. "India Studying the 'Accidental' Deaths of Hindu Wives." *New York Times,* January 15, p. 4.

Curvin, R., and B. Porter. 1978. "The Myth of Blackout Looters." *New York Times,* July 13, p. 21.

D'Altroy, T., and T. K. Earle. 1985. "Staple Finance, Wealth Finance, and Storage in the Inca Political Economy." *Current Anthropology,* 26:187–206.

D'Altroy, T. 1992. *Provincial Power in the Inca Empire.* Washington, DC: Smithsonian Institute Press.

D'Andrade, R. 1992. "Cognitive Anthropology." In *New Directions in Psychological Anthropology,* edited by T. Schwartz, G. White, and C. Lutz (pp. 47–67). New York: Cambridge University Press.

———. 1995. *The Development of Cognitive Anthropology.* Melbourne, Australia: Cambridge University Press.

Dahl, R. 1981. *Democracy in the United States,* 4th ed. Boston: Houghton Mifflin.

Dalton, G. 1969. "Theoretical Issues in Economic Anthropology." *Current Anthropology,* 10:63–102.

Darwin, C. 1998. *On the Origin of Species.* New York: Random House. Originally published 1859.

Dasgupta, M. 1978. "Production Relations and Population: Rampur." *Journal of Development Studies,* 14(4):177–185.

Dasgupta, P. 1995. "Population, Poverty, and the Local Environment." *Scientific American,* February, pp. 40–44.

Davis–Floyd, R. 2005. "Gender and Ritual: Giving Birth the American Way." In *Gender in Cross Cultural Perspective,* 4th ed., edited by C. Brettell and C. Sargent (pp. 449–460). Upper Saddle River, NJ: Prentice Hall.

Dehavenon, A. L. 1989–1990. "Charles Dickens Meets Franz Kafka: The Maladministration of New York City's Public Assistance Programs." *New York University Review of Law and Social Change,* 17:231–254.

———. 1995. "A Cultural Materialist Approach to the Causes of Hunger and Homelessness in New York City." In *Science, Materialism, and the Study of Culture*, edited by M. F. Murphy and M. Margolis (pp. 111–131). Gainesville: University of Florida Press.

de Lisser, E. 1998. "The Corporate Jungle: Anthropologists Find Business Studying Company Inefficiencies." *Wall Street Journal,* September 28, p. 1.

Deloria, V. 1969. *Custer Died for Your Sins.* London, England: Collier-Macmillan.

DeMarrais, E., L. J. Castillo, and T. Earle. 1996. Ideology, Materialization and Power Strategies. *Current Anthropology,* 37:15–31.

De Mott, B. 1990. *The Imperial Middle: Why Americans Can't Think Straight about Class.* New York: Morrow.

Dentan, R. 1968. *The Semai: A Non-Violent People of Malaya.* New York: Holt, Rinehart and Winston.

Devereaux, G. 1967. "A Typological Study of Abortion in 350 Primitive, Ancient, and Pre-Industrial Societies." In *Abortion in America,* edited by H. Rosen (pp. 95–152). Boston: Beacon Press.

de Waal, F. 1999. "Cultural Primatology Comes of Age." *Nature,* 399:635–636.

Dewalt, K. M., B. R. Dewalt, with C. B. Wayland. 1998. Participant Observation. In *Handbook of Methods in Cultural Anthropology,* edited by H. R. Bernard. London, England: Alta Press.

Diamond, J. 1997. *Guns, Germs and Steele: The Fates of Human Societies.* New York: Norton.

Dickman, M. 1984. "Concepts and Classification in the Study of Human Infanticide: Sectional Introduction and Some Cautionary Notes." In *Infanticide: Comparative and Evolutionary Perspectives,* edited by G. Hausfater and S. B. Hrdy. New York: Aldine.

Dickson, D. B. 1987. "Circumscription by Anthropogenic Environmental Destruction: An Expansion of Carneiro's (1970) Theory of the Origin of the State." *American Antiquity,* 52(4):709–716.

Divale, W. 1972. "Systematic Population Control in the Middle and Upper Paleolithic: Inferences Based on Contemporary Hunters and Gatherers." *World Archaeology,* 4:221–243.

Divale, W., and M. Harris. 1976. "Population, Warfare and the Male Supremacist Complex." *American Anthropologist,* 78:521–538.

Divale, W., M. Harris, and D. Williams. 1978. "On the Misuse of Statistics: A Reply to Hirschfeld et al." *American Anthropologist,* 80:379–386.

Dole, G. 1966. "Anarchy without Chaos: Alternatives to Political Authority among the Kui-Kuru." In *Political Authority,* edited by M. J. Swartz, V. W. Turner, and A. Tuden (pp. 73–88). Chicago: Aldine.

Dominguez, B., and S. Mahler. 1993. *Alternative Enumeration of Undocumented Mexicans in the South Bronx.* Ethnographic Evaluation of the 1990 Decennial Census Report Series. Washington, DC: Center for Survey Methods Research, U.S. Bureau of the Census.

Donald, L. 1997. *Aboriginal Slavery on the Northwest Coast of North America.* Berkeley: University of California Press.

Drew, E. 1983. *Politics and Money: The New Road to Corruption.* New York: Macmillan.

Du Bois, C. 1944. *The People of Alor.* New York: Harper.

Dumond, D. 1975. "The Limitation of Human Population: A Natural History." *Science,* 1987:713–721.

Dumont, L. 1970. *Homo Hierarchicus: The Caste System and Its Implications,* translated by M. Sainsbury. Chicago: University of Chicago Press.

Duran, D. 1964. *The Aztecs: The History of the Indies of New Spain.* New York: Orion Press.

Duranti, A. 1997. *Linguistic Anthropology.* Cambridge, England: Cambridge University Press.

———. 2001. "Linguistic Anthropology: History, Ideas and Issues." In *Linguistic Anthropology,* edited by A. Duranti. Malden, MA: Blackwell.

Durkheim, E. 1995 [1912]. *Elementary Forms of the Religious Life.* New York: Free Press.

Dyson-Hudson, R., and J. T. McCabe. 1985. *South Turkana Nomadism: Coping with an Unpredictably Varying Environment.* New Haven, CT: HRAF (Human Relations Area Files) Press.

Dyson-Hudson, R., and D. Meekers. 1996. "The Universality of African Marriage Reconsidered: Evidence from the Turkana." *Ethnology,* 35:301–320.

Earle, T. 1978. *Economic and Social Organization of a Complex Chiefdom: The Halelea District, Kauai, Hawaii.* Anthropological Papers, no. 63. Ann Arbor: Museum of Anthropology, University of Michigan.

———. 1989. "The Evolution of Chiefdoms." *Current Anthropology,* 30:84–88.

———. 1997. *How Chiefs Come to Power: The Political Power in Prehistory.* Stanford, CA: Stanford University Press.

———. 2000 "Archeology, Property, and Prehistory." *Annual Reviews in Anthropology.* 29:39–60.

Earle, T., ed. 1991. *Chiefdoms: Power, Economy, and Ideology.* Cambridge, England: Cambridge University Press.

Eaton, S. B., M. Shostak, and M. Konner. 1988. *The Paleolithic Prescription: A Program for Diet and Exercise and a Design for Living.* New York: Harper & Row.

Edgerton, R. B. 1971. *The Individual in Cultural Adaptation: A Study of Four East African Peoples.* Berkeley: University of California Press.

Eliade, M. 1958. *Birth and Rebirth: The Religious Meaning of Initiation in Human Culture.* New York: Harper & Row.

Ember, C., and M. Ember. 1992. "Resource Unpredictability, Mistrust, and War." *Journal of Conflict Resolution,* 36:242–262.

———. 1997. "Violence in the Ethnographic Record: Results of Cross-Cultural Research on War and Aggression." In *Troubled Times, Violence and Warfare in the Past,* edited by D. L. Martin and D. W. Frayer (pp. 1–20). The Netherlands: Gordon and Breach.

Ember, C., M. Ember, and B. Pasternack. 1974. "On the Development of Unilineal Descent." *Journal of Anthropological Research,* 30:69–94.

Ember, M., and C. Ember. 1971. "The Conditions Favoring Matrifocal versus Patrifocal Residence." *American Anthropologist,* 73:571–594.

Engels, F. 1990. *Origin of the Family, Private Property, and the State.* New York: International Publishers. Originally published 1884.

Erickson, C. L., and K. L. Chandler, 1989. "Raised Fields and Sustainable Agriculture in the Lake Titicaca Basin of Peru." *Fragile Lands of Latin America: Strategies for Sustainable Development,* edited by J. O. Browder (pp. 230–248). Boulder, CO: Westview Press.

Errington, F., and D. Gewertz. 1987. *Cultural Alternatives and a Feminist Anthropology.* New York: Cambridge University Press.

Estioko-Griffin, A. 1986. Daughters of the Forest. *Natural History,* 95(5):36–43.

Estioko-Griffin, A., and P. B. Griffin. 1997. "Woman the Hunter: The Agta." In *Gender in Cross-Cultural Perspective,* edited by C. B. Brettell and C. F. Sargent (pp. 219–227). Upper Saddle River, NJ: Prentice-Hall.

Evans-Pritchard, E. E. 1940. *The Nuer: A Description of the Modes of Livelihood and Political Institutions of a Nilotic People.* Oxford, England: Clarendon Press.

Exter, T. 1991. "The Cost of Growing Up." *American Demographics,* 13(8):59ff.

Fausto-Sterling, A. 1993. *Sciences,* March–April, pp. 20–24.

Fei Hsiao-T'ung, and Chang Chih-I. 1947. *Earthbound China: A Study of Rural Economy in Yunnan.* Chicago: University of Chicago Press.

Feinman, G., and J. Neitzel. 1984. "Too Many Types: An Overview of Sedentary Prestate Societies in the Americas." In *Advances in Archaeological Method and Theory,* edited by M. B. Schiffer (pp. 39–102). New York: Academic Press.

Ferguson, R. B. 1984. "Introduction: Studying War." In *Warfare, Culture and Environment,* edited by R. B. Ferguson (pp. 1–61). Orlando, FL: Academic Press.

———. 1989a. "Game Wars? Ecology and Conflict in Amazonia." *Journal of Anthropological Research,* 45:179–206.

———. 1989b. "Ecological Consequences of Amazonian Warfare." *Ethnology,* 27:249–264.

———. 1992. "A Savage Encounter: Western Contact and the Yanomami War Complex." In *War in the Tribal Zone: Expanding States and Indigenous Warfare,* edited by R. B. Ferguson and N. Whitehead (pp. 199–227). Santa Fe, NM: School of American Research Press.

———. 1995. *Yanomami Warfare: A Political History.* Santa Fe, NM: School of American Research.

Ferguson, R. B., and N. Whitehead, eds. 1992. *War in the Tribal Zone: Expanding States and Indigenous Warfare.* Santa Fe, NM: School of American Research Press.

Ferraro, G. P. 1994. *The Cultural Dimension of International Business.* Englewood Cliffs, NJ: Prentice-Hall.

Ferraro, G. P., W. Travathan, and J. Levy. 1994. *Anthropology: An Applied Perspective.* St. Paul, MN: West.

Fessler, D. 1999. *Toxic Sex: An Essay on Incest and Other Things.* Unpublished manuscript, Department of Anthropology, University of California at Los Angeles.

Fessler, D., and C. D. Navarrete. 2002. *Third-Party Attitudes toward Incest: Evidence for the Westermarck Effect.* Unpublished manuscript, Department of Anthropology, University of California at Los Angeles.

Fessler, D., and D. Navarrete. 2004. "Third-Party Attitudes toward Sibling Incest: Evidence for Westermarck's Hypotheses." *Evolution and Human Behavior,* 25:277–294.

Fiske, A. P. 1999. *Learning a Culture the Way Informants Do: Observing, Imitating, and Participating.* Unpublished manuscript, Department of Anthropology, University of California at Los Angeles.

Fletcher, M. 1998. "Interracial Marriage Eroding Barriers." *Washington Post,* December 29.

Fortune, R. 1965. *Manus Religion.* Lincoln, NE: University of Nebraska Press.

Foster, G, M. 1967. *Tzintzuntzan: Mexican Peasants in a Changing World.* Boston: Little, Brown.

———. 1974. "Limited Good or Limited Goods: Observations on Acheson." *American Anthropologist,* 76:53–57.

Fouts, R. S., and D. H. Fouts. 1985. "Signs of Conversation in Chimpanzees." Paper given at meeting of AAAS, Los Angeles, May 28–31.

———. 1989. "Loulis in Conversation with the Cross-Fostered Chimpanzees." In *Teaching Sign Language to Chimpanzees,* edited by R. A. Gardner, B. T. Gardner, and T. E. Van Cantfort (pp. 293–307). Albany: State University of New York Press.

Franke, R. 1974. "Miracle Seeds and Shattered Dreams." *Natural History,* 83(1):10ff.

———. 1975. "The Green Revolution in a Javanese Village." Ph.D. dissertation, Harvard University.

Frayser, S. 1985. *Varieties of Sexual Experience: An Anthropological Perspective on Human Sexuality.* New Haven, CT: HRAF (Human Relations Area Files) Press.

Frazer, J. 1911–1915. *The Golden Bough,* 3rd ed. London, England: Macmillan.

Freedman, R. 1977. "Nutritional Anthropology: An Overview." In *Nutrition and Anthropology in Action,* edited by T. Fitzgerald (pp. 1–23). Amsterdam, The Netherlands: Van Gorcum.

Fried, M. H. 1967. *The Evolution of Political Society: An Essay in Political Anthropology.* New York: Random House.

———. 1978. "The State, the Chicken, and the Egg; or What Came First?" In *Origins of the State,* edited by R. Cohen and E. Service (pp. 35–47). Philadelphia: Institute for the Study of Human Issues.

Frisancho, A. R., J. Matos, and P. Flegel. 1983. "Maternal Nutritional Status and Adolescent Pregnancy Outcome." *American Journal of Clinical Nutrition,* 38:739–746.

Frisch, R. 1984. "Body Fat, Puberty and Fertility." *Science,* 199:22–30.

Fulton, R., and S. Anderson. 1992. "The Amerindian 'Man–Woman': Gender, Liminality, and Cultural Continuity." *Current Anthropology,* 33:603–609.

Gal, S. 1989. "Language and Political Economy." *Annual Review of Anthropology,* 18:345–367.

Galaty, J. G., and D. L. Johnson. 1990. *The World of Pastoralism: Herding Systems in Comparative Perspective.* London, England: Belhaven Press.

Galef, B. G. 1992. "The Question of Animal Culture." *Human Nature,* 3:157–178.

Gandhi, M. K. 1954. *How to Serve the Cow.* Ahmedabad, India: Navajivan Publishing.

Gardner, B. T., and R. A. Gardner. 1971. "Two-Way Communication with a Chimpanzee." In *Behavior of Non-Human Primates,* edited by A. Schrier and F. Stollnitz (vol. 4, pp. 117–184). New York: Academic Press.

———. 1975. "Early Signs of Language in Child and Chimpanzee." *Science,* 187:752–753.

Gaulin, S., and J. S. Boster. 1990. "Dowry as Female Competition." *American Anthropologist,* 92:994–1005.

Gay, J. 1986. "'Mummies and Babies' and Friends and Lovers in Lesotho." In *Anthropology and Homosexual Behavior,* edited by E. Blackwood (pp. 97–116). New York: Haworth Press.

Geertz, C. 1973. *The Interpretation of Cultures.* New York: Basic Books.

George, S. 1990. "Agropastoral Equations in India: Intensification and Change of Mixed Farming Systems." "Dimorphism and Stature among Human Societies." *American Journal of Physical Anthropology,* 53:441–456.

George, S., R. Abel, and B. Miller. 1992. "Female Infanticide in Rural South India." *Economic and Political Weekly,* 30:1153–1156.

Gibbons, A. 1991. "Deja Vu All Over Again: Chimp Language Wars." *Science,* 251:1561–1562.

Gilmore, D. 1990. *Manhood in the Making: Cultural Concepts of Masculinity.* New Haven, CT: Yale University Press.

Ginsburg, W. 1999. "Income and Inequality, Eight Years of Prosperity: Millions Left Behind." www.adaction.org/99incineq.html

Glazer, N., and D. P. Moynihan. 1963. *Beyond the Melting Pot.* Cambridge, MA: Harvard University Press.

Gmelch, G. 1971. "Baseball Magic." *Transaction* 8(8):39–54.

Goddard, V. 1996. *Gender, Family and Work in Naples.* London, England: Berg Publishers.

Goldschmidt, W. 1965. "Variation and Adaptability of Culture." *American Anthropologist,* 67:400–447.

Goldstein, M. 1987. "When Brothers Share a Wife." *Natural History,* 96:39–49.

Goliber, T J. 1997. "Population and Reproductive Health in Sub-Saharan Africa." *Population Bulletin,* 52(4). Washington, DC: Population Reference Bureau.

Good, B. 1994. *Medicine, Rationality, and Experience.* Cambridge, MA: Cambridge University Press.

Good, K. 1987. "Limiting Factors in Amazonian Ecology." In *Food and Evolution: Toward a Theory of Human Food Habits,* edited by M. Harris and E. Ross (pp. 407–426). Philadelphia: Temple University Press.

———. 1989. *Yanomami Hunting Patterns: Trekking and Garden Relocation as an Adaptation to Game Availability in Amazonia, Venezuela.* Unpublished doctoral dissertation, University of Florida.

———. 1995. "Hunting Patterns and Village Fissioning among the Yanomami." In *Science, Materialism, and the Study of Culture,* edited by M. F. Murphy and M. Margolis (pp. 81–95). Gainesville: University Press of Florida.

Goodall, J. *See* Van Lawick-Goodall, J.

Goodwin, M. H. 1990. *He-Said-She-Said: Talk as Social Organization among Black Children.* Bloomington: Indiana University Press.

Goody, J. 1976. *Production and Reproduction.* New York: Cambridge University Press.

———. 1986. *The Logic of Writing and the Organization of Society.* Cambridge, England: Cambridge University Press.

Goudsblom, J. 1992. *Fire and Civilization.* New York: Penguin.

Gough, E. K. 1968. "The Nayars and the Definition of Marriage." In *Marriage Family and Residence,* edited by P. Bohannon and J. Middleton (pp. 49–71). Garden City, NY: Natural History Press.

Gould, R. 1982. "To Have and Not to Have: The Ecology of Sharing among Hunter–Gatherers." In *Resource Managers: North American and Australian Hunter–Gatherers,* edited by N. Williams and E. Hunn (pp. 69–91). Boulder, CO: Westview Press.

Graber, R. 1991. "Population Pressure, Agricultural Origins, and Cultural Evolution: Constrained Mobility or Inhibited Expansion?" *American Anthropologist,* 93:692–697.

———. 1992. "Population Pressure, Agricultural Origins, and Global Theory: Comment on McCorriston and Hole." *American Anthropologist,* 94:443–445.

Gramby, R. 1977. "Deerskins and Hunting Territories: Competition for a Scarce Resource of the Northeastern Woodlands." *American Antiquity,* 42:601–605.

Gramsci, A. 1971. *Selections from Prison Notebooks* (Q. Hoare and G. Nowell Smith, eds.). London: Wishart.

Gregersen, E. 1994. *The World of Human Sexuality.* New York: Irvington.

Gregor, T. 1973. "Privacy and Extra-Marital Affairs in a Tropical Forest Community." In *Peoples and Cultures of Native South America,* edited by D. R. Gross (pp. 242–262). New York: Doubleday/Natural History Press.

———. 1977. *Mehinacu.* Chicago: University of Chicago Press.

———. 1985. *Anxious Pleasure: The Sexual Lives of an Amazonian Peoples.* Chicago: University of Chicago Press.

———. 1994. Symbols and Rituals of Peace in Brazil's Upper Xingu. In *The Anthropology of Peace and Nonviolence,* edited by L. Sponsel and T. Gregor (pp. 241–258). Boulder, CO: Lynne Rienneer.

Gregor, T., and D. Tuzin. 2001. "Comparing Gender in Amazonia and Melanesia: A Theoretical Orientation." In *Gender in Amazonia and Melanesia,* edited by T. Gregor and D. Tuzin (pp. 1–16). Berkeley: University of California Press.

Gulliver, P. 1955. *The Family Herds.* London, England: Routledge & Kegan Paul.

Haas, J. 1982. *The Evolution of the Prehistoric State.* New York: Columbia University Press.

Hakansson, N. T., and R. LeVine. 1997. "Gender and Life Course Strategies among the Gusii." In *African Families and the Crisis of Social Change,* edited by T. Weisner, C. Bradley, and P. Kilbride (pp. 253–267). Westport, CT: Bergin and Garvey.

Hamilton, S., B. Popkin, and D. Spice. 1984. *Women and Nutrition in Third World Countries.* South Hadley, MA: Bergin and Garvey.

Hammer, D. 1993. "Linkage between DNA Markers on the X Chromosome and Male Sexual Orientation." *Science* 261:321–327.

Hannerz, U. 1998. "Transnational Research." In *Handbook of Methods in Cultural Anthropology,* edited by H. R. Bernard. London, England: Alta Mira Press.

Haraway, D. 1989. *Primate Visions: Gender, Race, and Nature in the World of Modern Science.* New York: Routledge.

Harner, M. J. 1972. *The Jivaro: People of the Sacred Waterfalls.* Garden City, NY: Natural History Press.

———. 1977. "The Ecological Basis for Aztec Sacrifice." *American Ethnologist,* 4:117–135.

———. 1980. *The Way of the Shaman: A Guide to Power and Healing.* New York: Bantam.

———. 1984. *The Jivaro: People of the Sacred Waterfall.* Berkeley: University of California Press.

Harrington, C., and J. Whiting. 1972. "Socialization Process and Personality." In *Psychological Anthropology,* edited by F. Hsu (pp. 469–507). Cambridge, MA: Schenkman.

Harris, D. 1987. "Aboriginal Subsistence in a Tropical Rain Forest Environment: Food Procurement, Cannibalism and Population Regulation in Northeastern Australia." In *Food and Evolution: Toward a Theory of Human Food Habits,* edited by M. Harris and E. Ross (pp. 357–385). Philadelphia: Temple University Press.

Harris, H. 1995. "Rethinking Polynesian Heterosexual Relationships: A Case Study on Mangaia, Cook Islands." In *Romantic Passion,* edited by W. Jankowiak (pp. 96–127). New York: Columbia University Press.

Harris, M. 1974. *Pigs, Cows, Wars, and Witches.* New York: Random House.

———. 1977. *Cannibals and Kings: The Origins of Cultures.* New York: Random House.

———. 1979a. "Comments on Simoons' Questions in the Sacred Cow Controversy." *Current Anthropology,* 20:479–482.

———. 1979b. *Cultural Materialism.* New York: Random House.

———. 1984. "Animal Capture and Yanomami Warfare: Retrospective and New Evidence." *Journal of Anthropological Research,* 40:183–201.

———. 1985. *Good to Eat: Riddles of Food and Culture.* New York: Simon & Schuster.

———. 1989. *Our Kind: Who We Are, Where We Came From, Where We Are Going.* New York: Harper & Row.

———. 1994. "Cultural Materialism Is Alive and Well and Won't Go Away Until Something Better Comes Along." In *Assessing Anthropology,* edited by R. Borofsky. New York: McGraw-Hill.

Harris, M., and E. Ross, eds. 1987. *Death, Sex, and Fertility*. New York: Columbia University Press.

Harris, M., J. Gomes Consorte, J. Lang, and B. Byrne. 1993. "Who Are the Whites? Imposed Census Categories and the Racial Demography of Brazil." *Social Forces*, 72:451–462.

Hart, C. W. M., and A. R. Pilling. 1960. *The Tiwi of North Australia*. New York: Holt, Rinehart and Winston.

Hartung, J. 1985. "Review of Incest: A Bisocial View, by J. Sheper." *American Journal of Physical Anthropology*, 67:169–171.

Hassan, F. 1978. "Demographic Archaeology." In *Advances in Archaeological Method and Theory*, edited by M. Schiffer (pp. 49–103). New York: Academic Press.

Hawkes, K. 1993. "Why Hunter–Gatherers Work: An Ancient Version of the Problem of Public Goods." *Current Anthropology*, 34:341–361.

Hawkes, K., K. Hill, and J. O'Connell. 1982. "Why Hunters Gather: Optimal Foraging and the Ache of Eastern Paraguay." *American Ethnologist*, 9:379–398.

Hayden, B. 1987. "Alliances and Ritual Ecstasy: Human Responses to Resource Stress." *Journal for the Scientific Study of Religion*, 26:81–91.

———. 1992. "Conclusions: Ecology and Complex Hunter/Gatherers." In *A Complex Culture of the British Columbia Plateau*, edited by B. Hayden (pp. 525–559). Vancouver, Canada: University of British Columbia Press.

———. 1993a. *Archaeology: The Science of Once and Future Things*. New York: W. H. Freeman

———. 1995. "Pathways to Power." In *Foundations of Social Inequality*, edited by T. D. Price and G. Feinman (pp. 15–86). New York: Plenum.

Hayden, B., et al. 1986. "Ecological Determinants of Women's Status among Hunter/Gatherers." *Human Evolution*, 1(5):449–474.

Hays, T. E. 1988. " 'Myths of Matriarchy' and the Sacred Flute Complex of the Papua New Guinea Highlands." In *Myths of Matriarchy Reconsidered*, edited by D. Gewertz (pp. 98–120). Sydney, Australia: University of Sydney.

Headland, T. N., K. L. Pike, and M. Harris. 1990. *Emics and Etics: The Insider/Outsider Debate*. Newbury Park, CA: Sage.

Heider, K. G. 1991. *Grand Valley Dani: Peaceful Warriors*, 2nd ed. Forth Worth, TX: Holt, Rinehart and Winston.

Hendry, J. 1995. *Understanding Japanese Society*. New York: Routledge.

Herdt, G. 1984a. "Semen Transactions in Sambia Cultures." In *Ritualized Homosexuality in Melanesia*, edited by G. Herdt (pp. 167–210). Berkeley: University of California Press.

———. 1984b. "Ritualized Homosexuality Behavior in the Male Cults of Melanesia 1862–1983: An Introduction." In *Ritualized Homosexuality in Melanesia*, edited by G. Herdt (pp. 1–81). Berkeley: University of California Press.

———. 1987. *The Sambia: Ritual and Custom in New Guinea*. New York: Holt, Rinehart and Winston.

———. 1997. "The Dilemmas of Desire: From 'Berdache' to Two-Spirit." In *Two Spirit People: Native American Gender Identity, Sexuality and Spirituality*, edited by S. E. Jacobs, W. Thomas, and S. Lang. Chicago: University of Chicago Press.

Herman, E. S., and N. Chomsky. 1988. *Manufacturing Consent: The Political Economy of the Mass Media*. New York: Pantheon Books.

Hern, W. 1992. "Shipibo Polygyny and Patrilocality." *American Ethnologist*, 19:501–522.

Hewes, G. 1992. "Comment on McCauly." *Current Anthropology*, 33:162.

Hill, J. 1978. "Apes and Language." *Annual Review of Anthropology*, 7:89–112.

Hill, J., and B. Mannheim. 1992. "Language and World View." *Annual Review of Anthropology*, 21:381–406.

Hirschfeld, L., J. Howe, and B. Levin. 1978. "Warfare, Infanticide and Statistical Inference: A Comment on Divale and Harris." *American Anthropologist*, 80:110–115.

Hitchcock, R. K. 1999. "Resource Rights and Resettlement among the San of Botswana." *Cultural Survival Quarterly*, 22(4). http://209.200.101.189/publications/csq/csq–article.cfm?id=364&highlight=Hitchcock.

Hochschild, A. R. 1998. *Time Bind: When Work Becomes Home and Home Becomes Work*. New York: Henry Holt.

Hockett, C., and R. Ascher. 1964. "The Human Revolution." *Current Anthropology*, 5:135–147.

Hogbin, H. I. 1964. *Guadalcanal Society: The Koaka Speakers*. New York: Holt, Rinehart and Winston.

Holton, G. 1994. *Science and Anti-Science*. Cambridge, MA: Harvard University Press.

Hommon, R. 1986. "Social Evolution in Ancient Hawaii." In *Island Societies: Archaeological Approaches to Evolution and Transformation*, edited by P. Kirch (pp. 55–69). New York: Cambridge University Press.

Hopkins, K. 1980. "Brother–Sister Marriage in Ancient Egypt." *Comparative Studies in Society and History*, 22:303–354.

Horney, K. 1967. *Feminine Psychology*. New York: Norton. Originally published 1939.

Hua, C. 2001. *A Society without Fathers or Husbands*. New York: Zone Books.

Husain, T. 1976. "The Use of Anthropologists in Project Appraisal by the World Bank." In *Development from Below: Anthropologists and Development Situations*, edited by D. Pitt (pp. 71–81). The Hague, The Netherlands: Mouton.

Irwin, G. 1983. "Chieftainship, Kula and Trade in Massim Prehistory." In *The Kula: New Perspectives on Massim Exchange*, edited by J. Leach and E. Leach (pp. 29–72). Cambridge, England: Cambridge University Press.

Isaac, B. 1988. "Introduction." In *Prehistoric Economies of the Pacific Northwest Coast*, edited by B. Isaac (pp. 1–16). Greenwich, CT: JAI Press.

Itani, J. 1961. "The Society of Japanese Monkeys." *Japan Quarterly*, 8:421–430.

Itani, J., and A. Nishimura. 1973. "The Study of Infra-Human Culture in Japan." In *Precultural Primate Behavior*, edited by E. W. Menzell (pp. 26–50). Basel, Switzerland: Karger.

Izquierdo, C. 2001. *Betwixt and Between: Seeking Cure and Meaning among the Matsigenka of the Peruvian Amazon*. Ph.D. dissertation, University of California, Los Angeles.

Jacobs, S., and C. Roberts. 1989. "Sex, Sexuality, Gender, and Gender Variance." In *Gender and Anthropology*, edited by S. Morgan (pp. 438–462). Washington, DC: American Anthropological Association.

Janus, N. 1991. "Advertising and Global Culture." In *Applying Cultural Anthropology: An Introductory Reader*, edited by A. Podolefsky and P. J. Brown. Mountain View, CA: Mayfield.

Jenkins, J. H., and M. Karno. 1992. "The Meaning of Expressed Emotion: Theoretical Issues Raised by Cross-Cultural Research." *American Journal of Psychiatry*, 149:9–21.

Jenkins, J. H., et al. 1986. "Expressed Emotion in Cross-Cultural Context: Familial Responses to Schizophrenic Illness among Mexican Americans." In *Treatment of Schizophrenia*, edited by M. J. Goldstein, I. Hand, and K. Hahlweg (pp. 35–49). Berlin, Germany: Springer.

Jenkins, J. H., A. Kleinman, and B. Good. 1991. "Cross-Cultural Studies of Depression." In *Psychological Aspects of Depression*, edited by J. Becker and A. Kleinman (pp. 67–99). Hillsdale, NJ: Erlbaum.

Jitsukawa, M., and C. Djerassi. 1994. "Birth Control in Japan: Realities and Prognosis." *Science,* 265:1048–1051.

Johnson, A. 1978. "In Search of the Affluent Society." *Human Nature,* 1(9):50–59.

———. 1989. "Horticulturalists: Economic Behavior in Tribes." In *Economic Anthropology,* edited by S. Plattner. Stanford, CA: Stanford University Press.

———. 2003. *The Matsigenka.* Berkeley: University of California Press.

Johnson, A., and T. Earle. 2000. *The Evolution of Human Societies from Foraging Groups to Agrarian States,* 2nd ed. Stanford, CA: Stanford University Press.

Johnson, A., and O. Johnson. 1987. *Time Allocation among the Machiguenga of Shimaa.* New Haven, CT: HREF (Human Relations Area Files) Press.

———. 2001. "Introduction to the Updated Edition." In *Cultural Materialism: The Struggle for a Science of Culture,* by M. Harris (pp. vi–xiv). Walnut Creek, CA: Alta Mira Press.

Johnson, A., and D. Price-Williams. 1996. *Oedipus Ubiquitous: The Family Complex in World Folk Literature.* Stanford, CA: Stanford University Press.

Johnson, A., and R. Sackett. 1998. "Direct Systematic Observation of Behavior." In *Handbook of Methods in Cultural Anthropology,* edited by H. R. Bernard. London, England: Alta Mira Press.

Johnson, O. 1978. *Domestic Organization among the Machiguenga Indians of Southeastern Peru.* Unpublished doctoral dissertation, Columbia University, New York.

———. 1980. *The Social Context of Intimacy and Avoidance: A Videotape Study of Machiguenga Meals. Ethnology,* 19(3):353–366.

Johnson, R. 2001. "Unraveling Workplace Intrigue—Karen Stephenson Helps Organizations around the World Find Their Backstabbers, Visionaries and Unsung Workhorses." *Los Angeles Times,* June 16.

Jonaitis, A. 1991. *Chiefly Feasts: The Enduring Kwakiutl Potlatch.* Seattle: University of Washington Press.

Kaeppler, A. 1978. "Dance in Anthropological Perspective." *Annual Review of Anthropology,* 7:31–49.

Kang, E. 1979. "Exogamy and Peace Relations of Social Units: A Cross-Cultural Test." *Ethnology,* 18:85–99.

Karno, M., and J. Jenkins. 1997. "Cultural Considerations in the Diagnosis of Schizophrenia and Related Disorders and Psychotic Disorders Not Otherwise Classified." In *DSM-IV Sourcebook,* edited by T. Widiger, et al. (vol. 3, pp. 901–908). Washington, DC: American Psychiatric Association.

Katz, R. 1982. *Boiling Energy: Community Healing among the Kalahari Kung.* Cambridge, MA: Harvard University Press.

Keegan, W. F., and M. D. MacLachlan. 1989. "The Evolution of Avunculocal Chiefdoms: A Reconstruction of Taino Kinship and Politics." *American Anthropologist,* 91:613–630.

Keeley, L. 1996. *War Before Civilization.* New York: Oxford University Press.

Kelly, R. 1976. "Witchcraft and Sexual Relations." In *Man and Woman in the New Guinea Highlands,* edited by P. Brown and G. Buchbinder (pp. 36–53). Washington, DC: Special Publication No. 8, American Anthropological Association.

Kelly, R. L. 1995. *The Foraging Spectrum, Diversity in Hunter Gatherer Lifeways.* Washington, DC: Smithsonian Institution Press.

Kennickell, A., et al. 1992. *Technical Working Paper.* Washington, DC: Federal Reserve.

Kennickell, A., et al. 2000. "Recent Changes in U.S. Family Finances: Results from the 1998 Survey of Consumer Finances." *Federal Reserve Bulletin,* January.

Kertzer, D. 1993. *Sacrificed for Honor: Italian Infant Abandonment and the Politics of Reproductive Control.* Boston: Beacon.

Khare, R. 1984. *The Untouchable as Himself: Identity and Pragmatism among the Lucknow Chamars.* New York: Cambridge University Press.

Khazanov, K. M. 1994. *Nomads and the Outside World.* Madison: University of Wisconsin Press.

Kimbrell, A. 2002. *Fatal Harvest.* Covelo, CA: Island Press.

Kirch, P. 1984. *The Evolution of Polynesian Chiefdoms.* New York: Cambridge University Press.

Klass, M. 1979. *Caste: The Emergence of the South Asian Social System.* Philadelphia: ISHI.

Kleinman, A. 1980. *Patients and Healer in the Context of Culture: An Exploration of the Borderland between Anthropology, Medicine, and Psychiatry.* Berkeley: University of California Press.

Kleugel, J., and E. R. Smith. 1981. "Beliefs about Stratification." *Annual Review of Sociology,* 7:29–56.

Knauft, B. M. 1987. "Reconsidering Violence in Simple Human Societies: Homicide among the Gebusi of New Guinea." *Current Anthropology,* 28:457–500.

———. 1990. "Melanesian Warfare: A Theoretical History." *Oceania,* 60:250–311.

———. 1994. The Human Evolution of Cooperative Interest. In *The Anthropology of Peace and Nonviolence,* edited by L. Sponsel and T. Gregor (pp. 71–94). Boulder, CO: Lynne Rienneer.

Kogod, K. S. 1998. "The Bridges Process: Enhancing Organizational Cultures to Support Diversity." In *Applying Cultural Anthropology,* edited by G. P. Ferarro (pp. 74–83). Belmont, CA: Wadsworth.

Konner, M. 1991. "The Promise of Medical Anthropology: An Invited Commentary." *Medical Anthropology Quarterly,* 5:78–82.

Kottak, C. 1990. *Prime-Time Society: An Anthropological Analysis of Television and Culture.* Ann Arbor: University of Michigan Press.

———. 1994. *Cultural Anthropology.* New York: McGraw-Hill.

Kroeber, A. L. 1948. *Anthropology.* New York: Harcourt Brace.

Kroskrity, P. 2001. "Arizons Tewa Kiva Speech as a Manifestation of a Dominant Language Ideology." In *Linguistic Anthropology,* edited by A. Duranti. Malden, MA: Blackwell.

Kumagai, H., and A. Kumagai. 1986. "The Hidden 'I' in Amae: Passive Love and Japanese Social Perception." *Ethos,* 14:305–320.

Kusin, J., S. Kardjati, and H. Renqvist. 1993. "Chronic Undernutrition in Pregnancy and Lactation." *Proceedings of the Nutrition Society,* 52:19–28.

Labov, W. 1972. *Language in the Inner City.* Philadelphia: University of Pennsylvania Press.

———. 1973. Some Features of the English of Black Americans. In *Variations of Present Day English,* edited by R. W. Bailey and J. L. Robinson. New York: Macmillan.

Lakoff, R. T. 1990. *The Politics of Language in Our Lives.* New York: Basic Books.

Lalasz, R. 2004. "World AIDS Day 2004: The Vulnerability of Women and Girls." Population Reference Bureau, November. www.prb.org/Template.cfm?Section=PRB&template=/ContentManagement/ContentDisplay.cfm&ContentID=12019.

Lambert, P. 1997. "Patterns of Violence in Prehistoric Hunter Gatherer Societies of Coastal Southern California." In *Troubled Times Violence and Warfare in the Past,* edited by D. L. Martin and D. W. Frayer (pp. 77–110). The Netherlands: Gordon and Breach.

Lang, H., and R. Gohlen 1985. "Completed Fertility of the Hutterites: A Revision." *Current Anthropology,* 26(3):395.

Lang, S. 1997. "Various Kinds of Two Spirit People: Gender Variance and Homosexuality in Native American Communities." In *Two Spirit People Native American Gender Identity, Sexuality and Spirituality,* edited by S. E. Jacobs, W. Thomas, and S. Lang. Chicago: University of Chicago Press.

Lansing, S. J. (1991). *Priests and Programmers: Technologies of Power in the Engineered Landscape of Bali.* Princeton, NJ: Princeton University Press. www.nsf.gov/sbe/nuggets/015/nugget.htm.

Lappe, F. M., J. Collins, and P. Rosset. 1998. *World Hunger: Twelve Myths.* San Antonio, TX: Grove Press.

Lawrence, P. 1964. *Road Belong Cargo: A Study of the Cargo Movement in the Southern Madang District, New Guinea.* Manchester, England: University of Manchester Press.

Leacock, E. B. 1978. "Women's Status in Egalitarian Society: Implication for Social Evolution." *Current Anthropology,* 19:247–275.

Leavitt, G. 1989. "Disappearance of the Incest Taboo." *American Anthropologist,* 91:116–131.

———. 1990. "Sociobiological Explanations of Incest Avoidance: A Critical Review of Evidential Claims." *American Anthropologist,* 91:971–993.

———. 1992. "Inbreeding Fitness: A Reply to Uhlman." *American Anthropologist,* 94:448–449.

Lebra, T. 1992 "The Self in Japanese Culture." In *Japanese Sense of Self,* edited by N. Rosenberger (pp. 105–120). Cambridge, England: Cambridge University Press.

Lee, R. 1968. "What Do Hunters Do for a Living, or How to Make Out on Scarce Resources." In *Man the Hunter,* edited by R. B. Lee and I. DeVore (pp. 30–43). Chicago: Aldine.

———. 1979. *The !Kung San: Men and Women in a Foraging Society.* Cambridge, England: Cambridge University Press.

———. 1990. "Primitive Communism and the Origin of Social Inequality." In *The Evolution of Political Systems: Sociopolitics of Small-Scale Sedentary Societies,* edited by S. Upham (pp. 225–246). New York: Cambridge University Press.

———. 1993. *The Dobe Jo/'hoansi.* Fort Worth, TX: Harcourt Brace.

Lee, R., and M. Guenther. 1991. "Oxen or Onions? The Search for Trade and the Truth in the Kalahari." *Current Anthropology,* 32:593–601.

Lee, S., and B. Edmonston. 2005. "New Marriages, New Families: U.S. Racial and Hispanic Intermarriage." *Population Bulletin,* 60(2). www.prb.org/pdf05/60.2NewMarriages.pdf.

Leeds, A. 1970. "The Concept of the Culture of Poverty: Conceptual, Logical, and Empirical Problems, with Perspectives from Brazil and Peru." In *The Culture of Poverty: A Critique,* edited by E. Leacock (pp. 226–284). New York: Simon & Schuster.

Leo, J. 1993. "The Melting Pot Is Cooking." *U.S. News & World Report,* July 5, p. 15.

Lesser, A. 1968. "War and the State." In *War: The Anthropology of Armed Conflict and Aggression,* edited by M. Fried, M. Harris, and R. Murphy (pp. 92–96). Garden City, NY: Natural History Press.

Lett, J. 1991. "Interpretive Anthropology, Metaphysics, and the Paranormal." *Journal of Anthropological Research,* 47:305–329.

Lett, J. W. 1997. *Science, Reason, and Anthropology: The Principles of Rational Inquiry.* Lanham, MD: Rowman & Littlefield.

Levine, N. 1988. *The Dynamics of Polyandry: Kinship, Domesticity, and Population on the Tibetan Border.* Chicago: University of Chicago Press.

Levine, N., and J. Silk. 1997. "Why Polyandry Fails: Sources of Instability in Polyandrous Marriages." *Current Anthropology,* 38:375–398.

Lévi-Strauss, C. 1969 [1949]. *The Elementary Structures of Kinship.* Boston: Beacon Press.

Lewis, O. 1966. *La Vida: A Puerto Rican Family in the Culture of Poverty—San Juan and New York.* New York: Random House.

Lewontin, R., S. Rose, and L. Kamin. 1984. *Not in Our Genes: Biology, Ideology, and Human Nature.* New York: Pantheon.

Lieberman, P. 1991. *The Evolution of Speech, Thought, and Selfless Behavior.* Cambridge, MA: Harvard University Press.

Liebow, E. 1967. *Tally's Corner: A Study of Negro Street Corner Men.* Boston: Little, Brown.

Lindholm, C., 2001. *Culture and Identity, the History, Theory and Practice of Psychological Anthropology.* New York: McGraw-Hill.

Linton, R. 1959. "The Natural History of the Family." In *The Family: Its Function and Destiny,* edited by R. Anshen (pp. 30–52). New York: Harper & Row.

Lizot, J. 1977. "Population, Resources and Warfare among the Yanomani." *Man,* 12:497–517.

———. 1979. "On Food Taboos and Amazon Cultural Ecology." *Current Anthropology,* 20:150–151.

Lockard, D. 1986. "The Lesbian Community: An Anthropological Approach." In *Anthropology and Homosexual Behavior,* edited by E. Blackwood (pp. 83–96). New York: Haworth Press.

Lomax, A., ed. 1968. *Folksong Style and Culture.* AAAS Pub. No. 88. Washington, DC: American Association for the Advancement of Science.

Lomax, A., and C. Arensberg. 1977. "A Worldwide Evolutionary Classification of Cultures by Subsistence Systems." *Current Anthropology,* 18:659–708.

Long, B. 1987. "Reincarnation." In *Encyclopedia of Religion* (vol. 12, pp. 265–269). New York: Macmillan.

Lostson, P. 1995. *Theories of Human Nature.* Peterboro, Canada: Broadview Press.

Lowie, R. 1948. *Primitive Religion.* New York: Liveright. Originally published 1924.

Ludwig, H., et al. 1993. "Uncertainty, Resource Exploitation, and Conservation: Lessons from History." *Science,* 260(5104):17–21.

Lunn, P. G. 1988. "Malnutrition and Fertility." In *Natural Human Fertility: Social and Biological Mechanisms,* edited by P. Diggory, et al. (pp. 135–152). New York: Macmillan.

MacCormack, C. P. 1982. "Adaptation in Human Fertility and Birth." In *Ethnography of Fertility and Birth,* edited by C. P. MacCormack (pp. 1–23). New York: Academic Press.

MacLachlan, M. 1983. *Why They Did Not Starve: Biocultural Adaptation in a South Indian Village.* Philadelphia: Institute for the Study of Human Issues.

MacLaury, R. E. 1992. "From Brightness to Hue: An Explanatory Model of Color-Category Evolution." *Current Anthropology,* 33:137–186.

MacLeish, K. 1972. "The Tasadays: The Stone Age Cavemen of Mindanao." *National Geographic,* 142:219–248.

MacLeod, J. 1995. *Ain't No Makin' It: Aspirations and Attainment in a Low-Income Neighborhood.* Boulder, CO: Westview Press.

MacNeish, R. 1981. "The Transition to Statehood as Seen from the Mouth of a Cave." In *The Transition to Statehood in the New World,* edited by G. Jones and P. Kautz (pp. 123–154). New York: Cambridge University Press.

MacQueen, K. 1994. "The Epidemiology of HIV Transmission: Trends, Structure, and Dynamics." *Reviews in Anthropology,* 23:509–526.

Malhotra, A., R. Vanneman, and S. Kishnor. 1995. "Fertility, Dimensions of Patriarchy, and Development in India." *Population and Development Review,* 21(2):281–307.

Malinowski, B. 1920. "War and Weapons among the Natives of the Trobriand Islands." *Man,* 20:10–12.

——. 1922. *Argonauts of the Western Pacific.* New York: Dutton.

——. 1935. *Coral Gardens and Their Magic.* 2 vols. London, England: Allen and Unwin.

Maloney, W. 1987a. "Dharma." *Encyclopedia of Religion* (vol. 4, pp. 239–332). New York: Macmillan.

——. 1987b. "Karma." *Encyclopedia of Religion* (vol. 8, pp. 261–266). New York: Macmillan.

Maltz, D., and R. Borkero, 1982. "A Cultural Approach to Male Female Miscommunication." In *Language and Social Identity,* edited by J. Gomperz. Cambridge, England: Cambridge University Press.

Mamdani, M. 1973. *The Myth of Population Control: Family, Caste, and Class in an Indian Village.* New York: Monthly Review Press.

Marett, R. 1914. *The Threshold of Religion.* London, England: Methuen.

Margolis, M. 2000. *True to Her Nature.* Prospect Heights, IL: Waveland Press.

Markus, H., and S. Kitayama. 1991. "Culture and the Self: Implications for Cognition, Emotion and Motivation." *Psychological Review,* 98:224–253.

Marshall, D. 1971. "Sexual Behavior on Mangaia." In *Human Sexual Behavior,* edited by D. Marshall and R. Suggs (pp. 103–162). Englewood Cliffs, NJ: Prentice-Hall.

Massing, M. 1989. "Crack's Destructive Sprint across America." *New York Times Magazine,* October 1, p. 38ff.

——. 1996. "Crime and Drugs: The New Myths." *New York Review of Books,* January, pp. 16–20.

Maybury-Lewis, D. 1997. *Indigenous Peoples, Ethnic Groups, and the State.* Boston: Allyn & Bacon.

McCorkle, C. 1994. "The Cattle Battle in Cross-Cultural Context." *Culture and Agriculture,* 50:2–4.

McFalls, J. A., Jr. 2003. "Population: A Lively Introduction." Population Reference Bureau, December. www.prb.org/Template.cfm?Section=PRB&template=/Content Management/ContentDisplay.cfm&ContentID=13446.

McGrath, J., et al. 1992. "Cultural Determinants of Sexual Risk Behavior for AIDS among Baganda Women." *Medical Anthropology Quarterly,* 6:153–161.

McGrew, W. C. 1977. "Socialization and Object Manipulation of Wild Chimpanzees." In *Primate Bio Social Development,* edited by S. Chevalier-Skolinkoff and F. Poirier (pp. 261–288). New York: Garland.

——. 1992. *Chimpanzee Material Culture: Implications for Human Evolution.* Cambridge, England: Cambridge University Press.

——. 1998. "Culture in Nonhuman Primates?" *Annual Reviews in Anthropology,* 27:301–328.

McGrew, W. C., C. Tutin, and P. Baldwin. 1979. "New Data on Meat Eating by Wild Chimpanzees." *Current Anthropology,* 20:238–239.

Mead, M. 1928 [1961]. *Coming of Age in Samoa: A Psychological Study of Primitive Youth for Western Civilization.* New York: Dell.

——. 1935 [1963]. *Sex and Temperament in Three Primitive Societies.* New York: William Morrow.

——. 1970. *Culture and Commitment.* Garden City, NY: Natural History Press.

Mechanic, D. 1986. "Role of Social Factors in Health and Well Being: The Biosocial Model from a Social Perspective." *Integrative Psychiatry,* 4:2–11.

Meggitt, M. 1965. *The Lineage System of the Mae Enga of New Guinea.* New York: Barnes and Noble.

——. 1977. *Blood Is Their Argument: Warfare among the Mae Enga Tribesmen of the New Guinea Highlands.* Palo Alto, CA: Mayfield.

Mencher, J. 1974. "The Caste System Upside Down: Or, the Not So Mysterious East." *Current Anthropology,* 15:469–478.

Merson, M. 1993. "Slowing the Spread of HIV: Agenda for the 1990's." *Science,* 260:1266–1268.

Messenger, J. C. 1971. "Sex and Repression in an Irish Folk Community." In *Human Sexual Behavior: Variations in the Ethnographic Spectrum,* edited by D. S. Marshall and R. C. Suggs. New York: Basic Books.

Miller, B. D. 1981. *The Endangered Sex: Neglect of Female Children in Rural North India.* Ithaca, NY: Cornell University Press.

——. 1987a. "Wife-Beating in India: Variations on a Theme." Paper read at the Annual Meetings of the American Anthropological Association, November.

——. 1987b. "Female Infanticide and Child Neglect in Rural North India." In *Child Survival,* edited by N. Scheper-Hughes (pp. 95–112). Boston: D. Reidel.

——. 1992. "Wife Beating in India: Variations on a Theme." In *Sanctions and Sanctuary: Cultural Perspectives on the Beating of Wives,* edited by D. Counts, J. Brown, and J. C. Campbell (pp. 173–184). Boulder, CO: Westview.

Minturn, L., and J. Stashak. 1982. "Infanticide as a Terminal Abortion Procedure." *Behavior Science Research,* 17:70–90.

Mitchell, D., and L. Donald. 1988. "Archaeology and the Study of Northwest Coast Economies." In *Prehistoric Economies of the Pacific Northwest Coast,* edited by B. Isaac (pp. 293–351). Greenwich, CT: JAI Press.

Miyadi, D. 1967. "Differences in Social Behavior among Japanese Macaque Troops." In *Progress in Primatology,* edited by D. Starck, R. Schneider, and H. Kuhn (pp. 228–231). Stuttgart, Germany: Gustav Fischer.

Mooney, J. 1965. *The Ghost Dance Religion.* Chicago: University of Chicago Press. Originally published 1896.

Moore, J. 1987. *The Cheyenne Nation.* Lincoln: University of Nebraska Press.

——. 1990. "The Reproductive Success of Cheyenne War Chiefs: A Contrary Case to Chagnon's Yanomami." *Current Anthropology,* 31:322–330.

Moran, E. 1999. *Human Adaptability, An Introduction to Ecological Anthropology.* Boulder, CO: Westview Press.

Morgan, L. H. 1994. *Ancient Society.* Tucson: University of Arizona Press. Originally published 1877.

Morgan, M. 1995. "Theories and Politics in African American English." *Annual Reviews of Anthropology,* 23:325–335.

Moseley, M. 2001. *The Inca and Their Ancestors, the Archeology of Peru.* New York: Thames & Hudson.

Moynihan, D. P. 1965. *The Negro Family, the Case for National Action.* Washington, DC: U.S. Department of Labor.

Murdock, G. P. 1949. *Social Structure.* New York: Macmillan.

———. 1967. *Ethnographic Atlas.* Pittsburgh: University of Pittsburgh Press.

Murphy, M. F., and M. Margolis. 1995. "An Introduction to Cultural Materialism." In *Science, Materialism, and the Study of Culture,* edited by M. F. Murphy and M. Margolis. Gainesville: University Press of Florida.

Murphy, R. 1976. "Man's Culture and Women's Nature." *Annals of the New York Academy of Sciences,* 293:15–24.

Murphy, Y., and R. F. Murphy. 2004. *Women of the Forest.* New York: Columbia University Press.

Murray, G. 1984. "The Wood Tree as a Peasant Cash Crop: An Anthropological Strategy for the Domestication of Energy." In *Haiti—Today and Tomorrow: An Interdisciplinary Study,* edited by C. Fost and A. Valdman (pp. 141–160). Lanham, MD: University Press of America.

———. 1995. "Peasants, Projects and Anthropological Models." In *Science, Materialism and the Study of Culture,* edited by M. F. Murphy and M. Margolis (pp. 159–184). Gainesville: University Press of Florida.

Murray, G. F., and Bannister, M. W. 2004. "Peasants, Agroforesters and Anthropologists: A 20-Year Venture in Income-Generating Trees and Hedgerows in Haiti." *Agroforestry Systems,* 61:383–397.

Nag, M., and N. Kak. 1984. "Demographic Transition in the Punjab Village." *Population and Development Review,* 10:661–678.

Nag, M., B. White, and R. Peet. 1978. "An Anthropological Approach to the Study of the Economic Value of Children in Java and Nepal." *Current Anthropology,* pp. 239–306.

Nardi, B. 1983. "Reply to Harbison's Comments on Nardi's Modes of Explanation in Anthropological Population Theory." *American Anthropologist,* 85:662–664.

Naroll, R. 1973. "Introduction." In *Main Currents in Anthropology,* edited by R. Naroll and F. Naroll (pp. 1–23). Englewood Cliffs, NJ: Prentice-Hall.

National Urban League. 1990. *State of Black America.* Washington, DC: Author.

Netting, R. 1986. *Cultural Ecology.* Long Grove, IL: Waveland Press.

———. 1989. "Smallholders, Householders, Freeholders: Why the Family Farm Works Well Worldwide." In *The Household Economy: Reconsidering the Domestic Mode of Production,* edited by R. Wilk (pp. 221–244). Boulder, CO: Westview Press.

———. 1993. *Smallholders, Householders: Farm Families and the Ecology of Intensive, Sustainable Agriculture.* Stanford, CA: Stanford University Press.

Netting, R., R. R. Wilk, and E. J. Arnould. 1984. *Households: Comparative and Historical Studies of the Domestic Group.* Berkeley: University of California Press.

Neville, G. 1979. "Community Form and Ceremonial Life in Three Regions of Scotland." *American Ethnologist,* 6:93–109.

Newitt, J. 1985. "How to Forecast Births." *American Demographics,* January, pp. 30–33, 51.

Newman, P. L. 1965. *Knowing the Gururumba.* New York: Holt, Rinehart and Winston.

Nishida, T. 1987. "Learning and Cultural Transmission in Nonhuman Primates." In *Primate Societies,* edited by B. B. Smuts et al. (pp. 462–474). Chicago: University of Chicago Press.

Noah, T. 1991. "Number of Poor Americans Is Up." *Wall Street Journal,* September 27, p. A2.

Oboler, R. S. 1988. "Is the Female Husband a Man? Woman/Woman Marriage among the Nandi of Kenya." *Ethnology,* 19:69–88.

Ochs, E., and C. Taylor. 2001. "The 'Father Knows Best' Dynamic in Dinnertime Narratives." In *Linguistic Anthropology,* edited by A. Duranti. Malden, MA: Blackwell.

Odend'hal, S. 1972. "Energetics of Indian Cattle in Their Environment." *Journal of Human Ecology,* 1:3–22.

Odum, H. T. 1971. *Environment, Power, and Society.* New York: Wiley-Interscience.

Ohlemacher, S. 2006. "Women-Owned Businesses Growing in U.S." *Forbes.* www.forbes.com/feeds/ap/2006/01/26/ap2477723.html.

Oliver, D. 1955. *A Solomon Island Society: Kinship and Leadership among the Siuai of Bougainville.* Cambridge, MA: Harvard University Press.

‡Oma, M., Kxao, and A. Thoma. 2002. "Will Tourism Destroy San Cultures?" *Cultural Survival Quarterly,* 26(1).

Oppenheimer, V. 1982. *Work and the Family: A Study in Social Demography.* New York: Academic Press.

Orans, M. 1968. "Maximizing in Jajmaniland: A Model of Caste Relations." *American Anthropologist,* 70:875–897.

Ortner, S., and H. Whitehead, eds. 1981. *The Cultural Construction of Gender and Sexuality.* Cambridge, England: Cambridge University Press.

Otterbein, K. 1994. *Feuding and Warfare.* Amsterdam, The Netherlands: Gordon and Breach.

Pandian, J. 1992. *Culture, Religion and the Sacred Self: A Critical Introduction to the Anthropological Study of Religion.* Englewood Cliffs, NJ: Prentice-Hall.

Paredes, J. A., and M. Pohl. 1995. "Anthropology and Multiculturalism in a University Curriculum: A Case Study." *Critique of Anthropology,* 15:193–202.

Parenti, M. 1986. *Inventing Reality: The Politics of Mass Media.* New York: St. Martin's Press.

Park, K. 1995. "The Re-Invention of Affirmative Action: Korean Immigrants' Changing Conceptions of African Americans and Latin Americans." *Urban Anthropology,* 24(1–2):59–92.

———. 1996. "Use and Abuse of Race and Culture: Black/Korean Tension in America." *American Anthropologist,* 98(3):492–499.

Parker, R. 1987. "Acquired Immunodeficiency Syndrome in Urban Brazil." *Medical Anthropological Quarterly,* 1:155–175.

Parker, S. 1985. "A Social–Technological Model for the Evolution of Languages." *Current Anthropology,* 26:617–639.

Pasternak, B., C. Ember, and M. Ember. 1997. *Sex, Gender, and Kinship: A Cross-Cultural Perspective.* Englewood Cliffs, NJ: Prentice-Hall.

Paztory, E. 1984. "The Function of Art in Mesoamerica." *Archeology,* January–February, pp. 18–25.

Pelto, P., and G. Pelto. 1976. *The Human Adventure: An Introduction to Anthropology.* New York: Macmillan.

Pfaffenberger, B. 1992. "Social Anthropology of Technology." *Annual Review of Anthropology,* 21:491–516.

Pimentel, D., and M. Pimentel. 1985. "Energy Use for Food Processing for Nutrition and Development." *Food and Nutrition Bulletin,* 7(2):36–45.

Pimentel, D., et al. 1975. "Energy and Land Constraints in Food Protein Production." *Science,* 190:754–761.

Pinker, S. 1994. *The Language Instinct: How the Mind Creates Language.* New York: Morrow.

Pivnik, A., et al. 1991. "Reproductive Decisions among HIV-Infected, Drug-Using Women: The Importance of

Mother–Child Co-Residence." *Medical Anthropology Quarterly*, 5:153–169.

Plath, D., ed. 1983. *Work and Life Course in Japan*. Albany: State University of New York Press.

Plattner, S. 1989. "Introduction." In *Economic Anthropology*, edited by S. Plattner (pp. 1–20). Stanford, CA: Stanford University Press.

Podolefsky, A. 1984. "Contemporary Warfare in the New Guinea Highlands." *Ethnology*, 23:73–87.

Population Reference Bureau. 2003. *Transitions in World Population*. www.prb.org/Template.cfm?Section=Population_Bulletin1&template=/Content Management/ContentDisplay.cfm&ContentID=12488.

Posey, D. 1990. "Who Benefits from Traditional Resources?" IDRC Books Online. www.idrc.ca/en/ev–30122–201–1–DO_TOPIC.html.

———. 1998. "Biodiversity, Genetic Resources, and Indigenous Peoples in Amazonia: (Re) Discovering the Wealth of Traditional Resources of Native Amazonians." *AMAZONIA 2000: Development, Environment, and Geopolitics,* June 24–26. Institute of Latin American Studies University of London.

Pospisil, L. 1963. *The Kapauku Papuans of West New Guinea*. New York: Holt, Rinehart and Winston.

Post, J. 1985. *Food Shortage, Climatic Variability, and Epidemic Disease in Pre-Industrial Europe*. Ithaca, NY: Cornell University Press.

Price, D. 1995. "Energy and Human Evolution." *Population and Environment*, 16:301–319.

Pusey, A., and A. Wolf. 1996. "Inbreeding Avoidance in Animals." *Trends in Ecology and Evolution*, 11(5):201–206.

Quinn, N. 1996. "Culture and Contradiction: The Case of Americans' Reasoning about Marriage." *Ethos*, 24:391–425.

Radcliffe–Brown, A. R. 1935. "On the Concept of Function in Social Science." *American Anthropologist*, 37:394–402.

Ragone, H. 1994. *Surrogate Motherhood*. Boulder, CO: Westview Press.

Ramirez, F., and J. Meyer. 1980. "Comparative Education: The Social Construction of the Modern World System." *Annual Review of Sociology*, 6:369–399.

Rappaport, R. A. 1984. *Pigs for the Ancestors: Ritual in the Ecology of a Papuan New Guinea People,* 2nd ed. New Haven, CT: Yale University Press. Originally published 1968.

Renfrew, C. 1994. "World Linguistic Diversity." *Scientific American*, January, pp. 116–123.

Reyna, S. P. 1989. "Grudge Matching and War: Considerations of the Nature and Universality of War." Paper presented at the American Anthropological Association annual meeting, Washington, DC, November 15.

Richerson, P., and R. Boyd. 2005. *Not by Genes Alone: How Culture Transformed Human Evolution*. Chicago: University of Chicago Press.

Rickford, J. 1997. "Suite for Ebony and Phonics." *Discover*, 18(12):82–87.

Riddle, J., and J. W. Estes. 1992. "Oral Contraceptives in Ancient and Medieval Times." *American Scientist*, 80:226–233.

Riviere, C. 1987. "Soul: Concepts in Primitive Religions." In *The Encyclopedia of Religion* (pp. 426–430). New York: Macmillan.

Robbins, R. 2005. *Global Problems and the Culture of Capitalism,* 3rd ed. Boston: Allyn & Bacon.

Roberts, R., and D. Brintnall. 1982. *Reinventing Inequality*. Boston: Schenkman.

Roberts, S. 1993. "Fighting the Tide of Bloodshed on Streets Resembling a War Zone." *New York Times,* November 15, p. B12.

Robins, L., et al. 1984. "Lifetime Prevalence of Specific Psychiatric Disorder in Three Sites." *Archives of General Psychiatry,* 41:949–958.

Rodgers, J. R. 1994. "Female-Headed Families: Why Are They So Poor?" *Review of Social Economy,* 52(2):22–49.

Rohner, R. 1975. *They Love Me, They Love Me Not: A Worldwide Study of the Effects of Parental Acceptance and Rejection*. New Haven, CT: HRAF Press.

Roosens, E. 1989. *Creating Ethnicity: The Process of Ethnogenesis*. Newbury Park, CA: Sage.

Root, M., ed. 1992. *Racially Mixed People in America*. Newbury Park, CA: Sage.

Ross, P. 1991. "Hard Words." *Scientific American,* April, pp. 137–147.

Royce, W. F. 1987. *Fishery Development*. New York: Academic Press.

Rubel, A. 1998. "The Epidemiology of a Folk Illness: Susto in Hispanic America." In *Understanding and Applying Medical Anthropology*, edited by P. Brown. Mountain View, CA: Mayfield.

Sabato, L. 1989. *Paying for Elections: The Campaign Finance Thicket*. New York: Priority Press.

Sackett, R. 1996. *Time, Energy, and the Indolent Savage: A Quantitative Cross-Cultural Test of the Primitive Affluence Hypothesis*. Unpublished doctoral dissertation, University of California at Los Angeles.

Safa, H. I. 1986. "Economic Autonomy and Sexual Equality in Caribbean Society." *Social and Economic Studies,* 35(3):1–20.

Sahlins, M. 1978. "Culture as Protein and Profit." *New York Review of Books,* November 23, pp. 45–53.

Sakar, J. 1993. "Till Death Do Us Part: Dowries Contribute to a Rise in Violence against Indian Women." *Far Eastern Economic Review,* October 28, pp. 40–41.

Sanday, P. R. 1981. *Female Power and Male Dominance: On the Origins of Sexual Inequality*. Cambridge, England: Cambridge University Press.

Sanderson, S. 1991. *Macrosociology: An Introduction to Human Societies,* 2nd ed. New York: HarperCollins.

Sanjek, R. 1994a. "Introduction: The Enduring Inequalities of Race." In *Race*, edited by S. Gregory and R. Sanjek (pp. 1–17). New Brunswick, NJ: Rutgers University Press.

———. 1994b. "Intermarriage and the Future of Races in the United States." In *Race*, edited by S. Gregory and R. Sanjek (pp. 103–130). New Brunswick, NJ: Rutgers University Press.

———. 1998. *The Future of Us All*. Ithaca, NY: Cornell University Press.

Sanjek, R., ed. 1990. *Fieldnotes: The Making of Anthropology*. Ithaca, NY: Cornell University Press.

Sankar, A. 1986. "Sisters and Brothers, Lovers and Enemies: Marriage Resistance in Southern Kuangtung." In *Anthropology and Homosexual Behavior*, edited by E. Blackwood (pp. 69–81). New York: Haworth Press.

Savage-Rumbaugh, S. 1987. "Communication, Symbolic Communication, and Language: Reply to Seidenberg and Petitto." *Journal of Experimental Psychology: General,* 116:288–292.

Savage-Rumbaugh, S., and R. Levin. 1994. *Kanzi: The Ape at the Brink of the Human Mind*. New York: Wiley.

Scheffler, H. 1973. "Kinship, Descent, and Alliance." In *Handbook of Social and Cultural Anthropology*, edited by J. Honigman (pp. 747–793). Chicago: Rand McNally.

Scheidel, W. 1996. "Brother–Sister and Parent–Child Marriage outside Royal Families in Ancient Egypt and Iran: A Challenge to the Sociobiological View of Incest Avoidance?" *Ethology and Sociobiology,* 17:319–340.

Scheper-Hughes, N. 1979. *Saints, Scholars, and Schizophrenics: Mental Illness in Rural Ireland.* Berkeley: University of California Press.

———. 1984. "Infant Mortality and Infant Care: Cultural and Economic Constraints on Nurturing in Northeast Brazil." *Social Science and Medicine,* 19(5):535–546.

———. 1992. *Death without Weeping: The Violence of Every Day Life in Brazil.* Berkeley: University of California Press.

———. 1995. "The Primacy of the Ethical: Propositions for a Militant Anthropology." *Current Anthropology,* 36:409–440.

Schlegel, A., and H. Barry. 1979. "Adolescent Initiation Ceremonies: A Cross-Cultural Code." *Ethnology,* 18:199–210.

Schlegel, A., and R. Eloul. 1988. "Marriage Transactions: Labor, Property and Status." *American Anthropologist,* 90:291–309.

Schoepf, B. 2001. "International AIDS Research in Anthropology: Taking a Critical Perspective on the Crisis." *Annual Reviews of Anthropology,* 30:335–361.

Schwartz, S. K. 2000. "Working Your Degree, Anthropology Majors Can Capitalize on the Growing Global Marketplace." CNNfn. November 17. http://cnnfn.cnn.com/2000/11/17/career/q_degreeanthropology/.

Scoditti, G. 1983. "Kula on Kitava." In *The Kula: New Perspectives in Massim Exchange*, edited by J. Leach and E. Leach (pp. 249–273). New York: Cambridge University Press.

Scott, J. C. 1985. *Weapons of the Weak: Everyday Forms of Peasant Resistance.* New Haven: Yale University Press.

———. 1990. *Domination and the Arts of Resistance: Hidden Transcripts.* New Haven, CT: Yale University Press.

Scrimshaw, S. 1984. "Infanticide in Human Populations: Societal and Individual Concerns." In *Infanticide: Comparative and Evolutionary Perspectives*, edited by G. Hausfater and S. B. Hrdy. New York: Aldine.

Scrimshaw, S., and Hurtado, H. 1981. "Field Guide for the Study of Health Seeking Behavior at the Household Level." *Food and Nutrition Bulletin,* 6(2):27–45

Service, E. R. 1975. *Origins of the State and Civilization: The Processes of Cultural Evolution.* New York: Norton.

Shankman, P. 1991. "Culture Contact, Cultural Ecology, and Dani Warfare." *Man,* 26:299–321.

Shapiro, I., and R. Greenstein. 1999. "The Widening Income Gulf. Center on Budget and Policy Priorities." www.cbpp.org/9-4-99tax-rep.htm.

Sharff, J. W. 1980. *Life on Doolittle Street: How Poor People Purchase Immortality.* Final Report, Hispanic Study Project No. 9, Department of Anthropology, Columbia University, New York.

———. 1995. "We Are All Chickens for the Colonel: A Cultural Materialist View of Prisons." In *Science, Materialism, and the Study of Culture*, edited by M. F. Murphy and M. Margolis (pp. 132–158). Gainesville: University Press of Florida.

———. 1998. *King Kong on E Street: Families and the Violence of Poverty on the Lower East Side.* Boulder, CO: Westview Press.

Shepher, J. 1983. *Incest: A Biosocial Point of View.* New York: Academic Press.

Shostak, M. 1981. *Nisa, The Life and Words of a !Kung Woman.* Cambridge, MA: Harvard University Press.

Shreve, J. 1994. "Terms of Estrangement." *Discover,* pp. 57–63.

Silk, L. 1985. "The Peril behind the Takeover Boom." *New York Times,* December 29, Sec. 3, p. 1.

Simmons, R. C., and C. C. Hughes, eds. 1985. *The Culture-Bound Syndromes.* Dordrecht: D. Reidl.

Simoons, F. 1979. "Questions in the Sacred Cow Controversy." *Current Anthropology,* 20:467–493.

Skinner, G. W. 1993. "Conjugal Power in Tokugawa Japanese Families: A Matter of Life or Death." In *Sex and Gender Hierarchies*, edited by B. Miller (pp. 236–270). New York: Cambridge University Press.

Small, M. 1992. "The Evolution of Female Sexuality and Mate Selection in Humans." *Human Nature,* 3(2):133–156.

———. 1995. *What's Love Got to Do with It? The Evolution of Human Mating.* New York: Anchor Books.

———. 1999. "'Race' and the Construction of Human Identity." *American Anthropologist,* 100(3):690–702.

Smedley, A. 1993. *Race in North America: Origin and Evolution of a Worldview.* Boulder: Westview Press.

Smith, E. A., and S. A. Smith. 1994. "Inuit Sex-Ratio Variation." *Current Anthropology,* 35:595–624.

Smith, E. A., and B. Winterhalder. 1992. *Evolutionary Ecology and Human Behavior.* Hawthorne, NY: Aldine de Gruyter.

Snowden, C. T. 1990. "Language Capacities of Nonhuman Animals." *Yearbook of Physical Anthropology,* 33:215–243.

Soloway, J. S., and R. B. Lee. 1990. "Foragers, Genuine or Spurious?" *Current Anthropology,* 31(2):109–146.

Spencer, P. 1965. *The Samburu: A Study of Gerontocracy in a Nomadic Tribe.* Berkeley: University of California Press.

Spickard, P. 1992. "The Illogic of American Racial Categories." In *Racially Mixed People in America*, edited by M. Root (pp. 12–23). Newbury Park, CA: Sage.

Srinivas, M. N. 1955. "The Social System of a Mysore Village." In *Village India: Studies in the Little Community*, edited by M. Marriot (no. 83, pp. 1–35). Washington, DC: American Anthropological Association.

Stacey, J. 1990. *Brave New Families: Stories of Domestic Upheaval in Late Twentieth Century America.* New York: Basic Books.

Stack, C. 1974. *All Our Kin: Strategies for Survival in a Black Community.* New York: Harper & Row.

Stack, C. 2005. "Domestic Networks: 'Those You Can Count On.'" In *Gender in Cross Cultural Perspective*, 4th ed., edited by C. Brettell and C. Sargent (pp. 363–372). Upper Saddle River, NJ: Prentice Hall.

Stern, S. J. 1988. "Feudalism, Capitalism, and the World System in the Perspective of Latin America and the Caribbean." *American Historical Review,* 93:829–897.

Steward, J. 1955. *Theory of Culture Change.* Urbana: University of Illinois Press.

Stewart, O. 1987. *Peyote Religion: A History.* Norman: University of Oklahoma Press.

Stone, L., and C. James. 1997. "Dowry, Bride-Burning, and Female Power in India." In *Gender in Cross-Cultural Perspective*, edited by C. B. Brettell and C. F. Sargent (pp. 270–279). Upper Saddle River, NJ: Prentice-Hall.

Stone, L., and N. McKee. 2002. *Gender and Culture in America,* 2nd ed. Upper Saddle River, NJ: Prentice Hall.

Strauss, C. 1992. "What Makes Tony Run: Schemas as Motives Reconsidered." In *Human Motives and Cultural Models*, edited by R. D'Andrade and C. Strauss (pp. 197–224). New York: Cambridge University Press.

Suggs, D., and A. Miracle, eds. 1993. *Culture and Human Sexuality.* Pacific Grove, CA: Brooks/Cole.

Sugimoto, Y., and R. Mouer. 1983. *Japanese Society: A Study in Social Reconstruction.* London, England: Kegan Paul.

Suh, E. M. 2000. "Self, the Hyphen between Culture and Subjective Well-Being." In *Culture and Subjective Well-Being,* edited by E. Diener and E. M. Suh. Cambridge, MA: MIT Press.

Sullivan, L. 1987. "Supreme Beings." In *The Encyclopedia of Religion,* edited by M. Eliade. New York: Macmillan.

Susser, I. 1982. *Norman Street.* New York: Oxford University Press.

———. 1996. "The Construction of Poverty and Homelessness in U.S. Cities." *Annual Review of Anthropology,* 25:411–435.

Swanson, G. E. 1960. *The Birth of the Gods: The Origin of Primitive Beliefs.* Ann Arbor: University of Michigan Press.

Swasy, A., and C. Hymowitz. 1990. "The Workplace Revolution." *Wall Street Journal Reports,* February 9, pp. R6–R8.

Tannen, D. 1990. *You Just Don't Understand: Women and Men in Conversation.* New York: Ballantine Books.

Tefft, S. 1975. "Warfare Regulation: A Cross-Cultural Test of Hypotheses." In *War: Its Causes and Correlates,* edited by M. Nettleship et al. (pp. 693–712). Chicago: Aldine.

Thurow, L. 1995. "Why Their World Might Crumble." *New York Times Magazine,* November 19, pp. 78–79.

Titon, J. T., et al. 1984. *Worlds of Music: An Introduction to the Musics of the World's Peoples.* New York: Schirmer Books.

Tomasello, M. 1994. "The Question of Chimpanzee Culture." In *Chimpanzee Cultures,* edited by R. Wrangham, et al. Cambridge, MA: Harvard University Press.

Tornay, S. 1979. "Armed Conflicts in the Lower Omo Valley, 1970–1976: An Analysis from the Nyangatom Society." *Senri Ethnological Studies,* 3:97–117.

Turnbull, C. 1968 [1961]. *The Forest People.* New York: Simon & Schuster.

Turner, V. 1967. *The Forest of Symbols: Aspects of Ndembu Ritual.* Ithaca, NY: Cornell University Press.

Tylor, E. B. 1871. *Primitive Culture.* London, England: J. Murray.

Ubelaker, D. 1994. "Positive Identification of American Indian Skeletal Remains from Radiographic Comaridon." *Journal of Forensic Sciences,* 35:466–472.

Uhlman, A. 1992. "A Critique of Leavitt's Review of Sociobiological Explanations of Incest Avoidance." *American Anthropologist,* 94:446–448.

U.S. Bureau of the Census. 1994. *Statistical Abstract of the United States.* Washington, DC: U.S. Government Printing Office.

———. 2000. "Poverty." www.census.gov/hhes/www/poverty.html.

———. 2001. "The Hispanic Population." www.census.gov/prod/2001pubs/c2kbr01–3.pdf.

U.S. Department of Agriculture. 2005. "Expenditures on Children by Families." www.usda.gov/cnpp.

U.S. Department of Health and Human Services. (2005). "Population Characteristics." In *Women's Health USA 2005.* http://mchb.hrsa.gov.

Upham, S. 1990. *The Evolution of Political Systems: Sociopolitics in Small-Scale Sedentary Societies.* New York: Cambridge University Press.

Vaidyanathan, A., N. Nair, and M. Harris. 1982. "Bovine Sex and Age Ratios in India." *Current Anthropology,* 23:365–383.

Vaillant, G. C. 1966. *The Aztecs of Mexico.* Baltimore: Penguin. Originally published 1941.

Vandiver, P. B., et al. 1989. "The Origins of Ceramic Technology at Dolni Vestonice, Czechoslovakia." *Science,* 246:1002–1008.

Van Lawick-Goodall, J. 1986. *The Chimpanzees of Gombe.* Cambridge, MA: Harvard University Press.

Vigil, J. D. 1988. *Barrio Gangs: Street Life and Identity in Southern California.* Austin, TX: University of Texas Press.

———. 1997. *Personas Mexicanas: Chicano Highschoolers in a Changing Los Angeles.* Fort Worth, TX: Harcourt Brace College.

Villa, P., et al. 1986. "Cannibalism in the Neolithic." *Science,* 233:431–437.

Volkan, V. 1997. *Blood Lines: From Ethnic Pride to Ethnic Terrorism.* New York: Farrar, Straus & Giroux.

Vrana, D. 1997. "Women in Business Flex Their Muscles." *Los Angeles Times,* September 3.

Wade, N. 1973. "The World Food Situation: Pessimism Comes Back into Vogue." *Science,* 181:634–638.

Wagley, C. 1977. *Welcome of Tears.* New York: Oxford University Press.

Walker, P. L. 1988. "Cranial Injuries as Evidence of Violence in Prehistoric California." *American Journal of Physical Anthropology,* 80:313–323.

Wallace, A. F. C. 1952. *The Modal Personality Structure of the Tuscarora Indians as Revealed by the Rorschach Test.* Bureau of American Ethnology Bulletin No. 150. Washington, DC: Smithsonian Institute.

———. 1961. *Culture and Personality.* New York: Random House.

———. 1966. *Religion: An Anthropological View.* New York: Random House.

———. 1970. *Culture and Personality,* 2nd ed. New York: Random House.

Warner, R. 1985. *Recovery from Schizophrenia: Psychiatry and Political Economy.* London, England: Routledge and Kegan Paul.

Watson, R. 1990. "Ozymandius, King of Kings: Postprocessual Radical Archaeology as Critique." *American Antiquity,* 55:673–689.

Weaver, T. 1994a. "Latino Legacies: Crossing National and Creating Cultural Boundaries." In *Handbook of Hispanic Cultures in the United States: Anthropology,* edited by T. Weaver (pp. 15–38). Houston: Arte Publico Press.

———. 1994b. "The Culture of Latinos in the United States." In *Handbook of Hispanic Cultures in the United States: Anthropology,* edited by T. Weaver (pp. 38–58). Houston: Arte Publico Press.

Weber, P. 1994. "Safeguarding Oceans." In *State of the World,* edited by L. Brown (pp. 41–59). New York: W. W. Norton.

Weil, P. 1986. "Agricultural Intensification and Fertility in the Gambia (West Africa)." In *Culture and Reproduction: An Anthropological Critique of Demographic Transition Theory,* edited by W. P. Handwerker (pp. 294–320). Boulder, CO: Westview Press.

Weiner, A. 1987. *The Trobrianders of Papua New Guinea.* New York: Holt, Rinehart and Winston.

Weinstein, M. 1995. "Why They Deserve It." *New York Times Magazine,* November 19, pp. 102–103.

Weisman, S. 1978. "City Constructs Statistical Profile in Looting Cases." *New York Times,* August 14, p. 1.

Weismantel, M. 1989. "Making Breakfast and Raising Babies." In *The Household Economy: Reconsidering the Domestic Mode of Production,* edited by R. Wilk (pp. 55–72). Boulder, CO: Westview.

Weisner, T. 1979. "Urban–Rural Differences in Sociable and Disruptive Behavior of Kenya Children." *Ethnology,* 18(2):153–172.

Weisner, T., and L. Bernheimer. 1998. "Children of the 1960s at Midlife: Generational Identity and the Family Adaptive Project." In *Welcome to Middle Age! and Other Cultural Fictions,* edited by R. Shweder (pp. 211–255). Chicago: University of Chicago Press.

Weisner, T., and R. Gallimore. 1977. "My Brother's Keeper: Child and Sibling Caretaking." *Current Anthropology,* 18:169–190.

Weiss, G. 1977. "Rhetoric in Campa Narrative." *Journal of Latin American Lore,* 3:169–182.

Weller, S. C. 1998. "Structured Interviewing and Questionnaire Construction." In *Handbook of Methods in Cultural Anthropology,* edited by H. R. Bernard. London, England: Alta Mira Press.

Westermark, E. 1894. *The History of Human Marriage.* New York: Macmillan.

Westoff, C. 1986. "Fertility in the United States." *Science,* 234:544–559.

Weston, K. 1991. *Families We Choose: Lesbians, Gays, Kinship.* New York: Columbia University Press.

———. 1993. "Lesbian/Gay Studies in the House of Anthropology." *Annual Review of Anthropology,* 22:339–367.

Weyer, E. 1932. *The Eskimos.* New Haven, CT: Yale University Press.

White, B. 1982. "Child Labour and Population Growth in Rural Asia." *Development and Change,* 13:587–610.

White, D. 1988. "Rethinking Polyandry Co-Wives, Codes and Cultural Systems." *Current Anthropology,* 29:529–572.

White, L. 1949. *The Science of Culture.* New York: Grove Press.

White, T. 1997. Quoted in ABCNEWS.com. www.abcnews.com/sections/scitech/cannibals827/index.html.

Whitesides, G. 1985. "Nut Cracking by Wild Chimpanzees in Sierra Leone, West Africa." *Primates,* 26:91–94.

Whiting, B., and C. Edwards. 1988. *Children of Different Worlds: The Formation of Social Behavior.* Cambridge, MA: Harvard University Press.

Whiting, J., and I. Child. 1953. *Child Training and Personality: A Cross-Cultural Study.* New Haven, CT: Yale University Press.

Whiting, J., and B. Whiting. 1978. "A Strategy for Psychocultural Research." In *The Making of Psychological Anthropology,* edited by G. Spindler (pp. 41–61). Berkeley: University of California Press.

Whyte, M. K. 1978. *The Status of Women in Preindustrial Societies.* Princeton, NJ: Princeton University Press.

Williams, L. M., and D. Finkelhor. 1995. "Paternal Caregiving and Incest: Test of a Biosocial Model." *American Journal of Orthopsychiatry,* 65:101–113.

Williams, T. 1989. *The Cocaine Kids: The Inside Story of a Teenage Drug Ring.* Reading, MA: Addison-Wesley.

Willigen, J. V. 1991. *Anthropology in Use: A Source Book on Anthropological Practice.* Boulder, CO: Westview Press.

Wilmsen, E., and J. Denbow. 1990. "Paradigmatic History of San-Speaking Peoples and Current Attempts at Revision." *Current Anthropology,* 31:489–524.

Wilson, E. O. 1975. *Sociobiology: The New Synthesis.* Cambridge, MA: Harvard University Press.

———. 1978. *Human Nature.* Cambridge, MA: Harvard University Press.

Wilson, M. 1963. *Good Company: A Study of Nyakyusa Age-Villages.* Boston: Little, Brown.

Winkelman, M. 1990. "Shamans and Other 'Magico-Religious' Healers." *Ethos,* 18:308–351.

Witowski, S., and C. A. Brown. 1978. "Lexical Universals." *Annual Review of Anthropology,* 7:427–451.

———. 1985. "Climate, Clothing, and Body-Part Nomenclature." *Ethnology,* 24:197–214.

Wolf, A. P. 1995. *Sexual Attraction and Childhood Association.* Stanford, CA: Stanford University Press.

Wolf, A. P., and C. S. Huang. 1980. *Marriage and Adoption in China, 1845–1945.* Stanford, CA: Stanford University Press.

Wolf, E. 1994. "Perilous Ideas: Race, Culture, People." *Current Anthropology,* 35:1–12.

———. 1998. *Envisioning Power: Ideologies of Domination and Crisis.* Berkeley: University of California Press.

Wolf, M. 1972. *Women and the Family in Rural Taiwan.* Stanford, CA: Stanford University Press.

Wolff, E. 2003. "The Wealth Divide: The Growing Gap in the United States between the Rich and the Rest." *Multinational Monitor,* 24(5). http://multinationalmonitor.org/mm2003/03may/may03interviewswolff.html.

———. 2004. "Changes in Household Wealth in the 1980s and 1990s in the U.S." The Levy Economics Institute of Bard College. Working Paper no. 404.

Wood, J. 1990. "Fertility in Anthropological Populations." *Annual Review of Anthropology,* 19:211–242.

Wood, J. T. 2005. *Gendered Lives: Communication, Gender, and Culture.* Belmont, CA: Wadsworth/Thomson Learning.

Woodburn, J. 1982. "Egalitarian Societies." *Man,* 17:431–451.

World Health Organization. 1968. *Statistics Reports,* 21:529–551. Geneva, Switzerland: WHO.

———. 1979. *Schizophrenia: An International Follow Up Study.* New York: Wiley.

Worsley, P. 1968. *The Trumpet Shall Sound: A Study of "Cargo" Cults in Melanesia.* New York: Schocken.

Wrangham, R., and D. Peterson. 1996. *Demonic Males, Apes and the Origins of Human Violence.* New York: Mariner Books.

Yamashita, L. 2005. Personal communication.

Yanagisako, S. J. 1979. "Family and Household: The Analysis of Domestic Groups." *Annual Reviews in Anthropology,* 8:161–205.

Yuan, L., and S. Mitchell. 2003. "Matrilineal Kinship: Walking Marriage in China." In *Conflict and Conformity,* 11th ed., edited by J. Spradley and D. McCurdy. Boston: Allyn & Bacon.

Yan, Y. 1996. *The Flow of Gifts: Reciprocity and Social Networks in a Chinese Village.* Stanford, CA: Stanford University Press.

———. 1997. "The Triumph of Conjugality: Structural Transformation of Family Relations in a Chinese Village." *Ethnology,* 36:191–212.

———. 2003. *Private Life under Socialism: Love, Intimacy, and Family Change in a Chinese Village, 1949–1999.* Stanford: Stanford University Press.

Zentella, A. C. 1990. "Returned Migration, Language and Identity: Puerto Rican Bilinguals in *Dos Worlds/Two Mundos.*" *International Journal of the Sociology of Language,* 84:81–100.

Basic Assumptions of Cultural Materialism

Cultural materialism assumes that the various parts of society are interrelated (the universal pattern) and that when one part of the sociocultural system changes, other parts will also change. *Infrastructure*, however, has theoretical priority as a research strategy. Cultural materialism advocates that the first step in understanding a widespread practice or belief is to look at infrastructural practices.

Infrastructure refers to how people make a living without depredating the environment and without causing destructive increases or decreases in population size (how populations strike a balance between population size and the consumption of energy from a finite environment under a given technology).

Infrastructure is divided into two parts:

- The mode of *production* (derived from Karl Marx—but without dialects) relates to people's ability to utilize natural resources and technology to satisfy basic needs.

- The mode of *reproduction* (derived from Thomas Malthus but without the pessimism of ultimate doom) relates to the behaviors that stabilize population growth (or decline) in relation to the availability of the food supply.

Structure refers to the organized patterns of social life involved in the economic processes that allocate labor and the products of labor to individuals and groups.

Structure is divided into two parts:

- The *domestic economy* refers to household activities, family relations, and the division of labor by age and sex. This includes domestic hierarchies, discipline, sanctions, voluntary organizations, and some religious groups.

- The *political economy* consists of groups and organizations that regulate production, reproduction, consumption, exchange, and defense between groups. These groups include political organizations, redistribution organizations, education, taxation, stratified hierarchies, and the military.

Superstructure refers to ideational, normative, and symbolic processes that influence the patterned ways members of society think, conceptualize, express, and evaluate behavior.

Superstructure is divided into two parts:

- *Behavioral superstructure* includes artistic expression (art, music, dance, narratives), rituals, sports and games, and science.

- *Mental superstructure* refers to beliefs such as ideology, kinship, ethnobotany, subsistence lore, ethnic and national identity, magic and religion, and taboos.

There is feedback among the components of the universal pattern.

- *Change:* The most effective sociocultural change releases more, rather than less, energy from the environment and affects individual cost–benefit decisions regarding work, family size, and living standards.

- While infrastructure is considered to have primary influence on sociocultural process, social structure and superstructure are not mere reflections of infrastructure. Changes in structure and superstructure may not always be compatible with infrastructure, but they are unlikely to be retained over time if they impede the efficiency of the infrastructural process.